WITHDRAWN
UTSA LIBR
D0426296

PRACTICAL TURFGRASS MANAGEMENT

PRACTICAL TURFGRASS MANAGEMENT

John H. Madison

Department of Environmental Horticulture
University of California
Davis, California

Van Nostrand Reinhold Company

New York *Cincinnati* *Toronto* *London* *Melbourne*

To Patsy

Van Nostrand Reinhold Company Regional Offices:
New York Cincinnati Chicago Millbrae Dallas

Van Nostrand Reinhold Company International Offices:
London Toronto Melbourne

Library of Congress Catalog Card Number: 74-122677

Manufactured in the United States of America

Published by Van Nostrand Reinhold Company
450 West 33rd Street, New York, N.Y. 10001

Published simultaneously in Canada by
Van Nostrand Reinhold Ltd.

15 14 13 12 11 10 9 8 7 6 5 4 3 2 1

Preface

The turfgrass manager welcomes scientifically developed information. But his goals do not always permit him to grow grass in a manner consistent with values provided by research. Demands of the game and beauty of the grass come first. Management art and skill require balancing continual changes in moisture, fertility, and weather to provide quality grass. Judgement is used to adapt principles to achieve goals.

Many will come to this book looking for *The* answer. This book provides information. There are many ways the information can be used. There are many ways to grow good grass and none is *the* one right way. This is one reason I have emphasized principles. This book has no beautiful color pictures of well-kept grass. You see the real thing every day. There are no glossy pictures of fine mowers. You will see the latest mowers at the next turfgrass trade show. It is what you do with a mower that makes your reputation good or bad.

In the pages that follow I have reviewed the research on turfgrasses. In that information I have tried to find the underlying principles. In expressing the principles I have often given a personal philosophy of management, or given a personal view of their use. Many readers will disagree with my viewpoint. And I welcome that because it is the continuing conversation over our disagreements that keeps turfgrass management an exciting and growing study. Science will continue to provide new data. With new data we will revise the principles from time to time.

John H. Madison

Davis, California
October 1970

Contents*

*Turfgrass botany, soils, fertility, irrigation, drainage, and related topics are presented in *Principles of Turfgrass Culture.*

1

INTRODUCTION

Psalms 104:14 He causes grass to grow for the cattle and herb for the service of man.

Turfgrass lawns forming a decorative background for man's activities are a natural product of the climate of northwestern Europe and the grazing of animals. Today's lawns result from a tension between the natural growth tendencies of the turfgrasses and the management activities of man.

The importance of a cool moist climate may be seen by comparing how the game of bowls has evolved in the Mediterranean climate of Italy as compared to the Channel climate of Scotland. Bocce ball is played on bare ground, on sea shells, on gravel, in alleys, and generally on rough ground. Bowling is played on a kept green of exacting turf where a stray pebble may excite violent emotion. The cool temperatures and plentiful and well-distributed rainfall of northern Europe will result in forests. When forests are cleared and their regrowth prevented by grazing, a turf results and it would be difficult to maintain an area bare against grass encroachment. In the Mediterranean climatic region, annual grasses flourish during winter rains, but in summer the ground is sere.

The famous lawns of England, which are mowed today, historically have been kept with the aid of sheep, rabbits, and scythe. An earlier golfer comments: "On one course at least the greens rarely require any attention beyond brushing away the rabbit droppings!"[1]

The frequent comparison of a well-kept lawn to a carpet is apt. The lawn mower is an adaptation of a 19th century rotary shear for shearing the nap on carpets. A textile engineer, Edwin Budding, adapted the machinery to shearing grass. In 1830 he received a patent on such a machine, which, in addition to mowing grass, was able to provide country gentlemen with "an amusing, useful, and healthy exercise")see Fig. 1.10.

In America, Captain John Smith wrote in 1612, "Virginia doth afford many excellent vegitables and living creatures, yet grasses there is little or none but what groweth in lowe marshes. . ." Farther north, however, correspondence of 1630 indicates, "There is grass aplenty though very long and thick stalked." In this New England a new concept

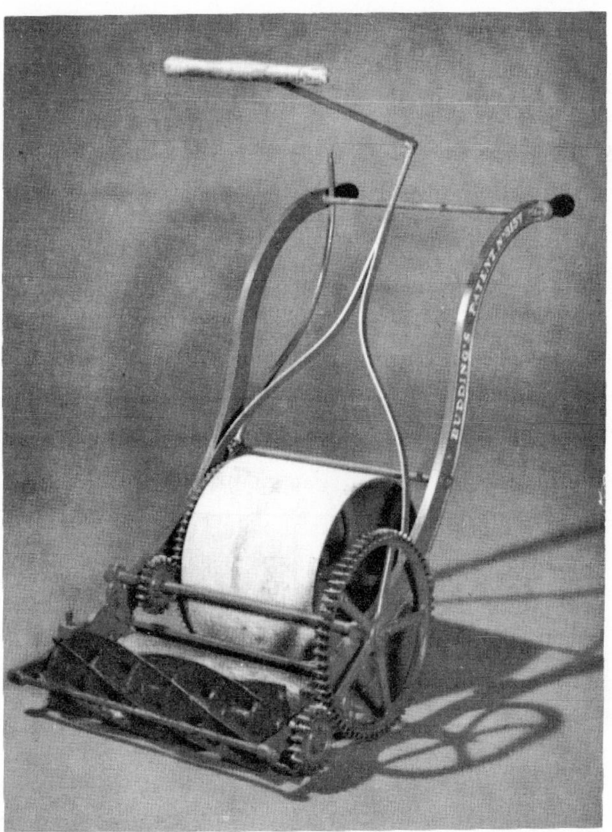

Figure 1.1 Budding's patent mower, 1830.

of a yard grew up. English towns had had the village green or common. But the European garden was private and walled, though in ordered and lawful communities the wall might give way to a hedge. New-world neighbors depended on each other and preferred to be able to keep a lookout without interrupting barriers behind which an Indian could hide, and the open yard developed. Even in Revolutionary times this was noted as an American idiosyncrasy. With continued settlement hedged and walled gardens appeared, but open yards or "homestead meadows" continued to be favored.

The open yard appeared in Victorian England but was imported from China, not America. Chinese aristocrats had favored the open yard as early as the 12th century and a Victorian fashion for gardens in the Chinese style led to tearing out hedges and sinking fences.

In keeping with his theories, Thorstein Veblen proposed that the open lawn is part of the "code of pecuniary beauty" in which we display our rich pastures in a bid for social recognition. But even unpastured lawns are quite practical, and the home lawn serves all three of the principal uses of turf. *(1)* It provides an attractive surrounding. *(2)* It softens the harshness of the environment by controlling dust, mud, erosion, and summer heat and glare. *(3)* It provides an arena for play.

The grassed area has always been preferred for sporting, and the greatest demands on turf result from the extreme maintenance requirements of the golf green, the bowling green, and the tennis lawn.

Whereas the perfect carpet, each blade alike, is pleasing to most, to others it seems sterile—too precise, too demanding. A more informal turf can be found in Europe where the daisies and blue star grass are given a chance to flower, and three of four mowings a year are sufficient to keep a turf controlled, yet allow seasonal variation in flowers. The greater knowledge and more demanding skill required by the perfect carpet is the subject of this book. Yet I am sympathetic to the informal turf and hope it will not be overlooked.

Golf and other British habits have led to the introduction of well-groomed grass in areas of the world where a lawn would otherwise be unknown. As the ultimate turf, the golf green too often becomes the example by which other turfs are judged or the ideal toward which they are maintained.

The word turf (torf, torfa) is common throughout Europe and derives from Sanskrit *darbhus,* a tuft of grass. A turf is a piece of the upper soil layer with the matted vegetation growing on it. Grass is most often the vegetation though it need not be. A second use of the word *turf,* is for the blocks of peat often used in Europe as fuel.

Where peat is burned this is the readily recognized use of the word, *turf.* In England and the United States turf also refers to horseracing.

The word lawn originally meant an open space between two woods and later an open space covered with grass. The word in its present sense appeared in the United States after the Civil War and has replaced such terms as "front meadow," "grass yard," "home green," "yardway," or "homestead meadow." Lawn carries the connotation of decorative home turf. Research papers have tended to avoid connotations of ornament as it is less productive of support funds than words of a more practical ring. Hence *turf, turf grass,* and *turf-grass* have been the preferred words for technical use. In 1952 Charles Wilson proposed to the Northern California Turfgrass Council that *turfgrass* be a single word and a resolution was adopted to that effect and presented to the Turfgrass Committee of the American Society of Agronomy. In 1953 the committee report published in the Agronomy Journal "recommends the use of the single word "turfgrass" as a descriptive term whenever appropriate."[9] Since then the U.S. and English Literature has used *turf* as referring to the growing, clipped sod, and the word *turfgrass* to refer to grasses used to produce turf.

Anyone working with grass becomes awed by the significance of grass for man. No book on grass can begin without respectful tribute to grass as a source of food, fiber, and shelter; of daily bread and of rice for Spain and China; of meat and beer; of bourbon and rum; and of a bowl of cornflakes with the cane sugar and milk of pastured cows poured over. The lowly grass underfoot truly supports man.

Lao-tse comments, "We come into the world soft and yielding and leave it hard and stiff." Life is softness and yielding; rigidity is synonymous with death. If when we fall we would fall safely we must give ourselves to the ground for in resisting we break bones. Drop a rubber ball, it bounces—a tea cup, it breaks. We compromise to create law and agreement, stand firm to battle and hate. Softly the grasses yield and bend. The trees tower over them, snows bury them, animals tread them, but in bending they succeed and cover the face of the earth, beloved by man.

The significance of grass is seared into man's subconscious and preserved in his culture. Psychologists have probed man's earliest memories and find they are of grass and trees.[12] And so when a man has finished his week's work in the city, it may be a hidden drive, a subconscious nostalgia for the youthful freedom of running barefoot through the secure fields of home that leads him to a weekend of toil in the yards of suburbia.

Through recorded history man has had a god in his culture to symbolize the grass. In Egypt and before then, in Sumer, there was a god identified with the grain. It was only as the youthful god died (the grain ripened and the leaves turned brown) that the people could live. He gave his life that they might find life in him. And among wonders, when the hard dead remains of this god, as found in the seeds of grain, were buried, he rose from his burial spot and reappeared as a new green shoot. He was reborn and hungry mankind was saved for another year.

Today in our culture the story has been turned around. Instead of a god to symbolize the life-giving grass, the reviving grass shoot at Easter symbolizes a dead and resurrected God.

The horticulturist or crop scientist skilled in growing plants in rows or beds will find that growing turf presents new problems. In horticulture plants from many parts of the world can be grown together in the same garden. Clues that help the horticulturist succeed with foreign plants are found in ecology. Every living wild plant exists today because there is some spot, some combination of climate and soil where it can successfully compete with other plants. The first step then in growing a difficult exotic plant is to reproduce as closely as possible that environment where it outperforms other plants. But when plants from Alpine, Mediterranean, and tropical areas all grow vigorously in the same garden, one seeks another reason. That reason lies with the tool that created civilization, the hoe. In hoeing away weeds and other plants, the stress of competition is removed. The struggling plant from the wild burgeons.

Competition is strong in the wild and a hundred and more plants compete to occupy the space, and use the water, nutrients, and sunlight that are adaquate for only one plant. Competition can be illustrated by an experience of my own. One spring a large sugar maple was cut down in an Ohio sugarbush where I frequently visited. The stump was about a yard across and the sunshine streaming in through the hole in the forest canopy covered about one third of an acre. When I first saw the stump, sap was flowing from it and hundreds of bees were harvesting the sugared juice. A week later I returned. The sap was fermenting and the stump was covered with drunken bees unable to fly. Sotted and dead bees lay on the forest floor where maple seedlings were beginning to push up through the litter. I made some seedling counts a month later and found over 200 seedlings of maple in each square yard. About 300,000 seedlings were coming up in the space that had been occupied by one tree. If ultimately one tree were to occupy that space again, all but one of those seedlings would die in the competition.

This example is not extreme; it is in fact quite the rule. Each elm tree produces hundreds of thousands of seeds during each of its reproductive years. If only two seeds from each tree were to survive, millions of seeds and seedlings from each tree would die, yet the population of elms would be doubled.

When we give a lone plant space, water, nutrients, and sunshine without any competition, it readily grows to a specimen plant. The agriculture supporting our civilization is based on reduction of the competition among plants; by providing optimum spacing in one garden, plants from all continents may flourish together.

In turfgrass culture we reverse this procedure. We work to increase the competition, to pack more and more smaller, weaker, splindlier plants into the same space—to make not two but ten grow where one grew before (Fig. 1.2). Then we irrigate, fertilize, and spray with fungicides and insecticides to keep the weakened plants alive.

An ultimate putting green may contain 20,000 innovations or plantlets per square foot (about as many leaves per square foot as a Persian carpet has tufts). The grazed pasture from which the lawn historically derived may have about 200 innovations per square foot.

Turf culture differs from other agriculture (except pasture management) in this deliberate creation of competition. This results in the enigma of turf culture. The more successful the grower is at producing a fine carpet of turf, the less successful he is at producing healthy, vigorous,

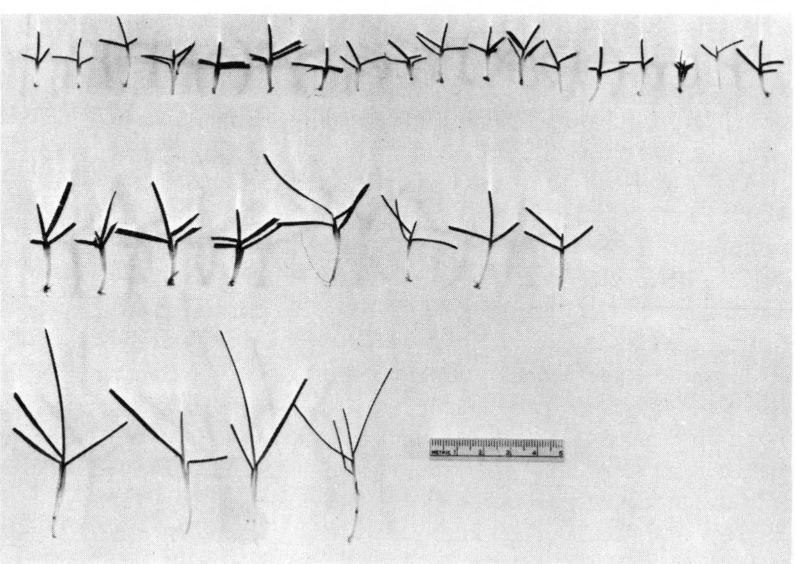

Figure 1.2 Kentucky bluegrass plants from one square inch mowed at 1/2, 1, and 2 in. In turfgrass culture, increasing numbers of smaller plants are grown in the same space.

individual plants. Each practice imposed to increase beauty calls for other practices to further control diseases, pests, desiccation, etc.

Throughout this book the philosophy of management is based on two concepts: *(1)* Competition provides a key to understanding and evaluating management practices. *(2)* Because of the competitive stress, management practices form a network. Each operation is related to and affects each other operation in the management plan. To illustrate, suppose we have a predominantly bluegrass turf which is mowed at 2 1/2 in. every ten days to two weeks, and which is rather thin, weedy, and neglected. A modest application of fertilizer may be expected to cause the turf to fill in more densely and crowd out many of the weeds. But the increased numbers of plants occupy space not previously utilized to the full, or used by weeds. Hence, competition is hardly increased. The resulting turf may be deeper rooted and better able to withstand drought. The overall apearance will have been improved without greatly affecting management demands.

Suppose that, pleased with the result we go into a moderately heavy fertilizer program. Again the turf becomes more dense, but since growth has filled in the bare areas, the new shoots crowd, not weeds, but each other. Competition is increased. The amount of roots per shoot are decreased and the turf runs out of water and nutrients sooner. Irrigations need to be more frequent and with increased moisture in the soil, compaction is increased and aeration decreased, resulting in further reduction of the root system. The surface soil stays wet longer. Water enters the compacted soil more slowly. As a result, disease attacks are more frequent and more severe, which increases the need for control. Loss of grass from disease or from infrequent irrigation may open up space to the invasion of weedy grasses such as crabgrass and *Poa annua.*

The management nexus is like a spiderweb in which a pull on one strand causes movement and changed tension on every other stand. Because of this net-like relation among practices, much of turfgrass management is an art. This book sets forth the scientific principles and explores the research findings, but it does not give answers to the basic management question: "At what level shall a given turf be managed?" The turf manager has pressure on him to please his public by producing beautiful turf, but to produce it with economy. Costs will increase as maintenance goes up. And the more like a beautiful carpet he keeps the grass, the greater the risk that the increasingly expensive turf will be lost during adverse weather, and the uglier damaged areas will appear by contrast. Thus he ends up in the position of working against himself, often with no way of deducing where he should stop. Science provides no good or bad, right or wrong, better or worse answers until we state our goal exactly;

until we define what we want to accomplish. Once we have decided our philosophy and our goals, we have, I think, information to make the decisions needed for achievement. We have the know-how to do the job.

There is art in the application of science. Science explains weather conditions leading to dollar spot, but art and experience are at work when a superintendent wakes in the night and knows from the change of the wind that he must spray for dollarspot in the morning. It is art and experience when the superintendent knows from the sound of a golf ball falling on the green that he will have to irrigate within two hours. Art and experience are needed for skillful application of scientific principles. Each area of turf has its own exposure, soil, and other characteristics, and while the principles of management remain constant, the application of them varies from site to site. When there is neither skill nor experience, even knowledge may result in failure, but experience is soon acquired. Without knowledge experience may be unreasoned and without benefit. I have seen an untrained school-grounds keeper set his mower low and his automatic irrigation system to apply one-half inch of water every night, for no other reason but that the equipment had that capability. In a year he turned a fairly decent turf into a field of crabgrass and knotweed.

Science in turfgrass management has been largely developed by the Agricultural Experiment Stations, the U.S. Department of Agriculture, and by the Sports Turf Research Institute in England. Work is beginning or is planned in other countries. Private research is conducted by several sod and seed producers, and by manufacturers of agricultural chemicals.

Turfgrass research in the U.S. probably began after 1906 when Dr. W. S. Harban of Columbia Golf Course went to the nearby U.S. Department of Agriculture office for technical assistance.[14] There he met and interested two outstanding grass scientists, C. V. Piper and R. A. Oakley, in the problems of turf. In 1908 while building the National Links at South Hampton, L.I., Charles B. McDonald realized there were not adequate answers to some of the problems encountered and that research was needed. He too went to the Department of Agriculture. There were no funds for such research, but a plan was made for cooperative work, with Piper and Oakley supplying direction and interpretation for trials carried out by the cooperator.

Such cooperative work provided the basis for continuing articles by Piper and Oakley which were carried in *Golf Magazine* from January 1913 on.[14]

In 1915 the United States Golf Association (U.S.G.A.) requested work of the Secretary of Agriculture, David F. Houston, and in 1916 a limited number of turf plots were established at the Arlington Experimental Farm of the Bureau of Plant Industry.

In 1922 the need for an authoritative body of information was again expressed and resulted in a meeting between Piper and Oakley with Hugh Wilson and Alan D. Wilson representing the U.S.G.A. A proposal was made for cooperative effort between the Department of Agriculture and the U.S.G.A. The Department of Agriculture accepted the proposal, and acceptance by the U.S.G.A. was accompanied by formation of the Green Section to administer the program. Work was set up at the Arlington turf gardens with C. V. Piper as director and with regular publication of the U.S.G.A. Green Section *Turf Bulletin* during the next thirteen years until the depression ended support. In 1942, the Pentagon replaced the turf gardens and research was moved to Beltsville. Work continues today at Beltsville under Felix V. Juska and A. A. Hansen.

In 1926 Oakley listed some contributions of work at Arlington which included the following:[18]

1. Grasses being sold were examined and their adaptation tested. Many were found expensive, undesirable, and seeded at excessive rates. Identification of redtop and bentgrass seeds was worked out since redtop was frequently used to adulterate bent seed.

2. "Secret" fertilizer mixes were analyzed and standard programs were worked out.

3. Proprietary compounds for worm control were analyzed and mercurous chloride was found to be the best active ingredient.

4. The sale of peat as "commercial humus" for top-dressing was fought.

5. Layer-cake construction of greens was largely stopped.

6. Anatomical basis of different mowing-height requirements was established.

7. Annual production of roots by perennial grasses was established.

8. Top-dressing need was established.

9. Vegetative establishment of bents was taught as a step in grass improvement.

10. Causes and means of control of diseases and pests were investigated.

11. Fertilizer needs were established.

These contributions were quickly accepted and contributed to steady improvement of turfgrass culture. Not all contributions were accepted by everyone though. In 1929 when reporting of fertilizer nitrogen was changed from percent ammonium to percent nitrogen, a survey found that 26% of users felt they could judge fertilizer quality by the smell.

Other contributions were accepted too readily.

From 1906 to 1916 the newly recognized significance of pH resulted in a decade of "whitewashed" greens. In 1917 work at Rhode Island showed colonial bentgrasses were favored by an acid soil while lime favored dandelion, plantain, and some other weed pests. This led to heavy sulfating during the ensuing decade with the pH of greens getting as low as 3.5.

While recognized work on a national level may be considered as having begun in 1920 with the establishment of the Arlington turf gardens and publication of the *Turf Bulletin,* local work had begun earlier.[20]

In 1885 J. B. Olcott began collecting superior grass strains privately at South Manchester, Connecticut. He later received some help from the Connecticut agricultural experiment station. His vegetatively propagated selections of red fescue and bentgrasses were his "thoroughbreds"; seeded grasses he regarded as mongrels.

In 1905 E. S. Garner began a turf program at the Rhode Island experiment station where he tested fertilizer use and turfgrass adaptability. Other early programs included those of the Florida experiment station begun in 1922,[8] and that at Massachusetts Agricultural College started in 1923 by L. S. Dickinson, who is honored today as much for his pioneering teaching efforts as for his research.[2,8] In 1924 beginnings were made at Kansas under J. W. Zahnley and at Ottawa, Canada, under G. P. Restis. In 1925 two outstanding agronomists lent additional efforts. Dr. Keim supervised student work on weed control and fertilizer at Nebraska, and H. B. Sprague initiated a full program at the New Jersey experiment station.[8]

Work at Pennsylvania began in 1929 under H. B. Musser and was stimulated by industry support organized and led by Joe Valentine, Superintendent at the Merion County Club. Research is expensive. Financial support of research by the turf industry in Pennsylvania has been outstanding and has resulted in one of the leading programs over the years.

Teaching of turf management was begun by Dickinson in 1926, and by 1930 half a dozen universities offered short courses in turf management.[2] A description of turf courses taught at twenty-six state agricultural colleges was published in 1967.[4]

Another prominent name during the early years of turf research is that of John Montieth, Jr., who was in charge of the U.S.G.A. Green Section research program beginning in 1928. He was a frequent contributor to the *Turf Bulletin* and made the first definitive study of turfgrass diseases.

In March, 1946, twenty turfgrass research men met in Columbus, Ohio to consider means of organizing themselves to further their work. A proposal for a turfgrass section of the American Society for Horticultural Science was rejected by that organization. The American Society of Agronomy approved formation of a turfgrass section on a trial basis and in November of 1946 the turfgrass research men met with the Agronomy Society at Omaha, Nebraska. By 1955 the turfgrass section was fully accepted, and meets annually as Section 5 of the Crop Science Society of America. Much turgrass research is also reported at annual meetings of the Weed Society of America.

An international turfgrass research conference was held at Harrogate, England in July of 1969. It was attended by eighty representatives of fifeen countries. Action was taken for the formation of an *International Turfgrass Society.*

Educational meetings are held across the U.S. (Fig. 1.3). In 1965, 124 such meetings were held with meetings in every month of the year and every region of the country, but with a preponderance in the north central and northeastern United States.[21] Additional related meetings are held by organizations representing parks, schools, nurseries, contractors, sod growers, gardeners, equipment suppliers, local golf associations and chapters, regional weed conferences, and the Sprinkler Irrigation Association.

Today most state experiment stations have turfgrass research programs. Some of these depend for support on grants from federal highway or urban beautification programs, etc. Some programs are offshoots of pasture work. Support has often been slow to come as turfgrass culture does not produce any "thing." Its product is the green of a park, the song of a bird, or the laughter of children. Little value was placed on such intangibles in the 1950s by marketing-oriented agricultural economists.

Figure 1.3 Turfgrass meetings across the country provide an opportunity for education and interchange of ideas.

Today's economists are sufficiently more sophisticated; they can deal with crops such as grass, that, without filling a single warehouse, inject billions into the economy and appreciably affect the gross national product. Perhaps in another decade economists will even be able to assign economic values to open grassy areas in the city as some tax assessors have already done. At present parks and golf courses do not have respected market value, and are sought as sources of land for freeways and schools because, in the condemnation, there are no buildings to be paid for. And if your city council is sufficiently naive (or corruptible) they will be persuaded to give a few acres of downtown park to a hotel chain in exchange for the hope that the city will become a convention center.

Fortunately, the growing multimillion-dollar sod industry is now providing a crop that can be evaluated in the traditional sense. Turf can be evaluated in terms of its cost of installation or its present cost of replacement (e.g., it supports a large sprinkler irrigation industry). The annual maintenance cost of turfgrass represents dollars directly entering the economy (for agricultural chemicals or turf machinery, for example). Additional turnover in the economy results from ancillary activities such as golf, bowling on the green, baseball, etc., and the cost of associated equipment such as balls, clubs, shoes, uniforms, gloves, nets, picnic and camping equipment, etc.

A 1954 survey of turf in Los Angeles country showed a replacement value of $262,000,000 and an annual maintenance expenditure of $90,000,000.[13] In 1956, Florida found $24,000,000 a year was being spent just to control chinch bug on St. Augustine turf. Such figures have created interest and led to surveys in New Jersey,[3] Florida,[8] West Viginia,[10] Colorado,[22] Pennsylvania,[19] and Texas.[11] In 1965, Nutter took these surveys as a base and made extrapolations to the country as a whole.[17] His findings showed a four-billion-dollar annual maintenance expenditure. This included the value of sod and seed but not other installation costs. No estimate of replacement cost was made, though surveys would suggest this to be two or three times the annual maintenance expenditure. Tables 1.1–1.3 from the *Turf-grass Times* give the distributions of this four billion dollars by type of turf installation, region of the country, and by maintenance practice.*

Those working with turfgrass know that not all construction and maintenance money is wisely spent. Much public money (school, park, etc.) is wasted. Specifications for construction are obsolete; maintenance is less than optimum; and trained men are too few.

*In her column of May 23, 1969, Sylvia Porter gave golf as a $6 billion annual enterprise, with 1/2 billion spent on course maintenance, and a course value of 2.8 billion.

Table 1.1. National Annual Turfgrass Maintenance Expenditures by Selected Facility[a]

Facility	*Annual National Expenditure ($)*	*Percent of Total*
Airports	34,606,352	0.8
Cemeteries	363,366,704	8.4
Churches	25,954,764	0.6
Colleges and universities	17,303,176	0.4
Golf courses	237,918,674	5.5
Highways	471,511,556	10.9
Lawns, Residential	3,002,101,097	69.4
Lawns, commercial	25,954,764	0.6
Parks, municipal	60,561,117	1.4
Schools, public	38,932,147	0.9
Miscellaneous[b]	47,583,735	1.1
Total	4,325,974,086	100.0

[a]From *Turf-grass Times,* Oct. 1965

[b]To include sod and seed production; municipal, state, and Federal government building lawns; state and Federal parks; private school facilities; professional athletic facilities; and others. Very conservatively estimated. For example, Florida alone grows approximately $10,000,000 worth of commercial sod yearly.[12]

Education is our weakest link and our greatest challenge. Many of today's skilled professionals developed their skill over the years, improving turf quality as they increased their own abilities. That opportunity no longer exists (Fig. 1.4).

Yet skilled men must be found to manage installations, many of which are valued at a quarter of a million dollars with annual budgets near $100,000. The universities can train the men but it has been difficult to attract university-calibre men to turf maintenance careers.

Limited numbers of trained men and rising maintenance costs may create a new kind of turf maintenance in the next decade. This will be a turf-contracting service for golf courses and industrial grounds, managed by an agronomist. The advantages will include these: the contractor can hire a plant pathologist, can maintain a small diagnostic lab, can hire a top equipment maintenance man, and can thus provide services his customers could not afford individually. By owning the equipment he can provide such tools as tree root pruners which a single golf course could not economically own. He can afford to mechanize every possible operation, and to train men to specialize in such operations as weed control, fertilization, etc. The golf course will receive good management at reasonable cost. It will have an accurate accounting of costs, with turf care separated

Table 1.2. National Annual Turfgrass Maintenance Expenditures by Region[a]

Region (U.S. Census Bureau Divisions)	Annual Expenditures ($)	Percent of National Total
New England Maine, Vermont, New Hampshire, Massachusetts, Rhode Island, Connecticut	183,271,396	4.2
Mid Atlantic New York, New Jersey, Pennsylvania	496,657,562	11.5
East, north central Wisconsin, Michigan, Illinois, Indiana, Ohio	772,188,186	17.9
West, north central North and South Dakota, Minnesota, Iowa, Nebraska, Kansas, Missouri	378,750,526	8.8
South Atlantic West Virginia, Virginia, Maryland, Deleware, Washington, D.C., North and South Carolina	742,864,584	17.2
East, south central Kentucky, Tennessee, Mississippi, Alabama	374,687,236	8.7
West, south central Oklahoma, Arkansas, Louisiana, Texas	570,179,610	13.2
Mountain Montana, Idaho, Wyoming, Nevada, Utah, Colorado, Arizona, New Mexico	199,073,182	4.6
Pacific Alaska, Washington, Oregon, California, Hawaii	609,474,712	14.1
Total—(U.S.A.)	4,326,546,994[b]	100.2

[a] Projected from 1960 census figures and the Texas Survey and adjusted, corrected, and updated to current evaluations. From *Turf-grass Times, Oct. 1965.*

[b] Although a discrepancy exists between the national evaluation totals appearing in Table 1.1 and Table 1.2, this difference is due to rounding off basic calculations at the second decimal place. Actually, the difference amounts to only one one-hundredths of one percent (0.01%).

from clubhouse operations. A principal disadvantage will be that the men on the course will be working for the contractor, not the club.

Already developing along similar lines is the administrative position of turf agronomist and horticulturist for the corporation that owns several golf courses, retirement cities, and other turfed areas.

In the first edition of his book, Musser took note of 124 grass species.[15] Today there are significant turf plantings of twenty to twenty-four species. Of these only three are considered in full detail in this book. *Poa pratensis,* Kentucky bluegrass, is still the first grass considered for a lawn in the United States. Of four bentgrass species planted, creeping bentgrass, *Agrosis stolonifera* outweighs the others in importance if not in acreage. It is the grass of golf greens; the grass

Table 1.3. Percentage Breakdown of National Residential Lawn Maintenance Expenditures by Selected Maintenance Practices[a]

Maintenance Practice	*Expenditure ($)*	*Percent of Total*
Topsoil, compost, top-dressing	165,115,560	5.5
Commercial fertilizer	210,147,076	7.0
Chemicals	75,052,527	2.5
Water	1,086,760,596	36.2
Equipment	795,556,790	26.5
Labor	705,493,758	23.5
Total	3.038,126,307	101.2

[a]Based on residential lawn total from Table 1.1 and percentage from Texas Survey (Table 1.8). From *Turf-grass Times, Oct. 1965.*

most able to withstand the most severe maintenance. Where temperatures require a subtropical grass, bermudagrass, *Cynodon dactylon* and its hybrids, lead all others for turf use. The secondary species are acknowledged throughout the book, and important differences in their management are considered.

I regard all turf uses as important. Yet it is impossible to write a book such as this without appearing to give undue emphasis to putting green turf.

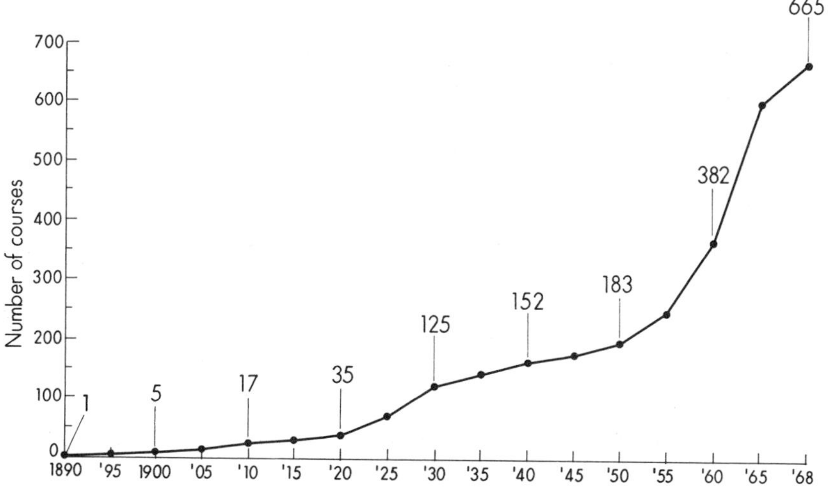

Figure 1.4 Growth of golf courses in California. During the depression and WW II almost no young men were getting training and experience. In the last decade the growth has been exponential, but the men trained by experience are reaching retirement age. *Courtesy W. B. Davis*

Turfgrass on greens receives the ultimate in care, the ultimate in abuse, suffers the most competition, is most subject to the ills and problems of all turf, and costs the most to build and maintain.*[6,7]
More examples can be drawn from experiences with greens; more kinds of machines are used in greens maintenance; more skill is needed to manage greens. Consequently putting greens turf is most discussed, and an assumption is made (though not always justly) that if one understands and can manage bentgrass under greens conditions, then one should be able to adequately care for other grasses; to manage for other uses.

References

1. Anon., 1929, *U.S.G.A. Green Sect. Bull.* **9**(1), 106.
2. Anon., 1930, *U.S.G.A. Green Sect. Bull.* **10**(6).
3. Anon., 1956, "In New Jersey Turf is big business," *Golf Course Reptr.* **24**(8), 10–12.
4. Anon., 1967a, "Turfgrass management training." *Weeds, Trees, and Turf,* Part I, **6**(2), 8–11; Part II, **6**(4), 24–26; Part III, **6**(6), 6–7; Part IV, **6**(7), 12–13.
5. Anon., 1967b, "Golf course operations: how does yours compare," *Florida Turfgr. Assoc. Bull.* **14**(1).
6. Bengeyfield, W. H., 1964, "Course maintenance centers on the putting green," *U.S.G.A. Green Sect. Rec.* **1**(6), 2–3.
7. Davis, W. B., 1966, "California's 50,000 acre golf course," *Calif. Turfgr. Cult.* **16**(1), 2–4.
8. Enlow, C. R., et al., 1928, "Turf studies at the Florida Experiment Station," *U.S.G.A. Green Sect. Bull.* **8**(12), 246–256.
9. Grau, F. (Chairman), 1953, "Report of the Turfgrass Committee," *Agron. J.* **41**, 650.
10. Henderlong, P. R., 1968, "The turf industry in West Virginia," *West Va. Turfgr. Conf. Proc., West Va. Agr. Expt. Sta. Misc. Pub.* **5**, 3–10.
11. Holt, E. C., W. W. Allen, and M. H. Ferguson, 1964, "Turfgrass maintenance costs in Texas," *Texas Agr. Expt. Sta. Publ. b* **1027,** 19pp.
12. Kelly, B., 1956, "This modern world—challenges and opportunities in a developing environment," *Lands. Arch.* **47**(1), 261–4.
13. Kimball, M. H., 1955, "Turfgrass by the thousands of acres," *Southern Calif. Turfgr. Cult.* **5**(1), 1.
14. Montieth, J. Jr., 1928, "The Arlington turf garden," *U.S.G.A. Green Sect. Bull.* **8**(12), 244–5.
15. Musser, H. B., 1950, *Turf Management,* McGraw-Hill Book Co., Inc., New York.

*Bengeyfield quotes a figure for a Southern California eithteen-hole golf course of 130A where three acres in greens used 25% ($28,000.00) of the budget.

16. National Golf Foundation, Chicago Ill., The Foundation keeps records and publishes information about golf, golfing, golf courses, and golf course construction.
17. Nutter, G., 1965, "Turfgrass is a four billion dollar industry," *Turf-grass Times* **1**(1), 1 ff.
18. Oakley, R. A., 1926, "Contributions to greenskeeping by the trained investigator," *U.S.G.A. Green Sect. Bull.* **6**(7), 155–160.
19. Pennsylvania Crop Reporting Service, 1966, *Turfgrass Survey*, Penna. Dept. Agr., Harrisburg, 36 pp.
20. Piper, C. V., 1921, "The first turf garden in America," *U.S.G.A. Green Sect. Bull.* **1**(2), 23.
21. Roberts, E. C. (Chairman), 1966, "Report, Committee on coordination of turf conferences and field days, Div. C-5," *Crop Sci. Soc. Am. Mimeo.*
22. Rydstrom, A. G., 1965, "The economic value of turfgrass in Colorado," *Colorado State Univ. Turfgr. Conf.*

2

TURFGRASS VARIETIES

There have been various codes for naming cultivated plants. The code now regulating the fancy names of cultivated plants was drawn up by committees from the International Botanical Congress and the International Horticultural Congress and was adopted at their meetings in 1952 and 1953.[59] This was of such interest to agriculturists in general that the code was extended to cover agriculture and forestry as well as horticulture. A copy of the code is available in the United States from the American Horticultural Society, 2401 Calvert St. N. W., Washington D.C. 20008, or elsewhere from the International Bureau for Plant Taxonomy and Nomenclature, Uithof, Utrecht, Netherlands. Some of the more important of the provisions are reviewed in the following sections:

The words "cultivar" and "variety" are used interchangeably and a variety (cultivar) is defined as "an assemblage of cultivated individuals which are distinguished by any characters (morphological, physiological, cytological, chemical, or others) significant for the purposes of agriculture, forestry, or horticulture, and which, when reproduced (sexually or asexually), retain their distinguishing features." Cultivars, or varieties, are further defined as to four types:

(A) A clone (cl.), consisting of uniform material reproduced asexually, as for example 'Arlington' bentgrass, reproduced by stolons, or 'Merion' bluegrass, reproduced by apomictic seed.

(B) A line, consisting of a sexually reproducing population of uniform appearance propagated by seeds, its stability maintained by selection to a standard. An example would be 'Raritan' velvet bentgrass, the parents of which are continually selected for five turf characteristics: seedling vigor, seed production, disease resistance, vigor, and turf adaptation.

(C) An assemblage of individuals showing genetic differences but having one or more characteristics by which the individuals can be differentiated from those in other cultivars. This is illustrated by 'Holfior' bentgrass which consists of a population without or with very short stolons.

(D) A uniform group which is a first generation hybrid (F_1) reconstituted on each occasion by crossing two or more breeding stocks maintained either by inbreeding or as clones. This is approximated by 'Tifhi 1' bahiagrass where seed is obtained by planting two clones which are highly self sterile and highly cross fertile, so that seed is essentially F_1 hybrid seed.

After establishing the meaning of cultivar or variety, the rest of the code is largely taken up with problems of nomenclature. The following high points are worth noting: New names shall be fancy names quite different from Latin forms used for scientific names. Thus, a new grass might be named 'Smith's dwarf' but should not be known as *compacta,* or *densa.* The variety name should be attached directly, or by implication, to a scientific name or a clearly understood common name. Thus, in an article about the variety 'Congressional' it should be first mentioned as *Agrostis stolonifera* 'Congressional' or as 'Congressional' creeping bentgrass. With the cultivar name properly established at its first use, it may be used alone in the rest of the article. That is, we may then write about 'Congressional' without further reference to the fact that it is a creeping bentgrass.

The code provides that the same name shall be used for only one variety in a genus. Thus, it would be inadmissible to name a colonial bent 'Congressional' when that name is already used for a creeping bentgrass. Since this provision (in fact the whole code) is directed to clarifying names, and to preventing confusions, it would appear best not to use the same name for more than one turfgrass. For example, there is no clear-cut separation in the use of blue- and bentgrasses by region or by climatic zone, and giving the name 'Supergreen' to both a bluegrass and a bentgrass would sooner or later result in confusion, even though the grasses were of different genera. Therefore, even though the code allows using the same name for more than one grass, turf workers should avoid the use of the same fancy name for more than one turfgrass. Of course, if a variety is no longer grown and is of no historic interest, the code permits the name to be reused.

New names shall consist of one or two words, or at the most, three words. They should be words and not numbers and should not be ambiguous. U-3 would no longer be an acceptable new name but will continue to be used by custom established before the code. The name should not be excessively long nor should it be one that exaggerates the qualities of the plant. For example, it would not be desirable to call a bermudagrass 'Hardiest,' for even though it were the hardiest at the time of introduction, it might no longer be so with the introduction of a new variety.

One practice has grown up in conflict with the spirit of the code. This is the practice of using the same introductory syllable for a series of varieties. Names such as Tifway, Tifgreen, Tiflawn, and Tiffine, and Pennlu, Pennlawn, and Penncross have the advantage of identifying the source of the variety as produced at Tifton, Georgia or at Pennsylvania State. However, repeated use of the same key syllable is confusing to the novice or to the occasional user. The code only prohibits the use of the same initial word in a series, but the intent, *clarity,* is such as to discourage repeated use of the same syllable.

A method is set up for establishing legitimate names. This is by publication of the name and a description of the plant. For convenience certain journals are agreed to be the official registration journals for certain plants. For turfgrasses the official journal of registry is *Crop Science,* Journal of the Crop Science Society of America.

In proper use, a variety name is capitalized and enclosed in single (never double) quotes. In lieu of single quotes the abbreviation cv., for cultivar, may be used. Thus we may speak of 'Delta' Kentucky bluegrass or of Kentucky bluegrass cv. Delta.

The code presents many more details of concern to those responsible for naming varieties of cultivated plants.

The problem of common names was studied by a Turfgrass Nomenclature Committee of Division C-5, the turfgrass division of the Crop Science Society of America (formerly Division XI of the American Society of Agronomy). This committee was concerned primarily with establishing a uniform code of spelling for various grass names. As an example, bermudagrass has also been spelled Bermuda grass, Bermudagrass and bermuda-grass. The turfgrass Nomenclature Committee has followed a pattern of combining words, and uses a lower case initial letter for the combined word, e.g., bermudagrass, bahiagrass, fescuegrass. The committee was not able to achieve complete uniformity.

Several common names involved three words and the combined form is too long and awkward. For these grasses the last two words are combined, but the first word is kept separate and capitalized if a proper name. Examples are Kentucky bluegrass, (not kentuckybluegrass), St. Augustinegrass, African bermudagrass, Bradley bermudagrass, etc.

The committee recommended that in a series of grasses the suffix be detached and appear at the end in plural form (bermuda, bent, zoysia, and fescue grasses). Also in publication the first mention of a grass should be of the full name, after which the suffix may be omitted. For example, *"We now use principally bermudagrass. We have used both bermuda and bentgrass for many years but find that for our purposes bermuda is better than bent."*

The committee compiled a list of about 400 grasses, clovers, and weeds associated with turf, and the list was adopted by the Nomenclature committee of the American Society of Agronomy.

Crop Science has been the registration authority for grasses since 1962. Previous varieties still currently grown are described in a U.S. Department of Agriculture publication by A.A. Hanson, *Grass Varieties in the United States.*[25] This chapter is concerned with varieties frequently used or discussed, but in general varieties indentified by a collection number are not discussed.

Criteria for selecting new turfgrasses become ever more sophisticated, and grasses may be selected for use only in a specific management program. Criteria may include the following:

1. Resistance to pests, including disease and insects.
2. Low spreading growth so mowing will produce a minimum of injury.
3. Tolerance of smog, salinity, compaction, heat, cold, traffic (wear), and other environmental adversities.
4. Density.
5. Rapid recovery from injury, which, with (4) provides minimum weediness.
6. Good color over a long season.
7. Adaptability to a specific management program. High-maintenance grasses that respond to high nitrogen levels with vigorous growth, etc., or low-maintenance grasses tolerant of drying, of low fertility, infrequent mowing, shade, etc.
8. Adaptibility to a specific use, as grasses for golf tees with a rapid recovery by runners, etc.
9. Adaptable to a wide range of climates or to a specific climatic niche.

Optimum achievement in selecting new varieties requires development of standards for evaluation. 'Merion' has a high nitrogen requirement and performs poorly when nitrogen is low.[31] 'Merion' and similar varieties have rated poorly in England where lower nitrogen levels are used. Similarly, varieties that perform well with some water stress may fail to stand out when regularly irrigated, and so on. Many varieties are excellent grasses in limited areas of adaptation (which suggests that many regional varieties are desirable), yet 'Merion' has been outstanding in many environments (which suggests that search for an ultimate and universal variety may succeed). In either case, unless we know the management under which the grass was evaluated, and evaluation of performance under other managements, we may waste the breeder's efforts and the producer's costs by failing to correctly study the potential of a variety. At the same time, failure of the breeder to select grasses for performance under stresses such as turf receives, may produce a *dud* that wastes everyone's efforts.

When early settlers landed in North America there was no bluegrass nor English bentgrass, but on the boats was hay for the cattle and hay as a packing material. Some of the hay came ashore as feed, in the animals, and as sweepings washed ashore. Both bluegrass and bentgrass seeds found their way ashore. A few years after settlement, colonial bentgrass was a "native" grass of Rhode Island and coastal New England.

The story of colonial bentgrass is interestingly told by Malte (see Ref. 49, Chap. 3). In the fall dried bentgrass is curly and soft and excellent for stuffing mattresses. When settlers in New England and Canada shook out their old bedding they planted colonial bentgrass. Colonial bent was quickly naturalized along the coast of Nova Scotia, Prince Edward Island, and Rhode Island.

Some settlers from Nova Scotia emigrated to New Zealand. Soon after they changed their bedding, colonial bentgrass was a "native" around the bays and along the coasts of New Zealand where it was called New Zealand browntop. The urge to resettle brought colonists from Rhode Island across the Oregon trail, accompanied by colonial bent. Bentgrass was soon at home in Oregon and it would be a romantic ending to say that the grass industry of Oregon got its start from a hitchhiker across the Oregon trail. But mixed German bent was brought to Oregon and planted and is a more likely source of the variety of bents that adopted Oregon as a home state. Creeping bent is found around the towns of Seaside and Coss Bay; colonial bent near Astoria; and highland bent in the hills behind the coast.

Kentucky bluegrass was not present in the U.S. in the early 1600s. That is to say there are no records of it, nor is there any Indian name for bluegrass recorded at that time. It did come, in hay and as seed, and in 1685 William Penn recorded sowing it. By 1750 mention of it was common and Franklin noted that it appeared naturally when land was drained. When settlers crossed the Appalachians, they found bluegrass and white clover in the meadows of Kentucky, Ohio, and Indiana, and the Indian name for it was *white man's foot grass.* The most reasonable explanation of its presence is that it was introduced by the French missionaries who traveled from Canada down the Ohio and Mississippi rivers and who had poultry and cattle at Vincennes, Ill., ca 1720. The missionaries brought seeds and agricultural tools to the Indians along with the Bible.[9,47]

A person raised in our automated age can hardly appreciate the influence of the horse. A day's travel meant stuffing the saddlebags with hay or grain, and when the horse was fed there was some spillage of seed. If a natural meadow was found and the horse relished a particular patch of grass, seeds would be gathered and taken home. Wherever the calvary went, letters sent home often contained seeds of grasses that seemed to be relished by the horses, or which gave promise of more hay or richer pasture.

It has often been remarked that all one had to do in these new lands of the west was to clear the land, and meadows of bluegrass and white clover sprang up. This has been taken as an argument that they were native plants and the seeds were already there. But all we need to know is that bluegrass seed passed through the horse and buffalo as readily as clover seed and we have adequate explanation for the universal presence of this introduced plant only 100 years after its introduction.

The story of bermudagrass is similar. Its first recorded introduction into the U.S. were ca 1750.[32] A century later settlers in Arizona found it flourishing as a "native" grass.

Of our other grasses, only St. Augustinegrass is truly native. It is a subtropical plant native to the Gulf Coast. Zoysia and centipedegrasses have been brought in by collectors from the U.S. Dept. of Agriculture. Bahiagrass has been imported, but has probably been an immigrant also for it appears spontaneously around some of the southern ports, a passenger, perhaps, on cattle boats from South America.

AGROSTIS STOLONIFERA L.

Creeping bentgrass is highly variable, and almost everyone who has studied the species has ended up recognizing varieties in the taxonomic sense rather than the horticultural.

Originally creeping bent was available in the U.S. only in mixed south German bent, where it comprised from 0 to 15% of the mixture.

Interest in creeping bentgrass in the U.S. waited for better knowledge of the grasses. In 1916 C.V. Piper, R.A. Oakley, and Lyman Carrier began to select little patches of outstanding grass from greens planted with south German bent. The selections turned out to be largely creeping bentgrass with a couple of velvet bents. They planted these selections at the Arlington turf gardens and by the fall of 1917 had developed 8 ft x 8 ft plots of the best. In the fall of 1918 test plantings were made on the E. Potomac Public Golf Course. At the same time Dr. Walter Harban started a nursery at the Columbia Golf Course, and in the following fall, 1919, he planted the first green of vegetatively propagated bentgrass. By the fall of 1922 stolons were available from commercial sources and over 125 greens had been planted. 'Washington' and 'Metropolitan' were the first two varieties released by the U.S. Department of Agriculture Research Service and the U.S. Golf Association cooperatively. 'Washington' had improved disease resistance and is still grown today. 'Metropolitan' was a vigorous selection and soon earned a reputation as a thatch builder and as susceptible to Helminthosporium melting out.

Previously, many greens had been built after the English manner using colonial bentgrass and Chewings' fescue. Annual reseedings of fescue were added. This formed a turf of erect grass, free of grain, and of excellent putting quality. Wearability and disease resistance were low, and in the U.S. climate such greens were difficult to hold during the summer. Consequently, improved creeping bentgrasses were eagerly sought. As stolons were the only source of planting materials, stolonized varieties were regularly used though seed would have been welcome.

In response to this need, Lyman Carrier resigned from the U.S. Department of Agriculture and went to Oregon. There natural stands of Seaside bent were cut for hay from tideland marshes in Coos Co. Carrier purchased hay, threshed the seed, and sold it under the name of 'Cocoos' bent beginning in 1923. Soon natural stands were being harvested from Revere Beach, Mass., Prince Edward Island, and from Seattle and Bellingham, Washington. Bent from Revere Beach was called 'Seaside' and this name has endured and become a generic name for creeping bent in the United States.[1]

Once seed was available, vegetatively planted strains lost favor. Among named varieties which appeared in the literature of the day and which are no longer used are the following: 'Inverness,' 'Columbia,' 'Flossmoor,' 'North Woods,' 'Vermont,' 'Virginia,' and from Australia: 'Albert Park,' 'Duncans 23,' 'Heidelberg,' 'Ivanhoe,' and 'Sydney.'[2,39] Varieties of current interest are listed in Table 2.1.

In the early 1930s the U.S. Golf Association built a device to hit a ball with a standard mechanical putt.[4] Different varieties were tested and putted differently. Faster greens gave a longer putt but with more drift. There was more difference between varieties than there was between the same grass two days after mowing and just mowed.

Today the first quality rated in a creeping bentgrass variety is disease resistance, and secondly, the factors which contribute to putting turf quality, such as density, thatchiness vs compactness, grain, etc.

AGROSTIS CANINA L.

A. canina (velvet bentgrass, brown bent) was one of the constituents of mixed bent seed shipped from Europe. It was quite at home around the drowned river mouth which forms the State of Rhode Island. Varieties have been developed at the University of Rhode Island and other coastal locations, but have never done well away from the northern coast.

Variety names include, Acme, Piper, Kernwood, and Raritan. In England, velvet bent is available from the wild and selections may be picked up for increase and subsequent stolonizing.

Velvet bent is described as the most beautiful of the turfgrasses. Its demands are high, even where it is adapted. Outside of its region of adaptation it is seldom grown successfully.

AGROSTIS TENUIS Huds.

A. tenuis is also known as Colonial bentgrass, browntop, New Zealand bent, Astoria, and Waipu.

Until recently the only strain of colonial bent was 'Astoria'. Engbretson and Hyslop made collections of plants along the Oregon coast near the mouth of the Columbia River. From these they determined fields which naturally contained pure stands of uniform types of colonial bent. Seed from these fields was harvested and sold as 'Astoria' though as with seaside, the seed is wild type and variable, and Astoria has almost become a generic term used more to distinguish colonial bent from highland bentgrass than to designate a variety. Washington state certifies the seed simply as *colonial bentgrass.* In 1964 Rhode Island released 'Exeter,' a product of twenty-four years of selection at that station. 'Exeter' is claimed to green earlier, hold better summer color, be winter hardy, and show leaf spot resistance.

HIGHLAND BENTGRASS

Elsewhere I have indicated taxonomic difficulties in placing highland bentgrass in an accepted species (see *Principles of Turfgrass Culture,*

Table 2.1. Bentgrasses [1,2,15,18,22,25,41,44-46]

Variety	*Source*	*Disease Resistance*	*Susceptibility*	*Remarks*
		Varieties of Creeping Bentgrass		
'Arlington' C-1	Selected by J. Montieth; collected at Northfield, N.J. 1928	Dollar spot; *Helminthosporium*	Brown patch	Swirls; good at 3/4 in. (tees?) Heat tolerant
'Berkshire'	Commercial selection	Snow mold		Not better than other varieties
'C-52'	Selected by R.R. Bond; collected at Old Orchard Grass Nursery, 1934	Dollar spot		Vigorous; best in spring and fall; builds thatch
'Cohansey' C-7	Selected by E.R. Steiniger; collected at Blementon, N.J., Pine Valley Golf Club, 1935	*Rhizoctonia; Helminthosporium*	Dollar spot	Apple green, aggressive, upright, competes with *Poa annua;* wide climatic tolerance
'Collins' C-27	Selected by J. Montieth; collected at Rosslyn, Va., 1937, Washington Golf and C.C.	Slight *Rhizoctonia* resistance		Dark green, upright, non-aggressive
'Congressional' C-19	Selected by R.P. Hines, Jr.; collected at Rockville, Md., 1936, Congressional C.C.	Snow mold	*Rhizoctonia*	Good blue-green color; early green up; upright, good surface, resists mowing damage
'Dahlgren'	Selected by F. Grau; collected at Dahlgren, Va., Naval Proving Grounds	Dollar spot; general resistance		Coarse yellowish color; not recommended for greens
'Evansville'	Selected by W. H. Daniel; collected at Evansville, Ind., Evansville C.C., 1958	Dollar spot; *Rhizoctonia* tolerant; *Helminthosporium*	Snowmold	Dense, good color into late fall; puffy, thatch former
'Metropolitan'	Selected by U.S.G.A. and U.S.D.A. cooperatively; New York seed sample, 1917		*Rhizoctonia; Helminthosporium*	Coarse; long ago superseded; of historic interest only

'Nemisila'	Ohio selection		Susceptible to pathogen not identified	Aggressive, dark green, upright growth, good texture, satisfactory in transition zone
'Norbeck'	Selected by J. Montieith, collected at Norbeck, Md. Manor Club, 1937			Never released
'Penncross'	Selected by H.B. Musser; collected at Penna. AES, Univ. Park, Pennsylvania	Dollar spot		Good color, uniform vigorous thatch builder, recovers fast, takes more HgC1, adapts in south.
'Pennlu' (Reg. #2)	Selected by H.B. Musser; collected at Lulu Temple Golf Course, Phila.	General resistance		Good density, texture, vigor; builds thatch, grain
Seaside	Wild seed from coastal stands		Susceptible	Lacks uniformity
'Toronto' C-15	Toronto Golf Club; Long branch, Ontario, Can.		*Rhizoctonia;* dollar spot	Thin, tight, and upright; it putts true; low summer vigor
'Washington' C-50	U.S.G.A.-U.S.D.A. cooperating; Collected at Rosslyn Va., Washington Golf and C.C.	Limited general resistance		Thin, tight, upright; putts true; heat resistant, slow grower in cold
		Varieties of Colonial Bentgrass [a]		
Astoria	Natural stands identified by Engbretson and Hyslop, 1926		Brown patch	Short determinate stolons; semierect

Table 2.1 cont'd.

Variety	*Source*	*Disease Resistance*	*Susceptibility*	*Remarks*
'Exeter'	J.A. DeFrance and C.R. Skogley; New England collections, 1940	*Helminthosporium*		Winter hardy, early green up, good summer color; leafy, adapted to cool north; poor at 1/4 in., good at 3.4 in.
'Holfior'	D.J. Van der Have from collection of S. Holland	Sl. Fusarium patch		Dense leafy growth with short stolons; not well accepted in U.S.; may be due to unfamiliar growth habit; better winter color
		Varieties of Velvet Bentgrass[b]		
'Acme'	P.I. 02541; 1919; collected from grounds of the U.S.D.A., Washington, D.C.			Not of sufficient fineness or disease resistance to survive
'Kernwood'	Selection from Kernwood, C.C. Salem, Mass.			Green early and late season
'Kingstown'	Selected by C.R. Skogley and J.A. DeFrance; from inbred selection from Piper by H.F.A. North, 1929	Dollar spot; some general resistance		Good vigor, texture, density; bright dark green color
'Piper'	P.I. 14.276; tested several years and released about 1938	General resistance		Fine, dense; good color, vigor
'Raritan'	Selected by H.B. Sprague; all sources of 1930	General resistance		High vigor and good turf quality

[a] Other Dutch varieties are available on the continent.

[b] Swedish and Dutch varieties are being tested in England. In the early 1930s the following additional velvet bent varieties were grown from stolons: 'Mountain Ridge,' 'Highland,' 'Yorkshire,' 'Newport,' 'Valentine,' 'Nykagyl,' 'Cunningham,' 'Elizabeth,' 'Nichol Ave. #1,' and 'Nichol Ave. #2.'

Chap. 2). For lack of a better alternative I am treating highland as an ecotype of *Agrostis tenuis,* highland as a common name, not a variety name.

There are no commercially available varieties of highland bentgrass. The University of Pennsylvania has developed a superior selection but seed is not being produced. Production would involve cleaning seed fields of wild strains. The Oregon Highland Colonial Bentgrass Commission has been working to reduce variability in the species by selecting to a type and using type plantings to produce breeders seeds. The problem of varietal seed is one of costs. Producing seed that costs $2.00/lb for an unknown market has higher risk than producing seed that costs 25¢ for a steady market.

Highland is an excellent grass for the Mediterranean climate of the west, but is not well liked in the eastern U.S. It recovers readily from drought injury. In England, highland is favored as a bottom grass for fescue. It is more resistant to Fusarium patch than *A. tenuis* and its excellent fall-to-spring color are appreciated though its indifferent summer color is objectionable.

AGROSTIS GIGANTEA

A. gigantea (A. alba, redtop, whitetop) is not a turfgrass but a pasture grass used to adulterate seed mixes or to compound cheap mixes for variety stores. Pasture varieties are available.

CYNODON DACTYLON (L.) Persoon

C. dactylon is also known as bermudagrass, couch, devil's grass, wire grass, Dhoob grass, Doob, dub, durba, durva, quick, florida grass, hariali, Kweek, Indian couch, manienie, neguil, scotch, scutch, serangoon, and yerba-fina. As a wild grass, the variable bermudagrass tends to be on the coarse and open side and for a high-quality lawn a selection rather than the wild type is very desirable. Also bermudagrass is amenable to hybridizing. The result is a number of hybrid varieties. Over ninety varieties of bermudagrass are under test at Arizona State, and Juska and Hanson have published a guide to the turfgrass varieties of bermudagrass which discusses forty named varieties and fifty unnamed introductions. All are vegetatively propagated. Even more introductions are being examined in the new collection at Stillwater, Oklahoma. A native of tropical regions of the world, bermudagrass was introduced into southern U.S. at an early date, the first recorded introduction being of its importation into Savannah, Georgia, in 1751 by Governor Henry Ellis.[32]

It is best adapted below the July 72° isotherm. North of this it does well at lower elevations where the summer nights are warm, but suffers cold damage in the winter. In hill and mountain areas where nights are apt to be cool it is not competitive.

Drought resistant, because of its deep root system, bermudagrass is said to reach its full development on deep, loose, well-aerated soil. In Africa it is a grass characteristic of ant hills where activity of ants in tunnelling and loosening the soil provides the loose well-aerated contidions required. Bermuda is now distributed throughout the warm regions of the world. A grass that colonizes as widely as bermuda is certain to adapt to all kinds of soils and conditions.

Table 2.2 characterizes the named turfgrass bermudas. Other selections such as Atlanta (once grown in Atlanta, Georgia) are no longer grown, and the many forage varieties are not given.[5,8,10,25,26,28,32,35,49,54]

CYNODON TRANSVAALENSIS Burtt-Davy

Cynodon transvaalensis Burtt-Davy, (Floridagrass, Ugandagrass) is a low-growing, fine-leaved, vigorous grass of good density that should make an ideal turf. I spent much time and money at Davis learning the management requirements of this grass for fine turf.

As it tends to appear nitrogen starved, I gave it increasing amounts of nitrogen up to one-half pound of nitrogen per week per 1000 ft^2. At all rates it appeared yellowish within a few days of applying nitrogen and the principal difference between rates was the amount of thatch built up. At high rates of nitrogen, thatch was measured in inches per season. Although weekly verticuting reduced thatch, plots appeared substandard. A second undesirable characteristic was seed head production. During hot weather great numbers of seed heads were thrown and even with daily mowing the texture was spoiled by the appearance of heads in the "boot" at the surface of the grass. I gave up the grass as not suited for fine turf, though the vigor with which it colonized a parking area suggests it may be useful for erosion control on land that has been strip mined. Uncared for, it was a very tolerable utility turf.

These three difficult characteristics, i.e., high nitrogen requirement, high thatch production, and high seed head production, have appeared in all of the hybrids I have tested. Consequently to date I have been reluctant to recommend hybrid bermudas for use where these characteristics would be objectionable. Additional breeding may clean up these present objections. Seed head production is affected by culture and climate, and is highest following a cold experience and following drought.[27,40] In the south, seed head production is much less a problem than in the colder transition zone.

Some of the following varieties have been selected from C. transvaalensis. In other instances an imported grass has been given a variety name, though it represents a species. In these cases a typical or a superior specimen has been imported and increased vegetatively so that a clone is represented and a varietal name can be correctly given.

'Bradley' *C. Bradleyi* Hurcombe	W. Bradley, ca 1910, veldt near Johannesburg S. Africa	Finer leaved than common; was identified by Hurcombe as *C. dactylon* x. *C. transvaalchsis* and given status as species because it was sterile; insect, nematode susceptible
'Elliot' P.I. 224146	Frankenwald Turf Res. Sta., Johannesburg S. Africa	One of their favorites; fine, good putting grass; slow spring recovery; cold intolerant
'Germiston'	S. African segregate	Like *C. Transvaalensis,* and probably is.
'Herrismith'	S. African segregate	Like *C. transvaalensis,* and probably is.
'Skaapplaas Fine' P.I. 224145	1935, D. Lorenz collected near water "pans" and used on two G.C.	Fine, aggressive, dense, drought tolerant grasses of medium green; considered superior to above two
'Sunturf' C. magennisii P.I. 184339 Magennis P.I. 213390	Selected by Magennes, 1922, as hybrid from patch of *C. transvaalensis*	Fine-leaved, slow growing; May be difficult to manage when mature, P.I. 184339 released in U.S. as Sunturf; dark green, spreading rapidly; few seed heads
'Transvaalensis' P.I. 213391 'Uganda' P.I. 183551	Introductions of *C. transvaalensis* from S. Africa and from Uganda via Cairo, Gezira Sporting Club, J. Plant	Fine-leaved; forms seed heads and dense thatch
'Waverly'	S. Africa	Probably *C. transvaalensis.*

POA PRATENSIS L.

Other names include Kentucky bluegrass, meadowgrass, smooth-stalked meadowgrass, spear grass, junegrass, greengrass, lawngrass, etc. Bluegrass was first harvested from wild stands in Kentucky, then later in Missouri, and then in the other midwestern states. Seed heads were stripped from hayfields before cutting. No varieties were developed, but seed was

Table 2.2. Bermudagrasses

Variety	*Source*	*Description*
Barberspan P.I. 183555 P.I. 283382	Lake Barberspan, W. Transvaal, S. Africa	Coarse, low growing, dense
'Bloupan' P.I. 213383	Jan Smuts Airport, Johannesburg, S. Africa	Fine leaved; used on greens and fine turf
'Brunswick'	Sea Island Golf Club, Sea Island, Ga.	
'Burning Tree'	Burning Tree C.C., Bethesda, Md.	Vigorous, spreading, dark green; leaves broad; cold tolerant
'Franklin' P.I. 213385	Mt. Edgecombe G.C., Natal, S. Africa	Fine, only slightly coarser than *C. transvaalensis*
'Hall's Selection' P.I. 183557 P.I. 213384 P.I. 224149	1933 by T.D. Hall from green of Germiston G.C.	Dark green, dense; tough sod, slow spreading
'Murray' P.I. 213386	Frankenwald turf Res. Sta. Johannesburg	Fine-leaved selection
'No-mow'	Florida selection FB 137	Low growth requires less mowing; has high shade tolerance
'Ohio'	Selected at C.C. near Cincinnati	Agressive, medium to coarse leaved, but of good cold tolerance
'Ormond' (Everglades #3)	Old fairway, 1946, R. Bair, Ellinor Village C.C., Ormond Beach, Fla.	Aggressive prostrate; good color; susceptible to dollar spot, mites
'Royal Cape' P.I. 224147 P.I. 283387	1930 Royal Cape C.C., C.M. Murray, Mowbray, S. Africa	Good texture, late and early color, wear resistance; does well in Imperial Valley, U.S.
'Santa Ana'	V.B. Youngner, U.C., Riverside, Calif.	Selected from a seedling of Roal Cape in 1956; released 1966; it has a deep blue-green color, is dense, free of grain, has early spring and late fall color; resistant to wear, smog, mites and salinity
'Texturf 1F' (Texas 35A)	E.C. Holt and J.R. Watson Golf Course in Texas, ca 1949-50	Fine texture; light green; rapid spring recovery; few seed heads; disease and drought susceptible

Table 2.2 cont'd.

Variety	*Source*	*Description*
'Texturf 10' (T-47)	E.C. Holt and J.R. Watson Corsicana C.C., Corsicana Texas, 1950	Medium texture, dark green, dense growth, early spring recovery, few seed heads; Sensitive to chlorinated hydrocarbon insecticides
'Tufcote' (Tuffy)	1942, Gen. Jan Smuts, Pretoria, S. Africa	Stiff leaves, rapid spread, few seed heads; released for athletic field use and erosion control
'U-3' Hall's superior	1936, L.D. Hall, Savannah G. C., Savannah, Ga.	A compact form, vigorous, slightly glaucous blue color; wear, disease, and insect resistant
x *Cynodon dactylon; crosses with C. transvaalensis unless otherwise noted*		
'Bayshore' 'Gene Tift'	1945, Roy Bair Bayshore G.C., Miami Beach, Fla.	Natural hybrid; light green, fine putting type
'Everglades 1; PeeDee	J.B. Pitner, Clemson AES mutant of tifgreen	Dark green, fine, dense, vigorous, fine stemmed; disease resistant
'Tiffine'	Glenn Burton, E.P. Robinson, Tifton Ga., E. Lakes G.C., Atlanta, released 1953	Light green, fine textured; male sterile; putting green type of turf
'Tifgreen' (Tifton 328)	Burton, Lathan, and Robinson, x superior clone Charlotte C.C., Charlotte, N.C. released 1956	Similar to above but darker green and better putting surface, susceptible to *Helminthosporium* summer blight
'Tiflawn' (Tifton 57)	Glenn Burton, released 1952, cross of two selected parents, F1' selection	Spread faster; denser; more weed-disease and cold resistant; more wear tolerant; requires less fertility
'Tifway' (Tifton 37) (Tifton 419)	Chance hybrid in seed from S. Africa, selected by Glenn Burton, Tifton, Ga.	Dark green, stiff leaves, aggressive, disease and weed resistant
'Tifdwarf'	Chance mutation or hybrid found in turf of Tifgreen at several locations, increased by Glen Burton and independently by Ray Jensen (8-10)	Extremely dwarf ground-hugging variety, withstands 1/8 in. mowing; deep green, few seedheads, low grain and thatch. dense, webworm susceptible; arsonate, chlorophenoxy acid injury

known by the state of origin. With the appearance of 'Merion' Kentucky bluegrass, seed production was moved to the west coast where no native bluegrass would contaminate the seed fields. The success of 'Merion' has encouraged development of other new varieties and the next decade should see the release of many new varieties with a strong trend to selection for a dwarf habit of growth. When dwarf and tall strains are both cut back a proportionate amount, reduction of tops, roots, and rhizomes is compatable. When both are mowed at the same height, dwarf varieties fare much better. Since low mowing is the more common practice, dwarf varieties are needed if bluegrass is not to be replaced as a turf grass by bentgrass and *Poa annua.*

When variety 'Newport' was released it proved to be an unusually vigorous seed producer. Instead of charging a premium, Oregon producers found they could undersell common seed. As a result bluegrass seed production moved to Oregon in the 60s and it is becoming increasingly difficult to buy wild-type seed. When common seed is purchased today it is most likely 'Newport' (or occasionally 'Merion'). This is unfortunate, for 'Newport' is not always a desirable variety and does not provide the broad genetic base expected from common seed. If common seed is wanted, it is necessary to buy seed with a known midwestern state of origin.

New varieties are being introduced by State Experiment Stations, by foreign producers, by commercial seed producers, and by sod producers. Sod producers prefer varieties that knit well. They will have to take care to use varieties that also continue to perform well over the years. If varieties fail to hold up for the consumer, sod will get a bad name. (Table 2.3 lists turf varieties of Kentucky bluegrass.)

POA ANNUA L.

P. annua is also called annual bluegrass and annual meadowgrass. There are many strains, some of them weakly perennial. Periodically the question is raised, "Can't we find a usable turf variety among all these races and types?" *Poa annua* withstands close mowing and produces a putting surface free of grain. For forty years a good *Poa annua* has been sought. To date all investigators have abandoned *Poa annua* and turned to other problems and *Poa annua* remains a weed. It is discussed as such in the chapter on weeds.

POA TRIVIALIS, L.

Poa trivialis or rough-stalked meadowgrass has some characteristics of *Poa annua.* It thrives under moist cool conditions but disappears into dormancy during long hot days. The dormant plants resist encroachment by better grasses and the browned spot is preserved until cooler weather. The quiescent crowns revive with autumn rains and form a dense, bright, yellow-green turf. *Poa trivialis* is often recommended as a grass for shady places but seldom serves well. Most shade resulting from tree competition is dry shade as the trees compete for water. *Poa trivialis* needs wet soil. Its yellowish color and season of growth favor it for overseeding as it blends with, masks, and crowds *Poa annua.* Varieties have not been developed.

FESTUCA RUBRA, L.

Other names include red fescue, creeping red fescue, and Chewing's fescue. In the United States, red fescue is used primarily as a complement to Kentucky bluegrass. The two are compatible and red fescue is tolerant of dry shade, bluegrass is not. *F. rubra* subsp. *commutata,* or Chewing's fescue is a bunch grass more tolerant of low mowing. In cool climates such as of northern Europe or northern New England, Chewing's can be mowed closely, e.g., to 3/16 in. in Great Britain. With warmer temperatures fescue does not tolerate the stress of close mowing. In milder climates *F. rubra* subsp. *rubra* is preferred. Chewing's quickly yellows with frost whereas the creeping red fescues tend to remain a beautiful green. The creeping fescues require mowing at over 1 1/2 in. during the warmer parts of the year. Creeping red fescue is coming into favor as a grass for winter overseeding, and Chewing's may have a place in seeding new greens to provide an earlier putting surface where the fescue will gradually yield to the bent as the bent matures.

Varieties of red fescue are listed in Table 2.4.

As a mainstay of fine turf in England, fescues are more closely examined there and evaluations will be found in the *Journal of the Sports Turf Research Institute.*

FESTUCA PRATENSIS HUDS.

Meadow fescue is also called *F. elatior* L.. Varieties of this have not been selected for turf. It is a coarse turfgrass which is often included in mixtures.

Table 2.3. Turf Varieties of Kentucky Bluegrass

Variety	*Description*
A-10	A variety developed by Warren's Turf Nursery; it is from a sexual line and propagated vegetatively.
Anheuser dwarf	Selected by W.H. Daniel in 1952 from Ahheuser Lawn in St. Louis; it is useful in breeding because of dwarfness and leaf spot resistance.
Aboretum	W.L. Brown at Shaw's Arboretum of the Missouri Botanic Garden selected this from a collection of plants from old Missouri lawns and pastures; grown as turf, this has not performed differently from common bluegrass
Arista	A variety from van Engelen in the Netherlands, it has been liked in early trials.
Belturf	This is a U.S.D.A. selection from A.A. Hanson and F.V. Juska; individuals were selected from old fields where early management experiments had been run; a vigorous, semiprostrate type with good rhizome development; tolerant of leaf spot and rust
Beaumont	Selected by O. M. Scotts, Marysville, Ohio, as a standard bluegrass type of good vigor; it is used by Scotts in blending
Cambridge	An older selection from England this is mentioned in trials but is little grown, coarse texture
Campus	From van Englen in the Netherlands; fairly susceptible to rust
Cougar	In a selection program at Washington State University, three varieties were sufficiently outstanding that one could not choose among them; the three were blended and released as 'Cougar'; good turf formers, they have leaf spot resistance but some susceptibility to rust; not especially suited to the transition zone (PN 205, 402, and 602 mixed)
Delft	A release of the Central Bureau (Cebeco) of Holland, this has been tried in England and is being observed in the United States
Delta	Selected by R. M. MacVicar at Ottowa, Canada, as a single plant selection from a local collection; 'Delta' has been controversial; an erect fine grass, it has contributed to mixtures in cooler areas but is less effective than common in warmer areas; susceptible to *Helminthosporium* and moderately susceptible to striped smut; it has good drought tolerance.
Fylking (0217)	A Swedish variety of Hogg and Lytle Sees, it has been tested and released in the U.S. by Jacklin Seed Co., Dishman, Oreg., it is a dwarf, high-maintenance grass with resistance to leaf spot and striped

Table 2.3 cont'd.

Variety	*Description*
	smut; slow spring greenup but late fall color; vigorous rhizome former; Fylking is a north European ecotype of frequent occurrence in Europe, less common in the U.S.; as a variety the number is appended
Golf	This Swedish variety is not an improvement over common in U.S. trials; highly susceptible to *Helminthosporium* disease.
Hope	An Alaskan variety (Acc. #282); this is much more tolerant of cold than continental varieties; varieties selected in the far north may go dormant ahead of winter in response to shortening day length
Merion	(Reg. No. 1) Developed from a single plant selection made by Joseph Valentine of the Merion Country Club, Ardmore, Penna.; it was extensively tested and released in 1947 by the U.S.G.A. and U.S.D.A. cooperatively; 'Merion' has had outstanding success and is still, twenty years later, the standard to which other selections are judged; in visiting plots across country 'Merion' plots could always be distinguished, even at a distance, because of their color and density; a low growing grass of good color. 'Merion' is tolerant of close mowing, resistant to *Helminthosporium,* requires high fertility, and is susceptible to rust and striped smut; disease susceptibility has decreased 'Merion's' desirability
Newport	(Reg. No. 2) Newport was selected at Plant Materials Center, SCS, Pullman, Washington, and used by Clausen and his co-workers at Carnegie Institute at Stanford in their collection; it was released in 1958 by the Washington AES, Oregon AES and the Plant Materials Center, SCS, cooperatively; a vigorous, highly productive, sod-forming grass of outstanding fall color; has a slow spring greenup and deteriorates rapidly in pure stands; at Davis deterioration is largely due to striped smut susceptibility; striped smut decimates stands during the winter, and in the spring there is no flush of growth except of weeds; a commercial production was certified separately as C-1 based on work that represents a low point in University turf research,[17] in my opinion.
Nudwarf	A Nebraska selection by R. H. Rasmussen chosen for its short aggressive growth and good color; has deep roots and rhizomes and is tolerant of hot dry weather; patented
Park	Released in 1957 by the Minnesota AES where it was selected by H. L. Thomas, Herman Shultz, A. R. Schmidt, and H. K. Hayes from a collection from old Minn. pastures; a mixture of fifteen superior strains; has high seedling and turf vigor; fairly rust resistant, but *Helminthosporium* susceptible; a good grass in areas where *Helminthosporium* is not a problem.

Table 2.3 cont'd.

Variety	*Description*
Pennstar (K-5[47])	This Pennsylvania selection by J. M. Duich and H. B. Musser has been extensively tested and has performed outstandingly save in seed production; low yields are apt to keep prices high; it is a dark green variety with good disease resistance
Prato	Developed by D. J. van der Have in the Netherlands from a Dutch collection of plants and released in the United States in 1964 by Northrop, King, and Co.; selected for rhizome production by dwarf plants; forms a dense tight sod and tolerates low mowing; moderate tolerance to rust; high density increases humidity in the sod and may aggravate *Helminthosporium* infections
Primo	A variety of Weibull's in Sweden it is described in English tests as a coarse type but a vigorous sod former; not yet tested in the U.S.
Sodco	W. H. Daniel of Purdue has released this multi-line selection in 1968 as a low-growing smut-resistant variety suited for sod production
Sydsport	Also from Weibull in Sweden it receives the same description as 'Primo'; a coarse vigorous sod former of promise in English tests but untested in the U.S.
Troy	Selected by R. E. Stitt at Montana AES from a Turkish collection P.I. 119684, 1955; a pasture selection; has not produced desirable turf
Windsor	Developed by the Research Division of O. M. Scott and Co., Marysville, Ohio, and released in 1962; moderate disease resistance; smut, rust, and *Helminthosporium* may appear but not at damaging levels; makes a dense turf of moderately fine texture; greater tendency to form stolons, lesser to tiller than 'Merion'; first patented turfgrass

In mixes it has the advantage of being cheap and germinating fast with a vigorous seedling. Thus it provides a quick response for the impatient homeowner. During the first year the leaves are about the color and width of Kentucky bluegrass and only later do the leaves become typically coarse. At this late date the seed merchant will hardly be blamed. Meadow fescue is not a turf former, and if sown thickly to produce a dense stand, it will tend to thin out in the years that follow. Of value in a utility turf, it is not a part of fine turf.

FESTUCA ARUNDINACEA Schreb.

Tall fescue is primarily a pasture grass, three varieties have been used for turf and work is being done to select types especially suited to turf. Tall fescue would ordinarily be considered too coarse for turf. However, it grows exceedingly well in the transition zone. Planted heavily (10–12 lb/1000 ft^2) in pure stands, tall fescue forms a uniform and acceptable turf. Planted in mixture with rhizomatous or stoloniferous grasses, plants of tall fescue tend to be isolated into clumps by the spreading grasses, and the appearance is of an old unkempt and weedy pasture. Where climate is cooler or warmer than in the transition zone, tall fescue deteriorates by invasion of blue or bermudagrasses. Within the transition zone it resists invasion and forms a good utility or athletic turf.

Tall fescue is vigorous during cool weather but has limited frost tolerance and winterkills in the north. Deep rooting of tall fescue makes irrigation less critical. The grass is disease resistant, but worn spots must be repaired by reseeding. Tall fescue should be mowed regularly, for if it becomes too mature it becomes difficult to mow. At Davis tall fescue performed well mowed to one inch but at shorter cuts it became subject to weed invasion.

Varieties of tall fescuegrass are listed in Table 2.5.

FESTUCA OVINA L.

Sheep's fescue may have some value, with red fescue, in sowing a ground cover at summer cabins where a grass soil cover is desired, but where it will be neglected.

LOLIUM MULTIFLORUM Lam.

Other names include Italian ryegrass, annual ryegrass, and domestic ryegrass. The sole turf use of annual ryegrass is overseeding dormant subtropical grasses in the winter. Annual rye has no place in a mixture—the concept of a nurse grass is false. Annual rye is not truly annual but has many perennial types in it which often endure for years as coarse weedy clumps. Several varieties are available but these have been developed for forage use. The primary requirement for overseeding use is disease resistance, and forage varieties Gulf and Tifton 1 have been favored because of

Table 2.4. Varieties of Red Fescuegrass [14, 16, 21, 23, 25, 29, 34, 45]

Variety	*Description*
	Commutata type
Boreal, Brabantia, Cascade, Chewing's, Erika, Highlight, Holy Cross, Koket, Oregon, Sceemter	
	Rubra type
Agio, Bargena, Clatsop, Cottage, Cumberland, Dawson (FR10), Duraturf, Golfrood, Lancashire, Norderney, Novorubra, Oasis, Polar, Reptans, Ruby, S-59, Sceempter, Sioux, Steinacher	
	Intermediate types
Illahee, Jamestown, Pennlawn	
	Other types
In Northern Europe these and many others are studied for turf, as the Chewings' type of fescue is the base for much fine turf; few of these are known in the U.S. at present; perhaps more will be tried as grasses for overseeding	
Brabantia	A selection of van Engelen in the Netherlands; has persisted well in England at turfgrass mowing heights
Cascade	A new Oregon selection of the Chewings' type; not yet widely planted
Dawson	A selection of the Sports Turf Research Institute named for their esteemed former director; while not outstanding it seems to have superiority in every test given it
Golfrood	This selection by van der Have in the Netherlands is of possible interest because of possible tolerance of a higher level of soluble salts; high density and superior performance in north
Highlight	A selection from van Engelen in the Netherlands; one of few that have impressed the staff of the Sports Turf Research Institute
Holy cross	A selection of native Alaskan red fescue from 62° 10' N latitude; high winter survival
Illahee	An Oregon selection of H. A. Schoth; it forms a dense uniform fine turf of good cold tolerance
Jamestown	A new release from Rhode Island; although the releases from Rhode Island have been of the highest quality, the climate of Rhode Island is too mild to pose the high stress needed to select varieties adaptable to a wide range of climates
Olds	This variety was selected and released by the School of Agriculture, Olds, Alberta; tolerant of cold winters; resistant to diseases of Alberta
Pennlawn	Developed by H. B. Musser, Penna., AES as a synthetic variety from three superior strains (F-55, F-74, and F-78); dense, spreads rapidly, tolerant of closer mowing; reduced leaf spot susceptibility; has been

Table 2.4 cont'd.

Variety	*Description*
	a superior grass in the east, and, for overseeding, in the south; in the west it has not been outstanding
Rainier	An Oregon selection H. A. Schoth; replaces 'Pennlawn' in the west and north though it has not been favored in the east
Ruby	An Alaskan selection from 64°44' N latitude; originates further north than any other variety; it has high survival by physiologically anticipating winter and being dormant when cold arrives

rust resistance (see Table 2.6). Florida has released its own rust resistant variety in which 90% of the plants are completely resistant.

LOLIUM PERENNE L.

Perennial ryegrass (English ryegrass) is one of the great grasses of the world. It requires cool temperatures and a high level of fertility and then becomes a leading pasture grass. Before selected varieties were available for turf in the U.S., Oregon perennial ryegrass was the type usually available. It was a poor turfgrass, formed clumps, was coarse textured and short-lived. Ryegrass has tough fibers and it is difficult to mow. Good ryegrass varieties are much like Kentucky bluegrass in color, leaf width, and appearance, differing in the shininess of the back (abaxial) side of the leaf. Under low fertility, ryegrass may clump, but with adequate nitrogen the good varieties form a solid turf.

Many varieties of ryegrass have been developed for forage. Those discussed below are late pasture types which have showed good persistance under turf conditions.

Until recently, ryegrasses have been classed as coarse. Pennsylvania Department of Agriculture has recently classed four varieties as qualifying for fine turf. These are 'Pelo,' 'Norlea,' 'NK-100,' and 'Manhattan.'[33]

Ryegrass has been mixed with 'Merion' where erosion control and suppression of weeds has been a problem. Ryegrass forms a cover weeks ahead of the 'Merion' without being suppressive as annual ryegrass and redtop have been.[19]

Some sod growers have used ryegrass with bluegrass to get better winter color and earlier spring greenup.[33] However, ryegrass is less hardy

Table 2.5. Varieties of Tall Fescuegrass

Variety	*Description*
Alta	Seed of three lines being grown at Corvallis by H. A. Schoth suffered severe winterkill in the winter of 1922-23. Survivors were put together to form a source of seed designated as 'Alta' and released in 1940. Similar to the other two varieties in appearance it has a high ability to survive summer drought. After 120 days of drought (on deep soil) at Davis, Cal. 'Alta' recovered a presentable appearance within two weeks after water was applied.
Kentucky 31	Selected by E. N. Fergus in 1931 from the Walter Suiter farm in Menifee County, Ky. A hillside pasture of the grass provided good forage well into the winter, and throughout the winter in mild years. Growth may fall off during heat.
Goar's	Goar's was selected by L. P. Goar at the Imperial Valley Experiment Station, El Centro, California and released in 1946. It is adapted for use on heavy textured alkaline soils, in regions of high summer temperature. 'Goar's' does not differ in appearance from the above two, but succumbed more rapidly to competition from bermudagrass in one test.

than blue and bentgrasses. Ryegrass is favored in the competition with other grasses by traffic and so is favored for athletic turf.

As with the fescues, ryegrass has a limited area of adaptation which does not extend south into the transition zone. There is more testing of ryegrasses in northern Europe, and tests are regularly reported by the Sports Turf Research Institute.

Table 2.7 lists ryegrasses that have shown some persistence in turf in tests.[19,21,23,25,29,33]

EREMOCHLOA OPHIUROIDES (Munro) Hack.

Centipedegrass was introduced from southern China ca 1919.* It is used as a turfgrass and it is hardy from Louisiana to N. Carolina and south. It is described as an acid-loving grass that will become yellowish and do poorly on alkaline soil.[25,43,49] The situation is more complicated, however, and chlorosis may be a response to bicarbonate or to sodium since it does well on some alkaline soils. Chlorosis may also result from nema-

*Seed was in Frank Meyer's collection when he disappeared in China in 1916 but it was not planted for test until about 1919.

Table 2.6. Varieties of Annual Ryegrass

Variety	*Description*
Gulf (Registration #8)	Gulf was selected from an introduction from Uruguay (P.I. 193145) and released in 1958 by the Texas AES and U.S.D.A. ARS. Its principle distinction is rust resistance with a uniform early maturity.
Tifton 1	Selected out of Westerwolds ryegrass by Homer Wills at Tifton, Ga. Rust-resistant individuals were selected through several generations to give high rust resistance.
Florida Rust Resistant	Selected at the North Florida Experiment Station by W. H. Chapman as an early maturing rust-resistant variety. Rust resistance enables it to endure longer into the spring and eases the transition.[11]

todes rather than pH. The fact is that we know little about this grass. Centipedegrass does well on neglect; high maintenance may result in its thinning and yielding to other species. Resistant to chinch bug and *Rhizoctonia,* it provides an alternate to the man no longer willing to fight the battle for St. Augustinegrass. It is damaged by ground pearls and nematodes. Moderately coarse, dense, and with large stolons, it is grown from seed with one variety available as this is written. The species is being worked on at Oklahoma State University and at Tifton, Georgia, and Florida has ten lines which vary greatly in hardiness.

One variety is Oklawn, which was released in 1965 by the Oklahoma AES as a variety adapted to Oklahoma. The variety has good cold and heat tolerance, drought tolerance, medium texture, and a medium green color.

PASPALUS NOTATUM

A grass of tropical America, bahiagrass is growing at its northern limit in the southern U.S. It is a somewhat coarse grass and more open textured than most southern grasses. Bahia is adaptable, growing on heavy or light soils, in shade or sun, with low fertility or high, in droughty locations or moist. Because of its character it may be weedy, and it is not tolerant of arsenate herbicides. At the same time there is the possibility of using *Poa annua* as a self-seeding winter grass by power raking and scalping bahia at the time *Poa annua* germinates. Fall raking may promote disease, whereas spring raking promotes greenup.[50] Bahia takes wear and is fairly pest free. Seed germinates over a period of years unless scarified. Several varieties are available. Common is generally too coarse to make a good

Table 2.7. Varieties of Perennial Ryegrass

Variety	*Description*
NK - 100	Developed by Northrop King from a cross between 'S-23' and Oregon perennial ryegrass. Turfgrass characteristics were sought. Leaves are narrow and deep green; the plant tillers heavily; Summer heat and drought are tolerated.
NK - 106	This is another Northrop King selection. It has not been widely tested by the public.
Norlea	Selected at Ottawa, Canada, by R. M. MacVicker with hardiness as a goal. It has good turf characteristics, but susceptibility to rust will probably limit further turf use.
Pelo	A variety from D. J. van der Have in the Netherlands selected from plants from old pastures. Selected for tillering and for survival under weekly harvesting. The variety has shown heat and drought tolerance and good tolerance to rust. It is one of the few varieties found to persist well in close turf in English trials.
S - 23	This variety from the Welsh Plant Breeding Station at Aberystwith was selected from a collection of plants from old grazed pastures. It has a dense, spreading growth, with high tiller production and persistence under grazing. Trials were made in the U.S. in the late '50s but at that time we may not have been ready to consider ryegrass for fine turf, for there was no response. I found it a superior turfgrass so long as fertility levels were maintained. Its ability to spread was excellent.
Manhattan	Developed for turf at the New Jersey Agricultural Experiment Station from selections of enduring plants in Central Park, New York City. It is reported as a fine textured, good colored, and persistant grass.
Stadium, Ileraf, Melle, and Sceempter	These other European varieties persisted as turf in England though none persisted at heights of cut less than one inch. New Jersey selections have performed better locally than the above.

turf. Bahia requires high mowing (2 1/2 in. or more) and seed heads are more easily cut with a rotary mower. Dollar spot is a problem of bahia. Table 2.8 describes varieties.[25,37,49,50]

STENOTAPHRUM SECONDATUM (Walt.) O. Kunze.

St. Augustinegrass or seaside quickgrass is a subtropical, stoloniferous American grass of coarse texture. It is favored for two characteristics. It is well adapted to the moist climate and coastal sands so prevalent in the Gulf Coast area. Secondly it is the most shade-tolerant subtropical grass. On the other hand, St. Augustine needs regular mowing for it becomes coarse and gets out of hand and in addition it is particularly subject to insect problems. A shy seeder, St. Augustine is normally sown vegetatively so that a program of selection should be rewarding. St. Augustine is a thatch builder.[25,28,42,49]

'Bitter Blue' is a variety of obscure origins along the Florida east coast. Probably a natural clone, it has closer internodes, more leaves that are shorter and narrower, and a closer growing habit than common. It has a good blue-green color and is frost tolerant. It forms a dense sod of good turf

Table 2.8. Varieties of Bahiagrass

Variety	*Description*
Paraguay	'Paraguay' is derived from patches found growing on the Gulf Coast, probably as escapes from early introductions dating to the Civil War. Leaves are shorter and hairier than 'Pensacola' and the variety does best in the drier regions so it is favored in Texas but not along the Gulf Coast. It is tough.
Pensacola	'Pensacola' was found along the docks at Pensacola, Fla. by E. Finlayson, increased by the Soil Conservation Service, and released by the Florida AES in 1944. It is one of the best turf varieties with narrow upright light green leaves that tend to brown early in the fall. It responds well to fertilizers.
Wilmington	Found growing near Wilmington, N.C. by Paul Tabor. It was collected and increased by the SCS because of its cold hardiness, being the only bahia tested at Chapel Hill that was not injured by cold over a twelve-year period. It has a narrow leaf and forms a dense sod of the best color, but is a shy seeder so that it may have to be planted from stolons.
Argentine	Selected by George Richey at the Florida AES from P.I. 148996 from Argentina. Selected as a pasture type it is coarse and hairy though finer than common. It is favored in southern Florida because it is close knit and maintains its color late in the season.
Tifhi 1	(Registration #1. Unfortunately the variety was registered in spite of a code recommendation that numbers shall not be part of a name.) 'Tifhi 1' was selected at Tifton by Glen W. Burton for a forage grass but it is denser and leafier than 'Pensacola'.
Paraguay 22 and Pensacola x common (a sterile triploid)	These are both broader leaved than the parent and I have not found records of these used for turf.

quality but not one of high wearability. The variety is a trade variety and uncontrolled so it is much mixed with common.

'Floratine' is a natural clone selected by Roy A. Blair and Gene C. Nutter and released by the Florida AES in 1959. Selected for turf use, it is fine leaved, has good color, and is more tolerant of close mowing than common. Certified sod is available.

Other varieties are being developed for turf use. 'Roselawn,' a pasture type, is sold for turf but shouldn't be.

PENNISETUM CLANDESTINUM Hochst. EX Chiov.

Kikuyugrass is grass from equatorial Africa. It is a grass of mild climates flourishing at high altitudes in the tropics. In the Americas it thrives at Bogota, Columbia where the temperature averages 68° the year around, at Mexico City with similar temperatures, and along coastal California where temperatures are 60–65°F.

Kikuyu has been introduced into California twice.[20,51] In 1916 it was planted by the U.S. Department of Agriculture for control of streambank erosion in southern California. In 1920, Dr. P. B. Denney of the University of California imported sprigs from the University of Pretoria. Of these two imports one is sterile, the other fertile though a shy seed producer. The grass is tolerant of a wide range of soils and moisture conditions, but not of temperature. With frequent, close mowing and heavy traffic, Kikuyu makes a presentable turf, but otherwise is a coarse thatch builder. In a neighborhood park in Los Angeles County, children playing in the grass were frequently cut by it and elderly persons stepping from the sidewalk onto the turf often suffered injury from turned ankles.

Where adapted, the grass is too vigorous and should be classed as a weed rather than a turfgrass. Bor says, "As if to make up for its reluctance to indulge in sexual reproduction it shows the utmost exuberance in vegetative activity." Certainly it is capable of spanning a sidewalk with pencil thick stolons in only a few days. Youngner has documented its spread. A stand of the fertile clone of less than half an acre covered 200 acres at the end of twenty-five years with twenty-eight scattered infestations within one mile. A thousand square feet of the sterile strain covered two acres in less than ten years.[51]

Kikuyu today is a major turf problem in coastal California. It extends north to San Francisco and holds more territory each year. Because it persists under extreme traffic, we may find we can live with it and can find it useful where other grasses fail. Low water, low fertility, and low mowing may help keep it manageable.

ZOYSIA[12,25,28,49]

Zoysia has been introduced into the U.S. on several occasions and was known to be in the U.S. by 1895. *Z. japonica* is a subtropical grass of great hardiness. Dorsett and Morse collected it for the U.S. Department of Agriculture in about 1929 near Kokai, Korea, a region where winter temperatures go to 40 below zero. The grass grew in rich sandy soil on the flood plains of the Deinonko River. Because of its hardiness it has been introduced as a suitable grass far north of the regions where it will grow well. At St. Louis, Mo. for example, it will thrive under the warm humid nights that make good "corn weather," but it is likely to be off-color seven months of the year. At Davis, California where days of 100°F may be followed by nights with temperatures between 50–60°F. *Zoysia* is slow to spread because of the low night temperatures. In spring, *Z. matrella* shows iron chlorosis when the air warms up in advance of the soil. *Zoysia* is a controversial grass. It grows with such density that a mature stand is likely to be weed free. At the same time a mature stand may be so dense that a lawn mower is apt to bounce or "float" over it without getting a good "bite." Thus with maturity the lawn surface may become more and more uneven. This condition is not improved by renovation, for then the turf is likely to look poorly for weeks while it recovers. When recovered it is again difficult to mow. Very close mowing is recommended to minimize this problem.

In Florida and Georgia, *Zoysia* has given trouble because its density makes it almost impossible to overseed. Homes with *Zoysia* have brown turf in the winter while the rest of the neighborhood is beautifully green with lawns of bermuda overseeded with ryegrass. About 1955, *Zoysia* was sold widely as 'Amazoy'; a heavy advertising campaign made extraordinary claims for the grass. When FTC action resulted in dropping many of the claims, the advertising became more modest and the rate of planting more reasonable for what must still be considered a grass under trial.

Although seed of *Zoysia* can be produced and has been available, plants from seed are variable and a patchwork turf results. For this reason only selected varieties are recommended and they are planted vegetatively.

As an introduction, *Zoysia* was free of pests for many years. This was a major point in its favor. However, it is now attacked by a rust, *Puccinia zoysia* Diet., which is so severe at times as to kill the turf if uncontrolled.

Table 2.9 lists varieties of *Zoysia.*

Table 2.9. Varieties of Zoysiagrass

Variety	*Description*
	Zoysia japonica
Meyer	'Meyer' results from introductions made in 1930 and selected at the Arlington farms of the Plant Industry Station in the 1940s by Ian Forbes, Marvin Ferguson, and Fred Grau. Tested as Z-52, it was released in 1951 as 'Meyer' in honor of plant explorer Frank H. Meyer. A tough grass, it matches bluegrass in leaf width and color and a mixture of the two has been recommended.
Midwest	Midwest was released in 1950 by W. H. Daniel at Purdue as an open faster-spreading type. The goal was to produce a noncompetitive type to mix with bluegrass. *Zoysia* would compensate for summer dormancy of bluegrass, bluegrass for cool-season dormancy of *Zoysia.*[12]
Z-73	A single plant selection from seed from 'Meyer' *Zoysia* selected by Fred Grau at Beltsville; it has not been released. A little broader leaved than 'Meyer' and less competitive, it produces good seed yields and might be of value in further breeding.
	Zoysia matrella
F.C. 13521	F.C. 13521 is a variety released by the "Alabama Agricultural Experiment Station without a proper name. It is described in Handbook 170 as having a fine dark green leaf with blades 3-5 in. long when not mowed. It is very dense and a good invader, as stolons creep under competing grasses. Stands considerable shade and has been fairly free of insects and disease.
	Z. matrella is also sold commercially under the name 'Flawn.'
	Zoysia tenuifolia
Mascarenegrass, Japanese temple grass	A very fine but tender grass, *Z. tenuifolia* can form a close turf without mowing if it is trodden to keep it compact. It forms as a very tight dense mat of stolons which in the sodbound condition buckle, or erupt, throwing up big folds of turf as much as a foot high.
	Zoysia matrella x *tenuifolia*
Emerald	An F_1 hybrid created by Ian Forbes at Beltsville, Md. It was selected from hybrids of all possible combinations of the three species. It was selected for fine leaf width, high density, good turf color, and winter hardiness. It was released in 1953, and its method of rating and selecting is described by Forbes, et al.

PRACTICUM

Grasses not discussed here are occasionally grown for turf. Examples are carpet grass (*Axonopus affinis* Chase[28] in the central states, and buffalo-grass (*Buchloe dactyloides* (Nutt.) Engelm.) in the unirrigated west. Although they serve in a limited region, such grasses are not of general value for producing quality turf. Outside of the north Atlantic countries, local grasses are often used for turf. In northern Europe much use is being made of procumbent, late flowering, heavy tillering forms of *Phleum pratense* L., timothy or cat's-tail, and P. *bertolonii* D.C., smaller cat's-tail.- These provide a wear-resistant and hardy turf for football fields in Sweden (ca 3000 stadia) and the Netherlands (ca 15,000 acres of sportsturf).

When purchasing grass varieties one does not always get the grass named on the label. In the case of certified seed and sod, a crop improvement association keeps check on the crop from the breeder stocks through foundation stock, on down to the material harvested. Uncertified stocks may have come from the named line originally, but may have undergone natural selection or contamination in the field, so a large percentage of the grass purchased is something else.

No one is responsible for maintaining some of the varieties and they are handed from one person to another with no guarantee that the stock is pure and uncontaminated. As an example of what may happen, I cite the following: In 1952 Charlie Wilson got from Jim Haines a plug of 'Cohansey' bentgrass from the old pie green at Denver Country Club and brought it to Davis where it has been part of our collection. One plot of Cohansey was abandoned and went to seed. About 1955 a Sunday visitor found the abandoned plot and picked up what was probably one of the seedlings, took it home, and propagated it. The seedling had the apple green color of Cohansey but was coarse, thatchy, puffy, and highly disease susceptible. Stolons from this plant were distributed to several golf courses as genuine Cohansey, "direct from the Denver Country Club," and greens were planted from it. Large parts of these greens died out within two years. Many golfers were inconvenienced, and the reputation of several good superintendents was put in jeopardy. Agronomists that travel widely report other examples of grasses that are not true to type.

Some grasses are distributed under a registered name by a private producer. Only the name is registered, not the grass. If you buy from the producer you will get the grass he sells under that name. But the grass can be changed from year to year by the producer. This is not to say that this does happen. It can happen, and in the past it has happened with some varieties of nursery stock. Usually the producer upgrades and improves

Table 2.10 Guide to Selection of Turfgrasses

Sub-tropical or warm regions	short tight turf under 1/2 in.	High maintenance[a] Bermudagrass Zoysiagrass
	Inter-mediate or deep turf	High maintenance Zoysiagrass Bermudagrass St. Augustinegrass Bahiagrass
		Low maintenance Centipedegrass Bahiagrass
	Green all year	Use any of the above; open up in the fall and sow red fescue, annual ryegrass, etc.
Transition zone	short tight turf	High maintenance Bermudagrass; in time bermuda invades and dominates other grasses; the takeover is faster with short cuts and warm night temperatures Creeping bentgrass
	Inter-mediate turf to 1-1/2 in.	High maintenance Bermudagrass Highland bentgrass; sown on clean ground highland may persist many years in a mediterranean climate Zoysiagrass Tall fescuegrass
		Low maintenance Bermudagrass Tall fescuegrass
	Deep turf over 2 in.	High maintenance Tall fescuegrass; sown on clean ground it resists invasion for a long time *Zoysia matrella*
		Low maintenance Tall fescuegrass Bermudagrass
Areas of temperate Climate	Short tight turf	High maintenance Creeping bentgrass Colonial bentgrass
	Inter-mediate turf	High maintenance Colonial Bentgrass Selected bluegrasses and red fescuegrass
		Low maintenance Selected bluegrasses and red fescue and clover
	Deep turf	High maintenance Bluegrass-creeping red fescuegrass Ryegrass (selected varieties)

Table 2.10 cont'd.

	Low maintenance
	Meadow fescue-red fescue-bluegrass-white clover
	Bluegrass-white clover

[a]High maintenance: regular, scheduled irrigation, fertilization, and mowing; control of weeds, insects, and diseases to produce quality turf.

Low Maintenance: regularly mowed but some neglect of mowing and fertilization usually results in weedy ground cover. Mowed short it is usually dominated by crabgrass in summer, *Poa annua* in winter.

the stock over the years but keeps the name because it is well known and has a good reputation.

When stocks are suspect they can be tested.[3] Four to six plugs of certified material are planted along side of plugs of the questioned grass. They are grown alike. If differences do not show up in the vegetative growth, both are allowed to form seed heads. If stocks are different, differences will almost invariably show both in vegetative growth and in the flower stalks. Use of certified stocks is the best program.

A turfgrass trial that has been commonly made in various parts of the country is this: Plots of several grass varieties are quartered. One half is fertilized, the other is not. Going across the fertility trials, one half is mowed close, the other half tall. Each quarter of the plot gets a different treatment combination. In a short while the management will be seen to be more important than the selection of grass. Any turfgrass well managed is better than any grass poorly treated. Advantages from variety appear with stress from climate, insects, diseases, etc. Then superior strains are found superior to ordinary or inferior varieties and climatically adapted species are found superior to species outside of their optimum range.

In recent years a number of books and magazines have contained charts and tables of turfgrasses as a guide to the user in selecting a grass. I feel that the approach is wrong: we should not compare the grasses, choose the best, and then impose an indifferent management practice on it. Instead we should choose the management, then select a grass that will respond to that kind of care. Consequently W. B. Davis and I made up a table similar to Table 2.10. This encourages defining your climatic zone and your management practices, and selecting the grass best adapted. This table has been greatly extended by Youngner.[55]

Another approach to grass selection given by Dr. Youngner is reproduced in Table 2.11.[56] This arrangement also first calls attention to goals and then to the grass. In reading the chart one should recognize that the order is not absolute and that small changes may occur in different sections of the country. Also differences among grasses which are close

Table 2.11 Which is the Best Turfgrass?[5,6]

I. Texture — leaf-blade width

Coarse	Tall fescue
	St. Augustine
	Meadow fescue
	Perennial ryegrass
	Common bermuda
	Kentucky bluegrass
	Zoysia
	Improved bermudas
	Colonial bentgrass
	Creeping bentgrass
Fine	Red fescue

II. High-temperature tolerance

High	Zoysia
	Improved bermudas
	Common bermuda
	St. Augustine
	Tall fescue
	Meadow fescue
	Colonial bentgrass
	Kentucky bluegrass
	Red fescue
	Ryegrass
Low	Creeping bentgrass

III. Cool-temperature tolerance (winter color)

High	Perennial ryegrass
	Kentucky bluegrass
	Creeping bentgrass
	Colonial bentgrass
	Red fescue
	Tall fescue
	Meadow fescue
	St. Augustine
	Improved bermudas
	Zoysia
Low	Common bermuda

IV. Tolerance of close clipping[a]

Low cut	Creeping bentgrass, 1/4 in. or less
	Improved bermudas
	Common bermuda
	Colonial bentgrass
	Zoysia
	St. Augustine
	Tall fescue
	Red fescue

Table 2.11 cont'd.

	Meadow fescue
	Perennial ryegrass
High cut	Kentucky bluegrass, 1-1/2 in or more
	V. Nitrogen fertility requirement
Low	*Zoysia*
	Red fescue
	Tall fescue
	Meadow fescue
	St. Augustine
	Kentucky bluegrass
	Perennial ryegrass
	Colonial bentgrass
	Common bermuda
	Improved bermudas
High	Creeping bentgrass
	VI. Salinity tolerance
High	Improved bermudas
	Common bermuda
	Creeping bentgrass
	Zoysia
	St. Augustine
	Tall fescue
	Perennial ryegrass
	Meadow fescue
	Red fescue
	Kentucky bluegrass
Low	Colonial bentgrass
	VII. Drought tolerance
High	Improved bermudas
	Zoysia
	Common bermuda
	Tall fescue
	Red fescue
	Kentucky bluegrass
	Colonial bentgrass
	Perennial ryegrass
	Meadow fescue
	St. Augustine
Low	Creeping bentgrass
	VIII. Compacted-soil tolerance[a]
High	Tall fescue
	Improved bermudas
	Common bermuda

Table 2.11 cont'd.

	Zoysia
	Kentucky bluegrass
	Perennial ryegrass
	Meadow fescue
	St. Augustine
	Red fescue
	Colonial bentgrass
Low	Creeping bentgrass
	IX. Disease tolerance
High	Tall fescue
	Zoysia
	Improved bermudas
	Common bermuda
	St. Augustine
	Meadow fescue
	Perennial ryegrass
	Red fescue
	Kentucky bluegrass
	Colonial bentgrass
Low	Creeping bentgrass
	X. Shade tolerance
Shade	Red fescue
	Zoysia
	St. Augustine
	Colonial bentgrass
	Tall fescue
	Creeping bentgrass
	Meadow fescue
	Kentucky bluegrass
	Perennial ryegrass
	Improved bermudas
Sun	Common bermuda
	XI. Wear resistance
High	*Zoysia*
	Improved bermuda
	Tall fescue
	Common bermuda
	Perennial ryegrass
	Meadow fescue
	Kentucky bluegrass
	Red fescue
	St. Augustine
	Colonial bentgrass
Low	Creeping bentgrass
	XII. Recovery from moderate wear[a]
Fast	Improved bermudas

Table 2.11 cont'd.

	Common bermuda
	Creeping bentgrass
	St. Augustine
	Tall fescue
	Kentucky bluegrass
	Perennial ryegrass
	Meadow fescue
	Red fescue
	Colonial bentgrass
Slow	*Zoysia*

XIII. Recovery from severe injury[a]

Complete	Improved bermudas	
	Common bermuda	
	Zoysia (but slow)	
	Creeping bentgrass	
	Kentucky bluegrass	
	Colonial bentgrass	
	Red fescue	Tends to become bunchy
	Meadow fescue	
	Tall fescue	
Partial	Perennial ryegrass	

XIV. Rate of turf establishment[a]

Fast	Improved bermudas (stolons)
	Common bermuda
	Creeping bentgrass (stolons)
	St. Augustine
	Perennial ryegrass
	Meadow fescue
	Tall fescue
	Kentucky bluegrass
	Bentgrasses (seed)
	Red fescue
Slow	Zoysia

XV. Cold tolerance (freezing injury)

Low	St. Augustine
	Centipedegrass
	Bahiagrass
	Bermudagrass
	Perennial ryegrass
	Tall fescue
	Bentgrass
	Red fescue
High	Kentucky bluegrass

[a] Position changes with changed climatic zone. Table is based on assumption of some climatic stress.

together may be minor differences while grasses separated by four or five places on the table are probably real. The best guide to new varieties and to varieties within a species is local experience. Local trials should be judged in terms of the management given. If a fescue variety does poorly under daily irrigation it may reflect an improper use of water rather than a poor variety, but it is still a poor variety for that kind of management.

The following example is of turfgrasses matched to a particular management scheme. In Great Britian the preference is for golf courses with nominal fees and light play and this can be got only with very economical maintenance. Red fescue (subsp. *commutata*) is resistant to wear and is the basic grass on the course. As red fescue is somewhat open and prone to weed invasion, browntop *(A. tenuis)* is planted with the fescue as a "bottom grass" filling in spaces and crowding out weeds. Both grasses tolerate acid soils, but fescue persists only at lower fertility levels. Consequently small amounts of acid residue fertilizers are used, and usually used infrequently. The acidity decreases numbers of dandelions, plantains, and several other weeds, and favors fescue and bent over blue and ryegrasses.

United States practice differs. Wearability is not achieved by use of a tough grass under low maintenance. Instead abundant fertilizer and water are used on a high-maintenance grass to get rapid growth so worn or damaged grass is rapidly replaced by new growth. (In the U.S. few areas have a climate suited to the fescue–bentgrass combination.)

Youngner studied grasses for wearability by use of a machine providing both shearing and scuffing actions.[52,53] For all varieties short clipping and either high or low irrigation resulted in decreased wear compared to higher mowing and average irrigation. The presence of *Poa annua,* crabgrass, clover, or broad-leaved weeds reduced wearability. Related to wearability was ability to recover from wear, and only stoloniferous grasses were able to recover fast enough to keep down weeds. Bentgrass withstood the least wear, then bluegrass. Grasses of high wear resistance included *Zoysia,* tall fescue, and bermudagrasses with Sunturf and U 3 the most resistant of varieties tested. *Zoysia* and tall fescue had poor ability to recover from wear.

The turf manager always has some seeding to do, so when a new variety becomes available a small plot should be tried. Almost any grass looks good the first season. The real test of a grass is whether it is better than your regular varieties after five or six years in the same location. With a small trial you can make observations under local conditions; then after a few years you can decide whether to use that variety extensively. In other words, to keep abreast, be in a hurry to make a small trial of what is new, but take your time and be sure before you stake your reputation on a new variety.

References

1. Anon., 1924a, "Strains of creeping bent," *U.S.G.A. Green Sect. Bull.* **4**(9), 210.
2. Anon., 1924b, "Named strains of creeping bent," *U.S.G.A. Green Sect. Bull.* **4**(10), 240.
3. Anon., 1929, "Green section summer meetings," *U.S.G.A. Green Sect. Bull.* **9**(9), 158–163.
4. Anon., 1933, *U.S.G.A. Green Sect. Bull.* **13**(3), 74–81.
5. Baltensperger, A. A., 1962, "Evaluation of bermudagrass varieties and strains," *Univ. Ariz. Agr. Expt. Sta. Rep.* **212,** 17.
6. Burton, G. W., 1960, "Tifway bermudagrass," *U.S.G.A. Green Sect. J. Turf. Management* **13**(3), 28–30.
7. Burton, G. W., 1966, "Tifway (Tifton 419) bermudagrass (Reg. #7)," *Crop Sci.* **6,** 93.
8. Burton, G. W., 1966, "Tifdwarf bermudagrass (Reg. #8)," *Crop Sci.* **6,** 94.
9. Carrier, L. and K. S. Bort, 1916, "The history of Kentucky bluegrass and white clover in the United States," *J. Am. Soc. Agron.* **8,** 256–266.
10. Clarke, S. E., Jr., 1966, "Tifdwarf evaluation," *Univ. of Florida Turfg. Management Conf. Proc.* **14,** 69–70.
11. Cooper, J. F., 1966, "Rust resistant ryegrass released by University of Florida," *Turf-grass Times* **2**(1), 5.
12. Daniel, W. H., 1965, 'Midwest' Zoysia: second report," *Midwest Reg. Turf Foundn. Turf Conf. Proc.,* p. 650.
13. Daniel, W. H., 1968, "Sodco bluegrass," *Midwest Reg. Turf. Foundn. Turf Conf. Proc.,* p. 79.
14. Elliot, C. R., 1968, "Registration of 'Boreal' red fescue (Reg. #6)," *Crop Sci.* **8,** 398.
15. Engel, R. E., 1967, "A comparison of colonial and creeping bentgrass for one half and three quarter inch turf," *Rutgers Univ. N.J. Agr. Expt. Sta. Bull.* **816,** 45–58.
16. Engel, R. E., and C. R. Funk, 1967, "Performance of red fescues," *Rutgers Univ. N.J. Agr. Expt. Sta. Bull.* **816,** 68–71.
17. Frakes, R. V., 1961, "Seedling vigor and rate of emergence in two sources of 'Newport' Kentucky bluegrass," *Crop Sci.* **1,** 306–307.
18. Funk, C. R., R. E. Engel, and P. M. Halisky, 1967, "Performance of bentgrass varieties and selection," *Rutgers Univ. N.J. Agr. Expt. Sta. Bull.* **816,** 41–44.
19. Funk, C. R., R. E. Engel, and H. W. Indyk, 1967, "Ryegrass in New Jersey," *Rutgers Univ. N.J. Agr. Expt. Sta. Bull.* **816,** 59–67.
20. Garner, E. S., 1925, "Kikuyu grass," *U.S.G.A. Green Sect. Bull.* **5**(11), 252–253.
21. Halcrow, J. G., 1966, "Grass variety trials," *J. Sports Turf Res. Inst.* **41,** 40–47, (1965).
22. Halton, D. F., 1966, "Golf course management in Australia," *J. Sports*

Turf Res. Inst. **41,** 25–31 (1965).

23. Handoll, C., 1967, "Grass variety trials," *J. Sports Turf Res. Inst.* **42,** 49–53 (1966).
24. Handoll, C., 1968, "Grass variety trials," *J. Sports Turf Res. Inst.* **43,** 12–22 (1967).
25. Hanson, A. A., 1959, *Grass varieties in the United States.* Agr. Handbook 170, U.S. Dept. Agriculture, ARS, 72 pp.
26. Hein, M. A., 1961, "Registration of varieties and strains of bermudagrasses 3 – *Cynodon dactylon* (L) Pers. Tifgreen (Reg. 5)," *Agron. J.* **53,** 276.
27. Horn, G. C., 1966, "Improving plants for turf with amendments," *Univ. Florida Turfgr. Conf. Proc.* **14,** 24–37.
28. Horn, G. C., 1967, "Turfgrass variety comparisons," *Univ. Florida Turfgr. Conf. Proc.* **15,** 91–99.
29. Jackson, N., 1965, "Further notes on the evaluation of some grass varieties," *J. Sports Turf Res. Inst.* **40,** 67–75 (1964).
30. Juska, F. V. (Chairman), W. H. Daniel, E. C. Holt, and V. B. Youngner, 1961, "Nomenclature of some plants associated with turfgrass management," *Turfgr. Nomenclature Comm., Div. II, Am. Soc. Agron. Mimeo.,* 21 pp.
31. Juska, F. V., and A. A. Hanson, 1961, "The nitrogen variable in testing Kentucky bluegrass varieties for turf," *Agron. J.* **53,** 409–410.
32. Juska, F. V., and A. A. Hanson, 1964, "*Evaluation of Bermudagrass* Varieties for General-Purpose Turf," U.S. Dept. Agriculture ARS, Agr. Handbook 270, Washington, D.C., 54 pp.
33. Kaerwer, H., 1968, "New ryegrasses for turf," *Turf-grass Times* **3**(6), 1 ff.
34. Klebesadel, L. J., A. C. Wilson, R. L. Taylor, and J. J. Koranda, 1964, "Fall growth behavior and winter survival of *Festuca rubra* and *Poa pratensis* in Alaska as influenced by latitude of adaptation," *Crop Sci.* **4,** 340–341.
35. Kneebone, W. R., 1965, "Notes from the bermudagrass breeding program, 1965," *Univ. Ariz. Agr. Expt. Sta. Rep.* **230**, 3–6.
36. Law, A. G., J. L. Schwendiman, and J. Clausen, 1964, "Registration of 'Newport' bluegrass (Reg. #2)," *Crop Sci.* **4,** 115.
37. Lewis, W. F., 1965, "Bahiagrass for industrial use," *Agron. Abstr.* **132.**
38. Long, J. A., 1965, "Bluegrasses today and tomorrow," *Midwest Reg. Turf. Foundn. Turf Conf. Proc.,* pp. 54–60.
39. Macbeth, N., 1928, "Bent putting greens in California," *U.S.G.A. Green Sect. Bull.* **8**(3), 58–60.
40. Moncreif, J. B., 1968, "Popular bermudagrass strains; requirements and peculiarities," *U.S.G.A. Green Sect. Rec.* **5**(7), 12–14.
41. Monteith, J. Jr., 1930, "Classification of redtop and the common bentgrasses," *U.S.G.A. Green Sect. Bull.* **10**(3), 44–50.
42. Nutter, G. C., and R. J. Allen, Jr., 1962, " 'Floratine' St. Augustinegrass. A new variety of ornamental turf," *Univ. Florida Agr. Expt. Sta. Circ.* S-123A.
43. Piper, C. V., and W. E. Stokes, 1925, "Centipedegrass *(Eremochloa ophiuroides),*" *U.S.G.A. Green Sect. Bull.* **5**(9), 196–197.

44. Radko, A. M., 1968, "Bentgrasses for putting greens," *U.S.G.A. Green Sect. Rec.* **5**(6), 11–12.
45. Roberts, E. C., 1965, "Turf-grass varieties, Part I, Northern," *Turf-grass Times.* **1**(2), 3 ff.
46. Schery, R. W., 1963, "The curious case of Highland bentgrass," *Garden J.* (N. Y. Botan. Gard.), **13**(5), 171–173.
47. Schery, R. W., 1965, "The migration of a plant," *Natural Hist. Mag.* **74**(11), 40–45.
48. Skogley, C. R. (Ed.), 1965, "Turf annual," *Park Maint.* **18**(7), 29 ff.
49. Thompson, W. R., Jr., 1966, "Turfgrass varieties, Part 2, South," *Turf-grass Times* **1**(4), 8 ff.
50. Whitton, G. M., 1968, "Bahia Grass," *Florida Turf.* **1**(2), 1ff.
51. Youngner, V. B., 1961a, "Observations on the ecology and morphology of *Pennisetum clandesinum,*" Phyton **16,** 77–84.
52. Youngner, V. B., 1961b, "Accelerated wear tests on turfgrasses," *Agron. J.* **53,**217–218.
53. Youngner, V. B., 1963, "The effects of traffic on turf," *Calif. Turfgr. Cult.* **13**(4), 28–29.
54. Youngner, V. B., 1966, "Santa Ana, a new turf bermudagrass for California," *Calif. Turfgr. Cult.* **16**(3), 23–24.
55. Youngner, V. B., 1967, "Adaptability of grasses for various types of turf," *Calif. Turfgr. Cult.* **17**(2), 13–14.
56. Youngner, V. B., J. H. Madison, and W. B. Davis, 1966, "Which is the best turfgrass," *Univ. Calif. Agr. Exten. Serv.* AXT-227, 2 pp.

****

57. *International Code of Nomenclature for Cultivated Plants,* 1969, Formulated and adopted by the international commission for the nomenclature of cultivated plants of the international union of biological sciences, Utrecht, Netherlands.

3

SOD AND SEED SELECTION AND PLANTING

The turfgrass seed industry has developed gradually with the demand for seed. Pastures and lawns have often been sown with sweepings from the barn floor where good hay had been handled. In the late 19th century Kentucky bluegrass seed began to be harvested in Kentucky. It was a desirable crop as it provided cash income and still left hay for the internal economy of the farm. Not only was seed harvested on the farm, but women and children hand harvested seed from the roadsides as a source of pin money.

Seed was harvested by machines that stripped heads from the plant. A head contains seeds in all states of development, and a curing period in the field or barn was used to dry green seed. When respiration of tissues slowed so seed heads no longer heated and moisture dropped to where mold would no longer be a problem, field seed was sold to a cleaning plant where it was threshed and cleaned.

Since the industry depended on and centered around the seed-cleaning plant, production was localized. When soils of Kentucky were depleted and insects further reduced yields, the industry moved to southern Iowa and northern Missouri. There has been some production at one time or another in most of the states from North Dakota south to Missouri and east to the Appalachians.

Production of bentgrass seed on the east and west coasts has been noted in Chapter 2. Production of bentgrass seed has centered on the west coast and principally in Oregon. When 'Merion' bluegrass seed was released, production was moved out of the midwest to reduce problems of contamination. As Oregon was already equipped to grow and process grass seed, production of 'Merion' was primarily in Oregon. Oregon has continued to produce named varieties of bluegrass. 'Newport' is a high seed producer and its release coincided with several poor seed years in the midwest. As a result, Oregon captured a major part of the market, selling surplus Merion and Newport seed as seed of common Kentucky bluegrass. I feel this has been unfortunate and that legal protection may be needed. True common bluegrass seed carries a broad genetic base of which the purchaser is deprived when pure lines are substituted under the label of "common."

A result of the change may be to allow a quality producer of midwest seed to survive by being able to charge a premium for his "wild" seed.

In Oregon, harvest is usually by combine, but the harvested seed is still of all ages and must be cured and recleaned to make a marketable seed. The straw is burned as a disease-control measure.[68]

Oregon is a major world source of turf seeds of bluegrass, bentgrasses, fescues, and ryegrasses. Other important sources are Denmark, New Zealand, Canada, and the Netherlands. Over 100,000,000 pounds of turfgrass seed are used annually in the U.S.[13,36] In one test, foreign seed performed as well as domestic, except it had more *Poa* weed species.[36]

Seed quality has usually been a problem to the consumer. Before seed trade was regulated, adulteration was common.[38] Good seed was diluted with dead seed and high-priced bentgrass seed was adulterated with various amounts of redtop.[39] It was not uncommon for the seed traders in Hamburg, Germany, to buy redtop seed from New England, relabel it mixed German bent or creeping bent, and send it back without even opening the bag.

Seed control began in England in 1869 with an act to control adulteration of seeds.[52] The act prohibited dilution with either dead seed or seeds which had been dyed to resemble other species. By 1880 the Agricultural Society of Britain was testing seeds for farmers. Hunter's, seedsmen in Chester, were the first to guarantee purity and germination of seeds they sold beginning in 1883. By 1914 most European countries were regulating seed trade. The U.S. passed a seed importation act in 1912 which did not regulate turf seeds unless they contained more than 10% redtop, which then made them agricultural seeds.

In 1918, Piper and Hillman published guides for distinguishing redtop and other commercial species of *Agrostis.*[38] Once the distinction could be made, seed could be evaluated. By 1926 when the seed act was amended to include turf seeds, shady practices had decreased. In 1917–1918, of thirty-five lots imported, fifteen were 100% redtop and four others contained appreciable redtop. Ten years later (1927–1928) sixty-seven samples of bent were tested and only two were adulterated.

Seed trade is regulated today by both federal and state laws.[93] A recommended uniform state seed law requires seed to be labeled as to the accepted name of the kind and variety; lot number; state or country of origin; percent by weight of all weed seed; name and frequency of each noxious weed seed present; percent by weight of crop seeds; and percent by weight of inert matter. For each named agricultural seed the label must state percent germination exclusive of hard seeds; percent of hard seeds if present; and month and year the test was completed. If turf seeds are mixed and packaged in lots of fifty pounds or less the label must also contain the word *mixed* or *mixture;* kinds must be separated under the headings: *fine textured grasses* and *coarse kinds:* agricultural grasses present in excess of 5% must be named. All grasses are considered coarse except *Agrostis tenuis* (including highland), *A. palustris* (i.e., *A. stolonifera), A. canina, Cynodon dactylon, Poa trivialis, P. pratensis,P. compressa, P. nemoralis, Festuca rubra* (including subsp. *commutata*), and *F. ovina*).

This labeling fails to resolve the fate of *Lolium perenne.* Perennial ryegrass has many coarse varieties but new varieties of significance are indistinguishable from Kentucky bluegrass in fineness.

Other reforms are desirable and being worked on. Bluegrass from Oregon, northern Europe, and parts of Canada may contain appreciable numbers of seeds of *Poa annua* and P. trivialis. Both are usually considered weeds. Some states are regulating the amount of seeds permitted of these weed *Poas.* Seed of the two weed *Poas* is difficult to separate from harvested seed. However, periodic fumigation of seed fields and regular roguing can clean up bluegrass seed and free the fine fescues of seeds of tall fescue and ryegrass before harvest. The clean seed would be more expensive, of course.

Weed and crop seed content has been regulated in terms of performance of agronomic crops. Its significance needs to be redefined for turf. Some noxious crop weeds are without effect on turf where regular mowing destroys them (bedstraw—*Galium spp.,* for example). On the other hand, crop seeds such as timothy and tall fescue are of no concern as impurities in a pasture mixture but are obnoxious weeds in a lawn.[76]

Certified seed is certified by a crop improvement association as being true to type. However, other quality standards are also applied to certified seed. Fields are examined for freedom from weeds and certified seed can generally be counted on to be pure as well as true to type. Certification was designed to protect purity of improved varieties. Recently, however, North Dakota has begun certifying common bluegrass seed. Certification means that the consumer is getting the wide variability of common seed.

The premium paid for certified seed is often quickly recovered in the reduced weediness when high-quality turf is grown on weed-free soil.

Seeds carry diseases. Not only should we buy the best seed possible, but it is advisable to have seed treated for disease control. Semesan, Ceresan, and Panogen are organic mercurials applied as dusts or slurries and are effective in controlling many seed-born diseases. For protection of seed against soil-borne diseases, seed may be treated with captan or thiram.

When seed of one species is thought to be contaminated by seed of another species of the same genus, such as creeping bent with colonial, or Kentucky bluegrass with Danish bluegrass *(Poa trivialis),* a determination is often difficult to make. Seeds vary widely within the species and many seeds must be examined. Separations are made on averages rather than individuals.[40,62] Seeds of some common turfgrasses are illustrated in Figure 3.1.

MIXTURES

Most grass seed is planted as part of a mixture. The historical tendency is to begin a new use or practice with many mixtures of many grasses and legumes and evolve to a few mixes of a few species or to a monoculture. This is illustrated in a recent study by Boeker.*
In Germany, regulations for seeding along the autobahnen called for 110 mixtures involving twenty-seven grasses and twenty forbs. Studies showed these mixtures could be replaced by two mixtures of four species, *Agrostis tenuis, Festuca rubra, F. ovina,* and *Poa pratensis.* These grasses establish a turf in a variety of soils and environments. More fescue is used in the mix where the environment is droughty. From a cover of these grasses a number of natural plant communities can arise.

A mixture of grasses may be made for several reasons. At times, part of the mixture has been considered a nurse crop. The idea of a nurse crop is that a few quick-germinating, fast-growing grasses can emerge ahead of

*P. Boeker, 1969, First International Turfgrass Conference, Proceedings, in press.

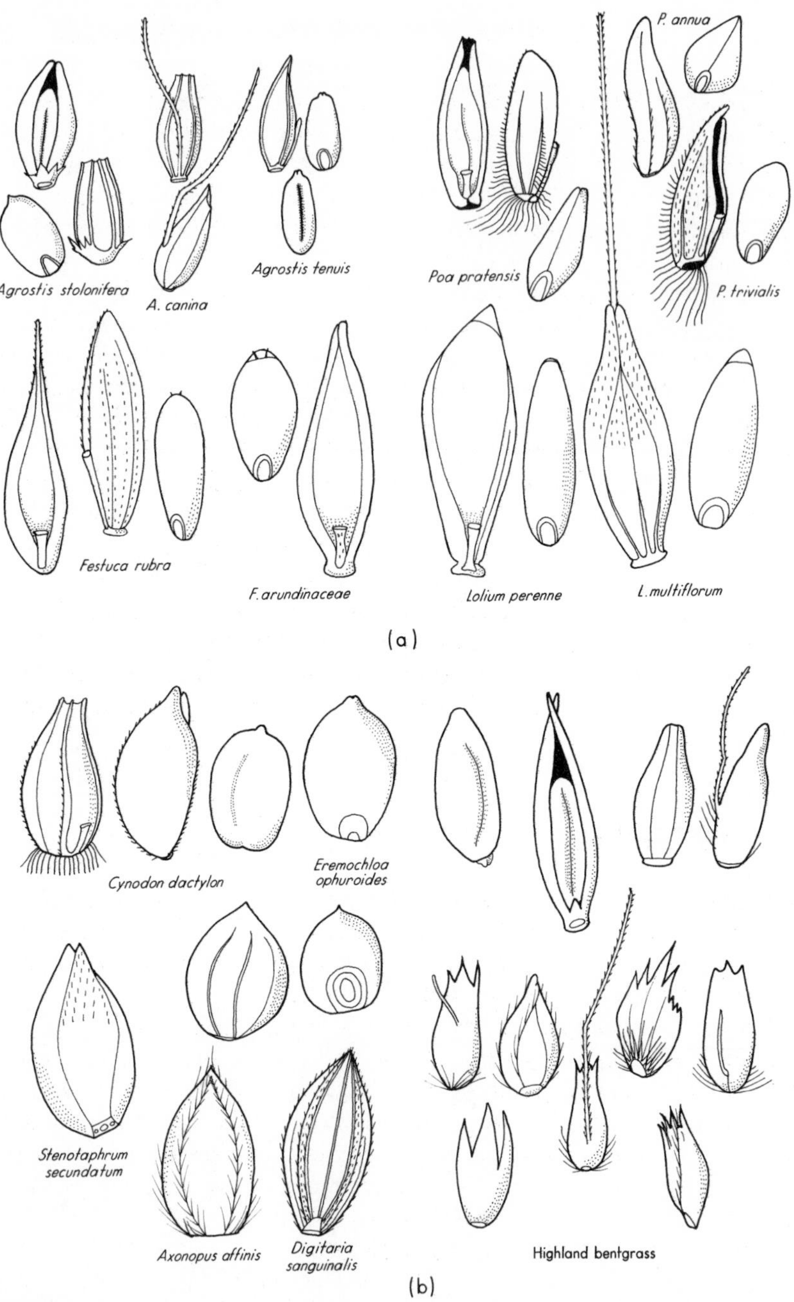

Figure 3.1 Turfgrass seeds. The larger seeds are drawn larger, but true proportions are not maintained. Also there is great variability among seeds. Many degrees of hairiness exist with a species and plants shown with awns may have a high percentage of seeds without awns in some lots and vice versa. Highland bentgrass seeds (b) illustrate to a degree the amount of variability.

the desired grasses and ameliorate the severity of the climate for finer grasses to follow. The nurse grass shades the soil and reduces temperature extremes. It slows wind movement, and increases thickness of the water boundary layer, so evaporation is retarded. Unfortunately, nurse grasses also compete vigorously with the desired grasses for water, minerals, and light and reduce stands of the better grasses. When soil can be kept adequately moist during germination, nurse grasses are a detriment and undesirable.[26,46] If nurse grasses are used they should be a small percent of the mixture.[60,65]

A second kind of mixture is made by the commercial seedsman. A person buying seed in a drug or hardware store seldom knows what he wants and store personnel are not qualified to advise him. A mix is blended to cover a variety of contingencies. A typical quality lawn mix will contain 50–75% Kentucky bluegrass, some of which is likely to be of named varieties. Bluegrass is the standard quality lawngrass in the United States and is the basic grass in the blend. The mix contains 25–40% red fescue as a shade grass and usually part of the fescue is as Chewing's and part as creeping red fescue. Chewing's is a name the public has heard and it may be included because of familiarity rather than performance. As the above two grasses need higher mowing and the consumer may mow closely, 5–10% of colonial or highland bentgrass may be included. Under a close cut, bentgrass may form the final lawn, but at higher cuts it ends up a weed in a bluegrass lawn. These three grasses form a basic seed mix for the temperate climate. In some sections of the country some white clover may be added to this. The above mixture is often cut with about 20% meadow fescue which germinates quickly and provides an immediate reward to the homeowner for his efforts. The first-season seedling meadow fescue has a texture and color that blends with bluegrass and it doesn't become coarse till later. Under good management meadow fescue is only weakly persistent.

The above kind of mix may be further cut with seeds of meadow fescue or ryegrass to produce a series of mixtures of different price. Price of home seed mixes is illusory. For example I took the entire line of one quality seed house and recalculated price in terms of price per one million seeds. On this basis there was a difference of a penny a million, but for the extra four cents quality seeds could be obtained; the other three grades contained increasing amounts of meadow fescue. Five pounds of the quality line sowed 2000 square feet whereas five pounds of the utility mixture sowed 800 square feet at an equivalent seeds per square foot rate. As an extreme example of low price, achieved by using improper seeds, I picked a bag from the shelf of a supermarket in Iowa. The five-pound bag sold for 98¢ and was next to mixtures selling from $1.00 a pound up. The name was similar to *Kentucky Lawn Mix.* Over 10% of the mixture was of weed and crop seeds and of inert. The grass seeds were 2% bluegrass and 88% timothy.

A segment of the public is becoming increasingly knowledgeable and wants bluegrass–fescue mixtures uncontaminated by bents and broad-leaved grasses. But price continues to be a factor limiting this market.

The professional turf manager generally prefers to select the grass suited to his planned use and to sow it without mixing. The finest lawns are of a single species of grass. The professional still finds good reasons for mixing grasses, however. In England mixtures may be of a tough, tillering grass, such as ryegrass or fescue, with a "bottom" grass to fill in and give good density.

Varieties of bluegrass are often mixed. Performance of such a mixture is below that of the best variety in the mix but better than of the poorest variety. The mixture may have a better disease response than that of the individual varieties. 'Merion' bluegrass, for example, is extremely subject to rust in pure stands but in mixtures it does not show unusual amounts of rust. Beard has noted the same effect when mixing species.[8] In a mixture, effects of disease on a single species were reduced.

Sod growers mix bluegrasses to include varieties they have found to knit rapidly. Number and length of stolons and rate of emergence and initiation of a new cycle are characteristics affecting sod.[51]

With present varieties of bluegrass divided between dwarf and standard types there is a question as to whether a mix should contain one or both types. As each will thrive under a different management, mixing would tend to be wasteful. When a dwarf variety is included in mixtures of standard varieties it tends to increase density of stand. Increased density is not always good, however. A dense bluegrass retains a higher humidity and may be more subject to *Helminthosporium* or other diseases than a more open turf.

Red fescue is commonly mixed with Kentucky bluegrass because of its compatibility of color and texture and its increased tolerance to shade. When a landscape contains appreciable shade, up to half the mix may be fescue. In new landscapes less than 10% fescue will provide a sufficient start, with the fescue quite able to spread as rapidly as shade from growing trees.

When large areas having a variety of environments are sown a mixture may be used to provide grasses adapted to the situations encountered. With several moist shady pockets at the base of slopes, one might include some seed of *Poa trivialis* in the mixture, etc. This approach is often used in highway work where rapid changes in elevation and exposure result in a variety of growing environments.

In the transition zone, tall fescue grass is used for school football fields and play yards. As tall fescue is a bunch grass it has seemed reasonable to mix blue or bermudagrass with it to fill in worn spots. In practice this does not work. As a pure stand tall fescue makes a good even turf.

But creeping grasses mixed in tend to separate tall fescue into clumps to produce an uneven and undesirable turf. Reseeding of worn spots is preferable.

Over the years there have been efforts to find a two-component mix for subtropical areas, so that winter overseeding would not be necessary.[59] Bermuda has been tried with highland bentgrass, *Poa bulbosa,* and *Poa annua.* When bermudagrass is opened up in the fall *Poa annua* develops a satisfactory winter turf.[100] At present there are several successful areas of mixed C-52 bentgrass and 'Tifgreen' bermudagrass. Both are extremely vigorous and each manages to persist in the presence of the other. As seasons change, shift in dominance from one variety to the other is so rapid that no long period of transition results as with other combinations noted above. No recommendation are made, but the possibility of a successful combination is noted.

GRASS SELECTION

When pure stands of grass are well grown at favorable seasons, all look excellent and there is often little to choose among them. Grown in mixtures, differences in survival and performance appear, and the more extreme the environment the more selective. If such selection were positive one would need only to sow a mixture of seeds and survival would be of the best adapted grass. In practice, when a mix is sown, individuals of each species manage to survive and compete so that a turf of motley shades and textures results. Grasses best adapted to the environment will predominate, however, and management will be easier and more effective if only those are grown.

Sometimes climate is an overriding environmental factor. In Rhode Island, Great Britian, or coastal Oregon, for example, colonial bentgrass is so favored that if it is not grown, it will still come to dominate whatever grass is sown. Management is simplified if colonial bentgrass is accepted as a principal grass. Similarly, other climates will favor bermudagrass, bluegrass, or ryegrass, among others.

Where climate is favorable, mineral status of the soil may become important. Perennial ryegrass and Kentucky bluegrass require good calcium levels and high fertility whereas colonial bent is indifferent to pH and sheep's fescue *(F. ovina)* needs an acid soil and tolerates low fertility.[21,7,43] In Great Britain a turf of colonial bent and mat grass *(Nardus stricta)* will often yield to perennial rye when limed.

Soil physical condition affects competition. Colonial bentgrass persists in sandy soils but is dominated by red fescue on heavy soils. With adequate fertility present, both red fescue and colonial bent will yield to ryegrass under the intense compacting traffic on sports turf. On extremely compacted soils, *Poa annua* may be the most persistant grass if moist conditions exist.[66]

Effects of management on competition may be difficult to anticipate. Bermuda is a summer grass in California whereas bent is favored by winter temperatures. Several persons have reasoned that winter fertilization would favor bent, summer fertilization bermudagrass. Tested experimentally, winter fertilization did not affect the competition; summer fertilization favored bentgrass.[56] Bentgrass has many shallow roots whereas bermudagrass has deep roots that are more widely spaced. Bentgrasses could get more nitrogen than bermuda from summer fertilizer and since competition is most active in summer, bent was favored. In the winter when there was no competition, fertilizer was of no advantage to bentgrass. Similarly, bermudagrass withstands closer mowing than bluegrass. When closely mowed, bermuda invaded bluegrass at a slower rate because stolons were cut back.

There have been studies of the competitive relations of turfgrasses in various mixtures.[25,59,63] At this point I do not think we have sufficient data from these studies to draw generalizations except that climate, soil chemistry, and soil physical condition may significantly favor one species or another and that shaded and wet areas often have a different composition than surrounding turf. When a species is in a favored environment, a small percent of seed in a mix is sufficient to establish the species. In a less favored spot, degree of establishment may depend on the percent of seed.[36]

Although management is easier with adapted grasses, other grasses are often chosen. Bluegrass is generally the grass of first choice for decorative turf and may be generally planted even in bermudagrass country. In a region where it is not adapted, even improved varieties of a grass will do poorly. This leads to dissatisfaction in their performance compared to anticipation.

Selection of grasses has been discussed in Chapter 2. Let me call attention again to two alternatives. We may select the grass and adapt the management program, or we may select the management program and then choose the best adapted grass. The latter is often the more successful approach.

A recent study has suggested selecting an athletic turf for its ability to absorb shock. More energy was absorbed with grass present, with dense bermudagrasses, with wet soil, and with sawdust-amended soil. Ability to absorb shock is proposed as a safety feature.[33] Trainers and coaches consider that the ability of turf to absorb shock is important for chronic knee and ankle ailments that arise from running on hard ground. Acute and severe injuries arise when activity has put tension on muscles and joints, and then a sudden impact, especially a twisting motion, overextends the already stressed parts. Safety requires there be no tight network of stolons that could catch cleats and fail to release them under torque.

GERMINATION OF SEEDS[91,92]

Longevity of seed is limited. The embryo is a bit of living tissue and as such continues to use energy and respire. In time, stored reserves are used to a point where growth is no longer possible. Any factor that increases respiration decreases longevity and vice versa. For best longevity seed should be stored at low temperatures and low moisture. Samples buried in the soil lost viability after the third winter for Chewing's fescue, perennial rye, and Kentucky bluegrass.[70] Highland bent and annual rye still germinated a bit less than 20%. *Zoysia* seed stored dry and cold (40°F) germinated 70% after six years and continued to germinate for four more years.[69]

When seed is freshly harvested it may be dormant and fail to germinate during a ripening period. During this time bluegrass may germinate at lower temperatures (5°C night, 10°C day).[81] Light, as well as cold, will help relieve dormancy and increase germination.[29,56] In testing seed, 0.1% KNO_3 solution is used to wet the seed and helps to overcome dormancy.[90] After six months seed is no longer dormant. A dormancy of bahia and bermudagrasses is due to a tight impermeable hull and hulled seed should be used for good germination.

Seed viability is affected by conditions of harvest.[30] When heads were windrowed germination was little affected by age of seed heads at harvest.[22] Combined seed became heated in the bag and lost germinability unless combined when seed was too dry to heat.

Temperature affects germination and most grass seeds other than fescues germinate best when temperatures alternate daily between higher and lower values.[27] Blue, bent, and bermudagrasses all require fluctuating temperature for effective germination. In various tests using differing day and night temperatures, optimum germination has been reported at 15–25 °C for rye, fescue, and bluegrass;[37] 12–25°C for ryegrass;[11] 13–30°C and 10–26°C for bluegrass;[44] 5–21°C for *Poa annua;*[42] and 10–38°C for bermudagrass.[61] Differences in optimum temperatures were found among ecotypes.[42,44]

Oxygen is generally needed for germination but some grasses can germinate under essentially anaerobic conditions (rice, e.g.). Bermudagrass has germinated satisfactorily under water and in air-dilution experiments germination was optimum with 8% oxygen in the atmosphere.[61]

Limited availability of water often limits germination. Under such conditions, germination and stand have been improved by use of suitable mulches. Hexaoctadecanol has been used to retard evaporation.[3] Sprayed on seed it slowed germination, but an emulsion applied to the soil at 225 pounds per acre improved germination and rate of cover.

In a test of drought tolerance, Rainier red fescue was found to tolerate more drying during germination than 'Ilahee,' 'Pennlawn,' or 'Chewings' but common was almost as tolerant as 'Rainier.' Of bluegrasses 'Merion' and 'Park' were more tolerant than 'Newport,' 'Windsor,' 'Delta,' 'Arboretum,' 'Geary,' or common.[99]

Various other factors affect germination. Seed quality varies year to year as a result of climate. Schery has compared light and heavy fractions of bluegrass seed.[75] Heavy fractions germinated well but variability was observed in the performance of the light fractions. Fresh sawdust in the seed bed may produce inhibitors of germination.[45] Genetic factors may affect seedling vigor,[35] and there are species differences given in Table 3.1. Bluegrass requires the longest time to germinate. Seeding depth is treated later.

SEEDBED

A turf may be grown by raking seed into the surface soil. That deep tillage is of benefit however, is well demonstrated by the often superior performance of turf seeded over irrigation lines where trenching machines have thoroughly stirred the soil to eighteen inches or more of depth. Tillage may increase noncapillary porosity. In addition deep tillage may break up impervious layers in the soil, bring mineral-rich soil to the surface, carry organic matter deeper into the soil, and stimulate nitrification.

Subsoiling is sometimes used to fracture plow-pans or other soil layers. This is most effective on a dry soil but unless the soil is settled with several inches of water before final grading it may settle later into alternate hollows and ridges which make mowing and other maintenance practices difficult. (See *Principles of Turfgrass Culture,* Figure 5.10.)

Turf soil is most commonly tilled with rototillers or discs. Both produce a fine seedbed if soil is at a suited moisture level; both set up clods when used on soil that is too moist or too dry.

In addition to tillage there are three important practices in preparing a good seedbed; fertilizing, controlling weeds, and amending the soil to limit crusting and encourage seedling emergence.

On weedy land, weed-control costs are largely recovered in more rapid establishment of the turf and lowered costs during the establishment period. After the land is prepared, a few weeks of fallow to germinate seeds will give some weed control if the soil is not stirred again. To avoid cultivation, germinated weeds can be controlled with a contact herbicide of short life such as a light oil.

Calcium cyanamide gives excellent but not complete weed control along with seedbed nitrogen. Fifty pounds of calcium cyanamide per thousand square feet is used. Half is tilled into the top two to three inches of soil. The remaining half is spread on the surface and lightly raked in. The soil should be moist as the reaction is a hydrolysis (See also *Principles of Turfgrass Culture,* Chap. 7). Planting is delayed one to four weeks.

Soil fumigants are available for use with or without tarpaulins and for professional or common application (see Chap. 9).

Nitrogen and phosphorus need to be readily available in the soil solution to get rapid establishment of turfgrass seedlings. Phosphorus is readily fixed by the soil and soluble phosphorus will give a response even in a soil that gives a good test for available phosphorus.[55] Without soluble phosphorus the seedlings stand still until the root system matures sufficiently to supply phosphorus. Nitrogen is needed for rapid establishment and on sterile or worn-out soils establishment may be directly proportional to the nitrogen supplied, not only in the seedbed but during the first few months. This is particularly true on highway cuts where sterile subsoils are exposed. I have often seen jobs where turf establishment would have been greatly improved if half as much seed had been used and the money spent on nitrogen fertilizer instead. If the weather is suited, monthly applications of nitrogen can be used with advantage until the soil is covered by grass, and looking straight down one sees only leaf blades and no areas of bare ground. Seeds, stolons, and sod benefit equally from seedbed nitrogen and phosphorus.

Because both nitrogen and phosphorus are needed, a soil test is seldom used to guide seedbed application. Instead a complete fertilizer is used to insure good growth and rapid development.

When fertilizer is placed on the surface of the seed bed there is possibility of salt injury. When a 5–10–5 was used in New Jersey, 5–10 lb/M (1/4–1/2 lb of N/M) placed on the surface did not affect seedlings; but growth was halved by salt injury when 20–40 lb/M were used (1–2 lb N/M). A heavy application of fertilizer in the seedbed could be made safely by tilling in all except 5 lb/M which was spread on the surface.[53]

When amendments are used to lessen soil crusting and increase seed emergence only a small amount is needed to mix in the top quarter inch. Best results in a trial were obtained by replacing soil over the seed with a material that did not crust.[32] Successful materials included vermiculite and coke. A sixteenth to an eighth inch of sand is an effective surface

Table 3.1. Seeding Data of Various Species

Grass Species	*Approximate Seeds per lb*	*Rates to Sow (lb/M-lawn)*	*Rates to Sow (lb/acre-field)*	*Days to Germinate*	*Av Germination*	*Av Purity*	*July Mean (°F) Favorable Climate*	*Comments*
Agrostis canina velvent bent	8-11,000,000	1-4	40-50	5-12	90%	95%	65	Not commonly available in the U.S.
A. tenuis highland bent	8,000,000	1-4	40-60	5-12	90	95	68-70	Mediterranean climate
A. stolonifera creeping bent	6-7,000,000	1/2-3	30-50	5-12	90	95	68	Coastal climate
A. tenuis colonial bent	7-8,000,000	1-4	40-60	5-12	90	95	68	Coastal climate
Cynodon dactylon bermudagrass	1,750,000	1/2-3	10-40		85	97	76+	Use hulled seed, or increase rates by 50%.
C.X. transvaalensis hybrid bermuda	stolons						78+	
Eremochloa ophuroides centipedegrass	410,000	1/2-1	15-25		70	50	80+	Availability limited

Festuca arundinacea tall fescue	230,000	10-15	400	6-12	90	97	74 —	Performs best alone; don't use in mixes
F. pratensis meadow fescue	230,000	2-6	60-80	6-12	90	97	72 —	Meadow and red fescue are used in mixtures and do not form a tight turf alone
F. rubra red fescue	615,000	2-6	60-80	5-12	80	97	68 —	
Lolium multiflorum annual ryegrass	230,000			5-8	90	97	65 —	Used only as overseeded turf at from 2-5 lb/M for greenup to 40-80 lb on greens
L. perenne perennial ryegrass	230,000	2-6	60-80		90	97	65 —	
Paspalum notatum bahiagrass	165,000	1/2-1	15-25		70	70	80 +	Availability limited; usually sprigged
Pennisetum clanestinum kikuyugrass	stolons						68 —	Cool subtropical; no seed
Poa annua annual bluegrass	2,200,000	1/2-2	20-40		60	80		Basically a winter grass; seed not normally harvested but available by advance contract
P. pratensis Kentucky bluegrass	2,200,000	1-4	40-80	6-30	80	85	72 —	

Table 3.1 cont'd.

Grass Species	*Approximate Seeds per lb*	*Rates to Sow (lb/M-lawn)*	*Rates to Sow (lb/acre-field)*	*Days to Germinate*	*Av Germination*	*Av Purity*	*July Mean (°F) Favorable Climate*	*Comments*
P. trivialis roughstalked bluegrass	2,500,000	1-4	40-80	6-30	80	85	60−	
Stenographrum secundatum St. Augustinegrass	stolons						80+	Sod and stolons
Zoysia japonica Japanese lawngrass	1,300,000				24		75+	Variable from seed; stolons used
Z. matrella manillagrass	680,000				50	90	80+	Variable from seed; stolons used
Z. tenuifolia	stolons mascarenegrass						80+	Vegetatively propagated

mulch aiding emergence and retarding drying. Readily decomposed organic matter helps aggregation of surface soil, and organic matter of low activity such as peat dilutes surface soil and limits the crust to small disconnected areas a seed can dislodge. A straw (or equivalent) mulch breaks the force of water drops and reduces crusting, and by keeping surface soil moist and plastic, it aids emergence.

RATE OF SEEDING

A seedling catch of one to fifty seedlings per square inch will give a mature turf, with time to maturity unaffected by numbers in this range. One half pound of seed per 1000 square feet and four pounds per 1000 square feet are of essentially the same order of magnitude and are hardly to be argued over. Seedlings spaced more widely grow more vigorously and form a mature turf in the same time as those spaced closer and in a shorter time than seedlings that are overcrowded.[57,60,67] When conditions in the seedbed are so severe as to result in high attrition of seedlings, high rates may be needed to get even a small stand. Such a situation is unusual, and a preferred solution to the problem is to modify the environment rather than sow high rates.

In the early years of this century seed quality was often poor and seed houses recommended 10–20 lb/M of seed that germinated as low as 10 to 20%. As seed sources improved, the research men at Arlington recommended 5 lb of bent seed per 1000 ft^2 as a maximum, and noted, "Heavier rates of seeding than that indicated are never justifiable and will not increase the chance of getting a perfect stand."[67]

Madison investigated rate and depth of seeding of blue and bentgrasses.[57] At rates of 8 lb/1000 ft^2 seedlings were too dense and maturation was delayed. Maturation could only take place when numbers were reduced, usually by disease, and if a fungicide was used, maturation of bentgrass seedlings was delayed for an entire growing season. Rates used were from 1 to 8 lb/1000 ft^2. After five months of growing weather, final populations were the same in all plots. But the final population was by attrition at high rates, by tiller production at low rates. Although 1 or 2 lb of seed per 1000 ft^2 were found adequate for optimum stands, Madison worked on clean ground.

Weeds compete with turf. Kemmerer and Butler found a 3-lb rate in the spring better unless crabgrass was controlled.[47] Then 1 1/2 lb was as good as 3 with common bluegrass and 1/2 lb was as good as 3 with 'Merion.'

While studying control of seed-borne diseases, Smith found disease to be higher when seed was thickly sown.[80] His heavy rate was equivalent to about 5 lb of red fescue seed per 1000 ft.^{2}

Seeding rates are suggested in Table 3.1. When tall fescue is used for turf, it is deliberately sown at high rates to crowd seedlings and cause them to grow with a finer and narrower leaf. When putting-green turf is overseeded with annual ryegrass, high rates are used, which keep the grass in seedling condition all winter. The seedlings die in the spring without developing mature leaves. Rates actually used have sometimes exceeded 100 lb/M (150 seeds/square inch). More disease was found on over-seeded rye at 80 lb/M than when seeded at 40 lb/M.[88]

DEPTH OF SEEDING

A seedling can emerge from a depth which depends on seed size and vigor. A simple but valuable test can be made as illustrated in Figure 3.2. Soil is placed in a flat and firmed to form a seedbed that runs on a diagonal from the flat bottom at one end to the flat top at the other end. Rows of seed are sown and the flat is filled and struck level. The result

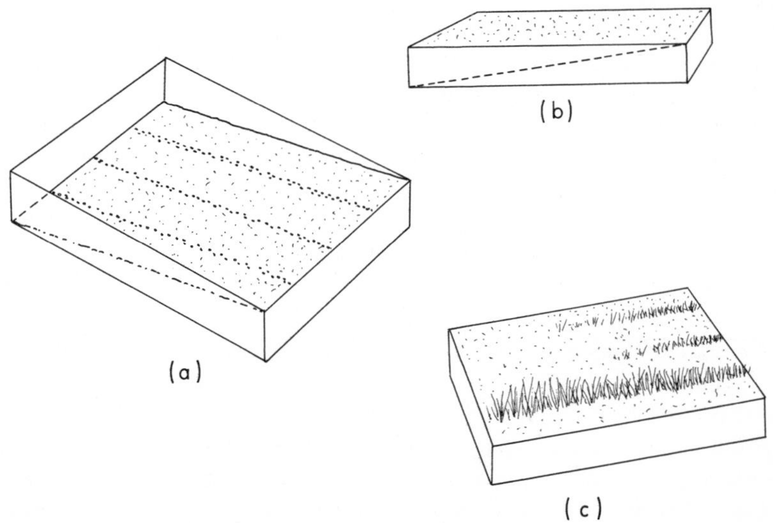

Figure 3.2 This simple test illustrates differences in vigor of seeds of different species or varieties. A wedge of soil is placed in the flat **(a)** and rows of seeds are sown. When the flat is filled **(b)** the row is covered at a depth which varies from 2 to 2 1/2 in. at one end of the flat to 0 in. at the other end. Few seeds emerge from the deeper end **(c)** unless the seeds have very high vigor. There will also be more rapid growth where fewer seeds come up, as there will be less crowding.

is seed sown at depths from 0 to about 2 in. Seeds of fine turfgrasses seldom emerge from depths greater than 1 in. This test is useful for comparing vigor of seeds in different lots.

Madison found bluegrass emergence unaffected at 0–1/4 in. depth in the field. At 1/2 in., emergence was reduced, but seedlings which emerged were more vigorous. Bentgrass produced the largest stand when firmed into the surface but emerged when covered 1/8 in. With more cover, emergence was reduced but again resulting plants were more vigorous.[57]

Van Slijken found with a mixture of colonial bent and fescue that emergence was halved when seed was sown deeper than 10 mm (0.4 in.).[94]

Seed depth was a problem when agricultural drills were used. Dropping seed between the rolls of a cultipacker has been effective. Today several machines are available especially designed for seeding turfgrasses. The special equipment does a good job and may disc, seed, firm, and mulch in a single operation.

SEASON OF SEEDING

Subtropical grasses are favored by heat. Seed, sod, and stolons are best planted in early summer. Temperature-season grasses are best sown at favorable seasons which vary with the geography. In California the best time is mid-October, and each succeeding month is less desirable; after late April or early May climate is no longer favorable. In the middle states, fall seeding is preferred; the season extends from late August to the third week in September. In northern states fall seeding is critical and seed sown after the first week in September may not mature sufficiently to prevent winter injury. Seeding should be sufficiently early to cover soil with grass as this prevents frost heaving. In the northern half of the U.S. a second choice is to sow on frozen ground in late winter. Early spring months provide the remaining favorable time.

Turf is in fact sown every month of the year. The reason for favoring fall months are: fall temperatures favor the grass and damping off is less of a problem than with warmer temperatures; evapotranspiration is about half the summer peak so less attention to water is needed and often fall rains reduce any need for hand watering; and weeds which germinate with a fall seeding are of species which are usually easily controlled compared to spring and summer weeds, many of which are difficult of control. Fall-germinated grass develops a better root system before summer temperatures limit further root growth. In brief, success is easier to achieve with a fall seeding.

Time of sowing has been studied at Massachusetts. Seed was sowed at two-week intervals from April to September. The following lists dates from best to poorest grouped by Duncan's test:[15]

Best	Sept. 1
	Sept. 15
	May 1, May 15
	June 1, Aug. 15
	June 15
Poorest	July 1, July 15, Aug. 1

In their trials, moisture availability was a limiting factor during some summer periods.

In the southern part of the transition zone it is often difficult to know whether to sow in midwinter or wait till spring. A midwinter sowing germinates slowly and seldom outgrows the green fuzz stage. Tips are apt to get frosted and if a period of overcast persists some damage occurs from *Fusarium* patch. When growing days arrive in late February, seedlings have already put down a root system and grow rapidly. Chances of a washout are greater in winter but only areas washed out need to be reworked and resown, and these areas would have to be resown anyway. With luck, seed will germinate rapidly enough to be of some help in controlling erosion. There are possible losses and gains, but in general persons who have taken the risk of winter sowing have been satisfied with their choice.

STOLONS AND SOD

Seedbeds may be treated the same in all respects for stolons and sod as for seed, with the exception that the grade should be lowered 1 1/2 to 2 in. for sod, and soil should be stockpiled for covering stolons and truing sod. Stolons are sown at from 2 to 6 bushels/1000 ft^2; for rapid cover, over double that rate should be used. Rates depend in part on the equipment available to plant the stolons as well as rate of cover desired. Various pieces of local equipment are used to sow stolons and vary from adapted row planters, to discs to cut the stolons in, to rollers to press them in (see Fig. 3.3). Machinery for handling sod and stolons is currently in a state of rapid development.[64] Small areas may be hand planted by: *(1)* raking to raise ridges and furrows; *(2)* spreading stolons; *(3)* rolling; *(4)* spreading topdressing and rerolling; and *(5)* immediately irrigating.

Careful scheduling is needed when planting sod and stolons. These materials cannot sit around on the job; deterioration is rapid. Irrigation

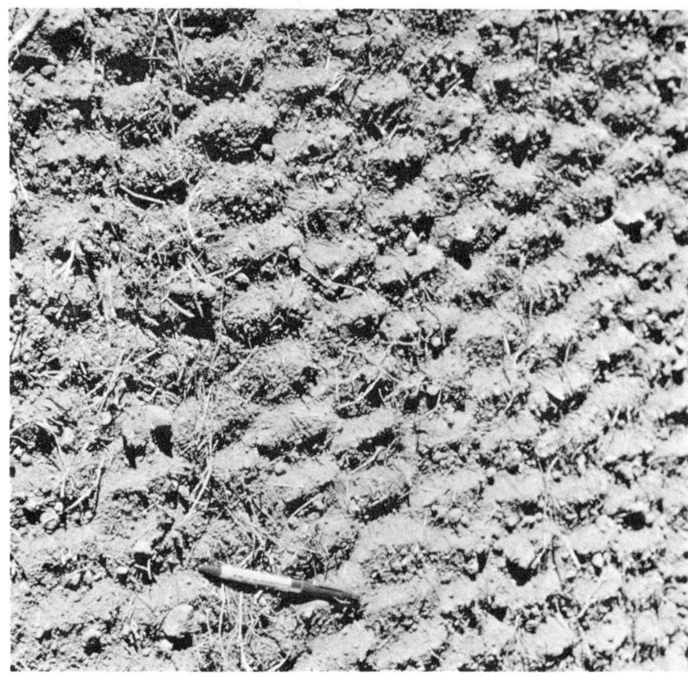

Figure 3.3 "Seedbed" with stolons planted by one of several machines available for such planting.

systems should be operable, and grade and seedbed established before these are delivered on the job. Careful estimation of sod will facilitate spotting of pallets, resulting in a minimum of carrying.

STOLONS

Stolons are preferably grown in a sandy soil that will shake loose. A foot row of stolons in the nursery will grow in one season to cover about 4–7 ft^2, sufficient to plant about 500 ft^2. This is harvested and cut to provide pieces that are 2–3 in. long with about 1–3 buds per piece. Stolons are respiring and will heat if deeply piled. Usually they are cooled by icing, by spraying with cold water, or by placing in a vacuum chamber and cooling by evaporation. If temperatures are high, a fungidical dip may be used for added protection.[82] Dry stolons may be held for several weeks at 31°F. They are soaked on coming out of storage. Received on the job, stolons should be piled so they are ventilated, so they can be sprinkled, and so they are protected from sun and wind. In hot weather they can be iced, the melting ice both cooling and wetting the stolons. If kept shaded, moist and ventilated, stolons can be held on the job up to six days. One planting machine uses sod, shredding it into stolons in the machine. Sod is hardier and easier to care for prior to planting.

Planting patterns should follow irrigation patterns, and as soon as a section is planted it should be irrigated. Grether suggests that at 100°F springs should be watered within 15 min of planting, within 20 min at 90 °F, 1/2 hr at 80°F, 1 hr at 70°F, and 2 hr at 60°F.[34] Under high heat, planting should be done only early and late in the day. If the planting machine does not sufficiently firm the soil, rolling is in order. Until it germinates, the stolon needs firm contact to get water from the soil. Frequent light sprinkling rather than deep irrigation is desired during the 7–10 days of germination. During the growing season 10 bushels/M will give a playable surface in two months, give or take a week.

Studies have been made on bermudagrass stolons. Stored on concrete or damp sand for 16 days, germination dropped from 90% to 35% but if stolons were turned and sprinkled on alternate days, germination remained at 90% throughout the 16 days.[20] Coastal bermudagrass harvested between October and February germinated an average of 96%; after 20 days in storage 94.7% germinated. If stored in a 70°F greenhouse, tender sprouts developed that were too fragile for machine planting.[10] Dormant stolons harvested March 1st were compared to stolons in active growth harvested May 22. After 24 hr of drying in air at 80% relative humidity, dormant stolons germinated 86%, active 100%. After 48 hr, dormant grew 33%, active 40%; but after 3 days, dormant still germinated 27% whereas active stolons failed to germinate.[97] At Mississippi, *Zoysia* and Tiflawn stolons were dug and planted in October, December, and February. Survival was sufficient to warrant a conclusion that *Zoysia* could be planted during its dormant season.[89] Survival was higher from plugs than from stolons, and a mulch reduced erosion.

When bermudagrass stolons were planted 0, 1, or 2 in. deep, emergence was complete in 16 days, but at 4 in. emergence took 31 days.[20]

SOD [CD]

Growing lawns from sod has been long practiced on a small scale. Sharp practices gave the potential industry a bad name early in the century. With production and promotion of high-quality sod, including certified sod, the industry has grown rapidly in the decades since 1950. Production centers in the states of California, Florida, Illinois, Maryland, Michigan, New Jersey, New York, Ontario, and Wisconsin and is primarily of bluegrass, bermudagrass, and St. Augustinegrass, with minor production of bents and *Zoysias.* By 1968 there were estimated to be about 80,000 acres in sod, producing an annual value of about $125,000,000.

Sod is produced largely on peat or loam soils. Sandy soils do not hold together during operations of cutting, rolling, and transporting sod. Soils used for sod raise a primary objection to sod. When the root zone of heavily trafficked areas has been extensively modified, use of sod may introduce a layer of compactable soil that nullifies benefits from soil modification. When soil must be laid over a modified root zone, it is common practice to go over the area in a week or ten days with a hole puncher, remove cores, and top dress with the root-zone material. This is repeated several times in the first few months.

Sod is an effective means of producing turf (see Fig. 3.4). Good sod is skillfully grown from good seed and has weeds under control. It is quickly laid to provide a turf of immediate visual satisfaction and one that can be used within two weeks to a month. Sod can be laid at any season

Figure 3.4 A well-laid sod from a good grower provides an almost instant turf, free of weeds, and of good quality. *Courtesy W. B. Davis.*

—at times when seed would fail. Although sod costs more, cost can often be recovered. Seeded turf can lose its cost advantage from the expense of dealing with one extensive weeding. Months earlier use of sodded turf may obviate any cost considerations.

One California landscape contractor has figured a breaking point at 45 days of maintenance. If a contract calls for him to maintain a new turf for 45 or more days after seeding, he finds it cheaper to lay sod instead. A principal benefit to the contractor is that he pleases his customer with a bonus while completing his contract early. When he uses sod on a 60-day maintenance contract for seed, his money is due and payable 60 days sooner. This has the effect of increasing the contractor's working capital. When interest is high and loans are hard to get, this is a valuable asset.

Sod is cut in various sizes. It may be cut 18 in. x 6 ft, so each roll contains one square yard. It may be cut 2 ft wide in long rolls, so the resulting turf has a minimum number of seams when laid. Or it may be cut 1 ft x 2 ft to provide many small sods which are light and easy to push around into place. This is largely a personal matter and may depend on how crews were trained.

Sod should be cut thinly. Adhering soil provides a reservoir for moisture during transport and establishment, and probably has no other value. Establishment is by production of new adventitious roots rather than branching of old cut roots. New roots soon emerge from thin sod, whereas roots from thick sod (ca 2 in.) may fail to penetrate the soil interface and remain largely in the sod layer.

In a study, sod was cut at 1/2, 1, and 2 in. One week later the 1/2 in. sod had a firm hold; after two weeks the 1/2-in. sod was firmly attached and roots were emerging from the 1-in. sod; after seven weeks the 2-in. sod was still unattached.[2] Rooting has been increased by laying sod on moist soil as compared to laying on dry soil, even when adequate irrigation followed.[48] Rooting has been increased on clay subsoil by tilling in sandy loam.[73] In one test sod from organic soil produced more roots than sod from mineral soil.

As with seed and stolons, irrigation is critical during sod establishment.

Weed-free sod will generally bury and suppress weed seeds in the seedbed. However, quackgrass, bermudagrass, and, to some extent, *Poa annua* will appear in the new turf if they were present in the seedbed. When sod is top dressed to fill in and level out cracks and joints, weeds can be introduced unless clean top dressing is used.

Warren calculates that once the soil is ready a man should lay

500–600 yards a day on rough work such as highway work, unless the sod is cut thick and heavy.[96] On home lawns 300–350 yards a day can be laid. On a putting green he considers that a man laying more than 100 yards a day is not taking sufficient pains. In the case of putting greens, cost estimates should include one top dressing; on highway work, costs should include hauling water.

In Michigan and Florida organic soils are used for growing sod. Research has not shown important differences between sod from organic soils and that from mineral soils, but users tend to prefer that from mineral soils, claiming better long-term performance. Sod from organic soils has a lower shipping cost, and holds more available water during shipment.[48] Florida mucks are low in minor elements and growers give special attention to copper, zinc, iron, and manganese fertility. Rolling is used prior to cutting organic sods to increase their ability to hold together.[88]

The goal in sod production is to produce a strongly knit turf in a minimum time. The crop is based on rhizome production rather than leaf production, and mowing and fertilizer practices are modified accordingly. Mowing is higher, nitrogen levels are kept relatively low, and phosphorus and potassium levels are normal or high.

Nitrogen is used in sod fields at rates of 1 lb/M/mo until seedlings begin to cover. Rates are then reduced to encourage root and rhizome production. Rates may be on the order of 1/3–2/3 lb/M/mo for 'Merion' or 1/4–1/2 lb/M/mo for common bluegrass.[73] Rates may be reduced in the summer, and doubled in September. Sod may be greened with nitrogen just prior to cutting. Nitrogen released from organic soils during warm weather may encourage top growth and slow the harvest.[73a]

There are reports that cutting sod on an old turf and permitting it to reroot in place stimulates and improves the turf.[74] A study by Hodges failed to show benefit though his experiment was not conducted at the most favorable season.[41] He cut the sod in June. September or October would be considered optimum months.

PLUGGING

Small spaced sods are sometimes used to establish a turf, or to introduce a new variety into established grass.[58] For good establishment, a little fertilizer should be placed beneath each plug and the plugs should be regularly irrigated during the first couple of weeks.

In using plugs to change grass species, the original stand can be first inhibited by spraying with such herbicides as MH-30 or sodium arsenate.

HIGHWAY SEEDING

Highway seeding is specialized and has different goals and different approaches. Steep slopes, sterile soils, varied exposures, and lack of irrigation result in severe microclimates.[54] Grass on shoulders and medians is largely decorative, but plantings on slopes may be primarily for erosion control, secondarily for appearance. Species intended to be permanent may be planted, or a temporary cover may be established for replacement by native cover. The established cover may be regularly maintained or completely neglected.

Steep slopes are difficult to work on. In about 1938 the Connecticut State Highway Department developed a method of spraying seed onto steep slopes (and elsewhere) in a water slurry.[19] This is now an accepted method of large-scale seeding, and several companies make hydroseeders.

In addition to water and seed, fertilizer has been added in the tank.[78] A further effort to get one-step operation resulted in a hydromulcher, which contains pumps, nozzles, and the rest of the equipment to handle mulching materials, or to spray on either grass stolons or seed. Although this permits a one-step operation, best results are often obtained by using two steps. In the first operation, no mulch is used and the seed is sprayed to make direct contact with the soil. Mulch is then applied over the seed. In a one-step operation some seed is mixed into the mulch and rate of establishment reduced. A hydromulcher may take about 20 min to fill and 20 min to empty and can cover 2–4 acres a day. A dye may be used in the tank to show area covered and intensity of cover. A typical load for a hydromulcher might be 1000 gal water, 20 lb of seed, 100 lb of 16–20–0, and 300–400 lb of cellulose fiber; this material should cover 15,000 ft^2.

Sturkie finds roadside failures the highest where there is no seedbed preparation. With liming and rough preparation, failures are reduced. If preparation is good and lime and fertilizer are used success is high.[83]

PLANT MATERIALS[1, 12, 23, 49, 72, 86, 102]

A single species having success over the widest geographical range is tall fescuegrass. Other plant materials successfully used in highway work include the following: Kentucky and Canada bluegrasses, red fescue, sheeps' fescue, common and 'Coastal' bermudagrass, lovegrasses (*Eragrostis* spp.), wheatgrasses (*Agropyron* spp.), wild rye (*Elymus* spp.), reed canarygrass (*Phalaris arundinacea*), blue grama *(Bontelous gracile)*, and *Bromus inermis.* Legumes are included for soil enrichment, especially when native vegetation is expected to invade. Legumes used include Lespedeza, *(L.*

cuneata), crown vetch *(Coronilla varia)*, birdsfoot trefoil, *(Lotus corniculatus)*, and on the very steep rocky slopes in the south, kudzu vine *(Pueraria thunbergiana)*.*

Daylily *(Hemerocallis)* tolerates a wide variety of microclimates. Honeysuckle *(Lonicera)* on steep rocky slopes develops much organic trash in which natives can get a foothold.

Birdsfoot trefoil provides a low cover. Crown vetch takes three to four years to establish and benefits from a light nurse crop, lime, and cool exposure.[13] Button suggests that a variety of materials should be used and changed with exposure, season, soil, etc.[19]

When salt is used to de-ice roads, salt tolerance may be a problem on shoulders. Among grasses tested, K-31, sand lovegrass, and blue grama have shown tolerance in Iowa.[102]

In northern Europe red fescue and colonial bentgrasses are primary roadside grasses.

FERTILIZER

Continuing nitrogen availability is needed until a dense cover develops that controls erosion. In hydroseeding, up to 1 lb of soluble fertilizer salts per gallon of water has not affected seed in 15–30 min exposures.[17] Lower rates are generally used and up to 2 lb of soluble nitrogen per thousand or 8 lb of slightly soluble nitrogen have been recommended.[78] Recommendations have been made for splitting applications to provide both soluble and insoluble nitrogen sources.[12,71,78] Some investigators have found no carryover from UF fertilizers into the second year.[71] In the southeast annual fertilization has kept bermudagrass as a cover for an extended period. Without added fertilizer native plant encroachment replaces bermudagrass in two to three years. When the cover is mowed, fertilizer may be needed to keep a high density for erosion control.[72] With a single application of 2 1/2 lb of N/M in the seedbed most of the increased growth was in the first month. But two years later plots receiving the highest initial nitrogen still had more cover and fewer weeds.[28]

MULCHES

Mulches are used in highway planting. They ameliorate the extreme temperatures (to 10°F difference), reduce erosion, conserve water, and in-

*Use of legumes attractive to bees is to be avoided. Bees are a serious hazard to traffic at times. Other legumes may attract herbivores such as deer.

crease density and vigor of stands.[5,18,14] Not all mulches do all these things. Modifying environment is apt to be most important in the summer, and erosion control is more important in winter and spring. Mulches of natural organic materials tend to contain weed seeds which may be objectionable or may be desirable for erosion control because of vigorous growth.

In most studies native straw has given high performance, has both controlled erosion and improved stands, and has been low in cost but also weedy.[5,6,9,13,23,24,83,84,77,78,86] Straw is bulky and laborious to handle and Button found that wood fiber at four times the cost of straw was cheaper, applied on the ground, because of reduced labor.[19] Wood fiber has generally rated well, but not always.

Woven nets of various materials have had various effects. If the ground was rough so there were channels under the fabric, nets and excelsior have failed to stop erosion. When they make good contact with the ground, nets control erosion to a degree depending on slope, soil, rate of precipitation, and thread gage.[31]

Straw, cobs, hay, hulls, pine needles, and other organic residues have performed better than mulches of paper, fiberglass, asphalt, or cellulose, but sawdust has floated and blown away. Fiberglass and asphalt have been easy to apply.[83]

Asphalt emulsions have tended to rate low because associated high temperatures reduce stands.[66] However, asphalt has been useful as a tack to keep other materials such as straw from blowing, and in place. A variety of industrial wastes are offered as mulches from time to time. On some highly erodable soils, mulches fail to arrest erosion.[4] In cold weather plastic sheets have been effective in conserving water.[16]

Some managers cut roadside grass when seeds are mature and use the hay (with seeds) to mulch areas where stands are thin.

SAND DUNES

Dunes cover twice the area of agricultural land in the world. Active sand engulfs good land, roads, and buildings, and creates other problems. Active sand may be controlled by vegetation, but where man's activities break the cover, blowouts start, and sand begins to engulf the land.

Control involves five steps. *(1)* Source of the sand must be controlled. If sand from a blowout threatens a building, the building cannot be protected without also stopping the blowout. *(2)* The sand must be brought into topographic conformity with the rest of the land. High dunes will catch the wind and must be knocked down so wind is no worse than in the rest of the landscape. *(3)* An initial cover of sand-resistant grasses must be established to still the sand. *(4)* Permanent vegetation should be planted in the protection of the sand-controlling grasses. *(5)* Land management must protect the cover from damage. Various plants may be used at different stages in different regions. The subject is covered in the 1948 U.S. Department of Agriculture Yearbook, *Grass.*[91]

Sometimes in the second stage (step *4*) it is desired to have a turf for the final cover. This will require first, that sand be controlled from coming into the area; second, that irrigation water be available; and third, that a regular fertilizer program be used.[86,101]

Establishing a perched water table is helpful to success. A plastic sheet can be placed beneath the sand root zone or an asphalt layer can be sprayed 18 to 24 in. beneath the surface. Irrigation frequency and fertilizer leaching will be reduced by using the interface.

If beachgrasses are growing, turf is seeded among them and in their protection. Alternatively seed is protected with a straw mulch. Potentially successful grasses are tall fescue, 'Clatsop' red fescue, and as a possible addition, colonial bentgrass; in the south, St. Augustine is adapted to sand. Fertilizer should be applied regularly in amounts sufficient to maintain a close cover. Clovers used in the turf will help. Such protective lawns should not be too closely mowed, and traffic should be low, as worn spots lead to new blowouts.

PRACTICUM

The manager is fortunate if he can be in on development of new turf from the beginning. Where new construction is taking place, construction workers will spread out over a large area. They will abuse the soil by driving heavy equipment on it when it is wet, by burying trash, by burning wastes at temperatures that fire the soil, and by washing out cement and plaster mixers at a dozen different spots.

Hold the construction area to a suitable size by fencing it. Fence around trees to be saved. Prohibit burning and burying. Use future parking areas for concrete washout. Each job has a *change order* which each subcontractor is required to read and initial. Put waste disposal instructions on the change order.

Soil may be protected from compaction by a mulch of several inches of wood chips or other wastes. These are flammable, however, and a cigarette butt may cause them to smolder for several days then break into flame when no one is around.

Advance knowledge permits advance weed control. Control measures can encourage germination of weed seeds existing in the soil, and prevent setting a new crop of seeds.

During grading and preparation of the land, see that the soil is worked on the contour. Repair of washouts is tedious and expensive. Working on the contour will reduce washing. Check surface drainage with a builder's level. Don't trust eyeball methods. When all trenching, subsoiling, grading, and preparation is done, see that it is settled by five to six inches of rain or irrigation. Then regrade where it is needed.

Where artificial soils are being mixed for special use, personally oversee the operation. Make sure mixing is complete, that grades are correct before laying the mix, and that depths of mix are those specified. I have seen two instances where the truck driver took it upon himself to change the sand order. His truck was getting stuck in the sand he was dumping so he asked the pit operator for something a little firmer, a bit tighter. The result was sand with a high silt content. Personal supervision by the manager caught these changes before damage was extensive.

Good planning keeps the work on schedule. Seed, fertilizer, weed control chemicals, and so on should arrive in advance of need, and good storage should be waiting. Seed should be appropriate to the management planned. Make sure seed is good quality, and that bluegrass is not full of *Poa annua* or *Poa trivialis,* and that the red fescue isn't 5% ryegrass. Don't plant weeds. If funds are limited, buy the best seed and use less of it.

Check to see if you should be using stolons or sod. A few hundred feet of sod on steep slopes of erodable soils may provide a good savings. If soil is washing from a slope onto sidewalks, sodding next to walks and keeping the walks clean may prevent slips, falls, and injuries.

Bringing it Up

Bringing up seed is largely a matter of water management. With soil at field capacity only light sprinkles are needed to replace evaporation losses from the surface. From October through March a single sprinkle of a few minutes each day may be adequate. A windy June day on the other hand may require constant patrolling and frequent sprinkling, and hand sprinkling of dry spots. It is desirable to have the surface dry once each day. This shrivels mycelium of soil-borne diseases. With warm temperatures expect dampening off diseases. Use a mercury fungicide spray on the soil surface. Once grass is up, roots are down, and intervals between irrigations should be stretched. With grass one to two inches high irrigation should be on the order of once every other day but depending on season and soil. The grass will indicate exceptions and often the exceptions will be small dry areas that are best hand-watered.

During the initial week a watering program is often established and then not changed. A week or two later grass is up and wet and damping off disease is at work.

If the irrigation system was not checked out before seeding, you may wish it had been. Once you have begun to water, seed needs to be kept moist. Irrigation errors are often corrected by wading out ankle deep in mud and spoiling the nice grade. As heads are to be reset later, installers may have been careless with the first setting. Cocked heads give the most trouble. On the low side the nozzle digs out the seed and soil and washes it up into a mound. The high side is dry and the stand is feeble.

First Mowing

When grass is ready for its first mowing, the soil should be firm and dry and the grass well rooted. The grass should be cut with a sharp mower, and clippings removed. First mowing has not been studied and time and height are a matter of judgement. There should be no hurry to mow, but the turf should not be allowed to get too much longer than the height at which it will be maintained. An informal decorative turf to be mowed at 2 in. can be mowed when it reaches between 3 and 4 in. and can be mowed at 2 in. On the other hand, a turf that is to be a putting green would be too severely injured if it were first mowed at 1/4 in. There one might mow it at 1/2 in. when it reaches 1 in. and then decrease the height and increase frequency over the last couple of months before play.

Early mowings are best done with a reel mower, as machines that mow by impact can be damaging to soft seedlings.

After the grass is up there are apt to be some bare spots that need to be reseeded. Common sense tells us to correct the problems that cause the bare spot. If it is a low wet spot, raising the grade with fill may be simple and permanent compared to draining the spot. If a bare spot is a dry spot, the sprinkler system may need attention before reseeding is practical.

Sooner or later we are all forced to sow at the wrong time of the year. It's a gamble. If we make it, we are in luck. But if heat and rain result in loss to damping off we should admit we lost the gamble. Instead of immediately reseeding into soil heavily infested with damaging organisms we should draw back. Optimum procedure might be to spray the soil with a fungicide, rake it so the crust can dry out, then when the season changes and temperatures begin to decrease, seed again.

As many diseases are seed borne, treatment of seed with a fungicide is a good precaution and may be particularly valuable when sowing at the wrong season.

Seeding is like many other practices. If we do the right thing at the right time of the year, the grass grows itself.

When sodding, plan and schedule the operation thoroughly. Don't sod a large area until you have had experience with an area of less than an acre.

References

General References

A. Crocker, W., and L. V. Barton, 1957, *Physiology of Seeds,* Chronica Botanica Co., Waltham, Mass., 267 pp.

B. Wheeler, W. A., and D. D. Hill, 1957, *Grassland Seeds,* D. Van Nostrand Co., Inc., Princeton, N.J., 734 pp.

C. *Golf Course Reporter,* 1965, **33**(2); an issue devoted to the role of sod in turfgrass culture.

D. International Turfgrass Conference and Show, 1967, *Proc.* **38,** 50 ff; a series of papers presented on sodding.

Cited References

1. Andrews, C. N., Jr., and C. L. Murdoch, 1965, "Evaluating grass and legume species for roadside turf," *Agron. Abstr.,* p. 48.
2. Anonymous, 1925, "How thick to cut sod for putting greens," *U.S.G.A. Greens Sect. Bull.* **5,** 172–173.
3. Astratt, P. R., and L. S. Bliss, 1963, "Some effects of emulsified hexaoctadecanol on germination, establishment and growth of Kentucky bluegrass," *Agron. J.* **55,** 533–537.
4. Augustine, M. T., 1965, "Vegetative slope and channel stabilization," *Agron. Abstr.,* p. 122.
5. Barkley, D. G., R. E. Blaser, and R. E. Schmidt, 1965. , "Effect of mulches on microclimate and turf establishment," *Agron. J.* **57,** 189–192.
6. Barnett, A. P., E. G. Diseker, and E. C. Richardson, 1967, "Evaluation of mulching methods for erosion control on newly prepared and seeded backslopes," *Agron. J.* **59,** 83–85.
7. Bradshaw, A. D., and R. W. Snaydon, 1959, "Population differences within plant species in response to soil factors," *Nature* **183,** 129–130.
8. Beard, J. B., 1965, "Factors in the adaptation of turfgrasses to shade," *Agron. J.* **57,** 457–459.
9. Beard, J. B., 1965, "A comparison of mulches for turf establishment on light soils," *Agron. Abstr.,* p. 48.
10. Beaty, E. R., 1966, "Sprouting of 'Coastal' bermudagrass stolons," *Agron. J.* **58,** 555–556.
11. Beever, L., and J. P. Cooper, 1964, "Influence of temperature on growth and metabolism of ryegrass seedlings. I. Seedling growth and yield components. II. Variation in metabolites," *Crop. Sci.* **4,** 139–146.
12. Blaser, R. E., 1968, "Establishment and maintaining turf and soil cover along newly constructed highways," *West Va. Agr. Sta. Misc. Publ.,* No. 5; *Proc. West Va. Turfgr. Conf.* pp. 11–16.
13. Blaser, R. E., and D. G. Barkley, 1963, "The effect of various mulches on microclimate and turf establishment," *Agron. Abstr.,* p. 117.
14. Bosshart, R. P., and W. H. McKee, Jr., 1966, "Grass seedling response to moisture and soil surface temperature stresses as affected by wood cellulose mulch," *Agron. Abstr.,* p. 25.

15. Bredakis, E. J., and J. M. Zak, 1966, "Timing of seeding," *Turf Bull. (Mass.)* **3**(1), 18–19.
16. Brock, J. R., 1964, "Grass under plastic," *Golf Course Reptr.* **32**(10), 63–64.
17. Brooks, C., R. E. Blaser, and W. W. Moschler, 1959, "The effects of fertilizer solutions on seed germination," *Agron. Abstr.,* p. 88.
18. Burrows, E. C., and W. E. Larson, 1962, "Effects of amount of mulch on soil temperature and early growth of corn," *Agron. J.* **54,** 19–23.
19. Button, E. F., 1966, "Hydroplanting highway turf," *Turf-grass Times* **1**(4), 1ff.
20. Chiles, R. E., W. W. Huffine, and J. Q. Lynd, 1966, "Differential response of *Cynodon* varieties to type of sprig storage and planting depth," *Agron. J.* **58,** 231–234.
21. Davies, W., 1937, "Modern concepts of grassland improvement," *Herb. Rev.* **5,** 194–199.
22. DeWitt, J. L., C. L. Canode, and J. K. Patterson, 1962, "Effects of heating and storage on the viability of grass harvested with high moisture content," *Agron. J.* **54,** 126–129.
23. Dudeck, A. E., N. P. Swanson, and A. R. Dedrick, 1966, "Protecting steep construction slopes against water erosion. II. Effect of selected mulches on seedling stand, soil temperature, and soil moisture relations," *Agron. Abstr.,* p. 38.
24. Dudeck, A. E., N. P. Swanson, and A. R. Dedrick, 1967, "Mulches for grass establishment on fill slopes," *Agron. Abstr.,* p. 51.
25. Engels, R. E., 1961, "Competition on turfgrass species in mixture," *Agron. Abstr.,* p. 74.
26. Erdmann, M. J., and C. M. Harrison, 1947, "The influence of domestic rye-grass and red top upon the growth of Kentucky bluegrass and Chewing's fescue in lawn and turf mixtures," *J. Am. Soc. Agron.* **39,** 682–689.
27. Frazier, S. L., and W. H. Daniel, 1960, "Turfgrass seedling development under measured environment and management conditions," *Agron. Abstr.,* p. 70.
28. Foote, L. E., 1967, "Fertilizer aids turf, reduces weeds and erosion," *Turf-grass Times* **3**(1), 1ff.
29. Gardner, W. A., 1921, "Effect of light on germination of light sensitive seeds," *Botan. Gaz.* **71,** 249–288 (1916).
30. Garman, H., and E. C. Vaughn, 1916, "The curing of bluegrass seeds as affecting their viability," *Kentucky Agr. Expt. Sta. Bull.* **198,** 16 pp.
31. Gilbert, W. B., and E. E. Deal, 1964, "Temporary ditch liners for erosion control," *Agron. Abstr.,* p. 101; also seen as an untitled mimeo, Turf Project, N. Carolina State Univ.
32. Gowan, K., 1964, "Soil crusting and seedling emergence," *Soil Water and Fert.,* No. 26; Mimeo., Agr. Expt. Serv. Soils Dept. Univ. Calif., Davis.
33. Gramckow, J., 1967, "Is your athletic field safe," Rept, Cal-Turf Inc., Camarillo, Calif., Mimeo, 48 pp. Also reported by R. Morrow, 1968, *Turf-grass Times* **3**(1), 2.
34. Grether, T., 1967, "Stolons and vegetative reproduction of turfgrass," *Northwest Turfgr. Conf. Proc.* **21,** 59–63.

35. Hanson, A. A., and F. V. Juska, 1962, "Seedling vigor of Kentucky bluegrass sources," *Agron. Abstr.,* p. 103.
36. Hanson, A. A., and F. V. Juska, 1964, "Turf quality of imported Kentucky bluegrass and red fescue seed," *Park Maint.* **17**(5), 22 ff.
37. Hart, C. A., 1966, "The effect of temperature and stimulators on the laboratory germination of some common turfgrass seeds," Unpubl. Rept, Dept. Environ. Hort., Univ. Calif., Davis.
38. Henry, H. H. 1928, "Changes in the bent grass seed market as viewed by the seed analyst," *U.S.G.A. Greens Sect. Bull.* **8,** 226–231.
39. Hillman, F. H., 1921, "South German mixed bent seed described," *U.S.-G.A. Greens Sect. Bull.* **3,** 37–39.
40. Hillman, F. H., 1930, "Identifying turfgrass seed," *U.S.G.A. Greens Sect. Bull.* **10,** 39–43.
41. Hodges, T. K., 1960, "Factors influencing the rooting depth of *Poa pratensis,*" M.S. Thesis, Univ. Calif., Davis, 53 pp.
42. Hovin, A. W., 1957, "Germination of annual bluegrass seed," *S. Calif. Turfgr. Cult.* **7**(2), 13.
43. James, D. B., 1961, "The influence of some edaphic factors on the growth and distribution of grasses," *Rept. Welsh Plant. Breed. Sta.* **1960,** 120–124.
44. Jurhen, M., W. M. Hiesey, and F. W. Went, 1953, "Germination and early growth of grasses in controlled conditions," *Ecology* **34,** 288–300.
45. Juska. F. V., and A. A. Hanson, 1959, "Evaluation of cool-season turfgrasses alone and in mixtures," *Agron. J.* **51,** 597–500.
46. Juska, F. V., J. Tyson, and C. M. Harrison, 1955, "The competitive relationship of 'Merion' bluegrass as influenced by various mixtures, cutting heights and levels of nitrogen," *Agron. J.* **47,** 513–518.
47. Kemmerer, H. R., and J. D. Butler, 1962, "Establishing spring seeded lawns," *Illinois Res.* **14**(3), 5.
48. King, J. W., and J. B. Beard, 1967, "Soil and management factors affecting the rooting capability of organic and mineral grown sod," *Agron. Abstr.,* p. 53.
49. Knowles, R. P., 1961, "Comparison of grasses for dryland turf.," *Can. J. Plant Sci.* **41,** 602–606.
50. Leggatt, C. W., 1946, "Germination of seeds of three species of *Agrostis,*" *Can. J. Res.* C **24,** 7–21.
51. Lobenstein, C. W., 1964, "Sod forming characteristics of Kentucky bluegrass as affected by morphological and physiological factors," Ph. D. Thesis, Purdue; *Dissertation Abstr.,* **25**(3), 3159.
52. Lyle, W. C., 1966, "History of the seeds act," *Gard. Chron.* **160**(21), 20–21.
53. McCrea, C., and R. E. Engel, 1960, "The effect of fertilizer rates and placement on turfgrass seedlings," *U.S.G.A. Greens Sect. J.* **12**(7), 28–29.
54. McKee, W. H., Jr., R. E. Blaser, C. K. Curry, and R. B. Cooper, 1964, "Effect of microclimate on adaptation of species along Virginia highway banks," *Agron. Abstr.,* p. 102.

55. McVey, G. R., 1967, "Responses of turfgrass seedlings to various phosphorus sources," *Agron. Abstr.,* p. 53.
56. Madison, J. H., 1962, "The effect of management practices on invasion of lawn turf by bermudagrass (*Cynodon dactylon* (L.) Pers.)," *Proc. Am. Soc. Hort. Sci.* **80,** 559–564.
57. Madison, J. H., 1966, "Optimum rates of seeding turfgrasses," *Agron. J.* **58,** 441–443.
58. Mahdi, Z., 1956, "The use of plugging for changing grasses in turf," *S. Calif. Turfgr. Cult.* **6**(3), 5.
59. Mahdi, Z., 1956, "The bermudagrass–bentgrass combination for an all year putting or lawn bowling green," *S. Calif. Turfgr. Cult.* **6**(2), 6.
60. Morgenweck, G., 1940, "Comparative seeding rate trials in pure sowings of grasses," *Pflanzenbau* **17,** 24–30, 33–64, 75–92 (seen in abstract).
61. Moringa, T., 1926, "Effect of alternating temperatures upon the germination of seeds," *Am. J. Botany* **13,** 141–159.
62. Musil, A. F., 1963, "Identification of crop and weed seeds," *U.S. Dept. Agr. Handbook* 219, Washington, D.C., 171 pp. 43 pl.
63. Musser, H. B., 1948, "Effect of soil acidity and available phosphorus on population changes in mixed Kentucky bluegrass–bentgrass turf," *J. Am. Soc. Agron.* **40,** 614–620.
64. Nutter, G. C., 1966, "Sod production expands and mechanizes," *Turfgrass Times* **1**(3), 12 ff.
65. Perron, W. H., 1961, "Mélanges a gazon," *Agriculture (Montreal)* **18**(2), 49–52.
66. Pietsch, R., 1965, "Phytosociological and ecological investigations into football ground turf (in German)," *A. Acker-Pflanzenbau* **119,** 347; seen in abstract in *Sports Turf Res. Inst. J.* No. 41, 1965 (1966).
67. Piper, C. V., R. A. Oakley, and L. Carrier, 1923, "Seeds and seeding for new greens and new fairways," *U.S.G.A. Greens Sect. Bull.* **3,** 159–161.
68. Pumphrey, F. V., 1965, "Residue management in Kentucky bluegrass (*Poa pratensis* L.) and red fescue (*Festuca rubra* L.) seed fields," *Agron. J.* **57,** 559–561.
69. Radko, A. M., 1955, "*Zoysia* seed storage and germination tests," *U.S.G.A. Greens Sect. J.* **8**(6), 25–26.
70. Rampton, H. H., and Te May Ching, 1966, "Longevity and dormancy in seeds of several cool-season grasses and legumes buried in soil," *Agron. J.* **58,** 220–222.
71. Richardson, E. C., and E. G. Diseker, 1961, "Control of roadbank erosion in the Southern Piedmont," *Agron. J.* **53,** 292–294.
72. Richardson, E. C., and E. G. Diseker, 1965, "Establishing and maintaining roadside cover in the Piedmont Plateau of Georgia," *Agron. J.* **57,** 561–564.
73. Rieke, P., 1968, "Forcing sod development," *Midwest Turf Foundn. Turfgr. Conf. Proc.,* pp. 43–47.
73a. Rieke, P., and J. B. Beard, 1969, *1st Intern. Turfgr. Conf., Proc.,* in press.
74. Rockefeller, W. J., 1929, "Cutting, moving, and relaying sod," *U.S.G.A.*

Greens Sect. Bull. **8,** 137–139; see also Welton, p. 142, same issue.
75. Schery, R. W., 1959, "Bluegrass sprouting under stress," *Agron. Abstr.,* p. 91.
76. Schery, R. W., 1967, "Select seed wisely," *Golf Supt.* **35**(10), 14 ff.
77. Schmidt, B. L., G. S. Taylor, and R. W. Miller, 1965, "Roadbank stabilization and vegetative establishment with corn steep liquor solutions and straw mulch," *Agron. Abstr.,* p. 49.
78. Schmidt, R. E., 1967, "Hydraulic vegetative planting of turfgrass," *Golf Supt.* **35**(3), 10 ff.
79. Simpson, S. L., and C. Y. Ward, 1964, "Manufactured mulches compared with grain straw for mulching roadside seedings," *Agron. Abstr.,* p. 103.
80. Smith, J. D., 1957, "Seed dressing trial, 1957," *Sports Turf Res. Inst. J.* **33,** 369–372.
81. Sprague, V. G., 1940, "Germination of freshly harvested seeds of several *Poa* species and of *Dactylis glomerata,*" *J. Am. Soc. Agron.* **32,** 715–721.
82. Stith, W., 1967, "Care of harvested grass," *Intern. Turfgr. Conf. and Show. Proc.* **38,** 62.
83. Sturkie, D. G., 1964, "Mulches and land preparation in establishing roadside turf," *Agron. Abstr.,* p. 103.
84. Swanson, N. P., A. R. Dedrick, and A. D. Dudeck, 1966, "Protecting steep construction slopes against water erosion. I. Effects of selected mulches on seed, fertilizer, and soil loss," *Agron. Abstr.,* p. 38.
85. Swanson, H. P., A. R. Dedrick, and A. D. Dudeck, 1967, "Protecting steep fill slopes against water erosion," *Agron. Abstr.,* p. 55.
86. Tabor, P., 1962, "Permanent plant cover for road cuts and similar conditions by secondary succession," *Agron. J.* **54,** 179.
87. Tatge, J., 1962, "How John Verdier builds sand dunes," *Park Maint.* **15**(3), 10–16.
88. Thomas, F. H., 1966, "Management of organic soil for sod production," *Univ. Florida Turfgr. Management Conf. Proc.* **14,** 149–152.
89. Thompson, W. R., Jr., and C. Y. Ward, 1063, "Summer turf may be set in the winter," *Miss. Farm. Res.* **26**(3), 6.
90. Toole, E. H., 1923, "Problems of germinating the various bluegrasses," *Seed World* **14,** 23–30.
91. U.S. Dept. Agr., 1948, Yearbook, *Grass*, Washington, D.C., 892 pp.
92. U.S. Dept. Agr., 1961, Yearbook, *Seeds,* Washington, D.C., 591 pp.
93. U.S. Dept. Agr., 1963, "Rules and regulations under the federal seed act," *Agr. Mktg. Serv. and Reg. Announcement, 156,* Washington, D.C., 79 pp.
94. Van Slijken, A., "Significance of sowing depth (Dutch)," *Land-en Tuinbouw jaarb.* **18,** 313; seen in abstr. in *Sports Turf. Res. Inst. J.* **41,** 85.
95. Waddington, D. V., W. C. Lincoln, Jr., and J. Troll, 1967, "Effect of sawdust on the germination and seedling growth of several turfgrasses," *Agron. J.* **59,** 137–139.

96. Warren, B., 1966, "The business of sod installation," *Turf-grass Times* **2**(1), 9 ff.

97. Webb, B. C., 1959, "Comparison of water loss and survival of 'Coastal' bermudagrass stolons harvested at two stages of growth," *Agron. J.* **51,** 367–368.

98. Wells, H. D., and B. P. Robinson, 1954, "Important diseases of ryegrass greens," *U.S.G.A. Greens Sect. J.* **7**(5), 25–27.

99. Wood, G. M., and L. W. Buckland, 1966, "Survival of turfgrass seedlings subjected to induced growth stress," *Agron. J.* **58,** 19–23.

100. Youngner, V. B., 1968, "Vertical mowing—aerification—and *Poa annua* invasion," *Calif. Turfgr. Cult.* **18**(1), 6; also in *U.S.G.A. Green Sect. Rec.,* 1965, **5**(3), 6–7.

101. Zak, J. M., and E. J. Bredakis, 1965, "Sand dune erosion control at Provincetown, Mass.," *Agron. Abstr.,* p. 126.

102. Zybura, E. L., and E. C. Roberts, 1965, "Comparison of foliar and root development of ten coarse grasses for roadside turf," *Agron. Abstr.,* p.

4

MOWING

"... Between these and the walks and drives, is everywhere a belt of turf (which, by the way, is kept close cut with short, broad scythes and shears and swept with *hair-brooms,* as we saw)."

Frederick Law Olmstead*

Grasses have evolved largely under the selective pressure of grazing animals so that removal of a portion of the leaf surface is a normal occurrence for grasses. However, the normal is not always the most desirable. Consider plants which grow on saline soils and which are called halophytes. Halophyte means salt lover. On good low-salt soils, with good garden care, scraggly halophytes burgeon into huge lush bushes and thrive. Halophytes are not lovers of salt; they have developed a tolerance of, and adaptation to salt. So grasses have developed a tolerance of, and adaptation to defoliation. They tolerate extensive defoliation and survive and compete without ever achieving their full growth potential. But full development may require some defoliation because of the specialized adaptation.

*Walks and talks of an American farmer in England, University of Michigan Press, Ann Arbor. p 54 (no date but ca 1850, speaking of the "People's Garden" or park at Berkenhead.)

Grasses have developed differently in response to grazing. Some grasses carry the growing point high where it is removed by grazing. The grass may then require over 10 days before it is actively growing again. In dry areas, this slow response can favor survival during drought. Other grasses have low protected growing points, store reserve foods in rhizomes or stolons, and quickly generate new growth. Grasses used for turf are in the second group.

In the early 1800s mechanical mowing devices appeared which permitted the gentleman with a small estate to participate in a little mild exercise while trimming his lawn. Without requiring the skill needed for a scythe, the mechanical device permitted him to mow with great uniformity. For the man with a large estate and no wish to keep a team of workhorses there was available in 1890 a steam-driven mower. Its great weight (1 1/2 tons) was turned to a virtue by using wide wheels to roll the turf as it was mowed. Although there was no dripping gasoline to make brown spots on the grass, I presume the same effect was achieved by occasional hot coals slipping through the grates. By 1914, Worthington produced a gang mower and ushered in the current era.

Early mowing of ornamental turf was without doubt patterned after grazing and haymaking practices, cuts being made from three to four times a year to monthly during the growing season. Such a schedule is still followed in some European parks. In crowded U.S. suburbs there is a kind of mind that finds even a little disorder disquieting. This, combined with an early 20th century passion for sanitary sterility, demands uniform lawns, free of weeds, evenly edged, and mowed as quickly as any new growth mars the uniformity of clipped ranks and rows. These views represent the extremes of mowing practice.

When a turf is mowed, the obvious result is that the leaf surface of the grass plant is reduced. There are other less obvious consequences: (a) There is a temporary cessation of root growth. (b) A moderate clip stimulates a burst of top growth. (c) The ratio of tops to roots is changed. (d) Carbohydrate production and storage is reduced. (e) Wound hormones are released. (f) Competition is reduced between larger and smaller plants. (g) Shading of lower leaves is reduced. (h) A port of entry for disease organisms is opened. (i) As the older portion of the leaf is removed, the remaining turf is younger, less matured. (j) Water loss (from cut ends) is temporarily increased. (k) Water uptake is decreased. (l) Species tolerant of mowing are favored over those intolerant. (m) There is less dew fall and more dew is produced by distillation. (n) Temperatures at the soil surface are more extreme.

With repeated mowing: (o) Population density increases (sod formation). (p) Yield decreases. (q) Fertilizer utilization changes.

The literature of grasses reports many experiments on defoliation. These are in good agreement and may be summed as follows: Many tropical species grow exhuberantly and soon shade out their lower leaves. They are benefitted by fairly frequent defoliation and may yield more with mowing at intervals as short as one month. As an example, 'Pensacola' bahiagrass produced the greatest regrowth when a sward was clipped at 5 cm (2 in.) or less, and clipping at 2.5 cm (1 in.) three to four times a year did not seriously reduce growth.[41] 'Coastal' bermudagrass is favored by mowing at 6-wk intervals.[4]

Temperate-season grasses differ in having a more limited season of growth. Except for an annual harvest, the more severely these are defoliated, the more severely total growth is limited.

Extent of damage varies with species. Differences based on height of growing point are important, but more important is the weight of the grass and its distribution. Grasses with thick heavy crowns close to the soil and with extensive rhizomes or stolons may have a large percent of their total weight in the zone extending one inch above and one inch below the soil line. Mowing such a plant removes relatively little total weight. A bunch grass without stolons or rhizomes, and with leafy stems, may have a large percent of its weight removed by mowing. This latter group contains important range grasses.

The following listing groups grasses according to bulk distribution:[40]

Top grasses

Tall oat grass	*Avena elatior*
Timothy	*Phleum pratense*
Meadow fescue	*Festuca pratensis*
Marsh *Poa*	*Poa palustris*

Bottom grasses

Red fescue	*Festuca rubra*
Kentucky bluegrass	*Poa pratensis*
Perennial ryegrass	*Lolium perenne*
Redtop	*Agrostis stolonifera gigantea*
Roughstalked meadowgrass	*Poa trivialis*

I prefer Klapp's list in which he rates grasses from least tolerant to most tolerant of mowing. The following is a selection of European grasses from Klapp:[25]

Least tolerant

Marsh *Poa*	*Poa palustris*
Smooth bromegrass	*Bromus inermus*
Cocksfoot	*Dactylis glomerata*
Meadow fescue	*Festuca pratensis*
Roughstalked meadowgrass	*Poa trivialis*
Bentgrass	*Agrostis*
Red fescue	*Festuca rubra*
Kentucky bluegrass	*Poa pratensis*

Most tolerant

Perennial ryegrass	*Lolium perenne*

In studying this list it is well to remember that these grasses were evaluated under pasture conditions in a cool climate. If I were to draw a list based on grasses under turf conditions in California, I should offer the following as a first approximation (based on tolerance to mowing):

Tolerates:

High mowing
Centipedegrass
Creeping red fescue
Meadow fescue

Medium high mowing
Chewing's fescue
Tall fescue
Kentucky bluegrass
Perennial ryegrass
Bahiagrass

Medium low mowing
Highland bentgrass
Colonial bentgrass
St. Augustinegrass
Zoysia grass

Low mowing
Bermudagrass
Creeping bentgrass

Klapp has noted that when pasture-type grasses are grown alone and not clipped, their capacity to spread and develop is weakened. Among pasture types favored by mowing, bluegrass was four times, ryegrass thirty-three times as frequent in pastures as in meadows. Only half as many species are able to grow in pastures as compared to meadows. Roberts notes that moderate mowing makes a denser turf[38] and Juska et al. found tillering and density promoted at one-inch mowing of bluegrass, though there was also more disease.[22,23]

The principal management choices when mowing turf are; height of cut, frequency of mowing, when to mow, patterns of mowing, equipment to be used, and sometimes whether to remove clippings or let them lie.

Mowing practices have been evaluated in terms of yield, effects on root and rhizome production, appearance, and verdure(Table 4.1). Yield data have been important in pasture studies. Results, however, cannot be generalized for turf, for when one is growing turf, the desired crop is what remains after mowing, not what is taken off. There is a point, as we lower the cut, where yield no longer measures turf qualities, and *verdure* is the more appropriate measurement. I have defined verdure as the living green plant material left growing *after* mowing.[38] Differences between yield and verdure are illustrated in Figure 4.1 and Table 4.2.

In this example yield indicates 1/2-in. mowing producing more yield than 1 or 2-in. mowing. Verdure shows 2-in. mowing producing a greater weight of turf able to take more wear.

DEFOLIATION AND YIELD

Yield has been used as a measure of response in many investigations. Graber found yields of 2660 lb of dry matter from a single cut of bluegrass; this yield decreased until with thirteen mowings at 1/2 in. annual yields were about 500 lb/acre. Close mowing one year reduced yields in following years.[13,15] Schery on the other hand found differences in mowing were soon without effect when all plots were returned to a common program of management as turf.[39] With a vigorous tropical grass, 'Coastal' bermudagrass, Clapp et al. found that fall defoliation had no effect on yield the following spring.[5]

Lovvorn worked with both blue and bermudagrasses, and although yields of bermuda were higher at higher temperatures, he found that with all grasses the greatest reduction from frequent mowing occurred at high temperatures and high fertility.[29]

Thompson, looking at 'Tifgreen,' found yield and carbohydrate production affected by an interaction between mowing height and season with

Table 4.1. Mowing and Mowing Interactions and Effects on *Poa pratensis* turf

Factor	*Yield*	*Verdure*	*Competition*	*Rooting*	*Rhizome Growth*	*Carbohydrate*
Mowing height lowered	Decreased (may increase at scalp-heights)[13-15,17,18,22-24,27,31,33,45]	Decreased (increased if lowered from hay heights)[14,22,23,33,35,45]	Increased—more, smaller plants[22-24,31-33,35,38]	Temporary decrease in growth, stopped growth, or loss of roots; higher oxygen requirement[1,6,10,17,18,22,27,28,35,36,38,45]	Decreased[3,17,18,22,45]	Decreased[3,36,38]
Mowing frequency increased	Decreased[9,15,18,22,23,31-33]	Increased slightly for that height[10,17,22,23,33,35]	Some increase[22,23,31-33,35]	Shallower and decreased rooting[3,6,10,22,34,38]	Decreased[15,22]	Decreased[3,15]
Mowing stress increased as temperature exceeds optimum.	Growth retarded; recovery set back if neat continues[29]	Decreased	Decreased; weaker plants lost	Root quality decreased then loss of roots[1,29]	Growth stopped; may be some loss[29]	Storage decreased; reserves used[1]
Mowing x N; fixed mowing stress as N increases	Increased[33,35]	Increased then decreased at very high stress[17,33,35]	Increased then lessened at high stress[33,35]	Large decrease[17,24]	Growth and number decreased[17,24]	New equilibrium between growth and storage; less storage[29,31,32]
Mowing x N x T; mowing and N stress fixed as *T* exceeds optimum	Drops; Recovery slow[17,18,29]	Decreased; loss of smaller plants	Decreased; loss of smaller plants	Growth stopped; severe loss[17,18,29]	Death of rhizomes[17,18,29]	Loss of reserves[17,18,29]
Mowing x irrigation; slight water stress between irrigations	Decreased[34,35]	Decreased[33-35]	Decreased[33-35]	Rooting may increase[33-35]	Rhizome survival enhanced[17,18]	Increased[3]
	Ineffective use of nitrogen fertilizer—irrigation stress dominates					
Mowing x season	Spring: Temperatures favor growth and storage takes place if stresses are not too severe Fall: Cool temperatures and short days favor storage and procumbent growth; less growth is removed by mowing; same mowing program is less severe in effect in fall Summer: During heat stress, rhizomes and crowns are protected by dormancy if N is low and irrigation is only at high tension: with high N and water there is loss of rhizomes and innovations					

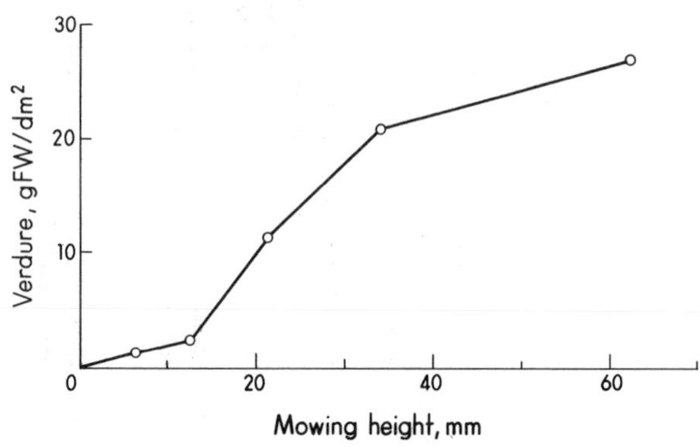

Figure 4.1 Kentucky bluegrass mowed at five heights. As the mowing height increases, verdure increases. Thus there is more turf "crop" at higher cuts, more grass to take the wear and abuse of the public.

1/4-in. mowing giving high spring yields, 1-in. mowing, high October yields.[42] Low heights led to more winter injury. Holt noted that as mowing practices were maŋaged to maximize yield there was less stubble, crown, and root.[19] Johnson used 1/2-in. mowing of bahiagrass to reduce yield of seed heads.[21]

Addional effects of mowing practices on yield are noted throughout the chapter.

DEFOLIATION AND ROOT AND RHIZOME PRODUCTION

Rooting measurements have often been used to evaluate effect of mowing on grasses. When a grass plant is cut, manufacturing of carbohydrate is

Table 4.2. Mowing Data for Merion Bluegrass

Mowing Height (in.)	*Av. Yield in g D.W./ft²/day*	*Average Verdure g/ft² D.W.*
1/2	0.683	17.3
1	0.670	24.1
2	0.216	27.7

In this example yield indicates 1/2 in. mowing producing more yield than 1 or 2 in. mowing. Verdure shows 2 in. mowing producing a greater weight of turf able to take more wear.

reduced and a burst of new leaf growth is stimulated at the expense of stored carbohydrate.[36] Supplies to the root diminish and root growth is slowed, stopped, or roots are even lost depending on the severity of the clip.

Bluegrass is characterized by an ability to begin new growth while calling on a minimum of reserves. Though reduction of roots is taken as an indication of injury or stress put on the plant by mowing, the effect is not simple. Crider has examined the effect in terms of percent of tops removed by a single clip followed by maintenance at that height by three clips a week.[6] With 90% of the foliage removed no further root growth took place. With 80% removed, growth had stopped by the 10th day, with 60% by the 28th day, and with 50% removed, 35% of the roots were producing growth after 33 days. With up to 40% of the foliage removed, root growth was slowed but not stopped.

Effects of this kind are seasonal and Brown found that even after mowing twice a week at 1 in. bluegrass grew well and stored carbohydrates during the early spring and throughout the month of October.[3] This may be partly a temperature effect of season. Beard reduced roots of bentgrass by one-half by mowing at 1/2 in. until temperatures reached 90 °F.[1] At that time temperature effects were overriding, and mowing did not further reduce limited roots. Put differently, carbohydrate content fell with rising temperatures except when grass was mowed close; then mowing was already limiting carbohydrate. Harrison found clipping reducing roots and rhizomes, but when nitrogen levels were low the effect was minimal.[17,18] When both temperature and nitrogen levels were high, defoliation resulted in death of rhizomes and loss of roots. Differences between 2 and 3-in. mowing heights of bluegrass were small, but 1/2-in. mowing greatly reduced roots, rhizomes, and yield. Madison found higher cuts increased deeper rooting but height of cut had little effect on verdure if nitrogen and irrigation were high.[33,35] When nitrogen levels were low, close mowing reduced verdure of bentgrass, and when irrigation was weekly, verdure was reduced by low mowing irrespective of nitrogen level.[34]

Mowing and soil oxygen are in interaction.[28] Mowed at 2 in. bluegrass reached full root production with 5% oxygen in the soil air whereas 10% oxygen was required for full production of roots by grass mowed at 1 in.

When root growth of bermudagrass varieties was evaluated, Kneebone found an increase in rooting when turf was mowed at 5/16 in.[26] He thought this due to an absence of thatch at cuts of 5/16 in. and its build up at higher cuts.

Rooting of pasture grasses has been thoroughly reviewed by Troughton.[43] Other aspects of turf rooting are discussed in *Principles of Turfgrass Culture,* Chap. 8.

HEIGHT OF MOWING

Choice of mowing height may be limited by use. Putting greens are mowed as high as 3/8 in. and as close as 1/8 in. but generally at 1/4 in. Decisions are most often made as to whether to go from 1/4 in. to 7/32 or 9/32 in. in response to season or other pressures. At the same time, opportunity for choice often is not used. An informal picnic area in a park may be most appealing mowed at 3 or 4 in., but be mowed at 1 in. because that is the height used on the park ball diamond a quarter of a mile away. Many home lawns are mowed at the height at which the mower was assembled when purchased.

Evidence shows better root and rhizome growth and increased storage of reserves when the height of the cut of a close-cut turf is raised. If mowing height is further increased there is a transition into a hay type of growth. That interval where the grass is too tall for good turf and too short for good hay has not been explored and we have little data to characterize it.

Related to the decrease of verdure with lower mowing (Fig. 4.1) is the decrease in leaf area index (LAI), the number of unit areas of leaf over a unit area of ground. We have seen how LAI is affected by height of cut (see *Principles of Turfgrass Culture*). Uncut grass will have about 7–8 ft^2 of leaf displayed above every square foot of soil. Mowed at 4 in., the LAI drops from 7+ to 4.9, and to 2.3 in grass mowed at 2 in. Ability of the plant to intercept and use sunlight drops off.

At the same time when Madison examined turf, not from the standpoint of a leaf area index, but a chlorophyll index in which he measured the weight of chlorophyll over a given area of soil, the change with mowing height was less severe.[35] Fertile highland bentgrass displayed an average of 9.38 mg of chlorophyll/dm^2 mowed at 1 3/8 in. (33 mm) and 9.05 mg at 1/2 in. (12.5 mm), which is not a significant difference.

The more important result of lowered height of cut is an increase in population. For example, highland bentgrass mowed at 33 and 12 1/2 mm had populations of 625 and 909 innovations/$dm.^2$ At the same time verdure dropped from 33 to 22 g/fresh wt/$dm.^2$ As grass weight decreased, population increased, so that real significance of lowered mowing appears when we express the effects on a per plant basis. As numbers increase each plant becomes smaller. As we went from 33 to 12 1/2 mm, plant size dropped in half from 50 mg per shoot to 23 mg and chlorophyll dropped from 14.2 μg per plant to 9.9 μg.

Height of mowing is in interaction with other factors as is noted throughout this chapter. The pattern of interactions shows that lower mowing increases plant numbers and competitive stress. When irrigation, fertilization, and climate also impose stress, a point is reached where smaller plant size is no longer offset by increased numbers. Numbers and size both decrease and the turf is thinned.[33]

Mowing and climate in interaction is illustrated by the following: In the climate of Great Britian and Denmark, red fescue and bluegrass are commonly mowed to 1/2 in., bentgrass to 1/8 in. In most of the U.S., neither fescue nor bluegrass long endure at 1/2 in. In the early years of the century when greens were of colonial bent and Chewing's fescue in imitation of those in England, they required annual fall overseeding to restore them. Red fescue was lost and bentgrass thinned by disease during summer's heat. A change to creeping bentgrass was necessitated by failure of colonial bent—fescue to survive.

The only grass for which we have found an optimum turf height is Highland Bentgrass. Goss notes its superior performance mowed at 3/4 in. as compared to 1 1/2 in.[12] In an analysis of growth at Davis we found that performance increased up to 3/4 to 1 in. Above 1 in. the grass began to form false crowns and then, with further height increase, there was a new increase in growth and production from the false crowns. As this latter growth forms inferior, puffy, or thatchy turf, an optimum mowing height is just below 1 in., just below the height where false crowning begins.

The kind of adaptation of turf to various cutting heights was explored at Davis. Grass mowed weekly at various heights was mowed down in increments and the distribution of the weight and chlorophyll was examined.

Fig. 4.2 shows the distribution for 'Seaside' and bluegrass. The following can be noted:

1. As the cut is lowered the amount of verdure dry weight is reduced more than chlorophyll. The capacity to make food remains moderately high (chlorophyll) but the capacity to store it is less (D.W.).

2. Amount of dry weight removed in the clippings is little affected by clipping height, but the amount of chlorophyll removed at low cuts is a large percent of the total at those cuts.

3. At high cuts the chlorophyll is carried higher in the plant than the dry weight.

The figure for Highland bentgrass shows the double peak at high cuts. The lower peak is for soil rooted innovations, the upper peak for false crowns.

Figure 4.3 shows percent of turf removed by weekly mowing at different heights. Of interest here is the nature of the curve. Small changes of height cause large effects when mowing is close. Above 1 3/8 in., changes in height have relatively little effect on percent removed (however, populations are higher, innovations smaller at lower cuts).

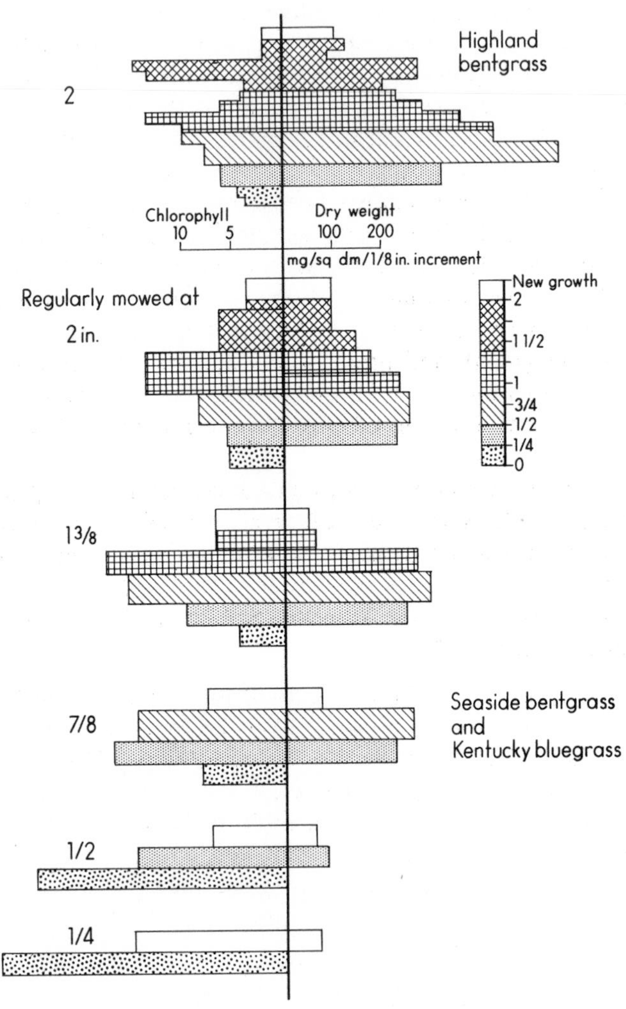

Figure 4.2 The vertical distribution of dry weight and of chlorophyll content in swards regularly mowed at various heights. Highland bentgrass illustrates the false crown that occurs when highland is mowed higher than 1 in. Data from seaside bent and Kentucky bluegrasses are also shown.

MOWING FREQUENCY

If the popular notion is true that less frequent mowing is more damaging because more clippings are removed, the slope of the curve would become more shallow with longer mowing intervals. In fact, with a two-week interval the curve becomes deeper, indicating that more weight is added below the cutter bar than above.

The following bluegrass data are typical results of studies of mowing intervals on meadows:[14]

Times cut in season	*Yield in lb/acre*
1	2660
6	960
7	520
22-24	500

With a more vigorous grass, 'Coastal' bermudagrass cut every six to twelve weeks produced maximum yield.[4] Production dropped when the interval was either longer or shorter.

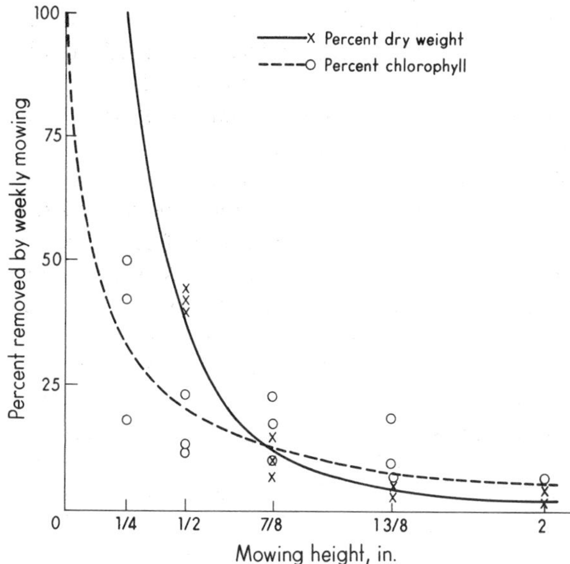

Figure 4.3 Percent of turf (or chlorophyll) removed by weekly mowing at various heights. Because of the difficulty of measuring the amount of living grass between 1/4 in. and the soil, 1/4 in. is taken as the base line for dry weight measurements.

Under turf conditions Juska and Hanson found that more frequent mowing (five times a week rather than once a week) reduced yield, rooting, rhizomes, and food reserves of both common and 'Merion' Kentucky bluegrass.[22] Only verdure was increased by more frequent mowing. This resulted in part from increased population which however, also increased the stress of competition.

In 1955–56 we imposed a series of random mowing intervals on a putting green, and measured clipping yield. When we analyzed the results we found an interesting pattern. When being mowed, daily yield was depressed by daily mowing. If one day were skipped, there was little production of clippings on that day, but there was a jump in production the following day. After the skipped day, mowing on two consecutive days depressed growth to its original low level. A single mowing did not completely overcome the stimulation of the skipped days. On the basis of this analysis we proposed to the Northern California Golf Course Superintendents Association that if greens were mowed two days and mowing was skipped the third day, slowed growth on the third day would not produce a noticeable change in the putting surface yet the rest from mowing would benefit and stimulate the grass. To fit the work week, it was proposed that Sunday and either Wednesday or Thursday be skipped. The program has proved satisfactory for several who used it.

The proposed program was criticized by individuals who felt that the grass adapted to mowing seven days a week and was upset by the introduction of irregular days. The experimental work was repeated with care and ojbections of technique were met.[32III]

The effect of small-interval differences was examined on 'Seaside' receiving putting-green maintenance. Greens were mowed seven days a week, six days, five days, etc. We found the effect of skipping one day a week was negligible but skipping two days made a significant difference in growth, whether it was two days at once or two days scattered through the week. Skipping three consecutive days was still better, but when three skipped days were spread through the week they were little better than two. Where one has a Monday closing a good program would be to skip Sunday and Monday and mow the other five days. Next best to skipping two consecutive days is a pattern of mow two, skip one, mow three, skip one, and then repeat. Skipping three consecutive days was favorable but is not often likely to be practical.

These programs all produced a fine-bladed turf of good putting quality. Programs with more than three skipped days resulted in more vigor leading to a coarser-bladed grass. The coarser grass affects appearance but does not necessarily affect putting quality.

To examine mowing intervals on decorative turf we used mowing intervals from daily to twenty-one days; and the longer the mowing interval the greater was the grass vigor as measured by its ability to produce yield.[31,32II] We used Seaside and Highland bentgrasses and 'Alta' fescue, each mowed at three different heights and in every instance the vigor of the grass was enhanced by a longer mowing interval. Some of our data are ullustrated in Figure 4.4. Of interest is the inflection point on the curve between intervals of four and five days. We found that regrowth during the first four days after mowing was largely due to continued growth of young emerging leaf blades which had been cut. By the fifth day new blades had emerged and subsequent growth was largely due to growth of new uncut blades.

The objection is usually made that longer periods between mowings cause an increasingly severe setback to the grass. This was not borne out for intervals to twenty-one days, which we examined. We tested this by measuring extent of growth on the day following a regular periodic mowing.

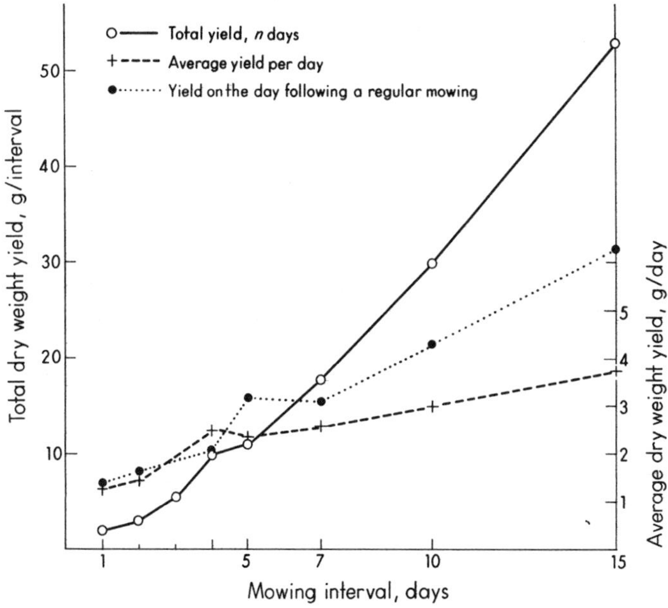

Figure 4.4 The effect of mowing interval on turfgrass vigor as expressed in terms of yield. The solid line illustrates the total yield when different mowing intervals are used. During the first four days yield is from growth of cut blades, after which growth of new blades predominates. Average growth per day is also increased by longer intervals (dashed line = yield in n days/n). Yield on the day following a regular mowing $[(n+1) - n]$ was appreciably increased with longer intervals, showing that removing more grass did not cause a greater setback (dotted line).

As an example of the results, when Seaside bentgrass was mowed at fifteen-day intervals, it produced an average daily growth of 15.8 g/100 ft^2 D.W. On the first day after mowing it produced 28.2 g/100 $ft.^2$ In other words, one effect of mowing was to stimulate rapid regrowth, and food reserves were readily available. When the grass was mowed at four-day intervals the average daily growth was 10.6 g/100 ft^2, but on the first day after mowing average growth was 7.86 g/100 $ft.^2$ In other words, at the more frequent interval mowing did not stimulate growth; in fact, the turf was not able to make its "daily quota" on the day following mowing. Only when the interval between mowings was five days or longer was there no setback from mowing but rather a stimulation of growth. (In the case of tall fescue a two-week interval was needed.)

In Great Britain mowing was tested at weekly and thrice weekly intervals at 1/8 and 3/8 in.[9] In this instance the reduced vitality produced by mowing three times a week was laid in part to decreased root system (86% as large) and the reduced ability of plants to forage for minerals, water, etc. Dawson concluded, however, that interval was less important than height and that it was better to mow at 3/8 in. three times a week than at 1/8 in. once a week.

Rules of thumb are often given for mowing frequency; mow when there is 1/2 in. of new growth; mow when new growth is one-third the height of clip; etc. I do not find these satisfactory. Among reasons, I note one based on data above. When grass is in a vigorous condition there will be a burst of growth from young cut leaves, then a delay before new growth emerges. The rules of thumb do not distinguish between these and I should find such rules more acceptable if they were based on growth of new leaves.

Figure 4.5 is based on counts we made from a bluegrass turf which had been mowed weekly. The experimental period began the day after a mowing and fresh areas were mowed each day. Clippings were divided into length intervals of 0–1 cm, 1–2 cm, 2–3 cm, etc., and separated as to whether the tips had been previously cut or were new and uncut. Only after the sixth day were more than 50% of the harvested blades from new growth. The median clipping length was in the 1–2 cm interval until the tenth day and in the 2–3 cm length until the eighteenth day. The longest clippings fell into the 4–5 cm class from the sixth through the sixteenth day, and only then did large numbers of very long clippings appear.

CHOICE OF MOWING INTERVAL

Thorough consideration of effects of different mowing frequencies brings us again to conflicts between esthetic and agricultural considerations. With relatively frequent cuts (two to three times a week) we have turf of good

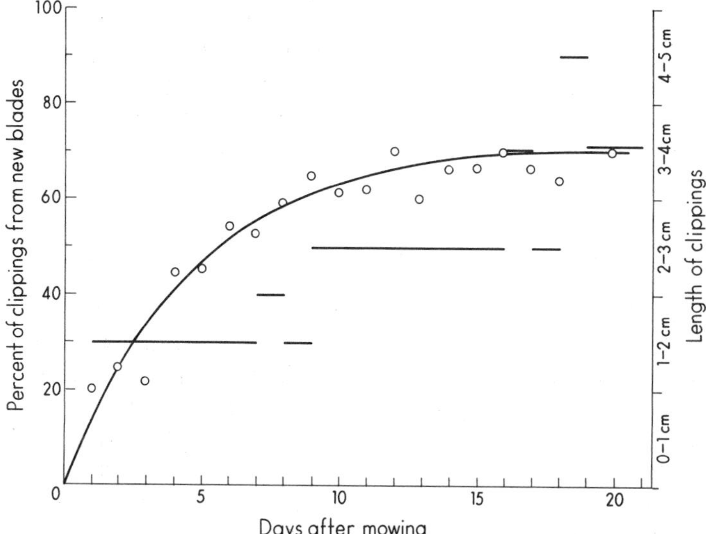

Figure 4.5 The increased contribution to clippings from new leaves is illustrated. The curve is based on the percent of clipping from wholly new leaves. The bars give the size class of the modal clipping based on length.

density. As the season progresses, each cut produces a smaller yield, and there are other evidences of stress. If we cut at a long interval of say two weeks, we get vigor, and a heavy burst of growth follows mowing, so in a couple of days the grass looks as if it hadn't been mowed. Depending on other factors, long interval may result in increased yield at each mowing. So at one extreme we have a neat, tight turf of decreasing vigor, at the other, a vigorous turf of coarser, more open character, and having long clippings that tend to stay on the surface. When wet they smother the grass below, and the long browned clippings accumulate near the surface and in time give a brown cast that detracts from the turf. The practical basis for choosing a mowing interval may be the size of clippings and whether they fall down out of sight. When clippings may be caught a longer interval can be used.

As shorter growing varieties of grass are developed and used, a longer interval can be used for the same amount of clipping regrowth.

Mowing height and frequency are in interaction. Deal found frequent mowing enhanced turf quality, close mowing reduced it.[10]Similar observations have lead to the proposal that frequent mowing would reduce the stress of close mowing. The thought is that removing a little bit frequently would hurt less then removing a longer clipping less often. Juska and Hanson investigated this using bluegrass.[22] They found frequent mowing less productive of stress than low mowing, but both reduced root, rhizome, and yield. Effects were additive, so the most stress was from low and frequent mowing. Frequent mowing did result in greater turf density (which implies stronger competition). Harrison proposed that the best way to get a turf of a certain *average* height would be to mow higher and more frequently.

SEASON AND MOWING

The value of interval changes with season. In summer's heat, temperature may depress growth so that it takes longer to produce the same growth of clippings. Increasing the interval benefits the heat-stressed grass.

In the fall growth is low and compact and frequent mowing is less injurious, but then there is less need for it. In the fall mowing height can also be lowered with relatively little stress on the grass. Fall scalping may be used to mow out duff and trash that may have accumulated. With highland bentgrass, it is especially desirable to scalp the grass in the fall to remove fluff and reduce false crowning. As temperatures warm to stress levels, grass survives better at higher cuts. Lowering cuts at such a time can increase stress to damaging levels. Increased susceptibility to disease from lowered cuts is noted under *Rhizoctonia* (Chap. 8). If cuts are to be lowered the reduction should be made when temperatures are favorable.

The effects of season can be illustrated by comparing a suggested optimum bluegrass mowing program in England with one in the California transition zone (Table 4.3).

In England temperature increases to a summer optimum, then decreases. In the transition zone, temperatures pass the optimum in the spring and fall. During the three hot summer months one may be more concerned with survival than beauty.

The above is directed to temperate-season grasses, of course, and bermudagrass and other tropicals are favored by summer temperatures. Cuts can be lowered then with little stress and raised in the fall to promote winter hardiness.[92]

A new choice confronting management is when to mow during the day.[30] With increased play on golf courses and the installation of lights for night play, some superintendents have used night mowing. Comments have been favorable and have noted that the grass stands to the cutter bar when turgid at night and does not lay down as it may on a hot day. It would seem reasonable to expect less injury when mowing will be followed by several hours of favorable temperatures rather than by several hours of heat and water stress. However, a full experimental evaluation of night mowing has not been made.

MOWING AND KIND OF GRASS

Mowing responses vary with the grass used.[24] Davis found Kentucky bluegrass and creeping red fescue both favored at 2-in. mowing, whereas 'Astoria' was eliminated at 2 in., favored at 3/4 in.[7,8] In coastal Washington, where climate favors bentgrasses, mowing results in bentgrass domination, but at 3/4-in. mowing, thatch buildup and weediness are both reduced as compared to higher cuts.[12]

Varietal differences in response to mowing occur within species. Law evaluated bluegrass root growth and found 'Merion' and 'Fylking'

Table 4.3. Effect of Seasons on Mowing Practices

California		*England*
75 °F	Mean July temperature	57 °F
45 °F	Mean January temperature	40 °F
	February 15-April 1	
Good growth; can mow as low as 1 in.		Frost; mow 1 in. to reduce injury
	April 1-June 1	
Vigorous growth; mow 1-1/4 in. or higher every five days		Good growth; begin to lower cut when days are sunny
	June 1-Sept. 15	
Growth slow; do not mow when daily temperatures exceed 95°; after each long hot spell resume mowing at 1/4 to 1/2 in. higher to reduce stress and keep soil and crowns cooler; mow late in day and irrigate before following noon; by end of last hot spell height may be 2-1/2 to 3 in.		Vigorous growth; mow 3/4 in. depending on use, mow when dry if possible; may need to mow twice a week
	Sept. 15-Nov. 15	
Growth vigorous, but spreading fall growth; lower cut to encourage dense turf-type growth		Growth slowing; raise height to insure vigorous condition during winter
	Nov. 15-Feb. 15	
Mow occasionally at 1-1/4 in. to remove frosted tips		Winter; mow occasionally at 1-1/2 in. to prevent excess accumulation of tops; do not mow when frozen

relatively little affected by 1/2-in. mowing as compared to 1-in. mowing, whereas 'Cougar,' 'Newport,' and 'Delta' had root growth severely depressed at 1/2 in.[27]

In another trial, yield, in response to mowing, differed among varieties. 'Merion' was less affected by 1/2-in. mowing than 'Newport,' 'Park,' or 'Delta.'[45]

Engel suggests mowing *Zoysia* in the north at 1/2–3/4 in. to minimize thatch.[11] Thatch insulates the grass from the warmth of the soil and increases winterkill.

In selecting bluegrass varieties, Law finds dwarfness and prolificacy of tillering are good indicators of tolerance to low mowing, whereas length of sheath is valueless.

Sometimes, close mowing is used to reduce grass vigor deliberately. Bermudagrass may build thatch so rapidly in the southwest that close mowing is used to reduce the rate of buildup. Similarly, *Zoysia* forms such a thick sod that a mower bounces around on top of it and fails to run true. A close cut is used to keep the machinery nearer the ground.

Under ordinary treatment, kikuyugrass in a favorable climate will overrun a landscape and produce a puffy thatch. But if mowed short, often, and held back by low fertility, low water, and high traffic, it forms a usable turf.

REMOVAL OF CLIPPINGS

A choice which may still be argued on the basis of the little evidence available is whether to remove or leave clippings. In an experiment in England clippings were consistently removed or left. After a period of several seasons differences developed as follows:[9]

Clippings returned	*Clippings removed*
More *Poa annua* (26%)	Less *Poa annua* (6%)
More earthworms	Fewer earthworms
Softer turf	Harder turf
Moister, more drought resistant	Dried out sooner
Greener in winter	Browner in winter
No moss	Moss present

Clippings are thought to be a possible reservoir for disease, but no more disease appeared than where clippings were removed.

Thatch is a reservoir of disease according to all expert opinion, and increases the difficulty of irrigation. Fall raking of bluegrass produced only 20–25% as much trash where clippings had been caught all season.

Thatch, however, is primarily from stolons and is so closely correlated with nitrogen use that clipping effects may be considered secondary. The decision to remove or leave clippings may well rest on other factors. If *Poa annua* is the problem then seed heads should be caught. If high temperatures and inadequate moisture are problems then perhaps one may best let the clippings fly. Recovery from drought, however, is favored by catching clippings and removing thatch. This program favors rooting in the soil. Roots are deeper in soil than on thatch and few roots may penetrate thatch that is allowed to accumulate (Chap. 5).

MOWING PATTERN

The turf manager may also choose a mowing pattern. One effect of mowing is to direct all leaves the same way to create a pattern. Grain results in grass mowed continually in the same direction. Hence on a green, direction is changed with each mowing. This decreases grain and also creates an interesting crossed pattern. Away from the green, however, directions are seldom changed. Institutional mowing is often rigid. The first cut is made next to the sidewalk and the same pattern is repeated over and over until the tractor tires form compacted strips or even ruts that then assure that the wheels will follow in the same track time after time (see *Principles of Mangement,* Chap.5; ref.31).

It would be desirable to rotate the direction of travel of large mowers just as with small ones, but most large areas are not circle shapes as greens are. Long axes are favored directions of travel as there is less turning. Landscape design also influences patterns.

There is an opportunity to profitably study mowing patterns. On golf fairways, for example, mowing along the long axis of the fairway requires minimum turning. Turns, however, are made in front of the tee and the green. During turns the spinning wheels and reels act like a gyroscope. When turning to the left the gyroscopic action tends to raise the left side of the mower and depress the right side. Right turns depress the left side. The cut will be uneven on the turn with the outside of each reel digging in and scalping. The faster the reel and the sharper the turn, the deeper the dig. As a consequence, a critical playing area in front of the green suffers, looks poorly, and tends to lose grass. One solution is to design the green (or tee) area so the mower turns by circling behind the green (or tee). A second solution it to use controls to engage and disengage the reel so turns can be made with the reel idle. A third possibility is to mow across the fairway. In practise the latter is not as consuming of time as one might think. Cross mowing can often be continued without interrupting the player or tractor driver, especially if the mower can move back and forth between two parallel fairways. A driver mowing with the long axis may be stopped 30% of the time waiting on play. In practice, mowing across fairways has added 5% to the mowing time on one golf course. Long, slanting mowing paths, angling 15 or 20° from the fairway axis will concentrate turns at the side of the fairway and allow alternate mowing in two directions.

Poor landscape design is difficult to cope with. Groves of trees should be closely planted with no grass or the trees should be separated by three to four feet more than the width of a gang mower. Odd trees should be replaced. Roughs should not be planted with solid tree rows. Occasional open areas between fairways can offer interesting vistas and allow the tractor driver to spread his work between two fairways when traffic is slowing him down. Damage of trees by mowers and vice versa can be avoided by keeping grass away from trees. At least one reel mower is built with a guide that keeps it away from tree trunks and allows the tractor-mower to circle the trees at a fixed distance.

KINDS OF MOWERS

Mowers themselves fall into four types: the reel, rotary, flail, and side bar.[16] The reel mower produces the finest mowing and is the standard mower to use for fine turf.

Reel mowers may drive from power applied directly to the reel or by gearing from wheels set outside the reel or from a roller behind the reel. This latter allows cutting closer to buildings, etc., and gives good maneuverability. With the driving roller behind, the front support may be either two caster wheels or a roller traveling ahead of the reel. Unless the turf is stiff and turgid, it may be pressed down by the front roller and fail to cut well. Consequently caster wheels are often preferred.

The clip of a reel mower is the forward distance it travel between cuts.[2] Practice indicates the best clip equals the mowing height. A mower mowing at a height of one inch should move forward one inch between scissorings of the blade across the bed knife. To mow at two inches a two inch clip would be desirable. As the clip exceeds the height, the grass appears ribbed. When the clip is less than the height, efficiency of the reel blade in gathering grass for the cut is reduced.

In a reel turning at constant speed, the clip will depend on the number of blades. Doubling the blades will halve the clip. When the number of blades is constant the clip will depend on the speed of the reel. If the reel spins twice as many times in the same forward distance the clip will be halved. As the energy depends on the square of the velocity, a reel turning twice as fast suffers four times the impact when hitting a foreign object. There is another effect of a fast reel. Energy expended at the bedknife results in a tendency of the mower to rotate around the bedknife. When you hit a clump of ryegrass in a bluegrass turf, the extra energy used at the bedknife causes the mower to dip, and dig in the turf. The extent of this dip is also increased by rotating the reel faster. Where clippings are caught, sufficient speed is needed on the reel to kick the clippings into the catcher. Beyond that there is no advantage to speed. The true advantage of more blades on a reel is that they permit the reel to turn at slower speeds with less wear on the bearings, less scalping on turns, and less damage from hitting twigs, pebbles, or cans.

The bedknife is lubricated by grass juice, and spinning the reel without cutting grass may increase wear and even result in seizing between blade and bedknife.

A reel mower produces the finest surface and is preferred for all quality turf. One reason is that a shearing cut is made perpendicular to the line of travel, parallel to the axle. If a wheel drops, a small trough is cut; but if a wheel drops on a rotary, a large circular area is scalped. A reel mower cannot mow tall grass.

A second type of mower is the rotary in which a spinning knife depends on the force of inertia of the grass blade to cut it off by impact. The main advantage of the rotary is economy. The knife is often mounted directly on the engine shaft without gears, belts or even a clutch. The blade is simple to sharpen. A second advantage is that it can reduce tall grass, fallen leaves, and weeds to a chopped mulch. Disadvantages include a high power requirement, high velocities of the blade with attendant danger, and wear concentrated to an inch or two of cutting edge with a need for frequent sharpening. Various blades are available for different cutting jobs.

A second version of a knife operating by impact is the hammer knife mower. Knives are rapidly rotated around a horizontal axle to cut against the direction of travel. There is only a small clearance between the blades and the housing and cut trash is recut until it is small enough to clear the housing. The principal advantage of the hammer knife is its ability to handle leaves and tall weeds and reduce them to a ground-up mulch. The knives are pivoted. In operation they are held out by centrifugal force. When they hit a rock or obstruction they pivot out of the way so there may be less danger from flying stones than with a rotary mower.

The sickle bar mower is suited to occasional mowing of grass and weeds of hay height. It operates with less power than the hammer knife but does not cut up the leavings.

For all mowing equipment, good maintenance is of the essence (see Fig. 4.6). To study mowing, men at Toro Manufacturing Co. took time-lapse moving pictures of grass blades after mowing. One finding was that leaves cut with a sharp mower began to grow again a few hours after mowing.[2] Cut with a dull mower leaf blades required over a day before growth resumed, and the area of injury spread, so more of the leaf browned off. A dull mower used regularly produces a turf with a yellowish or brownish cast. The amount of clippings in the basket decreases, and the turf fails to respond to fertilizer or other treatments to improve its appearance and growth. The problem is easily diagnosed by the ragged or frayed cut and the extent of the brown injured area at the end of the leaf.

The frequency with which mowers need to be sharpened depends on conditions of use. The more sand, pebbles, and twigs that go through a

Figure 4.6 A well-kept maintenance area. *Courtesy W. B. Davis.*

mower the more often it will need attention. With a reel-type mower, the reel needs to be sharp, the bedknife needs to be sharp, and the two need to be mated. After sharpening, the reel and bedknife are mated by lapping. A mixture of detergent, water, and fine emery powder is brushed over the blades while the mower is roating backward. If necessary, the bedknife is adjusted to compensate for the metal lapped off. An oil and emery combination is sometimes used as a lapping compound instead of suds and emery. However, the oil mixture is difficult to wash off and there is increased risk of getting emery into bearings or moving parts.

Lapping can also be used between sharpenings to increase the keenness of the cut but it is not capable of correcting dullness when the edge of the blade is abraded, rounded, and worn.

Rotary mowers are readily sharpened with a few strokes of a file and should be frequently filed as all wear is of the tip inch or two of the blade. Where a mower is being used all day, it is appropriate to stop for touch up every two hours.

A hammer knife mower is also readily filed, but has many more blades to be individually sharpened. A sickle bar mower is sharpened by grinding the blades on a specially shaped wheel. This can be done without special equipment.

Mowers should be cleaned reguarly. Mowers should be hosed after use with a soft stream of water (Fig. 4.7). A nozzle or air blast forces dirt into bearings. An air hose can be used advantageously to remove clippings from air-flow channels in the engine housing. This, clean oil, and clean-air filters are properly part of engine maintenance. When different grasses are mowed, as bentgrass and bermuda for example, the mower can be hosed off between areas to prevent cross contamination by carrying clippings from one area to the other.

In addition to increasing machine life, cleanliness develops pride. When a man works with a sharp, clean machine and personally tends to keeping it clean, washed, and painted he becomes more than a mower jockey. A man with pride in his work and in his machine will do a better job and will increase the life of the machine because of better care; but in the beginning he has to be taught to care for his machine.

When grass disease is present, mowing should be from the healthy grass to the diseased; the mower should then be washed. This will help lessen spread of the infection.

A goal of mowing is a uniform surface, and good mowing should produce that uniformity. A number of factors can result in irregular surfaces. If the clip of the mower is too great for the height being mowed, the surface will appear ribbed. The correction is to mow higher, use a different mower, or change the sprockets or gears so the reel runs faster.

Figure 4.7 Cleanliness and care of equipment are also part of growing good grass. *Courtesy W. B. Davis.*

If the height of the cutter bar is not uniform end to end, the mower will mow unevenly; the low end will expose grass more yellow in color. The result is a turf that is both uneven in height and in color. Uniform adjustment will correct the problem. Usually the roller is lower on one end though a low side may be due to uneven inflation of the tires on a side-wheel mower. When bearings are worn the cut may be ribbed or wavy and bearings must be replaced.

Some mowing problems are operator problems. We have already remarked on the gyro action of the reel. Some men take pleasure in the physical skill needed to spin a rapidly mowing mower so it comes back exactly in the next track. If this is done, the digging in from the gyro action will soon result in an off-color edge around a green. This is followed by loss of grass from environmental stress. To turn a mower properly, the reel is disengaged and the turn made off the green. The operator should not lean on the machine. On some mowers the handle is pivoted so one can't put weight on it, but on other mowers the height of cut varies as the operator leans more or less heavily on the machine. The operator should grip the mower handle with his palms facing up and his thumbs to the outside.

The environment also effects small changes in mower action. When we start mowing early on a summer day the grass is turgid and erect. It supports the mower higher than later in the day when the day's heat results in a limp soft grass blade that no longer holds the mower high. At the same time increasing temperatures expand the air in mower tires. When soil is wet and soft a mower may cut lower than when the ground is hard. On hard dry ground the mowers may bounce around more as the wheels hit obstacles. On greens the weight of clippings in the basket affects the actual height of cut. The basket should be emptied when about half full to prevent short cutting when the basket is full and heavy.

Efforts are made at times to improve the overall quality resulting from greens mowing. A reciprocating engine naturally vibrates as the piston changes direction at the end of each stroke. This increases soil compaction. Battery-operated electric mowers that avoid this problem are available. Although they haven't gained general acceptance yet, there is no reason why they shouldn't be increasingly used.

Brushes and combs have been added to mowers as accessary equipment. Their action is to agitate the grass so stolon ends and recumbent plants stand up where they can be mowed. This reduces graininess of greens. Combs and brushes, in particular, should be kept clean. When disease is present they should not be used as they can spread disease. They can be decontaminated by washing in fungicide diluted to normal spray strength. A household bleach solution diluted 10:1 is effective and cheaper.

MOWING PRACTICUM

There are two purposes of mowing. One is to provide grass of the correct height for play. The second is to increase the beauty of a sward by providing a uniform surface, and height is not significant to the purpose.

Although data from many sources show more turf vigor at higher cuts, and with a longer interval between cuts, there has been a tendency to mow ever shorter and more frequently. In the midwest in particular some superintendents mow fairways five times a week. Their intention has been to present a finer turf to their public. The results have been otherwise. Good grasses have been replaced by weedy species, especially *Poa annua.* This increased weediness has been obtained with increased cost of labor and machines for mowing. The cost of maintaining *Poa annua* through the summer is high. Fungicides (at about $2000–3000 per spray) and syringing must be used on the entire course instead of just the greens.

Municipal-course superintendents with budgets and equipment too limited for excessive maintenance have often had a better program. It appears again as if the better program is one providing the lowest level of maintenance consistent with the use to be made made of the grass. (I assume a liberal interpretation or *use* and *low-level maintenance* that takes due cognizance of the value of beauty and vigor of the turf. One does not need a manager to produce a starved, weedy, and erratically mowed turf.)

One approach to mowing is to assume you have a stress budget, i.e., that the grass can take just so much stress before it fails. If you put more stress on the grass with one practice, then you apply less stress from other sources. The shorter and more frequent the mowing the greater the stress. In Great Britain the weather is nearly perfect for bentgrasses. There is little or no stress from heat, water, or nematodes, and there has been less stress than in the U.S. from traffic. The British greenskeeper uses nitrogen fertilizer at a lower level so he does not build up stress from crowding too many short-rooted plants in a unit area. Consequently, the British turf man can mow greens two to three times a week at 1/8 in., bluegrass at 1/2–3/4 in., and have his grass survive except when disease stress is high.

While parts of New England have a climate almost as favorable as Great Britain the growing season is interrupted by occasional hot spells. Also there is more use of nitrogen fertilizers. One can mow greens at 3/16 in., but 1/4 in. would be preferable during the heat of summer. When mowing stress is frequent and traffic stress exceeds 1500 rounds a month, 1/4 in. becomes a minimum greens height.

Going south and west from the New England coast, summer stress from heat and water increases and less mowing stress is allowable. One-quarter inch should be a minimum greens mowing height, and as temperatures rise mowing frequuency should be reduced. Preventive disease sprays on greens are needed to avoid stress from these pests. Syringing becomes important. In the transition zone, summer climatic stress is so great that all stress from other sources needs to be minimized. One uses preventive sprays, syringes, and fertilizes with the greatest care to avoid any flushes of nitrogen, and holds back on mowing when the heat is severe. If you are not getting the clippings in the basket during a hot spell, mow less frequently. Consider raising the greens cut to 9/32 or 5/16 in. Bluegrass decorative turf should be appropriately higher–to two or more inches under heat stress.

To an extent, grass will provide its own measure of environmental stress by the amount of clippings produced. This is a good criterion to use. Clippings may drop off in July because of excess heat, or because of a buildup of nematodes. In either case, and without knowing the cause, a reduction in mowing frequency will aid grass survival. When a change in the weather favors the grass, increased clippings will tell you it is again time to mow more frequently. One superintendent compensates for mowing stress on tees by mowing only the teeing area to 3/4 in., the rest of the tee is mowed to 1 in. To change areas he mows down the new area and rests the old one at a higher cut.[37]

Mowing and irrigation operations should be planned to dovetail. Wet grass is difficult to mow. As mowing causes a temporary reduction of root growth, water uptake may be reduced following mowing. Stress will be minimized if irrigation follows shortly after mowing.[20]

Mowing, as other maintenance practices, should have its reasons. If you are mowing decorative turf just to keep it even and uniform, then height and frequency may be determined by the species of grass you wish to favor. If the turf is for erosion control, cuts can be high and just frequent enough to keep weeds from going to seed and contaminating nearby land. Under shade, stress is already high and mowing needs especial care.

Mower maintenance and operator training are management responibilities that cannot be neglected. If you can't afford a mechanic , then have one man to clean air filters, change oil, and grease all points; this limits the supervision needed. If a mower gets dull the superintendent should notice it at once in the ragged leaf ends and not wait until poor growth calls attention to trouble. The efficiency of the man doing the mowing can also change from day to day.

An economic study of large-scale turf operations indicates that 60% of the labor budget is used mowing, 15% of the supply budget (gas and oil), and 25% of the equipment repair and replacement budget. This is about 43% of the total budget. This indicates mowing is an operation where good management can save money, poor management can waste money.

There is considerable opportunity for the manager to study mowing programs both from the standpoint of mowing patterns and mowing frequencies. Improvements and economies should often be possible.

When several areas having different grasses and serving different uses are mowed alike little management is being exercised.

The turf manager may well sit down with top management from time to time and define the kind of operation being run. On some championship courses greens are mowed seven days a week and fairway mowers are always in motion. On the other hand, there are some neighborhood courses where conditions are excellent, and greens are mowed three times a week. The greens turf is a bit coarse perhaps but it putts well, there is no grain, collars are as good as the rest of the green. We need to ask which green represents our goal, both in terms of available budget and needs of the players. Is it enough that the green putt well or must it also impress guests with its closeness, fineness, texture, high color, etc.?

When we have fully defined our own goals we can operate a program to achieve them. Without goals we are in danger of copying the programs of other managers in the neighborhood.

Have a goal, watch the grass, watch the budget, and keep the mowers sharp, and you have the backbone of a good program. Keep an eye on the thermometer, budget your stresses, and keep the program in tune with the season.

Dawson has expressed himself thus: "Mowing is not the simple operation of removing excess growth as many imagine, but a process having far-reaching effects and therefore worthy of the most careful study and control."[9]

References

1. Beard, J. B., and W. H. Daniel, 1965, "Effect of temperature and cutting on the growth of creeping bentgrass (*Agrostis palustris* Huds.) roots," *Agron. J.* **57,** 249–250; see also *U.S.G.A. J. and Turf Management* **12**(3), 30–31 (1959).
2. Benson, D. O., 1963, "Mowing grass with a reel type machine," *Calif. Turfgr. Cult.* **13**(2), 11–14.
3. Brown, E. M., 1943, "Seasonal variation in the growth and chemical composition of Kentucky bluegrass," *Univ. Missouri Col. Agr. Expt. Sta. Res. Bull.* **360,** 56pp.
4. Burton, G., J. E. Jackson, and R. H. Hart. 1963, "Effects of cutting frequency on nitrogen yield, *in vitro* digestibility, and protein, fibre, and carotene content of 'Coastal' bermudagrass," *Agron. J.* **55,** 500–502.
5. Clapp, J. G., Jr., D. S. Chamblee, and H. D. Gross, 1965, "Interrelationships between defoliation systems, morphological characteristics, and growth of 'Coastal' bermudagrass," *Agron. Abstr.,* p. 34.
6. Crider, F. H., 1955, "Root growth stoppage resulting from defoliation of grass," *U.S. Dept. Agr. Tech. bull.* **1102,** 23 pp.
7. Davis, R. R., 1958, "The effects of other species and mowing height on the persistence of lawn grasses," *Agron. Abstr.,* p, 64.
8. Davis, R. R., 1967, "Population changes in Kentucky bluegrass–red fescue mixtures," *Agron. Abstr.,* p. 51.
9. Dawson, R. B., 1939, *Practical Lawn Craft,* Crosby Lockwood and son Ltd., London, pp. 96–99.
10. Deal, E. E., 1963, "Regulating growth of 'Merion' Kentucky bluegrass (*Poa pratensis* L.) turf with cultural and management techniques," PhD Thesis. Rutgers; *Dissertation Abstr.* **24**(3), 2643.

11. Engel, R., 1962, "What it takes to make a fabulous lawn," *House Beautiful* **104**(5), 188–191.
12. Goss, R. L., and A. Overland, 1965, "Effect of cutting height and fertilization on thatch formation and weed population in bentgrass turf," *Agron. Abstr.* p. 23.
13. Graber, L. F., 1933, "Competetive efficiency and productivity of bluegrass *(Poa pratensis* L.) with partial defoliation at two levels of cutting," *J. Am. Soc. Agron.* **25,** 328–334.
14. Graber, L. F., N. T. Nelson, W. A. Leukel, and W. B. Albert, 1927, "Organic food reserves in relation to the growth of alfalfa and other perennial herbaceous plants," *Wisconsin Agrc. Expt. Sta. Res. Bull.* **80,** 100–120.
15. Graber, L. F., and H. W. Ream, 1931, "Growth of bluegrass with various defoliations and abundant nitrogen supply," *J. Am. Soc. Agron.* **23,** 938–944.
16. *Grounds Maintenance*, 1966-date; publishes articles describing mowing and other turf-maintenance equipment; see for example Dec. 1966 and Dec. 1967 issues.
17. Harrison, C. M., 1931, "Effect of cutting and fertilizer applications on grass development," *Plant Physiol.* **6,** 669–684; see also *U.S.G.A. Greens Sect. Bull.* **11**(11), 210–217 for a more informal treatment of the same and additional data.
18. Harrison, C. M., and C. W. Hodgson, 1939, "Response of certain perennial grasses to cutting treatments," *J. Am. Soc. Agron.* **31,** 418–430.
19. Holt, E. C., and J. C. McDaniel, 1963, "Influence of clipping on yield, regrowth, and root development of dallisgrass, (*Paspalum dilatatum,* Poir.) and kleingrass (*Panicum coloratum,* L.)," *Agron. J.* **55,** 561–564.
20. Jantti, A., and P. J. Kramer, 1956, "Regrowth of pastures in relation to soil moisture and defoliation," *7th Intern. Grasslands Conf.*, pp. 33–42.
21. Johnson, J. T., and G. W. Burton, 1967, "Managing bahia for turf," *Agron. Abstr.,* p. 52.
22. Juska, F. V., and A. A. Hanson, 1961, "Effects of interval and height of mowing on growth of 'Merion' and common Kentucky bluegrass (*Poa pratensis* L.)," *Agron. J.* **53,** 385–388.
23. Juska, F. V., and A. A. Hanson, 1963, "The management of Kentucky bluegrass on extensive turfgrass areas," *Park Maint.* **16**(9), 22 ff.
24. Juska, F. V., J. Tyson, and C. M. Harrison, 1955, "The competitive relationship of 'Merion' bluegrass as influenced by various mixtures, cutting heights, and levels of nitrogen," *Agron. J.* **47,** 513–517.
25. Klapp, E., 1938, "Principles governing the value of herbage plants for hay and pasture," *Herbage Rev.* **6,** 57–63 (translation of a paper given before the 4th Intern. Grasslands Cong. Aberyswyth, 1937).
26. Kneebone, W. R., 1966, "Rootgrowth of bermudagrass varieties at three mowing heights in 1966," *Univ. Ariz. Agr. Expt. Sta. Rept.* **240,** 15–17.
27. Law, A. G., 1965, "Performance of bluegrass varieties under two heights of clipping," *19th Ann. Northwest Turfgr. Conf. Proc.*, pp. 27–32; also in *Weeds, Trees, and Turf* **5**(5), 26–28 (May 1966).
28. Letey, J., L. H. Stolzy, O. R. Lunt, and N. Valoris, 1964, "Soil oxygen

and clipping height," *Golf Course Reptr.* **32**(2), 16–26.

29. Lovvorn, R. L., 1945, "The effect of defoliation, soil fertility, and temperature, and length of day on the growth of some perennial grasses," *J. Am. Soc. Agron.* **37,** 570–582.
30. Lyons, W., 1962, "Night Maintenance," *Golfdom* **36**(7), 30 ff.
31. Madison, J. H., 1960, "The mowing of turfgrass, I. The effect of season, interval, and height of mowing on the growth of seaside bentgrass turf," *Agron. J.* **52,** 449–452.
32. Madison, J. H., 1962a, "The mowing of turfgrass, II. Responses of three species of grass. III.The effect of rest on seaside bentgrass turf mowed daily," *Agron. J.* **54,** 250–252 (II); 252–253 (III).
33. Madison, J. H., 1962b, "Turfgrass ecology. Effects of mowing, irrigation, and nitrogen treatments of *Agrostis palustris* Huds. 'Seaside' and *Agrostis tenuis*; Sibth. 'Highland' on population, yield, rooting and cover," *Agron. J.* **54,** 407–412.
34. Madison, J. H., and R. M. Hagan, 1962, "Extraction of soil moisture by 'Merion' bluegrass (*Poa pratensis* L. 'Merion') turf as affected by irrigation frequency, mowing height and other cultural operations," *Agron. J.* **54,** 157–160.
35. Madison, J. H., and A. H. Andersen, 1963, "A chlorophyll index to measure turfgrass response," *Agron. J.* **55,** 461–464.
36. Parker, K. W., and A. W. Sampson, 1931, "Growth and yield of certain *Gramineae* as influenced by reduction of photosynthetic tissue," *Hilgardia* **5**(10), 361–381.
37. Radko, A. M., 1967, "Useful tips," *38th Intern. Turfgr. Conf. and Show. Proc.,* pp. 40–41.
38. Roberts, E. C., and E. J. Bredakis, 1960, "Turfgrass root development," *Golf Course Reptr.* **28**(8), 12 ff.
39. Schery, R. W., 1966, "Remarkable Kentucky bluegrass," *Weeds, Trees, and Turf* **5**(10), 16–17.
40. Schlipf, 1941, *Practisches Handbuch der Landwirtschaft,* 27th ed., Berlin, in A Voisin, 1960, *Better Grassland Sward.* Crosby, Lockwood and Son, London, p. 22.
41. Stanley, R. L., E. R. Beaty, and J. D. Powell, 1967, "Effect of clipping height on forage distribution and regrowth of 'Pensacola' bahiagrass," *Agron. J.* **59,** 185–186.
42. Thompson, W. R., Jr., 1966, "The influence of potassium nutrition and clipping management on growth patterns, carbohydrate, and winter hardiness of 'Tifgreen' bermudagrass," Ph. D. Thesis, Miss. State Univ., *Dissertation Abstr.* **27B** (3), 1687.
43. Troughton, A., "The underground organs of herbage grasses," *Commonwealth Bureau of Pastures and Field Crops Bull.* **44,** 94–100; Commonwealth Agrc. Bur., Farnham Royal Bucks, England.
44. Wilkins, F. S., 1935, "Effect of overgrazing on Kentucky bluegrass under conditions of extreme drouth," *J. Am. Soc. Agron.* **27,** 159.
45. Wood, G. M., and J. A. Burke, 1961, "Effect of cutting height on turf density of 'Merion', 'Park', 'Delta', 'Newport', and common Kentucky bluegrass," *Crop Sci.* **1,** 317–318.

5

AUXILIARY MANAGEMENT PRACTICES

This chapter covers hole punching, top dressing, verticutting, thatch control, rejuvenation, renovation root pruning, overseeding, poling, brooming, syringing, plugging, mulching, nursery, composting, dyeing, etc.

HOLE PUNCHING (AERIFICATION)

Today, hole punching is considered essential for high-maintenance turfgrass. Empirical evidence has favored the practice. Hole punching may result in greening of grass around the hole within a few days. In turf with few roots, a lush growth of roots will be found in the holes. Hole punching is most commonly referred to as aerification. This may or may not be correct use of the term. Hole punching affects other factors in the management program and in some instances may be as effective in letting out carbon dioxide and toxic soil vapors as in letting in oxygen.[19,21,25,60] Hole punching may improve wetting of dry soils and drying of wet soils. Thompson and Ward found frequent hole punching (six times per year) resulted in earlier spring greenup and higher quality of 'Tifgreen' by the third year.[65]

Morgan used it to increase water penetration on hillside turf so half as much water was applied in a third fewer applications.[53] Over a ten-year period, Engel and Alderfer found cultivation decreasing thatch and increasing soil oxygen though top dressing was even more effective in increasing soil oxygen.*[15]

Soil oxygen above minimum levels is essential for germination,[31] root growth,[5.8.46.59.63] moisture uptake,[10.32.42.43] top growth,[37.40.43] and mineral uptake,[38.41.42] and levels may affect general vigor (Table 5.1).[40] In one instance with an ODR of 9 (gX10^{-8}/cm^2/min) germination was limited by moisture tensions over 3 bars but not by oxygen.[33] Below 2 1/2%, tomato roots could not penetrate a dense layer.[59] Root initiation stopped at an ODR of about 20[63] and 'Newport' root growth stopped at an ODR near 10.[46.47] In poorly aerated soils oxygen may move to roots in the intercellular space of the cortex.[13.34]

Table 5.1. Putting Green Condition and Oxygen Diffusion Rates at Different Soil Depths[40]

Condition of Putting Green	*Depth of Measurement (in.)*	*Oxygen Diffusion Rate[a]*
Good	2	51.6
	4	27.1
	12	3.8
Bad	2	10.0
	4	10.2
Declining	2	13.6
	4	14.7
	12	4.1

[a]Measured in g/cm^2/ min x 10^{-8} (av. of twenty measurements). A value of 20 is considered the critical level. Growth of grass roots is not satisfactory below this level.

In peas the first response to low oxygen was loss of turgor of the root tips.[10] Tomato roots changed their rate of water uptake within an hour of oxygen reduction.[32] Barley roots with adequate oxygen took up more water than roots in reduced oxygen[45] on the same plant. Reduced turgor may be the reason for reduced top growth. Kubota[37] found yield depressed with low oxygen and Letey et al. found Newport unable to make growth after mowing when ODR was low.[76.47] An ODR of 50–60 was needed before a good regrowth took place and intermediate values resulted in intermediate re-

*Aeration is most commonly measured electochemically with a platinum electrode and expressed as ODR (oxygen diffusion rate). The units of ODR are grams of oxygen x 10^{-8} per square cm per minute.[68] For simplicity, units will be dropped during most of the discussion.

growth. Similarly, mineral uptake was better with higher ODR.[41,42] In citrus, root oxygen affected levels of N, P, K, Ca, Mg, Zn, Cu, Mn, B, and Fe, though there were also seasonal effects.[38] With 'Newport' nitrogen uptake was affected more critically than phosphorus uptake, and that of potassium was confounded with sodium uptake.

Minimum levels of oxygen for good root growth have been found to be about ODR 20, with 40–60 optimum. However, the minimum level is higher at higher temperatures, and in wet soils. It varies slightly with the species [10,44] and with the carbon dioxide level in the soil.[9]

Stolzy et al. found root initiation stopped as the ODR dropped from 23 to 18 g x 10^{-8}/cm^2/min,,[63] and Letey et al. found growth stopped below 10;[64] however, tomato roots required 20 before they penetrated a dense layer.[54] Growth of bermudagrass roots was related to both oxygen and carbon dioxide content of the soil but dry weight showed the closest relation to $0_2/CO_2$ ratio.[7] Top growth was also related to soil oxygen and carbon dioxide during periods of heat stress. When soil oxygen levels were in the critical range, sunflower growth was reduced less at lower soil temperatures but when air temperatures exceeded 95°F there was a complete reduction of root growth irrespective of soil temperature and oxygen.[44]

Moisture affects soil aeration in two ways. Oxygen moves rapidly in air-filled pores but when the root is surrounded with a film of water, oxygen moves into the water and through it but slowly and the film of water limits oxygen uptake.[36,58] Root elongation was found limited by the water film until water tensions reached 20 mb.[24] Oxygen was found to limit root growth of cotton up to 500 mb, at which point water became limiting.[20] Due to moisture and tortuosity, a root 1 mm distant from adequate soil oxygen could still be limited by inadequate oxygen.[45]

Water also limits plant growth by competing with air for pore space. Air movement is related to water movement[1] and aeration is a function of air-filled porosity and irrigation practices. Compaction, as we know, reduces air-filled porosity and aeration but so does irrigation. After irrigation there is no aeration until tension exceeds the bubbling pressure of the soil.[24] Barley germination increased with air-filled pores in the 0–3 in. layer of soil.[37] Root penetration and depth has been found to be a function of bulk density and related to air-filled pores rather than to soil strength.[64] When soil was kept wet 'Merion' rooted on the surface.[66]

Factors influencing movement of oxygen also influence movement of carbon dioxide out of the soil. Sprinklers used in agriculture crust and seal the soil surface, which results in buildup of carbon dioxide. If temperatures are high this may result in death of the roots. Hence the agriculturist lightly tills the soil after sprinkler irrigation.[60] Root growth is affected by soil carbon dioxide, and whereas CO_2 depresses growth of barley,[21] corn roots recover rapidly as CO_2 is reduced.[23] In compaction experiments when bulk density was raised from 1.1 to 1.7, the soil accumulated in excess of 10% carbon dioxide at densities above 1.4.[31] Studies suggest that increasing CO_2 levels reduces root growth when aeration is good. If aeration is poor, other factors are limiting and carbon dioxide levels are without influence.[64]

To examine possible effects from soil produced vapors, we grew corn and tomato plants in solution culture. Some treatments were not aerated. Some treatments were aerated with clean air filtered through activated carbon. For other treatments air was first passed through soil, through soil mixed with grass clippings, through compost or other materials. When the solution was aerated with pure air, tops and roots grew better than in non aerated solution. Plant growth was reduced when solutions were aerated with air passed over garden soil. When air was passed over soil mixed with grass clipping, growth was depressed, leaves were chlorotic, and roots were short and brown.

We feel this demonstrates the possibility that hole punching may benefit turf by letting undesirable gases escape from the soil.

Hole-Punching Practicum

At the practical level, hole punching is as much associated with water relations as with aeration, though of course the two are related. Without hole punching greens tend to become a layer cake with alternate layers of partly decomposed thatch and top dressing. Water does not penetrate this layer very readily, nor do roots. Coarse sand layers from top dressing have a more severe effect on water and rooting than do finer-textured layers.[66] Hole punching removes cores of the layered soil which can be replaced with uniform material through which water can percolate unrestricted by interfaces.

When surface compaction limits water infiltration, hole punching may help get water in. Sides of the holes provide additional surface area through which water may move. With low infiltration rates and short irrigation cycles, islands of drought can appear between the holes.

Byrne et al. have tested effects of hole punching on water infiltration on a bowling green.[9] Infiltration improvements from hole punching lasted only a few weeks unless holes were large, close, and deep (7/8, 2, and 6 in.). Even then benefit was of limited duration unless holes were connected with lower soils of good conductivity.

"To relieve compaction" is a reason often given for hole punching. This reason is not exact. The hole can't be compacted, but the degree of compaction of the soil between the holes is not lessened. If the holes are filled with a material that resists compaction, and if holes are punched regularly on a monthly basis, compaction can be relieved in six to ten

Figure 5.1 The response of grass roots, here shown growing from "aerifier" holes, is accepted as justification for the operation of hole punching. *Courtesy the University of California Agricultural Extension Service.*

years. This method is used to upgrade greens soils by removing cores and backfilling with the improved soil mixture.

Many fertilizers perform better when raked into holes than when scattered on the soil surface. Moisture, temperature, and biological activity are all more uniform beneath the soil surface.

Hole punching assists thatch control. In a study of individual management practices made at Davis we found hole punching and top dressing were two practices reducing thatch accumulation. With hole punching, thatch destruction took place in a pattern. A cone of destroyed thatch surrounded each hole. We thought withdrawal of the spoon might have pulled up a tuft of thatch where it would be mowed off. Observation showed this was not the case. Decay may have been favored by changed water relations, or saprophytic insects that took up residence in the holes may have had an effect. If true, hole punching would affect thatch less when insecticides were regularly used. Possible effects of hole punching on insects need study. Thompson and Ward found aerification reduced thatch but the small effects were overridden by other management practices.[65]

Hole punching is used in association with adding seed or overseeding. Seed needs to contact soil for seedlings to survive and become established. Cores removed in hole punching can be used to provide a seedbed. Cores are broken, for example, by dragging a mat over them, or some soils can be allowed to "melt" under the impact of irrigation. Many seeds can germinate in the holes and reach the surface successfully. Injured turf can be restored with minimal disruption by hole punching and seeding, especially if some grass has survived. The area is protected from washing by the old grass. A freshly rototilled area is more subject to erosion and weed invasion.

Punching deep holes for rejuvenation of turf is discussed later under rejuvenation.

Hole punching or its equivalent has been done with a variety of equipment. English gardeners used a spading fork. The fork was inserted four to six inches, raised just enough to slightly lift and fracture the soil, then withdrawn; the process was repeated every four to six inches. If one tries this, it is best to have an English style fork in which the tines are square in cross section and taper, becoming larger near the top.

A spiked roller first gave a continuous operation. Such equipment is still available, along with equipment which pokes knife blades into the soil to slit it. As such equipment produces holes by squeezing the space from the soil between the holes, the effect is to compact the soil. This raises the question as to whether the benefit from the holes outweighs the damage from compaction. At present I know of no basis for proposing an answer.

Making the spike hollow to cut and remove a core, as in present machines, reduces compaction but does not eliminate it altogether. The hollow spoon is larger than the core produced and the difference measures the extent to which the soil between holes is squeezed and compacted.

Hole punching is also criticized because on a dry soil the machine rides high on the ground. To make an effective hole the soil must be so moist that it is in a compactable state and there is danger of slicking the sides of holes, which would render them less effective for gas exchange or water infiltration.

These objections are met by a machine which in effect saws a series of slots through the soil instead of punching holes. This works most effectively when the soil is dry and resistant to compaction. The parallel cuts tend to give grain to a green. On soils which swell and shrink there is some difficulty refilling the slots exactly level, and grain results. One California superintendent opens the slits on the morning of the day the course is closed. As the soil dries and shrinks during the day the slits open wide. He fills and levels the slits in late afternoon. In this way he avoids the settling that would give a washboard effect to the green.

When spoons rotate about an axle, the ends of the spoon travel a greater distance than the upper shanks. If the spoon pivots at the soil surface, the bottom end digs and cultivates the soil in this hole, but at the expense of some compaction.

If the soil is soft the spoon may pivot about the center of its insertion and dig at the bottom and compact at the top. Some machines avoid rotation and its cultivating effect, and use a vertical punching action in which forward travel is compensated for, and the spoon withdrawn at the same angle as it is entered.

TOP DRESSING — THEORY

Agrostis stolonifera is a highly variable species. Some creeping forms are naturally adapted to sandy coastal areas where wind-driven sand continually buries old stolons. By creeping, the plant continually mounts the sifting sands and new growth rises above. It is understandable then that top dressing finds a place in management's program. An important part of early greens maintenance, top dressing survived World War II labor shortages for a different reason: to true the surface of greens. A buildup of stolons under the surface may result in uneven greens. A layer of sand worked among the surface stolons firms the surface and gives a true roll to the ball.

Top dressing was the most effective treatment tested by Thompson and Ward for reducing thatch.[65] They reduced thickness of thatch under 'Tifgreen' from 27 mm to 5 mm.

Engel and Alderfer[15] also examined top dressing as a means of reducing thatch. Not only did they find it effective, but top dressing resulted in high soil aeration, high water infiltration, and, at the end of ten years, top-dressed turf rated highest in quality. Its only weakness was increasing incidence of dollar spot. They found measuring thatch thickness as reliable as ignition methods.

At Davis we have studied individual maintenance practices. We found that greens turf receiving only top dressing steadily improved in quality. At the end of two years it rated as high as any treatment and appeared as vigorous as plots receiving preventative fungicides and insecticides. Top-dressed plots had the least thatch. Top dressing was light and frequent so there would be no layering.

In another study we carried bentgrass plots five years under high nitrogen to build up thatch. We finally achieved a sod-bound condition where the grass was of poor color and failed to respond to fertilizer. Irrigation was difficult as water penetrated the thatch with great difficulty. *Curvularia* was continually present. Of treatments imposed on these plots, we got no response from wetting agents, fungicides, or fertilizers. There was limited response to hole punching but it did not result in recovery. Only top dressing gave full rapid recovery.

During the next two years several top-dressing materials were studied. We used sand with varying amounts and kinds of organic matter. We found sand or sand with 5–10% organic compost was satisfactory, but the greater the content of organic material the greater the risk from summer diseases. We also compared mineral and 100% organic top-dressing materials such as peat and sawdust and found only mineral materials gave a tight true surface. Peat and sawdust caused the stolons to "unravel," i.e., to knit loosely into a puffy soft surface.

Top Dressing Practicum

If top dressing is done only once or twice a year to firm and true the surface, a layered green results. Layers of top dressing alternate with layers of peaty thatch. The history of a green can often be read in such layers. Each superintendent uses a different texture top dressing and top dresses more or less frequently so that layers are closer or farther apart.

Where a green is built of good materials top dressing should be of the same material to prevent interfaces and interrupted drainage. Where green soils are unsatisfactory and being replaced gradually by hole punching and backfilling, top dressing should be of the new soil. It is almost axiomatic that when building new greens 20–30 yards of the greens soil should be stockpiled for truing the greens and providing initial top dressings. If the greens soil can be reproduced from available materials, stockpiling is not necessary. But it is still helpful to have sufficient top dressing for truing the greens as this job will come at a time when the work load is heavy. When getting ready to open new greens, one does not need the extra chore of mixing and preparing top-dressing materials.

Top-dressing materials should be weed and disease free. A pile can be covered with a plastic tarpaulin and fumigated with methyl bromide, or mixed with calcium cyanamide and stacked for three to four weeks. Allowance should be made for the nitrogen fertility content of the cyanamide.

When top-dressing materials are clean they have an advantage over some other operations in that they decrease weediness by burying weed seeds. A good top-dressing program in which dressing is frequent and the material used contains seeds of good grasses should do more to suppress *Poa annua* than almost any other program.

I feel that top dressing has more potential for good than we presently recognize. But we will have to change some viewpoints about it. As presently done, top dressing is a major golf course operation carried out about twice a year. Large amounts of sand are used and the operation is accompanied by hole punching and verticutting (to make sure *Poa annua* seeds are brought to the surface again?). The operation involves a crew of several men for several days, and costs run $200–500 per green.

A possible new approach to top dressing would be to make a smaller operation out of it and combine other practices with it, or use it to replace other practices. Top-dressing materials could contain sand, a fertilizer, a granular or dry form of insecticide, and a dry fungicide. Iron could be contained in it, and seeds of bentgrass added. A light dressing could then be run on with a spreader every ten to fourteen days. If it were light enough to sift down without matting and dragging that operation could be eliminated. The top dressing could replace the operations of fertilization, spraying for pests, treating with iron, reseeding, and weed control. In addition, top dressing keeps the infiltration and aeration rate high so hole punching can be eliminated. Need for verticutting could be reduced.

A clever superintendent using top dressing could, I feel, maximize his management effectiveness, and minimize his cost by such a program.

We can effectively add 2 in. per year of top dressing to the surface, though 1 in. gives results as good. One-half inch is a minimum effective amount. To examine the practice, consider 1/2 in. on 1000 ft.^{2}

$$\frac{1000 \text{ ft}^2 \text{ x } 1/2 \text{ in. deep}}{12 \text{ in./ft}} = 41.7 \text{ ft}^3 = 1.5 \text{ yd}^3 \text{ of top dressing/1000 ft}^2$$

To put this in terms of a 5000-ft^2 green, we would need from 7 1/2 yd minimum to 15 yd optimum per year. Twenty applications would require between 1/3 and 2/3 yd for each top dressing.

For purposes of example only, 1/2 yd of material might be formulated as follows:

Fine sand	1/2 yd	
Seed	2 lb	
Iron sequestrene	1/4 lb	
Dolomite lime	1/2 lb	
Single superphosphate	1/2 lb	
Potassium sulfate	2 lb	make allowance above for
Nitrogen from source of choice	2 1/2 lb	materials contained in the nitrogen source
Zinc sequestrene	1 oz	

Run these in the mixer and add just enough water to dampen particle surfaces so materials mix thoroughly. Mixed dry, seed will tend to "float" out. Then add: (a) insecticides in season of need, for example,

Diazinon to provide 1/2 oz active ingredient; (b) Fungicide, for example, Thiram to provide 9 oz active ingredient plus Semesan to provide 2 oz active ingredient.

The above should be used as soon as dry enough to spread. For safetys sake it should not be stored nor should children be allowed to play in it. Many other sources could be used to provide the same ingredients and the pesticides should be changed from time to time. The above example used Diazinon because of its systemic action and the Thiram-mercury combination because it is wide spectrum and specific for dollar spot. A dust mask should be worn when adding these materials, and the top dressing handled with rubber gloves once they are added. There are problems. If a soluble nitrogen source is used, the material will have to be watered in, which will reduce the effectiveness of the pesticides. It is probably best to use an insoluble source and not irrigate until the morning of the day following application. Be sure you recognize that the above program is experimental and is based on a synthesis of several individual experiments and of the experiences of superintendents as reported over half a century.

VERTICAL MOWING

The Verticut or vertical mowing machine was originally designed to control grain on putting or bowling greens. Vertical rotating knives were set to just nick into the surface. This raised loose stolons to where the mower removed them and cut through other stolons, stimulating them to form branches which would grow at angles to the parent stolon, thereby reducing grain. Frequent light use of the machine controls grain. It has often been used infrequently, resulting in reduced effectiveness, or set so deep that it injured the turf.

Set deeply with no power on the reel the machine has been used to slit turf, cutting through stolons and giving a mild form of hole punching. Set deep and with power the vertical mower has been used to cut thatch out of bermuda and bentgrasses though this is a severe treatment for bentgrass. The machine has been further used to cut up cores after hole punching and to help true the surface after top dressing.

Our attempts to evaluate regular vertical mowing during two growing seasons were not successful. Sooner or later someone adjusted the machine a bit too deep for the temperatures and injury resulted.

Tested on 'Tifgreen,' frequent verticutting (every two weeks) helped reduce thatch. Meyers used several verticutting and fertilization programs on 'Ormond' and concluded that no one program was best throughout the season.[52] More nitrogen and less verticutting was better after September. Up to September monthly verticutting and 1 1/2 lb of NH_4NO_3 per month rated best. Fairway vertical mowers are now available; their action is considered under thatch removal.[11]

THATCH REMOVAL

We need to distinguish between mat and thatch. Stoloniferous grasses have interlaced living stems above the surface of the ground. *Mat* is this network of living material.[17] Some mat is desirable. On greens mat obsorbs the shock of flying balls and takes much of the wear. A firm compact mat is no problem but a mat that is loose and fluffy is not playable.

As stolons in the mat die, they, along with fallen clipping, form *thatch,* a layer of interlaced dead material resistant to decay. At deeper levels partial decay reduces the stolons to a peaty fiber.[39] Thatch tends to hold water like a sponge, and may keep the crown area too wet. When thatch dries the surface becomes hydrophobic, difficult to wet. On a slope dry thatch sheds water like a thatched roof. When Morgan removed thatch from a hillside turf he increased water absorption and decreased application time.[53]

Grasses without stolons do not form a heavy thatch and thatch comes only from fallen clippings. Soft, juicy, thin-walled cells of bluegrass, red fescue, or ryegrass clippings decay, leaving threads of thick-walled fiber cells.[39] The threads form a felt-like layer over the soil surface. This peaty, felt-like thatch is thinner but is similar to the thatch of stolons in its effects. In time, stolons also break down to a fibrous peat, but near the surface solons are undecayed and thatch is coarse.

As thatch provides a home for insects, and food for facultative parasites, it has been implicated as a source of disease and of undesirable insects. Thatch affects water infiltration and may be a limiting factor in irrigation, irrespective of the soil or soil mix beneath it. Thatch is suspected of affecting soil aeration by limiting gas exchange, and contributing carbon dioxide. Thatch accumulation has been laid to acid soils, but results primarily from high nitrogen use which stimulates growth of the interlacing stolons which form the main body of thatch. Contributing to failure of the thatch to break down are excessive wetness and the use of fungicides and insecticides. Use of sugar, calcium, and nitrogen to stimulate bacterial growth in the thatch layer increased dollar spot but failed to decrease thatch.[29]

We found regular use of a preventative fungicide resulted in increased thatch accumulation. Alternate drying and wetting has contributed to thatch breakup and decay.

Bentgrass will build up thatch at the rate of about 5–10 mm/yr when receiving about 1 lb of N/1000 ft^2/mo. Bermudagrass will build thatch at a slightly faster rate, due in part to a longer growing season where bermudagrass is grown. At the extreme, Kikuyugrass has been known to raise the grade 1 ft per decade in Los Angeles.

Initially, thatch was removed from bermuda lawns in the south so ryegrass could be overseeded for the winter. The bermudagrass rake was developed for this purpose. The rake rests on the curved backs of a series of knives and is slid back and forth. The angle at which the handle is held determines how deeply the knives will cut on the backstroke. Later, knives were added to a rototiller type machine and thatch was cut, ripped, and torn out by the knives. This is the essential design of a thatching machine today. Refinements in the knife pattern result in a cleaner job.

Thatching is still done primarily to prepare bermudagrass for overseeding, though it is also done to aid water penetration, disease control, or to make a firmer turf.

Thatching is a severe operation and should only be done at a time when conditions favor recovery or when the overseeded grass will fill in until recovery takes place. Thatching prepares a seedbed and if it is not followed by overseeding, the weed population may jump.

When buildup of bermudagrass thatch became a problem at UCLA, T. Fuchigami (viva voce) used a sod cutter to cut the grass and thatch off about 1/4 in. above ground level. The material was rolled up and dumped. New growth broke readily from remaining rhizomes and stolons and recovery was satisfactory.

A variant of a thatching machine consists of a power rake in which rotating spring tempered wires scratch out duff and trash.

We did not find value from the use of such a machine in California. The rake produces a satisfying amount of trash and one has a feeling of real accomplishment from using it. When we used it in the spring or fall, the effect was to increase weediness of the grass. Summer injury of temperate-season grasses was less severe than we had anticipated. Following treatment grass was thin and leaves were abraded. We noted no difference between treated and untreated areas except for the increased weediness of the treated area.

In discussing these results with Richard Schmidt of Virginia (VPI) he suggested my failure was due to use of irrigation in California. Where natural rainfall is used, unraked grass has shallow roots in the thatch[39] and suffers more from drought than raked grass. Where raking has removed the accumulation of trash and thatch, roots are in the soil and extend through a greater volume of root zone. This agrees with data from an earlier experiment in which we had used water stress as a variable.

Thatch has been burned out in an experimental approach by Meszaros.[51] Fairways were slit with a verticut, then a burner producing a 2500 °F flame was taken over the dry turf at 1 mph. The verticut grooves were burned out to 1/2-in. width and remaining thatch soon broke up and decayed. The hope was to reseed in the fall without severe *Poa annua* contamination. Compared to other treatments *Poa annua* and *Fusarium* patch were both reduced by flaming along with spring seed-head production by Kentucky bluegrass.

A fairway verticut has been introduced for large turf areas but this is intended more as a thatching machine and provides sufficient power on the blades to cut deeply. In one report 3/4 acres/hr were thatched removing 30 yd^3 of trash per acre with blades spaced 1 in. apart and set 1/2 in. deep (below mowed surface).[11]

In any thatching operation pickup and disposal of the trash must be figured as a significant part of the operation.

REJUVENATION

I am using rejuvenation to refer to rehabilitation of a turf by the use of deep holes. This has often been called renovation, but renovation refers to a different series of operations. There is no reason why rejuvenation could not be used on any turf area. But again, I shall discuss it in terms of putting greens because they are most able to carry the cost, and are likely to show the most benefit.

When a putting green is chronically in such bad condition that rebuilding is contemplated, rejuvenation may be considered as leading to the same end but at one-third to one-half the cost. If rejuvenation is to be of benefit several factors must be present: *(1)* the present problem should be due to surface compaction and associated surface wetness with dry spots and poor infiltration; *(2)* a good soil that will drain well should be close enough to the surface that the holes will penetrate and make contact with it; and *(3)* there should not be associated problems of tree roots, or inadequate irrigation capability, etc.

When these conditions exist, deep (6–12 in.) large (1-in. diam), closely spaced (2–3 in. on centers) holes, backfilled with a suitable soil mix may correct the troubles without rebuilding.[27,54] Rejuvenation requires much labor. Don't underestimate the size of the job. If the backfilling soil has a high infiltration rate, about 15% noncapillary porosity when compacted, and makes contact with adequately drained soil at the bottom of the hole, the folowing benefits may be expected in some degree: *(1)* reduced wetness; *(2)* reduced dry spots; *(3)* reduced total irrigation time;

(4) some breakdown of thatch between the holes from better aeration and improved wetting and drying cycles; and *(5)* healthier grass, which was the main goal in the first place.

Hemstreet and Dorman made a detailed study of the rejuvenation of a 35-yr-old green where problems resulted from buildup of thatch and layers.[27] They needed 26 man-hours/1000 ft^2 to make 3/4 in. x 6 in. holes 2 in. on center with a soil tube. They backfilled with a sandy mix having 25% redwood sawdust and adequate fertilizers. Results included decreased resilience of the green (i.e., more give to the green), an infiltration rate of 2.5 in./hr, reduced surface wetness, reduction of irrigation time.

Morgan et al. treated a green having 1 in. x 6 in. holes 3 in. on center. They found recovery within two weeks; disappearance of standing water; no summer loss of grass on treated areas, severe loss on untreated areas; increased surface porosity (from 36 to 47%); and grass seed included in backfill material reduced *Poa annua* .[54]

Byrne et al. used a regular aerifier and compared it to 1 in. x 6 in. holes, 3, 6, or 9 in. on center.[9] They found the improvement linear with spacing; i.e., the closer the holes, the better the results. The green was a clay loam over drainage rock. Initially the rejuvenation increased the infiltration rate but after four months only plots with holes 3 in. on centers still had a significantly better infiltration rate. Seed was included with the top dressing but the green remained essentially *Poa annua*. They concluded that under the conditions, rejuvenation by this technique was not enough by itself to greatly improve the green. Other practices and conditions also would have to be changed.

RENOVATION

The goal of renovation is to change an existing turf containing weeds and mixed species and sometimes thatch or other undesirable conditions into a quality turf, without plowing and completely rebuilding the turf.

Renovation is not sufficient by itself to achieve this goal. Unless other management changes are made, it will take only a season or two to return to the same conditions that existed before renovation. Renovation should be followed by improved irrigation, mowing, and fertilization practices designed to favor the grass desired.

To renovate one must *(1)* control weeds; *(2)* kill existing grasses or reduce their competitive activity; *(3)* create a seedbed without disturbing the trash too severely as the trash serves as a mulch and controls erosion; *(4)* seed and fertilize; and *(5)* irrigate to bring up the grass.

When the existing turf consists of a thin weedy stand of desirable grasses, a selective herbicide can be used on the weeds, and the grasses can be stimulated by the fertilizer used in the seedbed. If existing grasses are of no particular value a contact herbicide is used. The turf is mowed as short as possible before spraying the herbicide to increase the efficacy of the herbicide. The shorter the cut the smaller the volume needed to wet and the more effective the kill of the weakened grass.[14]

Herbicides that have been used include sodium arsenite and Paraquat, (both are highly toxic—observe precautions).[8] Dalapon, Ammate, and Vapam have also been tested.[6] Sodium arsenite at 4–8 lb/acre, especially if temperatures are high and the soil dry, will severely scorch grasses and kill or reduce crabgrass, *Poa annua,* goosegrass, dallisgrass, and other grasses which are subject to arsenic toxicity. Bent and bluegrass make a fair recovery Where use of sodium arsenite is restricted, cacodylic acid will give a complete kill. Use at 5–20 lb/100 gal and spray to wet. Close such areas to the public for five days, then reseed and use.

Paraquat is a contact herbicide with rapid soil breakdown so planting can follow almost immediately after its use. There may be a fair survival of crowns after Paraquat, particularly of dormant grasses such as winter dormant bermuda.[26,29] If complete kill of the existing grasses is demanded, fumigation with methyl bromide materials may have to be used. As methyl bromide is not translocated, trees with roots in the treated area will be root pruned but not otherwise injured or killed. Such root pruning is of value in rebuilding greens.

Maleic hydrazide has been used just before seeding to slow growth of mature grasses so the seedlings have a better chance. The seedbed is prepared by various combinations of aerifying, scarifying, thatching, raking, vacuuming, dragging, and matting so that the new seed can fall on soil.

Seed falling on thatch will not make a stand, that falling on soil should grow normally. After seeding, dragging may be used to cover the seed, and then the whole irrigated to bring the seed up. Machinery is now available which will sow seed at suitable depths in coulter cuts, three inches on center. This greatly simplifies operations and once-over application is sufficient.

In the northern part of the country fall renovation will give a new stand with minimum weediness, but in the warmer sections it is difficult to find a season when weeds would not be germinated, particulary if one begins with a weedy turf which has spread its seeds on the soil. If weeds threaten to be a problem seeding may be delayed; the weeds can be brought up first, and the area resprayed to kill weeds before spreading the grass seed.

Using moderate methods a turf can sometimes be appreciably improved without taking it out of play. The grass is sprayed with maleic hydrazide to hold it back and seed is placed in by machine as described above. When major renovations are contemplated it is good to renovate a small area first. The experience will be valuable in scheduling the big operation. One must have the renovation program fully in mind with complete scheduling of men and machines and all chemicals on hand if the operation is to be done effeciently.

To repeat, the new turf must receive a more favorable management than the old if it is not to revert to the same or worse condition.

ROOT PRUNING

Tree and grass roots compete with each other. The best turf cannot be grown where tree competition exists. A tractor-mounted blade is available for root pruning. Small ditching machines have also been used to root prune by digging a one-inch trench one foot deep around the area to be protected. In some soils roots could be pruned by a vertical knife blade on a sod cutter. I have seen brown fairways turn green right to the pruning line the week after root pruning. The irrigation practices were not supplying enough water for both grass and trees, but as soon as tree roots were cut the grass had plenty. Tree roots need to be pruned only once every year or two.

When roots running into a green are pruned the first time, growth of grass on the green may be depressed. Dead tree roots in the green are attacked by decay fungi which may form a mycelial mat in the soil that ties up nitrogen or acts as a barrier to water penetration. Depressed growth may persist for more than a year. Calcium-containing fertilizers may speed the breakdown.

OVERSEEDING AND INTERSEEDING

Overseeding has been practiced for many years on bermudagrass turf. In late fall the turf was raked and 20–80 or even 100–200 lb of annual ryegrass seed was sown per 1000 ft^2. At the higher rates used on putting greens the ryegrass remained in seedling condition for the entire winter season. Enlow[16] reported on overseeding trials in 1925 but found no test grasses that were better than *L. multiflorum* (annual, domestic, or Italian ryegrass). During the sixities changes led to reinvestigation or overseeding.

Some changes on golf courses include: use of hybrid bermudagrasses of finer texture; extended seasons of play in resort areas; and higher standards so finer-textured, better putting grasses are desired for greens. Further more, overseeding has moved further north where transition periods are more gradual; ryegrass contrasts unfavorably with increased *Poa annua;* and long-standing turf may be permanently infected with *Pythium* cottony blight and nematodes, so resistant grasses are needed for overseeding.

Fall seeding has been particulary affected by cottony blight (see Chap. 8). After ryegrass has germinated a warm period will result in decimation by cottony blight. To avoid this the manager waits as late as possible to sow ryegrass. If he waits too long a cold snap may delay the ryegrass. Playing games with the weather is difficult, particularly if you have to win 100% of the time. Nematodes damage roots without visibly affecting tops during the moist cool winter period.[55]

In spring the transition period gives trouble. In the far south bermudagrass comes rapidly into growth. A competing grass weakens bermuda so the best grass is one that fades rapidly with the first few warm days. In the transition zone, bermudagrass turns green over a period of six to eight weeks and a winter grass should slowly yield to the bermuda to make a gradual transition from one to the other.

Top performing grasses are red fescue and *Poa trivialis.* Bentgrasses are slow to establish themelves.[18] Redtop is subject to disease and is unsatisfactory.[18] Seaside is slow to start but performs well in the spring.[56] Highland has not been rated satisfactory.[18] Kentucky bluegrass is too slow to start.[16] Red fescue has started fast, been dense[35,36], and made a gradual transition in the spring. Of the red fesuces 'Pennlawn' has been favored in the eastern U.S.[56,61,62] Other varieties such as 'Illahee' have been used in the Southwest.[22] Chewing's has also done well.[18] *Poa trivialis* has performed well and blends in color with *Poa annua*,[35,61] but seed has been difficult to get and weedy. It suffers spring disease.[62] I have one reservation about *P. trivialis*; it tends to go dormant in the spring without yielding to the summer grass. Annual ryegrass is still the most used and is well suited to home lawns, schoolyards, football fields, etc., where a green color at low cost is the goal.

Noer et al. recommend a mixture of grasses:[56,57,62] 'Pennlawn' for an early start and for stffness; *Poa trivialis* to mask *Poa annua;* and bents with or without bluegrass for slow late transition.[16] Similar mixtures are favored by other workers. These are used separately or collectively[56] to provide about 25 million seeds/1000 ft^2 or half that.[62] Such high rates give a good appearance quickly, though differences from lower rates disappear by spring.[61] Fine and coarse seeds may be sown separately for more even stands. Rye continues to be best in the far south and for rough use.

As with renovation, seeds must contact the soil to become adequately established. Consequaently mowing, hole punching, and verticutting may precede overseeding and top dressing. On greens, hole punching is done two to four weeks in advance of seeding. Some healing prevents an uneven tufting as when seeds concentrate in the holes.[61] Linderman sows seed hydraulically at 100 psi to assure contact between seed and soil.[48]

Seeding should be accompanied by fertilization with material containing both nitrogen and phosphorus. Less fertilizer is needed for red fescue mixtures than for rye or bent. Preventative fungicide sprays should precede sowing where dampoff is serious, and should follow germination.[48]

Overseeding is used on centipede and St. Augustinegrasses too. The principal difference between grasses is texture, and the overseeded grass masks the base grass best, if textures are similar (e.g., rye on St. Augustine, red fescue on 'Tifgreen'). For utility grass, short mowing has been shown to be important in preparing for overseeding.[22]

At the northern limit of overseeding, sowing is done in late September. In Southern Florida seeding is done in early December. In each climate the latest date that one can sow with confidence is preferred.[61] Ryegrass germinates the first week, and other grasses except bluegrass show the second week. Bluegrass requires twenty or more days.

Overseeded grasses remain as young tender seedlings during their life. They suffer from wear and during warm spells tend to fade away as disease cuts them down.

Heating cables will no doubt replace overseeding in some installations.[57] The bother and expense of overseeding would be eliminated. Bermudagrass greens suffer from traffic during their dormant season and often make a poor spring recovery.[22] Long ago this resulted in the recommendation that for year-round play the winter green should be separate from the bermudagrass summer green.[28,2] If soil were heated bermudagrass could be kept actively growing all winter so it could replace wear by growth and in the spring could develop without competition from overseeded grasses.

INTERSEEDING

Adding seed may be used to maintain strong stands of grass. Properly, stands should be strengthened by correct mowing heights, a good fertilizer, practice, etc. This cannot always be done, however. As traffic and close mowing take their toll, *Poa annua* and crabgrass move into turf. These weeds are heavy seeders. One way to offset competition from seed of these weed grasses is to provide seeds of desirable grasses. Aerifying, top dressing, or other operations can be accompanied by applications of seed, or seed can be a regular part of the top-dressing mixture. Observations have shown that regular use of seed reduces *Poa annua* in greens. Seaside bent is the seed most used to interseed putting greens but red fescue can be used in the fall in the south or in early spring in the north. It will germinate strongly to crowd *Poa annua,* though later as it fades it may open the way to other seeds unless the bentgrass is growing strongly.

Interseeding should be continually used to keep turf in repair when the principal grasses are bunchgrasses such as tall or meadow fescues or ryegrass. On heavely used paths where the problem is of severe compaction, reseeding is of little value. To grow grass in such places is difficult. One approach is to use redwood boards or bricks stood on edge with about 3-in. spaces between. The boards take the wear, and the grass grows between and covers the boards or bricks part of the time.

As trees grow up in a landscape, a fall interseeding of red fescue will help to adapt areas that are becoming shaded by new growth. The point should be obvious without further illustration that occasional additions of seeds of desirable grasses to turf will favor higher population of that grass.

POLING

Switching greens with a bamboo pole to remove dew is a common practice. The practice hastens drying of greens, breaks up mycelia of fungi, and facilitates mowing. Poling is important in disease control, particularly when the "dew" consists of water of guttation that contains nutrients in which fungi flourish. Poling is discussed under diseases (Chap. 8). The same result can be obtained by a short sprinkle to wash off the dew or by dragging a hose over the green.

BROOMING

A stiff broom run over greens lifts loose leaves and stolons to where they can be mowed. Brooming helps control grain, but the broom can be an instrument in the spread of disease.

SYRINGING

Syringing is done when water loss exceeds water uptake. It prevents severe wilting by supplying water through the leaves and by reducing loss through increased humidity around the leaves (Fig. 5.2); see *Principles of Turfgrass Culture* p. 310.

SOIL HEATING

Effects of heating on turf disease are discussed in Chap. 8; see also Chap. 4 in *Principles of Turfgrass Culture,* p. 146.

Figure 5.2 Syringing or showering the grass is often necessary to prevent severe wilt on sunny afternoons. Here both the green and collar are being syringed. *Courtesy the University of California Agricultural Extension Service.*

PLUGGING

Plugging is sodding on a small scale. Pluggers of different sizes and shapes are available. Plugs are used to repair damaged turf. The damaged area is plugged out. A corresponding plug of good grass from a nursery is cut and placed in the hole. As in sodding, a little fertilizer should be sprinkled in the hole before setting the plug and the plug should be watered regularly until established. On a new green plugging may be used to remove small areas of *Poa annua* before they go to seed.

MULCHING

Primary use of mulches is to protect highway slopes from erosion during turf establishment. Winter mulches are used to protect turf from cold. When straw or similar materials are used, damage from disease tends to be as great as the benefit from mulching.[5] Branches are better as they collect and hold snow without holding moisture or restricting sunshine.

Mulches of fiberglass or fibers have not proved desirable due to low light and high disease.[67]

Polyethylene mulches have been favored for trial recently. Large sheets of polyethelyne 30 ft wide and 6 or 4 mil in thickness are carefully tacked around the edges and pinned to the soil with nails. If wind gets under the plastic, the plastic is repidly destroyed.

Black polyethylene holds moisture, but excludes light and fluctuates widely in temperature. It is not used on turf. Clear polyethylene and plastic screen have both been used (see *Principles of Turfgrass Culture)* p. 146.

In early spring the plastic cover can be slit by running a verticut over it without power on the knives. This ventilates the grass, reduces temperature buildup and hardens the grass somewhat. When outside temperatures reach 70°F the plastic should be removed at once to prevent injury from heat and disease.

TURFGRASS NURSERY

This provides for replacement to turf damaged by disease, chemicals, vandalism, etc. In addition, when cups are changed new cups can be cut in *Poa annua* and the old cup filled with a plug from the nursery.

Where sod is readily available, there is probably no advantage to having a nursery for most park, school, athletic or other grounds. For golf courses it is desirable to have at least 1000 ft^2 available, cared for under near putting-green conditions.

When new construction can be planned in advance, a nursery can be planted to supply one's own stolons or sod. Even if savings in money are small, the stolons can be held in the ground until the day and hour they are needed. This assists survival. Sod can be grown on the same soil on which it is to be laid, and can be cut thinner than when it is shipped.

A nursery provides an opportunity to test new products and try new grasses before investing heavily in them. A grass bred, developed, or selected in a different climatic zone should be tested for four or five years before deciding on its suitability in your climate. Disease susceptibility or other weaknesses often don't appear until after the turf has become fully sodbound.

COMPOST

When mowers were horse drawn, composted manure was both top dressing and fertilizer for greens. That day is gone but many persons still find compost a good way to utilize fallen leaves and clippings. Compost is useful in preparing top dressing; is an excellent mulch for newly planted shrubs and trees, and increases workability of the soil, which is an advantage for flower beds.

In the traditional method, compost was formed of alternate layers of vegetable wastes and manure with a little lime and soil sprinkled on each layer. Piles were built 5 ft high and 6–10 ft wide and any length. If piles are kept moist and aerated, microbiological breakdown begins and in a few days temperatures in the pile rise to as high as 160°F. After a few weeks the pile is turned so the outside layers are now on the inside of the pile. The material goes through a second heat and is then ready for use. Heating presumably destroys weed seeds and disease organisms.

Since manure is seldom available today calcium nitrate (or lime plus a nitrogen source) can be added to provide about 2–2.5 lb N/yd.[3]

Milorganite can effectively replace horse manure and is said to result in a good heat. When compost is to be used in top dressing, De France suggests mixing the wastes to be composted with 13 lb of calcium cyanamide per cubic yard (Chap. 7). The cyanamide will kill most weed seeds. The compost should be protected from recontamination.

Fallen tree leaves make good compost, but grass clippings are poor unless diluted with large amounts of other material. Used alone, grass clippings tend to form a slimy layer that prevents suitable circulation of air and water, and which attracts flies that lay eggs in it.

DYEING GRASS GREEN

Brown spots in grass have often been dyed for weddings, or other ceremonial occasions. The film industry uses dyes to hide distracting spots in the background of outdoor movie sets. In the late 1950s interest arose in dying bermudagrass rather than overseeding for winter color. Today blemishes in sports turf receive cosmetic treatment to appear uniform on color TV. Costs of dyeing may vary from less than 1¢ to over 10 ¢/ft². The first step is to mow the grass to be treated short. This reduces the area to be dyed and hence the cost. Bermudagrass should be dyed when growth has essentially stopped. Late fall growth needs to be redyed, but early spring growth usually indicates change to a natural green color.

Youngner and Fuchigami[69] tested five materials in 1957 and found only one of the five to rate well after eight weeks. That was *Green Stuff.* Green Stuff is a green plastic coating material rather than a dye. In the decade since Youngner's test, dyes were abandoned and plastic coating materials became universal. Some of these are listed by Deal[13] and by *Grounds Maintenance* magazine.[2]

ROLLING

In the United States turf is rolled in the northern states after winter heaving has occurred. Only enough weight is used to press the heaved crowns back into firm contact with the soil. Rolling is done as soon as thawing is completed and the soil has become firm.

Rolling is also used in seeding, sodding, and stolonizing to press the seed material into firm contact with the seed bed.

In Great Britain where the turf is kept fine, rolling has been used to keep the turf smooth and press down uneven spots after traffic. There is less of this use today, but the roller is still used extensively on sports turf. Bowling and tennis greens and cricket pitches are rolled and rolled, and even a football turf will be rolled after its final mowing to give a "face" to the turf. When soil receives no traffic at all, rolling may be used to replace traffic in firming the soil.

MISCELLANEOUS PRACTICES

Although cart paths are not turf, they are the turf manager's problem. Holmes has reviewed construction problems.[30] He notes the need for a sound base of 4 in. of gravel, need for header boards to prevent breakdown from the edge, need for drainage, need for immediate repair of chuckholes and cracks, and need for periodic sealcoat; he warns against heading paths straight downhill or toward water.

With night lighting there is also the opportunity for night maintenance, and Lyons[50] states that night mowing may take some of the stress from mowing practices. It is done when temperatures are cool, moisture is up, and leaves are turgid so they cut cleanly.

Winter greens as an alternate to overseeding is attractive. The principal green escapes frost damage, escapes wear at a time when it does not readily recover, and enters the spring season with less *Poa annua* and with greater vigor.[2,28]

References

1. Aljibury, F. K., and D. D. Evans, 1965, "Water permeability of saturated soils as related to air pereability at different moisture tensions," *Soil Sci. Soc. Am. Proc.* **29**, 366–369.
2. Anonymous, 1966, "The case for temporary greens," *U.S.G.A. Green Section Record.* **3**(5), 11–12.
3. Anonymous, 1967, "Applying turf colorants," *Grounds Maint.* **2**(12), 63.

4. Aubertin, G. M., and L. T. Kardos, 1965, "Root growth through porous media under controlled conditions. II. Effect of aeration levels and rigidity," *Soil Sci. Soc. Am.* **29,** 363–365.
5. Beckett, H., 1929, "Covering bermuda greens for winter protection," *U.S.G.A. Green section Bull.* **9**(10), 175–178.
6. Bickowski, E. R., and V. B. Youngner, 1956, "Chemicals for lawn renovation," *Calif. Turfgr. Cult.* **6**(1), 3.
7. Brooks, C. R., 1966, "Growth of roots and tops of bermudagrass as related to aeration and drainage in stratified golf greens," Ph.D. Thesis, Texas, *Dissertation Abstr.* **27B**(5), 3371.
8. Burt, E. O., 1966, "Paraquat, an exciting new herbicide for all turf," *Turf-grass Times* **2**(1), 1ff.
9. Byrne, R. G., W. B. Davis, L. J. Booher, and L. F. Werefels, 1965, "A further evaluation of the vertical mulching method of improving old greens," 1965, *Cal. Turfgr. Cult.* **15**(2), 9–11.
10. Cannon, W. A., 1925, "Physiological features of roots with especial reference to the relation of roots to aeration of the soil," *Carnegie Inst. of Wash. Publ.* **368,** 168.
11. Clark, S., 1964, "Panel: Fairway verticutting," Univ. of *Florida Agr. Expt. Sta. Turfgr. Management Conf. Proc.* **12,** 88–89.
12. Crafts, A. S., 1961, *Transolocation in Plants,* Holt, Reinhart and Winston, New York, pp. 50–52.
13. Deal, E. E., 1967a, "Grass dyes, coloring compounds," *The Golf Supt.* **35**(1), 71–72.
14. Deal, E. E., 1967b, 'Tufcote' bermuda established using preemergence herbicides," *Agron. Abstr.,* p. 66.
15. Engel, R. E., and R. B. Alderfer, "The effect of cultivation, topdressing, lime, nitrogen and wetting agent on thatch development in 1/4 inch bentgrass turf over a ten-year period," *Rutgers Univ. N.J. Agr. Expt. Sta. Bull.* **818,** 32–48.
16. Enlow, C. R., 1928, "Winter grass experiments at Gainesville, Florida," *U.S.G.A. Green Sect. Bull.* **8**(11), 224–225.
17. Ferguson, M. H., 1964, "Mat and thatch—cause, effect, and remedy," *U.S.G.A. Green Sect. Record* **1**(5), 10–13.
18. Folkner, J., 1962, "Overseeding trials, 1961–62," *Ariz. Expt. Sta. Rept.* **212,** 26–29.
19. Fulton, J. M., and A. E. Erickson, 1964, "Relation between soil aeration and ethyl alcohol accumulation in xylem exudate of tomatoes," *Soil Sci. Soc. Am. Proc.* **28,** 610–614.
20. Gardner, H. R., and R. E. Danielson, 1964, "Penetration of wax layers by cotton roots as affected by some soil physical conditions," *Soil Sci. Soc. Am. Proc.* **28,** 457–460.
21. Geisler, G., 1967, "Interactive effects of carbon dioxide oxygen in soil on root and top growth of barley and peas," *Plant Physiol.* **42,** 305–307.
22. Gill, W. J., W. R. Thompson, Jr., and C. Y. Ward, 1967, "Species and methods for overseeding bermudagrass greens," *Golf Supt.* **35**(9), 10 ff.

23. Grable, E. R., and R. E. Danielson, 1965, "Influence of CO_2 on growth of corn and soybean seedlings," *Soil Sci. Soc. Am. Proc.* **29,** 233–238.
24. Grable, E. R., and E. G. Siemer, 1968, "Effect of bulk density, aggregate size and soil water suction on oxygen diffusion and elongation of corn roots," *Soil Sci. Soc. Am. Proc.* **32,** 180–186.
25. Guenzi, W. D., and T. M. McCalla, 1966, "Phytotoxic substance extracted from soil," *Soil Sci. Soc. Am. Proc.* **30,** 214–216.
26. Hansen, C. O., 1964, "Control of winter annual weeds in southern turf with paraquat," *Abs. Weed Soc. of Am.* p. 93.
27. Hemstreet, C. L., and F. Dorman, 1964, "Reviving old putting greens," *Calif. Turfgr. Cult.* **14**(3), 20–23.
28. Hinman, T. P., 1929, "Double bermuda greens and their treatment," *U.S.-G.A. Green Sect. Bull.* **9**(10), 196.
29. Holifield, E. L., and R. E. Frans, 1964, "Winter weed removal from dormant turf," *Proc. 17th S. Weed Conf.*, pp. 127–131.
30. Holmes, J. L., 1967, "Cart paths," *U.S.G.A. Green Sect. Record* **4**(5), 1–5.
31. Horton, M. L., and J. T. Ritchie, 1963, "Effect of compaction on soil gas composition as determined by gas chromotography," *Agron. Abstr.*, p. 7.
32. Huck, M. G., and A. E. Erickson, 1967, "Biochemical changes in tomato roots during brief periods of flooding," *Agron. Abstr.*, p. 66.
33. Hughes, R. D., J. F. Stone, W. W. Huffine, and J. R. Gingrich, 1966, "Effect of bulk density and soil water pressures on emergence of grass seedlings," *Agron J.* **58,** 549–553.
34. Jensen, C. D., and D. Kirkham, 1963, "Increased diffusion rate through soils containing growing corn roots," *Science* **141,** 735–736.
35. Kneebone, W. R., and G. L. Major, 1966, "Bermudagrass variety effects on winter overseeding in 1965–1966," *Ariz. Agr. Expt. Sta. Rept.* **240,** 1–3.
36. Kristensen, K. J., and S. R. Lemon, 1964, "Soil aeration and plant root relations, III. Physical aspects of oxygen diffusion in the liquid phase of the soil," *Agron. J.* **56,** 295–301.
37. Kubota, T., and R. J. B. Williams, 1967, "The effects of changes in soil compaction and porosity on germination, establishment, and yield of barley and globe beet," *J. Agric. Res.* **68,** 227–233.
38. Labanauskas, C. K., L. H. Stolzy, L. J. Klotz, and T. A. DeWolfe, 1965, "Effects of soil temperature and oxygen on the amounts of macronutrients and micronutrients in Citrus seedlings. *(Citrus sinensis* var. *Bessie),"* *Soil Sci. Soc. Am. Proc.* **29,**60–64; also in *Cal. Agr.* **20**(12), 12–13.
39. Ledeboer, F. B., and Skogley C. R.,1967, "Investigations into the nature of thatch and methods for its decomposition," *Agron. J.* **59,** 320–329.
40. Letey, J., 1961, "Aeration, Compaction and Drainage," *Calif. Turfgr. Cult.* **11**(3), 17–21.
41. Letey, J., O. R. Lunt, L. H. Stolzy, and T. E. Szuszkiewicz, 1961, "Plant growth, water use, and nutritional response to rhizosphere differentials of oxygen concentration," *Soil Sci. Soc. Am. Proc.* **25,** 183–186.

42. Letey, J., W. F. Richardson, and N. Valoris. 1965, "Barley growth, water use, and mineral composition as influenced by oxygen exclusion from specific regions of the root system," *Agron. J.* **57,** 629–631.
43. Letey, J., L. H. Stolzy, T. E. Szuszkiewicz, and N. Valoris, 1962, "Soil aeration essential for maximum growth," *Calif. Agr.* **16**(3), 6–7.
44. Letey, J., L. H. Stolzy, N. Valoris, and T. E. Szuszkiewicz, 1963, "Low soil oxygen most damaging to plants during hot weather," *Calif. Agr.* **17**(5), 15.
45. Letey, J., L. H. Stolzy, and D. E. Birkle, 1964, "Root oxygen supply as affected by distance to gas phase," *Agron. Abstr.,* 13.
46. Letey, J., L. H. Stolzy, O. R. Lunt, and N. Valoris, 1964a, "Soil oxygen and clipping height. Effects on the growth of Newport bluegrass," *Golf Course Reptr.* **32**(2), 64; reprinted in *Calif. Turfgr. Cult.* **14**(2), 9–12.
47. Letey, J., L. H. Stolzy, O. R. Lunt, and V. B. Youngner, 1964b, "Growth and nutrient uptake of Newport bluegrass as affected by soil oxygen," *Plant and Soil* **20**(2), 143–148; see also *Golf Course Rept.* **32**(2), 1964.
48. Linderman, H. O., H. Phillips, and T. M. Baumgertner, 1966, "Overseeding panel; bentgrasses," *Univ. Florida Agr. Expt. Sta. Turfgr. Management Conf. Proc.* **14,** 73–76.
49. Lunt, O. R., 1956, "A method for minimizing compaction in putting greens," *Cafif. Turfgr. Cult.* **6**(3), 1–4.
50. Lyons, W., 1962, "Night maintenance," *Golfdom* **36**(7), 30 ff.
51. Meszaros, J. P., 1967, "Burn thatch out," *The Golf Supt.* **35**(5), 51 ff.
52. Meyers, H. C., 1964, "Effects of nitrogen levels and vertical mowing intensity and frequency on growth and chemical composition of 'Ormond' bermudagrass," *Univ. Florida Agr. Expt. Sta. Turfgr. Management Conf. Proc.* **12,** 77–79.
53. Morgan, W. C., 1962, "Observations on turfgrass aeration and vertical mowing," *Calif. Turfgr. Cult.* **12**(2), 12–13.
54. Morgan, W. C., J. Letey, and L. H. Stolzy, 1965, "Turfgrass renovation by deep aerification," *Agron. J.* **57,** 494–496.
55. Nigh, E. L., Jr., 1966. "The influence of nematodes on winter development of overseeded annual ryegrass *(Lolium multiflorum)*," *Ariz. Agr. Expt. Sta. Rept.* **240,** 4–6.
56. Noer, O. J., C. G. Wilson, and J. M. Lathan, 1960, "Winter grass overseeding on bermuda putting greens," *Agron. Abstr.,* p. 71.
57. Nutter, C. (ed.), 1965, "Overseeding winter grass (a panel discussion)," *Turf-grass Times* **1**(1), 1ff.
58. Ohmura, T., and R. W. Howell, 1960, "Inhibitory effect of water on oxygen consumption," *Plant Physiol.* **35,** 184–188.
59. Rickman, R. W., J. Letey, and L. H. Stolzy, 1966, "Plant response to oxygen, supply and physical resistance in the root envirnoment," *Soil Sci. Soc. Am. Proc.* **30,** 304–307; also in *Calif. Agr.* **19**(3), 4–6.
60. Russell, E. W., 1961, *Soil Conditions and Plant Growth,* 9th ed., John Wiley & Sons, Inc., New York, p. 370.
61. Schmidt, R. E., and R. E. Blaser, 1961, "Cool season grasses for winter turf on bermuda putting greens," *U.S.G.A. Green Sect. J. Turf. Management* **4**(5), 25–29.

62. Schmidt, R. E., and J. F. Shoulders, 1964, "Overseeding bermudagrass with cool season grasses for winter turf," *Agron. Abstr.*, p. 102.
63. Stolzy, L. H., J. Letey, R. E. Szuszkiewicz, and O. R. Lunt, 1961, "Root growth and diffusion rates as a function of oxygen concentration," *Soil Sci. Soc. Am. Proc.* **25,** 463–467.
64. Tackett, J. L., and R. W. Pearson, 1964, "Effect of carbon dioxide on cotton seedlings root penetration of compacted soils," *Soil Sci. Soc. Am. Proc.* **28,** 741–743.
65. Thompson, W. R., Jr., and C. Y. Ward, 1966, "Prevent thatch accumulation," *The Golf Supt.* **34**(9), 21 ff.
66. Waddington, D. VanP., 1964, "Influence of soil aeration on the growth of three grass species," Ph.D. Thesis, Amherst, *Dissertation Abstr.* **26**(2), 1852.
67. Watson, J. R., Jr., H. Kroll, and L. Wicklund, 1960, "Protecting golf greens against winterkill," *Golf Course Reptr.* **28**(7), 10ff.
68. Wiegand, C. L., and E. R. Lemon, 1963, "Correction in paper 'A field study of some plant-soil relations in aeration,'" *Siol Sci. Soc. Am. Proc.* **27,** 714–715.
69. Youngner, V. B., and T. Fuchigami, 1958, "Colorants for dormant bermuda and other subtropical grasses," *S. Calif. Turfgr. Cult.* **8**(1),

6

PEST CONTROL*

Pest-control practices should be approached with thought. The turf manager needs especially to be aware of the interrelatedness of all elements of his program. The untrained and unobservant man asks, "What chemical can I use to kill this pest?" The sophisticated manager looks beyond gross symptoms and asks, "How can I modify my program to reduce or eliminate this problem?" His program may include the same chemical but as only part of the program for he will be treating the problem, not just the symptoms. Pest problems are, in fact, often indicative of management deficiencies.

To illustrate, let me describe a common experience. A consultant receives a call for help. He arrives at the turf site and finds it overrun with crabgrass. The manager desperately wants a (cheap) chemical to control

*"The following chapters use trade names of many agricultural chemicals. These are named on the basis of reports in the literature except that no materials reported by code number have been included. When many conflicting reports have appeared only materials giving the most consistent results have been noted, and some reports may have been overlooked. Omission of a proprietary chemical from any list may be due to oversight, to information that has been since superseded, or to other causes and is not to be taken as an implication of unsuitability. When a chemical occurs under several trade names, no effort has been made to list all names and the name used has been the one in most common use by turfgrass workers. Materials that have been listed as ineffective in some tests may sometimes be effective in other locations or under other test conditions."

it. On inspection the consultant finds not only 90% crabgrass; he also finds that the grass is thin; that it has never been fertilized; that it is mowed unnecessarily short; that it is overirrigated; and that wetness and traffic have resulted in severe compaction.

The manager is managing to *favor* crabgrass. If he kills it, the ground will be almost bare until a new cover develops. But with his program the new cover will be weeds, largely crabgrass. Before he applies a weed killer he should fertilize. Turfgrasses should be seeded in and encouraged. The mower should be sharpened and reset. A reasonable irrigation program should be initiated. Then use of a herbicide as part of an overall program will help remove remaining crabgrass under conditions where turfgrasses will fill in the holes.

The example is of a weed problem, but disease and insect control too should only be part of a complete program. Each organism in the universe strives to multiply and increase itself. In the struggle we wish to operate to favor turfgrasses, to weaken competitors.

Working from such a viewpoint will not free us of contradictions and problems. A compacted soil favors *Poa annua.* But use of a hole puncher to relieve compaction may provide an improved seedbed for *Poa annua.* (A possible solution may be to remove plugs and top dress the holes with weed-free dressing containing turfgrass seeds.)

There is little question that if we could eliminate all insects, all fungi, all weeds, all competing life forms, we could grow superior grass. Except in laboratory examples, this cannot be practically done. In the realistic view, control does not mean extermination. Control is often simple; extermination may be expensive, ridiculous, or impossible. A dense vigorous turf containing an occasional dandelion or crabgrass plant has weeds under control if weeds are few and fail to increase from season to season. A single spring spraying with MCPP might give such control, for example. If one were to use repeated sprays of various chemicals to remove remaining weeds and were to keep cost records, the cost of removing additional weeds would increase. One would soon reach a point where hand weeding would be the cheaper control for remaining weeds. Also, a second or third herbicide spray might reduce turf vigor to a point where disease could open up new areas to weed invasion.

When we realize how costly the effort is to completely eliminate pests, we may accept a broader viewpoint and regard our turf as a pasture. We can pasture ten to fifteen head of cutworms or other moth larvae per square yard of vigorous turf without concern. Their depredations will hardly add to the severity of the defoliation we are already giving with our mowers. To spray these few may be hardly worth the cost. Also a few larvae in the turf provide food to the wasps and other predators of cutworms and so favor a certain amount of natural control. If cutworm numbers do not increase we may consider we have natural control without elimination. But if the cutworm population goes to twenty or more head per square yard, overgrazing may require we act to reduce numbers.

Again our goal should be control, not elimination. Our costs increase if we saturate the landscape with insecticides in an effort to eliminate the problem. And we fail, for within the hour moths fly in from neighboring properties to lay their eggs. If our spray has been too effective and killed the predators of cutworms, the next generation may quickly build up to damaging levels.

Many insects in the landscape are working with us. Tunneling insects improve infiltration.* Thatch is broken down most rapidly in the gut of an insect. Insects predators control many potential pests. Twenty-two insects have been listed as parasites or predators on firey skipper in Ontario.[8] As a result, infestations of firey skipper seldom endure for longer than a month. Natural control reduces their numbers unless we spray too effectively and kill the predators.

Our job is to grow good turf. We occasionally need chemical controls to do this effectively. We can generally use chemicals with good success when we are growing good grass. As obvious as this may seem, there are many people who expect good turf to result naturally if pests are eliminated. Their approach to management is to attack and destroy the enemy. Having won a few skirmishes they expect the grass to thrive without further help. We must grow the grass. The biocides are only there to help, to supplement our other efforts when necessary.

In the two decades following World War II we have been presented with a host of chemicals that almost work miracles. Not all of the miracles have been beneficial, and we are still learning how to make best use of these chemicals.

Prior to the war, weed control was one of the most expensive of turf operations, and it is still a leading problem. The most effective cultural practice for weed control was to grow bentgrasses using fertilizers with acid residues, a method still favored in Great Britain. Chemical weed control with sulfuric acid or kerosene burned the vegetation away from clear areas. Solutions of iron or ammonium sulfates sprayed on grass and weeds burned them. Grass recovery was favored. Arsenates were used to

*Our first job each morning was brushing the putting greens with birch brooms to get rid of the wormcasts. We started using chemicals to get rid of the worms and succeeded, but then we had to use forks to do exactly the job the worm did for us. Jim Thompson in *The Golf Superintendent,* Aug. 1968, p. 35.

reduce crabgrass and *Poa annua.* PMA effectively controlled crabgrass but at great expense.

A variety of mercury compounds were used for disease control, with control and cost both closely related to the actual mercury content of the spray.

Compounds of arsenic, antimony, or tellurium were used as insect stomach poisons. Pyrethrum, rotenone, nicotine, mowrah meal, and other natural materials were used as contact poisons or repellents.

The miracle biocides are exemplified by DDT and 2,4-D. The latter herbicide selectively removes broad-leaved weed plants from grasses. Minute amounts act as a hormone and stimulate certain plant tissues to "grow themselves to death." As an insecticide DDT doesn't even have to hit an insect to kill it. DDT places a long lasting residue where the insect will walk through it and absorb it through the feet. DDT enabled the U.S. to finally rid itself of malaria. After feeding in the early morning, the blood gorged mosquito rests on the wall above the bed. There it absorbs DDT from residues on the wall paper, dies, and fails to carry and spread the malaria to another patient.

The miracle compounds bring practical problems however, which include the following:

1. Dosages are often small and critical. Dosages may consist of only ounces per acre. More or less may be ineffective. This requires accurate spraying.

2. Drift can cause damage off the property. A 100-micron droplet, mist size, can drift several hundred feet while falling to the ground in a wind on only 2–3 mph.[50]

3. Equipment may be hard to clean. Small amounts of herbicide adhering to the tank and equipment may be sufficient so a later spraying unintentionally injures sensitive plants.

4. Response may be critically affected by temperature, soil moisture, and other variables.

5. Materials are long lasting and accumulate in the environment.[35]

6. Materials often have high toxicity.

7. Uptake and poisoning occur readily through the skin. Instead of thinking of the skin as a barrier we must think of it as an organ of uptake. This means protective clothing and trained applicators.

8. Wastes and tank washout may be difficult to dispose of without causing pollution.

9. Containers require special disposal.

10. Herbicide damage may also result in failure of replant.

11. Some biocides have undesirable side effects on turf.

Of these I will give attention to some effects of long-lasting biocides, and to toxicity problems. Not listed above are some biological problems that will be noted.

Microbiologists have thought that all organic materials were ultimately broken down. However, amber and pollen grains have survived intact for millions of years, and perhaps soil humates are an example of products little subject to further breakdown. Some of our biocides are resistant to biological breakdown. Simazine is still found in the soil after over eighteen months, chlordane after twelve years.[2,35] This long life has important consequences. One consequence is that materials accumulate in the normal food chains of animals.[10,49]

The example most commonly cited is of robins and earthworms. In one study during the season following a DDT spray, the top two inches of soil contained 5–10 ppm of DDT and DDE (its conversion product). This accumulated in the earthworm population to an average of 120 ppm. Robins eating the earthworms accumulated the material to hundreds of parts per million, lethal amounts.[10] Also familiar are examples where spraying agricultural crops has resulted in runoff into streams, concentration of the hydrocarbons by algae, and further concentration by herbivorous fish, resulting in death of birds and fish eating the minnows.[40]

A second consequence of the long life of present biocides is that this years's program may influence our future program. The preemergence herbicide we apply this spring may prevent the establishment of bentgrass in bare areas next fall. Chlordane affects grass rooting. Heavy rates of chlordane applied for crabgrass control have resulted in drought injury to turf over five years after application in New Jersey.[23] In Colorado, both chlordane and calcium arsenate applied in 1954–55 caused injury from drought in the winter of 1963–64.[24] I certainly should not choose to put a limit on my activities ten years from now.

There is recent evidence that as DDT moves into the biosphere—into the bodies of plants and animals—it is conserved and protected from further breakdown. Thus accumulation goes in only one direction, it increases.

We cannot always foresee the consequences of applying such long-lasting materials in the environment. We need therefore to use such chemicals with caution and thoughtfulness.

Rachel Carson in the book *Silent Spring* has effectively publicized the thesis that we should use intelligent caution in dealing with materials that may affect our environment in the future, or in ways not fully understood.[19] Limits or our present understanding are set forth by Rudd.[40] We benefit greatly from pesticide use.[31] We now have enough experience to anticipate most of the side effects. However, we suspect from individual examples that there must be a limit above which continued accumulation in the biosphere would be injurious. This favors restraint in our use. When you read the label, remember, this is the minimum statement of danger. The producer makes it because he is required to by law.

Alternatives to using chemical biocides are possible. Not all are economical but here is an example: An Illinois scientist controlled mites on apples with a spray of flour and water. The sticky spray stuck the mites down so they couldn't move about and function.

The mite problem resulted, incidentally, from use of DDT in orchards. DDT doesn't hurt mites. They are resistant. But DDT kills insects that prey on mites. So with their natural enemies gone, mites have become a new pest on many crops where DDT is used.[29]

Puncture vine, a serious weed in Arizona and California, is being controlled by a weevil which feeds on the plant.[22] Control is being achieved within a few years of the introduction of its natural pest.[16] Klamath weed in northern California, and *Opuntia* cactus in Australia, have similarly been controlled by the introduction of insects feeding specifically on the weed, and parasites of rhodesgrass scale are being introduced in Arizona[18] and Florida.

Bermudagrass mite is controlled as readily by thatch removal as by insecticides.[30]

Soil fungi continually act and interact on each other. The addition of oak sawdust to the soil has shifted fungal activities and resulted in suppression of large brown patch.[45]

Complete control of screwworm has been effected in the southeast without the use of a single chemical.[4,22] Laboratory-reared males were irradiated to make them sterile. Released in the field they mated with normal females who laid sterile eggs. Since the flies mate only once, this method was effective.

Excellent progress is being made in the development of baits which attract certain insects from a large area to traps. Some insects which lay their eggs at night are attracted to light traps and are caught before they lay their eggs.[9,22,42] Natural enemies of the Japanese beetle have reduced it from a major turf problem to a minor one.[21]

A nematode known as DD136 is host for a bacterium which destroys insects.[6] The nematode is easy to raise and store, and sprayed on plants it lethally infects any bug that walks across it for periods up to three months.

A remarkable relationship is that of a beetle which feeds on banana roots and which secretes a chemical which protects the banana against Panama disease.[38]

During the past twenty years the total environment, sea to mountain, pole to pole, has become contaminated with chlorinated hydrocarbon insecticides. Many of our patrons are unhappy about this, and will object to our contributing to this pollution in an area which is presumably for enjoyment of the amenities of life. It becomes increasingly easy to cooperate with this viewpoint as insects become resistant to many of the chemicals and as biological methods become more practical. A number of companies have entered the field of biological control. The pharmaceutical companies use their know-how to provide bacterial controls, and new companies are supplying insect parasites such as the *Trichogramma* wasp.* The wasp effectively controls moth larvae.

A few pages ago I listed some practical operating problems of using pesticides. Below are some biological problems. Many of these problems arise in connection with one of the observed laws of biology: *the environment is used to its full capacity to support life.* As soon as we remove one life form from the landscape, another moves in to take its place. The change is sometimes beneficial, sometimes not. An extreme example of the operation of this principle is often seen with pasteurized greenhouse soils. Pasteurization reduces the total fungal population and eliminates the disease population. Normally, fungi produce chemicals that limit growth of other fungi. With the population greatly reduced by steam treatment, those remaining are no longer inhibited and grow vigorously. Their growth may sometimes suppress growth of the crop for several weeks. A disease fungus introduced in such a soil may run unchecked through a greenhouse bench.

These fungal interactions often result in inconsistent performance of fungicides. In one instance we may suppress the disease organism and get control. At another time we may kill a fungus which is suppressing the disease. Then the disease gets worse as a result of our spray. In still a third instance, the fungicide may give control, not by killing the disease organism, but by killing a fungus which is inhibiting a normal suppressor of the disease. With the inhibition eliminated the second fungus grows normally and the disease is suppressed.[1]

Herbicides depress yields, but so do weeds. Economically better yields are obtained by the use of a herbicide, but maximum yields are obtained by removing weeds by hand.[27] Weeds ultimately return to treated land but weeds killed by herbicides tend to be replaced by resistant, difficult-to-kill weeds. Here the expression of result may occur a season or two after the treatment. Often use of 2,4-D on turf results in rapid replacement of dandelion, wild lettuce, etc., by veronica and knotweed. Supression of *Poa annua* has resulted in its replacement by goosegrass. Control of goosegrass results in increased clover.

*"Bug business boom," *The Wall Street Journal,* 6 Sept. 1968, p. 1.

Similar results obtain with insect populations. I have already remarked on the increase of mites as a crop pest following use of chlorinated hydrocarbons.[29] Other examples are the appearance of infestations of Baker mealybug on pears after use of DDT[21] and the development of soft brown scale into a major pest after use of parathion on citrus.[20]

A slightly different phenomenon is that of resurgence. Often, an insecticide is more effective against the predators of a pest than the pest itself. The result of spraying is a temporary drop in the pest numbers followed by a jump in population as the pest increases, unchecked by natural predator control. As an example, Malathion used to control aphis on alfalfa in California resulted in an increase in aphis damage. Aphis predators are almost completely removed by malathion.[46]

A more familiar biological phenomenon is development of resistance to a chemical. At the end of World War II we hoped to use DDT to rid the world of flies and mosquitos. Twenty years later every fly and mosquito carries a burden of DDT on its body fat, but we are still swatting. Disease-producing organisms have developed resistance to fungicides, bugs to insecticides, and weeds become tolerant of herbicides. Thus we cannot place our trust in the chemical that works for us this year. Next year we may have a strain of brown patch resistant to PCNB, a sod webworm unaffected by chlordane, and a dandelion that is stimulated by 2,4-D. Present practice is to switch among several materials to prevent building a population resistant to one. These problems are diagrammed in Figure 6.1, which is part of the larger Figure 6.2.

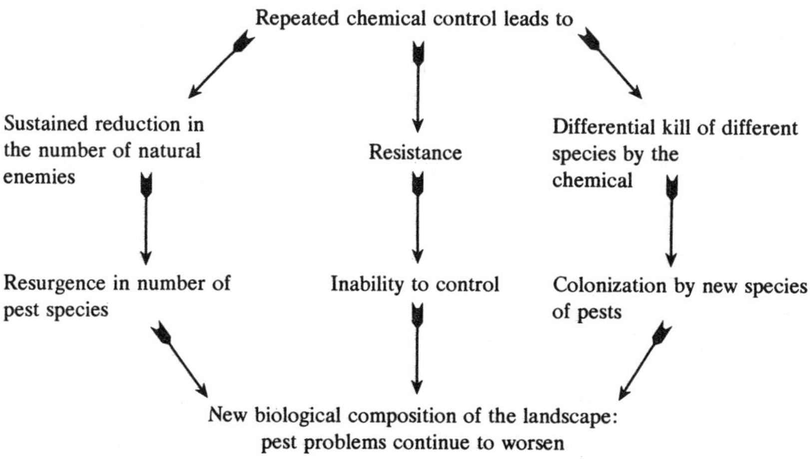

Fig. 6.1. The biological problems of pest control (After Rudd).

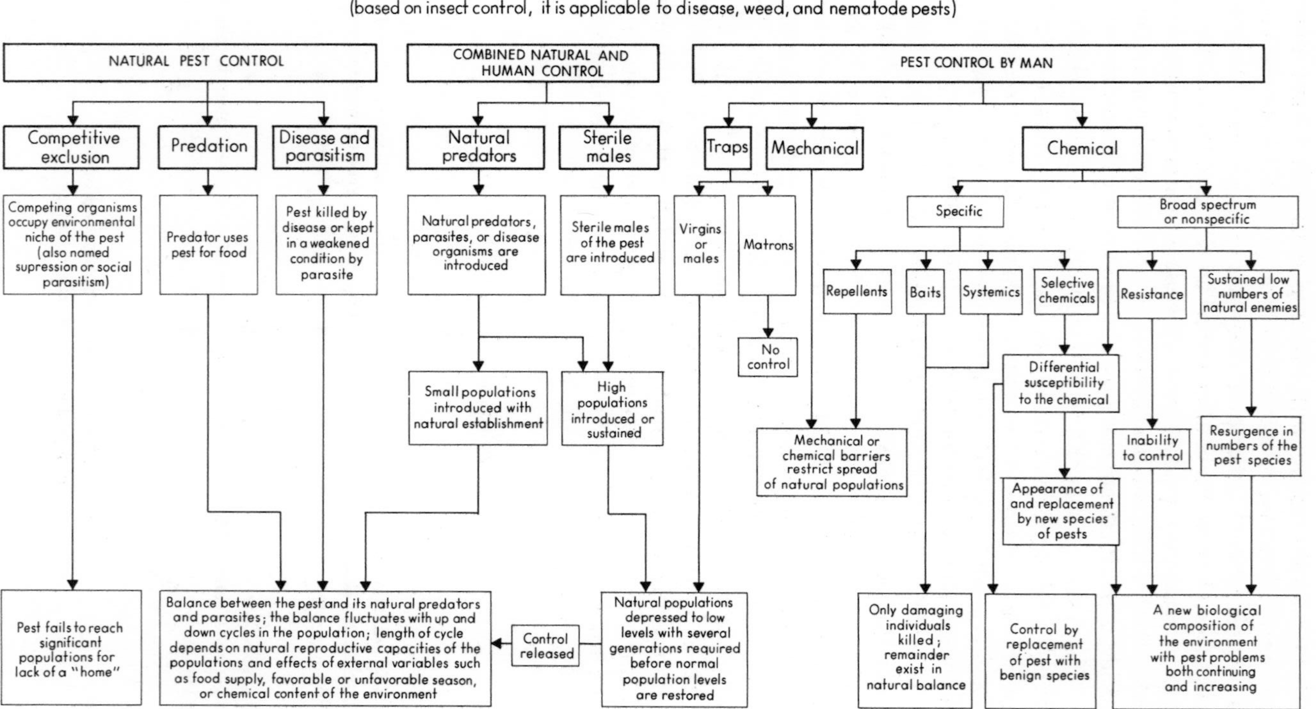

Figure 6.2 Schematic diagram of pest control.

Resistance also works for us. 'Merion' is a *Helminthosporium*-resistant variety of bluegrass. Different bluegrass varieties have different resistance to sod webworm damage.[39] A strain of St. Augustinegrass at the University of Florida appears somewhat resistant to chinch bug.[33] *Cynodon transvaalensis* and its hybrids are more resistant to mite than varieties of common bermudagrass, *C. dactylon.*[30] In the north, hairy chinch bug prefers bent and red fescuegrasses[43] whereas rye and bluegrasses are more resistant. We are not yet able to avoid all pests by choosing the right strain of grass. But we know we have the potential of increasing resistance and decreasing the effort needed for pest control.

Plant resistance is partly cultural. Chinch bugs prefer fertilized St. Augustinegrass and are not a problem when the grass is unfertilized.[28] Sod webworm survives poorly on bluegrass until fertilization and irrigation increase its succulence.[42] Similarly diseases such as *Fusarium* patch attack fertilized turf more severely, whereas weak parasites such as those causing dollar spot are less of a problem on vigorous turf of good fertility. Disease susceptibility and weed invasion both go up as mower height goes down.

We have noted practical and biological consequences of using biocides. We also need some knowledge of toxicity problems. In 1967, *Bioscience* carried an article by an officer of a company producing pesticides.[36] At one point he deplored the use of the term *biocide* as it created a bad public image, a public fear of useful and needed insecticides, fungicides, etc. He made a good case, but the day his article appeared, afternoon papers carried the story of scores of people killed in Tijuana. They died from eating bread made with sugar transported in a truck where parathion had spilled. We are, in fact, dealing with biocides. This was not the first example of deaths from casual contamination, and since then, the tragedy has been repeated elsewhere. I favor use of the term *biocide* if it will lead to respect for these chemicals and to care in their use.

The public is shocked by the occasional innocent or accidental death by acute poisoning. But the greatest number of persons injured by biocides are those who use them professionally, and who suffer, not death, but less spectadular chronic dissabilities, usually involving gradual degeneration of a tissue or a function.[25] To a degree, the consumer is protected by the Department of Health, Education, and Welfare, which regulated use of poisons on food. The applicator's welfare is the concern of the Department of Labor and the Department of Labor has seemed little concerned to date.

Chemical toxicity is generally expressed as the oral LD_{50} mg/kg. This is the least oral dose that will result in 50% mortality among a large population of test animals, usually rats, mice, rabbits, etc. It is given as milligrams of chemical per kilogram of animal body weight. For example if a man were to swallow a material with an LD_{50} of 400, he might expect to stand a 50–50 chance of dying if he swallowed 400 mg. for every kilogram of body weight. For a 160-lb man this represents a dose of just under one ounce (27.3 g). LD_{50} may on occasion be based on intake by other routes such as skin absorption, inhalation of fumes, etc. The LD_{50} mg/kg is equivalent to parts per million. It is inexact as it can vary by age, sex, and species.

In addition to the LD_{50} mg/kg there are two other kinds of information which tell us about toxicity. One is the effect of repeated doses. Some toxicants accumulate in the system until they reach toxic levels. Others result in creation of resistance with repeated doses so that a tolerance to the material is developed. The latter is almost harmless relative to the first.

Sometimes it is also desirable to know the toxicity when exposure is continuous over long periods. Continued inhalation of fumes from aromatic carbon compounds for a number of hours each week can, if continued over months and years, result in damage to organs such as the liver and kidney.

These various toxicity effects are translated by the agricultural research service of the U.S. Department of Agriculture into three kinds of labels. Materials that are safe enough for the average person to use with reasonable care receive a CAUTION label. Materials requiring more than average care in their use are labeled WARNING. Highly toxic materials requiring special care, special handling, or special clothing may be labeled POISON + WARNING + ANTIDOTE. Materials labeled poison are best left to the professional applicator, especially if they have toxic vapors or are taken up by the skin. Others of low solubility and low volatility can be safely used by the trained turf worker. As an example, turf men have used sodium arsenate for crabgrass control for years without recognized difficulty. Sodium arsenate is also sold for making poison baits and in this form is one of the leading pesticides causing child deaths. Restricting sodium arsenate use in California has resulted in a decrease of child poisoning.

Oral LD_{50} of many principle pesticides are given in the following pages. A clinical handbook on economic poisons by the U.S. Dept. of Health, Education and Welfare is available from the Superintendent of Documents, U.S. GPO, Washington 25, D.C., for a cost of 55¢[48] (PHS publication 476). Also available for 20¢ is a *Directory of Poison Control Centers.* This contains phone numbers of hospitals or doctors who maintain up-to-date information on treatments for poisoning.[3]

Persistence and toxicity of biocides requires that special efforts be taken to safely dispose of containers, washout, and surplus. Containers should be treated in a manner to prevent their possible reuse. Large metal containers can be sold to a reclaiming business where chemicals and high temperatures are used to clean and to reclaim them for secondary uses. Paper and plastic containers should be burned under such conditions that the smoke will rise and move away from human activities. Containers that have held organic phosphates or hormone-type herbicides should not be burned. Glass containers should be broken and metal ones punctured and then sent to a public dump telling the operator the nature of the materials.

Tânk washout or excess biocide cannot be legally or safely dumped in the sewerage system. Many biocides will kill or upset the bacteria that break down wastes at the sewerage farms. Many contaminate the waste waters. One suggestion is that wastes be dumped in a hole in soil where no plants will be grown in the next few years. Even here wastes should not be dumped in such quantity that ground waters are contaminated.

In the following pages I will outline a philosophy of pest control.

Our high-use, high-maintenance areas are under stress from both use and the management given them. This predisposes them to pest invasion. A management study at Davis produced the best bentgrass greens turf when preventative sprays of both fungicides and insecticides were used. On the other hand, injurious effects of herbicides were magnified under high maintenance.

Perhaps the optimum program uses fungicides and insecticides at levels that keep high-maintenance turf almost sterile except for the grass. An absence of insects will tend to keep off birds, and remove interest for pigs, skunks, and other insect eaters. Proposals have been made for building greens with long-term biocides mixed into and through the soil.[13.34]

For balance, however, we maintain other parts of the total area as biologically enriched areas. For instance, keep golf course roughs free of pesticides and so provide a reservoir of helpful predators such as birds, wasps, mantids, ladybird beetles, etc. Provide nesting boxes for birds whose nest sites are destroyed by clean-up operations that remove dead limbs, downed timber, and the like. An occasional brush stack in an out-of-the-way place provides cover for quail.Certainly the beauty of turf is enhanced by baby quail running across it after their mother.

Give intermediate protection to intermediate areas such as golf course fairways, park picnic grounds, institutional decorative turf, etc. Firstly, keep biocides off these areas except when need is demonstrated. When sprays are used they do not have to be general if only limited areas are suffering damage. If a careful diagnosis shows insect damage confined to areas near water, areas under lights, areas partly shaded, or areas of bentgrass, then limit spraying to those areas.

Secondly, try to find the right pesticide to kill the pest without killing predators in the area. For example, armyworm is a pest common on turf. It can be controlled with a parathion spray that requires protective clothing and kills predators. Or you can use a spray of a bacteria (*Bacillus thuringeinsis* Berliner) that makes armyworm and its relatives sick and which remains in the soil to infect others that come in later. When using the latter, predators continue to increase.

Thirdly, we may be able to control pests with a short-lived pesticide so its action does not extend beyond the desired control period. We have noted that chlordane as a preemergence crabgrass control has effects seven to ten years later and would therefore be less desirable than a material such as dacthal with action presumed limited to a single season.

These three cautions will help keep natural control as part of the program on the intermediate area though they propose goals we will only occasionally be able to achieve. To summarize my proposal I suggest using high-kill materials to control pests on high-maintenance turf combined with biological enrichment (no pesticides) of part of the landscape, and selective control on remaining areas.

A turf manager who works in the field (rather than at a desk) and who likes living things will find fun in the challenge to keep as many elements of the landscape as possible working for him.

PRACTICUM

The practical elements of pest control deal primarily with the control of materials and personnel, and with record keeping.

A person applying pesticides must be sufficiently trained so he appreciates the need for care in application, and the potential harm to himself and others if he doesn't do the job right. He needs skill to apply herbicides and fungicides without overlap or skips. Overlaps damage grass, skips weaken control. He must be willing to give up smoking and coffee breaks while making applications. Smoking takes vaporized poison directly into the lungs; eating takes it from the fingers to the stomach. He must wear goggles, as the eyes quickly absorb many poisons, and drift from mercurials can permanently cloud the vision. To prevent inhalation of spray, a mask is necessary. For pesticides that enter through the skin, gloves, long sleeves, boots, and other protective clothing must be worn. One way to be sure a man is protected is to supply the protective clothing and provide for its laundering. Not all precautions are needed for all materials. The label should provide information about precautions to be taken.

The manager should have a current phone number for a doctor he knows is prepared to handle poisoning cases.[3,5] If he is using highly toxic phosphates, he should have atropine on hand, and both he and the man's wife should be trained to give artifical respiration in case of collapse.[48]

You never expect to experience a problem from acute poisoning. Most never will. Your care will prevent it. Your preparation will enable you to cope with it if it happens. Lack of care and personal indifference (stupidity) of many of your workers will cause you to wonder why acute poisoning doesn't happen more often and to appreciate the care that is necessary to prevent chronic poisoning.

Records may well include the size of various turf areas; calibration of spray equipment; dates of last nozzle change and when the next change is expected; inventories of materials, amounts to be ordered, and when (let the supplier store the material for you as much as possible). For each material note temperature and time when it was used; The pest being controlled; rates used; degree of control obtained; and other chemicals applied to the turf within a week of the pesticide. This will enable you to evaluate effectiveness vs cost; conditions giving good control; and conditions resulting in turf injury.

The following is a check list of spray operations:

Label. Read the label, then read it again; reread it each time the material is used. Note whether protective clothing is required. Note the recommended first aid and be prepared to give it. Use a dictionary if needed. (When questioned in a Wisconsin survey, farmers, college students, and householders often didn't know, or poorly understood such words as: agitate, contaminate, foliage, hazardous, toxic, residue, residual spray, fungicide, and herbicide.)

Sprayer. The sprayer should be equipped with an agitator capable of keeping wettable powders in suspension. Use a disposable paper cup to catch a spray sample when the tank is full and again when it is near empty. Equivalent amounts of solids should settle out from each sample. After spraying there should be no solid residue on the tank bottom. The pump should handle a full range of pressures from low for herbicides to high for fungicides.

Nozzles. When spraying with a boom, use fan sprays and adjust the height of the boom so the fans just intersect at grass level. A uniform pattern is essential for spraying herbicides. You cannot get it with cone-pattern nozzles nor with partial overlap from adjacent nozzles.

Keep a close check on nozzle wear. Delivery rates increase as the hole wears. This can be partly compensated by reducing pressure, but with added wear the pattern loses uniformity. When any are worn, all nozzles shold be changed together to maintain uniformity of pattern.

Gun-type nozzles or sweep booms can be used to spray many fungicides and some noncritical insecticides or iron. Herbicides, many fungicides, and insecticides need a tractor or wheel-mounted boom for even application.

Calibration. Methods of calibration are given in appendix III.

Nozzle Pressure. With older contact poisons high pressures and small droplet size increased the number of hits, and you had to hit the insect to kill it. Present contact materials with residual action need not hit the insect so long as it walks through the material before the activity is lost. Lower pressures and larger droplets can be used, which reduces drift problems. To minimize herbicide drift the largest effective drop is preferred. However, too large drops may bounce off the leaf. Some fungicides extend their kill by forming fumes or vapors that diffuse throughout the turf layer. Others are effective only where they fall. The former can be applied under low pressures, the latter may need higher pressures to drive them into the turf.

Protective Clothing. Rubbers or boots, natural rubber gloves, and goggles may be of kinds that are available. Respirators depend on the material sprayed. U.S. Dept. of Agriculture publication ARS 33-76, *Respiratory Devices for Protection Against Certain Pesticides* list acceptable types.[7] Change respirator filters twice a day or more often. Change the cartridge after eight hours use, or if pesticide odor is noticeable. After use, wash the mask with soap and water and dry on a clean cloth. Protective clothing is needed not only while spraying but especially while opening cans or bags or pouring liquids or powders. At that time, drops of concentrated material are apt to splash on the skin or in the eyes.

Residue. It is difficult to wash herbicide residues from wooden tanks. Residues of phenoxy herbicides cling to even metal tanks and if there is a possibility of causing damage from the residue, the tank must be washed with care. Rinsing with water is sufficient for many compounds but phenoxy herbicides, and especially the esters, will need special attention. After the rinse use an alkaline solution. Ammonium hydroxide (laundry ammonia, 1 gal to 100 gal) or TSP (trisodium phosphate, 2 lb to 100 gal) are good. Allow the tank, hose, and nozzles to soak twenty-four hours in the solution then rinse them well with clean water.

Area Sprayed. Spray dosage based on the wrong area is a common cause of failure. If you don't know the area nor how to calculate it, hire a surveyor. Putting greens change size as the person mowing tends to mow out or in or to straighten curves or make them deeper. Greens can be checked from year to year by running lines between the sprinkler heads and checking the distance from the head to the edge green (Fig. 6.3). See appendix IV for a method of calculating area.

Check Up. It will be the manager's responsibility if anything goes wrong. He reads the label. He checks the dosage. He checks the operator for overlap. He sees that empty containers are properly disposed of. He sees that the operator has proper protective clothing for the material being used. He sees that any extra inventory of pesticide is stored in a locked and ventilated area away from areas of normal activities such as eating lunch, changing clothes, etc. If the label has become wet or loose,

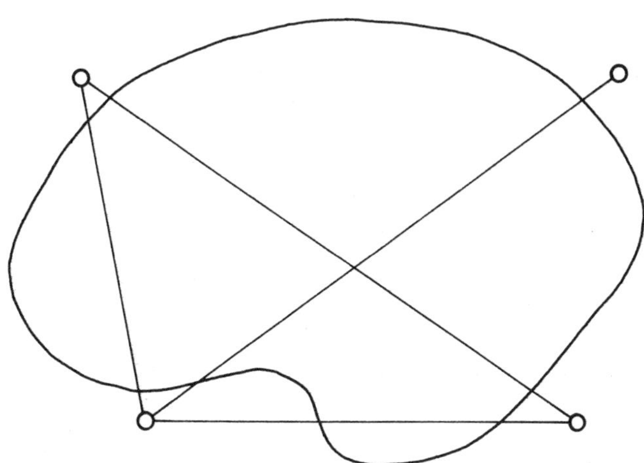

Figure 6.3 Sprinkler heads are permanent fixtures. If lines are stretched between them and distances measured to the edge of the green you can check to see if the green is changing size as a result of "mowing in" or "mowing out."

gummed tape should be wrapped around the container to hold the label in place. Unlabeled materials or materials in improper containers, e.g., coke bottles, should be destroyed. If there has been spillage in measuring the material, the spillage area should be decontaminated.

Mixture. Using several materials at once in the spray tank often saves costs. Compatibilities of chemicals are given in charts which are updated year to year. A current list may be available from your chemical supplier.

Data below are selected from *Excerpta Medica,* The Clinical Handbook on Economic Poisons)Table 6.1(, and from manufacturer's data.[48]

General Characteristics of Chemical Groups of Pesticides

The lists in the tables that follow are incomplete, listing only compounds commonly recommended for turf use. Materials not listed may be recommended for turf from time to time. Only the name considered to be the most common is used.

Organic Phosphates. Organic phosphates (Table 6.2) are readily absorbed through the skin, especially by the eyes, and most cases of poisoning result from skin absorption.

These compounds affect the enzyme cholinesterase. If phosphate insecticides are used regularly the applicator should have his blood cholinesterase level checked every two weeks.

Symptoms include headache, giddiness, nervousness, weakness, blurred vision, cramps, diarrhea, and chest discomfort. At low levels there may be mental depression, loss of memory, sleepwalking, or speech difficulty.[25]

Artificial respiration should be given as needed as a *first aid* measure. Death is usually from respiratory collapse. First aid should be ad-

Table 6.1. Probable Lethal Dose of Technical Material for a Human Adult[a]

Acute oral LD_{50} mg/kg	*Amount*
Less than 5	A few drops
5 to 50	A "pinch" to a teaspoonful
50 to 500	1 teaspoonful to 2 tablespoonsful
500 to 5000	1 ounce to 1 pint (pound)
5000 to 15,000	1 pint to 1 quart

[a]From the *Clinical Handbook on Economic Poisons,* U.S. Department of Health, Education, and Welfare.[48]

Table 6.2. Organic Phosphates

Name	*LD₅₀ mg/kg* Oral	Skin	*Comments*
Bay 20741 (Dasanit)	(2-5 estd.)		Skin absorption
Demeton	2.5	8.2	Ready skin absorption; long residue
Diazinon	103	455	Skin absorption; reacts with copper; long residue
Ethion	65	62	Skin absorption; reacts with copper; long residue
Malathion	1000	4444	Reacts with iron; safest of the group
Mocap	62	26	Skin absorption
Trithion	30		Absorbed through the skin
Parathion	3.0	6.8	Readily absorbed through the skin
V-C 13	270		Long residual action; limit use to once a year
Schradan	1.5	15.0	Readily absorbed through the skin

ministered for 24 hours following the onset of symptoms. When the patient is breating and conscious a 1/10 grain atropine sulfate pill should be given; the atropine sulfate should be obtained by prescription before using organic phosphates. If unconscious 1/30 grain should be given intravenously by a doctor. The patient should be decontaminated by removing clothing and washing the body all over, especially visibly contaminated areas. Use soap and plenty of water, then bathe again with ethyl alchohol. (If not available, use gin, vodka.) If the material has entered the stomach, induce vomiting.

Diazinon is recommended for several pests of turf. Less than 100 mg (2–3 drops) absorbed through the skin may cause symptoms and the illness lasts much longer than with the other phosphates. Many of these should be handled only by professional operators. Rates for the organic phosphates is in ounces per acre and recommended rates should not be exceeded. Phosphates are diluted and safer when used in granular form.

Children have a higher susceptibility than adults and 0.1 mg/kg has been sufficient to kill.

Chlorinated Hydrocarbons (Table 6.3). Except for DDT these are absorbed through the skin, respiratory tract, etc. They are insoluble in

Table 6.3. Chlorinated Hydrocarbons

Name	*Oral LD_{50}mg/kg*	*Comments*
Aldrin	38	Skin absorption
Chlordane	250	Skin absorption; accumulates in the soil
DDT	113	
Dieldrin	46	Skin absorption
Endrin	10	Skin absorption
Heptachlor	130	Skin absorption
Lindane	91	The active gamma isomer isolated from crude cyclohexachlorohexane
Methoxychlor	5000	Safest of those listed; baits made with Methoxychlor provide one of the safest forms of control for chewing insects
Toxaphene	90	Skin absorption

water and are formulated in various organic solvents which may aggravate toxicity. I again question whether there is any need to choose the most toxic of these for turf use, especially since residues are very enduring. DDT appears very safe with respect to human toxicity, but is damaging to birds and fish. Recent work shows DDT inducing hydroxylation of steroids (hormones). This interefers with egg-shell formation by birds.

Symptoms are usually directed to the nervous system. The compounds are fat soluble and are normally found in the body fat of animals. At toxic levels they also appear in the lipids associated with the nervous system and brain, and cause mental depression and convulsions. Early symptoms may include tremor, headache, and fatigue.

First Aid consists of removing any poison that may have been swallowed by inducing vomiting and by use of saline laxatives (salts, avoid oils). Wash contaminated skin with soap and water. Control convulsions with a relaxant and ventilate mechanically.

Carbamates. Oral LD_{50} mg/kg for Sevin (Carbaryl) is 500. It is absorbed through the skin. The oral LD_{50} for Azak is 34,600.

Symptoms are not known in detail but as carbamates inhibit cholinesterase, symptoms may be expected to be similar to those caused by organic phosphates.

First Aid is as for organic phosphates but recovery is very rapid.

Dithiocarbamates. These have low toxicity (Table 6.4) but cause irritation of the skin, eyes, and lungs.

Table 6.4. Dithiocarbamates

Name	*Oral LD_{50}mg/kg*
Ferbam	1000
Ziram	1400
Zineb	5200
Nabam	395

Compounds of Mercury. Data for mercury compounds are given in Table 6.5.

The last two compounds in Table 6.5 are usually used in combination as Calo–clor, Calocure, Fungchex, 2-1, etc. Do not mix with other turf chemicals.

Organic mercury compounds are somewhat more toxic than inorganic due to better absorption through both skin and digestive tract.

Acute *symptoms* are seldom recognized. Mercury is a protoplasmic poison and is injurious to blood, brain, liver, and kidneys. Kidney damage can accur without symptoms. Chronic symptoms usually appear with brain damage. Headaches, reduced coordination, and loss of side vision are early symptoms. Lack of coordination extends to speech, writing, and gait. Irritability may be present. Symptoms may progress to inability to act and mental stupor. Suspected poisoning can be confirmed by urine analysis.

Table 6.5[a]

Name	*Oral LD_{50}mg/kg*	*Comments*
PMA	40	Corrodes white metal-brass; don't use at temperatures over 80 °F
PMP(Metasol)	low	Avoid drift
Semesan	30	Avoid metal compounds in mixtures
Puraturf	30	
Metasol M turf spray	72	
Panogen	30	Reacts with metals
Emmi	148	
Memmi	155	
Mercuric chloride	37	Phytotoxic; not used alone
Mercurous chloride	100	

[a]Mercurics are toxic to 'Merion.'

Lack of effective treatments makes prevention essential. Goggles, masks, rubber gloves and protective clothing should be worn. If protective clothing has pockets removed, cigaretes, gum, candy bars, etc., can't be carried.

Cadmium Compounds. The cadmium compounds (Table 6.6) are used as fungicides almost exclusively on turf. As they are not used on food crops, the LD_{50} is not required. Cadmium ion complexes with sulfhydryl groups of body tissue. When inhaled, small amounts cause lung irritation, edema, and pneumonia. Taken by mouth, cadmium compounds cause vomiting so it is hard to ingest a lethal dose (estimated to be about 50 mg). However, very small doses cause gastroenteritis and result in liver and kidney damage. In test animals a subcutaneous injection of 0.01 mg/kg caused degeneration of the testicles and 0.25 mg/kg resulted in kidney damage.* Higher levels result in arterial hypertension and implicate cadmium as a possible contributor to heart attack. Cadmium compounds should not be allowed to contaminate pond or other water. Use of cadmium compounds has been discontinued in England because of their toxicity in the landscape.

Arsenicals. Data on arsenicals are listed in Table 6.7. Some skin absorption occurs, but the usual route of entry is through the mouth and nose. For years arsenicals have been the single most important cause of accidental death from pesticides. The principal victims, children; the principal cause, carelessness.

Symptoms include vomiting and abdominal pain. Profuse, painful diarrhea follows, and the body is dehydrated.

First aid is to induce vomiting with warm salt water.

Chlorophenoxy Herbicides. Data are listed in Table 6.8. Skin absorption is slight. Intake is through mouth and nose.

*This does not tell how much cadmium would have to be ingested to get such blood levels.

Table 6.6. Cadmium Compounds

Name	*Active Ingredient*
Caddy, Vi-Cad	Cadmium chloride
Puraturf 177	Phenylamino cadmium dilactate
Cadminate	Cadmium succinate, LD_{50} — 660 mg/kg
Cadox	Cadmium 8-hydroxyquinolinate
Crag turf fungicide	Cadmium calcium copper zinc sulfate-chromate

Table 6.7. Arsenicals

Name	*Oral LD₅₀mg/kg*	*Comments*
Lead arsenate	100	0.1 g lethal to man
Calcium arsenate	35	Phytotoxicity increases on soils containing sodium
Sodium arsenate	10	Phytotoxic; accumulates in the soil.
DSMA	600	
MSMA	700	
MAMA	720	
DMAA, cacodylic acid	830	
CAMA		
CPA	355	

Table 6.8. Chlorophenoxy Herbicides

Name	*Oral $LD_{50}mg/kg$*	*Comment*
2,4-D	375	
2,4,5-T	500	
2,4,5-TP	500	Eye irritant; absorbed through skin
MCPA	700	
MCPP	650	
2,4-DEP	850	

Symptoms may include skin dermatitis. Muscular weakness and fatigue are reported symptoms.

Phthalic Compounds. Data are listed in Table 6.9. Toxicity is low except for endothal, which is not used much on turf.

Symptoms of endothal are gastric inflammation, irregular gait, and convulsions. Symptoms are obscure.[26]

As a *first-aid* measure, feed cold milk.

Dinitrophenols. These are used to fortify oils and are not used much on turf. With even minor symptoms the operator should be removed from contact with the material for six weeks or more. The material is taken up and accumulated much faster than it can be excreted.

Table 6.9. Phthalic Compounds

Name	*Oral LD_{50}mg/kg*	*Comment*
Dacthal	3000	
Alanap	8200	
Endothal	35	An irritant

Symptoms include nausea, restlessness, flushed skin, sweating, a sensation of heat, and rapid breathing and heartbeat.

Urea Compounds. Siduron has an oral LD_{50} mg/kg of 7500. This is a group of low toxicity. It is used for brush control rather than on turf. Neburon is used on dichondra.

Heterocyelic Nitrogen Compounds. Data are listed in Table 6.10. Inhaled spray of paraquat may cause lesions in the lungs. There is some

Table 6.10. Heterocyclic Nitrogen Compounds

Name	*Oral LD_{50}mg/kg*	*Comment*
Diquat	400	An irritant
Paraquat	157	Skin absorption; irritating to skin
Simazine	5000	

Table 6.11 Miscellaneous Pesticides

Name	*LD_{50}mg/kg*	*Comment*
Acti-Dione	2.5	
PCNB	1650	
Captan	9000	A skin irritant
Difoltan	4600	
Dyrene	2710	A skin irritant
Daconil 2787	10000	
Thiram	865	A skin irritant
Dicamba	1040	

evidence that after a critical point lesions may continue to form and result in death even after the toxicant has been removed.

Solvents. Solvents used in formulating pesticides can cause appreciable discomfort to persons breathing fumes in an unventilated area. Headache, blurred vision, dizziness, and nausea can occur.

Micellaneous Pesticides. Data are listed in Table 6.11. These are of low toxicity except for Acti-dione, which has high toxicity.

Symptoms of actidione include salivation, diarrhea, stomach and gut pain, tremors, coma. No antidote is known.

References

1. Alexander, M., 1964, "Ecology of soil microorganisms," *The Cornell Plantations* **19**(4), 58–60.
2. Alexander, M., 1965, "Persistence and Biological reaction of pesticides in soils," *Soil Sci. Soc. Am. Proc.* **29,** 1–7.
3. Anon., "A directory of poison control centers," U.S. Dept. of Health, Education, and Welfare, Div. of Accident Prevention, Washington D.C.
4. Anon., 1958, "Screwworm vs screwworm," *Agr. Res.*, July, p. 8.
5. Anon., 1966, "Poisons," *The Golf Supt.* **34**(6), 30 ff.
6. Anon., 1967, "ARS Scientists working to exploit partnership of nematode–bacteria team to control insects," *West. Landscaping News* **7**(10), 2.
7. Agricultural Research Service, 1962, "Respiratory devices for protection against certain pesticides," U.S. Dept. of Agriculture ARS-33-76.
8. Arthur, A. P., 1962, "A skipper *Thymelicus lineola* (Ochs.) (Lepidoptera: Hesperiidae) and its parasites in Ontario," *Can. Entomologist* **94,** 1082–1089.
9. Baker, H., and T. E. Hienton, 1952, "Traps have some value," *Insects: Yearbook of Agriculture,* U.S. Dept. of Agriculture, Washington, D.C., pp. 406–411.
10. Barker, R. J., 1958, "Notes on some ecological effects of DDT sprayed on elms," *J. Wildlife Management* **22,** 269–274.
11. Beard, J. M., 1966, "Turf annual," *Park Maint.* **19**(7), 17 ff.
12. Bernard, J., 1962, "Rhodesgrass scale new Florida headache," *Golfdom* **36** (7), 54.
13. Brogdon, J. E., 1964, "Pest control on greens," *Univ. Florida Agr. Expt. Sta. Turfgr. Management Conf. Proc.* **12,** 84–86.
14. Brogdon, J.E., 1964, "Pest control," *Ibid.* **12,** 93–96.
15. Butler, G. D., Jr., 1962, "The distribution and control of the bermudagrass eriophyd mite," *Univ. Ariz. Agr. Sta. Rept.* **212,** 1–9.

16. Butler, G. D., Jr., 1962, "Biological control of puncturevine," *Ibid.,* p. 30.
17. Butler, G. D., Jr., and T. Scanlon, 1965, "Evaluation of materials for the control of bermudagrass mite," *Univ. Ariz. Expt. Sta. Rept.* **230,** 11–16.
18. Butler, G. D., Jr., and P. D. Johnson, "Life cycle studies of a Rhodesgrass scale parasite," *Univ. Ariz. Agr. Expt. Sta. Rept.* **230,** 21–23.
19. Carson, R., 1962, *Silent Spring,* Crest Books, New York, 304 pp.
20. DeBach, P., and B. Bartlett, 1951, "Effects of insecticides on biological control of insect pests of citrus," *J. Econ. Entomol.* **44,** 372–383.
21. Doutt, R. L., 1948, "Effect of codling moth sprays on natural control of the Baker mealy bug," *J. Econ. Entomol.* **41,** 116–117.
22. Department of Agriculture Appropriations for 1966, 1965, Hearings before a subcommittee of the Committee on Appropriations, House of Representatives, Part I, U.S. Government Printing Office, Washington, D.C., pp. 165–208.
23. Engel, R. E., and L. M. Callahan, 1967, "Merion Kentucky bluegrass response to soil residue of pre-emergence herbicides," *Weeds* **15,** 128–130.
24. Fults, J. L., 1966, "The crabgrass problem," *Proc. 37th Annual Turfgr. Conf. and Show Proc.,* pp. 37–41.
25. Gershon, S., and F. H. Shaw, 1961, "Psychiatric sequelae of chronic exposure to organophosphorous insecticides," *Lancet* **1,** 1371–1374.
26. Gleason, M. N., R. E. Gosselin, and H. C. Hodge, 1957, *Clinical Toxicology of Commercial Products,* Williams & Wilkins Co., Baltimore, Md.
27. Hodgson, J. M., F. P. Thrasher, and R. F. Eslick, 1964, "Effects of eight herbicides on yields of barley and wheat varieties," *Crop Sci.* **4,** 397–310.
28. Horn, G. C., and W. L. Prichett, 1962, "Chinch bug damage and fertilizer," *Florida Turfgr. Bull.* **9**(4), 3, 6–7.
29. Jacob, F. H., 1958, "Some modern problems in pest control," *Sci. Progr.* **46**(181), 30–45.
30. Jefferson, R. N., and J. S. Morishita, 1962, "Progress report on the bermudagrass mite and the frit fly," *Calif. Turfgr. Cult.* **12**(2), 9–10.
31. Jukes, T. H., 1962, "People and pesticides," *Am. Scientist* **51,** 355–361.
32. Kerr, S. H., 1959, "Turf insect problem is growing in south," *Parks and Rec.* **41**(7), 301–303.
33. Kerr, S. H., 1962, "Outlook on turfgrass insect studies in Florida," *Florida Turfgr. Bull.* **9**(2), 2–4.
34. Leach, B. R., and J. W. Lipp, 1926, "A method for grub proofing turf," *U.S.G.A. Greens Sec. Bull.* **6**(2), 34–39.
35. Lichenstein, E. P., and J. B. Polivka, 1959, "Persistence of some chlorinated hydrocarbon insecticides in turf," *J. Econ. Entomol.* **52,** 289–293.
36. McLean, L. A., 1967, "Pesticides and the environment," *Biosci.* **17,** 613–616.
37. Nutter, C. C., 1967, "Habits and control of chinch bugs in turf," *Turfgrass Times* **2**(5), 1 ff.

38. Park, D., 1967, "The importance of antibiotics and inhibiting substances," in, A. Burges & F. Raw, Eds., *Soil Biology,* Academic Press, New York, pp. 435–448.

39. Pass, B. C., R. C. Bunker, and P. R. Burns, II, "Differential reaction of Kentucky bluegrass strains to sod webworns," *Agron. J.* **57,** 510–511.

40. Rudd, R. L., 1964, *Pesticides and the Living Landscape,* Univ. of Wisconsin Press, Madison, Wisc., 320 pp.

41. Schread, J. C., 1967, "Newer insects, newer emphasis," *38th Ann. Turf Conf. and Show. Proc.*, p. 71.

42. Schuder, D. L., 1966, "Notes on the biology and control of sod webworms," *Midwest Regional Turfgr. Foundn. Turf Conf. Proc.*, pp. 53–54.

43. Streu, H. T., and L. M. Vasvary, 1967, "Control of the hairy chinch bug, *Blissus hirtus* Mont., in New Jersey," *Rutgers Univ. Coll. Agr. Environ. Sci. Bull.* **816,** 78–82 (1966 report).

44. Streu, H. T., and L. M. Vasvary, 1967, "Sod webworm control trials," *Ibid.*, 83–84.

45. Smith, L. R., and L. J. Ashworth, Jr., 1964, "Effect of organic amendments and PCMB upon innocculum potential of *Rhizoctonia solani* in field soil," *Phytopathology* **54,** 626 (abstr.).

46. Smith, R. F., and K. S. Hagen, 1959, "Impact of commercial insecticide treatments," *Hilgardia* **29**(2), 131–154.

47. Thomson, W. T., 1967, *Agricultural Chemicals,* Book I, *Insecticides,* 366 pp.; Book 2, *Herbicides,* 314 pp.; Book 4, *Fungicides,* 293 pp., Thomson Publications, Davis, Calif.

48. Wayland, J. H., Jr., 1963, "Clinical handbook on economic poisons," U.S. Dept. Health, Education, and Welfare Publ., Health Serv. Pub. **475,** 144 pp.

49. Woodwell, G. M., "Toxic substances and ecological cycles," *Sci. Am.* **216** (3), 34–31.

50. Youngner, V. B., 1966, "Some problems in herbicide application," *Calif. Turfgr. Cult.* **16**(4), 25–27.

7

INSECTS AND OTHER ANIMAL PESTS

Insects belong to the phylum *Arthropoda*, a group of over 2,000,000 kinds of animals which make up about 80% of all animal species. We are fortunate that so few are pests on turfgrasses. Members of the *Arthropoda* have their skeleton on the outside which results in a characteristic segmented body, and appendages with jointed sections.

Of several classes, the turf man finds the class of insects *(Hexapoda)* the most important. Insects have three main body sections: a head, a thorax, and an abdomen. They have three pairs of legs, a pair of antennae, and generally one or two pair of wings. Immature stages, however, often do not fit this description and may be wormlike.

Class *Arachnida* includes spiders, mites, ticks, and scorpions. The head is fixed to the chest section so only two main body sections result. They have four pair of legs and no wings or antennae.

Millipedes *(Dilopoda)* and centipedes *(Chibopoda)* are wormlike and may or may not have antennae. Centipedes have one pair of legs per body segment, millipedes have two.

The culinary class, *Crustacea,* of crabs and crayfish also includes sow bugs. Crustacea are jointed animals with the head merged into the thorax, with one or two pair of antennae, but many pairs of legs. Other animal pests will be noted later in the chapter.

Because of the exoskeleton, insects grow by shedding an old case and producing a new and larger skeleton. The change is called a molt; the between stages, instars. In a few insects all stages are alike except for size, but most insects metamorphose, or change between stages (Fig. 7.1). In some insects the instars change gradually, molt by molt, and the instars are called nymphs. In others, the instars are similar and called larvae. The larva ultimately gives rise to a resting stage, a pupa, from which the adult and recognizable insect emerges. Many adult insects feed but little. Nymphs and larvae have good appetites.

Our own classification of Arthropoda divides it into members that are pests and those that are not. Pests may be further classed as those which damage turfgrasses, such as chinch bug, and those, such as mosquitos, which are a nuisance to people using the turf.

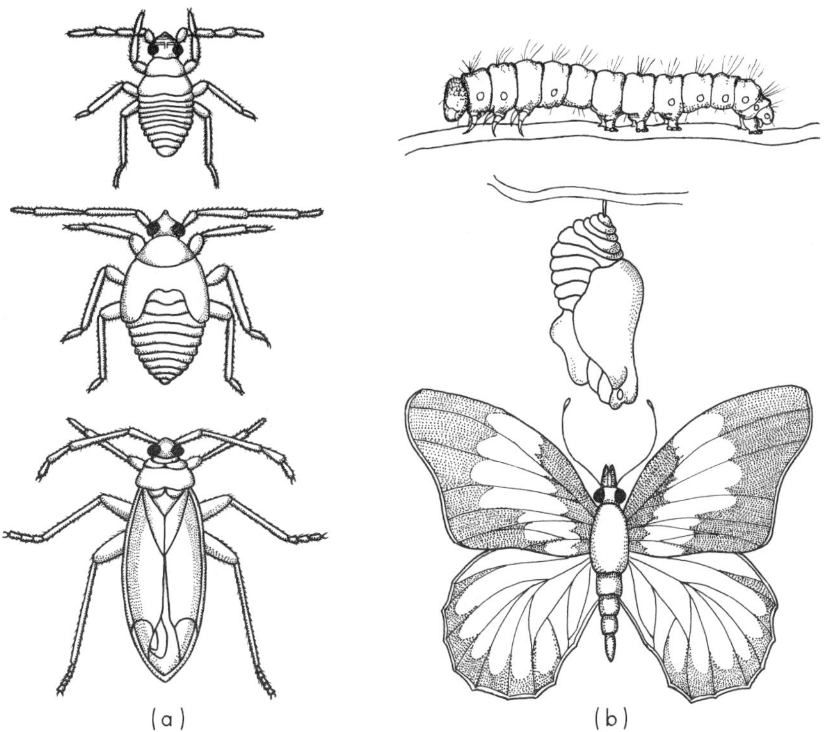

Figure 7.1 Incomplete (a) and complete (b) metamorphosis of insects.

There are also potential pests. As grain fields become lawns in suburbia, grain insects may try to survive on the turfgrasses and a few may succeed. An example is the frit fly. Other insects may be considered as low-grade pests. For example, major attacks of turf by aphis are rare. Yet I have seldom examined a plug of grass durig the growing season without finding an aphid or two present. Leafhoppers are common on turf in June, but are seldom treated for, though they may reduce turf vigor. Summer diseases often follow high population of leafhoppers, though a relationship has not been establshed.

As with other organisms there are interactions between insects and management practices. Insects, like all life forms, are chronically short of nitrogen. Nitrogen fertilizer makes turf attractive to pests and large crops of insects are encouraged by the use of nitrogen fertilizer.

In India a candy or confection is made from the honeydew excreted by a species of tree-dwelling mealybug. The yield of candy is increased by fertilizing the trees, which increases the numbers of mealybugs. (I found my sample of the candy intermediate between divinity fudge and molasses toffee.) St. Augustinegrass is little troubled by insects when grown at low fertility as a low-maintenance grass,[42] but at high fertility insect pests are legion. Similarly, sod webworm has not been a serious pest on bluegrass in the north until the grass is fertilized and irrigated.[85,75]

Irrigation directly affects insects by producing a succulent growth that is more subject to attack by some insects. In early stages sod webworm has difficulty getting enough to eat from the tough leaves of unirrigated low-maintenance bluegrass, and survival is low. Irrigation also has indirect effects. Many moths favor damp areas for laying eggs. Chinch bugs are attacked by a fungus in damp areas.[95] Regular periodic sprinkler irrigation washes moth eggs from leaves to the soil where many larvae perish. Bermudagrass mites require high humidity[18] but drown in surface water. In all likelihood the greatest effect of irrigation is to increase insects by providing suitably succulent food.

Low, frequent mowing also helps provide new soft growth of good succulence. At the same time low mowing reduces the total forage (verdure) so that equal amounts of grazing are relatively more damaging to the closely mown turf.

After hole-punching operations, insects are often found residing in the holes. There is no evidence that insect problems are affected one way or the other by providing these artificial burrows.

Many insects are found in thatch but these are often eating the thatch (e.g., pill bugs). Such insects may represent a normal population that would be found in the surface soil if there were no thatch. Nevertheless, thatch removal controls bermudagrass mite.[45]

The grass species affects insect problems. Some insects prefer or attack only one kind of grass. Within a species there may be more or less resistant strains. Southern chinch bug attacks St. Augustinegrass, for example;[121] billbugs attack *Zoysia* and Bermudagrasses; wireworms attack centipede and bahiagrasses; and rhodesgrass scale attacks St. Augustine and bermudagrasses. Preliminary tests of St. Augustinegrass varieties have encouraged some workers to attempt to breed varieties resistant to chinch bug.[54]

Insect infestations are subject to weather conditions.[96] As temperatures warm to an optimum, insects grow and reproduce more rapidly. Mild winters result in high survival so there are more adults to start the infestation the next year. Severe winters result in death of many pests and a reduced severity of problems. Japanese beetle has not survived in the far north. Some die at 22°F. Below15°F, most are dead; 0° with no snow cover causes very high mortality. Survival is poor in the hot dry southwest also. Use of heating cable to warm soil may affect severity problems by increasing winter survival.

Hairy chinch bug populations are reduced by wet and freezing weather. With a wet cool spring, large numbers drown and many are destroyed by a fungus. Hairy chinch bug reached damaging levels in the northeast during a series of hot dry summers.

Sod webworm does little egg laying during dull, cloudy, and rainy weather.

CONTROL OF INSECTS

Insect populations are controlled by natural predators and parasites, as well as by manipulation of the environment through trapping, fumigation, food poisoning, and external poisoning.

The significance of predation should not be underestimated. New insects introduced from abroad often become epidemic as they increase, unchecked by natural enemies they have left behind. Such introduced pests are not effectively controlled until natural predators are introduced. The Japanese beetle, for example, was trapped and poisoned for years in a massive effort to control it, but it steadily increased in numbers until natural controls were introduced. Today it is a lesser pest controlled by species of Tiphia wasps *(Tiphia popilliavora)*, a Centeter fly, and soilborne diseases of the grubs. Other insects have been similarly controlled. With a newly introduced pest, chemical control should be thought of as first aid until natural predation can can be established. One of the worst pests currently is the lawn chinch bug on St. Augustine which apparently has no effective population of active natural enemies.[59]

Use of the most effective form of environmental manipulation is denied to the turf grower. This is the plowing of the soil and rotation of crops. Managment practices which reduce thatch and which keep the grass hardened off rather than succulent will help minimize problems.

Fumigation usually controls weed, insect, and disease pests and may be used to produce quality sod or in construction of high-value turfed areas.

Trapping has been useful in some small areas.[7,98] Recent development of more effective attractants as baits should make this method more interesting in the future. Trapping begun early in the spring may keep populations at low levels all season.

Stomach poisons may be applied as baits to the surface of the leaves which the insect eats, or with systemics, to the soil or leaves so the poison gets into the sap stream where it kills both those insects that eat the leaves or those which, like the chinch bug, only suck the juices. Baits are seldom used on turf except for control of slugs, snails, mole crickets, and moth larvae. However, they offer us possibilities. When a suitable attractant can be found and placed in the bait, the insect will preferentially eat the bait. In this way small amounts of insecticide can be effective over a large area. This provides an economy. Also, the only insects affected are those eating the bait so predators are not destroyed.

The idea of systemic poisons is attractive. Any insect attacking the affected plant is killed, others are not. Demeton (Systox) is a highly toxic organic phosphate which is taken in through the leaves and has systemic effectiveness from two to six weeks. Diazinon has some systemic action, as do some other organic phospates.[20] Contact or systemic poisons are needed to control sucking insects as they cannot be controlled by stomach poisons. A good contact poison preferably has long residual action. If it endures in the environment, incoming insects will be poisoned and no buildup will occur. With a short-lived poison populations soon build up again, are again "gunned down" in direct attack, and again begin to build up. The result is a series of ups and downs in population with each buildup followed by a spray. The long-lasting contact poison tends to put control more on a seasonal basis rather than leaving it as a week-to-week battle.

The good contact poison leads to the paradox of the bad–good poison. The long-lasting contact insecticide tends to kill all susceptible insects, good or bad, which leads to the problem of resurgence. Long-lasting qualities also create residue problem on foods.

In addition to other controls we may mention legal controls. The problem of introduced insects is so great that movement of plant materials is regulated to prevent introduction of foreign pests, to prevent their spread, and to enforce control. Labelling and use of insecticides is also regulated.

THE TURF PESTS

Lepidoptera

The order *Lepidoptera* includes moths, skippers, and butterflies. It is a large order with about 150,000 species of which about 10,000 are found in North America. The order is characterized by relatively large membranous wings covered with shingled scales. Butterflies and months undergo a complete metamorphosis and the larvae are often called caterpillars. Caterpillars feed on plants, and most plants are eaten by one or more species of caterpillar. The caterpillar usually pupates inside of a case or cocoon which is spins from silken threads.

Capterpillars that eat turfgrasses are listed in Table 7.1.

Table 7.1. Moths with Larvae that Damage Turfgrasses

Lawn moths, species of *Crambus*	*Crambus bonefatellus* (Hulst.)[44,79,11]
	C. sprerryellus Klots[44,79,11]
	C. teterrellus [97,81,82,75]
	C. trisectus [97,81,82]
	C. mutabilis [81,82]
	Buffalograss lawn moth[11]
Skippers	*Hylephia phylaeus Drury,* firey skipper [79,11]
	Thymelicus lineda (Ochs), Essex skipper [83,85]
Armyworm	*Cirphis unipunctata* (Haw) *(Pseudoletia)* [38,79,11,109]
Fall armyworm	*Laphygma frugiperda* (Smith and Abbot) [79]
Beet armyworm	*L. exigua* (Hubner)[79]
Granulated cutworm	*Agrotis subterranea* (Fab) (Felta)[79,11]
Black cutworm	*Agrotis ypsilon* (Rott)[79]
Turnip moth	*A. segetum* [36a]
Hart and dart	*A. exclamationis* [36a]
Variegated cutworm	*Peridroma Margaritosa* Hay[79,11]
Garden dart	*Euxoa nigricans* [36]
Glassy cutworm	*Septis devastato* (Brace)[79]
Yellow Underwing	*Triphaena pronuba*[36]
Lucerne moth	*Nomophial noctuella* (D and S) [79,11]
Tropical sod webworm	*Pachyzanda phaeopteralis* [53]
Others	

These various worms are a considerable problem in milder climates. Winter survival is high and more generations are produced in the course of the longer growing season. In northern California, for example, one or two sprays a summer are usually sufficient to control caterpillars. At Los Angeles an additional spray is needed, and at San Diego a fourth spray may be required. In warm regions the numbers of one or another of the worms is apt to reach serious proportions every year. One year, populations of skipper may be prominent; the next year, lawn moth; then granulated cutworm; and so on. In cooler climates, damaging population of worms occur only in climatically favorable years. In northern Europe there may be a single generation in a year. Usually, problems occur only when a dry warm fall and a dry spring permit a large percentage of the larvae to winter successfully.[36]

Fortunately, the habits, diagnosis, and treatments are the same for all of these pests and we can adequately treat the group by describing any member of it.

Characteristics. The following description is based on Bohart's classic description of the lawn moth *Crambus bonefatellus*.[11] The moths tend to be nocturnal and can be seen flying over the grass at dusk. For about an hour at dusk they fly over grass, dipping down to drop eggs in the grass. They preferentially select humid areas in succulent grass and moths will congregate in such areas to lay most of their eggs—about two hundred. The eggs need moisture to develop, and if the area dries, mortality will be high. The eggs hatch in about 4 1/2 days at 75°F. The small worm produced leads a precarious existence. With its small mouth it can only skeletonize the soft interveinal surface parts of a leaf (Fig. 7.2). If the leaf is tough and hard it may starve to death at this stage. If a drop of rain or irrigation water hits the larva, it may wash off the leaf to the soil and be lost. The first and second instars are usually spent on a single grass leaf. By the third instar the worm is large enough to take bites from the edge of the leaf and leaves appear notched. During the fourth, fifth, and sixth instars the worm lives during the day at the soil surface in a silk-lined burrow camouflaged with bits of leaf and excrement. All feeding is at night. In these stages the worm eats entire leaves, eating about twice its own weight nightly. A hundred larvae per square yard at this stage can thin turf out at a rate where it seems to disappear overnight. As green leaves are removed the brown duff is exposed and the infested areas are straw colored. The worms stay close to their burrows and so tend to thin the turf in a circular area the size of a quarter or half dollar. From above the turf, these feeding areas appear as pock marks in the lawn and can be readily recognized once they have been pointed out.

After the sixth instar the larva usually pupates though there may be more instars. At 75°F it takes about 24 days from hatched egg to pupa.

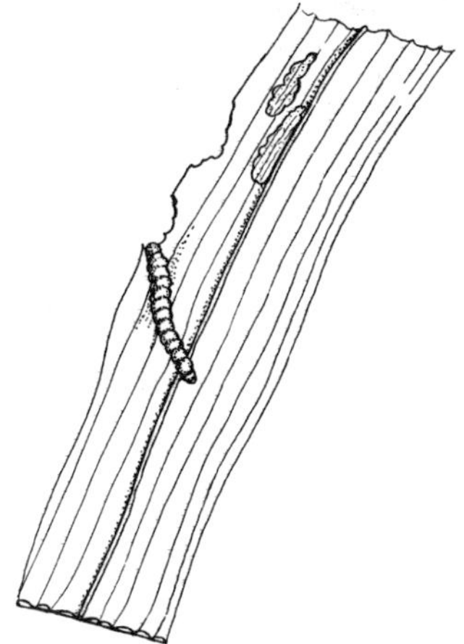

Figure 7.2 The first to third instars of caterpillars may live on a single leaf, at first feeding on softer tissues between the veins, then taking bites from the edge.

The pupal stage takes about a week. The 36-day life cycle described becomes about 130 days at 60°F and 33 days at 86°F.

The favored grasses are bluegrass and bentgrass. Bluegrass is susceptible to attack during its first year, after which it is too tough for a large population to build up unless fertilizer, irrigation, and close mowing result in soft growth.[11,82] Fescue and ryegrasses are not favored and bermudagrass infestations are slight and not important. Bentgrasses are the principal food. The buffalograss lawn moth attacks buffalograss and lives in a silk-lined chamber as deep as 18 in. below the surface. There it can survive the heat and drought as buffalograss is grown only under dry, nonirrigated conditions.[11]

The firey skipper is a less serious pest (Fig. 7.3). While it feeds on many turfgrasses, it is damaging only to bentgrasses. When skipper is present, masses like balls of white cotton are found in the grass and are kicked up by the mowers. These are the cocoon cases of a wasp (*Apenteles* sp.) that parasitizes skippers.[11]

The Lucerne moths prefer clover. Larvae are found in grass, but probably do not cause appreciable damage by themselves.

Cutworms (including armyworm) grow somewhat larger and may cut off the crown as well as leaves.[38] They prefer bent, rye, and bermudagrasses. They tend to hide deeper in the mat or soil than lawn moths. Various species may lay up to 1000 eggs.

Diagnosis. A false diagnosis for sod worms is often made. Numbers of moths fly up ahead of the mowers in the spring and then any loss of turf that occurs is laid to moth larvae. Every spring such flights result in the sale of large amounts of insecticide for brown spots caused by lawn

(a)

(b)

(c)

Figure 7.3 Caterpillar damage to turf. (a) Firey skipper adult. (b) Bentgrass turf damaged by firey skipper. (c) Stages of firey skipper, showing caterpillar, pupae, and cottony pupal cases of a wasp that has preyed on the caterpillars.

moths. This occurs in spite of the fact that lawn moths do not cause brown spots, nor do major infestations occur so early in the season. To diagnose for moth larvae a tablespoonful of pyrethrum extract is placed in a sprinkling can with one gallon of water and a test area of one square yard is sprinkled with the solution. Within two to ten minutes, the worms which have been hiding in the thatch and among the crowns of the grass plant come wriggling to the surface. If the area is measured and the worms counted, a census results. A population of one per square foot is tolerable; two per square foot becomes questionable; four per square foot indicates control is needed.

Most pyrethrum today is put up as light oil sprays for use around dairy barns, etc., and a suitable water-soluble extract is often not available. As a substitute we have successfully used household detergents in water to bring the worms out. Liquid detergents containing an added wetting agent (e.g., Vel) have worked well for us, but formulations change from time to time and you may have to try a couple of brands to find the best.

On one occasion the diagnostic treatment was used for control. On a severely infested green requiring immediate control, pyrethrum in water was poured on to make the worms surface. They were then winrowed and washed to the edge of the green with a hose. There, they were shoveled into a wheelbarrow and carted off.

Control. The various larvae are all attacked by parasites and predators[11,15,98] and there is considerable natural control. Trapping has been effective in reducing numbers for up to 75 ft. Baits containing DDT, Toxaphene, or both have been used successfully.[35,102] To control larvae with chemical sprays the turf should be mowed and irrigated. This minimizes the leaf area to be covered and maximizes the time the poison will be on the leaf before being washed off by the next irrigation. An insecticide is chosen that is effective as a stomach poison and is sprayed on at moderate to low pressures. A sticker spreader is used, and the goal is to wet the grass leaves on which the worms will feed that night. There is no virtue in using long-residue materials because the next irrigation will wash much into the soil, and mowing and regrowth will result in loss of the rest.

For natural control, sprays of *Bacillus entomocides* at 1 lb/acre of material containing 150 x 10^9 spores per gram have been effective. *B. thuringensis* has been reported both as adequate and disappointing.[44]

Chlorinated hydrocarbons are still extensively used but recent tests show reduced or little effectiveness.[100,69,98,81,44] Tolerance appears to have developed. There is good agreement on the effectiveness of Diazinon at 2 oz/1000 square feet.[110,98,81,44,8]

Other materials which have been recommended include: Carbaryl (Sevin),[81,44,8,12] Fenthion, 2 oz; Trichlorophon, 1 oz;[81] Ethion, 3 oz;[97] Trithion, 3 oz;[110] Baytex;[97] Toxaphene;[53,8] Baygon;[191] and Dursban.[98]

In the midwest a May or early June preventative spray has been recommended.[98] This reduces early populations to low levels so no large infestation builds up during that growing season.

Table 7.2. Beetles with Larvae that Damage Turfgrass

June beetle[87]	*Phyllophaga* spp.	2-3 yr life cycle; light to dark brown; 1/2-3/4 in. long
Green June beetle[53,119]	*Catinus nitida*	1-yr cycle; 1 in. flattened, velvety green bronzed edges; common in south but to L.I. and Ill.; grubs crawl on their backs
Northern masked chafer[88,115]	*Cyclocephala borealis*	1-yr cycle; 1/2 in.; chestnut brown with fine hairs; yellowish reddish head; nocturnal; fall grub 1 1/4 in. long; Most on rye and bermuda; common in southeast
Annual white grub[71]	*Ochrisidia villosa*	1-yr cycle; black to yellow in various patterns; Ohio and midwest in bluegrass
White grub[11]	*Spilosota hirta* (Lec.)	1-yr cycle; 3/5 in.; mostly yellowish brown with reddish head; grubs to 1 in.
Summer chafer, English June bug[36]	*Amphimallon solstitialis*	2-3 yr; 2/3 in.; light brown to yellowish; hairs; nocturnal
European chafer[36,4]	*A. majalis*	1/2 in.; light chocolate or tan; nocturnal; N.Y., Conn., W. Va., and spreading; bent and ryegrass preferred
Cockchafer[36] Maybug	*Melolonthera vulgaris*	3 yr; 1 in.; abdomen reddish brown, head and thorax black; white grub 1 1/2"; nocturnal
Garden chafer[60]	*Phyllopertha horticola L.*	1-2 yr; 1/2 in.; thorax metallic green; red-brown wing hairy; diurnal; favors Agrostis-fescue of dry areas in wet regions
Japanese beetle[38,88,118]	*Papilla japonica* Newm.	1-yr cycle; 1/2 in.; metallic green with wing cases coppery brown
Oriental beetle[118]	*Autoserica castanea* Arrow *(Maladera)*	5/8 in.; straw colored with dark markings; northeast
Asiatic beetle[34,118]	*Anomala orientalis* Waterh.	grubs to 2/3-1/4 in. long; chestnut-brown; short velvety hairs on bottom; nocturnal
Black beetle (Australia)	*Heteronychus sanctae-helenae* Blanchard	5/8 in.; parallel sided black beetle; annual cycle with spring and fall damage

Table 7.2 cont'd.

Billbug[50,11,53] Hunting billbug[58,51]	*Calendra* spp. *Sphenophorus benatis vestitia* (Chttn.)	1/4-3/8 in.; black-gray dark, reddish head and thorax; gray abdomen; 1/4-1/2 in. larva; 1/2-3/4 in. large in middle
Wireworms[33]	*Agriotes* spp. (*A. Mancus* (Say), *A. sputator* (L.), *A. lineatus* (L.), *A. abscura* (L.)	4-5 yr

In the southern U.S. the time of the first spray depends on the extent of the overwintering population. Numbers may warrant a spray as early as June or as late as August. After the first spray, up to three monthly repeat sprays may be needed depending on temperatures. In Florida control of the tropical sod webworm may be needed throughout the year and as often as every three weeks.[53]

Coleoptera

A second order of insects, *Coleoptera,* the beetles, is widely distributed and contains members damaging to turf. Among the beetles are many valuable predators such as the ladybird beetle; scavengers of offal (dung and carrion beetles); but also household pests such as cereal weevils, carpet beetles, and posthole beetles. Three families of beetles cause damage to turf. The most damaging are members of the *Scarabaeidae,* whose larvae are the white grubs that eat grass roots. A few members of the billbug family, *Cuculionidae,* find a home in turfgrass thatch and also have larvae that eat off roots. Larvae of the click beetles of family *Elateridae* are wireworms. They eat both dead and living vegetable matter. While they may help clean out thatch, the larger stages develop an appetite for subsurface roots and rhizomes. Flea beetles of family *Chrysomelidae,* are potentially damaging.[96,97,100]

Table 7.2 lists some of the commoner beetle pests of turf. There are 150 U.S. species of June bugs and the larvae of any of them may be found in turf at some time or another.

Beetle Grubs

In general, scarab beetles emerge in May or June from the soil where they have been pupating, though they may emerge as early as April in the south or July in more northerly regions. Adults eat foliage of trees and shrubs and within a month of emergence lay about 200 eggs in the soil and die. The eggs hatch to form grubs which are generally dark colored at the head end but which have a large white abdomen curled into a hook (Fig. 7.4). The grubs feed on turf roots until about October, molting and growing during this time. As the soil cools they go deep to spend the winter. Some species such as the northern masked chafer, complete their life cycle in one year. In the spring they come near the surface, feed a bit more, then pupate. The principal damage to grass is in the late summer when the grubs are large and still feeding. Other species have a life cycle of three years (two years in the south, four years at the northern limit). Their grubs are not damaging the first year but with all species the principal damage is in the late summer and early fall of the year of maturity. There is little or no spring feeding just before pupation and damage then is less common.

The green June beetle is the most prominent example of a few beetle grubs of nuisance value on greens. They do not injure the grass but eat dead vegetable material. However, they tunnel extensively and mounds of excavated trash are thrown out to form little dirt hills on greens.

Diagnosis. The diagnosis for beetle grubs is to dig out a volume of soil about a square foot in area and six inches deep. Select the sample from turf that is in the sun and appears unthrifty. The soil is crumbled and screened or sorted over to find and pick out the grubs. A dozen samples

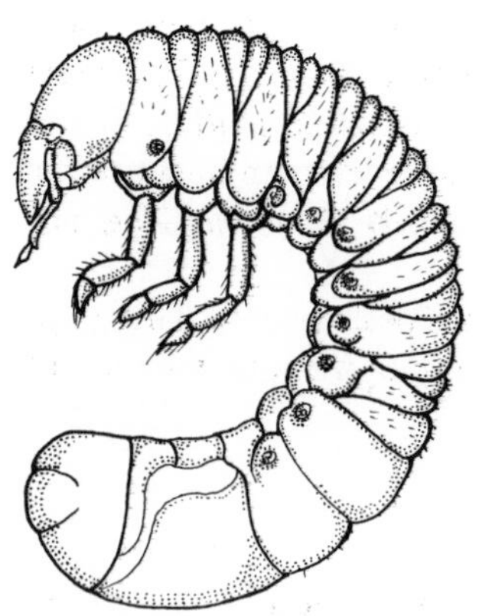

Figure 7.4 A beetle grub, showing the characteristic hook-shaped abdomen.

are counted. Fleming[32] suggests cutting a sod on three sides and folding it back on the uncut edge. The soil is worked over with a trowel and grubs are counted. The turf is then folded back in place, firmed, and watered. In severe infestations grubs have averaged as many as twenty five per square foot. One to five can probably be tolerated except on greens. Other symptoms are dead areas and grass that pulls up easily or rolls up because it is no longer attached by roots.

Control. Immediate control is difficult as it may take six weeks to get sufficient insecticide down into the soil. Hole punching does not seem to speed the process. Control is usually poor in the year of application, excellent the subsequent year. If immediate control is needed an insecticide with fumigant action such as dichlorodiethylether or DBCP should be tried. Grubs are seldom a problem on greens anymore. Chlorinated hydrocarbons used for surface insects have washed down into the soil and kept grubs under control. Lead arsenate or chlorinated hydrocarbons work well and both give control for periods up to ten years.[87,62,11] Materials may be applied as granules, dusts, wettable powders, or emulsifiable concentrates with equal success. Before applying the material, check for caterpillars. If present apply the insecticide as a stomach poison for moth larvae, then after two days irrigate to wash it down for subsequent control of grubs. Only a two-day exposure is used because breakdown of hydrocarbons is promoted by sunlight.

Lead arsenate is used at the rate of 10 lb/1000 ft^2. Expense may limit use of lead arsenate to greens. There it has value for limited control of *Poa annua* as well as grubs. DDT is an effective insecticide for grub control because of its long residual control. At 12.5 lb of active ingredient per acre, it has given control for three to four years; at 37.5 lb, for over ten years.[87] For soil high in organic matter higher rates may be needed; on sands, less is needed.

If the insecticide is applied in water, use a large volume and low pressure. Follow application with irrigation to apply about one inch of water but apply it slowly enough so there is no washing, puddling, or runoff. In 1926 Leach and Lipp[61] recommended grub proofing greens by working 35 lb/1000 ft^2 of acid lead arsenate into the top four inches of green soil in new construction. This is followed by 2 lb, 12 oz/yd of top dressing. The suggestion was brought up to date by Brogdon in 1964,[12] who recommended incorporating chlorinated hydrocarbon in soils of new greens.

Although insecticides are appropriate to high-maintenance turf, natural control will greatly reduce chances of grub problems on many large areas. To introduce diseases of insects such as the milky disease of Japanese beetle caused by *Bacillus pupilliae* or the insect disease caused by *B. entemocides* or

B. thuringensis, and be successful, some grubs should occur so the disease-producing organism can reproduce itself and remain alive in the soil. Consequently, disease-producing organisms are slow to establish on soils that have been treated with DDT, Chlordane, or other long-lasting materials. When spores are introduced, control gradually increases for two to four years until a natural equilibrium is reached. The heavier the initial infestation the sooner control obtains.

Billbugs

At present billbug damage is regional. *Sphenophorus phoeniciensis* is a pest on bermudagrass in the southwest, and *S. venatus vestita,* the hunting billbug, is a pest on Zoysiagrass. It was observed as a pest on *Zoysia* in 1959 in the mid-Atlantic states but as *Zoysia* is transported and planted as vegetative material, billbug is a potential pest throughout the range of *Zoysia.* Other billbugs appear through the southern states.

Billbugs are smaller beetles, generally in the neighborhood of 1/4 in. long. Mouth parts are formed into a snout but the snout is not formed for sucking (Fig. 7.5). It has well developed chewing organs at the tip. The adult may eat grass-blades or may work its snout into grass stems and eat out the softer interior parts. Adult beetles damage turf but the principal damage is from grubs that feed near the soil surface. They may feed above ground on leaves and stems or below the surface on roots. As they ma-

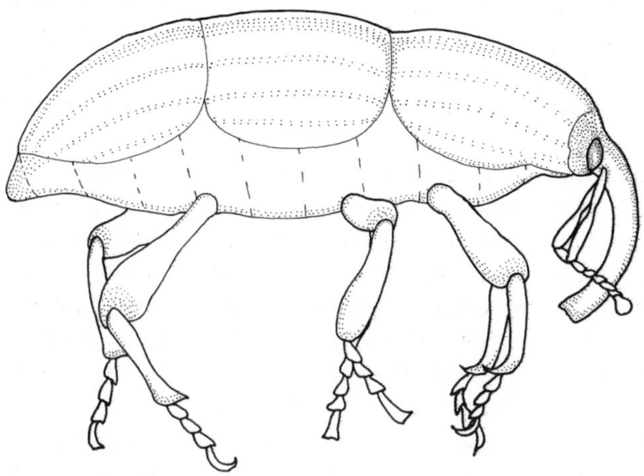

Figure 7.5 A billbug. The mouth parts are formed into a snout.

ture, they go below ground where they eat off roots. The grass dies of desticcation. Billbugs have a shorter life cycle than scarab beetles and may complete a generation in six weeks. Two or more generations a year may occur.

Diagnosis. Turf dries out from desiccation and brown areas result. Grass in these areas is easily pulled up. The insects have usually migrated from the dead areas and will be found in adjacent green turf. Mature larvae reach lengths of 1/2–3/4 in. and have a reddish head and white abdomen. Adults may be black to grayish to brown with black or dark reddish head and thorax. The snout gives a readily recognizable profile.

Control. Billbugs do not respond well to chlorinated hydrocarbons; this, together with the multiple generations, means that sprays for control must be repeated during the season. Diazinon has been used in conjunction with thatch removal, aeration, and fertilization, with successful results.[46] In Florida Kerr recommends Di-Syston or Thimet in turf nurseries or where these toxic materials can be safely used[58] (Oral $LD_{50.}$ 2.6 and 1.1 mg/kg). Baygon controlled billbugs but at high cost. Dichloroethyl ether can be used for control;[43] none of these give residual control. Juska[50] found that larvae could be controlled by chlordane; he used two applications of ten pounds per acre with a six-week interval.

Wireworms

The various species of *Agriotes* are seldom considered serious pests of turf in the U.S. though they are recognized as a problem in Great Britain, especially when turf follows pasture where large populations already exist. Controlling wireworms in Ontario increased pasture[33] yield to 50% and it is likely that wireworm control may assist turf improvement in marginal situations. The adult beetles are about one-half inch long, dark brown, gray, or black. The abdomen is hinged to the thorax and when placed on their back, beetles are able to snap the hinge with a click, pop up in the air, and turn over. The larvae, the wireworms, are from 1/2 to 1 1/2 in. long, hard, shiny, and dark brown (Fig. 7.6). The life cycle may take three or four years. During the last couple of years the older larvae feed on roots and rhizomes.

Diagnosis. Damage usually occurs in patches. A soil volume is dug out on the edge of an injured area and sorted over for grubs. More

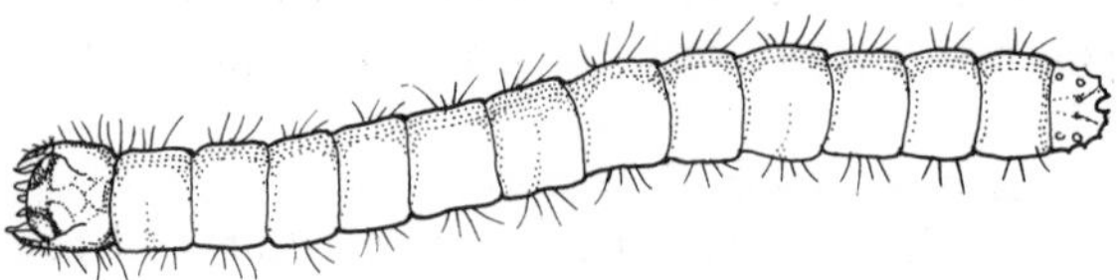

Figure 7.6 A wireworm. These are larvae of click beetles.

than two or three larvae per square foot may justify treatment if no other cause of damage is found.

Treatment. Animals, insects, and fungi prey on wireworms, giving some natural control. Control is as for grubs, i.e., use of chlorinated hydrocarbons, with better control the second year and control for seven to ten years.[33]

Flea Beetles

Flea beetles are found in turf on occasion and may become a pest with a shift in ecology. In Australia the couch flea beetle *Chaetocnema austraeica* badly damages bermudagrass.[100] The 1%16-in. beetle and its larvae feed on leaves, eating the mesophyll and leaving the epidermis, which dries and becomes silvery. The recommended control is 0.1% DDT.

Cereal Leaf Beetles

Oulema melanopa[1231] is found in Europe and Asia from Sibera to Spain. It is now in southern Michigan and Northern Indiana. It is a hard-shelled beetle, 5/16 in. long. Wing cover and head are metallic blues to black. Legs and front segment of the thorax are reddish to orange. The yellowish larva, up to 1/4 in. long, camouflages itself with a piece of moist fecal material onits back so it looks like a small gray slug. Damage is only potential and all stages are controlled with Sevin.

Clover Weevils

The clover weevil,[97] *Hyeroides* spp., is a 3/16-in. beetle that may lay eggs in grass crowns where the larvae feed. The beetle is metallic brown with a broad dark brown to black band on the outer wings. Larvae are grayish white and legless. Several damaging attacks have occurred on golf courses in New York and Long Island. In one case sprays of Diazinon in mid-June and late July provided control.

Hemiptera

The order Hemipterà, the bug order, is familiar to most gardeners. The principal member attacking turf, the chinch bug, is fortunately of regional rather than general distribution. The bug group is full of pests such as the stinkbug, squash bug, bedbug, spittle bug, and assassin bug. The kissing bug is a voracious predator with a painful bite.

Turf pests occur in two families in the order. The Miridae or plant bugs contains insects that damage grasses for seed, causing "silver top".

When plant bugs of the Miradae are a problem in seed fields of bluegrass or fescues, a contact insecticide is used in May, as the bugs are likely to feed on the developing seed head before emergence. Young seed heads should be torn apart in the field to see if the bug is present.

Chinch Bugs

The family Lygaeidae contains the chinch bug. ***Blissus insularis*** Barber, the lawn chinch bug is a pest only on St. Augustinegrass. The adult is relatively long-lived, females surviving an average of 70 days. They continue to lay over 250 eggs over a long period.[59] In southern Florida chinch bug is active throughout the year producing three generations and going into a fourth. Economically it is one of the most important turf pests; annual control in Florida is estimated to cost $24,000,000.[77]

Lawn chinch bug has long wings but walks rather than flies. Populations drop with the onset of cool weather, and population pressure is eased by wetness from frequent showers.

Just outside the range of the lawn chinch bug, the common chinch bug, ***Blissus leucopterus*** (Say) (Fig. 7.7), occurs on corn and grains and on turf of bermudagrass. The adults are shorter lived, 8–10 days, and in the spring there are large flights of adults.[3,42,77]

Blissus hirtus, hairy chinch bug, is a pest in the northeast, particularly from New Jersey to Connecticut to Ohio. The hairy chinch bug has short wing cases but commonly migrates by flying. In the spring there are flights as clusters of overwintering adults spread out. Hairy chinch bug favors bent, blue, and red fesuce grasses. A complete summer generation is produced. A second generation winters over.[3,94,77]

Eggs are tucked out of sight, often between tillers at the crown. Damage is primarily from the nymphs which grow from a red colored pinhead with a white band across the back to a brownish 1/5-in. long adult, taking six to eight weeks and passing through five (more or less) instars.

Chinch bugs are hot-weather bugs and thrive when it is hot and dry.[95] In wet cool years numbers decrease appreciably, and when the weather remains moist the bugs are attacked by a fungus disease. Chinch bugs have

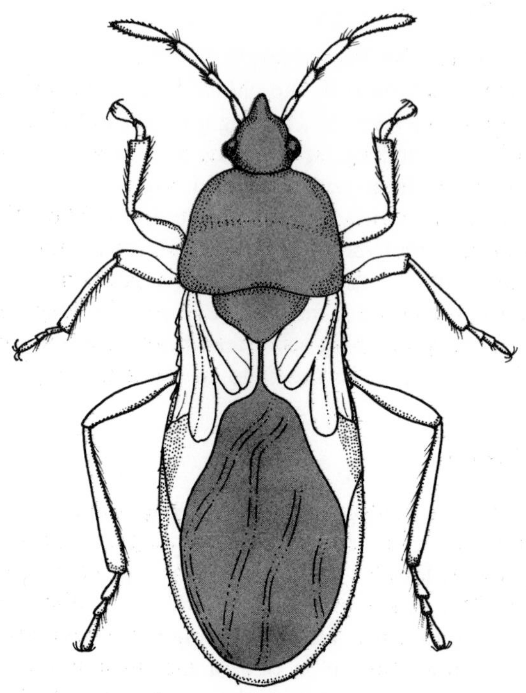

Figure 7.7 Common chinch bug.

occupied their present range for a long time[3] and have occasionally been a problem on greens. In recent years the problem has increased in severity due largely to a number of hot dry years, and partly to the use of chlorinated hydrocarbons, which has reduced competition of other insects with the resistant chinch bugs.[109] Increased damage is also due to higher levels of nitrogen fertilization. Horn and Prichett in Florida found a direct relation between damage and nitrogen fertility.[42] When no fertilizer was used, no damage occured. Damage increased with increasing nitrogen until at 16 lb N/yr/1000 ft^2 the turf was 63% dead. There was less damage when organic nitrogen replaced ammonium nitrate.

The decline of turf with chinch bug feeding suggests the possibility that the saliva is toxic.[53]

Diagnosis. Nymphs congregate. Feeding causes a small yellowish area of grass. At this stage, control is possible. As the grass dies, the bugs spread out and the browned patch becomes large. Diagnosis and evaulation are by means of a metal ring of a coffee can without a bottom which is pressed into the soil surface. This is kept filled with water for 10 minutes during which time chinch bugs float to the surface and can be counted and evaluated. Because of uneven distribution at least six to ten counts need to be made in the area. The can may be eased into the soil by cutting around it with a knife. Leakage is not important as long as the water level can be kept above the turf.

Control. Control of chinch bug is currently by organic phosphate materials or carbamates. When chlordane is used, chinch bug populations increase. Phosphaes and carbamates may be alternated to prevent buildup of resistance to either of them. Some recommended materials are listed in Table 7.3. Granular forms of insecticides are promising.

Diptera

The order Diptera is the order of flies. At present three flies are common pests of turf. Fly eggs hatch into wormlike larvae called maggots. The maggot of the frit fly, *Oscinella frit* (L.) lives in the stem of its host. The leatherjacket, exemplified by *Tipula paludosa* Meig, is a primary pest of turf in Great Britain. Eggs are laid in the soil. The maggot feeds at first on decaying organic matter, but later stages feed on turf roots. This pest has recently been introduced into northwestern U.S. The Australian sod fly or soldier fly, *Inopus rubriceps* (MacQuart), is a minor pest of turf in Australia and New Zealand and has been introduced into California. Fly maggots also occur in turf when blood, tankage, cottonseed cake, etc., are used for fertilizer. Maggots feed on the high-protein organic matter. In one instance at least, the maggots also ate feeder roots of grass causing a setback to the grass.[92]

Frit fly is a general pest of grain that manages to survive on turf. The fly is black and small, about 1/16 in. long (Fig. 7.8). Other stem-boring flies can make this transition to turf and 100 species of fly have been found on grass in the southwest. Only the frit has become a recognized pest on turf though. Several species are damaging in seed fields.[107] In England the frit fly has preferred bluegrass and perennial ryegrasses, and on mowed grass overwintering larvae of flies have averaged about eleven per square yard with little change year to year.[29,105] Larvae feed on stem tissue. On turf the larvae cause injury to the central leaf. The leaf survives at cool temperatures but dies in summer heat.[1] Three generations per year have been estimated in the east, four in the midwest, and more in the southwest.[45] When bluegrass lawns are irrigated, they yield flies throughout the growing season. As bluegrass growth slows flies may move in on greens where they are damaging. Flies often attack the collar first, then move gradually toward the center of the green.[45]

Table 7.3. Insecticides Recommended for Chinch Bug Control

	Type	LD_{50}*(mg/kg)*	*Rate/1000 ft²*	*Comments*
Aspon [77,58]	Organic dithiophosphate	851	3-4 oz in 25 gal	Contact poison; wash into soil before allowing turf activities; avoid drift and contamination of ponds and streams; 60-90 days control
Baygon [77,58,17]	Carbamate	95	2-3 oz to 1 gal	Contact poison; possibly some systemic action; avoid mixing with alkaline materials; long residual
Diazinon [77,100,53]	Organic thiophosphate	108	to 2 oz in 2 gal	Contact; two applications needed
Dursban [77,58]	Organic thiophosphate	135	1/2 to 2/3 oz	Contact and vapor action; short residual action on the leaf
Ethion [77,100]	Organic dithiophosphate	65 (uptake by skin)	2-4 oz in 2 gal (granular good also)	Contact; long residual action; do not mix with lime or copper
Sevin [109,7]	Carbamate	500 (uptake by skin)	1/5-1.0 oz in 2 gal	Contact; don't mix with alkaline materials; 5-30 day residual action; two applications needed; alternate with phosphates to avoid phosphate resistance
Trithion [77,109,17]	Organic dithiophosphate	30 (uptake by skin)	to 1 oz in 2 gal	Contact and stomach poison; long residual activity
VC-13 [77,17,53]	Organic thiophosphate	270	7 oz to 1 lb in water	Contact; also controls nematodes, caterpillars, and slugs; up to 8wk residual action

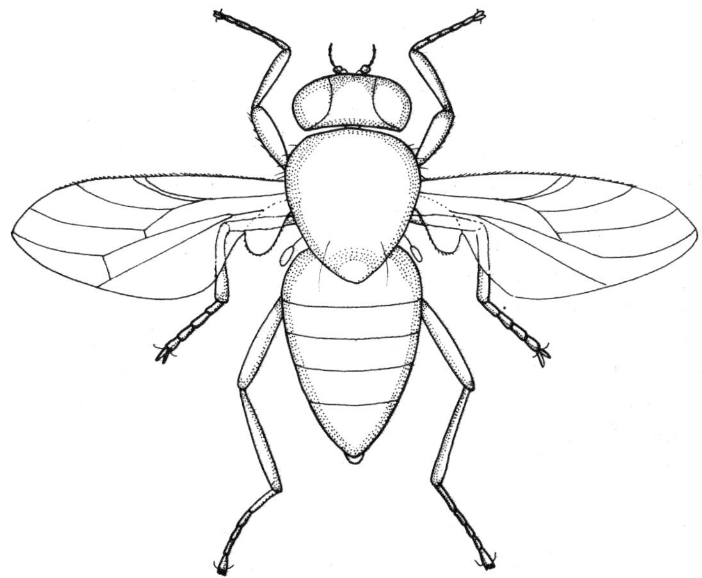

Figure 7.8 Frit fly.

Adult frit flies are attracted to white. If flies are present and the weather is warm and dry, flies will soon light on a handkerchief dropped on the ground. On a green, flies light on a ball as soon as it lands and thereby provide a ready clue to trouble. Grass appears unthrifty and retarded when fly larvae are at work. They may sometime be dissected out of the stem by cutting stems in half.

Control is with materials having contact or systemic action. Repeat applications are needed. There is no advantage to materials having residual action. Diazinon has been recommended. Its systemic action is probably valuable in killing maggots within the stem tissue. Although frit has been with us for half a century,[1] it has only recently been a severe problem. This may be due to resistance to DDT,[97] use of which has reduced predation.

The Australian sod fly or pasture soldier fly is a pest of mild climates where the larvae feed on cane, maize, grain, and pastures. Because of its adaptation to mild cool temperatures and moist soils the area of potential damage by this insect is limited. At present it is a common pest on the east coast of Australia. It has been introduced into California where, since 1948, it is found on the coastal side of the San Francisco peninsula south to Halfmoon Bay.[24] If it should cross the Golden Gate it could probably survive north through coastal Oregon.

Larvae feed on roots in the soil. Infested plants show pitted roots and decline in vigor. In a severe infestation a core cut with a cup cutter to 6 in. deep contained over 100 larvae. Fescue, rye, bent, and bluegrasses are all attacked, bent most severely. The generation time is probably at least two years. There is a principal flight in the fall at San Francisco(late September to early November) and a smaller flight in the spring.[24]

Diagnosis is by working over a soil core to find larvae which are up to 1/3 to 1/2 in. long. The head is dark brown, short, and broadly conical, and followed by twelve segments. Adults are slightly smaller than a housefly and the head of the female is red.

Control recommendations are not made. An infestation on a green at the Olympic Club in San Francisco was controlled with a drench of chlordane, rate and form not known. Saunders notes a preference of the fly for Kikuyu.[93] Hopefully this preference may make the fly an ally in the eradication of Kikuyu in parts of coastal California where both occur.

Leatherjackets are the larva of a crane fly, *Tipula* sp. The adult is seen flying slowly in damp sheltered areas where it resembles a large mosquito with an excess of legs hanging down. In Great Britain the adults fly in August and September, individuals living about ten days and laying 250 to 350 eggs soon after emerging. The larvae feed throughout the winter whenever temperatures support activity. The diet includes both dead vegetable matter and living roots. The full-size maggot may reach 1 1/2 in. is gray in color, and legless. When the maggot pupates it forms a brown skin. After two to three weeks the case slits down the back and the adult emerges, leaving the empty case protruding about 1/2 in. from the soil. This brown castoff skin has given the name *leatherjacket* to these pests.

Two species, *Tipula paludosa* Meig. and *T. oleracea* L., are the most widespread and damaging. Dawson lists six additional species which may cause damage,[27] three of *Tipula* and three of *Pales*.

Infestations are very subject to climatic changes and populations vary in severity from year to year. Within the turf, infestations are patchy rather than uniform. On greens infestations generally appear worst near the edges. In Europe ten to twenty maggots per square foot is considered a severe infestation. In Vancouver populations have exceeded 100 per square foot.[122]

Birds attracted by maggots may warn that the insect is present. The damage is a loosened turf which wilts and browns quickly under water stress. An emulsion of ortho-dichlorobenzene* diluted 400 to 1 can be

*This may be available from your janitorial supply house as a disinfectant for toilets.

applied at 1 gal/m^2 to cause the larvae to come to the surface. Gasoline also causes them to surface but kills the grass. Alternately the sod can be laid back and the soil worked over to search for maggots. These diagnostic acts should be repeated in several different spots because of the irregular distribution of the pests.

Use of arsenicals or chlorinated hydrocarbons for the control of any other insect should also provide control of leatherjackets. A 25% DDT emulsion at 1–2 oz/1000 ft^2 applied and washed in, is an example of a suitable control measure.[36] DDT or Aldrin at 3 lb/acre have been recommended for spring or fall spraying.[122]

A minor fly is *Hylemyia urbana* Mall., bermudagrass tip maggot, or couch tip maggot. The maggot of this fly, of housefly size, feeds on the terminal blade of bermudagrass. Control has been found necessary only after heavy top dressing or when stolonizing a new turf. It is currently recognized in Australia.[100]

Homoptera

The order Homoptera contains a range of pests which include aphids, leafhoppers, and the mealybugs and scales. They are sucking insects, many are wingless, metamorphosis is gradual so that the young resemble the adults, and many secrete a honeydew.

In general, *aphids* are not considered a serious pest of turfgrasses. I have almost never examined a grass sample during the growing season without finding a few aphids present. At the same time I have never seen a severe infestation though they do occur occasionally. I should choose to regard them as incipient pests that contribute slightly to the total stress on grass, but not sufficiently to economically justify separate control.

Aphids are a subsidiary pest of turf areas due to the honeydew they secrete. Cars parked under trees having aphids become spotted with the honeydew. Where the honeydew falls on sidewalks, picnic tables, etc., a mold grows on it producing black sooty spores that dirty clothing and are unattractive. If one wishes to control aphids, one should also control ants. Ants cultivate the aphids for the honeydew. If you spray a tree and kill the aphids, ants will just bring in a new population. Aphids are killed by contact sprays. Chlordane is specific for ants.

There are a number of different leafhoppers of the family Cicadellidae which are found on turfgrasses (Fig. 7.9). They feed by puncturing the leaf and sucking the juices. In the heat of the day they may move into shaded areas and damage may be more severe in the shade. Leafhoppers

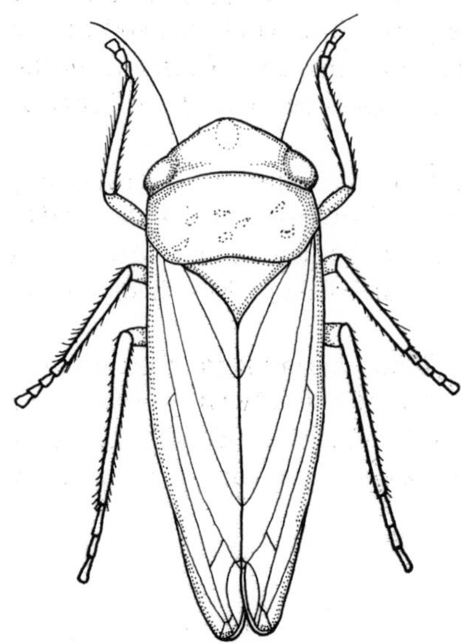

Figure 7.9 A leafhopper, many species of which may be found in turf.

are carriers of virus diseases, and may inject a toxin that reduces plant vigor. Leafhoppers are damaging to seed crops.

Diagnosis is visual. As one moves through the grass, the hoppers spring up in front. The blades of grass show dots where the leaf has been punctured in feedings.

Control is by contact poison; Malathion,[47] DDT, Diazinon, and Sevin[8] have been recommended.

Scale insects on turf are damaging where they occur and difficult of control. Turfgrass scale insects include, bermudagrass scale, *Odonaspis ruthae* Kot., rhodesgrass scale, *Antonina graminis* Mask., and ground pearls, *Margarodes meridionalis* Morr.

Ground pearls are a pest of centipedegrass and secondarily of bermudagrass (Fig. 7.10).[53] They feed on grass roots to which they are attached by their needle-like mouth parts. Not only are the young stages small and relatively undifferentiated but they are covered with a hard pale cover, whence the resemblance to pearls. Ground pearls are found in the southern tier of states but are only a potential pest in California. Size is up to 1/16 in. across.

The bermudagrass scale is found on bermudagrass rhizomes. It is small, reaching 1/16 in. in length. It is most damaging in shady areas.

The rhodesgrass scale was found in Texas in 1945 and by 1950 was in Florida.[89] It is damaging on both bermuda and St. Augustinegrasses, particularly of St. Augustine in Florida. It feeds on rhizomes and is larger than the bermudagrass scale, reaching 1/8 in. in length. In Florida it has a 60–70 day life cycle and can go through four to five generations in a year.[9]

Damage from these sucking underground insects is not obvious, and if serious, may result in a thin turf that fails to respond to fertilizer treatment. The turf should be lifted with a shovel and turned over. Because of the contrasting color, ground pearls are readily seen on the roots. A hand lens is helpful in looking for scales. Fish out pieces of older rhizome and peel back the sheaths. The most likely place to find scale insects is at a node protected by the sheath. New growth will not have had time for infestation and the larger more mature stages will be found on older rhizomes. The rhodesgrass scale is purplish brown with a cottony white secretion. The bermudagrass scale secretes a hard whitish clamshell-shaped cover.[14,118,12,121]

Underground scales are particularly difficult to control. Parasites have been introduced. A small wingless parasite, *Neodusmetia sangwani* (Subba Rao), was released in Tucson, Arrzona, in 1961 and recovered in scale collection made in 1964.[22] This indicates that the parasite has become established. The mature parasite lives for only forty-eight hours so that new introductions are best made by introducing mature larvae. The emerging adult can then spend its short adult life searching for new scales to lay its eggs on. In Florida the parasitic wasp, *Anagyrus an-*

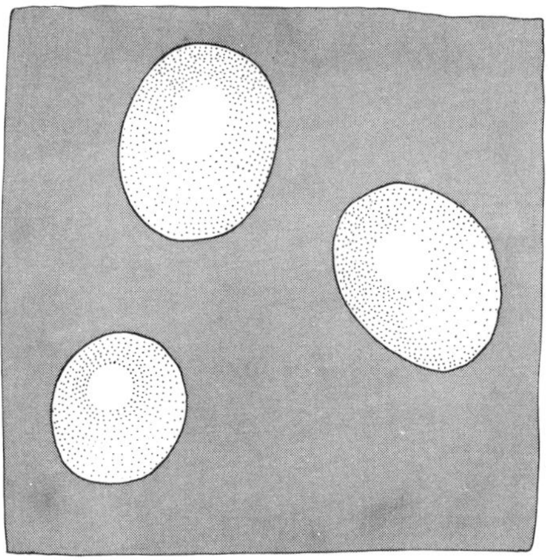

Figure 7.10 The waxy cover on ground pearls hides detailed features.

toninae, was released in 1954. It has become established in several locations and is spreading.[90]

The U.S.G.A. has recommended the use of the systemic insecticides Demeton and Schraden.[9] These are highly poisonous (1 drop toxicity) and are taken up through the skin. Residues are long lasting. If used it would be best to have the materials applied by a professional sprayman and to withdraw the turf from public use until it can be shown that surface residues are gone.

Control has been obtained on ground pearl with 4 lb/acre of Malathion used as a drench with extra water.[106] VC-13 used as a drench showed promise of control. Demeton and Dylox were ineffective in the same tests.

Florida recommendations are for 8–10 lb of Malathion per acre with 5 gal of summer oil, or, in areas where turf traffic can be controlled, a professional application of 4 lb of Parathion per acre with 5 gal of summer oil.[53] Sufficient water should be used to drench these into the soil.

Orthoptera

The order Orthoptera of cockroaches, grasshoppers, and crickets is of limited interest. The mole cricket is a soil pest in southeast U.S. and western Australia where it burrows in lighter soils and eats roots of grasses.[100,120] *Scapteriscus acletus* Rhen and Hebard is the principal species of mole cricket or "changa" in the coastal plain region of the U.S. along with *S. vicinus* Scud. Eggs are laid 3–8 in. deep in the soil where they hatch to form nymphs that burrow and feed in the soil. Adults live for several months and are fast runners and fliers.

Diagnosis. In making their runs, crickets loosen and push up the grass in streaks. Run your fingers through the grass and you can find the runs and tunnels beneath these pushed up areas.[120] Birds going after the nymphs are often damaging and may cut a furrow 1–2 in. long and 1 in. deep in digging them out.

Control. Chlordane is recommended as a standard control,[56,120] though other chlorinated hydrocarbons are also recommended. One-half pint of 75% emulsifiable concentrate or 1/2 lb of 40% wettable powder may be used in 20 gal of water for 1000 ft^2. Baits may be used for cricket control. Twenty-five pounds of bran is dampened and treated with 1 lb DDT as 20% WP or two oz of chlordane, 75% emulsion or equivalent. The bait is spread over 1–5 acres in the afternoon.

Auxiliary Pests

The auxiliary pests associated with turf include flies, mosquitoes, ants, chiggers, earwigs, wasps, clover mites, ticks, millipedes and centipedes, slugs and snails, and spiders and scorpions. These are discussed further[118] in U.S.D.A. Bulletin 53, available from the Superintendent of Documents for 15¢ and in the 1952 *Yearbook of Agriculture.*[117] Chlordane sprayed on building foundations or footing between the ground line and the wood will keep down invasion by ants, termites, millipedes, centipedes, earwigs, and pill bugs. If the problem is severe a bait of bran with chlordane, aldrin, or other chlorinated hydrocarbon can be used in addition to the spray. Baits containing metaldahyde are effective for snails and slugs. Metaldehyde is a strong attractant for these mollusks. Ticks, chiggers, and mites are arachnids. One-fourth pound of lindane or one pound of toxaphene per acre will control chiggers.[117] Ticks can sense warm-blooded animals and are attracted to paths and areas where people concentrate. These areas can be sprayed with DDT emulsion.[117] When the clover mite is present in large numbers it may enter buildings where its red color and spider shape are psychologically disturbing to some people. Invasions are stopped by spraying walks, foundations, flowers, shrubs, and lawns around the buildings with a miticide such as Dimite, chlorobenzilate, Aramite, or Kelthane. One quart of emulsifiable concentrate (1/2 lb active ingredient) per 100 gal is used at high pressure.[68]

Flies have quickly built up resistance to a number of compounds. Currently, the best control indoors is by use of pyrethrum, activated by synergists such as piperonyl butoxide or *n*-propyl isomer. Aerosols are convenient and the same ingredients are active against mosquitoes, gnats, wasps, centipedes, fleas, etc., and toxicity is low. DDT aerosols are effective against many of the same pests, but flies are generally resistant.[117]

An excellent material for the control of insects in buildings is silica aerogel.[28] The material is nontoxic and is used as a fine powder dusted about the premises. Roaches, earwigs, crickets, etc., that walk through the silica aerogel have the oil or wax stripped from their skeletons. They are then no longer waterproof and die in a few hours from drying out.

Malathion, fogged at high pressure in the afternoon, will keep down mosquito attacks during outdoor social functions that night.

The United States Department of Agriculture, Agricultural Research Service, publishes a weekly *Cooperative Economic Insect Report* which gives warnings and progress reports on the presence of damaging insects over the U.S. From time to time, various insects are reported causing damage to turfgrass species. Many more insects are reported as damaging turf species than are discussed here. However, many of these are small local outbreaks that subside without further attention. Other outbreaks occur in pastures and seed fields and are controlled in turf by mowing. The existence of these infestations does indicate thhough that good turf is nourishing food and may attract other pests over the years.

Arachnida

The second group of Arthropoda injuring grass are the mites of Class Arachnida. Many mites are predatory and when "fleas have little fleas upon their backs to bite them," the "little fleas" are apt to be mites. An examination of mites on bermudagrass in Arizona yielded twenty-two species in fifteen different families.[115] Some were predatory and most were minor in terms of direct damage. However, mites are important vectors of virus diseases of grasses, and are known to transmit viruses of turfgrasses.[103,104] The important turfgrass mite is an Eriophyid mite, *Aceria neocynodontis* Kiefer, infesting bermudagrass, particularly in the southwest, Florida, Georgia, and in Australia.[21,100,116] A related mite, *A. tulipae,* is associated with silver top disease in bluegrass seed fields.[11]

The mite is extremely small, the adult being about 200 microns long (about 1/125 to 1/150 in.). Magnification is needed for viewing. The mites cannot survive low humidity so they are not brought in on seed. They may blow in or be introduced, carried on thrips, leafhoppers, or other insects. The eggs are clear in color and hatch in about 5–6 days at 75°F. There are three instars and the life cycle is completed in 8–10 day at 75°F. The first nymphs are clear in color and one-third the size of an adult. The second instar is two-thirds of the adult size and whitish. The adult is whitish cream and wormlike with reduced legs near the minute sucking head. The mites live under the sheath with up to and over 100 per sheath. They require moisture and when relative humidity falls below 80%, mortality of both eggs and mites is high. When condensation occurs, mites drown. The mites can withstand heat, and temperatures of 120°F must persist for more than two hours before there are many dead. At low temperatures they are inactive.[19] Severe infestations may be suddenly reduced for reasons unknown. A mite,*Steneotarsonemus spirifex,* is frequently associated with the reduced populations, possibly as a social parasite.[23] Mite damage may be due in part to a toxin produced by the mites. The tufts have low vigor and become brown clumps which usually die. Internodes are shortened and leaves occur as a tuft or whorl. The distortion of plant parts continues to occur after the mites are dead, and affected lawns fail to resume active growth in the spring. Silver top of blue grass has been induced by the feeding of a single mite, which also suggest a toxin.[41] A summer *Helminthosporium* blight always appears associated with mite damage in Arizona. Mite damage is more severe in areas of poor sprinkler overlap and where mowing is short and infrequent. Fertilizer may increase infestation but also improves recovery. Bermudagrass varieties containing *C. transvaalensis* genes appear to be less affected than clones of *C. dactylon.* Observations indicate that resistant strains of common bermudagrass could be developed. At Arizona, Ormond and turf from seed of U-3 were the most severely affected of 96 varieties observed; Royal cape, *C. bradleyi, C. transvaalensis,* and the Tifton hybrids were little affected.[18]

Diagnosis. Short nodes and tufted leaves indicate the presence of the mite. Leaves may be light green and curl inward from the tip. The mite can be seen with the aid of a good ten-power lens when the sheath is pulled back. With *A. cynodontis* present, leaf tips remain clasped in the sheath of the previous leaf.

Control. Diazinon has given control as has dusting sulfur at 10 lb/1000 ft^2. In Florida, Trithion has been slightly better than Diazinon and Kerr[55] recommends 3 oz of active ingredient per 1000 ft^2 in 20 gal of water. Granular forms of Diazinon were more effective in Arizona.[17] The best treatment combined Diazinon, Captan, and ammonium nitrate,[17] though the Captan added little to the Diazinon–fertilizer combination. In California, thatch removal by vertical mowing and hole punching combined with fertilization was about as effective as Diazinon.[45] Insecticides of promise include Dursban, Banol, Baygon, and Ethion. Chemicals that did not give control included Bromyl. Kelthane, Dimethoate, Di-syston, Malathion, Dibrom, Meta-systox, and Tedion.[23] Summer sprays gave control; autumn sprays reduced spring damage; spring sprays didn't help damaged turf but aided summer control.[16]

Asiatic Clam

In Europe a mollusk, the Zebra clam, *Dreissena polymorpha,* has given trouble inside of water pipes since 1886. In the U.S. the Asiatic clam *Corbicula fluminea* Muller was first noticed in Washington State in 1938. Since then it has spread to a number of rivers in the U.S. With the popularity of mobile boats it should not take long to spread the clam throughout U.S. waters by carrying larvae in bilge. When irrigation water is drawn directly from infested streams, the free-swimming larvae are drawn in, attach themselves to the pipe, and grow. Within a short time pressures are reduced by friction and sprinklers are clogged.[80,101]

The larvae are released from May to September and the clams are controlled by introducing chlorine at the intake in amounts of 1 1/2 – 2 ppm, to provide 1/2 ppm residual. Slug dosing of the line has not controlled clams. Sand filtration has held back larvae of the zebra clam and may work for the Asiatic clam. Simple filtration is obtained by taking water from a drilled well a couple of hundred feet back from the stream or lake. Other pests in pipes may include snails, hydroids, and fresh-water sponges; control measures are the same.

Asiatic clams are edible but should be cooked.

Nematodes

Nematodes are small, transparent, unsegmented worms, most of which are free living and survive on decaying matter in the soil. A few are parasitic on plants and animals including man (pinworm, trichinaes, and hookworm, for example). At this time it is difficult to fully evaluate the significance of nematodes as a cause of turf disease.

Nematodes feed on plant roots and although they generally feed on individual cells, sufficient numbers of cells are killed that the root dies. When nematode damage has reduced the root system, no symptoms may appear until the turf is under stress. With high-maintenance turf regularly fed and watered, symptoms may never appear. Holmes[40] concluded that golf superintendents could grow grass well in spite of reduced root systems. We are hardly prepared to spend money or concern to control a pest when no visible or measurable differences result.

Where nematodes are a real problem evidence supports the hypothesis that the problem is not a reduced root system, but toxins in the plant from nematode feeding.[85] The nematode inserts its stylet into a root cell and injects a digestive juice, then sucks back the liquified contents of the cell. Toxins may be introduced into the plant with the saliva.

The great damage to turf throughout the coastal plains region has been largely due to a single nematode *Belonolaimus longicaudatis,* which causes damage at relatively low populations. As tops show injury without commensurate root damage, a toxin is implicated. A second nematode, *Hypsoperine graminis,* the pseudo–root–knot nematode, was found on St. Augustinegrass in 1959 and is increasingly damaging.

In the midwest, bluegrass is affected with a species of spiral nematode, *Helicotylenchus*.[84] When this was controlled in Wisconsin, there was no summer dormancy of the bluegrass and weed growth was suppressed by vigorously growing bluegrass. Dormancy resulting from nematode feeding again suggests the possibility of a toxin, The third disease related to nematodes is yellow turfs on bentgrass which has been related to the presence of several species of nematode between sheath and blade.[112,111] Again, a physiological disorder is related to feeding activities of nematodes and the likelihood of a toxin seems reasonable. In other instances damage results from numbers, the pseudo-root-knot nematode, *Hypsoperine graminis,* is damaging in large numbers. The nematode enters a root near the tip where it lives and feeds. Uptake or transport of water and nutrients is interfered with. As populations increase the root system is unable to supply the tops, which yellow and wilt.[86]

To summarize the present state of our knowledge, I should say we can generally grow turf in spite of injury to roots from nematodes except when populations are high. When toxins are involved, even small numbers of nematodes can be damaging.*

As with all organisms, nematodes are in a dynamic ecological relationship with their environment. Populations shift with the seasons; with changes in soil moisture, temperature, and fertility; and in interaction with other plants and animals in the soil.[68,78,88,37]

Nematodes are preyed upon by other nematodes and by fungi.[65] In turn, they carry fungal and virus diseases that-infect host plants.[89]

Of the fungi which attack nematodes, one type is of interest.[65,67,87,88] It forms a noose of several cells. When a nematode wanders into the noose, the cells are stimulated to swell, closing the noose and strangling the prey. Efforts have been made to stimulate the growth of such fungi as a nematode-control measure, but the ecology of the trapping fungi is itself complex.[66] In one trial additions of fresh organic matter stimulated growth of free-living nematodes.[59] This in turn favored growth of the trapping fungi and as nematodes were caught randomly, both free-living and parasitic, a reduction in parasitic kinds occurred. No reductions occurred, however, following applications of long-lasting organic matter.[65] Nutter and Christie[78] found an organic fertilizer, Milorganite, resulted in fewer nematodes and a slower buildup after treatment with a nematocide. UF also resulted in fewer nematodes than the soluble ammonium nitrate. In another trial a mulch of organic matter increased fungi in the soil and decreased nematodes. But when both a fungistat and a nematocide were applied, the fungi decreased and numbers of nematodes increased.[68]

Nematodes are favored by good aeration and require a higher critical level of oxygen in the soil than do grass roots. The critical level[37] is about 30×10^{-8} g cm^{-2} min^{-1}. Nematodes are favored by irrigation unless the result of irrigation is low soil oxygen. With increased nitrogen, reproduction of nematodes is favored so they build up at a much more rapid rate. In other words, high-maintenance turf favors nematode buildup and attack.

*What do we mean by small numbers? With over 20,000 per pint of soil reported,[2] numbers can get very large. When we speak of small numbers of nematodes, we are referring to fewer than 200–400 per pint of soil depending on species.

Temperature affects nematode populations. In the south where the nematode problem is severe, adults survive and are active the year around. In the northern tier states, populations are severely reduced in the winter and infestation must build up each year from survivors. In the south, winter activity is low. At Arizona, effects of nematodes on overseeded ryegrass were studied, and in the cool season when the ryegrass was active, rooting was stimulated by the presence of nematodes and there were 50% more roots on plants in infested soils.[74] Rooting of grasses was reduced by nematodes, however, during the warm growing season. The ryegrass may have been able to outgrow cool-season nematode injury yet have been sufficiently injured so root branching was stimulated.

Over forty species of nematodes have been found feeding on grass. The genera and species involved are summed in Couch[26] and Perry.[85] Nematodes are divided into two classes, ectoparasites and endoparasites. Ectoparasites live outside of the plant, feed on surface tissues, and can generally be controlled by nematocides. Endoparasites burrow at least part way into the host tissue, and are difficult to control. Root knot nematodes cause a knot of dividing tissue on the root where they house and are sometimes separated from the endoparasites as a separate class. Nematodes are further classified by mouth parts, appearance, and general feeding behavior into sting, awl, lance, stylet, pin, ring, spiral, dagger, cyst, stubby root, root knot, lesion, burrowing, grass seed, and leaf gall nematodes.

Diagnosis for nematodes can be divided ito two stages. First is the stage of suspicion. Second is the analysis for confirmation or denial. The reason for making this separation is that the second step requires expert help. If grass is growing on a light soil, if roots show scars or swellings. if bluegrass goes dormant or centipedegrass turns yellow, if the turf is thin, unthrifty, or yellowish, and if fertilizer response is poor, the presence of nematodes may be suspected.[76] The turf manager may then make a preliminary diagnosis, without help, in the following manner: Take a funnel, place about 3–4 in. of rubber tubing over the end, fold the end of the tubing over, and pinch it with a clothespin to seal it off. Hold the funnel upright by setting it in an empty quart mason jar, then fill the funnel with water. Fold a piece of screen to sit in the top of the funnel about 1/2 in. from the top, then place a handful of soil from the suspected nematode infestation on top of the screen. The soil will take up water and you will have to keep adding water to the funnel to keep the water high enough to touch the bottom of the soil on the screen. When the soil no longer takes up water, you can make a final addition of water so water and soil touch, and set the apparatus aside for twenty-four hours. During this time, nematodes will work down, pass through the screen into the water, and sink to the bottom where they will collect in the end of the tube. After twenty-four hours take a flat, dark-colored dish and draw off about a teaspoonful of water from the end of the rubber tube. Put this under a strong light and examine it with a 10-power lens. Any soil should yield a few nematodes which will appear as tiny translucent worms which may be drowned and inactive, or alive and flipping back and forth. If there are more than a couple of dozen, you may have a nematode problem. The nematodes may be harmless free-living forms that have built up in numbers because of moist soil and plenty of decaying clippings, or they may be parasites. To decide which, you need the help of an expert and this usually means sending a soil sample to a laboratory to have the kinds of nematodes identified.

Another approach to diagnosis is to treat a small area of unthrifty turf with a nematocide and observe to see if the treated area shows improvement during the next few weeks. Even better is to use several nematocides and treat several areas with each.[85] If the turf responds well to treatment, nematodes are likely to be a problem. (But, remember, some nematocides may also control scale insects.) However, if the turf does not respond, nothing has been proved. Either there may be endoparasites present which were not affected by the nematocide, or nematodes may not be a problem, or the nematocide may have been incorrectly applied.

The most direct approach to diagnosis is to make a composite sample of soil from a number of areas and send about a quart of the moist soil in a plastic bag to a laboratory for evaluation.

The pseudo-root-knot nematode which is increasing on St. Augustine turf in Florida, produces a visible swelling on the root. Living inside of the root is stimulates production of giant cells in the root.[86]

Control. There is a difference among grasses in susceptibility to nematodes.[35,39,91,74] Zoysias and bermudagrass are more affected than St. Augustine. Among bermudagrasses there are differences in susceptibility.[73]

A primary form of nematode control is crop rotation which the turfgrass grower cannot use. In the garden, plants can be grown which are toxic to, or excrete compounds which are toxic to nematodes. The great American Horticulturist, David Fairchild, grew plants of *Crotolaria spectabile* in his Florida garden to control nematodes.[31] Marigolds may be grown for the same purpose,[65] but we are not yet growing marigolds in our turf.

A temporary control is obtained on new plantings by starting clean. If the soil is fumigated, then planted with clean stock, the first infestation of nematodes will be delayed. In the south a valuable sod industry needs to ship clean sod. Workers at Tifton, Ga. have progranmed a control measure in which sod plugs are treated at 55°C (131°F) for fifteen minutes.[5] This pasteurization kills nematodes. Hopefully, the treatment can be developed on a large scale for field or sod use. If successful, I do not think it unreasonable to consider lifting and treating the turf in cases of severe infestations of greens with resistant nematodes. While the sod is off, the soil beneath can be fumigated.

Chemical controls for nematodes are not universally effective; endoparasites in particular are less effected. One of the oldest controls is dibromochloropropane (Nemagon, Fumazone). It gives good control of many kinds of nematodes at 5 gal/acre, and rarely causes phytotoxicity of the grass.

The remaining controls are all organic phosphates which generally control some insects as well as nematodes. VC-13 has been used for a number of years but has tied up in the surface soil and not moved down to where it could do the most good. It has been replaced by better performing products.

Sarolex is a formulation of Diazinon prepared especially for nematode control. It has performed well in Florida trials and is recommended at 30–40 lb/acre active ingredient. Mocap (VC 9–104) is a new compound that has performed well in Florida trials and is recommended as either an emulsifiable concentrate or granular material at 5 1/2 to 11 or/1000 ft^2. Dasanit has given the quickest control and has been used at 3–11 oz/1000 ft^2 (20–30 lb/acre). Both Mocap and especially Dasanit have the disadvantage of high human toxicity. Both should be applied by an operator wearing full protective clothing and may be safer in the granular form. The plant remains toxic for two days, the soil for ten days following application. However, only one application per year should be needed. Although one application per year of nematocide should control most nematodes, one stubby-root nematode recovers in two to four months. When irrigation water is pumped from lakes, awl nematodes may be pumped back on, lessening control. Nematodes are competitive and when a control kills only some species but not others, those remaining soon build up large populations.[85] The pseudo-root -knot nematode in an endoparasite and the only current recommendation is for a massive (20 lb/acre, active ingredient) application of granular Dasanit watered in with at least 1/2 in. of water. Other products show promise in tests at Florida.[85] Zinophos, effective on other crops, has not been satisfactory on turf.

If the soil is too wet, nematocides don't move in, and damage to the turf is likely. Soil should not be dry, however, but moderately moist. The materials should be applied in about 50 gal of water per 1000 ft^2 and watered in with a 1/4–1/2 in. irrigation. If thatch is heavy, try to control it before applying the nematocide. Nematocides should be applied at low pressures. Sprinkled in, there is little damage to the grass. With high pressures, damage to grass increases and the possibility of injury from drift is increased.[85,5]

Earthworms

Under favorable conditions earthworm populations may exceed 2,000,000 per acre,[98] with 1800 pounds of worms producing 25 tons of casts to the acre annually.[30] Activity of casting worms improves aeration, water penetration, nutrient availability, soil structure, and thatch breakdown.[49,64] European earthworms introduced into New Zealand pastures resulted in increased productivity without fertilizers.[72] Pastures containing 21% poverty grass and 10% moss, had high populations of good forage grasses and clovers free of poverty grass and moss after a European grassland worm. *Allolobophora caliginosa,* was introduced.

Statements such as the above have long convinced the husbandman that he was in partnership with the earthworm in producing good pastures. Turf, however, differs from pasture in receiving traffic, and traffic may cause worm casts to break down and seal the soil surface. Escritt reports (viva voce) that Dawson often cured drainage problems on British golf courses by controlling casting earthworms. On high-maintenance turf piles of casts are dirty and keep a ball from rolling straight. Thus the earthworm finds itself listed as a pest of fine turf, though where the grass is mowed higher, casts are unnoticed and the worm may be left to till the soil unmolested. Not all species make casts,[48] and heavy casting may be a response to poor nutrition or acid soils.[49] On our plots casting was much heavier on 'Cohansey' than on five other varieties of bentgrass. The use of chlordane and other chlorinated hydrocarbons for insect control and the use of arsenicals for crabgrass control has almost eliminated the worm as a pest of greens and worms are now seldom mentioned as a turf pest in the U.S. They continue as a primary pest in Northern Europe.

Earthworms are killed by ultraviolet light and when the sun comes out suddenly after a dark rain, many are killed before they can return to their burrows. When this happens with an imported oriental earthworm, *Pheretima hupeinsis,* an offensive stink results. The oriental earthworm, a stinkworm, occurs along the eastern seaboard and has been controlled[94] with 1 quart of 48% emulsified chlordane in 10 gal of water per 1000 ft^2. The insecticide is applied and the turf drenched on three consecutive days to wash it in as well as possible. Aldrin also gave control, but not the organic phosphates. On other worms, chlordane at 24 lb active ingredient/acre of emulsifiable concentrate or

16–32 lb active ingredient/acre granular gave control after two months that lasted for over four years,[63] with active residues still in excess of 2 1/2 ppm at that time.

Rodents

Tunnelling rodents make piles of dirt in unwanted places and cause depressions when old tunnels collapse. Gophers have been readily controlled in California with a special tool fitting on a three-point tractor hitch.[10,52] The tool makes a tunnel in the soil of the same size and depth as a gopher hole. While making the tunnel the tool drops a poisoned grain every 2–3 in. Gophers find it simpler to use the ready-made tunnel and to eat the provided grain. Populations are rapidly reduced. A tunnel around a turfed area limits invasion from nearby fields.

Cornell University developed a similar tool for making baited mouse runs in grass under the snow.

Rodents are also controlled by poisoned baits introduced in the tunnels or by poisoned gases. Use of methyl bromide as a fumigant has been effective but may kill grass over the runs. Calcium cyanamide may be less damaging of the turf. Gases are introduced into the burrow after all entrances have been closed. Baits are introduced by opening the burrow, scattering the bait and closing the burrow again or by using a 1/4–1/2 in. rod to probe for the burrow and dropping poisonus grain down the probe holes.

Trapping is effective and where gophers are a recurring pest, each man should be provided with a half dozen traps and instructed to set them anytime he sees burrowing activity. For trapping, the tunnel is opened. A trap is placed a foot or two down the tunnel using a trap in each direction. The hole is left open. When the gopher comes to repair the roof he will be trapped from whichever direction he comes.

Other Vertebrate Pests

Pigs, skunks, armadillos, moles, and perhaps other animals will tear up turf looking for grubs and insects to eat. These animals can roll up, or tear up a large area of turf in a single night. Control is to use an insecticide to kill the insects the animals are feeding on.

Depredations caused by the human animal are best controlled by fencing. High chain link fences with locked gates are the most effective means of controlling vandalism. When golf courses are contiguous to and part of a housing development, fencing may not be permitted. In this case the use of an automatic sprinkler system to shower the perimeters of the course immediately after closing may help somewhat to deter after-dark activities.

PRACTICUM

One of the difficult problems of insect control is one of personnel. The park, golf course, military establishment, veterans' hospital, etc., is often large enough that the turfgrass manager spends much of his time in the office. He depends on his help to keep him posted on turf conditions. It is difficult to get workers to report insect or other pest problems in the early stages before damage is done. Experienced men will often note a reduction in quality as soon as it occurs. But they will watch the change for a week or two until they are very sure before they will report it. By this time much damage may already be done.

On a large operation I would give serious consideration to hiring a college entomology student during the summer vacation of his junior year. Give him the last hour or two of the day to collect and prepare specimens for you. In this way you may get specimens of many pests in all stages from egg through instars and pupae to adult. Beneficial insects can be identified and the mounts will provide a good reference for future years. If he associates easily with the men he may get them interested in the "bugs" so that reporting is much more natural and done with some pride in their ability to recognize troubles.

Once again we find that the turf that is the easiest to maintain is the one maintained at the lowest level consistent with its use. On well-irrigated, well-fertilized turf the insects lay more eggs, more hatch, more survive, and they grow faster into adults that again lay more eggs and so on. On lower-maintenance grass, not only are pests fewer but their depredations are harder to see. The longer grass may hide a lot of small problem areas.

On high-maintenance turf our problem may not always be a single insect. A few aphids, a few leafhoppers, a few caterpillars, a few grubs may in the total add up to a problem, but it will take experience and judgment to decide when this is the case.

In meetings of the local turfgrass group it may be well to have as speakers persons from the state department of agriculture and from the university. It will help to know what services these organizations can offer. It will help to acquaint them with your problems and it is always helpful to know the man to whom to turn when trouble strikes.

If and when new pests occur in your area that are immigrants from other lands, remember, control will be difficult and demanding until natural predators are also imported. It will be to your advantage to work with your state or federal unit to help get such predators established.

In controlling insects you generally find several insecticides are available to control each pest. I propose two general rules to assist in making a choice among the alternatives. When the insect is a soil insect it will generally be difficult to get control chemicals down into the soil where the insect is. Hence, you benefit most from long lasting materials that will give control for the longest possible period. At the present this implies chlorinated hydrocarbons such as DDT or arsenicals such as lead arsenate.

When the insects are top feeders, mowing and regrowth of the grass will soon remove the insecticide from the area where the insect feeds. There is then no advantage to a long-lasting material, and as the long-lasting contact insecticides destroy predators and often result in a buildup or in resurgence of the pest, short-lived insecticides with a limited spectrum of kill are generally preferable.

The second general rule is, all else being equal, to choose from among several insecticides that have the lowest mammalian toxicity. It is difficult to keep people off turf they are used to playing on, for even a day.

Often I have not given rates of application. Each material is usually available in several formulations containing different percentages of active ingredients. Consequently the best procedure is to read the label on each material each time it is used, and follow the recommendations given, as they will be based on the amount of active ingredient and the form, i.e., granular, a wettable powder, emulsifiable concentrate, or a soluble salt.

The whole field of chemical control can always change overnight with the introduction of a new chemical. Of particular interest will be systemic insecticides as they are developed. They will be licensed for turf as turf is not used for feed, and ideally they kill only the pests feeding on the grass and allow the predators to build up to active levels.

Insect populations are very dependent on weather. So keep an open mind. A few wet, cold, hot, or dry years may result in damaging populations of an insect you have lived with for years without its ever having been a problem before.

When cost is important, baits are the cheapest form of control for chewing insects above ground. Mixed goods containing both a fertilizer and an insecticide usually cannot be recommended unless you are controlling a specific insect and the insecticide contained is specific for the insect to be controlled.

Contact poisons with a short life may need to be sprayed at high pressures to get good control as only those insects hit will be killed. With chlorinated hydrocarbons, residual action makes high pressures unnecessary as the insect has time to walk into the insecticide. Similarly, low pressures can be used for stomach poisons and for those organic phosphates that have systemic action or produce a toxic vapor.

The following summary of diagnosis is adapted from White:[121]

1. Grass thinned out. Birds feed actively.
Suspect moth caterpillars.
Wet a yard of turf with 1 tablespoonful of pyrethrum extract in a gallon of water. Look for worms wriggling to the surface. Favored by a warm and dry winter and spring.

2. All grasses show large distinct, irregular brown patches. Grass pulls loose easily.
Suspect grubs.
Lay back the sod and work over the soil looking for grubs and pupae. Favored by dry years.

3. Large distinct circular patches on blue, bent, or St. Augustinegrasses are yellowish and worst in the center.
Suspect chinch bug.
Drive metal ring in the soil and keep filled with water for ten minutes. Look for chinch bugs to float to the surface. Favored by hot dry weather.

4. Greens show an irregular patchy decline beginning at the edge and moving in.
Suspect frit fly (or leatherjackets).
Lay a white object down and watch to see if small black flies light on it. Favored by heat and irrigation.

5. Large irregular areas of St. Augustine or bermudagrasses show decline with slow growth and yellowish areas.
Suspect scales.
Pull up runners and pull back sheaths and look for scale insects at the nodes. Favored by hot dry weather.

6. Large irregular areas of bermudagrass have slow growth and contain yellowing or browned pads of witches broom growth.
Suspect bermudagrass mite.
Witches brooms occur with leaves drying and curling inward. Mites under leaf sheaths visible with magnification. Favored by hot dry weather.

7. Zoysia or bermudagrasses affected in small distinct circular areas where grass is yellowish or brown. Grass pulls out easily.
Suspect billbugs.
Look for adult billbugs. Dig up a sod and search the crown area for feeding grubs. Favored by thatch.

8. Centipede and bahiagrass show small distinct yellowed areas.
Suspect wireworms.
Pull up runners and look on bottom for pits and holes where wireworms have been feeding. Search thatch for wireworms. Favored by hot dry weather.

9. Southern grasses show streaks of brown or wilted grass. Grass in streaks pulls out easily.
Suspect mole crickets.
Run fingers through the grass and find burrows. Worst with dry weather and on new plantings.

References

1. Aldrich, J. M., 1920, "European frit fly in North America," *J. Agr. Res.* **18,** 451–474.
2. Alexander, P. M., 1964, "Nematode and Fairy Ring Control on 'Tifgreen' bermuda," *Golf Course Rept.* **32**(5),12ff.
3. Anon., 1926, "Injury to turf from chinch bug and other insects which attack grass leaves," *Bull. U.S.G.A. Green Section* **6**(4), 94–95.
4. Anon., 1967, "European chafer beetle continues to spread," *Turf-grass Times* **2**(4), 1ff.
5. Anon., 1968, "Hot water bath controls nematodes in sod," *Turf-grass Times* **3**(5), 18.
6. Arthur, A. P., 1962, "A skipper, *Thymelicus lineola* (Ochs.) *(Lepidoptera: Hesperiidae)* and its parasites in Ontario," *Can. Entomologist* **94,** 1082–1089.
7. Baker, H., and T. E. Hienton, 1952, "Traps have some value," *Insects, Yearbook of Agriculture,* U.S. Dept. Agriculture, Washington, D.C., pp. 406–411.
8. Beard, J. B., 1966, "Turf Annual," *Park Main.* **19**(7), 17 ff.
9. Bernard, J., 1962, "Rhodesgrass scale, new Florida headache," *Golfdom* **36**(7), 54.
10. Besemer, S. T., 1964, "Mechanical gopher control on golf courses," *Calif. Turfgr. Cult.* **14**(2), 16.
11. Bohart, R. M., 1947, "Sod webworms and other lawn pests in California," *Hilgardia* **17**(8), 296–308.
12. Brogdon, J. E., 1964a, "Pest control on Greens," *Proc. Univ. Florida Turfgr. Management Conf.* **12,** 84–86.
13. Brogdon, J. E., 1964b "Pest control," *Proc. Univ. Florida Turfgr. Management Conf.* **12,** 93–96.
14. Brogdon, J. E., 1965, "Diagnosing lawn problems: insects," *Proc. Univ. Florida Turfgr. Management Conf.* **13,** 98–99.
15. Bucher, G. E., and A. P. Arthur, 1961, "Disease in a field population of the introduced Essex skipper *Thymelicus lineola* (Ochs) *)lepidoptera: Hesperidae),*" *Can. Entomologist* **93,** 1048–1049.
16. Butler, G. D., Jr., 1962, "Control of eriophyid mite on bermudagrass," *Univ. Ariz. Agr. Expt. Sta. Rept.* **203,** 25–29.
17. Butler, G. D., Jr., 1963a, "The distribution and control of the bermudagrass eriophyid mite," *Univ. Ariz. Agr. Expt. Sta. Rept.* **212,** 1–9.

18. Butler, G. D., Jr., 1963b, "Variation in response of bermudagrass strains to bermudagrass eriophyid mite infestations," *Univ. Ariz. Agr. Expt. Sta. Rept.* **212,** 10–11.
19. Butler, G. D., Jr., 1964a, "The biology of the bermudagrass eriophyid mite," *Univ. Ariz. Agr. Expt. Sta. Rept.* **219,** 8–13.
20. Butler, G. D., Jr., 1964b, "Laboratory studies on the systemic action of Diazinon," *Univ. Ariz. Agr. Expt. Sta. Rept.* **219,** 29–33.
21. Butler, G. D., Jr., and A. A. Baltensperger, 1963, "The bermudagrass eriophyid Mite," *Univ. Ariz. Agr. Expt. Sta. Paper* **798.**
22. Bulter, G. D., Jr., and P. D. Johnson, 1965, "Life cycle studies of a rhodesgrass scale parasite," *Univ. Ariz. Agr. Expt. Sta. Rept.* **230,** 21–23.
23. Butler, G. D., Jr., and T. Scanlon, 1965, "Evaluation of materials for the control of the bermudagrass mite," *Univ. Ariz. Agr. Expt. Sta. Rept.* **230,** 11–16.
24. Campbell, R. L., 1968, "Biological studies of *Ionopus rubriceps* (Macquart): *Diptera: Stratiomyidae,*" Ph.D. Thesis, University of California, Berkeley.
25. Clement, R. C., 1968, "Pest control debates in court," *Science* 160, 1287.
26. Couch, H. B., 1962, "Nematodes," *Diseases of Turfgrasses,* Reinhold, New York, Chap. 3, pp. 132–155.
27. Dawson, R. B., 1939, *Practical Lawn Craft,* Crosby Lockwood & Son, London, pp. 185–190.
28. Ebling, W., 1961, "Physicochemical mechanisms for the removal of insect wax by means of finely divided powders," *Hilgardia* **30**(18), 531–586.
29. Emden, H. F. van, 1963, "A technique for the marking and recovery of turf samples in stem borer investigations," *Entomol. Exptl. Appl.* **6,** 194–198.
30. Evans, A. C., 1948, "The importance of earthworms," Farming Feb., in Voisin, A., 1959, *Grass Productivity.* Philosophical Library, New York, pp. 45–46.
31. Fairchild, D., 1947, *The World Grows Round my Door,* Chas. Scribner's Sons, New York, p 67.
32. Fleming, W. E., 1950, "Protection of turf from damage by Japanese beetle grubs," U.S. Dept. Agriculture Leaflet 290, 8 pp.
33. Fox, C. J. S., 1964,"Long-term effects of insecticides on wireworms *(Agriotes* spp.) of grassland in Nova Scotia," *Can, J. Plant Sci.* **44,** 32.
34. Friend, R. B., 1929, "The Asiatic beetle in Connecticut; *Anomala orientalis* as a lawn pest," *Conn. Agr. Expt. Sta. Bull.* **304,** 585–664, 4 pl.
35. Good, J. M., A. E. Steele, and T. J. Ratcliff, 1959, "Plant parasitic nematodes in Georgia turf nurseries," *Plant Disease Reptr.* **43,** 236.
36. Greenfield, I., 1962, *Turf Culture,* Leonard Hill Ltd., London, pp. 239–258.
37. Gundy, S. O. van, L. H. Stolzy, T. E. Szuszkiewicz, and R. L. Rackham, 1962, "Influence of oxygen supply on survival of plant parasitic nematodes in soil," *Phytopathology* **52,** 628–632.
38. Guppy, J. C., 1961, "Life history and behavior of the armyworm, *Pseudo-*

letia unipunctata (Haw.) *(Lepidoptera: Noctuidae)* in eastern Ontario," *Can. Entomologist* **93,** 1141–1153.

39. Hodges, C. F., D. P. Taylor, and M. P. Britton, 1963, "Root knot nematode on creeping bentgrass," *Plant Disease Reptr.* **47,** 1102–1103.
40. Holmes, J. L., 1966, "Status of nematodes in upper midwest," *Turf-grass Times* **1**(2), 11.
41. Holmes, N. H., G. E. Swailes, and G. A. Hobbs. 1961, "The eriophyid mite *Aceria tulipae* (Kiefer) and silver top in grasses," *Can. Entomologist* **93,** 644–667.
42. Horn, G. C., and W. L. Prichett, 1962, "Chinch bug damage and fertilizer," *Florida Turfgr. Bull.* **9**(4), 3, 6–7.
43. Jefferson, R. N., A. S. Deal, and S. A. Sher, 1959, "Turfgrass and Dichondra pests in Southern California," *S. Calif. Turfgr. Cult.* **9**(2), 9–15.
44. Jefferson, R. N., I. M. Hall, and F. S. Morishita, 1964, "Control of lawn moths in Southern California," *J. Econ. Entomol.* **57,** 150–152.
45. Jefferson, R. N., AND F. S. Morishita, 1962, "Progress report on the bermudagrass mite and the frit fly," *Calif. Turfgr. Cult.* **12**(2), 9–10.
46. Jefferson, R. N., F. S. Morishita, A. S. Deal, and W. A. Humphry, 1967, "Look for turf pests now," *Calif. Turfgr. Cult.* **17**(2), 9–11.
47. Jefferson, R. N., and J. E. Swift, 1956, "Control of turfgrass pests," *S. Calif. Turfgr. Cult.* **6**(2), 1–4.
48. Jefferson, P.; 1955, "Studies on the earthworms of turf. A. The earthworms of experimental turf plots," *J. Sports Turf Res. Inst.* **9**(31), 6–27.
49. Jefferson, P., 1958, "Studies on the earthworms of turf. C. Earthworms and casting," *J. Sports Turf Res. Inst.* **9**(34), 437–452.
50. Juska, F. V., 1965, "Another public enemy, Billbug injury in *Zoysia* turf," *Park Maintenance* **18**(5), 38–39.
51. Kelsheimer, E. G., 1956, "The hunting billbug, a serious pest of *Zoysia*," *Proc. Fla. State Hort. Soc.* 69:415-418.
52. Kepner, R. A., and W. E. Howard, 1960, "Gopher-bait applicator," *Calif. Agr.* **14**(3), 7.
53. Kerr, S. H., 1959, "Turf insect problem is growing in south," *Parks and Recr.* **41**(7), 301–303.
54. Kerr, S. H., 1962a, "Outlook on turfgrass insect studies in Florida," *Florida Turfgr. Assoc. Bull.* **9**(2), 2–4.
55. Kerr, S. H., 1962b, "Bermudagrass mite developments," *Florida Turfgr. Assoc. Bull.* **9**(4), 7.
56. Kerr, S. H., 1963, "Recommendations for commercial lawn spraymen," *Univ. Florida Agr. Expt. Sta. Circ.,* S-121 B, 10 pp.
57. Kerr, S. H., 1964, "Insect control by commercial lawn spraymen," *Proc. Univ. Florida Turfgr. Management Conf.* **12,** 112–115.
58. Kerr, S. H., 1965, "Chinch bug control studies," *Proc. Univ. Florida Turfgr. Management Conf.* **13,** 145–146.
59. Kerr, S. H., 1966, "Biology of the lawn chinch bug," *Florida Turfgr. Assoc. Bull.* **13**(4), 8, *Florida Entomologist* **49,** 10–18.
60. Laughlin, R., 1964, "Biology and ecology of the garden chafer *Phylloper-*

tha horticola (L). VIII. Temperature and larval growth," *Bull. Entomol. Res.* **54,** 45–759.

61. Leach, B. R., and J. W. Lipp, 1926, "A method for grub proofing turf," *Bull. U.S.G.A. Greens Sect.* **6**(2), 34–39.
62. Lichtenstein, E. P., and J. B. Polivka, 1959, "Persistence of some chlorinated hydrocarbon insecticides in turf," *J. Econ. Entomol.* **52,** 289–293.
63. Lidgate, H. J., 1966, "Earthworm control with chlordane," *J. Sports Turf Res. Inst.* **42** (Mar), 5–8.
64. Lunt, H. A., and J. G. M. Jacobson, 1944, "The chemical composition of earthworm casts," *Soil Sci.* **58,** 367–375.
65. Mankau, R., 1959, "Natural enemies of nematodes," *Calif. Agr.* **13**(9), 24.
66. Mankau, R., 1961, "Antagonisms to nematode trapping fungi in soil," *Phytopathology* **51,** 66 (abstr.).
67. Mankau, R., 1962, "Soil fungistasis and nematophageous fungi," *Phytopathology* **52,** 611–615.
68. Miller, P. M., and P. E. Waggoner, 1962, "Control of soil born fungi and incidence of *Pratelenchus penetrans*," *Phytopathology* **52**:926 (abstr.).
69. Milne, A., 1964, "Biology and ecology of the garden chafer *Phyllopertha horticola* (L). IX. Spatial distribution," *Bull. Entomol. Res.* **54,** 761–795.
70. Morris, O. N., 1961, "The development of the clover mite, *Bryobia praetiosa, (Acarina, Tetranychedae)* in relation to the nitrogen, phosphorus and potassium nutrition of its plant host," *Ann. Entomol. Soc. Am.* **54,** 551–557.
71. Neiswander, C. R., 1938, "The annual white grub, *Ochrosidia villosa* Burm., in Ohio lawns," *J. Econ. Entomol.* **31,** 340–344.
72. Nielsen, R. L., 1952, "Earthworms and soil fertility," *Proc. New Zealand Grassland Assoc.* **14,** 158–67.
73. Nigh, E. L., Jr., 1964, "Susceptibility of some turfgrasses in Arizona golf greens to the attack of a spiral nematode *Helicotylenchus erythrinae*," *Univ. Ariz. Agr. Expt. Sta. Rept.* **219,** 37–38.
74. Nigh, E. L., Jr., 1966, "The influence of nematodes on winter development of overseeded annual ryegrass *(Lolium multiflorum)*," *Univ. Ariz. Agr. Expt. Sta. Rept.* **240,** 4–6.
75. North, H. F. A., and J. A. Thompson, Jr., 1933, "Investigations regarding bluegrass webworms in turf," *J. Econ. Entomol.* **26,** 1116–1125.
76. Nutter, G. C., 1958b, "Nematodes, unseen enemy of turfgrass," *Parks and Recr.* **41**(9), 379–385.
77. Nutter, G. C., 1967, "Habits and control of chinch bug in turf," *Turf-grass Times* **2**(5), 1ff.
78. Nutter, G. C., and J. R. Christie, 1959, "Nematode investigations on putting green turf," *U.S.G.A. Green Section J. and Turf Management* **11** (7), 24–28.
79. Okamura, G. T., 1959, "Illustrated key to the Lepidopterous larvae attacking lawns in California," *Calif. Dept. Agr. Bull.* **48**(1), 15–21.
80. Otto, N. E., and T. R. Barthley, 1965, "Aquatic pests on irrigation systems," U.S. Dept, Interior Bureau Reclamation, Washington, D.C., 72 pp. (75¢).

81. Pass, B. C., 1966, "Control of sod webworms, *Crambus teterrellus, C. trisectus,* and *C. mutabilis* in Kentucky," *J. Econ. Entomol.* **59,** 19–21.

82. Pass, B. C., R. C. Bunker, and P. R. Burns, II, 1965, "Differential reaction of Kentucky bluegrass strains to sod webworms," *Agron. J.* **57,** 510–511.

83. Pengelly, D. H., 1961, *"Thymelieus lineola* (Ochs) *Lepidoptera Hesperidae)* a pest of hay and pasture grasses in Southern Ontario," *Proc. Entomol. Soc. Ontario* **91,** 189–197.

84. Perry, V. G., 1958. "A disease of Kentucky bluegrass induced by certain spiral nematodes," *Phytopathology* **48,** 397.

85. Perry, V. G., 1966, "Nematodes are a major nemesis to quality turf," *Turf-grass Times* **1**(2), 1ff.

86. Perry, V. G., and Kishwar Mirza Maur, "The pseudo-root-knot nematode of turf grasses."

87. Polivka, J. B., 1959, "The biology and control of turf grubs," *Ohio Agr. Expt. Sta. Res. Bull.* **829,** 30 pp.

88. Pramer, D., 1964, "Nematode trapping fungi," *Science* **144,** 382–385.

89. Protsenko, E. P., 1957, "New case of joint infection of grasses by fungi and nematodes," *Bull. Botan. Garden Moscow* **29,** 91–93; *RAM* **37,** 296, (1958).

90. Questel, D. D., and W. G. Genung, 1961, "Effect of a severe winter on survival of the recently established parasite of the rhodesgrass scale in Florida," *Florida Entomologist* **44,** 115.

91. Riggs, R. D., J. L. Dale, and M. L. Hamblen, 1962, "Reaction of bermudagrass varieties and lines to root-knot nematodes," *Phytopathology* **52,** 587–588.

92. Roberts, E. C., and R. Lavigne, 1959, "Fungus gnat found to inhibit development of turfgrass," *U.S.G.A. Green Sect. J. and Turf Management* **12(6),** 25.

93. Saunder, G. W., 1963, "Soldier fly attacks Atherton Tableland pastures," *Qd. Agr. J.* **89,** 217–219.

94. Schread, J. C., 1950, "Oriental earthworm and its control," *U.S.G.A. Green Sect. J. and Turf Management* **3**(1), 32.

95. Schread, J. C., 1863, "The chinch bug and its control," *Conn. Agr. Expt. Sta. Circ.* **223.**

96. Schread, J. C., 1964, "Weather affects insects," *Golf Course Reptr.* **32**(2), 40.

97. Schread, J. C., 1967, "Newer insects, newer emphasis," *Proc. 38th Intern. Turfgr. Conf. and Show*, pp. 71–73.

98. Schuder, D. L., 1966, "Notes on the biology and control of sod webworms," *Proc. Nidwest Regional Turfgr. Conf.*, pp. 53–54.

99. Sears, P. D., 1935, "Pasture growth and soil fertility," *New Zealand J. Sci. Technol.* **35A,** Suppl. 1.

100. Shedley, D. G., 1963, "Insect pests of lawns," *J. Agr. W. Australian Series 4* **4,** 507–514, 565–571.

101. Sinclair, R. M., 1964, "Clam pests in Tennessee water supplies," *J. Am. Water Works Assoc.* **56**(5), 592–599.

102. Skogley, R., 1965, "Turf annual," *Park Maintenance* **18**(7), 35 ff.

103. Slykhuis, J. T., 1959, "Current status of mite-transmitted plant viruses,"

Proc. Entomol. Soc. Ontario **90,** 22–30.

104. Slykhuis, J. T., 1962, "An international survey for virus diseases of grasses," *F.A.O. Plant Protection Bull.* **10,** 1–16.
105. Southwood, T. R. E., and W. F. Jepson, "The productivity of grasslands in England for *Oscinella frit* (L) *(Chloropidae)* and other stem-boring *Diptera,*" *Bull. Entomol. Res.* **53,** 395–407.
106. Spink, W. T., and J. R. Dogger, 1961, "Chemical control of the ground pearl, *Eumargarodes laingi,*" *J. Econ. Entomol.* **54,** 423–424.
107. Spink, W. T., and J. R. Dogger, 1962a, "Silver top of bluegrass," *J. Econ. Entomol.* **55,** 865–867.
108. Starks, K. J., and R. Thurston, 1962b, "Control of plant bugs on Kentucky bluegrass *(Poa pratensis)* grown for seed," *J. Econ. Entomol.* **55,** 993–997.
109. Streu, H. T., and L. M. Vasvary, 1967a, "Control of the hairy chinch bug, *Blissus hirtus,* Mont. in New Jersey," *N.J. Agr. Expt. Sta. Bull.* **816,** 78–82.
110. Streu, H. T., and L. M. Vasvary, 1967b, "Sod webworm control trials," *N.J. Agr. Expt. Sta. Bull.* **816,** 83–84.
111. Tarjan, A. C., 1955, "Occurrence of yellow tuft of bentgrass in Rhode Island," *Plant Disease Reptr.* **39,** 185.
112. Tarjan, A.C., and M. H. Ferguson, 1951, "Observations of nematodes in yellow tuft of bentgrass," *U.S.G.A. Green Sect. J. and Turf Management* **4**(2), 28–30.
113. Taylor, D. P., M. P. Britton, and H. C. Heehler, 1963, Occurrence of plant parasitic nematodes on Illinois golf greens, *Plant Disease Reptr.* **47,** 132–135.
114. Thompson, H. E., 1967, "Buffalograss sod webworm," *Turf-grass Times* **2,**(5), 7.
115. Thompson, H. E., 1963, "Mites associated with bermudagrass in Arizona," *Univ. Ariz. Agr. Expt. Sta. Rept.* **219,** 26–28.
116. Tuttle, D. M., and G. D. Butler, Jr., 1961, "A new eriophyid mite infesting bermudagrass," *J. Econ. Entomol.* **54,** 836–838.
117. U.S.D.A. (Dept. Agriculture), 1952, *Insects, The Yearbook of Agriculture,* USGPO, Washington, D.C., 780 pp, 72 pl.
118. Vance, A. M., and B. A. App, 1964, "Lawn insects, how to control them," *U.S. Dept. Agr. Home and Garden Bull.* 53, Washington D.C., 24pp.
119. Walton, W. R., 1921, "The southern green june beetle as a pest on golf links," *Bull. U.S.G.A. Green Sect.* **1,** 60–62.
120. Walton, W. R., 1921, "The changa or West Indian mole cricket as a pest on golf courses," *Bull. U.S.G.A. Green Sect.* **1,** 104–106.
121. White, R. W., Jr., 1965, "Relating the problem to the grass," *Proc. Univ. Florida Turfgr. Conf.* **13,** 84–88.
122. Wildinson, A. T., 1968, "Leatherjackets, new pest for golf greens," *U.S.G.A. Green Sect. Rec.* **6,**(1), 20–21.
123. Wilson, M. C., and G. E. Lehker, 1964, "Cereal leaf beetle," *Proc. Midwest Regional Turfgr. Conf.,* Suppl. 1–4.
124. Committee on Nomenclature, 1965, "Common names of insects," *Entomol. Soc. Am. Bull.* **11,** 304.

8

TURFGRASS DISEASES

We may recognize we have a turf disease by deviations from that which we recognize as normal growth. Among the deviations may be the following: change of color, the presence of lesions or spots, wilting, necrosis or death of parts of the plant, the destruction or loss of organs such as leaves or roots, or the rotting of tissue. The disease may be *systemic,* occurring throughout the plant, or *localized*, as in the various leaf spots where the infection is limited to an area which may be as small as 1/16 of an inch in diameter.

Couch[36] defines disease as an "aberrant form of metabolism, incited by agents of the biological and/or physical environment, and manifested by the altered physiological activity of one or more cells." Gould has simplified this to "disease is an abnormal condition."[91]

Heald[108] uses a different approach. Defining a healthy plant he then notes deviations as unhealthy. He states that for good vigorous plant growth we need the following: *(1)* the proper plant; *(2)* the proper environment; *(3)* freedom from mechanical injuries; and *(4)* freedom from infectious disease (parasitic plants, animals, or viruses).

Heald's definition gives us four convenient categories under which to discuss disease.

THE PROPER PLANT

The wrong plant may rapidly disappear from the turf, as occurs when red fescue is mowed at putting green height in the U.S., or may simply lack vigorous, thrifty growth, as when bluegrass or bermudagrass is shaded. The problem has been discussed but brief examples of the wrong plant include (a) use of Kentucky bluegrass in the bermudagrass zone where it is subject to long periods of temperature above 90°F. (b) use of highland bentgrass under conditions of high salinity; (c) use of 'Merion' in regions favorable to rust.

THE PROPER ENVIRONMENT

Among environmental factors leading to disease are: (a) nutritional deficiencies, (b) nutritional excesses or toxicities, (c) poor drainage, (d) dry spots, (e) shade, (f) poor circulation, (g) salinity, (h) chemical damage, (i) burning or scorching, (j) freezing, and (k) pH.

(a) Nutritional Deficiencies

Diagnosis is usually poor color of the grass, confirmed by clipping analysis or by test applications of nutrients to an experimental area. The problem is corrected by applying minerals to restore a good balance of nutrients in the plant.

(b) Nutritional Excess or Toxicity

Symptoms of excess are often discolorations similar to deficiencies except that with an excess, tip burning of the leaves is common along with early death of mature leaves. The problem is often helped by leaching the soil, by changing the water source, by removing clippings, or by liming acid soils. An example is toxicity resulting from copper-containing sprays (Bordeaux).[152]

(c) Poor Drainage

Symptoms include a yellowing of the grass, appearance of indicator weeds such as dallasgrass, sedges, and *Poa annua,* and the presence of surface water or wet spots. Among causes are low spots, faulty irrigation, and shallow soils (see *Principles of Turfgrass Culture,* Chap. 10). Hole punching, improved irrigation, and underground drainage may all help.

(d) Dry Spots

Symptoms consist of areas or varying size where grass wilts to a slaty gray-green. If water is not soon applied, the grasses dry and turn brown.

Many conditions may cause dry spots: an underground rock; a pan or subsoil coming near the surface; a fungus infection; or a high spot from which water runs off before it can penetrate. Hydrophobic areas of soil or thatch or heavily compacted areas may limit water penetration.[135]

If the condition results from poor infiltration, reduced application rates may correct it. Otherwise problem spots are likely to need individual attention. Use of a wetting agent may help initial penetration of a thatch.[135] Probing may reveal subsurface obstructions. In some instances it may be advisable to lift the sod, dig out, and replace the soil beneath the dry spot.

(e) Shade

Symptoms of shade are a yellowing of the grass followed by browning and decay. Sudden removal of the shade on a hot bright day may also result in browning. A continuous light shade may result in a thin deep green turf of soft growth that is difficult to mow.

Causes include temporary erection of bleachers, tents, or canopies; stacking of lumber; or the presence of dense tree growth. The treatment consists of removing the offending objects as soon as possible. Bleachers should be up as short a time as possible. Advance planning of construction will permit locating piles of lumber, sand, brick, etc., to destroy a minimum of turf. When shade is from a tree and both the tree and the turf contribute to the landscape, study may show a limb or two that can be removed without affecting the tree's appearance. Removal of lower limbs often lets in enough light to visibly benefit the grass. If the tree is the major landscape feature and grass is used only for soil cover, fair results are obtained by sowing red or sheep fescue in the shaded area and letting it grow wild with only two or three mowings a year.

(f) Poor Air Circulation

Even a short period of inadequate oxygen in the root zone has resulted in decreased photosynthesis, reduced carbohydrate content of leaves, and increased susceptibility to smog damage.[134,195] Letey found diseased areas of a green to have a lower oxygen diffusion rate than nearby healthy areas.[134] Poor surface air circulation results in grass remaining wet longer after an irrigation or after morning dew. This may cause a softer, more succulent growth but the principal evidence that it constitutes an unhealthy condition lies in the greatly increased susceptibility to fungus disease of the grass when there is poor air circulation.

A symptom is grass that remains wet late in the morning as compared to open grass.

To remedy, remove hedges, clear out underbrush, and cut lower limbs from trees so ground air circulates. When lack of air movement results from a low pocket in the terrain the problem may be difficult to solve. A pocket of several acres including golf or bowling greens, would justify installing an orchard wind machine.

(g) Salinity

Salinity was discussed in detail in *Principles of Turfgrass Culture,* Chap. 10. Symptoms are a tendency to wilt, tip burning of leaves, poor growth, and a high conductivity of the soil solution. The cause is a buildup of soluble salts in the soil which impairs water use by the plant.

To correct salinity one may heed the adage that if grass wilts it needs water. Water of sufficient quality must be applied in sufficient quantity to leach salts out of the root zone. One should obviously avoid adding additional salts (fertilizer, e.g.) to the soil.

(h) Chemical Damage

Symptoms vary greatly. Turf can be killed completely, can appear discolored, or seem only unthrifty (Fig. 8.1). Killed spots are often easily identified. Spots where fertilizer was spilled are green and overgrown around the edge. Stopping the fertilizer spreader without shutting it off, leaking gasoline across the grass, overlapping the spray pattern, etc., will create recognizable patterns of injury. On the other hand, when grass is slightly discolored and unthrifty, symptoms resemble those of mineral toxicity, low pH, or a dull mower. (See also Fig. 8.2.)

Chemical damage can be caused by spillage, by soluble fertilizer not washed in, by leaking equipment, by spray drift, or by poisoning from nearby industrial operations such as smelting. Free ammonia from diammonium phosphate can be toxic to germinating seeds.[5] Damage can result from not reading the fine print, e.g., applying PMA to 'Merion' bluegrass or using 2,4,5-T at temperatures that are too high. Included in chemical damage are urine burns and smog injury.

Smog injury results from products of combustion which may vary from place to place. A major portion of smog damage however, is as-

(a)

(b)

Figure 8.1 Chemical burns. In **(a)** PMA was used at high levels on a hot day and grass was burned severely where overlapping resulted in double application. In **(b)** a malfunctioning fertilizer spreader dumped fertilizer.

Figure 8.2 A fertilizer spreader skip has resulted in an orange rust-infested strip of bluegrass.

sociated with gasoline and the automobile, and now occurs in every sizable city in the world. The two most damaging products from gasoline are hydrocarbon peroxides and nitrogen oxides. Industrial operations contribute sulfur oxides and fluorides.[115] *Poa annua* is sensitive to smog damage, and can be used as an indicator plant for smog disease.[148] Bermudagrass also shows symptoms in the Los Angeles area. Damage appears as a bleaching between the veins. Newly matured leaf areas are most damaged and in grasses this appears as a bleached band across the leaf. The visible injury is from the collapse of mesophyll cells, mostly those surrounding the smaller veins.[111] Smog is no doubt damaging at levels too low to cause visible symptoms, and may be a predisposing factor for pathogenic diseases. Antipov[10] reports that grass near smog sources required more careful maintenance. He evaluated seventeen grass varieties for resistance and found that turf species were more susceptible to damage than weedy grasses.

Grass usually outgrows mild damage from chemicals. After severe injury replanting may be necessary. It may be necessary to leach spilled chemicals or even replace the soil before replanting. Smog damage becomes worse from year to year and legislated controls only slow the increase.

(i) Burning

Usual symptoms of burning is grass that is scorched brown on top but green underneath. The damage occurs in geometrical patterns related to the object causing the damage. Burn results when an object is laid on the grass in the full sun and heats up enough to injure the grass. A hose, a metal grass catcher, an empty metal pail, a doormat or other miscellaneous objects may be laid on the grass temporarily but long enough to cause burn. The treatment is to mow off the burned grass and encourage growth of the grass below.

(j) Cold Injury

Winterkill results in part from winter desiccation and is most common on high exposed areas subject to wind. Snow fencing and brush covers have been used successfully to promote snow cover; mulches of straw, etc., have decreased drying but increased disease;[45] aerifier holes to increase infiltration have increased drying in dry years; irrigation helps but systems are shut down for the winter. Use of plastic mulches has been noted in Chap. 5 and in *Principles of Turfgrass Culture,* Chap. 4. Plastic has been more beneficial following a fungicide spray.[29] Clear plastic has increased the 1/2-in. soil temperature 10° and the 3-in. soil temperature 5° with the increase persisting after removal of the plastic.[149] After appreciable work with plastic, Watson[208] concludes that it requires too much attention, and grass survival may be critical. With screen replacing sheet plastic or mulch, ten materials all gave better spring turf than the control. (Chap. 5).

Winterkill from other causes has been investigated by Beard,[19,20] Lebeau,[129-133] and Freyman and Brink.[79-81] Beard has worked on freezing injury for several years and categorizes our knowledge as follows:[20]

1. Direct low-temperature injury to hardened plant tissues. Injury depends on rate of freezing, rate of thawing, number of times frozen, the time frozen, tissue hydration, and experience after thawing. Grasses tested show decreasing resistance to direct injury from bentgrass through *Poa trivialis, Poa pratensis* ('Merion' being the most, 'Newport' the least hardy of those tested), *Poa annua,* creeping red fescue, tall fescue, perennial rye, *Zoysia,* and bermudagrass. The value of a snow cover in reducing direct injury is suggested by a comparison of temperatures during two winters. With never less than 6 in. of snow, soil was 17°F at 2 in., 26°F at 8 in. The following year snow was less than 2 in. and the 2 in. and 8 in. soil temperatures were -12°F and 4°F. Air temperatures were similar both years.[65]

2. Direct cold injury at reduced hardiness. After a December peak, hardiness decreases rapidly during February, and is low during March and April. At this time certain combinations of freezing and thawing are damaging when crown temperatures fall to 25°F or less. Most injured is *Poa annua,* followed by red fescue, tall fescue, and perennial ryegrass. Conditions leading to this type of injury are common along the Great Lakes from Chicago and into New England.

3. Desiccation has been treated above.

4. Toxic accumulation under ice. Ice is impermeable to some gases and Freyman and Brink have found CO_2 going to 19% under ice in the laboratory[80] and to over 8% in the field.[81] Turf under ice was flushed with nitrogen and survived without injury in the absence of oxygen, but when flushed with carbon dioxide the grass died in 21 days in the presence of CO_2. Lebeau found hydrogen cyanide gas accumulating in crowns under subfreezing conditions.[128] Survival was reduced with increasing concentrations of HCN. The HCN was the product of an unidentified snow-mold fungus.

5. Oxygen starvation under an ice sheet has been proposed as a possible cause of injury but no evidence exists to support the idea.

6. Leaching of tissues has also been suggested as a source of injury. In trials Beard was able to get some injury to bluegrass, but there was no significant amount of kill.

8. Heaving. Temperature gradients through a mature turf do not lead to serious heaving but heaving kills seedlings. Conditions for heaving occur in late fall when soil is wet and nights are clear and cool, leading to the formation of needle-ice. Heavier seeding rates or a mulch will limit heaving.[79]

9. Fungi. There are several psychrophylic (cold loving) fungi which attack turf in the winter. Temperature effects for fungal damage may be critical. Lebeau heated the soil to several temperatures. At 6°F or 3°F, turf was severely damaged by Fusarium patch. At 0°F turf came through the winter vigorous green and healthy. At -3°F it was attacked by an unidentified basidiomycete.[127]

Degree of injury from cold is influenced by a number of factors. Hydration of tissue is one of these. Tissue killed at 0°F when it contained 60% water was killed at 25°F when it contained 78% water.[19]

Winter injury is influenced by nutrition. In a study using bermudagrass there was little winter injury when nitrogen fertility was low. With nitrogen high, injury decreased as potassium levels increased.[2] At a given potassium level, injury increases as nitrogen levels increased. Nitrogen data from Carrol and Welton's study is given in Table 8.1.

Table 8.1. Turfgrass Survival as Affected by Temperature and Nitrogen Fertility

Temperatures	*23°F*		*14°F*		*5°F*		*4°F*	
Nitrogen Levels	*low*	*high*	*low*	*high*	*low*	*high*	*low*	*high*
Kentucky blue	100	90	80	60	25	5	20	5
Poa annua	80	50	40	10	3	1	5	0
Astoria bent	90	80	60	50	0	0	0	0
Red fescue	80	65	60	25	0	0	0	0
Perennial rye	70	20	0	0	0	0	0	0

Radko et al.[167] have called attention to other factors noted after a severe winter in the northeast U.S. in 1962–63. Much grass was lost, and the resulting bare spots distinguished areas of high traffic, of poor drainage, of close mowing, and of *Poa annua* invasion.

Thatch contributes to winterkill by insulating grass from the soil and by increasing desiccation.

Use of soil heating is discussed in *Principles of Turfgrass Culture,* Chap. 4.

To summarize, turf is killed in the winter by fungi, desiccation, and by direct cold injury. Management affects survival. The U.S. Department of Agriculture has developed a speedy test for cold hardiness.[201] Treatment consists of replanting areas that have been killed. Sometimes drainage can prevent the ponding that results in ice sheets.

Cold resistance can be bred into grasses (see *Principles of Turfgrass Culture,* Chap. 2).

(k) pH

High pH may result in symptoms of lime-induced chlorosis. Lime-induced iron deficiency appears readily in centipedegrass. Low pH results in symptoms which are also characteristic of mineral imbalance. The grass lacks the bright green color of good vigorously growing turf. It is fairly unresponsive to fertilizer and yields poorly. There may be a high proportion of brown leaves.

The immediate cause is the excessively high or low pH, but the resultant cause is probably unbalanced mineral nutrition. Aluminum and manganese often reach toxic levels at low pH. Ammonium sulfate would not be used as the exclusive fertilizer today, but it has been done. I have seen greens with a pH of 3.8, a foot of thatch, and a choking smell of sulfur when a cup was cut. This came from fifteen to twenty years of "sulfating."

Low pH is corrected by adding lime. However, conditions which produced a low pH have probably also resulted in a general nutrient imbalance so it may be necessary to add potassium, magnesium, or phosphorus in addition to lime. Smith[188] suggests that less disease may result if the pH is brought up by addition of a small amount of fine hydrated lime to cause an immediate small increase in pH and that this be followed by coarsely ground limestone so that the remaining change take place gradually rather than suddenly.

High pH is associated with alkaline irrigation waters and other problems of salinity and alkalinity (see *Principles of Turfgrass Culture,* Chap. 10). Of pathogenic diseases, *Ophiobolus* patch is favored by liming.

MECHANICAL INJURY

Mowing is itself a form of mechanical injury to the grass but as we do not have a turf without mowing, we have considered it separately. Under the heading of mechanical injury I shall discuss injury from: (a) dull mowers, (b) abrasion, (c) bruising, (d) scalping, (e) tearing, and (f) by stretching a point, lightning.

(a) Dull Mower

The symptoms of a dull mower are a reduction in yield and a color on the brownish side of green. The turf may fail to respond to fertilization. Ends of cut blades appear partly torn or shredded rather than cut, and the amount of dead tissue behind the cut is excessive, a quarter of an inch or more (see Benson, Chap. 4).

The cause is a dull or poorly adjusted mower which, instead of cleanly shearing the grass blade, squeezes, tears, or pulls the end off.

The remedy is to sharpen and correctly adjust the mower. Reduce the frequency of mowing until growth again produces a normal yield.

(b) Abrasion

Symptoms of abrasion are a dull, slaty, gray-green appearance as in wilt, followed by drying of the grass. The grass keeps a silvery gray color for a few days until the sun bleaches it to straw.

Abrasion is caused by a scuffing type of wear on the grass. The abrasion cuts through the protective cuticle and epidermis and exposes the internal leaf tissue to sudden drying. Abrasion is aggravated by sand (a turf by a beach, for example). The scuffing of the backyard pitcher before the wind up, or the gyrations accompanying a dance festival can cause this kind of damage.

As leaves are dead, regrowth from the crowns should be encouraged. If activity has worn the turf completely away, re-growth occurs from underground rhizome buds. If the grass is not a rhizome producer it may be necessary to replant.

(c) Bruising

Bruising (including frost damage) differs from abrasion in that the internal tissues rather than the epidermis are injured and there is not the immediate water loss. Tissues darken and turn brown. Bruising usually occurs in recognizable patterns. Round or elliptical ball marks, machinery tracks, and foot prints or heel prints are examples of familiar patterns.

Rupture of the internal cells occurs most easily when the grass is frosted. Simple pressures such as result from walking across the grass cause ice crystals to pierce cell walls.

Traffic should be prohibited on frosty grass until the frost has melted. If injury occurs, regrowth should be encouraged. Sprinkling may be used to remove frost when temperatures are above freezing.

(d) Scalping

Two slightly different forms of scalping occur. As false crowns of highland bentgrass are loosely attached, the mower can cut off or play can tear out pieces of the false crown to expose areas of brown thatch. With other grasses scalping is just short mowing which exposes yellow crowns or brown trash. Scalping is recognized by the color and often by the unevenness of the mowing. With low cuts slight variations in mowing height result in changes in color of the exposed crowns and the mower wheel traveling on the cut turf may be sufficiently lower than the other wheel to cause a yellow line on one side. Scallops and gouges appear whenever a mower wheel drops into a depression in the soil.

Reducing the height of cut to 3/4–1 in. will stop false crowing of highland. Scalped spots often result from mowing over uneven ground, or from a misadjusted mower. The most troublesome scalping results when a "mower jockey" spins his mower on the turn without slowing or raising it, or stopping the reel. One will too often see a green with the edge brown and bare from fast, scalping turns. Often diseases and insects first appear troublesome in the turning area.

(e) Tearing

The symptom of tearing (including divots) is an area of dry and dead turf caused by tearing grass loose from the soil. Sporting activities, especially those that use cleated shoes, are a main cause. With football played on wet soft soil it is not uncommon to strip one or two square feet of turf loose by evasive action or a tackle. The golf divot is familiar to all. Turning on the ball of the foot while wearing cleats will cut or tear grass loose as will spinning golf cart wheels.

Sods quickly replaced and watered may recover; otherwise replanting may be necessary. Deep-rooted and rhizomatous grasses of hardened growth withstand tearing better than soft, shallow-rooted or stoloniferous ones.

(f) Lightning

Montieth and Dahl[153] note lightning damage and describe it as a central burned area with forked projections extending outward. As it may take a day or two for the outer edges to turn brown, lightning damage may appear as a rapidly spreading disease. The center will require replanting.

Recovery from damage is by regrowth of the grass. Grass usually has an impaired ability to grow after damage. With limited carbohydrate, use cannot be made of fertilizer and root growth is reduced. Thus the first treatment is not to fertilize, but to be certain the injured area is adequately watered. After a couple days of regrowth and following a day of sunshine, a *light* application of fertilizer can be given. The data suggest a complete fertilizer.[22] Spreading growth will be encouraged, however, by applications of nitrogen.[116]

INFECTIOUS DISEASES

Infectious diseases are caused by biological factors in the environment, such as nematodes, bacteria, viruses, green plants (e.g., mistletoe), and nongreen plants (e.g., the fungi). Diseases caused by animals are treated in Chap. 7.Several plant diseases are bacterial, but fortunately we recognize no bacterial diseases on turfgrass.

Diseases Caused by Virus

This topic may be summed by quoting Couch.[36] "Viruses cause many plant diseases of economic importance. Such diseases are known for various turfgrass species, but information concerning them is not as yet sufficient to evaluate properly their importance." For example, bermudagrass is an alternate host for virus diseases of sugar cane,[76] rice,[214] and grapes.[196] Many of the turfgrasses are symptomless carriers of cereal yellow dwarf virus.[162] Kentucky bluegrass is diseased by bromegrass mosaic virus[181] and *Poa annua* and meadow fescue by ryegrass mosaic virus. Sugar cane virus has produced symptoms on 'Roselawn' St. Augustinegrass.[76]

Diseases Caused by Green Plants

Algae. Algae may grow on the soil surface so densely they form a mat which reduces soil aeration. The algae most commonly involved are the filamentous blue-green algae, which, despite their name, most often are seen as a black scum on the soil. Symptoms may include weak, poorly colored growth, and a yellowing of the grass from iron deficiency probably due to competition for the iron, or to production of root toxins. The iron deficiency occurs in algae-contaminated solution cultures as well as in the field.

Heavy algal growth results from excessive moisture, though at times use of organic fertilizers appears to promote their growth.

Control of blue-green algae is simple. Spraying with a 1:50 or 1:100 solution of household bleach and water, or with a half strength mercuric fungicide, or with 5 ppm copper sulfate solution, will control algae. The wet condition must be corrected, to prevent immdediate reinfestation. Aerifying may assist recovery by increasing water penetration and drying of the surface soil. Underbrush should be removed to improve air circulation and tree growth opened up to provide more light to the turf.

Moss. A heavy growth of moss may replace or smother the grass. The cause is conditions favoring growth of moss rather than grass.

Moss is usually indicative of poor nutrition, wetness, and shade. It is said to indicate an acid soil though this is not a necessary cause, and moss may also be found on neutral or alkaline soils.

Control involves pruning low branches to improve the light and ventilation, a modification of the irrigation program to reduce excess moisture, and a surface application of single superphosphate at about 3–5 lb of material per 1000 ft^2 to kill the moss. Old growths of some kinds of moss may be inches deep and all the duff may have to be raked out before grass will grow. As conditions improve, a complete fertilizer should be used to stimulate the turf.

Angiosperms. Higher plants parasitic on grass are not a problem. Mistletoe may be a problem in the associated landscape, and the orange threads of dodder (*Cuscata* sp.) may sometimes be found parasitizing clovers associated with grass.

Diseases Caused by Fungi

The remainder of this chapter is about fungal diseases. When the turf manager speaks of diseases, usually he means an infectious disease caused by a fungus. A few such diseases outweigh in importance all other diseases combined. The picture of such a disease in the minds of many persons is of a fungal spore alighting on a grass plant, germinating, growing outward, and feeding on the grass and destroying it. Most fungi are decay organisms growing only on dead matter, and performing a beneficial service. Disease-causing fungi are relatively few in number, but of such importance they receive all of our attention.

Growing fungi start when a *spore* or a *sclerotium* germinates. Spores are single cells, sclerotia are minute masses of dormant tissue, and both carry the organism through unfavorable seasons and reproduce it. The germinating spore or sclerotium produces a microscopic thread or *hypha.* A noninfective network of many hyphae is named a *mycelium.* Mycelium may often be seen as a cottony or cobwebby growth in the grass. Hyphae penetrate and digest dead clippings and plant debris. During infective stages they enter a stoma, wound, cut leaf blade, or penetrate cells directly. Inside the plant, hyphae enter cells and use the contents as food for their growth.

Decay fungi living on dead debris, and breaking down and recycling soil organic matter are called *saprophytes.* Some disease-causing fungi live only on live tissue, and must usually live on tissue of a limited kind, or from a limited species of plant. Such fungi are named *obligate parasites.* Rusts, smuts, and mildews are ready examples of obligate parasites. They can only live and grow in a living plant.

Many turf diseases belong to a third class of fungi, *facultative parasites.* These can be saprophytes or parasites, depending on conditions This is worth noting because in general, facultative parasites seldom cause serious diseases, but on turf they are responsible for most of the most damaging diseases.

Characterization of Fungal Diseases. Pathogenic fungal diseases have been characterized by meeting the criteria of Koch's postulates. The fungus must be isolated from diseased tissue, transferred to a healthy plant, made to incite the disease in that plant, and then the fungus must be recovered from the now diseased plant.

Most turf diseases meet the above criteria, but in recent years we have had large areas of turf killed by fungi under conditions where these criteria are not met. Technically the grass in these instances was not killed by a pathogenic fungus. Winter deadspot of bermudagrass is an example of such a disease. To characterize such diseases we need to consider conditions under which disease occurs.

Management Disease. Conditions which predispose a fungus disease are many and are discussed in later sections. What I wish to consider here is why we experience much turf damage from organisms that don't affect grass in the laboratory, i.e., that don't follow Koch's postulates, and why facultative parasites are so damaging to turf. To explain these I am proposing that we have, in fact, a *management disease.*

Competition among organisms is so keen that a change in elevation of a few millimeters may change the complex of fungi.[209] Among weapons in the struggle for existence are chemicals we may name toxins, or antibiotics. Excreted into the environment they inhibit other organisms, and protect the place of the organism excreting them.

Soil contains many such antibiotic residues. When plants are grown in sterile culture free from antibiotic compounds, roots are white, plump, turgid, and respire at a low rate.[164,168] In soil, similar roots are brown, often flaccid, and respiration is at a much higher rate.

A weakly parasitic fungus growing as a saprophyte in dead leaf cells often excretes toxins that kill adjacent cells which are then penetrated. The living cells in turn may produce toxins that restrain the fungus. We may ask, when is a cell dead, and in terms of the above we may say it is dead to the fungus when there is no resisting antibiotic. If environmental changes affect the plant so it is no longer making sufficient antibiotics, the former saprophyte may invade and destroy the plant. In our eyes the fungus has become a parasite. In the larger scheme of things, the fungus may have removed a poorly adapted plant in a natural fashion, i.e., cleared a space where a better adapted plant can compete.

A cause of changed plant chemistry may be our management program. Grass failure may be failure to funtion fully under the management we impose. Immature tissue differs from mature tissue. Frequent close mowing produces grass that is largely immature. High-nitrogen grass has a different composition from low-nitrogen grass, of both organic and inorganic materials. Regular irrigation increases grass hydration and chemicals are more dilute. Add to these changes introduced by high respiration due to stress, and changes produced by hormone-type weed sprays, and the composition of our grass plant is much modified. As part of its abnormal metabolism the grass may fail to maintain its chemical defenses. Weakly parasitic organisms may destroy grass in this state, yet not affect it in the laboratory. With grass lost and fungus present in the tissues we will name the condition a fungus disease, but perhaps the disease is the total state or condition and should be called *management disease.**

Curvularia is an example of a fungus often found infecting turf (usually in combination with other fungi) but which does not infect it in laboratory tests. Spring dead spot of bermudagrass contains a complex of fungi which are not pathogenic in the laboratory, and there is every evidence that it is in fact a management disease that cannot be brought under Koch's postulates. It is caused by high nitrogen, short mowing, traffic, wet spots in the fall, and favored by a period of dormancy followed by a warming trend, then a cold snap.[150,198] Some turf pathologists are of the opinion that we may expect to see management diseases increasing.

With management disease, the fungus is not important. When management practices have sufficiently reduced the vigor of the turf any weakly parasitic fungus that happen to be present will serve to restore the declining grass to a state of humus.

Disease Inoculum. When a suitable fungus is present, and when climate or management predispose the turf to disease, then disease begins. Most turf diseases produce local infections. Only a small area of tissue is damaged by each infection and a few hundred such injured spots per square meter do not noticeably weaken the turf. With thousands to many tens of thousands of plants per square meter, and multiple infections usually required for each plant, a heavy inoculation of spores or many hyphal penetrations are needed for a severe disease infection. Usually, conditions must sustain infection long enough to permit production of several generations. Most (sometimes all) spores are produced asexually, being pinched off at the end of a hyphae. (Sexual spores are often resting spores which carry the fungus through the season of stress.)

If a multiple infection is needed for disease, fungi are capable of producing the spores in necessary quantity. The 1953 U.S. Department of Agriculture Yearbook states that a severe rust infection in South Dakota could produce 2 x 10^{18} spores.[200] If one out of every 10,000 blew north into North Dakota there would be four spores for every wheat plant in North Dakota.

Stakeman has estimated that during peak of spore discharge, a single fruiting body of a fungus discharged 100 million spores an hour.[193]

Closer to the subject of turf, Gould states, "We have found about 50,000 spores in a one-fourth inch piece of *Fusarium* infested grass leaf."[91]

*Other hypotheses could be offered leading to the same conclusion; That given is only exemplary.

Spores are readily distributed. Splashing drops of water effectively spread spores out from a center of infection to adjacent areas; insects carry spores on their bodies; wind disperses them; and human traffic carries spores all over an area and from one area to another. There is twenty times the chance of getting disease from inoculum produced on our own property as from inoculum entering from nearby turf.[205] Spores are spread by turf maintenance operations. Hence work should proceed from the healthy area to the diseased area. The equipment is then cleaned.

Recognition of Fungal Diseases. When a disease breaks out it must be recognized or identified if effective controls are to be used. Positive identification of a disease may require the use of a microscope and other laboratory facilities, and may require a week or two to accomplish. Control of a disease cannot wait, but must begin at once. Initial sprays are often of mixtures of fungicide designed to control several possible diseases. After some experience, the turf manager can usually recognize the regional diseases with which he must cope and can use fungicides specific for the diseases. Recognition is assisted by experience which leads to knowledge of the time of year a disease occurs, the kinds of grass attacked, shape, size, and color of afected areas, and so on. Before he acquires the needed experience, the manager needs to be backed up by some authority to identify each disease. Then he can use his experience to learn to recognize its characteristics.

The best backing is of the state university, or state department of agriculture, or a commercial laboratory that can provide positive identification of the disease. After a few experiences the turf manager will get to know the regional diseases. He will not need further support from a laboratory except when he finds a new or unfamiliar disease.

Without the backing of a laboratory, the manager may have to rely on pictures or descriptive keys which are published in trade magazines or distributed by fungicide dealers. These do not give the feeling of certainty that comes from a laboratory report. Using pictures it may take longer to develop confidence in recognizing a disease. Aids to disease diagnosis are given in Figure 8.3 and Table 8.2.

One may often get valuable information from fellow turf workers, but such information should be questioned until it has been verified.

Control Programs. Disease outbreaks are controlled by spraying with a suitable fungicide. In addition management practices are modified to favor the grass at the expense of the disease organism. Mowing may be less frequent, and irrigation and fertility may be manipulated to provide

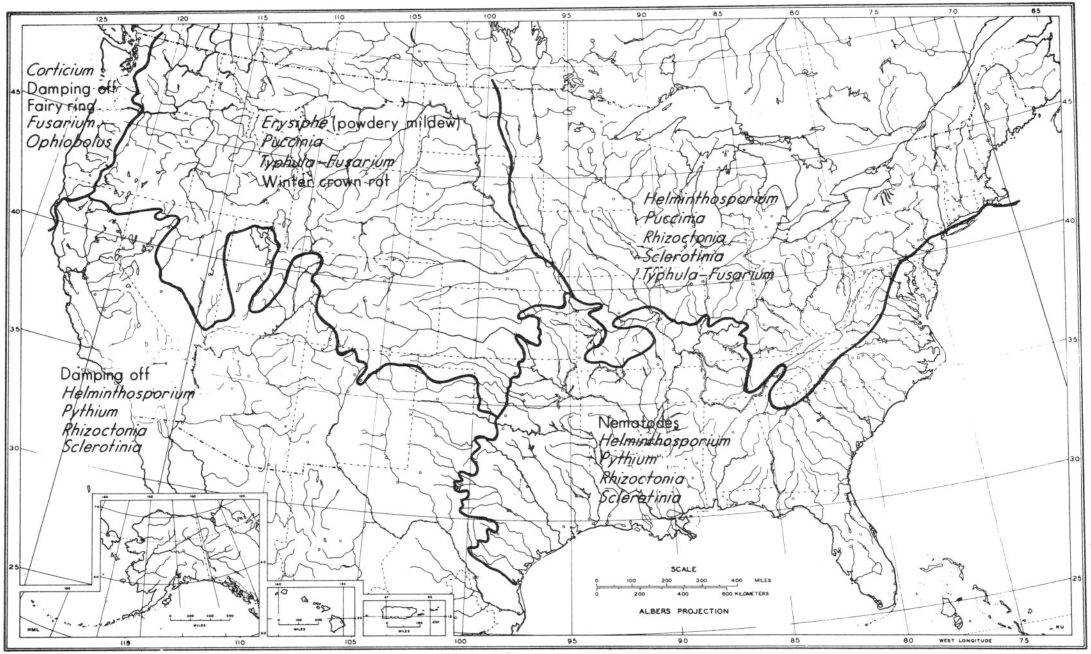

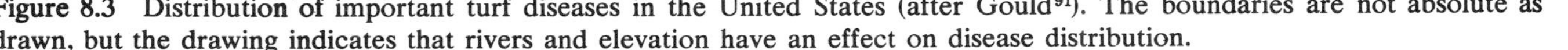

Figure 8.3 Distribution of important turf diseases in the United States (after Gould[91]). The boundaries are not absolute as drawn, but the drawing indicates that rivers and elevation have an effect on disease distribution.

Table 8.2. Some Common Turfgrass Diseases and Conditions Favoring Disease and Grasses Attacked

Disease	*Season*	*Grass Severely Attacked*	*Moderate Susceptibility*
Rhizoctonia; large brown patch	Summer; 75-85 °F; warming trend	Bentgrasses; bluegrasses; St. Augustinegrass; annual ryegrass	Centipedegrass; Bermudagrass; Bahiagrass; fescuegrasses
Helminthosporium; H. leaf spot; *H.* blight melting out	Summer; 80-95 °F; moist; overcast	Bluegrasses; fescuegrasses; bermudagrasses	Ryegrasses; St. Augustinegrass; bentgrasses
Sclerotinia homeocarpa; dollar spot	70-80 °F; low fertility	Bentgrasses; bermudagrasses	All other turf species; centipede and St. Augustinegrasses the least
Pythium blight; grease spot; cottony blight	Summer; late fall; 75-100 ° + F; hot-wet; high N	*Agrostis* species; Annual ryegrass; bluegrasses; fescuegrasses	Other turf species except St. Augustine, bahia, and centipede grasses
Typhula; snowmold	32-35 °F; requires a snow cover	Bentgrasses; *Poa annua*	Bluegrasses; fescuegrasses; ryegrasses
Fusarium patch; pink snowmold	36-55 °F; active in complexes to 75 °	Bentgrasses; *Poa annua*	Bahiagrass; bermudagrasses; some extent on fescue and ryegrasses
Fusarium rosem; Fusarium blight; *Fusarium* foot rot	June-Aug.; 77-87 °F; heat and drought	Bluegrasses; bentgrasses	Fescuegrasses; 'Meyer' *Zoysia*
Erysiphe graminis; powdery mildew	65 °F opt.; shade and humidity	Bluegrasses; bentgrass; red fescuegrass	
Ustilago spp.; smuts	When grass is in active growth	Bluegrasses; bermudagrass	Bentgrasses; fescuegrasses
Puccinia spp.; rust	70-75 °F; high lights intensity; humidity	Bluegrass; *Zoysia* grass; Annual ryegrass	Bermudagrass; Perennial ryegrass; St. Augustinegrass
Corticium; red thread	Cool wet; 55-72 °F	Festuca rubra	Bentgrasses; bluegrasses; ryegrasses
Ophiobolus patch	Cool wet overcast + lime	Bentgrasses	Bluegrasses; ryegrasses
Piricularia; gray leaf spot	Summer; high N; high humidity	St. Augustinegrass	

contitions favorable for disease control. These conditions are noted later for specific diseases.

Disease may also be controlled by a preventative program in which sprays are used in advance of any appearance of disease. On large areas and on utility turf, expense limits fungicide use to direct control of existing diseases. Even a single minimal spray for control is likely to cost over $20.00 and up to $100.00/acre. On valuable high-maintenance turf, a preventative program is usually desirable, but even here a control spray may be all that is used. Where climate favors the grass, a control program may be enough. Elsewhere, a preventative program is needed. In coastal Washington State for example, a preventative program is mandatory for growing high-maintenance bentgrass during weather favoring *Ophiobolus*.

A regular preventative spray is used to reduce populations of disease organisms to small numbers (Fig. 8.4). With thousands of infections per square foot needed to cause a disease, a fungus may need to go through several generations before there is sufficient inoculum to cause an epiphytotic or killing attack. If the buildup is interrupted by a spray which kills most of the inoculum, then the whole process must begin again from scattered survivors. Continuous interruption of the buildup by preventative sprays prevents disease outbreak even if the weather suddenly turns favorable for the fungus.

An example of a preventative program for a specific disease is one worked out by Shurtleff[179] for *Rhizoctonia*. He found the disease could be controlled in Rhode Island by three sprays applied during the time when

Figure 8.4 The right side of the plot received a preventative spray, the left side received none. The fungus illustrated is a saprophyte working in the thatch. The picture was obtained by scalping the plot with a mower to expose the thatch.

the spore-producing bodies which overwinter, the *sclerotia,* were germinating in the spring.

I began to support preventative programs when we found that two important summer diseases, *Rhizoctonia* brown patch and *Helminthosporium* melting-out, were active in Central California in December and January. The incipient infection was not visibly hurting the grass, but seaside bentgrass roots which normally grow vigorously at that time of the year were being killed on diseased plants.

Preventative spray programs can be classed as *specific* when aimed at a particular known disease, and *broad spectrum* when designed to control any of a number of possible known or unknown diseases. An example of a specific program is Shurtleff's program for *Rhizoctonia.* A fungicide is used which is specific for *Rhizoctonia* (Shurtleff used mercury sprays) and it is applied at the exact time of year that sclerotia are germinating.

Endo has given several broad-spectrum spray programs. An example of one follows.[60]

> *Group I* (effective against dollar spot, brown patch, red thread, *Fusarium* patch, and *Helminthosporium*-induced diseases). *(1)* PMA (phenyl mercuric acetate) with thiram (tetramethylthiuram disulfide); (Thiram mixed with mercurials has a limited shelf life and the mixture may be more effective if mixed in the tank).[13] *(2)* Emmi with thiram; *(3)* Panogen (methyl mercuric dicyanamide); or *(4)* Folpet with cadmium carbonate and thiram. *Group II* (effective against greasy spot caused by *Pythium* and rust caused by species of *Puccinia*). Zineb (zinc ethylene bisthiocarbamate), and cyclohexamide; or cyclohexamide with thiram. A group I spray is alternated with a group II spray, spraying every 7–14 days or every three weeks when disease activity is low.

Recovery from disease is by production of new grass to cover the ground. Successful control must keep the crowns alive and growing.

Predisposing Factors. Disease prevention by practicing good culture is emphasized throughout this book. Predisposing factors are examined here under one heading. Most important are climate, fertility, mowing, and irrigation practices. But compaction, thatch, air circulation, light, other organisms (e.g., insects), pH, salinity, freezing, etc., are also important. The turf manager often has at his fingertips the best source of information for him about the effects of the environment on disease. Since disease seldom removes an area of turf completely the question always exists as to why one area was affected while a foot away an area remained healthy. If keen powers of observation enable the manager to answer that question, he finds those weak spots in his own maintenance program which predispose grass to infection. Observation may require cutting plugs to examine the soil, setting cans to measure sprinkler applications, recognizing grass varieties, etc. On greens, surface drainage may carry soluble fertilizers into the low spots causing lush soft growth and leaving a slightly raised spot inches away stressed for both water and nutrients.[47]

1. Climate. Climate is the most important factor in disease management, for it determines which diseases will be problems and when. Secondly, we can do little to change the climate. The important climate is the climate at the ground which differs considerably in temperature and humidity from that at four feet. Occurrence of certain diseases at certain seasons provides a diagnostic characteristic. One usually need not worry about *Typhula* snowmold in the summer.

In the summer of 1962 a group of pathologists at a meeting in Oregon compared notes as to the most important diseases in the different sections of the country. With this and subsequently gathered data, Gould summarized the subject of climate and geography on disease. Figure 8.3 is based on information he developed. The information is biased for urban regions. In mountains or in unirrigated regions, problems may differ.

Climate affects both the disease and the grass (Fig. 8.5). The disease grows and multiplies rapidly enough to cause an epiphytotic within a fairly narrow range of temperatures. With a period of rain and heavy overcast the temperature range for infection may broaden as wetness

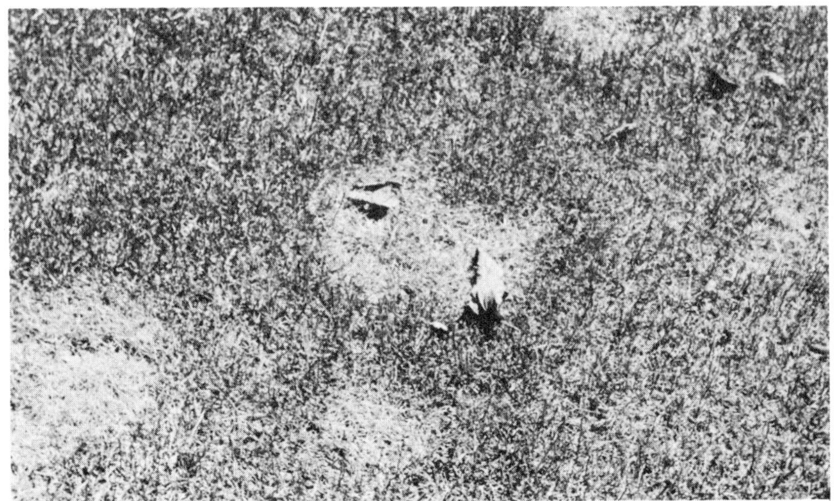

Figure 8.5 This plot was newly seeded in the fall. The following June, temperatures rose to over 100°F and patches of red fescue died. The disease was not identified, but obviously red fescue is not suited to such temperatures.

favors the fungus and overcast weakens the grass. Temperature interactions between grass and Fusarium have been noted. With *Rhizoctonia,* bentgrass damage occurs at temperatures which are above optimum for *Rhizoctonia* as bentgrass is weakened by the higher temperatures.[46] On subtropical St. Augustinegrass, however, *Rhizoctonia* causes damage at temperatures below optimum for the fungus, temperatures which are too cool for St. Augustine to be thrifty.[112,217]

Little can be done about extremes of high temperature. Top dressing seedings with lime or white sand can reduce soil temperature peaks two or three degrees (student data at Davis). Sprinkling grass may cool it temporarily, but then may result in increased leaf temperatures later (see *Principles of Turfgrass Culture,* Chap. 8). If sprinkling results in standing water, solar energy normally convected may heat the water to temperatures favoring *Pythium.*

Low temperatures are being modified by mulching and heating as previously noted.

2. Light. The turfgrasses are able to use full sunlight. A series of overcast days reduces photosynthesis and may increase susceptibility to disease.[139] Shade has a similar effect. Kentucky bluegrass in the shade is frequently mildewed and dollar spot first appears in the shady side of a green. When snow cover is prolonged in excess of forty days, snow molds increase rapidly and lack of light may be a factor in turf injury. Both fungal growth and sporulation may be affected by light. Mycelium of many fungi grows better in reduced or no light whereas light is often necessary for spore production.[32]

3. Moisture. Moisture problems bridge climate and management. Excessive rainfall must be tolerated, whereas a lack of rainfall is remedied by management's use of irrigation. Moisture is necessary for disease spread and irrigation management can favor or decrease its spread. Water of guttation affects increase of dollar spot, *Helminthosporium,* and *Rhizoctonia,*[61,58] and washing or poling guttation from the greens is a factor in disease control.[50] Damage from dollar spot is more severe when soil moisture is low.[39]

The question is often raised as to the best time to irrigate for minumun disease. There is a consensus that early morning watering is better because it removes water of guttation which can serve as a nutrient for fungi, and because the grass dries more quickly during the warming trend of morning. Monteith and Dahl[153] state that when greens are overwatered it doesn't make any difference when the water is applied; otherwise, if correctly watered, less disease appears when water is applied early in the morning.

With heavy dews during cool spring and fall weather, afternoon irrigation could prolong the number of hours grass is wet and so favor disease buildup.

Madison et al.[145] found that winter *Fusarium* patch on highland bentgrass was related to the irrigation pattern of the previous summer. With weekly irrigation, time of day made no difference, but when irrigation was more frequent, morning irrigation resulted in more disease than evening irrigation. On 'Seaside' bentgrass time of day was not important, frequency was.

The question also arises as to when in the management program irrigation should be practiced. Irrigation previous to mowing increases surface compaction of the soil. As cut ends of grass are a source of entry for pathogens, irrigation following mowing may favor infection.[55] Since mowing may cause a temporary stoppage of root growth, water stress often follows mowing. Janti and Kramer (Chap. 4) propose that irrigation should follow mowing. To reconcile these statements we suggest that irrigation follow mowing as soon as the cut ends of the leaves have dried. This subject could be studied further.

Irrigation during the heat of day reduces soil aeration and raises the humidity which leads to higher leaf temperatures. Both conditions are apt to favor disease. Standing water may heat and lead to a leaf scald.

When disease injures the root system we found that we could often recognize such areas before the appearance of visual symptoms. As these spots can take up less moisture for transpiration they may be felt as hot spots in the grass, photographed using infrared film, or seen in the early morning as spots lacking guttation water (Fig. 8.6).

4. Fertility.[6] In general, grass is most resistant to fungal attack when receiving balanced nutrition. Excessive nitrogen generally favors the disease. Late fall applications of nitrogen favor *Fusarium* patch, *Typhula* blight,[36] and spring dead spot.[198] *Sclerotinia* dollar spot is favored by low

Figure 8.6 The area of depressed growth results from root injury due to incipient *Rhizoctonia*. The short grass was 2°F warmer than grass on either side.

fertility,[39] whereas *Rhizoctonia* brown patch is favored by increased nitrogen,[36] especially if phosphorus and potassium are not also increased in a balanced fashion. Poor drainage has had overriding effects so that in wet areas nitrogen levels made no difference in *Rhizoctonia* incidence.[47]

Corticium red thread is decreased by bringing nitrogen up to a good fertility level.[41] Good nitrogen levels also aid recovery from *Ophiobolus* patch,[187] though Gould[92] finds urea may favor the pathogen. Rust is overcome by high nitrogen levels,[170] which stimulate growth so infected leaves may be cut off before the unsightly orange fruiting pustules develop and further spread the disease. Endo,[61] working on the range of composition of guttation water, finds its composition and its suitability for fungal growth changes with the fertility level.

In a continuing series of studies of the interactions of disease and nutrition Couch and his colleagues[22,37,39,41] find that after nitrogen, available calcium is the most important nutrient affecting disease severity. High available calcium decreases susceptibility whereas low levels of calcium result in total injury. He feels from his experiments that nitrogen is of most importance in keeping the grass growing so that a damaged leaf is replaced by a new one and rapid recovery is promoted. As long as potassium and phosphorus are available, high or low levels do not affect the course of the disease.

Nitrogen fertility levels may affect disease appearance. On experimental fertility plots we have had *Fusarium* patch appear on well-fertilized turf as a few well defined spots 4–8 in. in diameter. On plots receiving low nitrogen the appearance was more that of dollar spot. Spots were 2 in. across and numerous. On plots receiving no nitrogen the turf was peppered with spots about the size of a dime. The appearance was of three different diseases, and differences were so great that we couldn't collect data suitable for comparing the plots.

Altman[6] has reviewed nitrogen nutrition in relation to turfgrass diseases. One may conclude from a review by Christensen and DeVay that disease intensity can be affected by almost any mineral nutrient if a nutrient imbalance results.[31]

5. Mowing. Effects of mowing are fully discussed in Chap. 4. Data in Table 8.6 clearly show effects of mowing height on disease. At the U.S. Department of Agriculture turf plots at Beltsville it is standard practice to lower the height of cut to incite disease in resistance studies. Effects of mowing frequency are not so clear cut. Much of the entry of disease organisms into the plant takes place through ends of freshly cut leaves;[173] with more frequent mowing there are more fresh cuts.

With very high mowing (2–4 in.) a disease attack may often be so masked it is not noticed. Overarching leaves cover small areas defoliated by disease. But fewer rust pustules are matured when grass is mowed close.

6. Thatch. All authors have laid great stress on thatch as a contributing factor to disease, but little published work exists (Fig. 8.7).[48,55,59,94] During the noninfective stages, disease organisms may live and sporulate on clippings which serve as a source of inoculum for an epiphytotic.[179,182] However, sufficient clippings are present for this even without thatch. Thatch may act as a sponge and hold moisture around the crowns, thereby favoring fungal invasion. Thatch can interfere with air and water movement in the soil. On the other hand, returned clippings result in a more favorable nutrition. When clippings are regularly removed, nutrition tends to be less balanced and for best appearance it often becomes necessary to apply nitrogen at critical times when the free nitrogen would favor disease.

Associated with the problem of thatch is the question of removal of clippings. In one study of *Helminthosporium*[213] it made no difference if clippings were left when grass was mowed at 2 in. However, when grass was mowed at 1 in., leaving clippings predisposed the turf to disease. Certainly, leaving large clumps of sodden clippings during wet weather will shade and smother the grass.

Figure 8.7 Thatch-bound turf. Pale, "sick" areas did not respond to fertilizer, wetting agent, or other treatments. Only *Curvularia* was consistently isolated. The condition was corrected by top dressing.

7. Compaction and aeration. Compaction favors disease by holding water on the surface of the ground for longer periods.[134] *Pythium* melting out, a water mold, is often a symptom of bad compaction problems. The poorly developed root system under a compacted turf probably affects disease susceptibility because of the frequent short-term fluctuations of nutrient and water availability and frequent stress. In southern California, Endo found compaction of heavy soils the most common causes of turf failure. Compaction resulted in invasion by weakly pathogenic fungi not normally considered as problems on turf.[55]

In the last few years it has become standard practice in treating summer diseases in California to aerify greens and remove the cores, leaving the holes open. The observed improvement in disease control and grass recovery is justification.

8. Seeding rate. One of the most universal diseases in damping off of new seedlings, which is caused by several soil-borne fungi. Young seedlings are more susceptible to disease than mature plants and crowding from too much seed contributes to disease susceptibility. Smith[189] remarks that seeding should be light enough that there is air circulation between plants.

9. Other fungi. Soil contains many fungi, most of which are beneficial, acting to destroy dead waste materials in the soil. Many fungi produce substances which slow down or inhibit growth of other fungi.

When competition from other fungi in the soil is reduced, the fungi remaining, including disease-causing fungi, may be especially serious.[3] Corden and Young[34] found disease more severe on a soil that had its microflora reduced by previous use of fungicides. Use of methyl bromide in Washington State has been followed by severe infections of *Ophiobolus* patch and in New Zealand about one out of ten bowling greens treated with methyl bromide (to kill bermudagrass) had a severe disease problem.[9] In Canada, on the other hand, a fungus antagonistic to *Ophiobolus* took over the soil following sterilization and *Ophiobolus* was reduced thereby.[137]

Stevenson[194] finds *Helminthosporium sativum (H. sorokinianum)*[142] suppressed by eight species of soil actinomycetes, and Garrett[83] thinks increased bacterial activity at higher temperatures antagonizes development of *Fusarium nivale.* In the field *Fusarium nivale* is infectious at temperatures much below its laboratory optimum.

As turf diseases are more carefully studied, one seldom finds a disease attack due to a single species of fungus. Associations of several organisms are more the rule. These may be associations of major diseases[45,128,145] or of a major disease with weakly pathogenic fungi.[156]

10. Ventilation and pH. These unrelated predisposing factors have already been treated as part of the environment. Poor ventilation of greens

occurs more often than it should from a consideration of the disease problem. As the climax and target of a long vista, the green is often surrounded by landscape plantings. Overplanted shrubbery is kept because of a sentimental attachment by club members to the greenery and their unwillingness to admit they can have a dense copse or a good green but not both. Shrubs and trees do not have to be completely removed, but thinned so there is air movement across the green. When well done, the result may be increased beauty.

11. Biocides. What weakens the grass favors disease. Madison[146] has shown the use of herbicides to increase severity of *Rhizoctonia* on bluegrass. The insecticides tested showed no such effects, however, and a nematocide favored the grass. Other studies of the debilitating effects of herbicides on turf are being carried out.[27,84,169]

Anomolous responses to fungicides have been noted at Rutgers. Growth and sporulation of *Helminthosporium sorokinianum* has been stimulated by sprays of PMA; dollar spot has been stimulated by carbamate fungicides; copper spot by thiram sprays; and curvularia by Maneb.[107] These aberrations occur in the field and not in the laboratory and may be analogous to replacement phenomena of insects where death of one species results in colonization of that ecological niche by another organism.

12. Miscellaneous factors. As a suburbanite, I have had the opportunity to make observations on neighboring home lawns. I have seen diseased spots occurring year after year in exactly the same location. Spots often correspond to areas where the builder dumped trash, built fires, washed out cement and plaster mixers, or drove heavy trucks when the soil was wet.

Disease susceptibility may also be increased by the following which are discussed elsewhere: salinity (water stress favors dollar spot), traffic (cutting and bruising of the leaf favor entry and establishment), and other organisms (*Helminthosporium cynodontis* is found present in infestations of bermudagrass mite).[144]

CLASSIFICATION OF FUNGI

The fungi are classified into four groups on the basis of their sexually produced spores with a fifth group for those which produce only asexual spores and so cannot be related to the main groups. The five groups are: myxomycetes, the slime molds; phycomycetes, the algae-like fungi; ascomycetes, the cup fungi; basidiomycetes, mushrooms, puff-balls, bracket fungi, etc.; and fungi imperfecti, sexual phase unknown.

In Table 8.3 the fungi affecting turf are listed according to these groups. Those starred will be discussed. Those not starred are of secondary

Table 8.3. Classification of Fungi

Myxomycetes	
Mucilogo spongiosa *Physarum cinereum* and others	*Slime mold
Phycomycetes	
Pythium species*	Pythium blight; water mold, melting out, grease spot
Phialea temulenta	Blind seed
Ascomycetes	
Claviceps purpurea	Ergot
Epichloe typhinia	Choke
*Erysiphe graminis**	Powdery mildew
*Ophiobolus graminis**	Take all
*Sclerotinia homeocarpa**	Dollar spot
Phyllachora graminis *Phyllachora sylvatica*	Tar spot
Basidiomycetes	
*Corticium fusciforme**	Red thread, pinkpatch, corticium
Entyloma species	Blister smut
*Rhizoctonia solani**	Rhizoctonia brown patch, large brown patch, Rhizoc
*Typhula iotana**	Typhula blight, snow scald, winter scald
Ustilago species*	Smut
Puccinnia species*	Rust
Unidentified	*Winter crown rot
Sclerotinia rhizoides	Frost scorch, string of pearls
Uromyces jacksonii	Rust
Agaricus spp. *Amanita* spp. *Bolitus* spp. *Calva tia* spp. *Cantherellus* spp. *Clitocybe* spp. *Cortmarius* spp. *Discibeda subterranea* *Heceloma crustuliniforme* *Hydnelhum suaveolens* *Hydnum* spp. *Hygrophorus* spp. *Lactarius* spp. *Lepiota* spp. *Marasmius* spp. *Paxillus involutus* *Scleroderma verrucosum* *Tricholoma* spp.	*Fairy ring

Table 8.3 cont'd.

Fungi imperfecti	
Ascochyta spp.	Ascochyta leaf spot
Cercosporella spp.	Cercosporella eyespot, C. foot rot
Cercospora festucae	Cercospora leaf spot
Colletotrichium graminicola	Anthracnose
Curvularia spp.*	Fading out
Fusarium spp.*	Fusarium patch, pink snow mold, F. root rot, Silvertop
*Gloeocospora sorghi**	Copper spot
Gloeosporium	Root necrosis, G. Leaf spot
Helminthosporium spp.*	Melting out, leaf spot, zonate eyespot, blight, blotch
*Piricularia grisea**	Grey leaf spot of St. Augustinegrass
Septogloem	Char spot
Septoria spp.	Septoria leaf spot
Selenophoma spp.	Selenephoma leaf spot
Scolecotrichium graminas	Brown stripe
Spermospora subulata	Blast

importance and will be found discussed in other books such as that by Sprague[192] and particularly in the book by Couch.[36] The latter should be in the reference library of every professional turf man.

Myxomycetes

These are slime molds. A slime mold is the slimy ameboid body of any of a number of *Myxomycetes.* On turf the slime body moves through or over the turf, digesting dead clippings. On high-mown turf the slime body moving through the grass may be unnoticed. On fine turf however, the body moves over the turf and if it stays too long in one area it can smother or shade the turf so the grass is weakened and subject to attack by other diseases. Hosing the slime body away may break it up and spread it and the best control is to scrape up most of the fungus and then make up a little mercuric spray in a (plastic) sprinkling can and sprinkle the residue. Slime mold on a green is a symptom of overwatering.

Phycomycetes

Pythium species. This fungus causes *Pythium* blight, grease spot, and cottony blight. Several species of *Pythium* cause disease. In the south the most prominent is *P. aphanidermatum (P. butleri)* which causes cottony blight of overseeded grasses.[212] In the north *P. ultimum* or *P. arrhenomanes* cause grease spot or pythium blight of a number of turfgrasses.

Three primary factors serve to incite phthium blight: high temperatures,[155] high moisture, high nitrogen. With all three present, large areas of grass can be lost almost overnight. If any of the three is lacking, the disease tends to be confined to streaks and spots (Fig. 8.8).

When the disease is active it may appear as a dark greasy patch of disease surrounded by a dark ring where the infection is active. The greasy area rapidly turns reddish brown, then slowly fades to a straw color. If control is immediate, the grass may recover fairly rapidly, but if wet hot conditions continue or spraying is neglected, turf is soon killed.

Traffic spreads the disease and when it occurs on a green, a first step to control can be to cut a temporary green. In some instances, use of an aerifier may be needed to dry up the green. Couch[36] recommends that in addition to a fungicide, management should: *(1)* maintain satisfactory but not lush growth through light applications of a balanced fertilizer; *(2)* hold the soil in the acid range; and *(3)* provide irrigation intervals that hold the soil close to field capacity. Although wetness favors rapid spread of the disease, dryness increases the resulting injury.

Pythium has a special relation to bermudagrass turf because it affects the over-seeded ryegrass in southeastern U.S. Below 68°F cottony blight is not a problem on ryegrass. If temperatures reach 77° for two hours a day on three successive days, the disease is favored and the higher the temperatures and the longer they endure, the worse the disease. Two to four hours at 95°F may result in loss of 50% of the ryegrass.[72] Young seedlings are particularly susceptible.[73] Because of cottony blight, it is necessary to overseed bermudagrasses with annual ryegrass as late as possible to avoid warm spells, but not so late that one fails to get good growth before cold weather.

With ryegrass spreading *Pythium* through the turf one wonders what the effect will be on bermudagrass the following year. Freeman and Horn[77] examined this question and found all the subtropical turfgrasses resistant to *Pythium* except bermudagrass. They rated the bermudas and many varieties of temperate-season grasses for susceptibility to *Pythium aphanidermatum* on a basis of 0–5, where 0 is freedom from the disease. These ratings are presented in Table 8.4. Moore et al. got similar results.[154,155] They found only tall fescue, *Poa trivialis,* and improved bermudagrasses to be resistant.

When there is a previous history of *Pythium,* preventative spraying is urged. For control, fungicides are used at three to five day intervals. If mowing is continued, sprays should follow mowing. For control, Monteith[159] recommends mixtures of mercurous and mercuric chlorides; Couch[38] recommends Zineb; Endo[63] recommends panogen; and Freeman et al. recommend Dexon, Memmi, Panogen, Fore, and Terrachlor super X.[78] DD has controlled *Pythium* on pineapple and may be worth a test

Figure 8.8 *Pythium* disease. With high temperature, high moisture, and high nitrogen, an epiphytotic can occur in hours. The above three pictures trace the course of an epiphytotic over 48 hr. Spread of disease in mower tracks is characteristic of *Pythium.*

Table 8.4. Grasses Rated for Resistance to Infection by Phythium Ultimum[77]

Bermudagrass		*Agrostis*		*Bluegrass varieties*		*Fescues*	
Common	2.3[a]	Red top	5.0	Park	4.3	Alta	5.0
C. transvaalensis	2.0	Penncross	5.0	Delta	4.8	K-31	5.0
Tiffgreen	1.8	Seaside	5.0	Newport	4.5	Illahee	5.0
C. magenisii	1.8	Astoria	5.0	*P. trivialis*	4.5	Pennlawn	5.0
Bayshore	1.8	Highland	5.0	*P. annua*	5.0		
Uganda	1.5						
Ormond	1.3						
Tex. 22	1.0						
Tifway	1.0						
Tiffine	1.0						
Texturf	0.5						
Florida 50	0.8						
Tiflawn	0.5						
Everglades	0.5						

[a]0, resistant; 5, susceptible.

on turf.[7] Because of short life Dexon is used for control but not as a preventative spray.

Ascomycetes

Erysiphe graminis DC. (powdery mildew). Bermudagrass, bluegrass, red fescue and red top are subject to powdery mildew. While an individual mildew organism parasitizes a single leaf cell, infections are so numerous that infected leaves are colored gray by the spore producing *conidia* on the surface of the leaf. Mildew requires high humidity rather than free water for spores to germinate and penetrate the leaf. As a result it is a problem in areas having high humidity. It occurs infrequently in southwestern U.S. but is common through the north-central states and northern Europe. Yarwood et al.[215] find 65°F is the optinum air temperature. Shade is commonly associated with mildew on turf. Poor air circulation favors the necessary high humidity. Mildew is so common in shade that one is tempted to posit shade as an important predisposing factor per se. However, in the shade air temperatures are lower, relative humidity higher, and plants are weaker, so shade is probably a secondary cause in favoring these factors. 'Merion' bluegrass is more susceptible than common.[159]

Control is easy and should be applied early, for the disease spreads rapidly. Couch[38] recommends cycloheximide (Actidone), using a 60 ppm solution at 2 gal/1000 ft^2 of turfgrass. Gaskin and Britton recommend Karathane.[86]

Ophiobolus graminis Sacc. var. *avenae* E. M. Turner. The disease is *Ophiobolus* patch of turfgrasses. Variety *graminis* causes take-all disease of cereals.

Ophiobolus is widespread on grasses. It occurs as a disease on turfgrass in northern Europe and Australia, but in the United States it is reported only from the coastal regions of the Pacific Northwest.[89,96,97] It affects the various bentgrasses, *Poa annua,* bluegrass, and ryegrass.[187] Fescuegrass is resistant and one effect of *Ophiobolus* patch is to cause replacement of bentgrasses by fescues. It is favored by cool wet overcast conditions and higher pH, or perhaps by lime.[187,189] The disease is increased by either lime or calcium nitrate fertilizer.[9] Increasing phosphorus decreases the disease and use of ammonium sulfate or ammonium phosphate has reduced the disease, but nitrogen from other sources has had other effects.[89,96] Balanced fertilization using ammonium sulfate with good levels of both phosphorus and potassium has been very effective in minimizing the disease.[90,99]

In Australia, use of methyl bromide has resulted in severe destruction of turf by *Ophiobolus* patch in 20 of 200 instances of use.[9] Presumably antagonists of the disease were killed by the fumigation. On the other hand, *Trichoderma viride* became the dominant organism in soil pasteurized with steam. It so suppressed *Ophiobolus* that experimental work with the disease could not be carried out in the treated soils.[137]

Carbon dioxide appears to depress the disease, and fresh manure or chopped fresh alfalfa spread over the turf have slowed the progress of the disease. When the same materials were first composted they were without effect.[90]

Ophiobolus patch first appears as small brown spots. With cool wet overcast these rapidly enlarge. They may become several feet in diameter and may coalesce to form large areas of dead turf. As the grass is killed the dead areas fill back with weeds and must be replanted. In Australia *Ophiobolus herpotrichus* has been found as a component of the organisms of spring dead spot on bermudagrass.[185]

Moderate levels of balanced fertility and low pH have given the best control. Where the disease occurs, preventative sprays are essential.

Chlordane has been effective as a preventative material. In an extensive test Gould[99] found Chlordane and ammonium sulfate gave control superior to fungicides and in one year their repeated use eliminated the disease from an area. Fungicide control has been most effective with organic mercury sprays applied weekly.[89,118] Where liming becomes necessary a coarse ground limestone of slow availability has been found to increase the disease much less than finely ground materials.[187]

Scelerotinia homeocarpa F. T. Bennett. This fungus causes dollar spot. Dollar spot affects the turfgrasses except for tall and meadow fescue and ryegrasses. It is an important disease in three quarters of the United States, being minor northwest of the Missouri River. In Florida dollar spot is most prevalent on 'Ormond' and 'Tifway' bermudagrasses, on centipede and bahiagrasses, and on 'Emerald' Zoysiagrass. The Florida strain of *Sclerotinia* is more tolerant of heat than isolates from Ohio or Rhode Island. Dollar spot is found on *Ophiopogon,* the turfing lily,[76] and is highly pathogenic on nutgrass *(Cyperis rotundis)* in Mississippi.[15]

Most commonly recognized on greens as circular straw colored spots one-half to three in. in diameter, dollar spot has been of less concern on turf mowed higher where it occurs as larger spots. While damaging, these have not been accorded much attention.

Dollar spot occurs in mild humid weather with temperatures in the 70s, and experienced turf men readily learn to recognize "dollar spot weather." In the laboratory Endo found dollar spot to grow well between 50 and 88°F but produced toxins causing root necrosis between 60 and 80 °F. On bentgrass it was most damaging at 80°F.[56] Smith found seasonal spring and fall outbreaks to correspond to time of spore production in culture.[186]

Dollar spot does not penetrate healthy grass. A saprophyte on old yellowing blades, its mycelium grows on the inner surface of leaf sheaths. There guttation water caught in the blade–sheath axil may help nourish the fungus.

Endo finds guttation water favoring the disease.[58,63] Toxins produced by the fungus cause injury and death of roots and stunting and degeneration of tops.[62,122] Toxins released beneath the sheath may cause the leaf to weaken and die when it is penetrated by the fungus as a saprophyte. Mowing of the infected blade scatters and spreads the disease.

While Kentucky bluegrass shows decreased resistance to the disease with increasing nitrogen, in general, higher levels of nitrogen have been observed to reduce the disease on putting greens.[39] Endo finds the quality of the guttation water affected by the fertility program and fertilizer source may affect the severity of the disease.[58] Milorganite has reduced dollar spot compared to several other fertilizers,[33,171] and in two trials we have observed increased dollar spot with ammonium nitrate as compared to either nitrate or ammonium nitrogen alone. Endo suggests that an effect of nitrogen may be to increase the ratio of healthy green leaves to senescing and yellowing leaves (where infection begins).[58]

Ph is not important but disease susceptibility is greatly increased by water stress, and the soil should be kept near field capacity.[39]

Preventative sprays should be used on high-maintenance turf at two to three week intervals during dollar spot weather. As a "cure" sprays should be used at three to four day intervals. The cadmium sprays are specific.

As fungicide tests are affected by weather patterns from year to year, workers at Rutgers summed fifteen years of experience,[49] and listed the following as those of 220 sprays tested which have performed well over the fifteen years and which are available on the market: Actidione ferrated, Actidione-thiram, Caddy, Cadminate, Cadox, Calo-clor, Calo-clor with Tersan, Dyrene, Kromad, Panogen, and Semesan with Tersan. Also performing well but slightly less effective than the above were: Metasol P-6, Ortho Lawn and Turf, PMAS, Semesan, and Thimer. Other materials performed less well. Tests at other stations are in essential agreement with the New Jersey results. Daconil has given good control.[95]

Sclerotinia borealis, Bubak and Blengel. In the far north where the cold penetrates below the snow layer *Sclerotinia borealis* causes loss of turf of *Agrostis, Poa,* and *Lolium* species.[65,172] Development is favored by a long rainy autumn, slight freezing of the soil, a thick snow cover, and slow melting in the spring.[120] Four varieties of Kentucky bluegrass were protected in Alaska by sprays of PCNB. Thimer, Thiram, and mercurics gave only moderate control.[121] Soil warming can protect valuable turf.[130]

Basidiomycetes

Corticium fuciforme (Berk.) Wakef. The resulting disease is red thread, pink patch, or *Corticium.* Bent, rye, and bluegrasses are susceptible but *Corticium* is most familiar as a disease of red fescue and reaches serious levels on high-cut turf in the Pacific Northwest, along coastal California, and in northern Europe. It is less common on putting-green turf.

Corticium attacks leaves and leaf sheaths. Lesions, which appear water soaked, soon result in dead leaves which form patches of brown from a few inches to a few feet in size. The patches have many unaffected green leaves among the brown and the mixture looks "ratty." When moist overcast continues for several days the fungus may be seen as a pink gelatinous coating on the leaf with the coral pink "horns" of the fruiting body (ca 1/4 in. long). The fungus grows at temperatures from freezing to 80°F. Bennett reported an optimum between 59 and 77°F and Erwin narrowed this to 65–72°F.[64] The optimum temperature for infection appears to be lower than that for culture and Gould[91] found the disease worst at 58°F with very little development at 67°F, though Endo[56] got good infection from 60 to 70°F. Erwin shows different temperature optima for different strains of the fungus.[64]

Maintaining adequate nitrogen levels is most important as the grass normally seems to outgrow the fungus unless slowed by low fertility or heavy overcast. Muse and Couch[158] found calcium nutrition affecting the disease, a deficiency increasing disease proneness in Jan. and March, and excess decreasing disease in October. Turf treated with maleic hydrazide to retard growth was more severely infected with *Corticium* than turf not treated.[64] *Corticium* appears to respond to the same fungicidal program as dollar spot, which see. However, carbamates give better control than cad·mium carbonate. Carbamates are of less value on dollar spot.[95]

Rhizoctonia solani Kuhn (*Thanatephorus cucumerus* (Frank) Donk. (*Pellicularia filimentosa* (Pat.) D. P. Rogers). *Rhizoctonia solani* Kuhn was first identified as a turf pathogen in 1916, by Piper who identified the cause of the brown patches of turf as the fungus *Rhizoctonia solani.*[165,166] This was the first properly identified turfgrass disease. Field-trained men of the time did not immediately accept that turf was killed by fungal diseases. As late as 1926 Monteith found it necessary to offer evidence to convince golf course superintendents that the disease was not caused by spiders; that the web-like threads were the mycelium of a fungus.[152]

Rhizoctonia is the number-one turf enemy in the United States according to a survey of turfgrass diseases by Dr. Charles Gould. It affects over 100 species of grass including all turfgrasses,[91,192] and is an important disease in all areas of the country except the cool humid Pacific Northwest.

Rhizoctonia solani Kuhn names a broad group of fungi, the mycelial threads of which appear alike in the vegetative state. On occasion collected strains have fruited and produced sexual spores. These strains have generally been classified as *Thanatephorus cucumerus* (Frank) Donk., (*Pellicularia filimentosa* (Pat.) D. P. Rogers), a basidiomycete.[206] Recently, however, isolates classed with *Rhizoctoni* have fruited and found to be ascomycetes. Thus, even though the members of *Rhizoctonia* are grouped together because of similar vegetative structures, the group may contain unrelated members. Turf brown patch may be caused by closely related organisms but we cannot assume we are dealing with a single true species as some early investigators did.

Rhizoctonia solani (or rhizoc for short) is present as part of the flora of most soils. Although acid soils have been considered to favor *Rhizoctonia,* there is no lack of inoculum[192] in basic soils and the fungus grows at a wide range of pH values.[152] The fungus forms small hard bodies of compact mycelium, *sclerotia,* which survive unfavorable seasons and "seed" new infections.

The sclerotia are brown to blackish flattened discs of about 1/32–3/32 of an inch in diameter and may often be found embedded in the plant tissue or they may be in the soil. The fungus may also survive for long periods in the soil as a saprophyte living in dead clippings or thatch and in tests has survived two years in dry soil.[202] Infected clippings which miss the catcher provide a source of new infection for four months or more.[18] Top dressing applied to greens may also be a source of infection.[141] In addition, *Rhizoctonia* is seed borne[126] and may be sown with the seed unless the seed is treated. Seed-borne inoculum is especially important, as seedlings and young grass plants are very susceptible to injury.

The many strains of *Rhizoctonia* may vary as to the plant infected, the severity of the disease caused, the temperatures at which they are pathogenic, whether they grow down in the soil or on the soil surface, etc. A virulent strain however, is likely to infect several turfgrasses and Atkins, for example, cross inoculated rhizoc strains from tall fescue and bermudagrass.[12]

Over the years brown patch on bentgrass putting greens has been given most attention.

In 1930 Dickinson[50] gave a detailed description of the response of rhizoc on greens to temperature conditions, and offered evidence that the occurrence of brown patch was completely predictable from weather records. When warm temperatures dropped to the 60s, sclerotia germinated and produced short mycelial threads about 1/2 in. in length. Growth remained static in this condition, but if a warming trend then followed, the mycelia began to grow and became infective from the mid-70s to the mid-80s. While activity of the fungus practically stops above 90°F, the higher temperatures may weaken turf so that damage is more severe when temperatures fall again to the 80s. A drop to 65°F followed by a rise to 75–80°F could result in the appearance of the smoke ring within three hours. Dickinson offered evidence that the disease could be checked at this stage by poling, to break up the mycelium mechanically.

A study of this kind suggests that one is dealing with a fungus responding to a limited range of growth conditions, and it may be that a single ecotype comes to predominate in a large geographical area. At the same time many strains exist and one has been described from California which is pathogenic at temperatures near freezing and can cause brown patch in January, particularly on autumn seeded turf.[145] Variability is also indicated by Endo's work. Of thirty-four isolates he made of rhizoc, four were capable of infecting bentgrass.[55]

Rhizoctonia in the northeast U.S. is described as most damaging on putting greens during hot humid weather. In the spring, with warming temperatures, sclerotia germinate and are likely to first grow as soil saprophytes which reach a high level of activity in two to four days at favorable temperatures.[36,173,179] Development of brown patch is favored by soil nitrogen and by water levels in the lower ranges of availability.[163] With warming temperatures the fungus may infect first roots, then stolons and leaves.[110] The fungus enters more readily through cut ends of leaves. Rowell[173] found in a laboratory experiment that uncut grass inoculated with *Rhizoctonia* remained fairly free of the disease while cut grass was severely damaged. The fungus enters at the tip of the cut blade, through stoma, or by penetrating the leaf, and progresses downward to the center of the plant. Moisture from guttation water contributes to rapid spread of the disease, the mycelium bridging from one drop of water to another.[186] The guttation water (so-called dew) provides not only a moist medium at the cut ends, but may contribute nutrients and may be capable of inactivating the fungicide PMA.[173] With continuing moist, warm conditions, disease results in a brown patch of infected plants several inches to several feet in diameter (Fig. 8.9). The edge of the patch may be bordered, especially in the early morning, with a band of dark smoky or purplish color where the fungus is actively destroying the grass. The patch enlarges as much as several inches a day. The collapsed leaves containing masses of mycelium become dry and turn brown.

An early observation of the importance of moisture in the spread of *Rhizoctonia* during the infectious stage was made on a lakeside golf course in New York State.[175] Six men each mowed three greens starting regularly at 7:00A.M. As an aid to mowing, "dew from the lake" (guttation water) and worm casts were poled from each green before mowing. The six greens mowed first each morning were free of *Rhizoctonia,* the six mowed third were seriously affected. Early morning poling,dragging, or hosing of greens assists in *Rhizoctonia* control.[69]

The classic description of the dead patch of grass with the smoky ring of active infection to the outside describes a leaf infection which is readily stimulated by presence of surface water. In the dry southwest formation of "dew" or at least its persistence during the early morning hours is less common in the summer, and rhizoc in this classic form may occur only infrequently, and only under the short mowing and high moisture on putting greens.

Rhizoc is more commonly seen in the southwest in a second form which appears to have a more prominent effect on the root system.

As the disease appears in Davis, fungal growth begins during mild weather, moving outward in a circle from a center of infection, without visibly damaging the grass. Initial growth may be saprophytic or at too low a rate to be damaging. As the weather warms, the fungus, which has moved out from its center of infection, becomes active by damaging the grass in the form of a ring. Grass in the center of the ring appears fairly normal and the fungus does not move back into this area. Damage occurs to the root system and the ring of grass which turns brown and dies usually dies from desiccation due to a root system unable to supply adequate water. Frequent sprinkling or sprinkling and syringing during the period of infection may keep the grass green and alive.

Rhizoctonia disease appears in two symptomatic forms, and differences between them may be summed as follows:

Northeast Leaf Infection	*Southwest Root Infection*
Usually a leaf infection with mycelium visibly infecting the leaves when conditions are favorable for the disease	Primarily a root or crown infection
Produces a dead brown patch	Produces a brown ring (rings may coalesce)
Leaves usually die from fungal invasion	Leaves likely to die from desiccation
Disease travels in moist air from cut leaf to cut leaf (as well as in soil and thatch)	Disease travels in soil or thatch

The second type of infection has been observed in the field rather than studied in the laboratory. Laboratory study is needed.

In a study of brown patch in Rhode Island, Shurtleff[178] found he could control *Rhizoctonia* with a series of three carefully timed mercurial sprays. When spring soil level temperatures were over 60°F and the humidity over 98% sclerotia began to germinate. At that time he irrigated the turf and forty eight hours later sprayed it with mercuric chloride. The irrigation and spray were repeated three times at weekly intervals, at the end of which time the disease potential was minor. This proposed program has not been widely used.

The usual seeded bentgrass green is a patchwork quilt of lighter and darker green grasses and in the winter some of the patches become reddish. I had often pointed this out to students as a possible genetic difference in anthocyanin producing ability. When Aage Anderson was working with the turf program at Davis, his training as a plant pathologist led him to question my statement. He had often seen such reddish color associated with disease. During the winter of 1961–1962 he examined many such reddish clones and in every case found the grass infected with *Hel-*

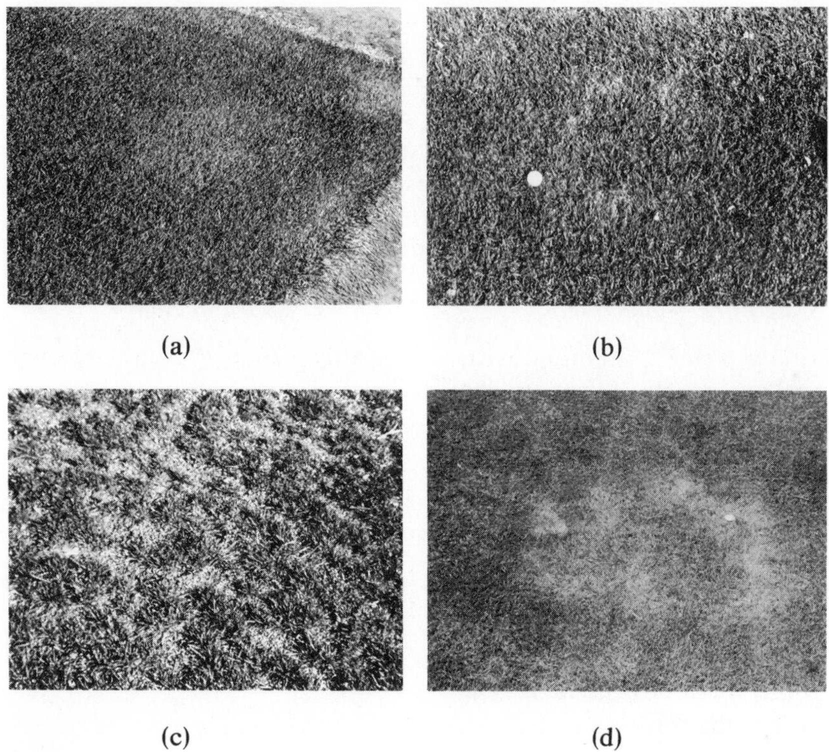

Figure 8.9 *Rhizoctonia solani* — large brown patch, (a) A cold weather strain on bluegrass in January at Davis, California. (b)-(d) Various degrees of severity of the disease.

minthosporium. At the same time he looked at many samples of green bentgrass for comparison. On a very large percentage of these samples he found *Rhizoctonia* to be active. On these plants emerging roots and new roots became necrotic and died when 1/2–1 in. long. While we noted the correlation between the presence of *Rhizoctonia* and the necrosis of roots we did not establish that the damage was caused by the fungus, nor whether the fungus was systemic in the roots.

Not all isolates of rhizoc are pathogenic to bentgrass.[55] Sherwood and Rindberg found evidence that rhizoc produced toxins[177] and Kerr[122] presented evidence that these toxins might cause root necrosis. Thus we may have been seeing root injury from toxins produced by saprophytic strains of *Rhizoctonia* growing in the thatch or on the dead sheath bases.

We had been assuming on the basis of studies in the literature and on the basis of our own observations that bentgrass reestablished a new vigorous root system every fall and winter when soil temperature favored root growth. Thus it was disappointing to find a summer disease damaging the root system even in the winter.

Hearn[110] found rhizoc in Texas was active from September to January though it caused no injury at that time. *Rhizoctonia* is infectious at lower temperatures.[46,112] In southern U.S. it appears in the spring and fall when nights are cool and during mild spells in the winter. The vigor of St. Augustine is low at such times.[217]

In mild climates then, it appears *Rhizoctonia* is present even in winter and new infections start not only from germinating sclerotia but from the old growths which carry over. Thus Shurtleff's program would not necessarily be effective in the South as it is in Rhode Island.

Organisms which injure roots, such as *Rhizoctonia,* can be detected before the appearance of brown grass. The reduced root system and attendant water stress provide clues. In the early morning, areas of infection may appear as areas where there is no dew (guttation water) while surrounding grass is covered. Infected areas fail to grow as rapidly after mowing as the healthy grass. At 2:00–4:00 P.M. infected areas may appear bluish or grayish due to water stress. At the same time water stress results in higher temperatures so the infection may be felt as a hot spot by running the hand over the grass.

Reduction and control of *Rhizoctonia* can be effected both by cultural practices and chemical sprays. Among the cultural practices importance of early dew removal has been discussed.

Bloom and Couch[22] explored the effects of fertility on *Rhizoctonia* infection in greenhouse tests. They recommend a normal level of nitrogen with balanced phosphorus and potassium. When N in their tests was low relative to P and K, the disease was less severe; but if N was high relative to P and K, severity was increased. When N was low, pH had little effect; but the disease was favored by alkalinity at high N and acidity when N was in balance.

Hearn[110] found excess N was more damaging if applied in the ammonium form.

Data from our field studies are given in Table 8.5. In this field experiment P and K levels were adequate. Low-N turf was badly starved and high-N provided about 2 lb of N/1000 ft^2/mo. Nitrogen fertility was in interaction with mowing and irrigation practices. Low fertility resulted in more disease; medium nitrogen resulted in the least disease. When irrigation was weekly there was a relatively high incidence of disease at all nitrogen levels, but when moisture was kept high, higher levels of nitrogen produced less disease.

More disease was associated with more frequent mowing. Further effects of mowing are given in Table 8.6

Table 8.5. Incidence of *Rhizoctonia* on 'Seaside' Bentgrass as Affected by Management[a]

Treatments[b]	*High N*	*Medium N*	*Low N*	*Total*
		Irrigation treatments		
5 irrigations per week	35.2	30.5	51.1	116.8
1 irrigation per week	53.8	53.2	64.6	171.6
		Mowing treatments		
5 mowings per week	55.6	48.2	63.4	167.0
1 mowing per week	33.3	35.4	52.3	121.0
Total	88.9	83.6	115.7	288.2

[a]Davis, 1963.

[b]All treatments produced highly significant differences, In addition there was an interaction between the irrigation and fertility treatments. When plots were irrigated once a week there was a high level of disease at all fertility levels. When soil moisture was kept high, higher levels of nitrogen produced less disease. Nitrogen was at 1/2, 1, and 2 lb/1000 ft^2/mo as UF.

These data were collected from plots originally mowed at 1/2 and 7/8 in. In early May the height of mowing was changed to give the series of heights listed in Table 8.6. Shortly thereafter *Rhizoctonia* became prevalent in the plots. On June 3, two of the four replications were aerified.

In general there was more disease at the lower cuts. The injury increased by aerification. This was probably an effect of drying. The plots were irrigated only weekly and when drying of the surface soil was increased by aerification, more plants with disease-injured roots died from drying. It was necessary to increase the irrigation to twice weekly to prevent even greater killing of grass.

There has been speculation as to why brown patch is favored by drying of the soil when it is a disease requiring moist conditions. One hypothesis suggests that the reduced air movement in a moist soil results in a buildup of carbon dioxide inhibits growth of the fungus. Drying may concentrate toxins to more damaging levels.

Soil organic matter influences rhizoc.[190] Oak sawdust added to the soil was twice as effective as PCNB (Terrachlor) in reducing rhizoc inoculum potential though rice hulls were without effect.

This can perhaps be attributed to fungitoxicity of lignin decomposition products or of polyphenols.

Use of disease-resistant grasses assists control. The two grasses first released by the Arlington turf gardens, Metropolitan and Washington bentgrasses, were chosen for brown patch resistance.[152] Shurtleff has evaluated twenty three grasses for their disease resistance,[178] and finds bents among the least resistant, fine fescues among the more resistant grasses (Table 8.7).

All turf pathologists have considered thatch control important in reducing disease. Endo[55] has noted that disease is generally associated with heavy or compacted soils. However, injury may be aggravated on sands because of their droughty nature. We have also found *Rhizoctonia* increased on bluegrass when an herbicide had been used previously.[146] *Rhizoctonia* affected 23% of untreated turf while plots sprayed with one of five herbicides had an average disease incidence of 29% and ranged as high as 41%.

Summing cultural factors, the best practices would include selecting a good grass variety, poling greens, using a balanced fertilizer at moderate rather than high levels, not lowering the mowing height after the seasonal temperatures have reached the 70s, and watching the irrigation to prevent drying of the soil or wilting of plants with damaged roots.

Effects of compaction could well be relieved by hole punching if accompanied by close attention to irrigation.

Bordeaux was the first chemical recommended for brown patch control,[166] but repeated use resulted in copper toxicity. Experiments soon

Table 8.6. Effect of Mowing Height and Aerification of *Rhizoctonia* Disease in 'Seaside' Bentgrass[a]

	Square feet of grass injured by *Rhizoctonia* (50 ft²/ plot)			
Height of Mowing (in.)	*May 31* *Replications 1 and 2*	*June 13* *Replications 1 and 2 Aerified*	*May 31* *Replications 3 and 4*	*June 13* *Replications 3 and 4*
2	1.9	3.5	1.4	1.2
1 3/8	9.4	33.8	14.7	22.4
7/8	6.2	21.4	15.3	21.4
1/2	10.7	25.1	15.2	35.0
1/4	16.1	47.3	17.6	26.3

[a] Davis, 1961.

Plots originally mowed at 1/2 and 7/8 in. were given different heights of mowing in early May, following which *Rhizoctonia* became prevalent in the plots. Two of the four replications were aerified on June 3rd. In general, aerification resulted in a greater increase in the disease and, at the lower cuts, a slower rate of recovery. Usually, plots were irrigated once per week though sometimes twice.

Table 8.7. Susceptibility of Turfgrasses to Brown Patch[a]

Grass	*Rating*[b]
Rhode Island colonial bentgrass	8.8
Highland colonial bentgrass	8.6
B-11 velvet bentgrass	8.5
Astoria colonial bentgrass	8.2
Seaside creeping bentgrass	7.6
Meadow fescue	7.6
Red top	7.4
Merion bluegrass	7.3
Perennial ryegrass	7.1
Annual ryegrass	7.1
Tall fescue	7.1
Poa annua	6.6
Illahee red fescue	6.1
Trinity fescue	5.8
Creeping red fescue	5.7
Poa trivialis	5.2

[a] After Shurtleff.[178]
[b] Rated 0 to 11, where 11 = 100% kill.

showed mercurials to be of value,[88] and they have been the basis of chemical control since. Their ability to act on the sclerotia makes them valuable in an early-season preventative program.

PCNB is consistently rated higher than other fungicides.[95] Early-season spraying with PCNB (Terrachlor) may also be used as a preventative program. PCNB is a fungistat which prevents the fungus from achieving full growth potential in the soil. However, PCNB is little effective once the disease becomes a leaf infection. At high levels or with warm temperatures PCNB may cause yellowing of the grass.

In the region where rhizoc is an annual problem, use of a preventative spray should be added to the list of cultural practices to be followed.

For control, a 1:1 mixture of mercurous and mercuric chloride is used at 2 oz/1000 ft.^{2} in 5–10 gal of water.[36] (Use goggles; do not use galvanized tanks.) At higher temperatures mercurous chloride (calomel) is used alone as it is less injurious to turf. Two ounces of Thiram and one-half ounce Semesan (active ingredient) was found an effective control by Bachelder and Engel.[13,49] (These chemicals are combined in Tersan OM). Couch et al.[41] tested twenty-two chemicals and found that all reduced severity of the disease but grass made the most rapid recovery when the following were used: Tersan OM, Ortho Lawn and Turf Fungicide, Dyrene, Dithane M-22, Actidione-Thiram, and Thimer.

The level of control from organic fungicides may decrease from year to year as the fungus builds up tolerance. In laboratory tests Elsaid and Sinclair[54] found *Rhizoctonia* becoming more and more tolerant of Captan, Dichlone, Maneb, PCNB, and Thiram. Thus the most effective program may be one which alternates organic with inorganic fungicides and which changes the organic fungicide from time to time.

As used, fungicides act on fungi growing on leaves and on the soil surface. The large reservoir of infection below the surface remains untouched. For this reason Lukens and Stoddard (141) have investigated the injection of fungicide into the soil and report a deeper heavier root system as well as rhizoc control for more than one season.

They have used Nabam (1:600) and oxyquinoline sulfate (1:1200) injecting into the soil at a pressure of 200 psi about 12 in. deep and 4 ft on centers. Also they have drenched greens with oxyquinoline sulfate at 1 oz/16 gal water to provide 1 pint/ft^2.

Together with other controls,[11] such drenches have given promise of preseason *Rhizoctonia* control, but they have not been fully evaluated in the field and it appears that *Rhizoctonia* is likely to remain the number-one turf disease in the United States for some time into the future.

Typhula iotana Imai. This fungus causes *Typhula* blight, snow scald, and winter scald. *Typhula* blight is most damaging to bentgrass greens, but also affects bluegrasses, fescues, and ryegrass. Congressional bent has shown resistance.

Active at 32°F, *Typhula* grows beneath a snow cover, and the longer the cover remains, the more turf is likely to be found damaged when a thaw occurs. During a long thaw with the surface of the ground cold and wet, and with frozen soil beneath preventing drainage, rapid expansion of the damaged areas can occur. With an open cold winter, damage from *Typhula* is likely to be slight. *Typhula* produces the most infections at 32–41°F and grows well to 54°F.[35,133]

Typhula first appears as straw colored spots a few inches across. If the infection continues these spread and coalesce to kill large areas. When the weather promotes active growth a greyish white mycelium may be found around the outer edge of the infection. In older infections the straw color turns to grayish white.

Typhula damage occurs principally in Canada, Alaska, and the northern third of the United States. In the southern part of its range, *Typhula* is generally found in association with *Fusarium nivale.* The complex is treated under *Fusarium*. *Typhula idahoensis* has an overlapping range, and in Alaska *T. idahoensis* may damage bluegrasses. Season, geographical range, and color, all supplement a principal diagnostic feature, the many sclerotia, or small compact masses of mycelium which serve as "seeds." These are found embedded in the dead plant parts (Fig. 8.10). About pin head size to a little larger, they are light to dark brown. Sclerotia are formed in light containing ul-

(a)

(b)

Figure 8.10 *Typhula* blight, **(a)** Close-up of dead leaves with sclerotia fruiting bodies of *Typhula* imbedded in the leaves. **(b)** *Typhula* on bentgrass combined with *Fusarium nivale,* forming the snow-mold complex.

traviolet.[32] Mycelium and infective hyphae are formed under the dark snow blanket.

Cultural practices which reduce susceptibility to the disease include thatch reduction and control of nitrogen at a fairly low level. In other words as the weather cools off in the fall the superintendent wants to have a sufficient level of nitrogen to keep dollar spot low, and to assist in quick recovery from thatch-removal operations. But by the time the snow flies, nitrogen should be at a low level.

Roberts[170] has listed varietal differences in susceptibility at Iowa. From the less to the more susceptible he listed Astoria, Congressional, Penncross, Old Orchard, Washington, Arlington, and Seaside bentgrasses.

In the region of injury from *Typhula* a preventative spray is mandatory on fine turf. Mercury sprays have generally been preferred, but good control has been obtained with any of a number of materials. The first spray should usually not be given before October, and the second one should be delayed as long as possible before the first snow. When the season has favored *Typhula* a spray should also be given during the January thaw, and again in the spring when the ground will permit traffic. Without a spring spray, a fivefold increase in the disease in a three-week period has been noted. A regular spray program controls the disease until weather favorable to *Typhula* passes.

Among the fungicides which have been tested and recommended for *Typhula* are the following: calcium propyl arsenate, Calocure, Calo-clor, Panogen, PMA, and Scut F-72. Materials less extensively tested or giving a lesser degree of control include: Tersan OM, Actidione–Thiram, Cadminate, and Kromad.[174]

Adams and Howard[1] noted that treatments of the previous year reduced the incidence of *Typhula* by 1/5 to 2/5. They had used Kromad, Otho Lawn and Turf fungicide, MF-96 (Nabam-cadmium), and V-PYM-3% (PMA–thiram).

Inorganic mercurics provide longer residual action than organic mercurics. Dyrene performance has varied. Carbamates perform less well than mercury or cadmium sprays.[95]

Ustilago striiformis (Westend.) Niessl causes striped smut; *Ustilago cynodontis* (Pass.) Henn causes bermudagrass loose smut; and *Urocystis agropyri* (Preuss.) Schrot. causes flag smut. A number of other smuts are diseases of flowers and seeds in particular and will not be treated here (see Couch or Sprague).

Striped smut appears to have moved from the position of a relatively insignificant disease to one of prominence in the last few years. This may be because we now have more plant pathologists looking at turfgrass. I think, however, there is another factor at work. With the release of 'Merion' bluegrass large areas of turf were planted to a pure strain of turf for the first time. In turf of common bluegrass susceptible individuals may be eliminated from the sward in a few years. But 'Merion' is a vigorous grass, and susceptible to striped smut. As smut got into 'Merion' lawns, grass was thinned in the spring but recovered later with the infestation enduring and becoming more extensive the following year. The way was opened for widespread epiphytotics. 'Newport' is a second susceptible grass and is very widely planted. As a result we now have in the spring season, not infested plants among healthy grasses, but infested lawns of wide extent.

In other words, the use of selected (and susceptible) varieties has helped promote striped smut to a ranking disease.

Spore germination is stimulated by horse and cow manure. Spores germinate to produce hyphae which enter seedling coleoptiles or penetrate young tillers. Halisky et al. have observed that dense tillering grasses are more severely infected than open spreading growers.[105,106]

As spring nitrogen levels increased, grass was better able to outgrow competition. Infected plants were more subject to loss from drought, insects, nematodes, and the disease but had a heavier infection the following fall.[106] Other studies have rated varieties for susceptibility or have tested chemicals for control of the disease.

Of the bentgrasses, Seaside, 'Penncross,' 'Washington,' 'Toronto,' 'Evansville,' and 'Pennlu' have been reported to have varying susceptibilities.[85,109,106] 'Pennlu,' 'Pencross,' 'Cohansey,' 'Arlington,' and 'Congressional' are reported as failing to show symptoms in one set of tests. All bluegrasses examined have had some degree of susceptibility, though it may be so low that some varieties may be called resistant.[105,106,124] Varieties that appear particularly susceptible are 'Merion,' 'Cougar,' 'Newport,' 'Troy,' 'Delta,' 'Arboretum,' and common. 'Newport' rated resistant at Beltsville, susceptible at New Jersey. At Davis I have found 'Newport' susceptible over a longer season. A characteristic of 'Newport' is its late fall and early winter growth and color. In the mild-California climate, smut on 'Newport' continues growing and fruiting later into the winter and begins earlier in the spring than on other varieties. By the time 'Merion' shows smut stripes in the spring, 'Newport' has already been decimated.

Smut is systemic, continuing within the plant tissues where it is protected from the action of externally applied fungicides. To be effective a fungicide must have some uptake, some systemic action.

Lukens reported that mild infections were controlled by a spring application of a 1:400 Nabam drench.[140] Urea at 8 oz in 10 gal/M gave better control than seven other fungicides he tested.[138] Gaskin and Simmons found 70–90% control in November after an earlier application of 1 lb/M of PCNB and better control at higher rates, to 4 lb/M.[87] Above that turf was injured. The greatest promise is held by a series of compounds under test as systemic fungicides. The first of these, "Plantvax," controls flag smut and striped rust and has been shown to inhibit striped smut on bluegrass.[101,103]

Flag smut is similar to striped smut in all essentials but infects colonial bent and red fescuegrasses in addition.[36] It is controlled by Plantvax with limited injury to the plant.[102]

Loose smut of bermudagrass is a disease of seed heads but is mentioned because of the frequency of seed head formation on bermuda turf. The fungus remains in the host plant without pathogenic effects until the apical meristem initiates an inflorescence.[30] The fungus invades the inflorescence and the result is a greasy black flower head. The disease can persist from year to year without need for reinfection.[143]

Smuts are carried on seed and it is worth treating seed to prevent introducing the disease on new turf. Ceresan or Semesan may be used as seed treatments.[117]

Puccinia species. This fungus causes rust. As grass generally survives, rust has been considered a minor disease, and has ranked tenth in importance in Gould's survey.[94] Rust has proven so severe on 'Merion' bluegrass, annual ryegrass, and on *Zoysia,* that it is an important consideration in grass breeding. Rust is treated in detail by Couch.[36] The complete life cycle of rust is complex, consisting of five distinct kinds of spores, each with its own requirement for growth and development of the next stage. In the complete cycle, grass is infected by aeciospores, usually from barberry, and itself produces teleospores, which are overwintering spores. If rust had to go through the complete cycle it would not be a problem on turf. However, the infection that results from the aeciospore can also produce (and does) urediospores, which infect more grass, resulting in more urediospores, etc. It is the asexual repeating cycle of urediospores that results in rust epiphytotics on turfgrasses.

Rust is seasonal and spore establishment has special requirements. The spore germinates and the germ tube enters a leaf stoma when there is a period of: *(1)* several hours of dark or low light; *(2)* high humidity; and *(3)* temperatures in the correct range (70–75°F for rust on 'Merion'). Following penetration, infection is established with a day of high light intensity, warming temperatures, and sufficiently high humidity that the leaf dries slowly.

An infection is localized. The orange fruiting pustule erupts at the site of the infection. If the infected area is cut off, the fruiting body is not seen, i.e., does not spread spores. As 'Merion' is tolerant of close mowing, the simplest management attack on the disease has been to supply good levels of nitrogen and water to keep the grass growing vigorously, and to mow at 3/4 to 1 in. Under these conditions growth is mowed off rapidly enough that infections are removed before they fruit. The unsightly appearance is avoided and reinfection is reduced. This is an effective program on grass growing in the sun, but grass in the shade may suffer worse infection.

The effectiveness of nitrogen in this program is dependent on irrigation practice. With adequate water 2 lb of N/yr reduced rust. Without supplemental irrigation, 10 lb of N/yr did not reduce the incidence of rust.[29]

Underwood has observed 'Merion' orange with rust while adjacent common bluegrass was unharmed.[199] Plots planted 50:50, Merion: common showed almost no rust on the Merion. California sod growers also favor a 50:50 mix of Merion as it is relatively rust free. Underwood speculates that in the mixture the resistance factor from common is excreted and taken up by Merion roots.

The fungus causing rust on Merion is *Puccinia graminia* Pers. F. sp. *agrostis* Erikss.[25] Bluegrass varieties 'Prato' and 'Delft' are also susceptible to this fungus. 'Park' is resistant. 'Delta' and common are moderately resistant, and 'Newport' is immune to this particular rust (though not to other rusts).[24]

Zoysia has recently been attacked by a rust, *Puccinia zoysiae* Diet.[125,113] The rust appears on grass in the shade at seasons when temperatures are cool and *Zoysia* is no longer growing vigorously. If not controlled the rust can kill *Zoysia.*

Chemical control of rust is an economic problem because of large areas involved. Cycloheximide (Actidione) or Zineb have been used for rust control. Nickel-containing sprays have shown promise but results have been erratic.[100] Plantvax has given systemic control of striped rust, *Puccinia striiformis,* and a dichlorotetrafluoracetone has controlled several rust species; ethyl parathion an insecticide, has controlled *Puccinia lolii* used at 10 g/100 liters (ca 1 oz/80 gal).[42]

Winter crown rot. Caused by an unidentified basidiomycete, which infests red top, red and meadow fescues, and Kentucky bluegrass, winter crown rot is known only in the colder regions (Canada). While *Fusarium* patch and *Typhula* blight thrive best on an unfrozen soil beneath a snow blanket, winter crown rot is most severe on frozen ground unprotected by snow.[127] Both are favored by 80–90% rh and at 100% rh growth is checked.[35] Steam distillation of the hydrocyanic gas from plugs of grass can be used to identify the disease.[131] In a saprophytic phase, the fungus produces poisonous hydrocyanic gas. If an ice sheet or frozen soil surface is present, pockets of the gas accumulate and may kill grass which then serves as food for further growth.[128] Where the disease occurs, one should use a mercurial fungicide as a preventative winter spray program as described under *Typhula* blight.[207,128]

Marasmius and many other genera of Basidipmycetes cause *fairy ring.* A fairy ring in the grass is always interesting even though common. Rings may be from inches across to 1/2 mile in diameter.[132] Caused by a great variety of fungi, fairy rings may be minor and ephemeral appearing for a while after the first fall rains, or they may be a major problem. They seem a more serious problem in the cooler moister regions such as coastal areas. Fairy rings may appear in any kind of turf.

Shantz and Piemeisel[176] classified fairy rings in three types: Type I kills the grass or badly damages it. Type II only stimulates growth of the grass. Type III does not affect the grass and is only recognized by the seasonal appearance of the ring of mushrooms. Three zones are recognizable in a typical type I fairy ring and these are diagrammed in Figure 8.11. In the case of type II fairy rings, the ring of lush growth in the turf creates a lack of uniformity and implies that the rest of the grass is not growing as well as it might. Such fairy rings can sometimes be masked by nitrogen fertilizer.

In a type I fairy ring turf injury may be caused indirectly. Competition for water and nutrients can result in turf injury. In some cases the mat of mycelium may be so tight and dense that water and air penetration are limited. In such a case, regular aerification may relieve the problem, and as the mycelium may offer a hydrophobic surface, the use of a wetting agent may also assist water penetration. Fairy ring may infect the grass and cause direct damage. In laboratory cultures *Marasmius oreades* has penetrated roots and spread through the cortex of Kentucky bluegrass, red fescue, and colonial bentgrass.[67] In addition the mycelium of the fungus is cyanogenic and may injure or kill grass by producing cyanide in the soil.[66,68]

Fairy rings are difficult to control. A large mass of mycelium extends through a large soil volume and perhaps into plant tissues. It is

Figure 8.11 A type I fairy ring. The outside of the ring is on the left. The advancing mycelium in the soil releases ammonium compounds, stimulating growth of a deep green outside ring. Grass is dead or dry over the main body of the mycelium so a dead ring appears inside of the outside green ring. In this region the mycelium releases toxins and large amounts of ammonium, and results in a dry soil, all inhibitory of growth. As the old mycelium decays, released nutrients stimulate growth and a second stimulated region forms an inner ring. Inside the inner ring, growth is normal.

difficult to kill the entire fungal mass without missing some. If any is left, the ring has not been controlled, just slowed. Proposed methods are fumigation, drenching with fungicides, digging out the infected soil, and combinations of digging and drenching. There is no evidence of the methods being successful.

Lebeau and Hawn have proposed a method of control. Rings watered daily for a month till the soil was really soggy were controlled.[132]

Fungi Imperfecti

Fusarium nivale (Fr.) Snyder and Hansen. This causes *Fusarium* patch (pink snow mold). *Fusarium* patch occurs on bent, blue, and bermudagrasses and less frequently on fescue and ryegrasses.[36,48] *Fusarium* is active over a wide range of temperatures. Tests of a British strain showed an optimum near 68°F in the laboratory.[21] The fungus survived subfreezing temperatures, and was active from about 4°F to near 90°F. In the field the disease is more damaging in years when snow falls before the ground freezes.[45] This is explained by data of Lebeau that there is no infection at 32°F, but much grass is lost with soil temperatures under snow of 37 or 43°F.[127,129] The fungus is damaging at higher temperatures and causes damage with wet cold overcast. In San Francisco it was found to be the active organism in an attack of "dollar spot" with temperatures in the 60s. In England it occurred on high-nitrogen turf in August, *Fusarium* is in fact a year around problem in England of greater extent than is recognized.[119] Garrett proposes that with warm temperatures, antagonistic microorganisms are more active and the disease is suppressed.[83] At warmer temperatures the grass may outgrow any injury.[36]

In the northern part of the country *Fusarium* is found in a complex with *Typhula* blight (Fig. 8.10**b**). As *Typhula* needs the dark of a snow blanket, it disappears from the complex where there is less than 20–30 days of snow cover in the winter. Elsewhere *Fusarium* patch has been found complexed with *Rhizoctonia,*[150] *Curvularia, Helminthosporium,* or nematodes,[55] and *Fusarium* patch may be a complex of *Fusarium* spp.[45]

When the fungus is active, it may appear as orangish yellow spots of dead grass several inches to over a foot in diameter (Fig. 8.12). The ring is surrounded by a smoky gray ring where grass is dying and outside of that a ring of whitish and pink mycelium. As the grass dries the pink and gray rings disappear and after a day of sunshine the dead spot bleaches to a pale straw. A couple of sunny days will often halt an infection.

In tight, well-fertilized, low-cut turf rings of disease are sharply defined and may grow to over a foot in diameter. At lower fertility and higher cuts the circle is ragged, poorly defined, and may even escape notice if surrounding grass is tip burned by frost.

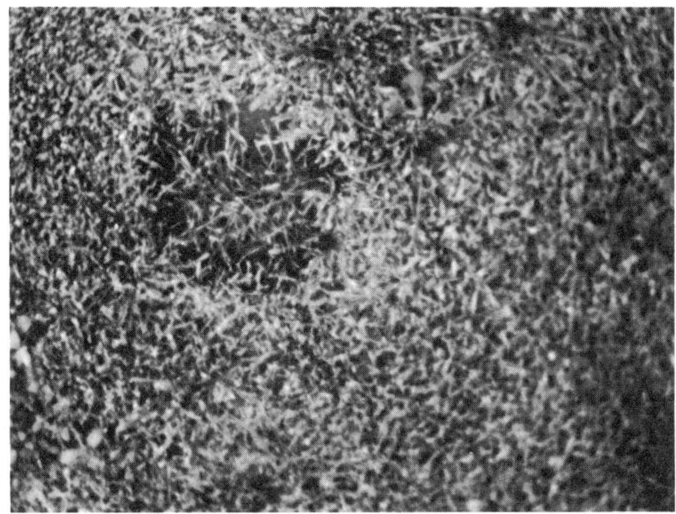

Figure 8.12 *Fusarium nivale.* A spot of *Fusarium* patch about 10 cm across that is active on bentgrass during cold wet weather.

Fusarium patch is favored by excess nitrogen fertilizer; by manure; by thatch (clipped leaves may carry dormant mycelium): and by straw mulches.[43,45,48] The latter have been used in the northeast to protect exposed grass. Mycelium of several species of *Fusarium* permeated every straw of an experimental mulch.[46] Iron appears to confer increased resistance, lime decreased resistance to *Fusarium* patch.[188] Bentgrass had less *Fusarium* patch when fertilized with urea than when fertilized with equivalent UF.[145]

Daily summer irrigation of bentgrass has increased *Fusarium* incidence the following winter. Weekly irrigations also increased *Fusarium* on Seaside as compared to twice weekly irrigations, but not on highland bentgrass. Highland had more *Fusarium* though when previous irrigation had been in the morning rather than the evening.[145]

Where *Fusarium* is a problem a preventative program is necessary. This is discussed under *Typhula.* Mercury sprays are specific.[36,98,94] In a thorough study at Washington State, organic mercurics were found generally superior to inorganic, and PMA was found the most reliable. [98] PMA is phytotoxic and has a short life; respraying every two weeks is therefore required for a preventative program. Burn was reduced by using 3/4 oz PMA in 10 gal/M rather than 5 gal. Additions of up to 2 oz of nitrate/M reduced phytotoxicity but more increased it. Cadmium compounds were less effective but resulted in a denser turf. Good control with minimum phytotoxicity could be obtained by alternating sprays of PMA and Caddy (1 oz of 20% in 5 gal/M). Smith found effectiveness of mercurous–mercuric choride at 2:1 improved with addition of 10% malachite green oxalate.

Fusarium roseum and *Fusarium* species. These cause *Fusarium* root rot. In his book Couch notes reports of *Fusarium* root rot on bentgrasses, red fescue, annual and perennial ryegrass, and annual and Kentucky bluegrasses. It was not then regarded as a serious disease. Endo has systematically isolated various fungi from grass roots and tested them for pathogenicity.[55] He found large numbers of *Fusarium* isolates, most of them pathogenic. He states that damage from *Fusarium* root rots is probably more widespread and more serious than is recognized. Gould found other species of *Fusarium* affecting turf when the weather became too warm for *F. nivale.*[93]

In 1963 Couch reported that a warm-weather disease of turfgrass on the eastern seaboard was found incited by *F. roseum.*[37,38] Several strains were isolated and all were found pathogenic. The fungus did not occur as a root rot but as a foliar fungus. Lesions originate at cut tips or on the leaf surface. An irregular dark green blotch fades to light green, reddish brown, tan, and finally white with a light brown margin. As the spot extends the width of the leaf, the leaf tip is cut off and yellows, and with many lesions the turf develops a yellow cast. In the crown rot stage light green patches 3–5 in. across may appear. If conditions remain favorable for the disease the spots enlarge, become reddish brown, then fade or bleach to light straw. The injury may appear as streaks, circles, or crescents, which may enlarge to 3-ft patches with a reddish border and green central patch, i.e., a frog eye. The large patches may coalesce and can kill large areas of turf within 10 to 14 days of first symptoms.[17] The disease has been found associated with *Helmintosporium sorokinianum, Pythium ultimum, Sclerotinia homeocarpa,* and *Fusarium tricinctum;* and with the weak pathogens *Alternaria, Penicillium,* and *Curvularia.*[38]

The disease has been observed as early as June and through August. The disease is aggravated by heat and drought, and is worst on south-facing slopes, along cement walks and drives, and in open areas where turf receives 12 to 14 hr of full sun. Optimum temperatures are 25–30°C with no activity above 35°C (95°F).[17]

The disease has infected bluegrasses, bentgrasses, and less severely, red fescue and 'Meyer' *Zoysia.* Of several bluegrass varieties tested, only 'Newport' was resistant to all isolates.

In laboratory tests the disease was more severe with high nitrogen, high fertility, or with low calcium. In the field hydrated lime has reduced severity of infections.

Couch got some control from Dithane M-45, but Bean used it without success. Weekly sprays of Dyrene, Difostan, and Tersan OM gave partial control for Bean, the Tersan OM being the most effective. The best control at the present would appear to be discontinuance of spring fertilizer applications and substitution of an application of lime. *Fusarium* blight looks like another disease of high maintenance.

Helminthosporium spp. This species causes melting out, zonate eyespot, helminth, *Helminthosporium* leaf spot, red leafspot, netblotch, *H.* blight, brown blight, and leaf blotch. *Helminthosporium* diseases affect most principal turfgrasses and share with *Rhizoctonia* the position of the most serious disease problem in the United States. Only in the northern tier of states from the Missouri River west to the Cascade Mountains are the *Helminthosporium* diseases of minor importance.

Whereas *Rhizoctonia* is most damaging to putting green turf, *Helminthosporium* is the foremost problem on home, school, and institutional turf. The disease is not reported on *Zoysia* or St. Augustinegrasses, and of the other grasses, colonial bent is little affected, bluegrasses and fescues the most.[52,55,154,160] The many bermudagrass varieties run the gamut of susceptibility with 'Tifway' and 'Royal Cape' among the most susceptible, 'Tifgreen' and 'Texturf 10' among the least susceptible grasses; helminth is a problem on overseeded ryegrass in the south.[160,210,211]

Of many species and strains of helminth *H. vagans, H. dictyloides,* and *H. sorokinianum* (*H. sativum*[142]) are most damaging to bluegrass.[18] *H. cynodontis, H. stenospilum, H. triseptatum, H. rostratum,* and *H. giganteum* may be found in any and all combinations as a disease complex on bermudagrass.[70] Helminth is also found in complexes with *Fusarium roseum,*[38] *Curvularia,*[123,156] *Pleosphaerulina,*[123] and, in the spring in dead spot complex. *H. cynodontis* occurs associated with bermudagrass mite in Arizona and California.[55]

There are regional differences in *Helminthosporium* disease. *H. vagans* is commonly found in the San Francisco bay region,[144] whereas on the southern California coast, where the climate is not too different, *H. sorokinianum* is more common.[55] *H. cynodontis* is not damaging on bermudagrass in southern California, but in Arizona, with summer rains, *H. cynodontis* can be serious. Along the humid gulf coast it may limit usefulness of bermudagrass.[44]

Most helminth diseases are similar in that they have several aspects and are favored by warm weather, though the organism is apt to be present the year around. With cool temperatures, or with fluctuating relative humidity the disease appears as leaf spots in which a necrotic bleached spot is surrounded by a purplish ring.[210] With more favorable disease conditions, the spot cuts off the leaf and the tip browns, or the spot girdles the leaf sheath killing the entire leaf. Sheath girdling thins the entire turf without causing dead spots (melting out). With continuous high humidity and temperatures from 80 to 95°F, the infection spreads to the crown and into roots.[51,210] Blighting is favored by shady overcast,[139] high nitrogen,[29] close mowing,[189] or other factors that deplete carbohydrate reserves. Severity depends on inoculation potential. Thousands of spores per square foot are needed for a serious infection.[18] Spore germination and establishment is favored by guttation water.[58] There is reduced penetration of 'Merion' bluegrass leaves, which may be the basis for its resistance to helminth.[156] With blighting sudden collapse and drying of leaves occurs, and grass acquires a slaty gray cast. Patches to several feet in diameter may die. Final death may be hastened or caused by desiccation following root injury. The most severe infections have occurred in either very wet or very dry soil.[210] Severe damage results when a period of wet overcast is followed by bright sun and drought. The wet period promotes spread of the disease and the following dry period stresses weakened plants so damage and death are increased. Where desiccation is a factor, syringing may keep turf alive until root activity is restored.

Cheesman and Roberts used solution culture to study *H. vagans* and found the highest infection with high nitrogen and low water stress.[29] In another study a good level of nitrogen fertility assisted recovery.[170] With low nitrogen there were five times as many infections and they resulted in death, while with 2 lb of slow-release nitrogen per 1000 ft^2 there was good recovery from injury. In a study by Elliott,[53] added fertilizer increased yield without increasing the number of infections so there was a lowered percentage of diseased tissue. In general, nitrogen promotes disease with overcast, and recovery with sunshine.

Course of the disease may also be affected by previous use of herbicides or insecticides.[169] Recovery from the disease has been more rapid on sandy soils than on heavier soils.[216]

Where clippings are left, Weiling et al. think they may contribute to continuous high humidity leading to crown rot.[210] On bluegrass, Williams and Schmidt[213] found clipping removal made no difference on grass mowed at 2 in. In the case of grass mowed at 1 in., there was less loss from *Helminthosporium* when clippings were removed. In England where temperatures remain below the optimum for helminth, the disease becomes serious only when bluegrass is mowed 1/2 in. or less.[189]

Endo notes that *H. sorokinianum* is seed borne on blue and bentgrass seed[57] and Muhle finds *H. vagans* on bluegrass seed.[157] Control should begin in the leaf-spotting stage with sprays every two weeks while the weather is favorable to the disease.

Various workers have listed the following among effective fungicides: (Those that have rated well in one test, however, are likely to have rated poorly in another test, in another year, or at another station.) Actidione, Kromad, Omadine, Captan, Terramycin, Dyrene, PCNB, Actidione RZ,[210,191] and Actidione-thiram, with control from mercurials being erratic and causing injury to bluegrass. On bermudagrass preferred controls include PMA, PCNB, Panogen, Emmi, and Memmi;[75] also Dithane M-45, Daconil 2787, Ortho Lawn and Turf.[23]

Lukens recommends a drench of Dyrene using 100 oz/M as giving control for 11 weeks.[139] Couch suggests that 2–4 oz/M of Kromad, 4–6 oz/m of Captan, or 200 g/M of Omadine results in more grass and better control of disease than some of the phytotoxic chemicals.[40] In preliminary trials Bean has found 3% DMSO (dimethyl sulfoxide) to increase activity of Dyrene and Dithane M-45 (30% against *Helminsthosporium*).[16] Across the country Gould finds that for leaf blights, mercury sprays give best control, Panogen rating highest. Carbamates gave an intermediate rating, cadmium compounds low. For foot rot, all did less well with mercury and Dyrene rated best.[95]

Gloeocercospora sorghi D. Bain and Edg. This causes copper spot and zonate leaf spot. A minor disease able to severely injure the bentgrasses, copper spot produces a pink spot. In size of spot, season of appearance, control measures, etc., it is similar to dollar spot and the two sometimes appear together. Cadmium and mercury sprays control[49] and organic compounds give poor response (see under dollar spot).

Other Fungal Diseases

Spring dead spot. This appears to be a management disease without a specific pathogen but to which a number of fungi may contribute. The only fungus consistently found is a species of *Helminthosporium.*[204] *H. spiciferum, Pythium, Ophiobolus,*[185] *Curvularia,*[150] and *Fusarium*[38,204] are species commonly found in the complex. Spring dead spot was present in the lower midwest as early as 1936 but became a recognized problem in 1956. The disease occurs on *C. dactylon, C. transvaalensis,* and varieties, such as 'U-3,' 'Tiffine,' 'Tiffgreen,' 'Tifway,' 'Tiflawn,' 'Sunturf,' and 'Texturf IF'; it has also been reported on 'Emerald' *Zoysia.*[198,204] It is most severe on the hybrid bermudas.

In the lower south, spring dead spot is not a problem; slightly further north it is worse on greens turf. Still further north more greens are of bentgrass and principal damage is to fairway and lawn turf.

There is no recognition of the area in the fall, but when new growth starts in the spring, grass fails to grow on patches several inches to several feet across. Grass in the area is dead and rhizomes and roots are black. The disease does not move out on the periphery of the spot the following year. The spot is not recolonized by grass for a year or more and the patch is host to weeds.[212] Associated with high disease incidence are maintenance practices such as close mowing, high nitrogen fertilization, and traffic which compacts the soil. Thatch is considered to contribute significantly to the problem as the disease does not occur on new turf but only on turf older than three or four years when thatch has begun to accumulate. Wet spots are likely to be damaged and disease is favored by warm spells in the spring which initiate growth and are then followed by cold snaps.[198]

At the present there is no control. Dieldren has reduced the disease in some areas, not others.[203] Nabam used in the fall in August, September, and October does not control but hastens recolonization of damaged areas the following spring.[183,184,150]

Damping off (seedling disease). Young seedlings are susceptible to diseases and may be readily killed by fungi that are unable to infect older plants. The fungi often girdle the seedling at the soil level. They are soil-borne fungi and include species of *Pythium, Phytophthora, Fusarium,* and *Rhizoctonia.* Uniform irrigation would assist greatly in control of the disease. When a seeded area dries unevenly one faces a dilemma. If one irrigates for the benefit of the dry areas the moist areas are too wet and damping off is favored. If one waits till all of the area is dry, drought kills seedlings in the drier areas. Drying the soil surface once a day is of great value in breaking up surface mycelium.

Readily available phosphorus and nitrogen in the seedbed is of importance for rapid establishment and maturing of the seedlings. Seeding at lower rates assists in more rapid establishment and allows more ventilation through the grass. Treatment of the seed will also assist in preventing seedling infection. Orthocide,[117] Semesan, Thiram, Ceresan, and Chloranil among others may be used for seed treatment.*
Fumigation of the soil is a control method that often has value but soil fumigation should be of the finished seedbed. When the competition between fungi is reduced by fumigation, an introduced disease can run wildfire through the area. Treated seed should be used on fumigated soil and dirty tools and equipment should be kept out of the seedbed.

Sowing seed in the proper season may help reduce damping off. Some of the most damaging organisms are hot-weather types. Seeds sown

*Semesan, Ceresan, and other mercurials are used to treat *seed-borne* diseases with some possible loss in germinability. Captan, Thiram, and other organic fungicides are usually used to treat seed for *soil-borne* seedling diseases.

in the fall and early spring escape the heat and do not need sprinkling several times a day as seeds sown in June often do. If one starts a fall seeding with the soil well irrigated, the seedling grass will need less water than is often thought. The seedling root will be exploring soil at, or near, field capacity even though the surface is dry. Under such conditions a sprinkle every other day may be quite sufficient depending on the soil and temperature.

Piricularia grisea (Cke.) Sacc. (gray leaf spot of St. Augustinegrass). Southern Florida, that cut-off northern outpost of the West Indies, not only evolved its own turfgrass, St. Augustinegrass, but evolved an insect to feed on it, lawn chinch bug, and a disease to infect it, gray leaf spot.

Gray leaf spot is a primary pathogen of St. Augustine but is a minor disease until St. Augustine is brought under high maintenance. With high nitrogen the disease increases to over 100% and with rain and high relative humidity in the summer it becomes highly destructive.[147] Spots may be from 2 mm to 2 cm long and with more than thirty lesions per blade when the grass dies. The fungus causes collapse of the mesophyll and appearance of a depressed blue-gray spot with a brown margin. There may also be marginal chlorosis.[75] On a new planting Freeman recorded a rate of cover of unsprayed grass that was only 65% of that sprayed weekly.[74] Crabgrass and bermudagrass are also hosts for the disease.[147]

Cercospora leaf spot may also be found on St. Augustine but produces smaller, rounder, darker spots, 1/2–3 mm in size and dark brown to purple in color.[71]

Thiram is used at 4 oz/M for control of gray leaf spot.

Yellow tufts. Yellow tufts was first described by Oakley in 1924 and it still is not fully characterized.[161] It generally occurs on bent or bermudagrass during cool seasons. A tuft of innovations from one crown is yellowish and the condition is persistent for several weeks, then disappears with new growth. The condition has not responded to fertilizer or iron. Tarjan and co-workers found it associated with the presence of nematodes feeding between the sheath and leaf of the grass[197] (Chap. 7). On bermudagrass in Africa the condition was found to result from an upset metabolism at certain temperatures which resulted in formation and accumulation of allantoin in the leaves.[14] Allantoin is toxic. (This suggests a lead to be explored in studying spring dead spot.)

A physiological yellowing of bluegrass often occurs in the fall. Grass on compacted areas that has been suffering during the summer may appear green in the fall while adjacent grass produces yellowed leaves that can be greened with iron sprays. The behavior suggests that with cool soils there is a decrease in iron uptake by mass flow, and that point contact uptake is inadequate except in the denser soil.

Curvularia lunata (Curvularia). Several species of *Curvularia* are ubiquitous on turf as saprophytes with the capability of being weakly pathogenic.[114] They are not normally primary pathogens but have been noted throughout the chapter as occurring in complexes with other pathogens such as *Fusarium roseum,*[38] *Helminthosporium,*[123,156] *Pythium,*[204] etc. On occasion *Curvularia* may be part of the complex I call management disease. In one example I have seen heavily thatched bentgrass showing a disease which appeared as arcs or rings of discolored grass (Fig. 8.7). Over several seasons the only pathogenic fungus consistently isolated from the turf was *Curvularia.* When thatch was controlled the disease disappeared.

At this state of our knowledge I should say that *Curvularia* is a fungus which is unable to cause disease on turf except when it has help, either from other fungi or from man.

Mycorrhiza. Some roots are colonized by fungi in a relation which may be noninjurious and in some instances is beneficial in aiding mineral uptake. *Endogone* has been observed to colonize bentgrass roots at certain seasons, and on blue and ryegrasses species of *Mucorales* and *Fusarium* and other imperfect fungi have been found colonizing. They are not in the soil but at the surface.[82]

New diseases. We may reasonably expect to find other diseases attacking turf. *Fusarium roseum* has only been recognized since 1963, for example, and within the same period Britton and Rogers have found bentgrass roots infected with *Olpidium brassicae* and with *Polymixa graminis.*[26]

Other Diseases

I have considered a number of leaf spot and other diseases as being minor at this writing, and for those and for diseases of flower and seed the reader is referred to more complete treatments as given by Couch[36] or Sprague[192] et al.

DISEASE PRACTICUM

The first step in the practical manager's program is to avoid, in so far as possible, creating conditions which favor disease, and to eliminate such conditions where they exist. Drain low wet pockets of soil. Important and heavily trafficked areas should receive good light and ventilation, and such shade as occurs should be high open shade. Use grass varieties which are the best adapted for the region, and when a variety is available with proven resistance to important diseases of the region, choose it. Some of the worst disease problems occur in the transition zone where summer temperatures are too high for temperate-season grasses and too low for the rest of the year for good performance by the subtropical grasses.

Treat seed to control seed-borne diseases. Plant seed at lighter rates to avoid crowding and when up, mow the grass often enough to allow ventilation through the turf. Plant seed during the most favorable season. The seedbed should contain phosphorus and nitrogen fertilizers to assure rapid establishment. Once the grass is up it should be watered as needed and spot watered on areas that dry fast. On mature stands of grass, mow at appropriate heights. Use a modest, balanced fertilizer program and avoid applying fertilizer when cloudiness, heat, wet, or cold would result in soft or disease susceptible growth. As the weather cools, the fertilizer level may be increased during weather favoring dollar spot; this will also aid in recovery from fall aeration, verticutting, or thatch removal. Fertility level can then be allowed to drop before winter snow or rains start. Management practices which could be deleterious should be avoided at critical times of the year. For example, lowering the height of cut or spraying with an herbicide should not be done during a heat spell.

A preventative spray program should be employed on fine turf. When spraying greens, include collars and aprons. The manager should anticipate diseases expected at each time of year. He should know the specific recommendation for the diseases and should either have an adequate stock of fungicide for a control program or be sure that adequate stocks are readily available from his supplier. Spray equipment should be available and in working order.

In addition to adequate supplies of fungicide the store room should have rubber gloves, goggles, respirators, and other appropriate protective clothing, and the men should have been trained in their use and importance. Spray equipment should be calibrated as to its rate of delivery, and the exact area of principal turf swards should be known.

There is a choice of preventative programs. If a manager is thoroughly familiar with a particular disease, the preventative spray can be with a fungicide specific for the disease. Alternatively, the preventative spray can be a broad spectrum spray designed to cover all contingencies. This is more expensive and could result in reducing the antagonists of a disease. A broad-spectrum program recommended by Endo is given on p. 246.

If fertilizer is being applied, a mixed product containing a fungicide is beneficial in a preventative program. Use of a mixed product just for control without need for the fertilizer would be a poor choice.

In the fall or spring when the grass is growing vigorously and disease is at a low level, attention should be given to thatch removal, scalping of puffy areas and, if necessary, spraying with herbicides. At other times, injury from these practices may predispose the turf to disease.

If algae and moss appear, attention should be given both to the watering program and to the improvement of light and ventilation by pruning or removing shrubs and trees.

Mowers should always be sharp, as a dull mower predisposes grass to disease.

A management program should be flexible. If there are several days of overcast and the amount of grass in the catcher begins to fall off, or if the yield drops for any reason, reduce the mowing to assist in rebuilding vigor. Change the irrigation practice with the season. Change fertilization programs according to the season and to the diseases expected. Don't depend on the calendar alone. Look at the grass, look at the sky, and use an appropriate program.

When disease strikes, study symptoms to make sure the disease appearing is the disease expected. If it is not recognized, a sample should

Figure 8.13 Because of poor turning practices, the weakened grass at the edge of the green is often the first place to show disease symptoms. In this picture both collar and green edge show injury.

be sent at once to a laboratory for identification. A plug is cut from the edge of the infection, wrapped in waxed paper (do not use a polyethylene bag for disease samples), and sent. Mail the sample so it will arrive on a working day. If you are not sure of the disease, use a broad-spectrum spray. Note differences between the diseased and adjacent nondiseased areas and see if you can discover clues to a better program of management. Wash off early morning guttation water, and check to see that mowers are correctly used (no skidding, turns, etc.) (Fig. 8.13). Mow from healthy turf to diseased turf, then wash the mower.

If the soil is wet and grass is still wilting, aerify and leave the holes open to help dry out the soil, and syringe the grass leaves to keep turf from wilting. Usually, any changes in the weather will work in favor of the superintendent. If a time comes when all practices are sound and there is still no abatement of the disease, a dry application of fungicide may be helpful. Thoroughly mix 2–4 oz of a mercurous–mercuric chloride fungicide in 1/4–1/3 yd of fine sand for every 1000 ft^2 of turf, and spread it on the turf. The mercury vaporizes and may penetrate areas that the fungicidal spray was not reaching. If white sand is used the reflectance can reduce temperatures a degree or two and increase the reflected light on the leaves.

Control must be followed by recovery and so the grass must be kept growing well, since the only recovery is by regrowth of grass over the area.

References

1. Adams, P. B., and F. L. Howard, 1963, "Residual control of grey *(Typhula)* snow mold of bentgrass," *Golf Course Reptr.* **31**(5), 20–22.
2. Adams, W. E., and M. Twersky, 1960, "Effect of soil fertility on winter killing of 'Coastal' bermudagrass," *Agron. J.* **52,** 325.
3. Alexander, M., 1963–64, "Ecology of soil microorganisms," *The Cornell Plantations* **19**(4), 58–60.
4. Allen, T. C., Jr., and A. H. Freiberg, 1964, "Symmetrical dichlorotetrafluoroacetone, a synthetic organic rust chemotherapeutant," *Phytopathology* **54,** 580–583.
5. Allred, S. E., and A. J. Ohlrogge, 1964, "Principles of nutrient uptake from fertilizer bands. VI. Germination and emergence of corn as affected by ammonia and ammonium phosphate," *Agron. J.* **56,** 309–313.
6. Altman, J., 1965, "Nitrogen in relation to turf diseases," *Golf Course Rptr.* **33**(5), 16–30.
7. Anderson, E. J., 1966, "1, 3-Dichloropropane, 1, 2-dichloropropane mixture found active against *Pythium arrhenomanes* in field soil," *Down to Earth* **22**(3), 23.
8. Anonymous, 1952, "Plant diseases—two diseases of turf," *Agric. Gaz. NSW.* **63,** 200–203.

9. Anonymous, 1962, "Ophiobolus patch disease," Grass Research, New South Wales, June 1962, as reported in *J. Sports Turf Res. Inst.* **38,** 467–468 (1963).
10. Antipov, V. G., 1959, "Gas resistance of lawn grasses, (in Russian), *Bot. Zurnal* **44,** 990–2. Cited by Gould.
11. Ashworth, L. J., Jr., B. C. Langley, and W. H. Thames, Jr., 1964, "Long-term inhibition of *Rhizoctonia solani* by a nematocide, 1,2-dibromo-3-chloropropane," *Phytopathology* **54,** 187–191.
12. Atkins, J. G., 1952, "Forage crop *Rhizoctonia* cross inoculation tests (Abstr.)," *Phytopathology 42,* 282.
13. Bachelder, S. and R. E. Engel, 1963, "1962 Turf fungicide trials," *Park Maint.* **16**(4), 38–44.
14. Badenhuizen, N. P., and E. N. Lawson, 1962, "Lethal synthesis in *Cynodon dactylon* growing in southern Africa," *Am. J. Botany* **49,**158–167.
15. Bain, D. C., 1964, "Sclerotinia blight on nutgrass in Mississippi," *Plant Disease Reptr.* **48,** 742.
16. Bean, G. A., 1965, "The use of dimethyl sulfoxide (DMSO) with certain fungicides for controlling *Helminthosporium* diseases of Kentucky bluegrass," *Plant Disease Reptr.* **49,** 810–811.
17. Bean, G. A., 1966, "Observations and studies on *Fusarium* blight disease of turfgrass," *Phytopathology* **56,** 583 (abstr.); see also *The Golf Supt.* **34**(10), 32 ff.
18. Bean, G. A., and R. D. Wilcoxson, 1964, *Helminthosporium* leaf spot of bluegrass. Pathogenicity of three species of *Helminthosporium* on roots of bluegrass," *Phytopathology* **54,** 1065–1070.
19. Beard, J. B., 1965, "Bentgrass (*Agrostis* spp.) varietal tolerance to ice cover injury," *Agron. J.* **57,** 513.
20. Beard, J. B., 1966, "Winter Injury," *The Golf Supt.* **34**(1), 24–30.
21. Bennett, F. T., 1933, "Fusarium species of British cereals," *Ann. Appl. Biol.* **20,** 272–290.
22. Bloom, J. R., and H. B. Couch, 1960, "Influence of environment on disease of turfgrasses. I. Effect of nutrition, pH, and soil moisture on *Rhizoctonia* brown patch."
23. Boyle, A. E., and A. D. Davidson, 1966, "Control of summer blight in common bermuda," *Univ. Arizona Agri. Expt. Sta. Rept.* **240,** 13–14.
24. Britton, M. P., and J. D. Butler, 1965, "Resistance of seven Kentucky bluegrass varieties to stem rust," *Plant Disease Reptr.* **49,** 708–710.
25. Britton, M. P., and G. B. Cummings, "Subspecific identity of the stem rust fungus of 'Merion bluegrass," *Phytopathology* **49,** 287–289.
26. Britton, M. P., and D. P. Rogers, 1963, "*Olpidium brassicae* and *Polymorpha graminis* in roots of creeping bent in golf putting greens," *Mycologia* **55,** 758–763.
27. Callahan, L., R. Ilnicki, and R. Engel, 1964, "Phenoxy compounds and turf injury," *U.S. Golf Assoc., Record* **2**(2), 12–13.
28. Carroll, J. C., 1943, "Effects of drought, temperature and nitrogen on turfgrasses," *Plant Physiol.* **18,** 19–36.

29. Cheesman, J. H., E. C. Roberts, and L. H. Tiffany, 1965, "Effects of nitrogen and osmotic pressure of the nutrient solution on incidence of *Pucinnia graminis* and *Helminthosporium sativum* infection in 'Merion' Kentucky bluegrass," *Agron. J.* **57,** 599–602; see also *Golf Course Reptr.* **32**(5), 18–20.
30. Chevalier, L., 1960, "Comportement du *Cynodon dactylon* vis-a-vis d'un parasite *Ustilago cynodontis* (Pass.) P. Henn.," *Naturalia Monspel, Ser. Bot.* **12,** 3–12.
31. Christensen, J. J., and J. E. DeVay, 1955, "Adaptation of plant pathogen to host," *Ann. Rev. Plant Physiol.* **6,** 367–392.
32. Cochrane, V. W., 1958, *Physiology of Fungi.* John Wiley & Sons, Inc., New York, 524 pp.
33. Cook, R. N., R. E. Engel, and S. Bachelder, 1964, "A study of the effect of nitrogen carriers on turfgrass disease," *Plant Disease Reptr.* **48**(4), 254–255.
34. Corden, M. E. and R. A. Young, 1961, "Changes in soil microflora following treatment with fungicides," *Phytopathology* **51,** 64.
35. Cormack, M. W., and J. B. Lebeau, 1959, "Snowmold infection of alfalfa, grasses, and winter wheat by several fungi under artificial conditions," *Can. J. Botany* **37,** 685–693.
36. Couch, H. B., 1962, *Diseases of Turfgrasses,* Reinhold Book Corp., New York, 289 pp.
37. Couch, H. B., and E. R. Bedford, 1964, "Influence of nutrition and soil moisture on the development of *Fusarium* blight of turfgrasses," *Phytopathology* **54,** 890 (abstr.).
38. Couch, H. B., and E. R. Bedford, 1966, "*Fusarium* blight of turfgrass," *Phytopathology* **56,** 781–786.
39. Couch, H. B., and J. R. Bloom, 1960, "Influence of environment on diseases of turfgrasses. II. Effect of nutrition, pH and soil moisture on *Sclerotinia* dollar spot," *Phytopathology* **50,** 761–763.
40. Couch, H. B., and H. Cole, 1957, "Chemical control of melting-out of Kentucky bluegrass," *Plant Disease Reptr.* **41,** 205–208. see also *Golf. Course Reptr.* **25**(7), 5 ff.
41. Couch, H. B., L. D. Moore, and E. R. Bedford, 1962, "Chemical control of *Rhizoctonia* brown patch of bentgrass," *Phytopathology* **52,** 923 (abstr.).
42. Courtillot, M., 1965, "Effectiveness of parathion against ryegrass rust," (in French), *Compt. Rend., Acad. Agr. France* **51,** 223–228.
43. Dahl, A. S., 1928, "Snow molds," *U.S.G.A. Green Sect. Bull.* **8**(10), 148–200.
44. Dahl, A. S., 1929, "Zonate eyespot disease of turfgrass," *USGA Green Sect. Bull.* **9**(4), 71–75.
45. Dahl, A. S., 1929, "Results of snowmold work during winter of 1928," *USGA Green Sect. Bull.* **9**(8), 134–6.
46. Dahl, A. S., 1933, "Effect of temperature and moisture on occurrence of brownpatch," *USGA Green Sect. Bull.* **13**(3), 53–61.
47. Dahl, A. S., 1933, "Relationship between fertilizing and drainage in the occurrence of brownpatch," *Ibid.* **13**(5), 136–139.

48. Dahl, A. S., 1934, "Snowmold of turfgrasses as caused by *Fusarium nivale,*" *Phytopathology* **24,** 197–214.
49. Davis, S. H., Jr., S. Bachelder, and R. E. Engels, 1967, "Control of dollar spot, copper spot, and brown patch diseases from 1948 to 1963, with various fungicides and combinations," *N.J. Agr. Expt. Sta. Bull.* **816,** 99–107.
50. Dickinson, L. S., 1930, "The effect of air temperature on the pathogenicity of *Rhizoctonia solani* parasitizing grasses on putting green turf," *Phytopathology* **20,** 597–608.
51. Dosdall, L., 1923, "Factors affecting the pathogenicity of *Helminthosporium sativum,*" *Minn. Agr. Expt. Sta. Tech. Bull.* **17.**
52. Dreschler, C., 1930, "Leaf spot and foot rot of Kentucky bluegrass caused by *Helminthosporium vagans,*" *J. Agr. Res.* **39,** 129–135.
53. Elliott, E. S., 1962, "The effect of soil fertility on the development of Kentucky bluegrass diseases," *Phytopathology* **52,** 1218 (abstr.).
54. Elsaid, H. M., and V. B. Sinclair, 1962, "Adapted tolerance to organic fungicides by an isolate of *Rhizoctonia solani,*" *Phytopathology* **52,** 731 (abstr.).
55. Endo, R. M., 1961, "Turfgrass diseases in southern California," *Plant Disease Reptr.* **45,** 869–873; see also *Calif. Turfgr. Cult.* **10**(3), 22.
56. Endo, R. M., 1963, "Influence of temperature on rate of growth of five fungus pathogens of turfgrass and on rate of disease spread," *Phytopathology* **53,** 857–861.
57. Endo, R. M., 1964, "Turfgrass disease situation in California in 1963," *Golf Course Reptr.* **32**(5), 27–30.
58. Endo, R. M., 1967, "The role of guttation fluid in fungal disease development," *Calif. Turfgr. Cult.* **17**(2), 12–13.
59. Endo, R. M., and A. H. McCain, 1961, "Fungus diseases of turfgrass and their control," *Calif. Turfgr. Cult.* **11**(2), 9.
60. Endo, R. M., and A. H. McCain, 1965, "Fungal diseases in "California: their nature, factors influencing their development and their control," *Calif. Turfgr. Cult.* **15,**17–24.
61. Endo, R. M., and R. H. Macher, 1962, "Induction of fungal infection structures by guttation fluid," *Phytopathology* **52,** 731 (abstr.).
62. Endo, R. M., I. Malca, and E. M. Krausman, 1964, "Degeneration of the apical meristem and apex of bentgrass roots by a fungal toxin," *Phytopathology* **54,** 1175–1176.
63. Endo, R. M., and J. J. Oertli, 1963, "Stimulation of fungal infection of bentgrass," *Nature* **201,** 313.
64. Erwin, L. E., 1941, "Pathogenicity and control of *Corticium fuciforme,*" *Rhode Island Agr. Expt. Sta. Bull.* **278.**
65. Ferguson, A. E., 1966, "Winter injury north of the 49th," *The Golf Supt.* **34**(8), 38–39.
66. Filer, T. H., 1965, "Damage to turfgrasses caused by cyanogenic compounds produced by *Marasmius oreades,* a fairy ring fungus," *Plant Disease Reptr.* **49,**571–574.
67. Filer, T. H., 1965, "Parasitic aspects of a fairy ring fungus, *Marasmius oreades,*" *Phytopathology* **55,** 1132–1134.

68. Filer, T. H., 1966, "Effect on grass and cereal seedlings of hydrogen cyanide produced by mycelium and sporophores of *Marasmius oreades,*" *Plant Disease Reptr.* **50,** 264–266.
69. Fitts, O. B., 1924, "Early morning watering as an aid to brown patch control," *USGA Green Sect. Bull.* **4**(7), 159.
70. Freeman, T. E., 1957, "A new *Helminthosporium* disease of bermudagrass," *Plant Disease Reptr.* **32,** 38–44.
71. Freeman, T. E., 1959, "A leafspot on St. Augustine caused by *Cercospora fusimaculaus,*" *Phytopathology 49,* 160–161.
72. Freeman, T. E., 1960, "Effects of temperature on cottony blight of ryegrass," *Phytopathology* **50,** 575 (abstr.).
73. Freeman, T. E., 1963, "Age of ryegrass in relation to damage by *Phythium aphanidermatum,*" *Plant Disease Reptr.* **47,** 844.
74. Freeman, T. E., 1963, "Grey leafspot reduces coverage rate of St. Augustine," *Florida Turfgr. Bull.* **10**(1), 6–7.
75. Freeman, T. E., 1964, "Influence of nitrogen on severity of *Piricularia grisea,* infection of St. Augustine grass," *Phytopathology* **54,** 1187–1189.
76. Freeman, T. E., 1966, "Turf disease research 1965–66," *Univ. Florida Turfgr. Management Proc.* **14,** 159–161.
77. Freeman, T. E., and G. C. Horn, 1963, "Reaction of turfgrass to attack by *Pythium aphanidermatum,*" *Plant Disease Reptr.* **47,** 425–427.
78. Freeman, T. E., and G.C. Horn, 1967, "*Pythium* fungicides," *Golf Supt.* **35** (2), 58 ff.
79. Freyman, S., and V. C. Brink, 1965, "Low temperature injury of turfgrass," *Ann. N.W. Turfgr. Conf. Proc.* **19,** 32–38.
80. Freyman, S., and V. C. Brink, 1966, "Ice sheet injury to turf," *Ann. N.W. Turfgr. Conf. Proc.* **20,** 64 ff.
81. Freyman, S., and V. C. Brink, 1967, "Nature of ice-sheet injury to alfalfa," *Agron. J.* **59,** 557-560.
82. Gadgil, P. D., 1965, "Distribution of fungi on living roots of certain *Gramineae* and the effect of root decomposition on soil structure," *Plant and Soil* **22,** 239–259.
83. Garrett, S. D., 1956, *Biology of Root-Infecting Fungi,* Cambridge Univ. Press, 252 pp.
84. Gaskin, T. A., 1964, "Effect of pre-emergence crabgrass herbicide on rhizome development in Kentucky bluegrass," *Agron J.* **56,** 340–342.
85. Gaskin, T. A., 1965, "Varietal reaction of *Agrostis stolonifera* to stripe smut," *Plant Disease Reptr.* **49,** 286.
86. Gaskin, T. A., and M. P. Britton, 1962, "The effect of powdery mildew on the growth of Kentucky bluegrass," *Plant Disease Reptr.* **46,** 724–725.
87. Gaskin, T. A., and J. A. Simmons, 1966, "Chemical control of stripe smut on Kentucky bluegrass," *Agron. Abstr.,* p. 38.
88. Godfrey, G. H., 1925, "Experiments on the control of brownpatch with chlorophenol mercury," *USGA Green Sect. Bull.* **5**(4), 83–87.
89. Goss, R. L., 1966, "Turfgrass research in the Pacific Northwest," *Midwest Regional Turf Foundn. Turfgr. Conf. Proc.* pp. 9–12.
90. Goss, R. L., and C. J. Gould, 1967, "Some interrelationships between fer-

tility levels and *Ophiobolus* patch disease in turfgrasses," *Agron. J.* **59,** 149–151.

91. Gould, C. J., 1963, "How climate affects our turfgrass diseases," *Ann. N.W. Turfgr. Conf. Proc.* **17,** 29–43.
92. Gould, C. J., 1963, "Current research on control of turfgrass diseases at the Western Washington Experiment Station," *Ibid.*, p. 43.
93. Gould, C. J., 1963, "Some practical aspects of disease control," *Golf Course Reptr.* **31**(5), 66–71.
94. Gould, C. J., 1964, "Turfgrass disease problems in North America," *Golf Course Reptr.* **32**(5), 36.
95. Gould, C. J., 1966, "Use of Fungicides in controlling turfgrass diseases," *Golf Supt.* **34**(10), 19 ff.
96. Gould, C. J., R. L. Goss, and M. Eglitis, 1963, "*Ophiobolus* patch disease of turf," *Golf Course Reptr.* **31**(5), 58–62.
97. Gould, C. J., R. L. Goss, and M. Eglitis, 1961, "*Ophiobolus* patch disease of turf in western Washington," *Plant Disease Reptr.* **45,** 296–7.
98. Gould, C. J., R. L. Goss, and V. L. Miller, 1961, "Fungicidal tests for control of *Fusarium* patch disease on turf," *Plant Disease Reptr.* **45,** 112–118.
99. Gould, C. J., R. L. Goss, and V. L. Miller, 1966, "Effect of fungicides and other materials on control of *Ophiobolus* patch disease on bentgrass," *J. Sports Turf Res. Inst.* **42,** 41–48.
100. Hardison, J. R., 1963, "Commercial control of *Pucinnia striiformis* and other rusts in seed crops of *Poa pratensis* by nickel fungicides," *Phytopathology* **53,** 209–216.
101. Hardison, J. R., 1966, "Systemic activity of two derivatives of 1.4-oxathiin against smut and rust diseases of bluegrass," *Plant Disease Reptr.* **50,** 624.
102. Hardison, J. R., 1966, "Chemotherapy of *Urocystis agropyri* in 'Merion' Kentucky bluegrass (*Poa pratensis* L.) with two derivatives of 1,4-oxathiin," *Crop Sci.* **6,** 384.
103. Hardison, J. R., 1967, "Systemic fungicides for stripe smut," *Weeds, Trees, Turf* **6**(5), 28–30.
104. Hardison, J. R., and W. S. Anderson, 1965, "effects of symmetrical dichlorotetrafluoroacetone on rust control, yield and germination of seed of *Poa pratensis* L.," *Phytopathology* **55,** 1337–1364.
105. Halisky, P. M., C. R. Funk, and S. Bachelder, 1966, "Stripe smut of turf and forage grasses, its prevalence, pathogenicity, and response to management practices," *Plant Disease Reptr.* **50,** 294–298.
106. Halisky, P. M., C. R. Funk, and S. Bachelder, 1966, "Stripe smut attacks 'Merion' bluegrass," *Weeds, Trees, Turf* **5**(12), 8–9.
107. Halisky, P. M., C. R. Funk, and S. Bachelder, 1966, "Occurence and pathogenicity of *Helminthosporium sativum* in the Rutgers turf plots in 1964 and 1965," *N. J. Agr. Expt. Sta. Bull.* **816**, 72–75.
108. Heald, F. D., 1943, *Introduction to Plant Pathology,* McGraw-Hill Book Co. Inc., New York, 603 pp.

109. Healy, M. J., M. P. Britten, and J. D. Butler, 1965, "Stripe smut damage on 'Pennlu' creeping bentgrass," *Plant Disease Reptr.* **49,** 710.
110. Hearn, J. H., 1943, "*Rhizoctonia solani* Kuhn and the brown patch disease of grass," *Proc. Texas Acad. Sci.* **26,** 41–42.
111. Hill, A. C., M. R. Pack, M. Treshow, R. J. Downs, and L. G. Transtrum, "Plant Injury induced by ozone," *Phytopathology* **51,** 356–363.
112. Holt, E. C., 1963, "Control of large brown patch on St. Augustinegrass," *Golf Course Reptr.* **31**(5), 48–50.
113. Horn, G. C., 1965, "Diagnosing turf diseases," *Univ. Florida Turfgr. Management Conf. Proc.,* **13,** 95–97.
114. Howard, F. L., and M. E. Davies, 1953, "*Curvularia* 'fading-out' of turfgrasses," *Phytopathology* **43,** 109 (abstr.).
115. Iglauer, E., 1964, "Fifteen thousand quarts of air," *The New Yorker.* **40**(3), 54 ff.
116. Jacklin, A. W., 1962, "Turf management, maintenance fertilization," *Ann. N.W. Turfgr. Conf. Proc.* **16,** 79–81.
117. Jackson, N., 1959, "Seed dressing trials, 1958," *J. Sports Turf Res. Inst.* **9,** 455–458.
118. Jackson, N., 1959, "*Ophiobolus* patch disease fungicide trial, 1958," *Ibid.,* 459–461.
119. Jackson, N., 1961, "Turf disease notes, 1960," *J. Sports Turf Res. Inst.* **10,** 171–175.
120. Jamalainen, E. A., 1949, "Overwintering of *Gramineae* plants and parasitic fungi. I. *Sclerotinia borealis* Bubak and Vlengel," *Mastaloust Aikakausk* **21,** 125–140; in *RAM* **30,** 45 (1951).
121. Kallio, A., 1966, "Chemical control of snow mold (*Sclerotinia borealis*) on four varieties of bluegrass *(Poa pratensis)* in Alaska," *Plant Disease Reptr.* **50,** 69–72.
122. Kerr, A., 1956a, "Some interactions between plant roots and pathogenic soil fungi," *Australian J. Biol. Sci.* **9,** 45–52.
123. Klomparens, W., 1955, "A study of *Helminthosporium sativum,* P. K. and B. as an unreported parasite of *Agrostis palustris,* Huds," PhD. Thesis, *Dissertation Abstr.* **15,** 951.
124. Kreitlow, K. W., and F. V. Juska, 1959, "Susceptibility of 'Merion' and other Kentucky bluegrass varieties to stripe smut *(Ustilago striiformis),*" *Agron. J.* **51,** 596–7.
125. Kreitlow, K. W., F. V. Juska, and R. T. Haard, 1965, "A rust on *Zoysia japonica* new to North America," *Plant Disease Reptr.* **45,** 185–186.
126. Leach, C. M., and M. Pierpoint, 1958, "*Rhizoctonia solani* may be transmitted with seed of *Agrostis tenuis,*" *Plant Disease Reptr.* **42,**2–10.
127. Lebeau, J. B., 1964, "Control of snowmold by regulating winter soil temperature," *Phytopathology* **54,** 693–696.
128. Lebeau, J. B., 1966, "Pathology of winter injured grasses and legumes in Western Canada," *Crop Sci.* **6,** 23–25.
129. Lebeau, J. B., 1967, "Recent advances in controlling winter injury to turfgrass," *Ann N.W. Turfgr. Conf. Proc.* **21,** 14–21.

130. Lebeau, J. B., 1967, "Soil warming and winter survival of turfgrasses," *J. Sports Turf. Res. Inst.* **43,** 5–11.

131. Lebeau, J. B., and W. M. Cormack, 1956, "A simple method for identifying snow mold damage on turf grasses," *Phytopathology* **46,** 298.

132. Lebeau, J. B., and E. J. Hawn, 1963, "A simple method for control of fairy rings caused by *Marasmius oreades,*" *Sports Turf Res. Inst.* **11**(39), 23–25.

133. Lebeau, J. B., and C. E. Logsdon, 1958, "Snow mold of forage crops in Alaska and Yukon," *Phytopathology* **48,** 148–150.

134. Letey, J., 1961, "Aeration, Compaction and Drainage," *Calif. Turfgr. Cult.* **11,** 17–21.

135. Letey, J., N. Welch, R. E. Pelishek, and J. Osborn, 1963, "Effect of wetting agents on irrigation of water repellent soils," *Calif. Turfgr. Cult.* **13**(1), 1–2.

136. Ludwig, R. A., 1957, "Toxin production by *Helminthosporium sativum* P. K. and B. and its significance in disease development," *Can. Botany* **35,** 291–303.

137. Ludwig, R. A., and A. W. Henry, 1944, "Studies on the microbiology of recontaminated sterilized soil in relation to its infestation with *Ophiobolus graminis* Sacc.," *Can. J. Res.* **21,** 343–350.

138. Lukens, R. J., 1965, "Urea, and effective treatment for stripe smut on *Poa pratensis,*" *Plant Disease Reptr.* **49**, 361.

139. Lukens, R. J., 1965, "Control of bluegrass foot rot disease with a single drench of fungicide," *Phytopathology* **55,** 708; see also "Low sugar disease "melts out" bluegrass," *Turf-grass Times* **3**(5), 1 ff (1968).

140. Lukens, R. J., and E. M. Stoddard. 1960, "Control of stripe smut on *Poa pratensis* with Nabam," *Plant Disease Reptr.* **44,** 672 pp.

141. Lukens, R. J., and E. M. Stoddard, 1961, "Wilt disease of golf greens and its control with nabam," *Phytopathology* **51,** 577 (abstr.); see also *USGA Green Sect. J.* **14**(4), 27–31.

142. Luttrell, E. S., 1955, "A taxonomic revision of *Helminthosporium sativum* and related species," *Am. J. Botany* **42,** 57–67.

143. McCain, A. H., and P. M. Halisky, 1962, "Infection of bermudagrass by *Ustilago cynodontes,*" *Phytopathology* **52,** 742 (abstr.).

144. McCain, A. H., T. G. Byrne, and M. R. Bell, 1965, "Melting out of bluegrass," *Calif. Turfgr. Cult.* **15**(4), 30–31.

145. Madison, J. H., L. J. Peterson, and T. K. Hodges, 1960, "Pink snowmold on bentgrass as affected by irrigation and fertilizer," *Agron. J.* **52,** 591–592.

146. Madison, J. H., 1961, "The effect of pesticides on turfgrass disease incidence," *Plant Disease Reptr.* **45**(1), 892–3.

147. Malca, M. I., and J. H. Owen, 1957, "The gray-leaf-spot disease of St. Augustinegrass," *Plant Disease Reptr.* **41,** 871–875.

148. Middleton, J. T., 1961, "Photochemical air pollution damage to plants," *Ann. Rev. Plant Physiol.* **12,** 431–448.

149. Miller, D. E., and W. C. Bunger, 1963, "Use of plastic covers in sweet corn production," *Agron. J.* **55,** 417–424.

150. Moncrief, J. B., 1968, "Enigma of spring dead spot," *USGA Green Sect. Rec.* **6**(1), 16–18.
151. Monteith, J., Jr., 1925, "The leaf spot of bluegrass," *USGA Green Sect. Bull.* **5,** 198–199.
152. Monteith, J., Jr., 1926, "The brown patch disease of turf; its nature and control," *USGA Green Sect. Bull.* **6,** 127–142.
153. Monteith, J., Jr., and A. S. Dahl, 1932, "Turf diseases and their control," *USGA Green Sect. Bull.* **12**(4), 87–187.
154. Moore, D., and H. B. Couch, 1961, "*Pythium ultimum* and *Helminthosporium vagans* as foliar pathogens of *Gramineae,*" *Plant Disease Reptr.* **45,** 616–19.
155. Moore, D., H. B. Couch, and J. R. Bloom, 1962, "Influence of pest infection air temp on *Pythium* blight of Highland bentgrass," *Phytopathology* **52,** 926 (abstr.).
156. Mowen, R. G., and R. L. Millar, 1963, "Histological relationships of *Helminthosporium vagans, H. sativum,* and *Curvularia lunata* in leaves of 'Merion' and common Kentucky bluegrass," *Phytopathology* **53,** 351.
157. Mühle, E., 1949, Möglichkeiten des Pflantzenschutzes in Grassamenbau," *Nachrbl. Dent. Pflanzenschutzdienst* (Berlin) **3,** 150–152; in *RAM* **30,** 274 (1951).
158. Muse, R. R. and H. B. Couch, 1965, "Influence of environment on diseases of turfgrass. IV. *Phytopathology* **55,** 507–510. Effect of nutrition and soil moisture on *Corticium* red thread," Phytopathology **55,** 507–510.
159. Myers, W. M., 1952, "Registration of varieties and strains of bluegrass *(Poa* spp.)," *Agron. J.* **44,** 155.
160. Nelson, R. R., and D. M. Kline, 1961, "The pathogenicity of certain species of *Helminthosporium* to species of the *Gramineae,*" *Plant Disease Reptr.* **45,** 644–648.
161. Oakley, R. A., 1924, "Mottled condition of bent turf," *Bull. of U.S. Golf Assoc.* **4,** 259.
162. Oswald, J. W., and B. R. Huston, 1953, "Host range and epiphytology of the cereal yellow dwarf disease," *Phytopathology* **43,** 309–313.
163. Papavizas, G. C., and C. B. Davey, 1961, "Saprophytic behavior of *Rhizoctonia* in soil," *Phytopathology* **51,** 693–699.
164. Park, D., 1967, "The importance of antibiotics and inhibiting substances," in A. Burges and F. Raw, Ed., *Soil Biology,* Academic Press, New York, pp. 435–448.
165. Piper, C. V., and H. S. Coe, 1919, "*Rhizoctonia* in lawns and pastures," *Phytopathology* **9,** 89–92.
166. Piper, C. V., and R. A. Oakley, 1921, "The brown patch disease of turf," *USGA Bull.* **1**(6), 112–15.
167. Radko, A. M., H. M. Griffin, L. Record, and R. E. Harman, 1963, "Winter-spring injury in the east," *USGA Green Sect. Rec.* **1**(2), 7–13.
168. Reuszer, H. W., 1962, "Axenic techniques in the determination of root functions and the interrelationships of microorganisms and plant roots,"

Soil Sci. **93,** 56–61.

169. Richards, L. T., 1957, "Effect of insecticides and herbicides applied to soil on the development of plant diseases," *Can. J. Plant Sci.* **37,** 196–204.
170. Roberts, E. C., 1963, "Relationships between mineral nutrition of turfgrass and disease susceptibility," *Golf Course Reptr.* **31**(5), 52–57.
171. Roberts, E. C., 1965, "What to expect from a nitrogen fertilizer," *Calif. Turfgr. Cult.* **15,** 1–5.
172 Roed, H., 1960, "*Sclerotinia borealis* Bub. and Vleng., a cause of winter injury to winter cereals and grains in Norway," *Acta Agr. Scand.* **10,** 74–82.
173. Rowell, J. B., 1951, "Observations on the pathogenicity of *Rhizoctonia solani* on bentgrasses," *Plant Disease Reptr.* **35,** 240–242.
174. Runnels, H. A., 1963, "Tests on dollar spot and snow mold," *Golf Course Reptr.* **31**(5), 42–44.
175. Schardt, A., 1925, "Brown patch control resulting from early morning work on greens," *Bull. U.S. Golf Assoc.* **5,** 254–5.
176. Shantz, H. L., and R. L. Piemeisel, 1917, "Fungus fairy rings in eastern Colorado and their effect on vegetation," *J. Agr. Res.* **11,** 191–245.
177. Sherwood, R. T., and C. G. Rindberg, 1962, "Production of a phytotoxin by *Rhizoctonia solani,*" *Phytopathology* **52,** 586–7.
178. Shurtleff, M. C., 1953a, "Susceptibility of lawn grasses to brown patch," *Phytopathology* **43,** 110 (abstr.).
179. Shurtleff, M. C., 1953b, "Factors that influence *Rhizoctonia* to incite turf brown patch," *Phytopathology* **43,** 484 (abstr.).
180. Shurtleff, M. C., 1955, "Control of turf brown patch," *Univ. Rhode Island Agr. Expt. Sta. Bull.* **328** (contrib. 862), 25 pp.
181. Sill, W. H., and R. J. Chin, 1959, "Kentucky bluegrass, *Poa pratensis L.,* a new host of the Bromegrass mosaic virus in nature," *Plant Disease Reptr.* **43,** 85.
182. Slana, L. and A. Boyle, 1964, "Resistance of bermudagrass (*Cynodon* spp.) to *Helminthosporium cynodontis* Marignoni," *Univ. Ariz. Agr. Expt. Sta. Reptr.* **219**; report on turfgrass research, pp. 29–41.
183. Small, W. A., 1964, "Spring dead spot of bermuda controlled by fungicidal treatment of the root-zone," *Agron. Abstr.,* p. 106.
184. Small, W. A., 1967, "Application of soil drench fungicides to large turf areas," *Agron. Abstr.,* p. 57.
185. Smith, A. M., 1965, "*Ophiobolus herpotrichus,* a cause of spring dead spot in couch turf," *Agr. Gaz. N.S.W.* **76,** 753–758.
186. Smith, J. D., 1955, "Fungi and turf diseases. Dollar spot disease," *J. Sports Turf Res. Inst.* **9**(31), 35–59.
187. Smith, J. D., 1956, "Fungi and turf diseases. VI.*Ophiobolus* patch disease," *J. Sports Turf Res. Inst.* **9**(32), 180–202.
188. Smith, J. D., 1959a, "The effect of lime application on the occurrence of *Fusarium* patch disease on forced *Poa annua* turf," *J. Sports Turf Res. Inst.* **9**(35), 467–470.

189. Smith, J. D., 1959b, "*Fungal Diseases of Turf Grasses,*" The sports Turf Research Institute, Bingley, Yorkshire, 90 p.
190. Smith, L. R., and L. J. Ashworth, Jr., 1964, "Effect of organic amendments and PCNB upon innoculum potential of *Rhizoctonia solani* in field soil," *Phytopathology* **54,** 626 (abstr.).
191. Smith, N. A., and G. Gayer, 1961, "Chemical control of Kentucky bluegrass leaf spot caused by *Helminthosporium vagans,*" *Quart. Bull. Mich. Agr. Expt. Sta.* **44,** 2.
192. Sprague, R., 1950, *Diseases of Cereals and Grasses in North America,* The Ronald Press Co., New York, 538 pp.
193. Stakeman, E. C., and J. G. Harrar, 1957, *Principles of Plant Pathology,* Ronald Press Co., New York, 549 pp.
194. Stevenson, I. L., 1956, "Antibiotic activity of actinomycetes in soil as demonstrated by direct observation technique," *J. Gen. Microbiol.* **15,** 372–380.
195. Stolzy, L. H., O. C. Taylor, W. M. Dugger, Jr., and J. D. Mersereau, 1964, "Physiological changes in and ozone susceptibility of the tomato plant after short periods of inadequate ozygen diffusion to the roots," *Soil Sci. Soc. Am. Proc.* **28,** 305–308.
196. Storer, W. N., L. H. Storer, and G. K. Parris, 1951, "Field and laboratory investigations indicate grape degeneration in Florida is due to Pierce's disease virus infection," *Plant Disease Reptr.* **35,** 341–344.
197. Tarjan, A. C., and S. W. Hart, 1955, "Occurrence of yellow tuft of bentgrass in Rhode Island," *Plant Disease Reptr.* **39,** 185.
198. *Turf-grass Times,* Panel, 1967, "Spring dead-spot is still a mystery," **2**(4), 6 ff.
199. Underwood, J. K., 1964, "Rust on Merion bluegrass," *Golf Course Reptr.* **32**(5), 22.
200. U.S. Dept. of Agriculture, 1953, Yearbook, *Plant Disease,* Washington, D.C., 940 pp.
201. U.S. Dept. of Agriculture, 1953, Agri. Res. Service, 1964, *A Speedy Test for Cold Hardiness. Agric. Res.* **13**(6), 15.
202. Vaartaja, O., 1964, "Survival of *Fusarium, Pythium,* and *Rhizoctonia* in very dry soil," *Bi-monthly Rept., Dept. Forestry (Ent., Path.), Can.* **20,** (6), 3.
203. Wadsworth, D. F., 1961, "Results of chemical drenches in the control of spring dead spot of bermudagrass," *Phytopathology* **51,** 646 (abstr.).
204. Wadsworth, D. F., and H. C. Young, Jr., 1961, "Spring dead spots of bermudagrass," *U.S. Golf Assoc. J.* **14**(6), 25–27.
205. Waggoner, P. E., 1962, "Weather, space, time and chance of infection," *Phytopathology* **52,** 1100–8.
206. Warcup, J. H., and P. H. B. Talbot, 1962, "Ecology and identity of mycelia isolated from soil," *Trans. Br. Mycol. Soc.* **45,** 495–518.
207. Ward, E. W. B., and G. D. Thorn, 1961, "Evidence for the formation of HCN from glycine by a snow mold fungus," *Can. J. Botany* **44,** 95–104.
208. Watson, J. R., Jr., 1966, "Frost protection," *Ann. N. W. Turfgr. Conf.*

Proc. **20,** 68–74.

209. Webster, J., 1956–57, "Succession of fungi on decaying cocksfoot culms," *J. Ecol.,* I, **44,** 517–544; II, **45,** 1–30.
210. Weiling, J. L., S. G. Jensen, and R. I. Hamilton, 1957, "*Helminthosporium sativum,* a destructive pathogen of bluegrass," *Phytopathology* **47,** 744–746.
211. Wells, H. D., and J. F. McGill, 1959, "NK-37 bermudagrass is highly susceptible to *Helminthosporium stenospilum,*" *Agron. J.* **51,** 625.
212. Wells, H. D., and B. P. Robinson, 1954, "Important diseases of ryegrass greens," *USGA Green Sect. J.* **7**(5), 25.
213. Williams, A. S., and R. E. Schmidt, 1963, "Studies on dollar spot and melting out," *Golf Course Reptr.* **31**(5), 36–40.
214. Yamada, W., and H. Yamoto, 1956, "Studies on the stripe disease of the rice plant, III," *Special Bull. Okayama Prefect Agr. Expt. Sta:* **55**35–56.
215. Yarwood, C.E, S. M. Cohen, and J. Santilli, 1954, "Temperature relations of powdery mildews," *Hilgardia* **22** 603–622.
216. (Youngner) Anon., 1959, "Recovery of diseased turf grown on sand and heavy clay soil," *Calif. Turfgr. Cult.* **9**(3), 24.
217. Zummo, N. and A. G. Plakidas, 1958, "Brown patch of St. Augustine," *Plant Disease Reptr.* **42,**

9

WEED CONTROL*

Unless chemical weed control is accompanied by a change in management program, it will only result in replacing an easy to kill weed with a weed more difficult to control.

Weeds have assured that Adam's burden would be carried down through the generations of man. Weeds are plants growing where they are

*Throughout the first of the book, rates are given as amounts of material per 1000 square feet, but weed control chemicals are used in very small amounts usually given as amount of active ingredient (ai) per acre. The convention will be followed in this chapter, and so if we speak of a 1-lb rate, 1 lb ai/acre is implied.

The possibility of effective, selective weed control since World War II has led to a host of investigations. Papers published on chemical weed control are numerous, often of limited scope, and no attempt will be made to review the literature completely. Much early work was carried out with chemicals that have been superseded. One superior chemical replaces several previous ones. Much of the literature is thus outdated. Research reports cited are often the ones nearest at hand. I apologize to those whom I thereby slight.

not wanted and have been an ever-present and therefore annoying problem in turfgrasses. In spite of much research, and development of superior chemicals, the Pennsylvania study, noted in Chapter 1, found weeds still to lead as a principal turf problem.

Nature does not favor a monoculture. Neither climate, soil, nor moisture remain the same for more than a few feet. Every square foot receives at least a few new weed seeds each year. Whether these seeds germinate and grow depends on several factors. If there is light and moisture at the right season they will germinate. If the seedlings tolerate mowing they will grow. If the more extensive root system of the weeds enables them to obtain more water and nutrition, weeds will crowd the grass. Management becomes important in control. To reduce germination and seedling survival, light can be cut off by a dense deep turf; careful irrigation can dry new seedling before the grass is stressed. Good moisture and nutrition in the root zone of the grass will enable it to compete with tap-rooted weeds. All turf will have a few weeds, but weediness is often a symptom of inadequate management.

We have noted (Chap. 6) that organisms will fully occupy the environment. When we remove a weed, the space vacated will come to be occupied by another organism. Control is successful if the weed is replaced by grass. This is the basis of the statement in the chapter head. This is the essence of weed control—replacement—replacement of an unwanted weed by grass. Good management is essential for replacement. Grass must be favored. Failure to fully appreciate the importance of vigorous replacement can lead to a sort of nightmare in which each additional spray results in a worsened weed problem. For example, if bluegrass is mowed at 1/2 in. and dandelions are removed with MCPP, bluegrass does not have the vigor to fill back, and spaces left by dandelions will fill in with crabgrass, knotweed, veronica, *Poa annua,* or other weeds depending on climate and season. If knotweed fills back and is removed with dicamba, bluegrass will be further weakened by the herbicide of the type used. The end of such a continuing program is replacement of the bluegrass by weeds. Many a *Poa annua,* goosegrass fairway got to be that way in just this manner. If higher mowing was not possible in that example, interseeding with bent or bermudagrass would have been an alternative.

Every turf has its areas of sun and shade, or higher and lower elevation. If irrigation is right in the low or shady areas, high and sunny areas are likely dry. If high or sunny areas are moist, low or shady ones are generally wet. And so even the good manager will have some weeds because there are spots of thin turf where grass cannot compete with full effectiveness.

METHODS OF WEED CONTROL

Chemical methods of weed control predominate to such a degree that we sometimes forget there are other methods. Not only is management important in growing good grass to replace weeds, management practices can affect weediness. Hole punching, thatching, and top dressing can all provide a seedbed for weed seeds, and top dressing can add weed seeds. Operations which disturb the soil need to be timed so they are done at a season when weeds are not germinating. For example, fall or early spring verticutting of greens can promote *Poa annua* whereas late spring verticutting can hasten its death.[174]

When seeds are germinating frequent irrigation can greatly favor weed survival. In April, I have counted up to 2000 crabgrass seeds per square foot. Only two to four per square foot needed to survive to make a weedy turf. When irrigation was stretched to two to three week intervals, an average of only four plants per 100 square feet survived.

When part of a nitrogen-starved turf is given a light application of fertilizer, it may soon appear starved again. But the treated area is readily recognized by reduced numbers of weeds and increased turf density. Suitable fertility is essential for effective weed control.

Turf weeds increase as mowing height is lowered. However, this is complicated by a seasonal effect. During the season of weed seed germination, seedling survival is reduced by high mowing which shades out tender seedlings with vigorous turf. Later in the season, among weeds that do survive, grass may tolerate shorter mowing than many weeds. Fewer weeds may survive in short mown turf at that season, depending on predominant weed species and the turf species. Bermudagrass invasion of cool-season grasses has been reduced by close mowing, which removed stolons so invasion was by tillers only.[120]

Without weed seeds there is little weed problem, and limiting introduction of seeds is an important method of weed control. Weed content of grass seed is limited by law, but control of weed content of top dressing, topsoil, manures, or similar materials that may be brought on the land is up to the turf manager. Weeds on the property should not be allowed to go to seed. A single *Poa annua* plant has produced a cupful of seeds in one season. A single plant of shepherd's purse has produced 2327 seeds.[144] When plants have gone to seed, equipment will spread seed over the property unless equipment is cleaned after use in weedy areas.

Sometimes weed control is assisted by insects. Insect control has been used in Australia to stop a takeover of the land by *Opuntia* cactus, and in California by Klamath weed.[3] During the present decade, introduction of a weevil is controlling puncture vine in the southwest.[100] Although effective, this is a limited method that requires a predator that is specific for the weed, and which will not adapt its appetite to desirable plant species.

Cultivation is an important means of weed control in agriculture, but in turf culture, we are apt to overlook mechanical weed control. Weeds are continually invading. What are we to do when only half a dozen weeds grow on a green? Wait until there are more so we can justify using a spray, or spud them out so we won't have to spray? Hand weeding an area is expensive, but when the man growing the green spends two minutes with a pocket knife lifting out a couple of weed seedlings, it may pay dividends. Early removal prevents establishment and seed production, and can reduce need for chemical control. Also the man who has been trained to stop for a minute or two to look over *his* green and to mend the blemish a weed causes is apt to develop greater pride in, and responsibility for his work. A little hand weeding can be an important adjunct to other weed-control practices.

The most significant turf weed control is by chemicals. I hope I have made it eminently clear that chemical control is only a management tool and cannot be separated from total management if it is to succeed. The rest of this chapter will be largely concerned with two subjects: weed plants and their chemical control.

HERBICIDES

Herbicides may be classified in several ways. We shall be most interested in classifications that divide them into: *(1)* foliage-applied vs soil-applied; *(2)* contact vs translocated; *(3)* selective vs nonselective; and *(4)* preemergent vs postemergent. These classes are not exclusive. An herbicide may be a soil-applied, translocated, selective, preemergent type.

Foliage Applied vs Soil-Applied Herbicides

Some foliage-applied herbicide will reach the soil; some soil-applied herbicide will fall on leaves. The classification however does describe the principal area of action. Foliage-applied materials must be able to enter the leaf and must be applied to contact and to wet the leaf. Soil-applied herbicides are taken up by the root or they may be fumigants which kill a variety of living material in the soil.

Soil fumigants are volatile compounds which are effective at warm temperatures, (over 65°F) in soils that are well aerated by tillage, and in soils with moisture levels favorable for biological activity. Fumigants noted include methyl bromide, Mylone, Vapam, Vorlex, and (by stretching a point) calcium cyanamide. On turf, fumigants are used in the seedbed before seeding.

Soil-applied herbicides include soil sterilants used beneath paths, parking lots, etc., to stop all growth for a number of years. Many herbicides listed can be used as soil sterilants at high rates (e.g., Simazine or Monuron). Sodium arsenite, borates, and sodium chlorate are compounds specifically used as sterilants.

I consider it a grave responsibility for a horticulturist to apply a long-term poison to his soil. The future is uncertain. Temporary buildings tend to remain in use 60–100 years. But a *permanent* parking lot is apt to become a new green next year. Sterilants should not be used where roots of desirable plants will penetrate, or where rain will wash or drain into planted areas. Many a green approach has been browned by water washing from a trap sprayed with a triazine (Fig. 9.1).

Herbicides intended to be taken up by the root must be applied with sufficient water to move them into the root zone. A number of soil-applied materials adsorb in the surface soil and are effective on seedlings emerging through the layer.

Leaves are covered by a layer of waxy protective material named cutin. Composition and thickness of cutin layers depends in part on the

Figure 9.1 A homeowner spot sprayed clumps of tall fescue with a triazine which later washed downhill and killed strips of turf.

plant species. It also depends on growing conditions. Tough, hardened plants tend to have a thicker protective layer whereas plants grown soft at high fertility and moisture levels tend to have thin layers of cutin. On some plants cutin prevents entry of herbicides which must enter through stoma. This is demonstrated by spraying plants kept in the light and in the dark. Only lighted plants with open stoma effectively take up the herbicide. On other plants there is movement of herbicides through the cutin or possibly through pores or cracks or interfaces in the cutin layer. Knowledge of herbicide entry through leaves is not complete. Some wetting agents (named adjuvants) greatly increase entry and effectiveness of herbicides, presumably by increasing movement through the cutin layer. Use of emulsifiable oils has increased effectiveness of entry.[97] Evidence suggests that if we could get effective entry of some herbicides through the cutin we could decrease our application rates by a factor of ten or a hundred.[159]

Some of the injury reported on greens turf may result from increased entry because of thin cuticle and many stoma, resulting from soft growth under moist conditions.

Contact vs Translocated Herbicides

Some herbicides such as weed oil, cacodylic acid, and others do not move in the plant very far beyond the point of contact. Only plant tissues touched by the spray are killed. Of course if a stem is killed, the leaves above will die. Roots and rhizomes protected by soil may regenerate the plant. Contact sprays are often used on paths, around buildings, fences, markers, and parking lots, and on road shoulders.

The part of a translocated herbicide which enters a plant moves in the plant and affects tissues and organs at a distance from the point of entry. Entry is generally through stems and leaves but may be through roots. Movement is through the vascular system to growing points of both shoots and roots. Examples of translocated compounds include chlorophenoxy compounds and DSMA and other arsenates. Translocated herbides may move in phloem or xylem or both. As movement in xylem is by mass flow, herbicides moving in xylem perform best when taken up in the soil solution and moved through the plant into leaves. It is possible for herbicides to move back in the xylem from leaves to roots but not likely. (The soil needs to be dry and the plant should be under water stress. Herbicide in appreciable amounts of water is sprayed on the leaves when the humidity is high. The water solution is taken in through the leaves and moved throughout the stressed plant.)

In contrast to xylem, phloem is a living tissue. To be moved in the phloem an herbicide must be of low toxicity for if phloem cells are killed by contact with the herbicide, movement stops. Materials that move in phloem move toward sinks and tend to concentrate in growing tips. The 2,4-D type of herbicide is of this kind. The above explains why doubling the rate of such herbicides may result in failure. At higher concentrations herbicides may injure phloem cells and therefore fail to translocate. Effectiveness is sometimes increased by halving the rate and repeating the spray after a few days. Phloem-translocated herbicides move most readily when soil is moist, skies are sunny, and temperatures are moderate, i.e., when photosynthate is high and the phloem active.

Selective vs Nonselective Herbicides

Nonselective herbicides are effective against all plant species and are used more in agriculture than turf culture. These include such materials as weed oils, sulfuric acid, and others. There is a high degree of overlap between contact and nonselective herbicides and nonselectives are often used to control weeds on shoulders, parking lots, and paths, and around buildings, traps, and monuments, etc.

Selective herbicides affect different species differently, by killing plants of one species, while plants of another species survive. Selectivity may be achieved in several ways. In row crops, selectivity may be obtained by placement. The spray is carefully regulated to wet soil or foliage between corn rows for example, with spray wetting only old basal leaf sheaths in the row.

Some selectivity is obtained by differential wetting. In wheat, for example, drops of spray may bounce off waxy leaves and stems of wheat while wetting leaves of wild mustard. To some extent differential wetting is probably a factor in selective turfgrass weed control.

Differences in development are useful on turfgrass. Much control of weeds in turfgrass is based on the great tolerance to herbicides of mature perennial grass and low tolerance of seedling stages of annual weeds. Some differential control on bermudagrass has been obtained experimentally by spraying dormant bermudagrass with a nonselective Paraquat, to kill winter weeds. The dormant bermudagrass is unaffected.

Biochemical differences in plant tolerance to herbicides is a basis for selectivity. Selectivity is receiving a great deal of attention today. A biochemical difference in tolerance between monocots and dicots enables chlorophenoxy herbicides to remove dicots from grass, and dalapon to remove grass from dicots. Such biochemical differences in tolerance are being explored to an increasingly fine line. Within the grasses, DSMA selects against some species. Within a single species such as *Agrostis stolonifera* individual clones respond differently to herbicides, though we cannot yet use such differences to maintain pure stands.

Selective herbicides are of greatest interest in turfgrass culture. They enable us to effectively use replacement phenomenon, replacing weeds with a desirable grass. With biochemical selectivity, the difference is often in degree of injury to different plants. The desired plant can be damaged too if herbicide is used at incorrect rates, or during periods of dry soil or high temperature.

Preemergent vs Postemergent Herbicides

Many weeds produce seeds with varying periods of dormancy so that germination takes place throughout the growing season. Crabgrass and barnyardgrass are examples of weeds that germinate over the entire summer. The 2327 seeds from one plant of shepherd's purse *(Capsella)* germinated over a period of 215 days. Actual germination took place on 96 of the 215 days, i.e., on days with rising temperature, especially in spring and fall.[144] Such weeds are most simply controlled by a preemergence herbicide which is applied to the soil. Most preemergence chemicals are adsorbed in the surface layer of the soil where they poison seedlings as they emerge through the soil crust. If the chemical lasts a suitable length of time without breakdown, a single spray can control weeds for an entire season. If life of the herbicide is too short, weeds germinate at the end of the season in time to grow seeds for the following year. If the life is too long then the herbicide may interfere with overseeding or germination of grass seeds sown in the future. Whereas preemergent herbicides interfere with germination of newly sown grass seed, they are useful to control weeds in newly planted stolons.[47]

Operations such as thatching or hole punching may disturb the soil surface and reduce effectiveness of preemergence chemicals.

In some tests, preemergence chemicals applied in the fall have been effective against weeds germinating the following spring. However, the preferable time to apply preemergence herbicides is a short time prior to germination of weeds to be controlled. This is usually early fall for winter weeds such as chickweed and annual bluegrass, and early spring for crabgrass and other summer weeds. DCPA and calcium arsenate have given better control applied 30–60 days ahead of crabgrass germination.[61] As time of spring germination of weeds varies from year to year, Engel suggests timing application by relating it to the bloom of an appropriate shrub in the landscape.

Where turf is thin following use of preemergence herbicides, work in progress at Rhode Island indicates that about 200 lb/acre of activated charcoal may "cancel" the herbicide and permit a safe seedbed for turfgrasses.*[121]

When effective, a good preemergent herbicide provides an almost ideal weed-control chemical. In some seasons they are not effective and postemergence herbicides need to be used. Postemergence herbicides are useful wherever weed seeds have succeeded in germinating and are most effective used soon after germination while weeds are still in the seedling stage.

FACTORS IN DEGREE OF CONTROL

Homeowners are apt to equate control with 100% elimination. We have already noted that we have control when weeds are few and their numbers are not increasing. Elimination is impossible except at great cost and then for only a single instant of time. The effectiveness of a spray in giving control is influenced by a number of factors including weed species and age; temperature, moisture, and sunlight; soil type and exchange capacity;[139] and use of wetting agents and other chemicals in formulation. These affect the amount of herbicide entering the plant and its effectiveness in the plant.

WEED SPECIES AND AGE

Seedlings of annuals are generally easily controlled. Perennials (including turf) are often controlled as seedlings, with control increasing in difficulty with age. Herbicides should not be used on new turf until it is 8–12 weeks old for translocated materials or 4–8 weeks for soil surface preemergent herbicides. Some chemicals are damaging for even longer periods than these.[27,37,51,104,126,134,146,149] Injury is increased by run-off into soil.[146]

When mixed species are present replacement may be of the killed weed by a resistant weed rather than by turf. For example, use of 2,4-D on a turf containing dandelion and veronica may result in replacement of dandelions with veronica instead of turf. To control weeds in such a mixture, the most economical advance will be made if the difficult-to-control weed is controlled first. Later any residual of easily controlled weeds can be readily cleaned up.

*See also S. W. Bingham, First International Turfgrass Research Conference, Proceedings (in preparation).

Weeds can develop resistance to herbicides and a once-useful herbicide may have to be replaced by a different formulation.

CLIMATIC FACTORS

Activity of herbicides increases with temperature. Herbicides applied in cold weather may give poor results. During mild weather when grass is growing well, control is apt to be good and damage to the grass quickly outgrown. Weed control may increase at high temperatures but injury to grass may also be increasingly severe and grass may fail to replace weeds. As temperatures increase rates of application are often decreased.

When using translocated herbicides, other elements of the climate should be such that plants are functioning normally with adequate levels of sugar (sunshine) and moisture. Soil moisture should be good, especially for effective use of herbicides taken up through roots.

Rain following foliar herbicide use may reduce its effectiveness. High humidity is desirable when herbicides are applied dissolved in water. If spray drops evaporate too rapidly, penetration may be low. Leaf penetration may be improved by slow evaporation accompanying night application.

MOWING

Mowing within 24–48 hr of applying a herbicide may increase turf injury. As effects are not predictable, simply avoid mowing.

SOIL FACTORS

Cation-exchange capacity changes effectiveness of many soil-applied herbicides. Clay colloids and organic matter adsorb herbicides and rates may have to be increased on soils of high organic or clay content and decreased on sandy soils. However, organic matter increases toxicity of trifluralin, presumably by adsorbing toxic vapors.[16] Preemergence herbicides that are adsorbed in the soil surface on clay colloids may leach into the root zone if used on sand. Need for soil moisture has been noted.

HERBICIDE FORMULATION

Most herbicides are complex chemicals which are mixed in proprietary formulations that increase their complexity. The following classes first list forms of herbicidal chemicals, then list secondary chemicals used with them.

Dry Formulations

Soluble Powders. Soluble materials such as the sodium methyl arsenates or dalapon, for example, are readily prepared by dissolving in water.

Wettable Powders. Materials of low solubility such as DCPA or diphenamid may be milled into a fine powder and suspended in water. Wettable powders require continuous agitation to prevent their settling out and to give a uniform level of chemical in the spray.

Granular. Preemergence herbicides in particular are often used fixed to the surface of an inert material such as expanded vermiculite, organic wastes, or clay pellets. Suitable particles will drop between leaves and fall on the soil surface where preemergence materials are most effective. A minimal amount is left behind on the leaf surface. In a test of eight granular materials, effectiveness has been increased 15–50% by watering in rather than waiting three days for rain. Light and heat tended to result in breakdown of chemicals that were not washed in.[43,112]

Volatile herbicides with toxic fumes may also be effectively applied in granular form. Granular preparations of foliage-applied herbicides are formulated but difficult to use. Moisture may be needed to make particles stick to leaves, and timing and spreader adjustment may be too critical for effective use.

Liquid Formulations

Soluble Concentrates. Materials such as dicamba and 2,4-D amines form soluble liquids which are easily added to water.

Emulsifiable Liquid Concentrates. Herbicides such as bensulide or 2,4-D ester are soluble in oil but not in water. They are prepared in a light oil with an emulsifying agent. Mixed in water they form a usually milky liquid which may separate unless the mixture is agitated from time to time. It is easier to keep an emulsion than a wettable powder in suspension.

Active-ingredient content of dry formulations is usually expressed as a percent. DCPA (Dacthal) can be purchased as a wettable powder having

75% ai (active ingredients). To put 15 lb ai in the tank will require 20 lb of the powder (15÷0.75). Liquid formulations express active ingredient as pounds per gallon. In order to have in the tank 2 lb 2,4-D amine containing 4 lb ai/gal 2 quarts of formulation will have to be added.

Carriers. Water is the cheapest and most readily available carrier. Not all herbicides are soluble in water and water has some undesirable characteristics. With high surface tension, water forms drops which ball up and roll off the surface of many leaves. Water is polar and fails to wet nonpolar waxy surfaces. Oil is sometimes used as a carrier, for contact herbicides in particular. Not only will oil wet the waxy surface of leaves but will creep along them, increasing the area of contact. As neither oil nor water are ideal carriers, a herbicide formulation may have other compounds added to increase effectiveness.

Amount of water used with herbicides is critical. Label recommendations give values that result in maximum retention of herbicide by the weed. Use of more or less water decreases efficiency.

Additional Substances

Oil emulsions may be made with oil as a *filming agent.* Forming a film on the leaf the oil aids penetration of herbicides of some molecular types. Horn used oil at 2 gal/acre and was able to use dicamba, DSMA, MSMA, and others at one-half the usual rate with equal effectiveness.[97] When water sprays are used on plants that are hard to wet, a *wetting agent* may be added. In some instances kind or concentrations of wetting agent may be critical for high effectiveness of an herbicide. With oil emulsions an *emulsion stabilizer* may be used to lower tension at the oil–water interface. This enhances dispersion of the oil and retards separation of oil from water. The same compound may serve as both an emulsion stabilizer and wetting agent. Some emulsion stabilizers also act as *penetrating agents* and increase movement through the cuticle.

Some compounds having low solubility in common solvents may be dissolved in a *coupling agent,* which is then dissolved in oil and the whole emulsified with water. A coupling agent may also be a filming agent. A *toxicant* may be added to herbicides of low killing power, as for example a dinitrophenol to a light oil.

The turf manager uses mixtures supplied to him. The manufacturer is the person concerned with the above intricacies of formulation. However, the above does indicate the inadvisability of tampering too much with herbicide instructions or of haphazard mixing of herbicides. Unless a herbicide mixture has been recommended by a reliable source, it should be first tried on an experimental basis only.

Different proprietary formulations contain the active chemical in different forms. As an example, an organic acid may be offered in the acid form or as a salt of potassium, sodium, lithium, or other metal. Alternatively, it may be conjugated with another organic moiety to form an amino salt or an ester. Herbicidal effectiveness against a certain weed may be enhanced by having the herbicide in a particular form, but such details will not be considered here unless they are of unusual significance.

An active search for new herbicides continues and we may expect future improvements in both herbicides and formulations. At the same time, there is a possibility of breeding grasses for resistance to herbicides of high effectiveness. Some grasses such as St. Augustine have an ability to metabolize trazines for example. If we could confer that ability on strains of bluegrass we could then use Atrazine to remove bermuda and bentgrasses from bluegrass along with a wide range of broad-leaved weeds.

Herbicides are often combined to give a broader spectrum of control. Some combinations which have been successful include these:

1. DSMA + a preemergence herbicide such as DCPA or Bensulide has been used for emerged crabgrass. DSMA gives contact control of emerged crabrass, but as germination continues all summer, addition of a preemergence herbicide limits germination during the rest of the season.

2. DSMA or other organic arsenate + 2,-4-D. DSMA controls several grasses, the 2,4-D controls broad-leaved weeds. Also, there are weeds which have some susceptibility to arsenic and to phenoxy compounds but neither herbicide alone kills the weed; the combination, however, is lethal. An example is bindweed, which succumbs to AMA + 2,4,5-T.

3. Dicamba + 2,4-D. These complement each other in giving a broader kill of dicot weeds. Other combinations of Dicamba with chlorophenoxy compounds have been tried. 2,4-D and MCPP give a wide spectrum of kill with Dicamba whereas Silvex tends to be effective against the same weeds as Dicamba.

4. Mixtures of chlorophenoxy herbicides, such as 2,4-D with 2,4,5-T or MCPP.

Other combinations have been tried and a number of mixtures are sold but the above exemplify commonly accepted mixtures for turfgrasses.

HERBICIDES AND TURFGRASS INJURY[37,136,167]

Plant poisons tend to affect all plants to some degree. The balance between injuries and benefits is put into perspective by studies on cereals. Plots treated with herbicides greatly outyielded untreated plots, but yields were less than in plots kept clean by hand weeding. Expense prohibits hand weeding. Chemical control gives us an advantage if we use the right chemical correctly.

To know if an herbicide is the right chemical for our use we do need a full evaluation of its subtleties. For example a number of herbicides injure grass root systems.[50,56,58,68,167] With high levels of irrigation and fertilization this may be of no concern, but may cause severe injury of unirrigated turf during a drought.

In many herbicide tests, turf injury is ignored if the grass makes a vigorous recovery in ten to fourteen days. In its region of greatest adaptation, quick recovery of a turfgrass is perhaps an adequate evaluation of suitability. Outside the adapted region, in the transition zone, for example, climatic stress added to chemical stress may increase significance of the latter. Chemical stresses of which we may be unaware may take several forms. Photosynthesis may be reduced (Atrazine); respiration may be increased (Dicamba) or decreased (Propham); the plant may be stimulated to use up reserves in a burst of growth (2,4-D); root morphology may be disturbed (Silvex);[30,32] rooting may be decreased (Chlordane); rhizome growth may be suppressed (DCPA);[73] tillering may be reduced (CAMA); cell divisions may be inhibited (MH); or other metabolic upsets may take place. Such changes may be quickly out-grown or may persist for years.[68] Effects of herbicides may appear in apparently unrelated ways. In one study herbicide use increased amounts of injury from large brown patch disease,[119] in another, from dollar spot.[125]

When metabolic injury occurs grass vigor may be reduced so that replacement is not by turfgrasses but by a resistant weed. When this happens our program results in a set-back rather then a benefit (Fig. 9.2). We have

Figure 9.2 These plots of highland bentgrass were sprayed with herbicides. Later in the season, under heat stress, damage appeared on some plots, indicating residual injury that was not apparent without stress.

already noted increased risks from herbicides used at high temperatures or on sandy soil.

In our laboratory we have found appreciable interaction between herbicides and nitrogen-induced yield. After application of some herbicides, grasses respond normally, and increased nitrogen increases yield. After application of a second collection of herbicides, grass responds to small nitrogen applications but yield falls off with high nitrogen use. A third group of herbicides limits growth and the reduced growth is not affected by nitrogen fertility. These responses raise a question as to the value of goods containing both fertilizer and herbicide. Use of such mixtures has been justified on the basis that fertilizer encouraged turf vigor. If the herbicide is one that stops nitrogen use by turf, we are not getting value from the fertilizer. We may even wonder if nitrogen is retarding instead of promoting turf recovery.

When herbicides are applied in late fall, cold may reduce growth and lengthen the recovery period. If freezing occurs soon after fall herbicide use, ice formation may concentrate a soil-applied herbicide to a level where it causes severe damage. This has happened when preemergence herbicides were applied late in the fall for control of spring-germinating *Poa annua.*

There is no need to tell the professional turfgrass manager that benefits from herbicide use are accompanied by risk. In the public mind however, even the most potent chemical is expected to confer only benefits. In dealing with the public, it is necessary to emphasize continually the attendant risks, particularly as many manufacturers neglect to do so, or do so only in fine print.

Different turfgrasses differ in their tolerance to various herbicides. Table 9.1 summarizes data from the literature.

HERBICIDES

Table 9.2 provides a cross reference between the many proprietary names of herbicides and the names used in this book. Proprietary formulations may differ from the type as to whether they are salts, acids, esters, amines, etc., and may vary in formulation. Herbicides listed are not necessarily recommended for turf use.

The following discussion includes many compounds of arsenic. These have high human toxicity and first aid is to induce vomiting while waiting for the doctor.

Acrolein (Aqualin, acrylaldehyde, 2-propenal; $LD_{50}=46$ mg/kg; toxic to fish; irritating to skin, eyes, and lungs; burns). Acrolein is a contact aquatic herbicide of high toxicity. Operators need protection. It is used up to 15 ppm. Water should not be used for irrigating for 2–3 days and then in accordance with instructions. Toxic to most plants, it is used on submerged and floating leaved plants, but fails to affect cattails. It is formulated as an 85% concentrate.

Table 9.1. Effects[a] of Some Common Herbicides on Turfgrass Species [23-26,30,31,110,168]

Herbicide[b]	[c]*Bluegrass*	*Bentgrass (greens)*	*Fescue-grass*	*Ryegrass*	*Bermuda-grass*	*Bahia-grass*	*Centipede-grass*	*St. Augustine-grass*	*Zoysiagrass*
Atrazine	x	x	x	x	x	x	ic	u	u
Balan	u	i	u	u	u	u	u	u	u
Bandane	u	u	i	u	i	u	u	u	u
Bensulide	u	u	u	u	i	u	u	u	i
Calcium or lead arsenates	i	i	i	0	i	0	0	i	0
2,4-D; 2,4,5-T	u	x	u	u	u	u	u	x	u
DCPA	u	x	x	u	u	u	u	u	u
Dicamba	i	i	i	0	i	u	i	i	i
Dicryl	0	0	0	0	u	x	x	x	u
Dephena-trile	u	u	u	u	u	0	0	0	0
Dipropalin	u	u	u	u	u	0	u	u	u
Endothall	i	x	x	0	i	0	0	i	0
MCPP	u	u	u	u	u	u	u	x	u
Organic arsenicals	i	i	x	u	u	x	x	x	u
Paraquat (dormant)	x	x	x	x	u	0	u	x	u
Picloram	0	0	0	0	x	u	u	u	u
Propazine	x	x	x	x	i	x	u	u	i
Siduron	u	i†	u	u	i†	u	u	u	u
Silvex	u	x	i	u	i	x	x	x	0
Simazine	x	x	x	x	x†	x	u	u	u
Terbutol	u	i	i	0	u	u	u	u	i
Trifluralin	u	u	u	u	i	u	u	i	i

[a]The above does not constitute a recommendation. It attempts to list some reports in the literature.

[b]x, not recommended.
u, has been used with safety.
i, used but some injury may occur.
0, insufficient data.
†, may depend on variety.

[c]The degree of injury indicated by i is from very slight to fairly severe. Some workers do not report injury when turf recovers rapidly.

Table 9.2. Herbicides

Herbicides	For Discussion in Text see under	Selective: Foliar-Contact	Selective: Foliar-Translocated	Selective: Soil-Contact	Selective: Soil-Translocated	Non-selective: Foliar-Contact	Non-selective: Foliar-Translocated	Non-selective: Soil-Applied	Uses: Preplant	Uses: Preemergence	Uses: Postemergence	Uses: Bare ground	Uses: Aquatic
ACP	*TCA*												
Acrolein	Acrolein					x							x
Acrylaldehyde	Acrolein												
Actrile	Ioxynil												
Aerocyanate	KOCN												
Agronox	MCPA												
Alanap	NAP												
AMA	AMA				x				x				
Amino triazole	Amino triazole						x		x			x	
Amitrol, Amitrole	Amino triazole												
Amizine	Amino triazole + Simazine												
Amizole	Amino triazole												
Amsol	2,4-D												
Ansar 138	Cacodylic acid												
Ansar 157	MAMA												
Ansar 160	Cacodylic acid												
Ansar 184	DSMA												
Ansar 170	MSMA												
Ansar 529	MSMA												
Ansar 560	Cacodylic acid												
Ansar 584	DSMA												
Antrol	AMA												
Aqua Kleen	2,4-D												
Aquathol	Endothall												
Aqualin	Acrolein												
Arsan	Cacodylic acid												
Arsinyl	DSMA												
3 AT	Amino triazole												
ATA	Amino triazole												
Atlas A	Sodium arsenite												
Atrazine	Atrazine				x			x		x	x	x	
Atratol A	Atrazine												

Table 9.2 cont'd.

		Selective				Nonselective			Uses				
Herbicides	For Discussion in Text see under	*Foliar-Contact*	*Foliar-Translocated*	*Soil-Contact*	*Soil-Translocated*	*Foliar-Contact*	*Foliar-Translocated*	*Soil-Applied*	*Preplant*	*Preemergence*	*Postemergence*	*Bare ground*	*Aquatic*
Azac, Azak	Terbutrol												
Azar	Terbutrol												
Balan	Balan			x						x			
Bandane	Bandane				x					x			
Banvel D	Dicamba												
Barweed	2,4-D												
Basphapon	Dalapon												
Benefin	Balan												
Bentrol	Ioxynil												
Bensulide	Bensulide			x						x			
Betasan	Bensulide												
Benzac 1281	2,3,6-TBA												
Binnell	Balan												
Blue copperas	Copper sulfate												
Bluestone	Copper sulfate												
Blue vitriol	Copper sulfate												
Borax	Borate												
Borate	Borate							x				x	
Bromacil	Bromacil	x		x				x		x	x	x	
Bromion	Bromoxynil												
Bromomethane	Methyl bromide												
Bromoxynil	Bromoxynil	x					x						
Buctril	Bromoxynil												
Butoxone	2,4-D; 2,4-DB												
Butyrac 118	2,4-DB												
Butyrac 175	2,4-DB												
Cacodylic acid	Cacodylic acid					x					x		
Calar	CAMA												

Table 9.2 cont'd.

Herbicides	For Discussion in Text see under	*Selective*				*Nonselective*			*Uses*				
		Foliar-Contact	*Foliar-Translocated*	*Soil-Contact*	*Soil-Translocated*	*Foliar-Contact*	*Foliar-Translocated*	*Soil-Applied*	*Preplant*	*Preemergence*	*Postemergence*	*Bare ground*	*Aquatic*
Calcium arsenate	Calcium arsenate		x		x					x	x		
Calcium cyanamide	Calcium cyanamide							x	x				
Calcium propyl arsenate	CPA												
Calcium acid methyl arsenate	CAMA												
CAMA	CAMA		x								x		
Caparol	Prometryne												
Casoron	Casoron			x						x			x
CDEC	Vegedex												
Certrol	Ioxynil												
CET	Simazine												
Chem-rice	Propanil												
Chem-Sen	Sodium arsenite												
Chip-Cal	Calcium arsenate												
Chlordane	Chlordane				x					x			
Chloro-IPC	CIPC												
CIPC	CIPC			x						x			
Clout	DSMA												
CMPP	MCPP												
CMU	Monuron												
Copper sulfate	Copper sulfate												x
Copperas	Copper sulfate												
CPA	CPA		x								x		
Crab-E-Rad	DSMA												
Crabex	Sodium arsenite												
Crabnot	KOCN												
Cyanamide	Calcium cyanamide												
Cyanol	KOCN												

Table 9.2 cont'd.

Herbicides	For Discussion in Text see under	*Selective*				*Non-selective*			*Uses*				
		Foliar-Contact	*Foliar-Translocated*	*Soil-Contact*	*Soil-Translocated*	*Foliar-Contact*	*Foliar-Translocated*	*Soil-Applied*	*Preplant*	*Preemergence*	*Postemergence*	*Bare ground*	*Aquatic*
2,4-D	2,4-D		x								x		x
Dacamine	2,4-D												
Dacamine 4T	2,4,5-T												
Daconate	MSMA												
Dacthal	DCPA												
Dacthalor	DCPA												
Dalapon	Dalapon		x							x	x		x
Dal-E-Rad	D SMA												
2,4-DB	2,4-DB	x									x		
2,4-D Butyric	2,4-DB												
DCPA	DCPA			x						x			
Dedweed	KOCN												
2,4-DEP	2,4-DEP				x					x			
DF Spray	Endothall												
Di AMA	AMA												
Dicamba	Dicamba		x		x					x	x		
Dichlor	Casoron												
Dichlorbenil	Casoron												
Dicryl	Dicryl		x								x		
DIMA	DSMA												
Dimet	DSMA												
Diphenamide	Diphenamide				x					x			
Diphenatrile	Diphenatrile			x						x			
Dipropanil	Dipropanil			x						x			
Diquat	Diquat					x					x		x
Disomar	DSMA												

Table 9.2 cont'd.

Herbicides	For Discussion in Text see under	*Selective* *Foliar-Contact*	*Selective* *Foliar-Translocated*	*Selective* *Soil-Contact*	*Selective* *Soil-Translocated*	*Non-selective* *Foliar-Contact*	*Non-selective* *Foliar-Translocated*	*Non-selective* *Soil-Applied*	*Uses* *Preplant*	*Uses* *Preemergence*	*Uses* *Postemergence*	*Uses* *Bare ground*	*Uses* *Aquatic*
Diuron	Diuron				x					x			
DMA, DMA-100	DSMA												
DMAA	Cacodylic acid												
DMPA	Zytron												
DMTT	Mylone												
Dowpon	Dalapon												
DPA	Propanil												
DSMA	DSMA	x									x		
Dual Paraquat	Paraquat												
Du-Sprex	Casoron												
Dybar	Fenuron												
Dymid	Diphenamide												
Emulsamine	2,4-D												
Endo	Endothall												
Endothall	Endothall		x								x		x
Endothall turf herbicide	Endothall												
Enide	Diphenamide												
Enz	CPA												
Eptam	Eptam				x				x				
EPTC	Eptam												
Erase	Cacodylic acid												
Fairlawn	CPA												
Falone	2,4-DEP												
Fenac	Fenac			x						x			
Fenoprop	Silvex												
Fenuron	Fenuron				x							x	
Gesafram	Prometone												
Gesagard	Prometryne												
Gesamil	Propazine												
Gesaprim	Atrazine												

Table 9.2 cont'd.

		Selective				*Non-selective*			*Uses*				
Herbicides	For Discussion in Text see under	*Foliar-Contact*	*Foliar-Translocated*	*Soil-Contact*	*Soil-Translocated*	*Foliar-Contact*	*Foliar-Translocated*	*Soil-Applied*	*Preplant*	*Preemergence*	*Postemergence*	*Bare ground*	*Aquatic*
Gesatop	Simazine												
Gramoxone	Paraquat												
Gr-Cyan	Calcium cyanamide												
Hedenol	2,4-D												
Herban	Norea												
Hormatox	2,4-D												
Hormosalt	2,4-D												
Hy-Cy	Calcium cyanamide												
Hydrothol 47	Endothall												
Hyvar-X	Bromacil												
Ioxynil	Ioxynil	x									x		
Iso-Cornox	MCPP												
Karmex	Diuron												
Karmex DL	Diuron												
Kleen-Up	CPA												
Kloben	Neburon												
KOCN	KOCN		x								x		
Krab	KOCN												
Kuran, Kuron	Silvex												
Kurosal	Silvex												
Lawnwood Parklane	CPA												
Maleic hydrazide	MH												
Maleric hydrazine	MH												
MAMA	MAMA		x								x		
MAM	MAMA												
Marmer	Monuron												
MCP	MCPA												
MCPA	MCPA		x								x		
MCPP	MCPP		x								x		
Mecopar	MCPP 2,4-D												
Mecopex	MCPP												
Mecoprop	MCPP												

Table 9.2 cont'd.

		Selective				*Non-selective*			*Uses*				
Herbicides	For Discussion in Text see under	*Foliar-Contact*	*Foliar-Translocated*	*Soil-Contact*	*Soil-Translocated*	*Foliar-Contact*	*Foliar-Translocated*	*Soil-Applied*	*Preplant*	*Preemergence*	*Postemergence*	*Bare ground*	*Aquatic*
Mediben	Dicamba												
Mephanac	MCPA												
Metasol 57	PMP												
Metasol P-6	PMP												
Methar	AMA												
Methoxone	MCPA												
Methyl bromide	Methyl bromide							x	x			x	
MH	MH		x								x		
MH-30, MH-40	MH												
MMA	MSMA												
Monuron	Monuron				x					x	x	x	
MSMA	MSMA				x						x		
Mylone	Mylone							x	x				
NaAs	Sodium arsenite												
NAP	NAP			x						x			
Naphthalan	NAP												
No-Crab	CPA												
Norea	Norea			x						x	x		
Orthoarsenate	Calcium arsenate												
Oust	DSMA												
Paraquat	Paraquat					x					x		x
Paraquate CL	Paraquat												
Paraquat dichloride	Paraquat												
PCP	PCP					x					x	x	
Penite	Sodium arsenite												
Phenox	2,4-D												
Phix	Cacodylic acid												
Phthalic acid	DCPA												

Table 9.2 cont'd.

Herbicides	For Discussion in Text see under	*Selective*				*Nonselective*			*Uses*				
		Foliar-Contact	*Foliar-Translocated*	*Soil-Contact*	*Soil-Translocated*	*Foliar-Contact*	*Foliar-Translocated*	*Soil-Applied*	*Preplant*	*Preemergence*	*Postemergence*	*Bare ground*	*Aquatic*
Phytar 138	Cacodylic acid												
Phytar 160	Cacodylic acid												
Phytar 560	Cacodylic acid												
Picloram	Picloram		x							x	x		
PMA	PMA	x									x		
PMAC	Cacodylic acid												
PMAS	PMA												
PMP	PMP		x								x		
Potassium cyanate	KOCN												
Prefar	Bensulide												
Pre San	Bensulide												
Primatol O	Prometone												
Primatol P	Propazine												
Primatol S	Simazine												
Prometon	Prometone												
Prometone	Prometone					x	x				x		
Prometryne	Prometryne		x		x					x	x		
Propanil	Propanil	x									x		
Propazine	Propazine		x		x					x	x		
Propon	Silvex												
2-Propenal	Acrolein												
Quicksan	PMA												
Radapon	Dalapon												
Reglone	Diquat												
Rogue	Propanil												
Runcatex	MCPP												
Sel-Tox	PMA												
Siduron	Siduron				x					x			
Silvex	Silvex		x		x					x	x		x

Table 9.2 cont'd.

		Selective				*Non-selective*			*Uses*				
Herbicides	For Discussion in Text see under	*Foliar-Contact*	*Foliar-Translocated*	*Soil-Contact*	*Soil-Translocated*	*Foliar-Contact*	*Foliar-Translocated*	*Soil-Applied*	*Preplant*	*Preemergence*	*Postemergence*	*Bare ground*	*Aquatic*
Silvisar 510	Cacodylic acid												
Simazin	Simazine												
Simazine	Simazine		x					x		x	x	x	
Sindone	Sindone			x						x			
Slo-Gro	MH												
SMDC	Vapam												
Sodium arsenite	Sodium arsenite		x					x			x	x	x
Spor-Kil	PMA												
Stam-F34	Propanil												
STCA	TCA												
Super Crab-E-Rad	AMA												
Surcopur	Propanil												
2,4,5-T	2,4,5-T		x								x		
Tag	PMA												
Tat-C-Lect	PMA												
TBA	2,3,6-TBA												
2,3,6-TBA	2,3,6-TBA		x								x		
TCA	TCA		x		x					x	x		
TCB	2,3,6-TBA												
TCBA	2,3,6-TBA												
Telvar	Monuron												
Terbutrol	Terbutrol		x		x					x	x		
Tordon, Tordon 22, Tordon beads	Terbutrol												
2,4,5-TP	Silvex												
2,4,5-T Propionic	Silvex												
Treflan	Trifluralin												
Tricalcium arsenate	Calcium arsenate												
Trichlorobenzine	2,3,6-TBA												

Table 9.2 cont'd.

		Selective				Nonselective			Uses				
Herbicides	For Discussion in Text see under	Foliar-Contact	Foliar-Translocated	Soil-Contact	Soil-Translocated	Foliar-Contact	Foliar-Translocated	Soil-Applied	Preplant	Preemergence	Postemergence	Bare ground	Aquatic
Tri-Fen	Fenac												
Trifluralin	Trifluralin			x						x			
Triox	Sodium arsenite												
Tryben 200	2,3,6-TBA												
Tupersan	Siduron												
Urox B, Urox HX	Bromacil												
Vapam	Vapam							x	x				
Vegedex	Vegedex			x						x	x		
Vorlex	Vorlex							x	x				
VPM	Vapam												
Weedanol	2,4-D												
Weedanol Cyanol	KOCN												
Weedar	MCPP												
Weedar 64	2,4-D												
Weed-B-Gon	2,4-D												
Weed-E-Rad	DSMA												
Weedez	2,4-D												
Weed-No-More	2,4-D												
Weedo	Sodium arsenite												
Weedone	2,4-D												
Weedone 2,4,5-T	2,4,5-T												
Weedone 2,45-TP	2,4,5-TP												
Zytron	Zytron				x					x			

AMA (Antrol, Methar, Diama, Super Crab-E-Rad, ammonium methanearsonate, disubstituted (octyl, dodecyl) ammonium methanearsonates; LD_{50} = 600 mg/kg). AMA is used as a postemergent crabgrass killer. It is also effective against chickweed, water sedge, dallisgrass, and others. Two applications at 5–7 day intervals are needed. The 16% solution is used to give 2 1/2–3 lb active ingredient (ai)/acre in 50–100 gal water. Soil should be moist and bentgrasses may be discolored; St. Augustine, fescues, and centipedegrasses are severely injured.

Amino Triazole (ATA, Amitrol, Weedazole, 3-AT, Amizol, AT, Amitrole, 3-amino-1,2,4, -triazole; LD_{50} = 14,7000 mg/kg). A nonselective postemergent, translocated herbicide, amino triazole is used for cleanup around fences and buildings and for control of emerged water weeds such as cattail. It is effective against poison oak or ivy. One to thirty pounds per acre in 30–300 gal is used to wet foliage without runoff.

Arsenic Trioxide (Sodite, Atlas A, Penite-35, As_2O_3; LD_{50} = 13 mg/kg). Arsenic trioxide is an insoluble poison applied as granules, dusts, or solutions at rates of 500–2000 lb ai/acre to sterilize soils for 5–15 yr. Life decreases as rainfall increases and soil colloids increase. Human toxicity is high. Monuron may be added to hasten initial kill.

Atrazine (Gesaprim, Primatol A, Atratol A, 2-choloro-4-ethylamino-6-isopropylamino-*s*-triazine; LD_{50} = 3080 mg/kg).[23,26,101] Available as granules and wettable powder, Atrazine at 10–40 lb ai/acre is a temporary soil sterilant of shorter life than simazine. At 1–4 lb ai/acre in 10–12 gal water it is a selective, postemergent spray for some grasses. Tolerant grasses are able to metabolize Atrozine into nontoxic compounds. Of turfgrasses, Atrazine may be used on *Zoysia,* St. Augustine, and centipedegrasses for control of chickweed, crabgrass, nutgrass, and others; it has been used to kill bermuda in St. Augustinegrass.[24] Its use is similar to simazine but simazine has generally proved safer. At turf rates Atrazine is not damaging to woody plants.[28] When used to control weeds in sprigged *Zoysia* it reduced stolon formation and spread of crowns.[62] Reports on toxicity of Atrazine to bermudagrass are not in agreement. *Festuca arundinacea* is reported as tolerant in one study.[110]

Balan (Benefin, Binnell, *N*-butyl-*N*-ethyl-*a,a,a*-triflouro-2,6-dinitro-p-toluidine; LD_{50} = 800 mg/kg). Balan is used as a preemergence herbicide on turf to control crabgrass, watergrass, and goosegrass, yellow and green foxtail, purslane, carpetweed, and others. It is used at 1–2 lb ai/acre. A long-lasting compound related to Treflan but of greater safety on turf, it may affect seed germination for a year. It is available as 2.5% granules and an emulsifiable concentrate (EC) of 1.5 lb/gal. The granules are used on turf as the EC is volatile and should be cultivated in. Apply only to fully matured grasses. Bentgrass is damaged; fescue thinned but other turfgrasses are considered tolerant.[129]

Reports of effectiveness of Balan and degree of injury vary widely.

Bandane (Polydichlordicyclopentadiene isomers: LD_{50} = 575 mg/kg; skin uptake).[24,26,27,51,53,73,110,134,150] Bandane is a chlorinated hydrocarbon herbicide with some insecticidal properties and is available as granular formulations or as an EC, containing 4 lb/gal. It is used on both mature and young turf in early spring as a preemergence crabgrass control chemical. It may be used on Dichondra. On young turf injury was caused at three days emergence but not at 7 days. At the 1 1/2 times rate, rhizome production by 'Merion' was reduced. Crabgrass control has been rated fair to excellent and in some instances Bandane has given good goosegrass control. Bandane has a long residual life.

Bensulide (Betasan, Pre San, Prefar, *S*-(*O*-*O*-diisopropyl phosphorodithioate of *N*-(2-mercaptoethyl)benzenesulfonamide; LD_{50} = 770 mg/kg).[26,46,84] Bensulide has been of particular interest as a preemergence control for *Poa annua,* but is also listed as controlling such weeds as crabgrass, watergrass, goosegrass, purslane, shepherd's purse, and others. It is used at 5–15 lb ai/acre in sufficient water to carry it to the soil. It is available as an emulsifiable concentrate (4 lb ai/gal) and as 7% granules.

When used to control *Poa annua* on a green one must be sure there is a good stand of bent present as the chemical may limit seeding for the entire following growing season, though seed has emerged when sown after 60 days.[19] Bermudagrass may be yellowed by Bensulide. Bensulide has been reported effective on the alkaline side of neutral but not the acid side. Reports of soil effects vary. One investigator indicates that rate of application depends only on time of year and length of season.[13] Other investigators report effectiveness decreased by organic matter and cation-exchange capacity.[117] A fall application on bermudagrass for control of *Poa annua* gave good residual control of crabgrass the following season. Although greens have a high degree of tolerance, summer wilt may be increased.[40] Used on newly sprigged bermuda Benuslide has limited spread and increased winterkill.[44,47] Bensulide has been reported most toxic to crabgrass when N. P, and S were applied in a 1:1:1 ratio.[81] Bensulide is among materials which may be effectively "cancelled" by activated charcoal at 4 lb/1000 ft.[2]

Borate (Boron, Borax, Borascu, Tronabor, Gerstly Borate; LD_{50} = 2500 mg/kg). Borates are used as nonselective soil sterilants. At 5–10 lb/acre, boron is an element necessary for plant growth. At higher rates it becomes toxic, first to trees and shrubs and to grass at higher levels. Boron compounds are used to control weeds in corporation yards, around buildings, etc., but they should be used with caution. Don't use boron compounds where you expect to grow good ornamental plants.

Bromacil (Hyvar X, Urox, 5-bromo-3-*sec*-butyl-6-methyluracil; LD_{50} = 5200 mg/kg). Bromacil at high rates is a nonselective soil sterilant. At 2–6 lb ai/acre it has selective pre and postemergence properties when applied to the soil. It has been used experimentally on turf. There have been some trials to see if it can discriminate between turfgrasses to take bent and bermuda out of blue. No recommendations are made at present for use of this phytotoxic chemical on turf.

Bromoxynil (Brominil, Buctrile, 3,5-dibromo-4-hydroxybenzonitrile; LD_{50} = 100 mg/kg). Available as an EC containing 2 lb ai/gal. Bromoxynil is being used experimentally on grass as a postemergent foliage spray since many grasses are tolerant in young stages. It is tested at 1/2–1 lb ai/acre, but no recommendations for turf use can be made in 1968. It can be used soon after seeding bent, blue, and fescuegrasses. Fescue and bent are more susceptible than blue to injury. For use on seedlings, Ioxynil appears even safer.[118,129]

Cacodylic acid (Ansar 138, Arsan, DMAA, Ansar 560, Silvisar 510, Phytar 560, Phytar 160, Phytar 138, dimethylarsenic acid; Ld_{50} = 830 mg/kg). Cacodylic acid is available as a 65% wettable powder (WP) or emulsifiable concentrate (EC) and is used at 5–20 lb/100 gal (spray to wet) as a nonselective, postemergent contact herbicide. It is also available on vermiculite. It is used in renovating turf. Five days after treatment, the dead turf may be thoroughly irrigated and reseeded. As it is not root absorbed, it may be used under trees. It may corrode bronze markers.

Calcium Arsenate (Chip-Cal, Kleen-up, orthoarsenate, tricalcium arsenate, $Ca\ (AsO_4)_2$; LD_{50} = 35 mg/kg).[52,110,129,158,64] Calcium arsenate is used at 500–1200 lb ai/acre to control crabgrass and *Poa annua* with incidental control of chickweed. When soil contains chemicals that increase the solubility of calcium arsenate, injury to turfgrass may result. For this reason it is usually better to split applications and to reduce levels of application in subsequent years. Calcium arsenate is used preemergence and should be applied in the fall before *Poa annua* emerges or in the spring before crabgrass emerges. As with arsenicals, it is effective when soil and plant phosporus is at low levels. Calcium arsenate reduces innovations and rhizomes and results in thinning of turf. It causes more injury to fescue and bent than to bluegrass.[50] It is best used in low amounts in cool weather and with turf seed used to thicken grass stands before the soil becomes too toxic. At control levels arsenic inhibits turf seedlings.[104] Bentgrass, 'C-52,' 'Seaside,' 'Arlington,' and "Pennlu" have been injured more seriously than 'Washington,' 'Cohansey,' or 'Congressional.'[105]

Calcium Cyanamide (Cyanamide, Aero-cyanamide). Cyanamide is not a fumigant but is similarly used as a preplant treatment. It is discussed under nitrogen fertilizers (see *Principles of Turfgrass Culture*, Chap. 6). It is used a month ahead of planting on a warm moist soil. Forty pounds/1000 ft^2 are tilled into the surface inch and a second 40 lb spread on the surface. The soil needs some clay content and use on sands may be questioned. Cyanamide provides sufficient nitrogen for the seedbed without other additions. Thirteen pounds per cubic foot controls weeds in compost and aids decomposition.

CAMA (Calar, calcium acid methyl arsenate; $Ca(CH_3A_sOHO_2)$; medium toxicity).[73,109,134] CAMA is used as 8–10% solutions to provide 2–4 lb ai/acre. The lower rate is used at emergence and seven days later. The higher rate is used on older crabrass. Dallisgrass and foxtail are also controlled. It is active for an entire growing season. At 2 lb/acre, it has reduced tiller and rhizome formation of 'Merion' and thinned bluegrass stands by a third.

Casoron (Dichlobenil, Di-chlor, Du-sprex, 2,6-dichlorobenzonitrile; LD_{50} = 2710 mg/kg).[82,84] Casoron is being tested as a soil-applied preemergence chemical to control crabgrass, watergrass, quackgrass, dandelion, purslane, plantain, clover, and other weeds and to control bracken fern, horsetails, smartweed, cattails, rushes, and others in associated nonturf areas. It has injured turf species. It is used at 1–10 lb ai/acre, and is available as 50% wettable powder or 4% granules. Casoron does not move extensively in the soil and is most effective if lightly stirred in since it breaks down on the surface of hot soil. For this reason it has been tested more on crop plants than turf. Granules, appled in March at 1–5 ppm, are used for preemergence control of aquatics.

Chlordane (Chlordan, Halts, Ortho-klor, octochlor, 1,2,4,5,6,7,8,8-octachloro-2,3,3a,4,7,7a-hexahydro-4,7-methanoindine; LD_{50} = 250 mg/kg; skin absorbed).[18,27,51,52,73,77,149,150] An insecticide, Chlordane has herbicidal properties at high rates. Used at 60 lb/acre it gives fair preemergence control of crabgrass but is less effective than other chemicals. Ant and grub control are auxillary benefits. We find treated bluegrass to grow well and with good rhizome growth, but with roots and tillers inhibited. Reduced rooting has resulted in drought injury to turf a decade after Chlordane was applied. There are conflicting results on safety studies of Chlordane on young turf. Reports vary from safe to damaging; one study indicated more injury to fall-seeded than to spring-seeded turf.[50,76] The principal damage reported is thinning of the turf.

CIPC (Chloro IPC, Chloropropham, isopropyl *N*-(3-chlorophenyl) carbamate; LD_{50} = 5000 mg/kg). A selective preplant and preemergence herbicide, CIPC is used in ornamental plantings at 2–4 lb ai/acre for control of grasses. Grasses tend to become resistant quickly.

Copper Sulfate (Copperas, bluestone, blue vitriol, blue copperas, copper sulfate pentahydrate; LD_{50} = 300 mg/kg). Copper sulfate is an algacide at 1 ppm. One-half ppm applied on several consecutive days may be more effective. Do not mix with wetting agents or other chemicals.

CPA (Kleen-up, No-crab, ENZ, Fairlawn, calcium propyl arsenate; LD_{50} = 355 mg/kg). CPA is formulated as 18–24% on vermiculite for spreader use, at 20–40 lb ai/acre for pre- or postemergence control of crabgrass with incidental control of purslane, carpetweed, pigweed, and others. It is recommended for use at crabgrass emergence on established blue, bent, rye, and fescuegrasses or dichondra. It may be applied at the time of turf seeding with only little reduction of turfgrass germination. Tests on turf have been limited but favorable.

2,4-D (Aqua Kleen, Barweel, Butoxone, Phenox, 2,4-DA, Weed-Rap, Formula 40, 2,4-D NaS, 2,4-DE, Dacamine, Emulsamine, Hedonol, Hormosalt, Hormotox, Am Sol, Weedar64, Weed-B-Gone, Weed-no-More, Weedanol, Weedone, Weedez, and no doubt others; 2,4-dichlorophenoxyacetic acid; LD_{50} = 375 mg/kg).[32,110,126,146,147] 2,4-D is a selective, translocated, foliar applied, postemergent hormone-type herbicide. The various formulations vary among simple salts, amine salts, and esters of high or low volatility. Granules are formulated for aquatic weed control. 2,4-D controls many common broad-leaved weeds when used at 1/4–4 lb ai/acre. Low volatile esters are preferred for spraying in the vicinity of sensitive plants. St. Augustine, centipede, and bentgrasses are injured and all turfgrasses may be injured as seedlings. In one study seedlings were resistant when ten weeks old. Rhizome growth of bluegrass may be significantly decreased.

Dalapon (Dowpon, Radapon, Basfapon, 2,2-dichloropropionic acid; LD_{50} = 3860 mg/kg; may cause skin and eye irritation). Dalapon is used pre- and postemergence as a selective, foliage-applied, translocated herbicide to control grasses in broad-leaf plantings. It is a soluble salt, 75–85% active, used at 4–8 lb ai/acre. It is most effective at low rates with repeat applications at 1–3 week intervals. In turfgrass management it is most often used as a spot spray to control growth around traps, markers, fences, monuments, etc. It is rapidly taken up but slow to act. It may leach into the root zone and injure ornamental plantings and inhibit growth for 60 days or more. It is slow to act and 2–3 weeks may pass before symptoms occur.

TCA. Trichloroacetic acid has been similarly used but has been largely replaced by Dalapon. Dalapon is used to control emerged aquatics. Dalapon damage to trees often resembles salt damage, but affects both old and young leaves whereas salt affects older leaves.

2,4-DB (2,4-D Butyric, Butyrac 118, Butoxone, Butyrac 175, 4-(2,4-dichlorophenoxy) butyric acid; LD_{50} = 500 mg/kg; Irritant). 2,4-DB is a selective, postemergent, contact herbicide, absorbed through the foliage. In the plant it is converted to 2,4-D, which is translocated. Grasses are resistant and 2,4-DB has been used experimentally on turf.

DCPA (Dacthal, phthalic acid, Oust, Dacthalor, DAC 893, dimethylester of tetrachloroterephthalic acid; LD_{50} = 3000 mg/kg).[24,26,49,50,53,84,110,115,129,136] DCPA has rated high as a soil-applied preemergence crabgrass-control chemical. It causes little damage to bluegrass but may injure red fescue or bentgrasses, and has been considered risky on greens. Available as 50 and 75% wettable powders and 2 1/2 and 5% granules it is applied at 4–14 lb ai/acre; still higher rates are used on high organic soils. DCPA is one of the most consistent herbicides in reducing goosegrass and is effective against spurge, chickweed, purselane, foxtail, and barnyard grass. The chemical is strongly absorbed and little leached. When applied in the fall, it gave control till the following July.[158] Use for two years at 15 lb created a persistent residue. DCPA resulted in severe reduction in rhizome and tiller production by 'Merion'; among several bentgrass varieties it was most injurious to Toronto.[73] It is reported as suppressing turfgrass germination for 60 days in one test, 100 in another.[51,158] Used to control weeds in sprigged bermudagrass it decreased winter survival.[44]

2,4,-DEP (Falone, tris(2,4-dichlorophenoxyethyl) phosphite; LD^{50} = 850 mg/kg). 2,4-DEP is a soil-applied preemergence herbicide which endures in the soil surface and under growing conditions breaks down into a 2,4-D precursor. It is available as 5 and 10% granules or a 2 or 4 lb/gal EC. It is used on turf for control of crabgrass, goosegrass, chickweed, foxtail, watergrass, purslane, and others. It is used at 1–8 lb ai/acre in two applications, the first 2 weeks before germination and the second 6 weeks later. 2,4-DEP is activated by 1/2 in. of water following application.

Dicamba (Banvel D., Mediben, 2-methoxy-3,6-dichlorobenzoic acid; LD_{50} = 1040 mg/kg).[57,23] Available as an emulsifiable concentrate of 4 lb ai/gal or as 10% granular, Dicamba is used at 1/4 to 2 lb ai/acre as a selective, translocated, postemergence herbicide. It may be used at higher rates for preemergence control.

Dicamba has had quick acceptance for turf because of its ability to control knotweed. Use of chlorophenoxy herbicides has often resulted in heavy stands of resistant knotweed, especially on compacted soils. Dicamba gives good control of knotweed but is sufficiently inhibitory of turfgrasses that replacement by grasses if often slow, especially since the compacted soil usually remains compacted.

Dicamba should not be used on bentgrass greens but has been effectively used on bentgrass fairways.[57] It is damaging when used in the root zone of ornamental plantings. It is relatively mobile in the soil and will move into the root zone, be taken up, and translocated. It is an effective herbicide but should be used cautiously to avoid damage.

Dicamba is favored for weeds resistant to phenoxy weed killers, such as knotweed, chickweed, white clover, curly dock, red sorrel, and ground ivy, as well as for species of medic, dandelion, henbit, purslane, and yarrow. It is often mixed with organic arsenicals or 2,4-D to extend the range of control to nutgrass, johnsongrass, bindweed, star thistle, crabgrass, and others. Veronica. plantain and some docks are not controlled.

Dicryl (*N*-(3,4-dichlorophenyl) methacrylamide); LD_{50} = 1800 mg/kg).[113] Dicryl is a pre- and postemergent herbicide of limited soil life which has been tested on turf. Present data indicate that 1 lb ai/acre increases effectiveness of herbicides used for crabgrass control on bermudagrass.[24,160] The mixture may aggravate arsenic damage on St. Augustine and centipedegrasses.

Diphenamide (Dymid, Enide, *N,N*-dimethyl-2-diphenylacetamide; LD_{50} = 1050 mg/kg). Diphenamide is a selective preemergence herbicide used to control grasses in ornamental plantings. It is available as a wettable powder, granules, or a fluid. It is used on dichondra turf, ice plant, and on bermudagrass for control of annual grasses, knotweed, and a few other broad-leaved weeds. Colloid adsorbed, its effectivenness is reduced on muck soils. Rates to 6 lb ai/acre may be used on heavy soils but not more than 4 lb on sandy soils. Life is 6–8 mo but it may leach in sandy soils and require a repeat application. All temperate-season turf species have been injured and bermudagrass has suffered chlorosis from use of dophenamide at 2–4 lb.[51,84,163]

Diphenatrile (Diphan, diphenylacetonitrile.[27,33,134,163] This preemergence spray has been tried and found to give crabgrass control without injury on bermuda, Kentucky blue, bent, fescue, and rye grasses. Applied to the soil before seeding, it has caused a reduction in emergence of turfgrass seedlings for a period of 40 days.[51] In Florida it has not given crabgrass control for a full season. It is used at 30 lb ai/acre[49]

Dipropalin (2,6-dinitro-*N,N*-dipropyl-4-methylaniline).[26,110] A preemergence soil-applied herbicide this gives good control of crabgrass and is being tested on turfgrasses. In trials 8 lb ai/acre has been tolerated by tall fescue, *Zoysia,* bermuda, St. Augustine, and centipedegrasses but in other tests the same rate has injured blue, bent and fescue grasses. Dipropalin is an analog of Trifluralin and is safer on turf.[37]

Diquat (Reglone, 1,1-ethylene-2,2-dipyridilium dibromide; LD_{50} = 400 mg/kg; irritating to skin; may cause lung lesions): Diquate is a nonselective, postemergence, contact herbicide recommended for aquatic weed control. It is sprayed on emerged leaves at 1/2–1 lb ai/acre; for submerged aquatics it is used at 1/4–1 ppm. Experimentally, this may serve like Paraquat to scorch existing turf in a renovation and replant program. Perennial weeds regrow from the root.

Diuron (Karmex, Momer, Karmex-DL, 3-(3,4-dichlorophenyl)-1,1-dimethylurea); LD_{50} = 3400 mg/kg; irritating).[84,101] This is not to be considered as an herbicide around turf as it is injurious to grasses and has extremely long residual effects, i.e., for two years and more. It is used in grass seed fields as a directed spray between rows at rates of 1/2–2 lb/acre. Do not use on light soils or near desirable plants and avoid repeat applications. It has been used on dormant bermudagrass where it gave control of *Poa annua* and winter weeds, and controlled crabgrass the following summer, but with injury to turf.

DSMA (DMA, Sodar, Dimet, Clout, Crab-E-Rad, Disomar, Ansar 184, DIMA, Oust, Methar, Arsinyl, Dal-E-Rad, Weed-E-Rad, DMA-100, Ansar 584, disodium methyl arsenate; LD_{50} = 600 mg/kg).[26,109,160] DSMA is formulated as emulsifiable concentrates of 1 and 2 lb ai/gal; as 50–80% wettable powders; as 2–5% granules; and on vermiculite. It is used at rates of 4–5 lb ai/acre in 20–50 gal water and usually repeated after 10–14 days. It is used primarily to control emerged crabgrass but is also effective against dallisgrass, nutgrass, velvetgrass, goosegrass, watergrass, johnson-grass, foxtail, and other grasses and against chickweed, knotweed, and others. The younger the weedy grass the more effective the spray.

As DSMA leaches readily, it has no preemergence activity. Turf soil should be moist when DSMA is used. DSMA may be combined with 2,4-D to increase the range of weeds killed, and the mixture is more effective in control of nutgrass. DSMA is toxic to St. Augustine, centipede, and carpet grasses, and damaging to fescue, but can be used to remove *Paspalums* from bermuda and *Zoysia* grasses.[26] Its use has reduced stands of bluegrass by a third. Tillers were reduced more than rhizomes.[73] When thatching operations were used at the same season as DSMA, turf recovery was reduced.[107]

Endothall (DF Spray, Endo, Hydrothol 47, Aquathol, Hydrothol 199, Endothall Turf Herbicide, disodium 3,6-endoxohexahydrophthalate; LD_{50} = 35 mg/kg; irritant; skin absorption). Endothall is a selective soil-applied pre- and postemergent herbicide, available as 5% granules or 1.5–2.0 lb/gal EC. It is used at 3–6 lb ai/acre and damages bent, fescue, and *Zoysia.*[110] It is used on turf as a specific control for *Veronica* and red sorrel though it controls other weeds too.[110] Soil should be moist, temperatures below 80°F, and the mature turf growing vigorously. Two applications two to three weeks apart are used. Endothall has controlled bromegrass in bluegrass seed fields.[35] Endothall is also used as an aquatic herbicide. The special aquatic formulations should be used to avoid fish kill. Used at 2 ppm, not more than two applications a year should be made. Endothall has a short residual life in the soil.

EPTAM (EPTC, *S*-ethyl dipropylthiocarbamate; LD_{50} = 1630 mg/kg). Eptam is not a turf herbicide but does have a special use in the control of nutgrass (*Cyperus* spp.). Its use is discussed under nutgrass. Available as 5 and 10% granules and 6 lb/gal EC, it is used at rates of 2–8 lb ai/acre; it should be rapidly incorporated into the soil to avoid break-down.

Fenac (Tri-Fen, 2,3,6-trichlorophenylacetic acid; LD_{50} = 3160 mg/kg). Fenac is a selective, translocated, soil-applied, preemergence herbicide and temperary soil sterilant. Fenac has a long residual action and is not recommended for turf. It has been used experimentally on highway turf. Leached into the soil. it controls weed emergence for a long period of time. It s particularly effective against deeprooted weeds.

Fenuron (Dybar, 3-phenyl-1,1-dimethylurea; LD_{50} = 6400 mg/kg; irritant).[131] Fenuron is not an herbicide to be used on turf as it is primarily a soil sterilant and kills woody plants. It has been used experimentally in the southwest where it has killed puncture vine with survival of bermudagrass.

Ioxynil (Certrol, Bentrol, Actril, 2,6-diiodo-4-cyanophenol; LD_{50} =305 mg/kg). Ioxynil is a selective, postemergence contact herbicide which is being tried experimentally on turfgrasses but for which no recommendations are made in 1968. a 50% soluble powder is used at 1/2–1 lb ai/acre in 10–20 gal. It is of interest because it kills a wider range of broad-leaved weeds than 2,4-D, and appears to be tolerated by seedling turf. A 1/2-lb rate was suitable and 1 lb maximum. It was most effective applied 4–5 weeks after emergence and injury was outgrown by 10 weeks in the spring. Among weeds controlled were mouse-ear chickweed, chamomile, buttercup, and speedwell. Dock required two applications for control.[112] Speedwell was controlled most effectively by a mixture with MCPP.

KOCN (Aerocyante, Crabnot, KRAB, Bonide Krab, Dedweed, Weedanol Cyanol, potassium sodium cyanate; LD_{50} = 85 mg/KG). KOCN is an older contact herbicide of some selectivity which is used for crabgrass control in turf; it is applied when crabgrass is in the seedling stage. As results are affected by humidity, rain, sunshine, and temperature, KOCN has been largely replaced by herbicides that have less critical requirements.

MAMA (MAM, Ansar 157, monoammonium methylarsenate; LD_{50} = 720 mg/kg). MAMA is a selective postemergence herbicide used essentially as DSMA except that applications are repeated within 5–7 days. It may be used at higher temperatures, and a surfactant is recommended with it . It is available as solutions containing 10 lb ai/gal for use at 1 1/2–2 lb ai/acre. It should not be used on St. Augustine or centipedegrass.

MCPA (MCP, Agroxone, Methoxone, Mephanac, Weedar, Bintrol, Raphone, 2-methyl-4-chlorophenoxyacetic acid; LD_{50} = 700 mg/kg; eye and skin irritation).[147] MCPA is a foliage-applied, selective, translocated herbicide. A variety of formulations are available for use in spring or fall at 1 oz to 2 lb ai/acre. MCPA helps control some difficult weeds such as sedges, bindweed, and puncture vine. Injury has resulted to St. Augustine, bent, carpet, and buffalograsses. MCPA should not be allowed to contaminate irrigation water.

MCPP (CMPP, Mecoprop, Mecopex, Runcatex, Iso-cornox, 2-(2-methyl-4-chlorophenoxy) propionic acid; LD_{50} = 650 mg/kg). MCPP is a foliage applied, selective, translocated herbicide. MCPP is safer than related compounds for use on turfgrasses and in addition effectively kills several weeds resistant to 2,4-D. These include clovers, chickweed, knotweed, and ground ivy in addition to more easily controlled dandelion, plantain, shepherd's purse, and mustard. Various formulations are used at 3/4–1 lb ai/acre in 20–40 gal. Do not use in hot weather or when soil is dry. It is best during the spring flush or growth. It may also be mixed with 2,4-D to increase number of weed species killed, but not on bentgrass.[29]

Methyl Bromide (Dowfume MC, Dowfume MC 33, Brozone, Bromo methane, Panobrome Cl., Picricide, Profume, Brom-O-Gas, Weedfume, and others). Methyl bromide is a highly toxic odorless gas and in the above formulations is mixed with varying amounts of chloropicrin (tear gas), which provides a warning as well as extending effectiveness.

Methyl bromide is used at 500 lb/acre for weed control or at 1000 lb for weed, disease, and nematode control. Methyl bromide is injected under a tarpaulin. Heavy vapors spread along the ground and descend into the soil. After 24 hours at soil temperatures above 60°F, the tarp may be removed and the soil planted three days later. One pound cans with a special applicator are available for treating small areas of noxious weeds or small lots of top dressing.

When an area is to be spot treated, a small trench may be dug around the area and filled with water to soak the soil beneath. Methyl bromide is then confined to the area treated. Roots within the treated area will be killed but as methyl bromide is not translocated, the effect is of root pruning. To avoid killing too much of the root system, the methyl bromide should be applied 3–4 ft from woody plants and on one side of the plant only.

Fumes do not move effectively into clods, and effectiveness is reduced on soils of high organic content. Average weed control has been improved in a mixture named Trizone which contains 61% methyl bromide, 30% chloropicrin, and 9% propargyl bromide.[79,88] The mixture named Weedfume has 2/3 chloropicrin. It controls weeds at greatly reduced cost, but disease control is reduced.

MH (MH-30, MH-40, maleic hydrazide, maleric hydrazide, Slo-Gro, 6-hydroxyl-3-(2H)-pyridazinone; LD_{50} = 4000 mg/kg). While MH has herbicidal properties it is most familiar on turf as a growth retardant. Where MH is used for controlling growth of turf around buildings, along roadsides, and around trees, monuments, and markers, it should first be used on a trial basis and careful notes taken. Performance varies appreciably with conditions and uptake is highest when the plant is turgid, making new growth at heights of 4–8 in., the air is humid (above 40% rh), and no rain or irrigation takes place during the following 24 hr.[21] MH has been used on bermudagrass to favor overseeded grasses.[48]

Monuron (Telvar, CMU, 3-(*p*-chlorophenyl)-1,1-dimethyl urea; LD_{50} = 3600 mg/kg).[148] Monuron is a soil sterilant and a somewhat selective preemergence herbicide. It is used primarily against grass. It has been used to control weeds in ice plant, and grass and oxalis in Dichondra. It has been used at rates up to 2 lb ai/acre on mature bermudagrass with and without apparent injury and with control of oxalis, clover, *Poa annua,* and other weeds.[84] At 3 lb/acre, growth was slowed and seed-head formation inhibited. Do not use on sandy soil, do not repeat applications until residual effects have worn off (2 yr or more),[9] and do not use around desirable ornamental plants.

MSMA (MMA, MSAMA, Ansar 170, Ansar 529, Daconate, monosodium acid methylarsenate; LD_{50} = 700 mg/kg). MSMA is put up as an emulsifiable concentrate of 4–6 lb/gal and used at rates of 2–5 lb ai/acre in 40–50 gal water. Use of MSMA on turf is still experimental and directed against nutgrass, dallisgrass, and other Paniceae. Check recent trade magazines for rates and details of use. It must be used with a wetting agent. Because of phytotoxicity use may be confined to spot spraying.

Mylone (DMTT, 3,5-dimethyltetrahydro-1,3,5-(2*H*)-thiodiazine-2-thione; LD_{50} = 500 mg/kg). Mylone is a granular soil fumigant that can be applied with a fertilizer spreader and tilled or washed into prepared soil. There it will volatilize and kill weeds. Soil is ready to plant after three weeks over 60°F. If irrigation has formed a crust, light tillage should be used to break the crust 5–7 days before planting. Mylone and Vapam were designed to be used without a tarp, but results may be improved by covering for a few days. This is particularly true where rhizomes of bermudagrass or quackgrass stick out above the soil surface. These are not killed otherwise. Five to six pounds ai/1000 ft² are used.

NAP (Alanap, Napthalan, *N*-1-naphthylphthalmic acid or *N*-1-naphthylphthalimide; LD_{50} = 8200 mg/kg). NAP is a soil-applied, selective, preemergence herbicide which has been used on turf. Available as granules, WP, and EC, it is used at rates of 2–4 lb ai/acre and moved into the soil with irrigation. Rates are reduced on light soils and high levels used on clay soils. It is not used on high organic soils. It controls many weedy grasses and some broad-leaved weeds. It has a short residual action and is effective for 3–8 weeks.

Neburon (Kloben, 3-(3,4-dichlorophenyl)-1-methyl-1-butylurea; LD_{50} = 11,000 mg/kg; irritant). Neburon is a preemergence soil-applied herbicide of some selectivity. It is used in Dichondra to control grass, chickweed, and other weeds. It has been used to spot spray mouse-ear chickweed. Its half life is 8–9 mo[148] and one should not use frequent repeat sprays.

Norea (Herban, 1-(*s*-(3a,4,5,6,7,7a-hexahydro-4,7-methanoindanyl))-3,3-dimethylurea; LD_{50} = 2000 mg/kg). Norea is a crop herbicide that is being used experimentally on turf. Among weeds controlled are crabgrass, goosegrass, watergrass, chickweed, spurge, and purslane. Weeds of *Malvaceae* and *Convolvulaceae* are tolerant. Available as an 80% WP and as granules it is used at 1–4 lb ai/acre. Irrigation should follow application of this herbicide. It should not be used on sandy soils.

Norea kills by affecting photosynthesis of young plants rather than killing seedlings and has the advantage that it may be used for a week after germination has begun. Hence if you were unable to make a preemergence spray in time, Norea gives you two weeks of grace. Dichondra appears tolerant.

Paraquat (Paraquat dichloride, Gramoxone, Paraquat CL, Dual Paraquat, 1,1-dimethyl-4,4-dipryidilium dichloride; LD_{50} = 157 mg/kg). Paraquat is considered safe because it leaves no residue on food crops, but it is not safe for the operator. In the body it forms free radicals which are high-energy catalysts of destructive reactions. Complete protective clothing should be used with this material.

Available as an aqueous solution containing 2 lb ai/gal, paraquat is used at 1/4–1 lb ai/acre. Used with a spreader sticker, its effect is immediate and not affected by subsequent rain. Activity is neutralized by anionic surfactants. Paraquat is broken down in the soil and does not accumulate. It is not recommended for sands. Paraquat has been used experimentally to kill winter weeds in dormant bermuda, centipede and *Zoysia* but has injured St. Augustine.[84,85,96,108]

Paraquat has been used in renovation to kill existing grasses before reseeding. Rhizomes are not killed. In one trial *Poa* was suppressed in favor of fescue, clover, and weeds.[108] In another trial *Agrostis* species recovered from April or October sprays but not a July treatment. There was some recovery of bluegrass and ryegrass from the July treatment.[10]

PCP (Pentachlorophenol is sold under many names to control termites, wood decay, etc.; LD_{50} = 78 mg/kg; irritant; skin absorbed; use protective clothing). PCP is a pre- and postemergence contact herbicide and its most likely use is to fortify oils used for contact control of weeds around buildings, parking lots, fences, and other bare areas. Preemergence effects last from three to five weeks.

Picloram (Tordon, 4-amino-3,5,6-trichloropicolinic acid; LD_{50} = 2000 mg/kg). Picloram is a foliage- and soil-applied, somewhat selective, translocated, pre- and postemergence herbicide of long residual life.[9] It has been used experimentally on turf where ornamental plantings are not rooted in the soil. It is an effective herbicide against poison oak and poison ivy.[86] Drift and contamination of ponds and water supplies should be avoided. Rates used have been 2–8 lb/acre, with some resistance of mature grasses to lower rates. Two pounds has injured bermuda but not St. Augustine, centipede, or *Zoysia*.[23,25] Good postemergent control of winter weeds has been obtained on dormant subtropical grasses with 1/4–1/2 ai/acre in October.

PMA (PMAS, Tat-C-Lect, Tag, Phix, Spor-Kil, Sel-Tox, Quicksan, PMAC, phenyl mercuric acetate; LD_{50} = 40 mg/kg; burns and irritates) (discussed below).

PMP (Metasol P-6, Metasol 57, phenyl mercuric propionate; relatively nontoxic). The above two fungicides have controlled crabgrass and constituted one of the earlier controls. They are relatively expensive unless also being used for their fungicidal properties. PMA is used at 2–6 lb ai/acre/week beginning with crabgrass germination; the dosage is increased up to 50% and the frequency to 5 days as the season goes on. Plants should be dry for 24 hr after treatment, grass should be mowed high to aid control, and treatment should be at temperatures under 80°F. Be reminded that 'Merion' is injured by mercurials. PMP is used at 12–14 lb ai/acre. Both may cause turf discoloration.

Prometone (Methoxy Propazine, Prometon, Primatol O, Gesefram, 2-methoxy-4,6-bis (isopropylamino)-*s*-triazine; LD_{50} = 2980 mg/kg). Prometone is a pre- and postemergence soil sterilant which is similar to Simazine in its use. Prometone, however, has shorter residual life though it is still active for over a year.

Prometone has been used on *Zoysia*, centipede, and St. Augustine grasses at 1–3 lb ai/acre, usually 2–3 mo after emergence. It should be kept from desirable plantings. It is not recommended, since other triazines are safer.

Prometryne (Caparol, Gesagard, 2-methyl mercapto-4,6-bis (isopropylamino)-1,3,5-triazine; LD_{50} = 3750 mg/kg). Prometryne is less phytotoxic than other triazines, has a shorter residual life, and is less damaging to grasses. It is used in fields of bluegrass planted for seed but not on turf except experimentally. It should prove safer than Simazine for edging traps. It is used at 1 1/2–4 lb ai/acre. It is used only on tolerant subtropical grasses. Various reports indicate injury, at one time or another to all grasses studied.

Propanil (Chem-rice, DPA, Rogue, Stam F-34, Surcopur, 3,4-dichloropropionanilide; LD_{50} = 1384 mg/kg). Propanil is a selective, postemergence, contact herbicide. It has been used experimentally on turf but probably should not be considered further. It breaks down in the soil to an azo compound (butter yellow), which is a cancer-inducing agent.

Propazine (Gesamil, Primatol P, 2-chloro-4,6-bis (isopropylamine)-1,3,5-triazine; LD_{50} = 5000 mg/kg). Propazine is a selective triazine which has been used for control of broad-leaved weeds in centipede, *Zoysia,* and St. Augustinegrasses with a degree of safety similar to Simazine or Atrazine.[26]

Siduron (Tupersan, 1-(2-methylcyclohexyl)-3-phenylurea; LD_{50} = 7,500 mg/kg).[25] Siduron is a preemergence, soil-applied herbicide. Siduron is not effective against broad-leaved weeds but when the 50% WP is used at 2–10 lb ai/acre it controls germination of crabgrass, watergrass, cheatgrass, nimblewill, and others. Bluegrass is tolerant and Siduron may be used in the seedbed with only moderate reductions in stand.[22] Among both bent and bluegrasses there are varietal differences in tolerance. 'Iagreen' bentgrass is sensitive, 'Cohansey' is not.[155] On soils of high cation-exchange capacity Siduron may persist a second season and dosage should be reduced the second year. Low rates are for sand, high for soils with high content of organic material.[93] Except for susceptible varieties of bentgrass, Siduron is considered one of the safest of preemergence herbicides.

Silvex (2,4,5-TP, Kuron, Kuran, Fenoprop, Propon, Weedone 2,4,5-TP, 2,4,5-T Propionic, Kurosal, Silvi-Rhap, 2,4,5-trichlorophenoxy-propionic acid; LD_{50} = 500 mg/kg; eye irritant; skin absorbed). Silvex is a translocated, selective, postemergence herbicide. Available as potassium and amine salts and as esters, it is used on turf to give control of some weeds resistant to 2,4-D. Used at 3–4 lb ai/acre it is applied only in the spring or fall when the weather is cool. It is not used on bent or St. Augustine, and it tends to thin tolerant grasses and reduce rooting.

Silvex is sufficiently toxic to turfgrasses that it may be difficult to get good vigorous replacement of weeds by turf.

Although it is sometimes used for aquatic weed control it should not be applied to water used for irrigation.

Injury from Silvex has been greatest at high temperatures, on acid soils, and during long days. Bent clippings have been reduced 0–59%, depending on season.[57] Seed yield of red fescue has been reduced 50%.[128] Silvex has caused seed-head abnormalities in rye, fescue, and bluegrass, and degeneration of roots and disruption of the pericycle in bentgrasses,[147] resulting in lowered drought tolerance.[132] Silvex has remained in the soil and killed 'Merion' seedlings four weeks after application. It has injured seedling grasses that are 4–5 mo old.

Simazine (CET, Gesatop, Primatol S or 2-chloro-4,6-bis (ethylamino)-*s*-triazine; LD_{50} = 5000 mg/kg). Simazine is a selective, soil-applied, preemergence herbicide and soil sterilant. It is available as 50 and 80% WP and 4, 8, and 10% granules. It may be used at 1–4 lb ai/acre and watered in to control watergrass, mustard, chickeweed, crabgrass, foxtail, purslane, Russian thistle, and other weeds in ornamentals.

St. Augustine has a high tolerance for Simazine but varying degrees of injury have been reported on other subtropical turfgrasses.[23,24,26,89,101] In one test granular applications to 8 lb did not affect young trees in turf but a spray application injured them.[28] Used in the landscape, Simazine may result in an interveinal chlorosis similar to boron injury. However, boron affects older leaves, Simazine both young and old leaves. Used on sprigged grasses, Simazine has reduced rate of spread and increased winter injury.[44,47] 'Meyer' *Zoysia* sprigs have been somewhat tolerant but 'Midwest' has been injured.[62] Tall fescue has been tolerant of Simazine in one test.[110] Simazine activity extends through a second growing season, often longer.[9]

Sodium Arsenite (Triox, Penite, Atlas-A, Chem-sen, Crabex, Weedo, Na_3ASO_2, sodium acid arsenite (Na_2HAs0_2): LD_{50} = 10 mg/kg; a leading poisoner of children; its salty taste appeals to pets, children, and cattle). Where use of this slightly selective, postemergence herbicide is permitted, it is used at 4 lb ai/acre to control emerged crabgrass. It causes tip burn of the turfgrasses but is favored for its low cost compared to organic arsenicals. It accumulates in the soil to give residual control of crabgrass and *Poa annua.* At double rate it has been used to set back existing turf in a renovation program. It is used at 4 ppm for aquatic weed control. At very high rates it completely sterilizes the soil.

Sodium Chlorate. This is a temporary soil sterilant, usually lasting less than a year. It is used at 1–3 lb/100 ft² as a solution or dust to spot treat areas of noxious weeds. It is not used to control weeds near buildings, as it increases flammability and creates a fire hazard.

2,4,5-T (2,4,5-TE, 2,4,5-Tlve, Dacamine 4T, Envert-T, Reddon, Tributon, Trinoxol, Phortox, Weedone 2,4,5-T, 2,4,5-trichlorophenoxyacetic acid; LD_{50} = 500 mg/kg). 2,4,5-T is a translocated, foliage-applied, selective herbicide. Because 2,4,5-T is injurious to ornamental planting it is generally used as a low volatile ester. It extends the effectiveness of 2,4,-D on herbaceous weeds to woody weeds and brush, and is most familiar on turf as a mixture with 2,4,-D when weeds to be controlled include woody brush such as poison ivy, etc. The mixture is specific for brush control. The salt is used for control of floating and emerged aquatics.

2,3,6-TBA (TBA, TCB, TCBA, Benzac 1281, trichlorobenzene, Tryben 200, 2,3,6-trichlorobenzoic acid; LD_{50} = 1370 mg/kg). TBA is a nonselective soil sterilant used at 10–30 lb/acre. As it is somewhat less toxic to grasses than to broad-leaved weeds, it has received some attention experimentally but has injured bermudagrasses at 4 lb/acre.[101] It affects cover a second growing season.[9]

TCA (STCA, ACP Grass Killer, trichloroacetic acid; LD_{50} = 5000 mg/kg; highly irritating protein precipitant). TAC is a selective, translocated, pre- and postemergence herbicide used to kill grasses. It is used much as Dalapon for spot treatment of weedy grasses such as johnsongrass. It is little used today.[141]

Terbutrol (Azak, Azac, Azar, 2,6-di-tert-butyl-p-tolylmethyl carbamate; LD_{50} = 34,600 mg/kg). Terbutrol is a selective, preemergence herbicide. Available as an 80% WP or as granules, terbutrol is applied at 10 lb ai/acre to control crabgrass. Application is followed by irrigation to wash it into the surface soil where it has a long residual life. At Davis it has reduced rooting of bluegrass and caused water stress a year after application. Bentgrass and fescue are injured and repeat applications injure even bluegrass.[129] There may be some thinning of turf and some discoloration of bentgrass. Toronto 'bentgrass' is unusually sensitive. Control of crabgrass is good.

Trifluralin (Treflan, trifluoro-2,6-dinitro-*n,n*-dipropyl-*p*-toluidine; LD_{50} = 3700 mg/kg).[17,24,26,27,110,173] Trifluralin is a selective preemergence herbicide available as an EC of 4 lb ai/gal or as 5% granules. It is used at 1/2–1 1/2 lb ai/acre in 40–50 gal water. As it is most effective incorporated into the top 2 in. of soil by discing, Trifluralin has not been much used on turf. However, it has been effective in some trials as a control for *Poa annua* and is listed as providing selective controls against a number of grasses such as goosegrass, watergrass, stinkgrass, sandbur, foxtail, bluegrass, crabgrass, and others. Very long lasting, it may increase susceptibility of remaining grasses to stress and may injure overseeded grasses sown several months later. Toxicity is increased by high organic content of the soil.[16]

Trifluralin causes injury to all turfgrasses and so its safer analogs, Balan and Dipropalin, are preferred for turf use.[44,73,75]

Vapam (SMDC, sodium methyldithiocarbamate, Chemvap, VPM; LD_{50} = 820 mg/kg; a soil fumigant). Vapam is used as a liquid to provide 6–9 lb ai/1000 ft^2. It may be tilled or washed in and sealed with a heavy irrigation. After a week of over 60°F the soil surface is tilled to break any crust, and is ready to plant a week later.

Vorlex (a mixture based on methyl isothiocyanate and chlorinated three-carbon compounds; LD_{50} = 305 mg/kg). Vorlex is a nonselective soil fumigant, with broad activity against insects, fungi, and nematodes in addition to weeds.

Vorlex is injected four to six inches deep with a chisel applicator and the soil is rolled to seal it. After four days above 60°F the surface is cultivated; planting is done after the fourth or fifth week. One to 1 1/2 gal/1000 ft^2 are used but the rate may be halved if a tarp is used.

Vegedex (CDEC, 2-chlorallyldiethldithiocarbamate; LD_{50} = 850 mg/kg). Vegedex is a selective preplant or preemergence herbicide which has been used experimentally for control of annual grasses in turf.[76] Recommended rates are 4–8 lb ai/acre.

Weed Oils. Many oils are in this broad class. They may be fortified with poisons to increase their effectiveness. Their principal advantage is economy, but they are environmental pollutants which create an offensive smell and appearance. Their use is generally incompatible with uses of turf. A number 1 or 2 fuel oil from paraffin- or naphthalene-based crude oils is one of the most effective contact oils. The oil will go further and be more effective if fortified with dinitro compounds, 2,4-D, TCA, PCP, or other herbicides.

Zytron (DMPA, *O*-(2,4-dichlorophenyl)-O-methyl isopropyl phosphoramidothioate). Considerable research has been done on this preemergence herbicide. Difficult to manufacture, its costs could not be brought into the range of equally effective compounds and its manufacture has been discontinued.

CLASSIFICATION OF WEEDS

Response of a weed to chemical control will depend in part on whether it is a monocot or a dicotyledonous species. Susceptibility to control further depends on whether the weed is an annual, biennial, or perennial.

Monocotyledonous plants include grasses, and have parallel veins—their leaves will tear in a straight line. Seedlings emerge as a single spear. Most species are herbaceous and have flower parts in multiples of three. Weedy monocots include species of grass, sedge, rush, and occasionally species of lily or its families. Dicot leaves have veins which form a network and tear in a broken line. Emerging seedlings present two leafy structures, cotyledons, one on each side of the stem. Plants may be herbaceous or woody, and flower parts are usually in multiples of four or five or are numerous. Dicot weeds belong to many families though a large share belong to the composite or daisy family.

Growth of a dicotyledonous plant is by two meristems. In a typical dicot, cell divisions in the growing point result in vertical extension in length. Later growth of a cambium layer results in increased girth, i.e., growth in diameter. The growing tip is the youngest part of the plant and encloses the growing point. In contrast, the growing point of grasses is carried low and leaves extend above it by a false stem of overlapping sheaths. Mowing removes the oldest part of grass leaves. Mowing typical dicots removes the growing point and young tissues and sets the plant back for two to several weeks. In this fashion mowing effectively controls many dicot weeds and those that survive and flourish under turf conditions are those in which the growing point grows horizontally, close to the ground, or is carried low as in rosetting plants. Dandelion and plantain are examples of rosette plants. Knotweed, spotted spurge, and *Veronica* are examples of procumbent, trailing, or prostrate plants which are weeds of turf.

Many herbicides, mostly chlorophenoxy compounds, select between monocots and dicots. It is more difficult to find herbicides selective between monocot species, or between dicot species.

Herbicides are most effective against young plants and are more effective against annual than perennial weeds. Annual plants are those that complete their life cycle in one growing season and depend upon seed to survive from year to year. Annuals may be further divided into cool-season and warm-season annual plants. Cool-season or winter annuals usually germinate in the fall and flower and set seed in the spring or early summer, though germination often extends from autumn through early spring. Warm-season or summer annuals do not germinate until the soil is warm and they flourish under warm summer conditions. Spotted spurge is an example of a summer annual. Herbicide application for winter annuals will be most effective during their cool season of germination. For summer annuals herbicides are most effective when applied during late spring.

Biennial plants complete their life cycle over two growing seasons. Many are rosetting plants the first year, producing stems, flowers, and seed the second. Perennial plants endure from year to year, producing seed and often spreading by vegetative runners. They are often difficult to kill. Selectivity of sprays is sometimes based on the greater tolerance of perennial plants for herbicides. Perennial plants often have underground growing points which survive contact sprays and reestablish the plant. In the seedling stage, perennials, biennials, as well as annuals are readily destroyed by low applications of herbicide and applications should be timed to coincide with this susceptible stage. When seeds germinate over a long season, preemergence sprays are apt to be most effective.

Subtropical grasses exhibit winter dormancy at the northern limits of their range. Control of winter weeds may seem of little importance on dormant turf at a season when it is not used and activities have moved indoors. However, vigorous weed growth sets back spring recovery, and winter weeds should be controlled. On dormant bermudagrass, Paraquat has killed winter weeds without damage to dormant grass[84,85,96,108] and preemergence herbicides applied as the bermudagrass browned off have effectively reduced winter weeds.[84]

In a recent questionnaire, golf superintendents ranked their weed problems as follows: *(1) Poa annua, (2)* knotweed, *(3)* crabgrass, *(4)*broad-leaved weeds, *(5)* goosegrass, and *(6)* miscellaneous.[129]

There is no way of making a complete list of weeds as many plants may appear at one time or another as weeds in turf. Weeds discussed are common turf weeds selected largely from those in the report of the Turfgrass Nomenclature Committee of Division IX of the American Society of Agronomy[103] (now Section 5 of the Crop Science Society of America). As major turf areas of the U.S. were represented on the committee, it is hoped the list will also represent all areas.

Grassy weeds are among those most difficult to control and a major unsolved problem is that of turfgrasses which are weeds in other turfgrasses.[71] Two principal grassy weeds, annual bluegrass and crabgrass, are discussed at length. Other monocotyledonous weeds of turf are listed in Table 9.3 by common name and discussed under their scientific name.

Table 9.3. Monocot Weeds or Grassy Weeds of Turf[a]

Common Name	*Botanical Name*
Annual bluegrass	*Poa annua*
Beargrass	*Cenchrus pauciflorus*
Barnyardgrass	*Echinochloa crusgalli*
Bentgrass	*Agrostis* spp.
Bermudagrass	*Cynodon dactylon*
Bluegrass	*Poa annua*
Bristlegrass	*Setaria* spp.
Bristly foxtail	*Setaria* spp.
Bromegrass	*Bromus* spp.
Burgrass	*Cenchrus pauciflorus*
Carpetgrass	*Axonopus* spp.
Chess	*Bromus* spp.
Chufa	*Cyperus esculentus*
Cocksfoot, cockspur	*Echinochloa crusgalli*
Cocograss, cocosedge	*Cyperus rotundus*
Couch	*Agropyron repens, Cynodon dactylon*
Crabgrass	*Digitaria* spp.
Creeping velvetgrass	*Holcus mollis*
Dallisgrass	*Paspalum dilatatum*
Devilgrass	*Cynodon dactylon*
Ditchgrass	*Echinochloa crusgalli*
Fingergrass	Spp. of *Digitaria, Cynodon, Paspalum,* and others
Foxtailgrass, foxtail millet	*Setaria* spp.
Garlic	*Allium vineale*
Goosegrass	*Elusine indica*
Green bristlegrass, green foxtail	*Setaria viridis*
Groundnut, ground almond	*Cyperus esculentus*
Hairy crabgrass	*Digitaria sanguinalis*
Hedgehoggrass	*Cenchrus pauciflorus*
Jungle rice	*Echinochloa colona*
Kikyuygrass	*Pennisetum clandestinum*
King's ranch bluestem	*Andropogon ischaemum*
Muhley	*Mehlenbergia schreberi*
Nimblewill	*Muhlenbergia schreberi*
Nutgrass, nutsedge	*Cyperus* spp.
Onion	*Allium canadense*
Pigeongrass	*Setaria* spp.
Purple nutsedge	*Cyperus esculentus*
Quackgrass, quickgrass, quitch	*Agropyron repens*
Rushnut	*Cyperus esculentus*
Sandbur, sandspur	*Cenchrus paucifloris*
Silver crabgrass	*Elusine indica*
Smooth crabgrass	*Digitaria ischaemum*
Snakegrass, stinkgrass	*Eragrostis cilianensis*
Tall fescuegrass	*Festuca arundinacae*
Velvetgrass	*Holcus* spp.

Table 9.3 cont'd.

Common Name	*Botanical Name*
Watergrass	*Ecninochloa crusgalli*
Wild garlic	*Allium vineale*
Wild millet	*Setaria* spp.
Wild onion	*Allium canadense*
Wiregrass, witchgrass	*Agropyron repens* (sometimes *Cynodon*)
Yardgrass	*Elusine indica*
Yellow bristlegrass, yellow foxtail	*Setaria lutescens*
Yorkshire fog	*Holcus lanatus*

[a]Weeds are discussed under the botanical name in the text.

WEEDY GRASSES

Poa Annua

Common names include annual bluegrass and annual meadowgrass (Fig. 9.3).

Poa annua probably ranks as the number one weed today in terms of numbers, range, and difficulty of control. At the same time it is a grass that is often encouraged and favored.

Poa annua has many characteristics of a desirable turfgrass. It forms a true putting surface and withstands low mowing and compacted soils. It seeds prodigiously and injured areas recover rapidly from seed. In many coastal and northern areas of cool mild climate, annual bluegrass crowds out other grasses, becomes the predominant grass, and is highly desirable.[127]

Away from areas of mild cool climate, annual bluegrass is unreliable and despised because it results in sudden failure of turf at critical times. Failure results from high disease susceptibility and low heat tolerance.

At almost any time during the past fifty years there have been articles which have said, "Annual bluegrass has many good features, so let us learn to live with it, let us improve it by selection." At the same time one can find articles which say, "We have tried to tame it, to live with it, but its treachery has destroyed us, let us destroy it." I choose to call it a weed because if it were to disappear from the earth tomorrow we should quickly resolve any resulting problems, but if it were to double tommorrow, our troubles would increase.

Poa annua is probably a fairly recent arrival on earth and is considered to have arisen as a hybrid tetraploid from a chance cross between *Poa infirma* H.B.K. of warm regions and *Poa supina* Schrad. of cool regions. The ranges of these could have overlapped during rapid climatic

Figure 9.3 *Poa anuua;* annual bluegrass.

changes at the close of a glacial period.[164,165] An autotetraploid has potential for wide variation and plants of annual bluegrass vary in color, attitude, degree of tillering, longevity, tolerance of mowing, etc. No clones appear to show notable disease resistance or heat tolerance. Gibeault reprints a list of 48 varieties or ecotypes from among those that have been described.[75] Timm, however, reduces European types to three principal ones: *(1)* An erect, bunch type which is strictly annual and predominates in Mediterranean regions. *(2)* A vigorous procumbent type having many biennial and perennial plants which predominates in Germany and parts of northern Europe. *(3)* A procumbent type similar to *(2)* in its longevity and root development, but much less vigorous.[161] It is found in northern Europe or at high altitudes in southern Europe. The first type appears to dominate in southwestern United States[38,99] but Youngner finds perennial strains occurring in closely mowed greens.[170] These perennial clones are relatively shy seeders, a desirable characteristic for turf. Present clones lose leaves during temperature stress and fail to grow replacements until the season is favorable for renewed growth. Dr. Youngner continues to evaluate perennial clones for improved genetic characters.

Poa annua generally begins germinating in the fall when daytime soil temperatures are less than 80°F, night temperatures are 50 to 70°F, and soil is moist.[35] Optimum temperatures for germination are reported as alternating between 59 and 86°F, and 40° and 70°F,[157] or as 60°F constant temperature.[38] Light is required for germination.[56] Plants grow rapidly and flower after six to eight weeks of growing weather.[172] *Poa annua* is largely self-pollinated and the seed is mature fourteen days after pollination.[99,102,157] Seed of annual lines is dormant for several weeks though seed from perennial strains can germinate immediately.[99,170] Dormancy is broken most rapidly under cool fluctuating temperatures.[159]

In regions of mild winters, germination and growth continue all winter and into spring. In cold regions many fall-germinated plants are killed in the winter. As weather warms in the spring, renewed germination and rapid growth reestablish the grass. Growth is optimum when shoot temperatures are 60–70°F and root temperatures are 50–65°F. Growth becomes increasingly vigorous until optimum temperatures are exceeded. At that time growth may appear white from seed heads which may form, even on grass mowed at 3/16 of an inch. Plants grow better at high temperatures when light intensities are also high (12,000 fc) and better at low temperatures with low light (3000 fc). There is more growth when days are long. Growth is most vigorous with 80°F days of 16 hours and high-intensity light, and with 62°F night temperatures.[106]

Annual bluegrass rapidly develops a good root system on good soils, but on compacted soils the root system is small and shallow. As annual bluegrass rapidly takes over on compacted soils, it has a reputation for being shallow rooted.[156]

When soil temperatures warm, *Poa annua* begins to suffer what Beard terms indirect heat stress.[15] Roots slow, then stop growth. No new roots are initiated; existing roots turn brown and are lost. Top growth slows. Leaves are smaller and appear at longer intervals.

Physiologically the protein metabolism is upset. The plant lacks recuperative powers, and is easily injured by stress or disease. In this condition a rise to 100°F for a few hours is sufficient to kill many individual plants and most are killed at temperatures only slightly higher.

The result is that a *Poa annua* turf weakened by indirect heat stress is quickly killed by direct heat stress on a hot day. This sudden dying is the most objectional characteristic of *Poa annua.* Soil temperatures are more important than air temperatures in producing stress.[15] *Poa* will survive longer in wet soil, as wet soil has a higher heat capacity. Ventilation is more important than syringing in reducing plant temperatures,[15] but syringing may help keep leaf and surface soil temperatures from going as high or from staying high for as long a time.

Poa annua responds to nitrogen and is favored by lime, but benefits slightly, if at all, from added phosphorus and potassium.[156] It has low tolerance for acidity or drought and occurs to a lesser degree when acid residue fertilizers are used.[76] It does not compete with tall grasses and is not tolerant of salinity.

Poa annua is susceptible to smog injury and is often used as a smog indicator. During high smog levels newly expanded cells are injured and a bleached appearing band appears across the emerging leaf.[20,106]

There is no simple control measure for *Poa annua.* Nevertheless, I consider that if control were a primary goal, it could be achieved. Control would result from several cultural and chemical practices designed to weaken annual bluegrass and at the same time encourage a dense growth of the favored grass. No practice alone appears sufficient to control annual bluegrass, but a combination of practices will control it. A principal difficulty in control is heavily compacted soil that limits growth of other grasses and makes replacement of *Poa annua* difficult. Factors in *Poa annua* control include the following:

Water. Annual bluegrass is more sensitive to drying than other grasses. Youngner obtained effective control by withholding irrigation.[172] Control is hardly possible when soil is kept continually wet. Cold-water irrigation may prolong summer survival.[14]

Seedbed Verticutting, hole punching, machine raking, and other operations, especially when carried out in the fall or early spring, provide a seedbed for *Poa annua* and help admit light which is necessary for *Poa annua* germination.[174] When the above operations on greens are replaced by frequent top dressing, seed is buried away from the light and germination is suppressed. Of course, the top dressing material must be clean or weeds can be introduced.

Fertilizer. Fertilizers of acid residue will reduce competitiveness of annual bluegrass with bentgrass.[156] A pH of 5.0–5.5 will favor bentgrass and limit annual bluegrass. Fertilizers low in phosphorus should be used during control.

Competition. Continual intraseeding will provide a reservoir of desirable seeds to more than offset the supply of *Poa annua* seeds in the soil. Bent can germinate at higher temperatures than annual bluegrass and will germinate and grow in the fall, a month before *Poa annua.*[56] *Poa annua* has been found less of a problem in bentgrass varieties which grow tight. It invades open-growing varieties more readily.[39]

Mowing. Annual bluegrass will withstand the shortest mowing you can give it, but on decorative or utility turf, a high dense turf depresses both germination and survival by limiting light at the soil level. Taller grass is deeper rooted and allows the longer intervals between irrigation that stress *Poa annua.*

Chemical Control. *Poa annua* is more sensitive to arsenicals than are many of the desired grasses. Continued and repeated use of arsenicals reduces both *Poa annua* and crabgrass but does not eliminate them.[172] There are many recommendations [14,42,45,76,118,127,143] based on successful practice. Unfortunately, such recommendations do not give the accompanying management practices, and arsenicals may get the credit when acid soils and good irrigation practice may have been equally important. Lead arsenate is generally recommended at rates from 20 lb/M/yr to 4 lb/M/yr applied 2 oz/M/wk during the growing season. There is a consensus that an initial heavy application is desirable followed by lighter applications at least once or twice a year to keep up arsenic levels. Arsenic is effective only when soil phosphorus is low.[105,142] Calcium arsenate is used as well as lead arsenate but the low solubility of lead arsenate makes it safer to handle. Arsenic also hurts bentgrass roots and reduces germination of bentgrass seed. Damage to bent is more frequent when the more soluble calcium arsenate is used. Calcium arsenate safety is increased by using small doses monthly rather than large doses annually or semiannually. Some observers feel arsenic will drive out bent before annual bluegrass.[79]

Selective preemergent herbicides are also useful provided there is sufficient good grass to effectively replace *Poa annua* without reseeding. Table 9.4 lists some chemicals tested and results obtained. Effectiveness has been reduced when the herbicide was accompanied by vertical mowing.[174] Of materials tested none have given suitable postemergence control of *Poa annua* without also causing some injury to the turf.

Partial Control of Poa Annua. Here I am proposing a changed viewpoint toward *Poa annua.* Where annual bluegrass forms a large part of springtime turf, the turf manager often adapts his program to get maximum survival to carry him through some important event such as Fourth of July. As an alternative I suggest he consider encouraging early demise of *Poa annua* so favored grasses may spread before the stress of summer's heat. Instead of trying to hang onto annual bluegrass he might begin to carry his turf on the dry side as soon as weather permits. This will cause surface soil to be warmer. When temperatures are in the 70's turf can be sprayed with sodium arsenite at two pounds per acre.[127] (There is also a possibility of using low rates of Endothal similarly.) this should knock out most *Poa annua* but vertical mowing can be used to further stress *Poa* by cutting

Table 9.4. Herbicides which have been used to control *Poa annua* in turfgrass[a]

Herbicide	*Rate (lb ai/acre)*	*Control (%)*	*Comments*
Avadex	1.0	0-90	Slight turf injury (bent, fescue)
Balan	1.5-3.0	95-100	Control at higher rate; slight turf injury (bent, fescue)
Bensulide	6-24	65-100	Long residual; no gross injury to young plants; established *Poa* not controlled
Bromacil	0.5-0.8	75-90	Mature turf severely injured
Calcium arsenate	360-720	75-93	Injury of bentgrass; coverage from bent and fescue seed reduced
Casoron	4-8	100	Severe injury to bent; two months injury to bermudagrass
CIPC	6-24	100	Long residual; three months injury to bermuda; not tested on other grasses
DCPA	2-10	75-98	No injury to dormant bermuda, some to bent and fescuegrasses
Diphenamide	4	100	High turfgrass injury (bermuda, fescue, bent)
Endothall	4-6		Tested only on dormant bermuda where it gave some postemergence control
Fenac	6	80-100	Some turf injury (bent)
Lead arsenate	360-720	26-45	Coverage from bent and fescue seed reduced temporary injury of bermudagrass
Monuron	2		Dormant bermuda only; significant control

[a]The above is a listing, not a recommendation.[25,38,39,64,76,80,82,84,98,105,169,173,174] Other materials showed low effectiveness, inconclusive results, or high turf injury in the particular tests reported. Chemicals tested included the following: Crag, Dicryl, Dipropalin, Falone, Ordram, MH, Neburon, Randox, Siduron, Simazine, TBA, Vegadex, and Velsicol B. MH has reduced seed head formation and 4-fluorophenoxyacetic acid has induced sterility.

and abrasion. As sodium arsenite reduces rooting of bents, water should be withheld to build up stress in advance of spraying. Water is used carefully after spraying.

Youngner proposes experimental spraying with gibberellin late in the fall or during spring thaws to stimulate new growth of *Poa annua* which would increase susceptibility to freeze injury. This could also aid early death of *Poa annua.*

In most areas a program could be developed that would kill off *Poa annua* by early or mid-May leaving about six weeks of growing weather before heat stress slowed growth of bentgrasses.

Crabgrass

Important species include *Digitaria ischaemum* (Schreb.) Muhl.(smooth crabgrass), and *Digitaria sanguinalis* (L.) Scop. (hairy crabgrass) (Fig. 9.4). Silver crabgrass is a name sometimes applied to goosegrass.

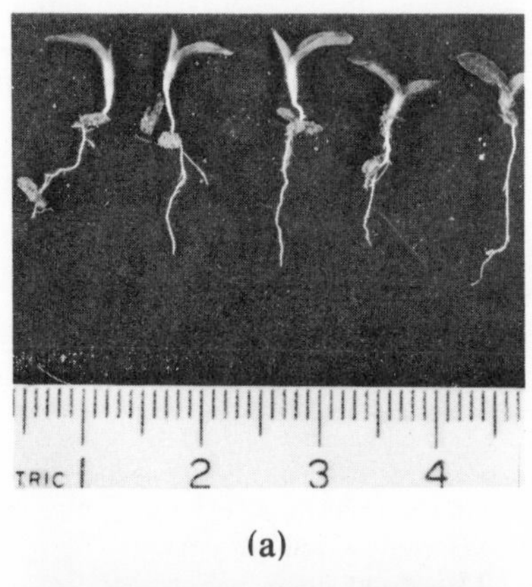

(a)

(b)

(c)

Figure 9.4 *Digitaria sanguinalis;* hairy crabgrass seedling and young vegetative stages.

Crabgrass is a tropical turfgrass that is weakly perennial in parts of southern United States but appears mostly as a hot-weather annual, germinating in the spring only after soil temperatures exceed 65 °F.[171] The persistence of the weed outside of the tropics is exemplified by a species of *Digitaria* which is one of only three angiosperm plants on the Antarctic continent. Most homeowners regard any weedy grass as crabgrass and apply crabgrass controls indiscriminately to tall fescue, dallisgrass, quackgrass, watergrass, and a host of others. Failure of control in these instances contributes to a legend of the invincibility of crabgrass.

Crabgrass may germinate as early as March in warm climates. It may first appear as late May in the northern states of the U.S. The first leaf is small, short, broad, and hairy with hair ends having a visible swelling. The leaf is subtended by a short coleoptile. The internode of the coleoptile phytomer may elongate several millimeters, in contrast to seedlings of *Festucae,* for which the first internode seldom develops (see *Principles of Turfgrass Culture,* Chap. 1).

Smooth crabgrass tends to be the predominant species outside of the northeast. The two species may hybridize to form an intermediate type. A single plant may produce up to 100,000 seeds.[68] Seeds germinate over the entire growing season. Plants rapidly form lax tillers which frequently root at the swollen nodes. Leaves have relatively short sheaths and blades. Blades have a rounded base, are fairly broad, and taper to a point. Ligules are 1–2 mm membranes. In flower, two to eight racemes are borne near the apex of the culm, spreading out to make the fingers. The lower glume and palea are much reduced.

Flowering begins in July. When days are short germinating seeds form flowers after only a few foliar nodes.

The swollen nodes of crabgrass break as a crab's legs break, at the joint, which makes hand weeding unprofitable.

As a subtropical plant, crabgrass may increase in a series of hot years, be reduced in a series of cold summers.[68] In the corn belt, where showers are frequent and nights are hot, crabgrass thrives and the region is known as the crabgrass belt and crabgrass as St. Louis bentgrass. Crabgrass often grows coupled with *Poa annua,* each germinating in the bare spots left by seasonal death of the other.

Crabgrass can seldom be controlled with chemicals alone. Control results from a combination of cultural practices. Control is most effective when a turf of dense grass is mowed at not less than two inches and irrigation frequency is reduced to allow drying of surface soil between irrigations. As height of cut is reduced, crabgrass increases in proportion.[66]

When summer temperatures are high, fertilizers may favor crabgrass over temperate-season grasses. Fertilizer is best used to produce a dense turf before crabgrass begins to germinate.

Chemical Control. With the development of effective preemergence herbicides, chemicals have greatly assisted control. They must be applied before germination begins and as they are effective in the surface soil, granular formulations are often more effective than liquid sprays. As crabgrass has a long season of germination, herbicides need to have several months of residual activity, or more than one application per year needs to be made. Some longer-lasting materials may be applied in the fall for *Poa annua* reduction and will still have sufficient residual action to control crabgrass all summer. Preemergence materials do not prevent germination but so inhibit root and shoot growth that death precedes establishment.[156]

Postemergence control is largely based on use of organic arsenicals. Control should begin by late June to control seed production. The mercurials, PMA and PMP, will also control crabgrass but cost is high unless PMA is also being used for disease control. As with other weeds, postemergence control is more effective when plants are young. Because of the long season of germination pre- and postemergent sprays may be used at the same time, one to knock down germinated weeds and the other to limit further germination and establishment.

Trials and tests of herbicides for control of crabgrass are too extensive to report. All herbicides used can cause injury to turf. Results of tests often show considerable variation from year to year. Turf may fail to outgrow injury in a dry spring and degree of moisture, sunshine, etc., can affect results. Again, note that on sand greens lowest rates should be tested before using any materials extensively. With high organic matter, the factor of safety is higher.

In general, early spring application has been more effective than fall or late spring applications.[7]

The following materials appear to best combine safety and effectiveness as of 1969.[8,11,18,43,55,58,60,61,63,64,72,90,94,109,112,113,123,125,129,130,133,138,145,153,162]

DCPA at 7 1/2–15 lb ai/acre has generally given 80–100% full-season control with minimum injury to bluegrass and some thinning of red fescue and bentgrasses. Best results were obtained when DCPA was applied 30–60 days before crabgrass germination.[61]

Bensulide at 10–15 lb ai/acre has given 80–100% control without injury to bentgrasses. Full season control is obtained.

Balan at 1–6 lb ai/acre has given to 100% full-season control without injury to blue, bent, and bermudagrass. It should be watered in at once.

Bandane at 30–40 lb ai/acre gives full-season control. Here reports vary from no injury to negligible injury. It is tolerated by all turfgrasses, but some injury to Tifgreen has been reported. It is reported as unsatisfactory on bermudagrass in Arizona.

Siduron at 9–18 lb ai/acre gives 80–100% control for less than a full season. A repeat spray is necessary.

I rate the following below the above either because of turf injury, poor crabgrass control, or inadequate testing.

Terbutrol at 10–15 lb ai/acre has given full-season control with little apparent injury, but it has long residual action and decreases rooting into the following year so that treated grass may suffer drought injury. Some injury has been reported on bentgrasses and on Tifgreen. Injury may result from repeat sprays.

Diphenatrile at 20–40 lb ai/acre has been reported safe and effective but some reports cite poor perfomance. More testing is needed before this compound can be rated.

Dipropalin at 4–8 lb ai/acre has given good control but reports of injury vary from no injury to thinning of turf. More testing is desirable.

The following have been extensively tested and are much used but have several disadvantages. Tricalcium arsenate, lead arsenate, and Chlordane. These are all used at high rates and have long residual action, injuring turf years after application.[68] These give mostly partial control. Control and degree of injury with arsenicals is variable depending on soil phosphorus and other factors; injury increases on light soils, infertile soils, and with water stress. Calcium propyl arsenate has not been tested enough to make generalizations.

Trifluralin and diphenamide have been fairly extensively tested and appear too damaging to turf for routine use.

Atrazine and Simazine may be used on St. Augustine, *Zoysia*, and centipedegrasses only.[24]

Table 9.5 summarizes preemergence herbicides used on crabgrass.

Postemergence Crabgrass Control. At the present all postemergence control is based on arsenicals which produce some scorching and injury of turfgrasses and which usually require repeat applications. These materials are all discussed on pages 327 to 342. Sodium arsenite is one of the cheapest forms and where its use is legal can give some control at 2–4 lb/acre. Organic arsenicals are somewhat more discriminating. DSMA

Table 9.5. Summary of the More Effective preemergence Chemicals Used for crabgrass Control in the Late 1960s[a]

Herbicide	*Rate (lb ai/acre)*	*% Control (%)*	*Comments*
Balan	3/4-3	32-100	Some injury to greens reported
Bandane	17 1/2-50	50-93	Some injury to fescue, Tifgreen
Bensulide	7 1/2-20	50-98	Safe but long residual action
Calcium arsenate	370-550	40-100	Control from good to erratic; injury frequent; thinning common; bent, fescue reduced
Chlordane	35-340	60-85	Frequently rated poor or variable; occasionally excellent; low injury; emulsion most injurious
DCPA	5-20	80-100	Good control; some injury to bent and fescue
Diphenatrile	20-40	80-100	Of promise but needs wider testing
Dipropalin	4-8	good-excellent	Thinned seaside; of promise but needs wider testing
Lead arsenate	400-1000	variable	Thinning of turf; injury at control levels
Siduron	5-20	70-95	Generally safe; does not last entire season; tolerated by seedling turf
Terbutrol	5-20	50-100	Injury to bent and fescue
Trifluralin	2-8	85-100	Used primarily on subtropical grass with temporary discoloration and thinning of grass

[a]Other materials appeared less effective or more injurious or had not been adequately tested for inclusion with the above.

is the most commonly used at 2–5 lbs. ai/A. Dicryl mixed with DSMA has improved its performance in some tests on bermuda and *Zoysia* grasses.[24]

Other Grasses

Agropyron repens (L.) Beauv. (quackgrass; perennial). In the field, quackgrass (Fig. 9.5) in Kentucky bluegrass has been killed by dicamba at 20 lb ai/acre and by Picloram at 3.5–7 lb.[166] Dalapon has been used as a preplant herbicide. At low rates it may only induce rhizome dormancy, from which the plant recovers; rates to 60 lb may be needed for rhizome kill.[67] Autumn resistance to Dalapon is high. Control is aided by cultivation which induces rhizome germination.

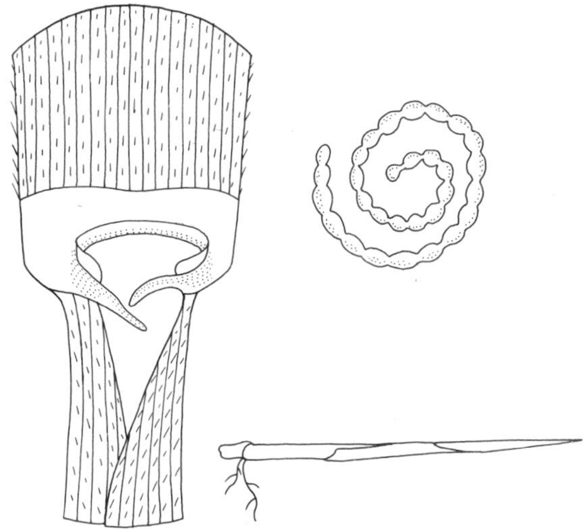

Figure 9.5 *Agropyron repens;* quackgrass. The vigorous pointed rhizome is characteristic.

Agrostis Spp. (bentgrass; perennial).[75] Bentgrass is a common weed in bluegrass turf. Control measures are being tested, but no recommendation can be made in 1968. One should, of course, avoid seed mixes containing bentgrass if one wants a bluegrass lawn. At present, spring applications of Silvex at low rates with repeat sprays of 2,4-D is as effective as other proposals.

Allium canadense. L. (wild onion; perennial) and Allium vineale L. (wild garlic; perennial) (Fig. 9.6). November and March treatments repeated to three times of 2,4-D, MH, or Dicamba have given control. Silvex has been less effective.

Andropogon ischaemum. L. (King Ranch bluestem; perennial). This has been reported as invading fine turf in the south central states. No control is reported but I cannot imagine this grass surviving long in well cared for turf.[122]

Axonopus affinis Chase. (carpetgrass; perennial) and *A. compressus* (Swartz) Beaus. (tropical carpetgrass; perennial) (Fig. 9.7). Carpetgrass is controlled ecologically by fertilizing and raising the management to moderate levels. Chemical control is obtained from a single spray of DSMA or AMA at 4 lb ai/acre, provided the grass to be favored is tolerant of arsenicals.[41]

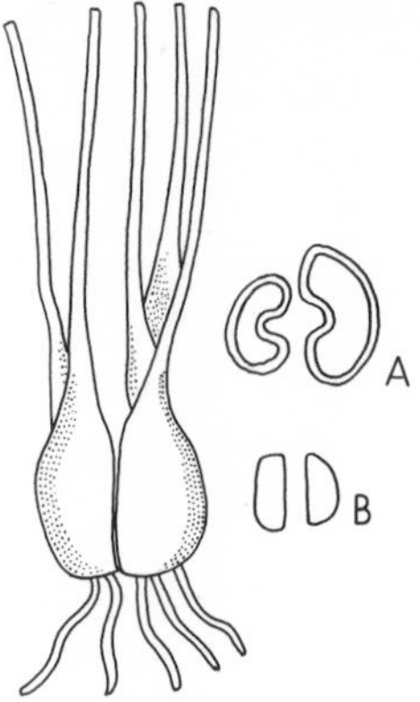

Figure 9.6 Leaf cross sections of wild garlic. (A) *Allium vineale*, (B) *A. canadense.*

Bromus spp. (bromegrass, chess; annual) (Fig. 9.8). For chemical control of bromegrass, preemergence herbicides would be favored. Brome has been controlled in fields of red fescue by 3.4–7 lb ai/acre of picloram.[166] Endothall has been used in fields of bluegrass for seed.[35]

Cenchrus pauciflorus Benth. (sandbur; annual) (Fig. 9.9). Cenchrus tends to be a problem in utility turf where cost of herbicides cannot be justified. In roadside turf arsenicals have given control with sprays repeated at 7–20 day intervals. Endothall has given control but at rates I should not consider safe on turf (32 lb ai/acre) Preemergence controls would be preferable.[135]

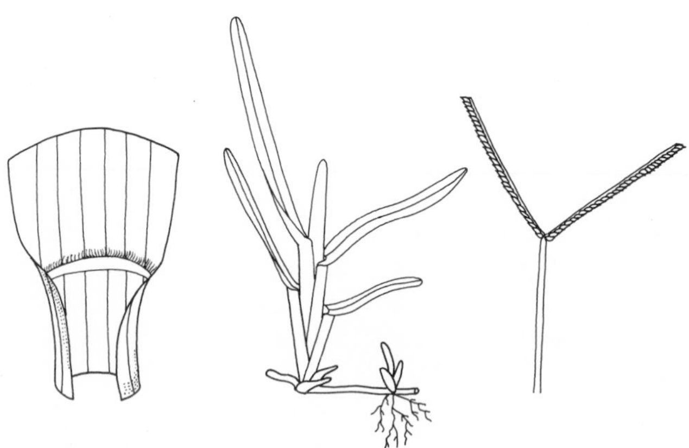

Figure 9.7 *Axonopus affinis;* carpetgrass.

Figure 9.8 Bromegrass.

Cynodon dactylon (L.) Pers. (bermudagrass; perennial). As a weed of other turfgrasses, bermudagrass is controlled with spot treatment using methyl bromide fumigation, or repeated sprays of Dalapon at less than 4 lb ai/acre until control is achieved. Atrazine controls bermuda in St. Augustinegrass. Monuron has been used to control bermuda in ice plant, and Dephenamide has given some control in Dichondra.

Bermuda has been kept out of bentgrass greens in the south by the following method of hand weeding. A vertical knife blade is fastened to a sod cutter and the green is ringed weekly, always cutting in the same track. Any shoots that have crossed the line during the week are cut off. The cut shoots are picked up by hand. If they have rooted, they are spudded out.

Cyperus esculentus L. (yellow nutsedge; perennial) and *C. rotundus* L. (purple nutsedge; perennial) (Fig. 9.10). These grassy sedges have been difficult of control. They produce rhizomes with tubers like small

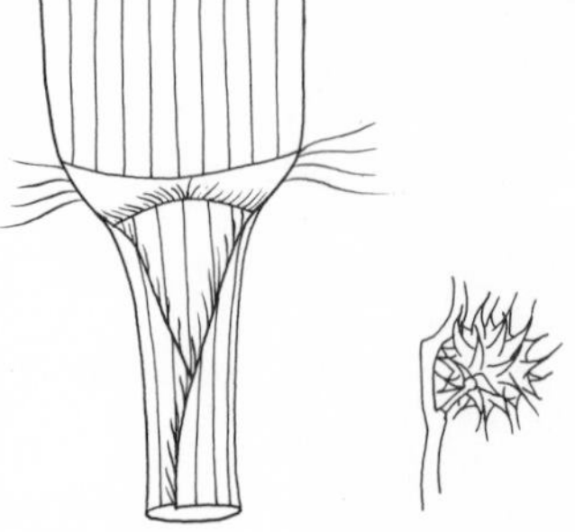

Figure 9.9 *Cenchrus pauciflorus;* field sandbur.

potatoes. The "eyes" are dormant and dormancy is released by injury or separation from the plant. Chemicals may kill the parent plant, the rhizome, and all of the tuber except the dormant eye which subsequently germinates to reestablish the plant. Tubers of this pest are often sold as a novelty for garden planting under the name of "ground nuts."

Amitrol and Eptam have been used with cultivation to control nutgrass prior to seeding.[89] In established turf up to 3.8 oz ai/M of AMA

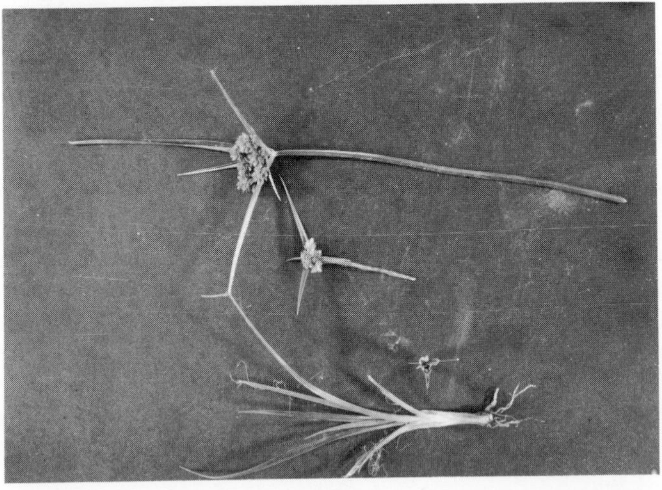

Figure 9.10 *Cyperus* spp. This is not nutgrass, but shows vegetative characteristics of the genus.

have been used.[65] Repeat sprays are used. Each spray kills new plants and releases dormant buds on remaining tubers. New growth is sprayed to kill it and release remaining dormant buds; spraying is continued until the "seed" supply is exhausted. Three to five applications of AMA the first year and one the second have been sufficient, especially if crowded by vigorous turf.[116]

Recently, control has been improved by a mixture of 2,4-D and AMA.

Echinochloa crusgalli (L.) Beauv. (barnyardgrass; annual) (Fig. 9.-11) and *E. colonum* (L.) Link (jungle rice; annual). Barnyardgrass is usually controlled by regular mowing. It will be controlled by the same controls as crabgrass. There are several biotypes and usually a few specimens will survive any selective herbicide.

Elusine indica (L.) Gaert (goosegrass; annual) (Fig. 9.12).[64,69] With the use of 2,4-D to remove spring weeds, goosegrass was able to move in and became an increasingly prominent weed in the 1950s. Preemergence control as for crabgrass is recommended but it is not as successful. For postemergent control, timing is very critical, and effective results are obtained only in the seedling stage. DSMA has reduced seed set and germination.[69,93]

Figure 9.11 *Echinochloa crusgalli;* barnyardgrass.

Eragrostic cilianensis (All.) Lutati (stinkgrass; annual). ICPA has given control along with other preemergence herbicides.

Festuca arundinacea Schreb. (tall fescue; perennial). One of the plants often mistaken for crabgrass, tall fescue seed is a frequent contaminant of red fescue and perennial ryegrass seeds. It is removed by hand digging or spot spraying with Dalapon or a contact herbicide.

Holcus lanatus L. (velvetgrass, yorkshire fog; perennial) (See Fig. 9.13) and *H. mollis* L. (creeping velvetgrass; perennial).[6] The former is being introduced as an impurity in Oregon-grown seed, the latter is coming into U.S. turf as an impurity in European seed. These are noxious weeds in turf and difficult to control.

H. mollis was present in one field with 7 tons/acre dry weight of rhizomes.[111] Field control is with 2–6 lb ai/acre of Eptam.[111] At high fertility levels bentgrass can crowd out much velvetgrass. Winter mowing at 4 in.

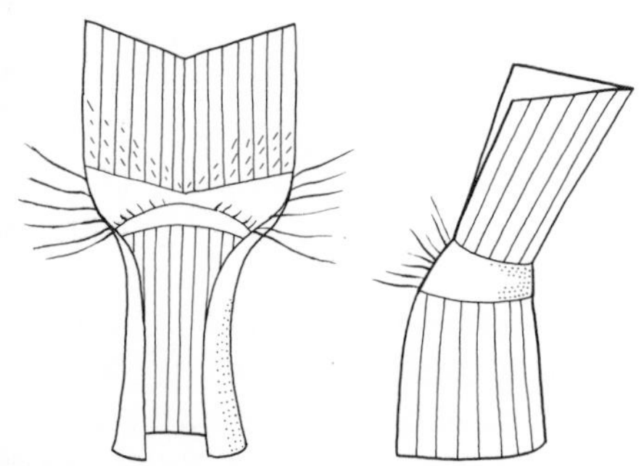

Figure 9.12 *Eleusine indica;* goosegrass; silver crabgrass.

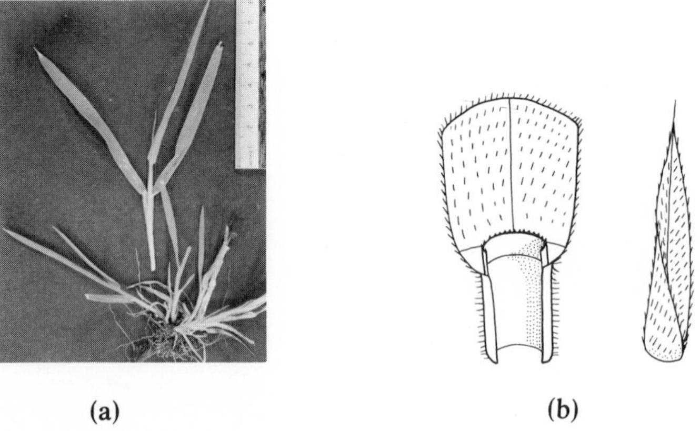

(a) (b)

Figure 9.13 *Holcus lanatus;* velvetgrass.

has reduced stands whereas 2 in. mowing increased them. In bermudagrass, a mixture of DSMA with 1 lb ai/acre of Diuron has controlled velvetgrass but this mixture should not be used around other plants. Spot spraying with translocated herbicides such as Dalapon is perhaps the best recommendation at present. Dalapon sprays have been more effective in July than in April or October.[10]

Mulhlenbergia schreberi Gmel. (nimblewill; perennial) (Fig. 9.14). Nimblewill has only recently become a pest of turf. Tolerant of some shade, nimblewill appears to have invaded turf when irrigation increased the soil moisture. This was aided by a series of moist cool summers in the midwest. Dicamba has retarded stolons when applied at 4 lb and reduced seed set at 6 lb.[34] These are both severe rates for turf. Picloram has shown promise. Both Picloram and Dicamba are injurious to trees, which are apt to be present wherever nimblewill is a weed.[137]

Paspalum dilatatum Poir (dallisgrass; perennial) (Fig. 9.15). Dallisgrass is a weed of wet spots and the first step in control is to drain or dry the area. Once that is done, repeated spraying with DSMA or other organic arsenicals at from 4 to as high as 32 lb ai/acre will control the weed. Higher rates are used only for spot spraying. Drying for as long as possible following the spray enhances control.[74] Dicryl added to DSMA has increased its effectiveness but has also resulted in injury to centipede and St. Augustine grasses.[160]

P. notatum Flugge (bahiagrass; perennial). Bahia can be removed from bermudagrass with repeated sprays of organic arsenicals.

Pennisetum clandestinum Hochst ex Chiov (kikuyugrass; perennial) (Fig. 9.16).[77] Arsenicals have been proposed for control, but no effective selective control exists at present. MH has reduced flowering. High concentrations of 2,4,5-T (1 lb in 40 gal) have given promise of eradication of kikuyu in one trial.

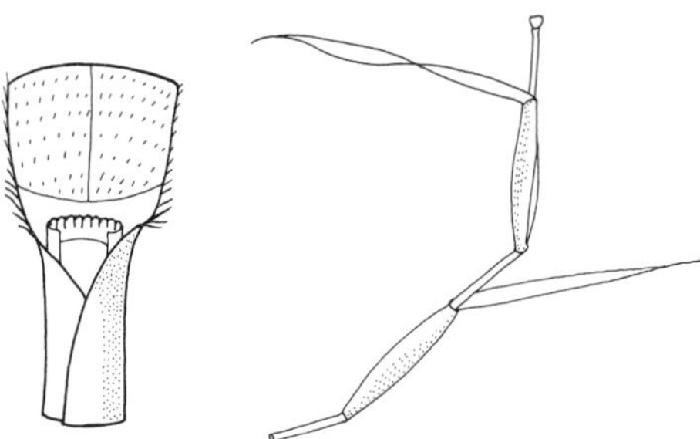

Figure 9.14 *Muhlenbergia Schreberi;* nimblewill.

(a) (b)

(c)

Figure 9.15 *Paspalum dilatatum;* dallisgrass.

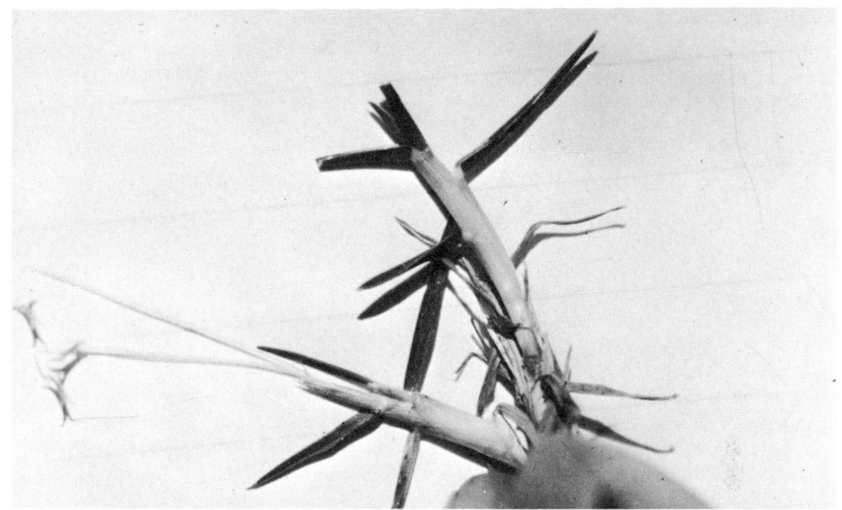

Figure 9.16 *Pennisetum clandestinum;* kikuyugrass plant in flower showing exserted floral organs.

Setaria glauca Beauv. (yellow foxtail; annual) and *S. viridis* (L.) Beauv. (green foxtail; annual) (Fig. 9.17). Preemergence control as for crabgrass will generally give effective control of foxtail.

Grasses other than the above frequently appear as weeds of new turf. They usually disappear soon with regular mowing and fertilizing unless they are being favored by some practice in the management.

DICOTYLEDONOUS WEEDS OF TURF

Some broad-leaved weeds commonly found in turf are identified by their common names in Table 9.6.

Most genera contain other weed species than the one listed, but the listed weed may be considered as fairly typical.

Achillea millifolium L. (Compositae) (common yarrow; perennial; Fig. 9.18). Leaves are pinnately dissected and have a pungent smell. The pubescent leaves are on the gray side of green. 2,4-D, 2,4,5-T, and Dicamba are used.

Amaranthus blitoides Wats. (Amaranthaceae) (prostrate pigweed; annual; Fig. 9.19). Pigweeds found in turf are prostrate arising from a usually fleshy red root. Leaves are simple with a limp texture. Preemer-

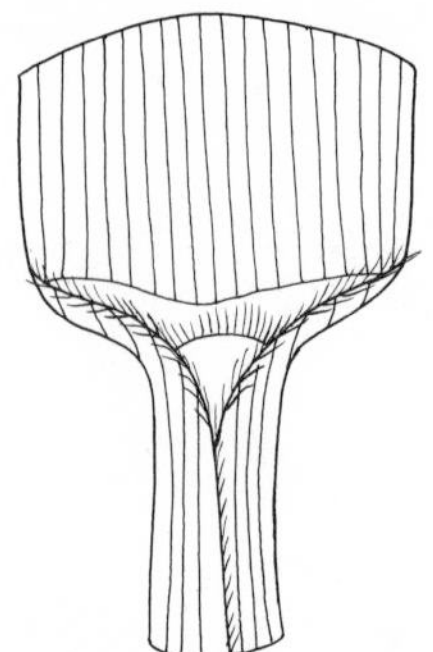

Figure 9.17 *Setaria viridis;* green foxtail.

Table 9.6. Dicotyledenous Weeds Commonly Found in Turf[a]

Alfalfa	*Medicago sativa*
Alkali mallow	*Sida hederacea*
Annual mouseear chickweed	*Cerastium viscosum*
Australian brass buttons	*Cotula australis*
Bindweed	*Convolvulus arvensis*
Birdseye pearlwort	*Sagina procumbens*
Birdsfoot trefoil	*Lotus corniculatus*
Black medic	*Medicago lupulina*
Black mustard	*Brassica nigra*
Brass buttons	*Cotula* spp.
Bristly mallow	*Modiola caroliniana* (but see *Malva*)
Broad-leaved plantain	*Plantago major*
Buckhorn	*Plantago lanceolata*
Burclover	*Medicago hispida*
Buttercup	*Ranunculus* spp.
Canada fleabane	*Erigeron canadense*
Carpetweed	*Mollugo verticillata*
Catsear	*Hypochoeris* spp. (see *Taraxacum*)
Cheeses	*Malva rotundifolia*
Chickweed	*Stellaria media* (*Cerastium* spp.)
Chicory	*Cichorium intybus* (see *Taraxacum*)
Cinquefoil	*Potentillia* spp.
Clover	*Trifolium* spp. (see also *Medicago*)
Coltsfoot	*Dichondra repens*
Cotton batting plant	*Gnaphalium chilense*
Creeping charlie	*Nepeta hederacea*
Creeping woodsorrel	*Oxalis corniculata*
Cress	*Coronopsis* (see *Brassica* spp.)
Crowfoot	*Ranunculus* spp.
Cudweed	*Gnaphalium chilense*
Curly dock	*Rumex crispus*
Cutleaved geranium	*Geranium dissectum*
Daisy	*Bellis perennis*
Dandelion	*Taraxacum officinale*

Table 9.6 cont'd.

Deadnettle	*Lamium amplexicaule*
Dichondra	*Dichondra repens*
Dock	*Rumex* spp.
Dwarf mallow	*Malva rotundifolia*
Dwarf pearlwort	*Sagina apetala*
English daisy	*Bellis perennis*
Field madder	*Sherardia arvensis*
Field bindweed	*Convolvulus arvensis*
Field sorrel	*Rumex acetosella*
Filaree	*Erodium* spp.
Fleabane	*Erigeron canadense*
Geranium	*Geranium* spp.
Gill-over-the-ground	*Nepeta hederacea*
Ground ivy	*Nepeta hederacea*
Groundsel	*Senecio vulgaris*
Healall	*Prunella vulgaris*
Henbit	*Lamium amplexicaule*
Irish moss	*Sagina subulata* (also *Minuatia verna*)
Knotweed	*Polygonum aviculare*
Lawn pennywort	*Hydrocotyl umbellata*
Lettuce	*Lactuca* spp. (see *Taraxacum*)
Lippia	*Phyla nodiflora*
Little cheeses	*Malva rotundifolia*
Little pickles	*Oxalis corniculata*
Loosetrife	*Lysimachia nummularia*
Madder	*Sherardia arvensis*
Mallow	*Malva* spp.
Matgrass	*Phyla nodiflora*
Milfoil	*Achillea millefolium*
Miner's lettuce	*Montia perfoliata*
Moneywort	*Lysimachia nummularia*
Morning glory	*Convolvulus arvense*
Mouse-ear chickweed	*Cerastium* spp.
Mustard	*Brassica* spp.
Narrow-leaved plantain	*Plantago lanceolata*
Nettle (dead)	*Lamium amplexicaule*
Pearlwort	*Sagina* spp.
Pennycress	*Thalaspi* (see *Brassica*)
Pennywort	*Hydrocotyl umbellata*
Pepperweed	*Lepidium* (see *Brassica*)
Perennial mouseear chickweed	*Cerastium vulgatum*
Pickles	*Oxalis corniculata*
Pigweed	*Ameranthus* spp.
Pimpernel	*Anagallis arvensis*
Pineappleweed	*Matricaria suaveolens*
Plantain	*Plantago* spp.
Poison ivy	*Rhus radicans*
Poison oak	*Rhus diversiloba*

Table 9.6 cont'd.

Poison sumac	*Rhus vernix*
Portulaca	*Portulaca oleracea*
Prostrate knotweed	*Polygonum aviculare*
Prostrate pigweed	*Amaranthus blitoides*
Prostrate vervain	*Verbena prostrata*
Puncture vine	*Tribulus terrestris*
Red sorrel	*Rumex acetocella*
Red woodsorrel	*Oxalis rubra*
Rocket	*Barbarea* (see *Brassica*)
Scarlet pimpernel	*Anagallis arvensis*
Shepherd's purse	*Capsella bursapastoris*
Smartweed	*Polygonum* spp.
Sida	*Sida hederacea*
Solvia	*Solvia sessilis*
Sorrel	*Rumex acetosella*
Sourgrass	*Oxalis* spp.
Sowthistle	*Sonchus* (see *Taraxacum*)
Speedwell	*Veronica serphyllifolia*
Spotted spurge	*Euphorbia maculata*
Spurge	*Euphorbia* spp.
Swine cress	*Barbarea* (see *Brassica*)
Thistle	Spp. of *Circus, Sonchus, Centauria* (see *Circus*)
Thymeleaf speedwell	*Veronica serphyllifolia*
Trefoil	*Lotus* spp.
Turf daisy	*Bellis perennis*
Vervain	*Verbena* spp.
Veronica	*Veronica* spp.
White clover	*Trifolium repens*
Wild lettuce	*Lactuca* spp. (see *Taraxacum*)
Wild Mustard	*Brassica* spp.
Winter cress	*Barbarea* (see *Brassica*)
Woodsorrel	*Oxalis* spp.
Yarrow	*Achillea millifolia*
Yellow rocket	*Barbarea* (see *Brassica*)
Yellow woodsorrel	*Oxalis corniculata*

[a]Herbicide data are discussed under the botanical name in the text.

gence herbicides, Dicamba, 2,4-D (butyl ester), 2,4-D + MCPP, are used.

Anagallis arvensis L. (Primulaceae) (scarlet pimpernel; annual; Fig. 9.20). A spreading plant with small (1/3 in.), oval pointed, smooth leaves in pairs and red axillary flowers on clear mornings. Effective herbicides include 2,4,5-T and Silvex.

Barbarea vulgaris (L.) R. Br. (Cruciferae) (winter cress; biennial; see *Brassica*).

Figure 9.18 *Achillea Millefolium;* yarrow.

Figure 9.19 *Amaranthus blitoides;* prostrate pigweed.

Bellis perennis L. (Compositae) (english daisy; turf daisy; perennial; Fig. 9.21). Leaves are oval, toothed, and in a basal whorl. Low white or pink daisy flowers are seen in the spring. These are part of the turf, or a weed, depending on taste. Herbicides used include MCPP + 2,4-D alkanolamine, 2,4-D + Dicamba, Silvex.[6]

Brassica campestris L. (Cruciferae) (wild mustard; biennial; Fig. 9.-22). I have referred all the mustards and cresses to this entry. These biennial weeds are all rosetting weeds common in new turf but soon disappearing. Leaves are usually dark green and incised with coarse teeth at the base though leaves of the flowering stem may be simple. Flowers are yellow (white), crushed leaves have a pungent smell, and all have the sprightly cress taste. Included are species of *Barbarea, Brassica, Draba, Lepidium, Thalspi,* etc. 2,4-D is an effective herbicide.

Figure 9.20 *Anagallis arvensis.*

Figure 9.21 *Bellis perennis;* turfing daisy.

Capsella bursapastoris (L.) Medic (Cruciferae) (shepherd's purse; Fig. 9.23). This crucifer is more persistent in lawns than the above. The rosetting, deeply cut, basal leaves soon support a stalk with the characteristic heart-shaped seed pods. 2,4-D is used.[144]

Cerastium arvense L. (Caryophyllaceae) (chickweed; see also *Stellaria*); *C. viscosum* L. (annual mouse-ear chickweed); and *C. vulgatum* L. (perennial mouse-ear chickweed; Fig. 9.24). Leaves are small, sticky haired, entire, and oval. More or less grayish in color the plant spreads to form a mat in turf. There are small axillary flowers. In *C. arvense* the flower petals are about twice as long as the sepals, rather than equal. In *C. vulgatum* the flower stalk is longer than the flower, rather than shorter. These are difficult weeds to control; MCPP, Dicamba, Dicamba + 1/4 lb/acre Picloram are used. Because of reinfestation from seed, preemergence sprays should also be used.[26,57]

Cichorium intybus L. (Compositae) (chicory; perennial; see *Taraxacum*).

Cirsium spp. (Compositae) (thistle; biennial). Thistles of *Cirsium* or annual *Centaurea* may occur in new turf. An effective herbicide is 2,4-D.

Convolvulus arvensis L. (Convolvulaceae) (field bindweed; wild morning glory; perennial; Fig. 9.25). This plant produces arrow-shaped grayish leaves on a vining stem when in the field. Heavy storage roots to 10 ft deep may be left in areas converted to turf. There the continual interruption of growth from mowing results in a cluster of trailing stems with small reduced leaves. Although 2,4-D may control seedlings, the old persistent plants are resistant. AMA + 2,4,5-T is very effective.

Cotula australis (Sieber) Hook. f. (Compositae) (Australian brass buttons; annual; Fig. 9.26). The dissected and aromatic leaves vary in

Figure 9.22 Examples of the mustard family (Brassicaceae).

shape. The species tolerates fairly close mowing and form small yellow flat heads of flowers without ray petals. Control is obtained with 2,4-D.

Dichondra repens Forst. (*Convolvulareaceae*) (coltsfoot; perennial; Fig. 9.27). Small rounded leaves may have an apical notch and arise from a creeping stem. 2,4-D is used.

Erigeron canadense L. (*Compositae*) (horseweed; annual or biennial; Fig. 9.28). A tall weed with daisy flowers it can survive in rough turf. Long linear leaves, usually hairy, are whorled about a stem that may rise a few inches or several feet with daisy flowers at the branched top. 2,4-D is used.

Erodium spp. (Geraniaceae) (filaree; annual; Fig. 9.29). Deep green, finely dissected leaves form a basal whorl and occur along creeping stems. There are pink geranium-like flowers which mature long beaked seed pods. 2,4-D is used.

Euphorbia maculata L. (*Euphorbiaceae*) (spotted spurge; annual; Fig. 9.30).[82,83,139] The prostrate spurges which form weeds of turf have small, oval, entire leaves on opposite sides of a creeping stem. Leaves are green to red with a dark smudge on each. A subtropical plant, it germinates late in the spring when the soil is warm. When days are hot, a seed may

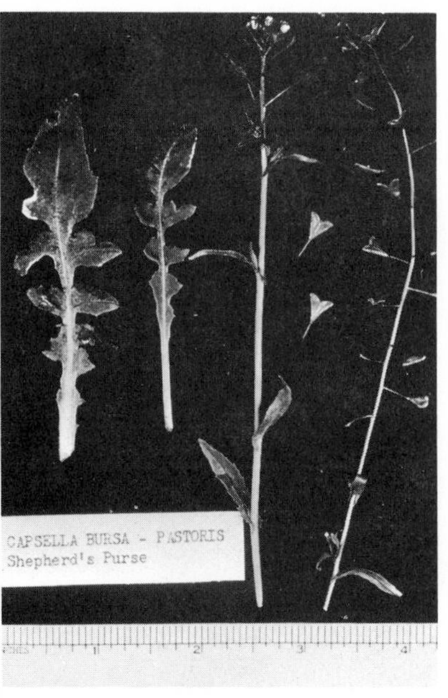

(a)

(b)

Figure 9.23 *Capsella bursa-pastoris;* shepherd's purse.

(a)

(b)

Figure 9.24 *Cerastium* spp.; mouse-ear chickweed.

Figure 9.25 *Convolvulus arvensis;* field bindweed.

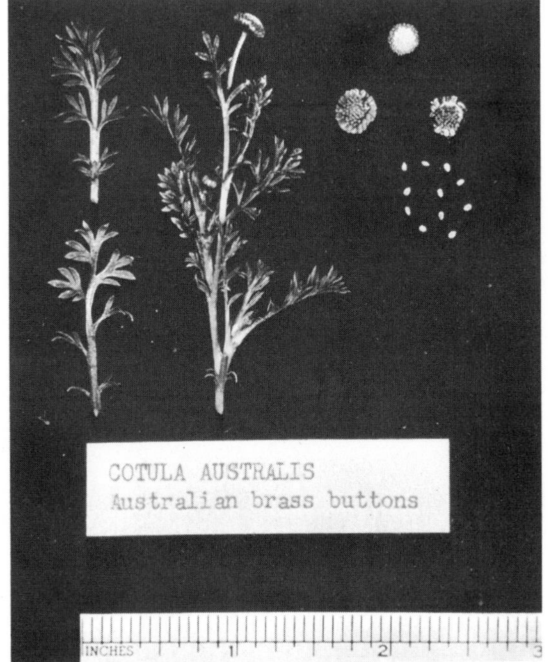

Figure 9.26 *Cotula australis;* Australian brass buttons.

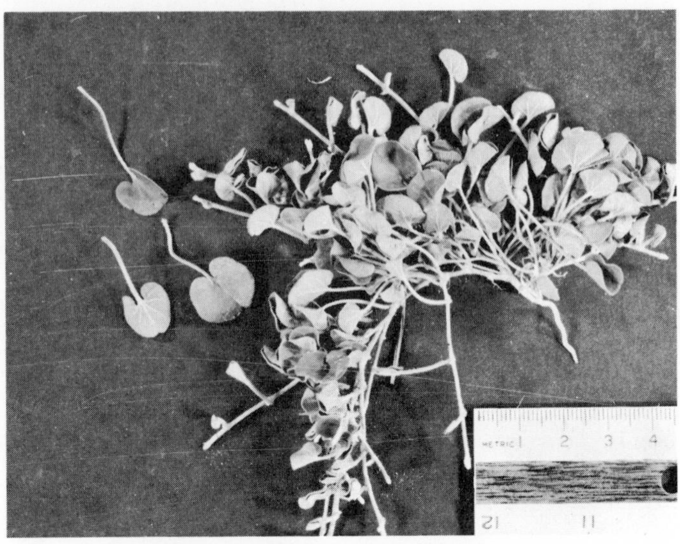

Figure 9.27 *Dichondra repens;* colt's foot.

Figure 9.28 *Erigeron canadense;* horseweed.

germinate and produce plant, flowers, and seed in 10 to 14 days. It is easily controlled, but since it has such a short life cycle herbicides need to be used every week or two at temperatures that would make them damaging to grass. Consequently, the only reasonable control is with preemergence herbicides, e.g., DCPA, Bandane, and Siduron; 2,4-D, MCPP, Dicamba and picloram are also used.

Geranium dissectum L. *(Geraniaceae)* (geranium; annual; Fig. 9.31). Geraniums have palmate, dissected opposite leaves and flowers with light pink petals. Plants may become diminutive with mowing and survive in turf. Effective herbicides are 2,4-D and 2,4,5-T.

Gnaphalium chilense Spreng. (Compositae) (cudweed, cotton batting plant; annual or biennial; Fig. 9.32). leaves are narrow and spatulate and almost white with hair. May have a single erect stem or several decumbent stems. Easily controlled by improved maintenance. Silvex or 2,4-D + DSMA or AMA are used.[41]

Hydrocotyle umbellata L. (Umbelliferae) (pennywort; perennial; Fig. 9.33). Small rounded leaves from a creeping stem, pennywort differs from Dichondra in having wavy leaf margins. The area should be drained before MCPP or 2,4-D are used.

Hypochoeris glabra L. (Compositae) (smooth cat's ear; perennial; Fig. 9.34). and *H. radicata* L. (hairy cat's ear). Refer to *Taraxacum.*

Lamium amplexicaule L. (Labiatae) (henbit; annual or biennial; Fig. 9.35). Leaves are rounded with rather deep cut teeth, arising from a procumbent stem. Only lower leaves are petiolate. Silvex, 2,4-D, 2,4,5-T, and Dicamba can be used but two applications may be needed.[33]

Lotus corniculatus L. (Leguminoseae) (birds-foot trefoil; perennial; Fig. 9.36). Leaves are pinnate with five leaflets on procumbent stems from a central taproot. Yellow pea flowers are borne on slender stems. This clover relative can form an enduring association with turfgrass much as clover does. In unfertile rough turf it may be a welcome addition to the cover. If unwelcome, use 2,4-D.

Lysimachia nummularia L. (Primulaceae) (moneywort; perennial; Fig. 9.37). Creeping and trailing stems bear smooth roundish leaves on small stems to form a low ground cover. Primrose yellow flowers occur near the ground in early summer, usually in a shady moist environment where grass will do poorly. Be sure you want to remove it before using 2,4-D.

Malva parvifolia L. (Malvaceae) (cheeseweed; biennial; Fig. 9.38); *M. rotundifolia* L. (dwarf mallow; annual or biennial); *Modiola caroliniana* G. Don. (bristly mallow; perennial); and *Sida hederacea* Dougl. (alkali mallow; perennial). These members of the family may be grouped together as all are difficult of control. Leaves are similar and are round, having palmate veins with shallow lobes and notches. Leaves of Sida are grey. Flowers are clustered in leaf axils. No firm recommendation for control can be made. Try 2,4,5-T + Dicamba or AMA.

Matricaria suaveolens (Pursh) Buch. (Compositae) (pineapple weed; annual; Fig. 9.39). *Matricaria* leaves are pinately issected and fine. The flowers form a yellow inconspicuous cone with no ray flowers. When

(a)

(b)

Figure 9.29 *Erodium cicutarium;* filaree. Part **(a)** illustrates size differences found in many weeds. A dwarfed plant from turf is smaller than a single leaf of a vigorous specimen.

(a)

(b)

Figure 9.30 *Euphorbia maculata;* spotted spurge.

Figure 9.31 *Geranium carolinianum.*

crushed, the head emits a sweet fragrance of pineapple. These are resistant to 2,4-D. Some preemergence herbicides are effective.

Medicago hispida Gaertn. (Leguminosae) (bur clover; annual; Fig. 9.40) and *M. lupulina* L. (black medic; annual). The medics differ from the clovers in that the middle leaflet of the three leaflets is extended on a short petiole. The yellow pea flowers are relatively inconspicuous. MCPP, Dicamba, Silvex, and Picloram are effective.

Modiola carolinina (L.) G. Don. (Malvaceae) (bristly mallow; see under *Malva*).

Mollugo verticillata L. (Aizoaceae) (carpetweed; annual; Fig. 9.-41).[140] A light stem, much branched, forms mats. At each node is a whorl of short thin spatulate leaves with small inconspicuous flowers. MCPP, Dicamba, 2,4,5-T, and 2,4-D can be used. If an infestation is serious, a preemergence herbicide should be used.

Montia perfoliata (Donn) Howell (Portulacaceae) (miner's lettuce; annual; Fig. 9.42). This is included as an example of several members of the family that can endure as a sparse part of low-maintenance turf. *Claytonia* and *Caliandra* can contribute lovely spring flowers to the informal meadow-like type of turf. 2,4-D is used.

Nepeta hederacea (L.) Trevisan (Labiatae) (ground ivy; Gill-over-the-ground; perennial; Fig. 9.43*a*). This has creeping or trailing stems with opposite leaves that are round-kidney shaped with crenate teeth. As is moneywort, this is apt to give a good ground cover in damp shady areas

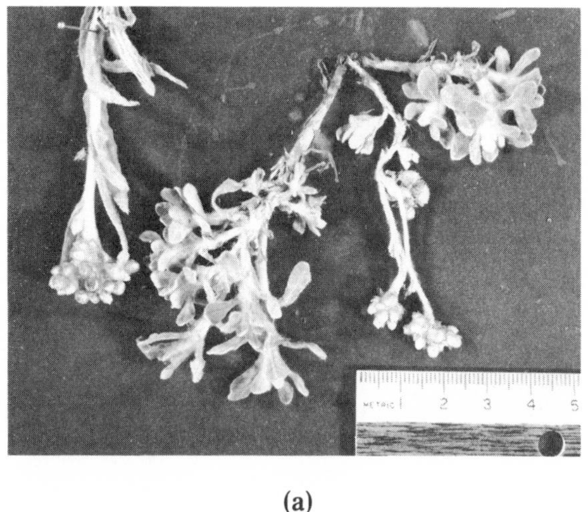

(a)

(b)

Figure 9.32 *Gnaphalium chileunse.*

Figure 9.33 *Hydrocotyle umbellata;* pennywort.

Figure 9.34 *Hypochoeris glabra;* smooth cat's ear.

Figure 9.35 *Lamium amplexicaule;* dead nettle.

Figure 9.36 *Lotus corniculatus;* bird's foot trefoil.

where turf might do poorly; it thus may be a "desirable weed." 2,4-D and Silvex can be used to control it.

Oxalis corniculata L. (Oxalidaceae) (creeping wood sorrel; perennial; Fig. 9.44). The compound leaves with three heart-shaped leaflets in green or red are well known as are the yellow flowers and sour "little pickle" fruits. Once there has been a large patch of oxalis, control is best obtained with preemergent herbicides. 2,4-D, 2,4,5-T, Silvex, and Dicamba are used. One pound active ingredient per acre of Monuron can be used to control oxalis in Dichondra if there are no ornamentals, shrubs, or trees. One pound of monuron has also been used for oxalis control on bermudagrass as has 1/4–1/2 lb ai/acre of Picloram.[29]

Phyla nodiflora Greene (Verbenaceae) (lippia; perennial; Fig. 9.45). Lippia has been used as a substitute ground cover for turf. It spreads rapidly and is extremely drought tolerant. The many small verbena flowers are attractive to bees. Three-quarter inch leaves are opposite, oblanceolate, thick, and serrate near the tip. 2,4-D is used.

Plantago major L. (Plantaginaceae) (broad-leaved plantain; perennial; Fig. 9.46) and *P. lanceolata* L. (buckhorn). The leaves are large and leathery, elliptic, more or less toothed with a deep channel over the midrib. In buckhorn the leaves are linear. These are familiar turf weeds. MCPP, 2,4-D, 2,4,5-T, Silvex, Dicamba, and picloram are used.

Polygonum aviculare L. (Polygonaceae) (prostrate knotweed; annual; Fig. 9.47). There are many common weed in genus *Polygonum.* All are similar, having small entire opposite leaves at a swollen node. This is

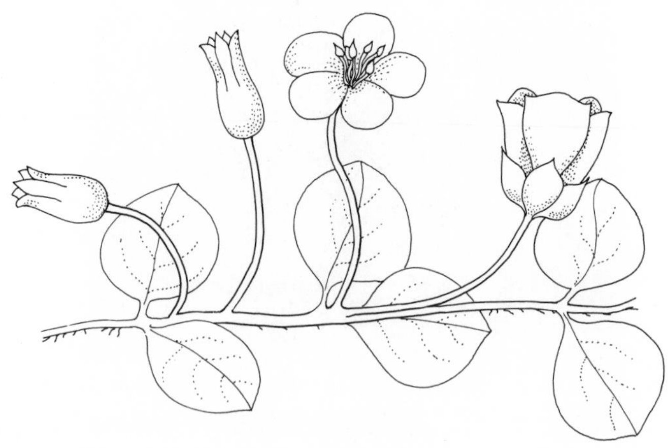

Figure 9.37 *Lysimachia Nummularia;* moneywort.

(a)

(b)

Figure 9.38 *Malva parviflora;* Little cheeses.

Figure 9.39 *Matricaria suaveolens;* pineapple weed.

a principal weed of highly compacted soils and its control may only leave a bare area which is unreceptive to turf and which will be recolonized by other weeds. Knotweed is a fairly resistant to the 2,4-D-type compounds and their use often results in an increase in knotweed. The favored post emergent herbicide is Dicamba. Use of Picloram in continental pastures has resulted in replacement of *P. bistorta* by *Poa, Agrostis,* and *Fescue* species.[152,12]

Portulaca oleracea L. (Portulacaceae) (purslane; annual; Fig. 9.48); *Portulaca* is a prostrate herb with a fleshy stem and fleshy, simple obovate leaves. 2,4-D, 2,4-D + MCPP, and Dicamba have been used.

Potentilla reptans L. and others (Rosaceae) (cinquefoil; false strawberry; perennial; Fig. 9.49). Species in turf have procumbent slender stems. Leaves are palmately three to five foliate. Leaflets are wedge shaped with serrate or dentate ends. A weed of dry infertile areas, it is usually controlled with proper management. 2,4-D and 2,4,5-T have been used.

Prunella vulgaris L. *(Labiatae)* (self-heal; perennial; Fig. 9.43*b*). This has a square stem, opposite leaves, and is generally soft and hairy, ovate, toothed, or entire. Rosy flowers are borne in clusters in leaf axils. 2,4-D can be used but foliage may be difficult to wet and old plants may survive.

Ranunculus repens L. and other spp. (Ranunculaceae) (buttercup.

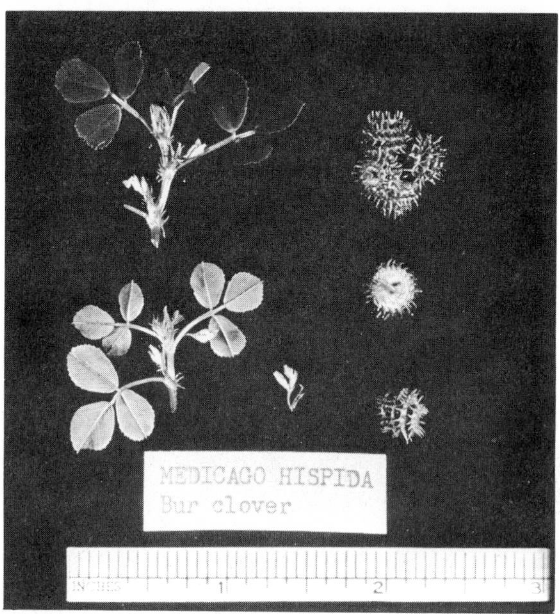

Figure 9.40 *Medicago hispida;* Bur colver. The short stalk on the middle leaflet distinguishes medies from clovers.

Figure 9.41 *Mollugo verticillata;* carpetweed.

(a)

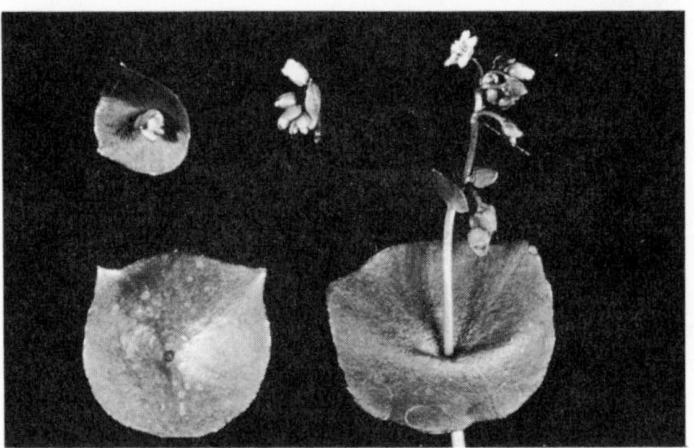

(b)

Figure 9.42 *Montia perfoliata;* miner's lettuce.

perennial; Fig. 9.50). Buttercups generally have pinnately dissected, toothed leaves, from a runner or underground stem. When pastures are converted to turf, old rootstocks in the soil may renew the plant for a time. If it persists it is apt to be because of wet conditions and improved drainage is needed. 2.4-D has been used for control.

Rhus radicans L. (Anacardiaceae) (poison ivy; perennial; Fig. 9.51). *R. diversiloba* T. & G. (poison oak);[140] and *R. vernix* L. (poison sumac). These woody vining shrubs often limit use and enjoyment of turfed areas

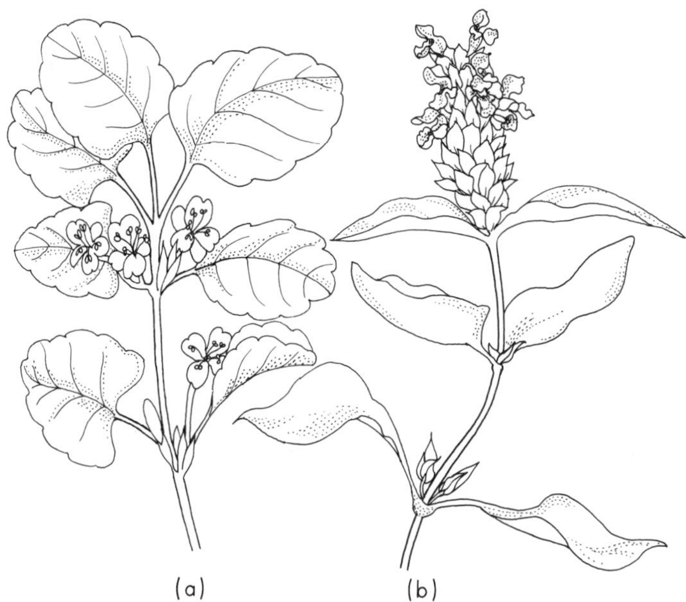

Figure 9.43 Plants of Labiatae. **(a)** *Nepeta hederacea;* gill-over-the-ground. **(b)** *Prunella vulgaris;* self-head.

and provide maintenance problems. When burned, smoke is severely poisonous to sensitive persons. Homeopathic solutions are available for building resistance in the work crew. Where infestations are severe, pasturing cattle, goats, or sheep will initiate control and open up paths where the work crew can go in. Herbicides used include amino triazole at 16–24 lb, and Picloram at 2 lb/100 gal; these should be sprayed till dripping. This treatment has given control for three years.[86] 2,4,5-T, and Dicamba have also been used.

Rumex acetosella L. (Polygonaceae) (red sorrel, sour grass; perennial; Fig. 9.52) and *Rumex crispus* L. and other spp. (dock). Dock is most familiar in turf as a rosette of large coarse, linear leaves from a perennial taproot. Sorrel spreads by rhizomes and produces arrow-shaped leaves which are often reddish. Dicamba will control sorrel and some dock species but fertilizer may be as effective. MCPP, 2,4,5-T, and 2,4-D have also been used.

Sagina apetala Ard. and other spp. (Caryophyllaceae) (pearlwort; perennial; Fig. 9.53). Sagina forms a moss-like mat in turf. Leaves are small and linear in opposite pairs. These are cousins of chickweed and

Figure 9.44 *Oxalis corniculata;* wood sorrel.

should be treated similarly. Regular use of PMA on greens controls it there. MCPP has also been used.

Scleranthus annus L. (Caryophyllaceae) (knawel; annual; Fig. 9.54). Knawel forms many small spreading branches from a tough taproot. Leaves are small, linear, entire, and in pairs clasping the nodes. Dicamba and Silvex have been used.

Senecio vulgaris L. (Compositae) (common groundsel; annual; Fig. 9.55). Leaves of this common weed are dark green and shiny above, paler beneath, and are pinnately incised and toothed. The flower head has no ray flowers and is not conspicuous. It is resistant to herbicides.

Figure 9.45 *Phyla nodiflora;* lippia.

Sherardia arvensis L. (Rubiaceae) (field madder; annual; Fig. 9.56). Madder has slender, procumbent, square stems, and lanceolate leaves in whorls of four to six. Silvex has been used.

Sida hederacea (Dougl.) Torr. (Malvaceae) (perennial). See *Malva.*

Soliva sessilis Ruiz. & Pav. (Compositae) (soliva; annual; Fig. 9.57). Leaves are fine and pinnately dissected on low stems with axillary flowers. It is not widespread; MCPP and 2,4-D have been used for control.

Stellaria media (L.) Cyrill. (Caryophyllaceae) (common chickweed; annual; Fig. 9.58). For other chickweeds see *Cerastium.* Leaves are small, green, ovate, opposite, smooth but with some hairy petioles. This genus constitutes a major turf weed. MCPP, Silvex, Dicamba, and Dicamba + Silvex.[6,36,154]

Taraxacum officinale Weber (Compositae) (dandelion; perennial; Fig. 9.59). Dandelion is a representative of the tribe Cichorieae of the Compositae family. Members of the tribe are characterized by a milky juice; chicory, wild lettuce, sow thistle, cat's ear, and hawkweed may all be referred here. In mowed turf, these are rosetting plants with toothed

Figure 9.46 (a) *Plantago major;* common plantain.

and incised lanceolate leaves. MCPP, 2,4-D, and Dicamba have been used. Picloram at 1/4 lb has been used for fall control.[6,29]

Tribulus terrestris L. (Zygophyllaceae) (puncture vine; perennial; Fig. 9.60). In the southwest this may be a troublesome weed associated with turf areas. Chemical control is difficult and a degree of natural control is now being achieved from one of two weevils introduced to control it.[100] Fenac at 4 lb has controlled young stages with fair grass survival. Amitrol and Atrazine have given control of puncture vine along with other vegetation.[131]

Trifolium spp. (Leguminoseae) (clover; perennial; Fig. 9.61). Clover and grass forms a natural association thriving on low maintenance. A principal objection to clover is its attractiveness to bees. Some persons have a severe and sometimes fatal reaction to bee sting poisons. MCPP, Silvex, Dicamba, and Endothall have been used.[6,57]

Figure 9.46 (b) *P. lanceolata;* lanceleaved plantain.

Verbena bracteosa Mickx. (Verbenaceae) (vervain, perennial; Fig. 9.62). Vervain may form a diffuse spreading weed in turf. Leaves are opposite with coarse serrations or incisions, and with a membrane along the petiole. 2,4-D has been used.

Veronica serphyllifolia L. (Scrophulariaceae) (thyme-leaf speedwell; perennial; Fig. 9.63). This and related species are persistent weeds of turf. It may be introduced as a contaminant of lawn seed. It is resistant to chemical and cultural control. Leaves are opposite, ovate, and crenulate on creeping stems. Blue flowers are freely born. To limit need for repeat control a preemergence herbicide can be used. The first chemical used for control was Endothall at 1–1 1/4 lb ai/acre in 150 gal. This is apt to scorch turf and there is regrowth of the weed in a couple of months. MCPP + 2,4-D in two applications separated by two weeks has given to 75% control. Mixtures with Picloram offer possibility of control.[6] A recent trial got kill from Ioxynil + MCPP (Soper, D., 1969, First International Turf Research Conf. Proc., in press).

AQUATIC WEEDS[70,95]

Aquatic weeds have a place in ponds as a source of food for fish and

Figure 9.47 *Polygonum aviculare;* knotweed.

Figure 9.48 *Portulaca oleracea;* purslane.

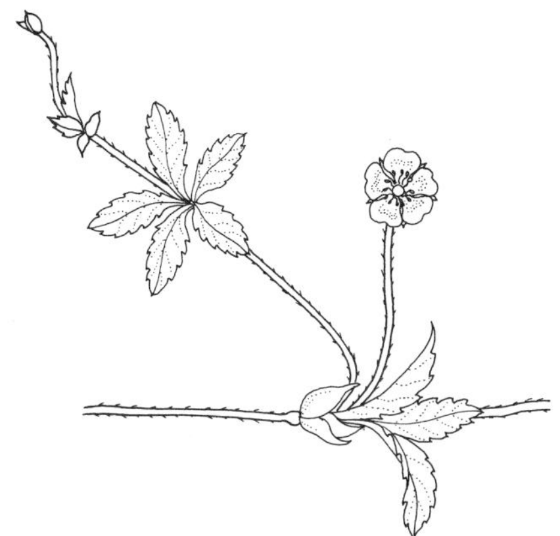

Figure 9.49 *Potentilla canadensis;* common cinquefoil.

Figure 9.50 *Ranunculus repens;* buttercup.

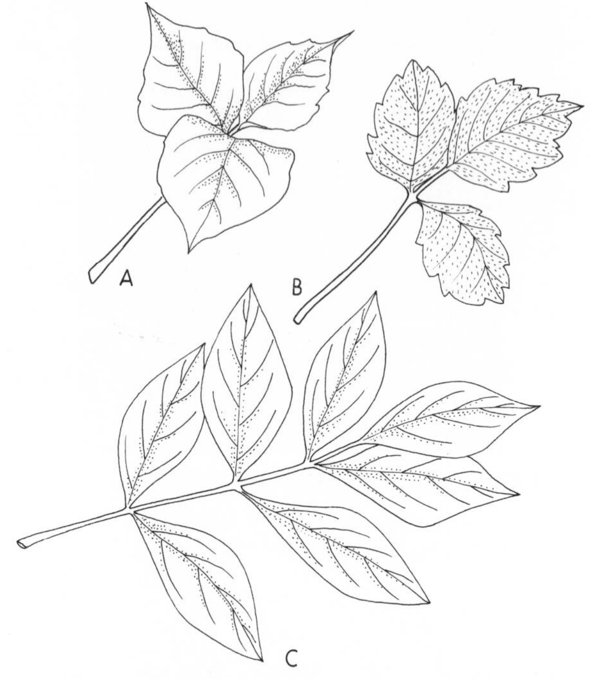

Figure 9.51 *Rhus* spp. Leaves are variable. **(a)** *R. radicans;* poison ivy. **(b)** *R. diversiloba;* poison oak. **(c)** *R. Vernix;* poison sumac.

ducks, and to provide protection for birds that nest in such places. When weeds choke the waters, rushes block the view, or when flow of irrigation water is impeded, weed control may benefit primary uses of the water. Problems may be of algae (small free-floating plants); submerged (underwater) plants; floating plants; or emersed plants which stick up out of the water, such as grasses, sedges, cattails, or bulrushes.

Biological control can be by foraging animals, and ducks, for example, can eat large amounts of some plants. Fish are less effective.

Environmental control can reduce weeds by making the pond a less favorable place for growth. Depth, temperature, and fertility of the water are primary environmental factors. Temperatures can be reduced by deepening the water and by use of shade trees. Shade will reduce available light energy and reduce growth. Deepening the water will create an environment unfavorable for emersed plants such as cattails. Fertilizer greatly increases aquatic growth, and irrigation should not

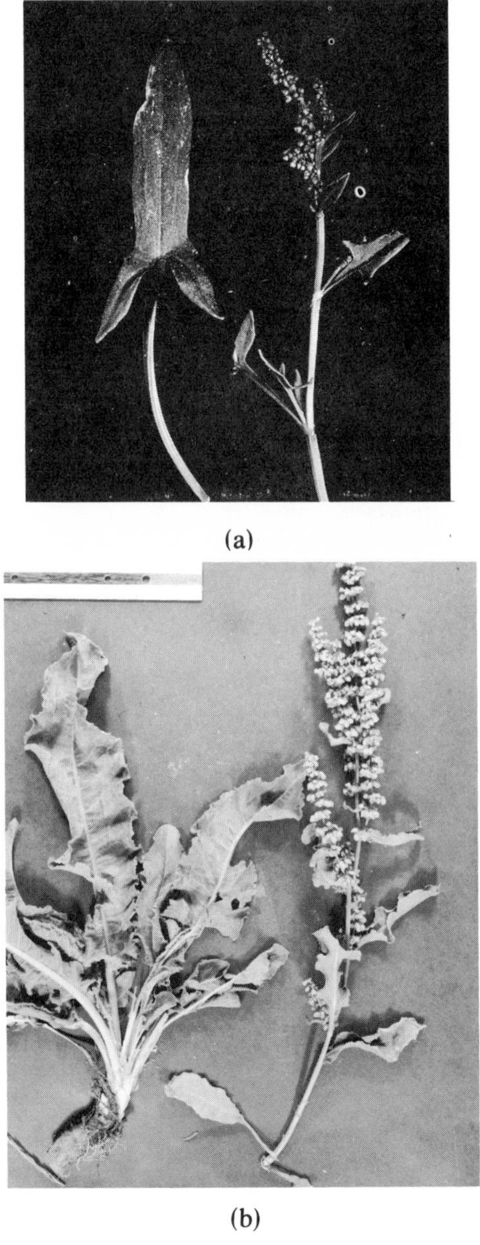

(a)

(b)

Figure 9.52 (a) *Rumex Acetosella;* sour dock. (b) *R. crispus;* curly dock.

Figure 9.53 *Sagina subulata;* Irish moss. Here the dense mat is picked apart.

wash fertilizers into the waters. At the same time, if the problem is one of impeded water flow from submerged aquatics, fertilizer can cause a dense growth of algae on the surface that will shade over the submerged plants.

Chemical control is most often based on parts per million (ppm) of active ingredient. One ppm by weight is supplied by 2.7 lb (2 lb 11 oz) of active ingredient per acre-foot of water; by volume, 1/3 gal ai/acre-ft. This can be expressed in the following formulas:

active ingredient (gal) = pond area x av. depth x desired ppm x 0.33

active ingredient (lb) = pond area x av. depth x desired ppm x 2.72

Herbicides are most often applied to emersed leaves on an area basis. In this instance it may be necessary to limit the application in order to avoid killing fish or to avoid making the water unfit for irrigation. The formulas may then be turned around and used to calculate the maximum allowable amount of herbicide that can be used.

Pond area x av. depth x maximum ppm x 2.72 = maximum pounds of herbicide permitted

Chemicals may be applied as sprays above the surface or just below the surface of the water. Below the surface, there is no drift,

Figure 9.54 *Scleranthus annus;* knawel.

and hazard to the operator is greatly reduced. Granular materials may be used to get even application or to apply some preemergent materials to the pond bottom. Other preemergent herbicides can be applied only by draining the pond and spraying the pond bottom. March is a preferred time for preemergent applications. Postemergent applications are made before seed set. Control of pond flora may require use of several chemicals over several years. Use only those herbicides licensed for aquatic control. Formulations for submerged aquatic weeds are usually based on salts as the auxiliary chemicals used in emulsifying esters greatly increase fish kill. Esters are used for better penetrations of floating or emersed leaves.

Rights of downstream users must be protected and you are liable for damage done them by your control practices.

Weed control is based on the weed, the chemical, and the rate.A manual illustrated in color, put out by the Bureau of Reclamation,* aids water weed identification. Some herbicides used for aquatic control are relisted in Tables 9.7 and 9.8.

*N. E. Otto and T. R. Bartley, 1965, *Aquatic pests on Irrigation Systems,* Department of Interior, Bureau of Reclamation, USGPO Item 841, $1.75.

(a)

(b)

Figure 9.55 *Senecio vulgaris.*

Aquatic weed control is secondary to turf management problems and no effort is made to develop complete information. For an extensive treatment of the subject, see Bureau of Reclamation publications.*

Weed Control on Ditch Banks

This closely follows control for emerged aquatic weeds. Mixtures may be used such as Dalapon and Silvex, or DSMA = Silvex. For drainage ditches care need be taken only that desirable plants are not injured and herbicides will not cause damage when washed off the property. With irrigation ditches care must be taken to use an herbicide that does not damage turf, or which deteriorates fast enough that water can be used after a day or two, or to have provision for wasting the water treated.

With water flowing in a ditch, herbicides are applied at the upstream side to provide a suitable concentration of chemical for a minimum length of time. Less chemical will be needed if flow can be reduced during the control period. Suitable additions include:

*U.S. Bureau of Reclamation, 1949, *Control of Weeds on Irrigation Systems* U.S. Dept. of Interior, Bureau of Reclamation, USGPO, Washington D.C., 140 pp. (35¢).

Figure 9.56 *Sherardia arvensis;* **field madder.**

1. Aromatic solvents such as naptha at 300–500 ppm for 30 min. An emulsifier is used at from 10% for temperatures up to 60°F to 5% above 70°F. This amounts to 4–6 gal of solvent plus emulsifier applied over 30 min for each cfs (cubic foot per second) of flow. If more than 1/2 mile of ditch is involved 2–3 gal of booster are added every 1/2 to 3/4 mile. Fish are killed.

2. Benchlor-3C is used to provide 500 ppm for one hour. Fish are killed.

3. Acrolein. Follow manufacturers directions. A toxic irritant and lachrimator, the operator needs protection. It kills fish.

Flow is calculated from a weir notch or:

$$\text{cfs} + \text{av. width (ft)} \times \text{av. depth (ft)} \times \text{av. velocity (ft/sec)}$$

Gallons of herbicide needed for control are given by:

$$\frac{450 \times \text{concentration in ppm} \times \text{minutes} \times \text{flow (cfs)}}{1{,}000{,}000}$$

PRACTICUM

There are two principal steps in chemical weed control. The first is to be certain that there is an adequate amount of a desirable turfgrass present which is adapted to the management given and that the management program encourages vigorous growth of that grass. The second step is to select a suitable chemical and apply it uniformly at the correct rate, at the right season, and with the soil suitably moist and the grass in a condition of growth that is resistant to the chemical. A principal cause of failure to control is still use of the wrong chemical applied in the wrong way.

Because herbicides cause at least some turf injury, we want to use a minimum amount and a minimum number of applications, which is also good economy. A way to minimize applications is to survey weeds that have to be controlled. Often if the chemical used is chosen to control a difficult weed, other weeds will be controlled also. If weeds cannot all be controlled by one chemical a tested mixture can be used. A mixed herbicide often extends the spectrum of kill to include most problem weeds.

The amount of herbicide used should be kept to a minimum; however difficult-to-kill weeds require follow-up sprays for effective control. If one spray of DSMA gives 35% control of crabgrass and two sprays give 95% control, use two or none. Thirty-five percent control will hardly affect turf appearance or amount of crabgrass seed produced.

With a program decided on paper, equipment should be checked. Nozzles should be of the correct type (fan), without wear, and must all deliver at the same rate. The boom should be at the correct height so spray patterns touch at the ground level without overlap. Check the calibration periodically. Calibration and other relevant information is given in Chap. 6 and Appendix III.

With equipment ready, the time to spray is selected so the weed is in a suitable stage of growth, soil is moist, grass is growing vigorously with some hours of sunshine previous to spraying, and temperatures are on the cool side of 75–80°F.If a liquid carrier is being used (as opposed to granular) put water in the tank first, then add herbicide. If herbicide is added first, some may leak down into the pump and come out at a high strength that kills grass. Remaining water is added and the mixture agitated until it is uniform. It is then sprayed uniformly over the area to be treated with no skips, no overlaps, no slowing, no repeats.

If the above is done, the turf manager in the regions where turf is adapted will have fair assurance of successful control. In the transition zone, potential for damage to turf is higher. Treated turf may be more

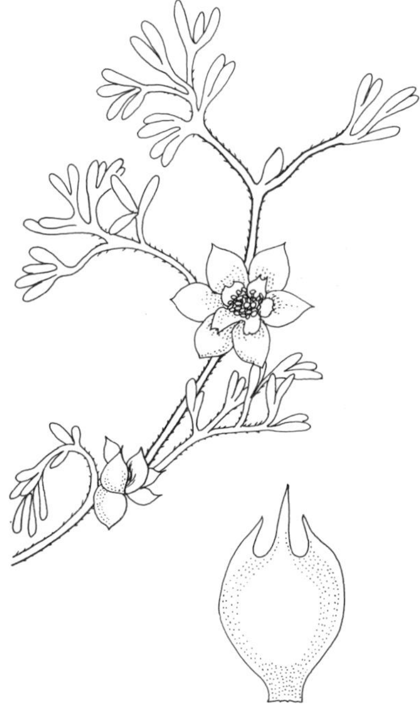

Figure 9.57 *Soliva sessilis.*

(a)

(b)

(c)

Figure 9.58 *Stellaria media;* common chickweed.

subject to damage from temperature extremes which can occur in many months of the year.

One can easily demonstrate that control is not always correctly and successfully applied. At a meeting of turf managers tell a story on yourself of how you damaged some grass by using the wrong herbicide. Chances are that your story will soon be topped by a dozen others.

Because of many variables in using herbicides, your own notes will be invaluable to you. Notes should include date, temperature, kind of grass, conditions of humidity and soil moisture, brand, rate, and formulation of chemical, date of following rain, and weeds controlled. Soil texture may also be of concern.

We have noted that herbicides are more effective on young plants and usually more effective on sandy soils. Many greens are built from sandy soil mixes, and mowing practices result in most of the leaf surface being of a very young age compared to grass mowed higher and less often. As a result, greens are often sensitive to chemicals that would not injure less highly maintained grass. This is another argument for using new chemicals at low rates on test areas until you have found the degree of tolerance under the existing conditions.

When annual weeds are being controlled with preemergence herbicides, initial planning should look ahead for as much as a year. Many preemergence chemicals have residual action that affects seed germination for more than one growing season. If there is likelihood that new seed will need to be germinated to strengthen the turf, a herbicide should be chosen that has a sufficiently short residual life.

Sooner or later a mistake is made and we should be prepared to deal with it. Most herbicides either tie to soil colloids or are leachable. Work currently under way at Rhode Island proposes use of activated charcoal to adsorb those herbicides that become fixed in the soil and to cancel their toxicity.[121] Although the work has not been published,* a tentative suggestion is made that 200 lb/acre of activated charcoal worked into the seedbed will permit germination of grass where preemergence herbicides have been used. The following recommendation for use of charcoal is untested but the rest of the program has been used with success.

As soon as you realize that herbicide damage to turf will result, immediately do as many of the following as you can in order given!

1. Apply activated charcoal to the surface to adsorb as much herbicide as possible.

*As of 1968.

(a)

(b)

Figure 9.59 Two composites of the Cichorieae tribe. (a) *Taraxacum officinale;* dandelion. (b) *Sonchus oleraceus;* sow thistle.

2. Give the turf a long heavy irrigation, trying to run at least two inches of water into the soil. This will be an effort to leach as much free herbicide as possible from the root zone.

3. If the soil will now support a hole punching machine, use it and remove cores; otherwise go to step four.

4. Top dress heavily (1/4 in.) to provide an uncontaminated rooting medium for new growth.

5. Stop mowing and fertilizing.

6. Spray with a fungicide and repeat at five-day intervals. Do not use fungicides which may be injurious to grass.

7. When new growth begins, mow, but only when necessary. Begin to fertilize new growth lightly. If the soil was too wet for step three, consider doing it now and follow by a second top dressing.

8. Keep traffic off the turf during this period and until recovery is assured.

The gardener has a maxim to be heeded; "One year's seeding—seven years' weeding." Weed control is a never ending task but we can make the task harder or easier. Effort used to prevent weeds from going to seed reduces future weed problems and preventing seed formation and introduction is a first line of attack. A second line of attack is to prevent seeds from germinating. Time operations so you don't provide a seedbed by hole punching, thatching, etc. Instead, keep a dense tight turf. Fertilizer is the cheapest and most effective form of chemical weed control. A dry soil surface at the time of seed germination is a form of preemergence control, to be used along with preemergence chemicals. The third line of attack is to use selective herbicides on weed seedlings so they are killed while small and susceptible. Those weeds that survive our third line of

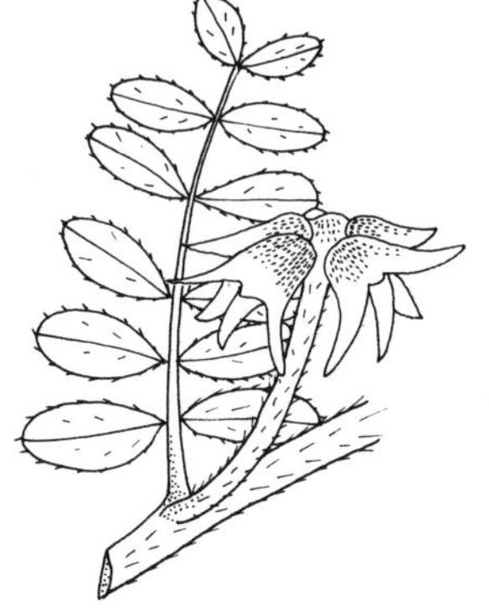

Figure 9.60 *Tribulus terrestris;* puncture vine.

Figure 9.61 *Trifolium repens;* white clover.

attack bring us full circle and we must begin again to prevent their setting seed.

The importance of all three elements in the program may take a monent's thought to appreciate. Every year, we shall have to repeat our weed-control program. There is no such thing as one-time control. We shall be fighting weeds the rest of our lives. When we can accept this, then we can see the value of a systematic and routine program that strikes at each step in the weed cycle. When control is routine and effective it makes little demand on us, but sometimes we have the notion that we can organize a big effort, control weeds, and then go on to other things. The weeds show up again next year and we have to mount a new effort. Because our program is new each time instead of routine from year to year, it makes renewed demands on us each year. In time it looms before us as a major unsolved problem. I suggest the problem may be one of attitude.

Often, our weed-control practices can be improved by better knowledge of the weeds being controlled. Several experiment stations have guides for identifying local weeds. If you have a man on your staff with an interest in plants and a knowledge of botany, have him spend rainy afternoons pressing and mounting weed specimens. The preparation and display of specimens should increase knowledge and interest in weeds by several of your staff.

Figure 9.62 *Verbena bracteata;* vervain.

Table 9.7. Classes of Aquatic Plants and Control Measures

Genus	*Common Name*	*Control and Remarks*
	Algae	
Many genera	Algae, plankton, green scum	Copper sulfate, 1 ppm; Hydrothal-47, 0.2 ppm; sodium arsenite, 2 ppm

Copper sulfate can give control with a minimum of equipment. Copper sulfate is placed in a cloth bag suspended from the middle of a rope. A man on each end of the rope on opposite sides of the pond can move the bag about over the area until the copper sulfate is dissolved.

Genus	*Common Name*	*Control and Remarks*
	Submerged Aquatics	
Ceratophyllum	Coontail	Sodium arsenite; Endothal; Silvex; Diquat
Myriophyllum	Water milfoil	Silvex; Endothal; Diquat
Heteranthera	Water stargrass	Silvex; 2,4-D (granular)
Potomogeton	Pondweed	Sodium arsenite; 2,4-D; Silvex
Vallisneria	Eelgrass	Sodium arsenate; 2,4-D (granular)
Anacharis	Elodea	2,4-D; Silvex; sodium arsenate
Cabomba	Fanwort	2,4-D (granular); Hydrothal-47, 2 ppm
Najus	Naiad	Sodium arsenite; 2,4-D; Diquat
Utricularia	Bladderwort	Sodium arsenate; Silvex
Ranunculus	Buttercup	Diquat

Sodium arsenite is used at about 4 ppm, Endothal at 2 ppm, Diquat at 0.5 to 1.0 ppm. 2,4-D and Silvex (as Kuron) are effective as granules at 4-8 lb ai/acre or 4-6 lb ai/acre. Granular Casoron can be used in March as a preemergent herbicide for many of the above. Endothal and 2,4-D are the materials of least fish toxicity. Best control is when weeds are young and growing actively.

Table 9.7 cont'd.

Genus	*Common Name*	*Control and Remarks*
	Floating Aquatics	
Alternaria	Alligator weed	Silvex; 2,4-D with water drained
Lemna	Duckweed	Endothal; Diquat; 2,4-D; 4,5-T
Eichhornia	Water hyacinth	2,4-D amine
Nymphaea	White water lily	2,4-D; 2,4,5-T esters
Nuphar	Yellow water lily	Silvex, 1 ppm
Brasenia	Water shield	2,4-D; 2,4,5-T esters
Hydrocotyl	Water pennywort	2,4-D; 2,4,5-T esters
Pontederia	Pickerelweed	2,4-D; 2,4,5-T esters

Leaves are sprayed with esters of phenoxy herbicides at about 2 lb ai/acre but this can be reduced to 1/2 lb by suspending it in 5 gal of kerosene. If an aquatic application is desirable, granular forms of the phenoxy compounds can be used at 4-8 lb ai/acre or Diquat can be used at 1/4-1 ppm using more as the water contains more organic matter.

Genus	*Common Name*	*Control and Remarks*
	Emersed aquatics	
Sagittaria	Arrowhead	Diquat; Silvex; 2,4,5-T; 2,4-D
Scirpus	Bulrush	2,4-D repeated; Silvex; Casaron preemergent
Typha	Cattail	Dalapon; amino triazole after flowering but before seeding; Diquat
Phragmites	Reed	Dalapon, 15 lb/acre, then amino triazole 15 lb/acre; Diquat
Juncus	Rush	Dalapon + 2,4-D or 2,4,5-T; Diquat
Eleochrus	Spike rush	2,4-D repeated; Silvex; Diquat
Jussiaea	Creeping water primrose	2,4-D; 2,4,5-T

Use ester forms of phenoxy acids at 2 oz/gal and spray to wet leaves without runoff. Control will be improved if water can be drained at time of spraying. Diquat is sprayed at 1/2 oz/gal. For aquatic control Silvex can be used as a granular material at 20 lb ai/acre. Dalapon is used at 15-20 lb/acre, or at 10 lb/acre with 2 lb of amono triazole added. Amitrol T contains ammonium thiocyanate as an activator for increased effectiveness against cattails. It should not be used along channels for irrigation water. Persons walking in treated areas, then walking on fine grass, can cause footprinting damage from such materials as Dalapon and amino triazole.

Table 9.8. Some Herbicides Effective Against Aquatic Weeds

Herbicide	*Amount*	*Safe for Swimming and Recreation*	*Safe to Use to Irrigate*	*Safe to Fill Spray Tank*	*Safe to Drink (cattle and human)*	*Fish Tolerance*
Acrolein	15 ppm	4 days	w	w	w	toxic
Amino triazole	5-10 lb/acre	several wk	w	w	w	—
Aquathol	2 ppm	24 hr	7 days	7 days	7 days	Don't eat fish for three days
Casoron	4-16 lb ai/acre	w	w	w	w	Don't eat fish for sixty days
Copper sulfate	1 ppm	safe	safe	1 ppm safe	7 ppm safe	1 ppm safe
2,4-D	2-2 1/2 ppm, 1/2 oz/gal	OK	w	w	w	100 ppm tolerated as salt; not ester
Dalapon	15-20 lb/acre	—	w	w	w	tolerated at rates used
Diquat	1/4-1 ppm	10 days	10 days	10 days	10 days	—
Endothal	2 ppm	14 days	14 days	14 days	14 days	Don't eat fish for three days
Hydrothal	2 ppm	14 days	14 days	14 days	14 days	Don't eat fish for three days
Silvex	2 ppm' 8 lb/acre	2 days	w	w	w	Some toxicity at higher rates
Sodium arsenite	4 ppm	2 days	2 days	2 days	When tests 0.05 ppm	Fish tolerate 4 ppm once a year
2,3,5-T	2 ppm, 1/2 oz/gal	24 hr	w	w	w	Salt tolerated, ester toxic

(—)Data not available.

(w) If water is to be used for this purpose consider a different spray. Before using, test water to make sure it is safe.

(a)

(b)

Figure 9.63 **(a)** *Veronica serpyllifolia;* perennial, **(b)** *V. persica,* annual.

As always, we come back to the management enigma. Chemical weed control will work best on turf that needs it least. Very weedy turf will benefit least from chemical control as the grass itself is not of sufficient vigor. We must grow better grass. Then, when the need for control has been diminished, chemical control will enable us to gain mastery over the fewer remaining weeds.

References

General References

1. Audus, L. J. (ed.), 1964, *The Physiology and Biochemistry of Herbicides,* Academic Press, Inc., New York, 555 pp.
2. Klingman, G. C., 1963, *Weed Control as a Science,* John Wiley & Sons, Inc., New York, 421 pp.
3. Robbins, W. W., A. S. Crafts, and R. N. Raynor, 1952, *Weed Control,* McGraw-Hill Book Co., Inc., New York, 503 pp.
4. Thomson, W. T., 1967 (rev. ed.) *Agricultural Chemicals,* Book II, *Herbicides,* Thomson Publications, Davis, Calif., 314 pp.
5. Warren, W., 1964, *Oregon Weed Control Handbook,* Oregon State Univ. Cooperative Exten. Serv., Corvallis, 253 pp.

Cited References

6. Adamson, R. M., 1961, "Weeds in turf," *Res. Rept. Western Sect. Natl. Weed Comm. Can.,* pp. 114–118.
7. Ahrens, J. F., R. J. Lukens, and A. R. Olsen, 1962, "Pre-emergence control of crabgrass in turf with fall and spring treatments," *N.E. Weed Control Conf. Proc.* **16,** 511–518.
8. Ahrens, J. F., and Olsen, 1961, "Comparisons of pre-emergence herbicides for the control of crabgrass," *N.E. Weed Control Conf. Proc.* **15,** 276–279.
9. Alexander, M., 1965, "Persistence and Biological reaction of pesticides in soils," *Soil Sci. Soc. Am. Proc.* **29,** 1–7.
10. Allen, G. P., 1965, "Seasonal ability of herbicides," *Weed Res.* **5,** 237.
11. Ames, R. B., and C. R. Skogley, 1962, "Pre- and Post-emergence crabgrass control in lawn turf," *N.E. Weed Control Conf. Proc.* **16,** 528–535.
12. Anonymous, 1964, "Control of knotweed," *Golf Course Reptr.* **32**(4), 70.
13. Antognini, J., R. A. Gray, J. D. Wright, and B. H. Lake, 1964, "Weed control in grass and Dichondra with Betasan," *Agron, Abstr.,* p. 104.
14. Bartlett, N., 1967, "Can you work with *Poa annua*?" *Golf Supt.* **35**(2), 30ff.
15. Beard, J. B., 1968, "Effect of temperature stress on *Poa Annua,*" *U.S.G.A. Green Sect. Rec.* **6**(2), 10–12.
16. Beardsley, C. E., K. E. Savage, and V. O. Childers, 1967, "Trifluralin behavior in soil. I. Toxicity and persistence as related to organic matter," *Agron. J.* **59,** 159–160.
17. Bingham, S. W., and C. L. Foy, 1967, "Use the right chemical tool for weed control in lawns," *Weeds, Trees, and Turf* **6**(4), 12ff.

18. Bingham, S. W., and R. E. Schmidt, 1964, "Crabgrass control in turf," *So. Weed Conf. Proc.* **17,** 113–122.
19. Bingham, S. W., and R. E. Schmidt, 1967, "Residue of bensulide in turfgrass soil following annual treatments for crabgrass control," *Agron. J.* **59,** 327–329.
20. Bobrov, R. A., 1955, "The leaf structure of *Poa annua* with observations on its smog sensitivity in Los Angeles County," *Am. J. Botany* **42,** 467.
21. Bohne, P. W., and B. S. Morgan, 1962, "The present status of MH-30 as a managment tool for highway turf," *Agron. Abstr.,* p. 101.
22. Brown, D., 1968, "Surveying the pre-emergent chemicals and ideas," *Midwest Reg. Turf Foundn. Turf Conf. Proc.,* pp. 20–22.
23. Burt, E. O., 1964, "Tolerance of warm season turfgrasses to herbicides," *So. Weed Conf. Proc.* **17,** 123–126.
24. Burt, E. O., 1964, "Control of grass weeds in Florida turfgrasses," *Univ. Florida Turfgr. Management Conf. Proc.* **12,** 47–53.
25. Burt, E. O., 1966, "Summary of South Florida research," *Univ. Florida Turfgr. Management Conf. Proc.* **13.** 160–163; **14,** 162–166.
26. Burt, E. O., 1965, "Warm season turfgrasses and pre-emergence herbicides," *Golf Course Reptr.* **33**(3), 54ff.
27. Burt, E. O., and J. A. Simmons, 1962, "Germination and growth of turfgrass seedlings following pre-emergence herbicides," *N. Central Weed Conf. Proc.* **19,** 52.
28. Burt, E. O., R. W. White, and J. A. Simmons, 1962, "Tolerance of some trees and shrubs in newly sprigged and established St. Augustinegrass to atrazine and simazine," *So. Weed Conf. Proc.* **15,** 119–120.
29. Byrd, B. C., and F. A. Nyman, Jr., 1966, "Progress report on highway vegetation control experiments using Tordon 101 mixture and Norbeck particulating agent," *Down to Earth* **22**(1).
30. Callahan, L. M., 1964, "The effects of three phenoxyalkylcarboxylic acid compounds on the physiology and survival of turfgrasses," Ph.D. Thesis, Rutgers, 129pp.; *Dissertation Abstr.* **25**(2), 2142.
31. Callahan, L. M., 1966, "Turfgrass tolerances do differ," *Weeds, Trees and Turf* **5**(11), 6ff.
32. Callahan, L. M, and R. E. Engel, 1965, "The effects of phenoxy herbicides on the physiology and survival of turfgrass," *U.S.G.A. Green Sect. Rec.* **3**(1), 1–5; see also *Agron. Abstr.*, 1963, p. 117.
33. Campbell, W. R., and R. K. Singh, 1963, "Henbit and chickweed studies," *N. Central Weed Control Conf. Proc.* **19,** 52–53.
34. Campbell, W. R., and R. K. Singh, 1963, "Notes on nimblewill control," *N. Central Weed Control Conf. Proc.* **19.**
35. Candoe, C. L., W. C. Robocker, and T. J. Muzik, 1961, "Annual grass seed control in grass seed production," *Washington State Weed Conf. Proc.*, pp. 38–39.
36. Cerns, W. G., 1960, "Effect of dextrorotary isomer of 4-chloro-2-methyl phenoxy propionic acid (Compitox) on chickweed," *N. Central Weed Control Conf. Proc.* **17,** 103–104.

37. Chappell, W. E., and R. E. Schmidt, 1962, "Phytotoxic effects of certain pre-emergence crabgrass control treatments on seedling turf grasses," *N.E. Weed Control Conf. Proc.* **16,** 474–478.
38. Cockerham, S. T., and J. W. Whitworth, 1967, "Germination and control of annual bluegrass," *Golf Supt.* **35**(5), 10ff.
39. Cornman, J. F., 1966, "Annual bluegrass—a turfgrass enigma," *Cornell Plantations* **21**(4), 66–68.
40. Corman, J. F., 1966, "Residual effects of R-4461 on perennial turfgrasses," *N.E. Weed Control Conf. Proc.* **20,** 552–553.
41. Couch, R. W., R. I. D. Murphy, D. E. Davis, and H. H. Funderburk, 1964 "The control of catsear, dallisgrass, carpetgrass, and other lawn weeds in bermudagrass turf," *So. Weed Conf. Proc.* **17,** 107–111.
42. Daniel, W. H., 1966, "I'm tired of *Poa annua,*" *Golf Supt.* **34**(8), 16ff.
43. Deal, E. E., 1967, "Crabgrass control chemicals," *Golf Supt,* **35**(1), 94ff.
44. Deal, E. E., 1967, "Tufcote bermuda establishment using pre-emergence herbicides," *Agron. Abstr.,* p. 66.
45. DeFrance, J. A., and J. R. Kollett, 1959, "Annual bluegrass control with chemicals," *Golf Course Reptr.* **27**(1), 14ff.
46. Dewald, C. L., L. W. Fancher, and B. H. Lake, 1963, "Betasan, a promising new herbicide for use on turf," *So. Weed. Conf.* **16,** 110–114.
47. Duble, R. L., and E. C. Holt, 1965, "Preemergence herbicides as they influence bermudagrass establishment," *Golf Course Reptr.* **33**(3), 55ff; see also M. S. Thesis, Texas A & M, 1965.
48. Dudley, J., 1963, "Experience with maleic hydrazide," *U.S.G.A. Green Sect. Rec.* **1**(3), 12.
49. Duich, J. M., 1962, "Pre-emergence crabgrass control needs further research," *Sci. for the Farmer* **9**(4), 8ff.
50. Duich, J. M., B. R. Fleming, and A. E. Dudeck, 1961, "The effect of pre-emergence chemicals on crabgrass, and bluegrass, fescue, and bentgrass turf," *N.E. Weed Control Conf. Proc.* **15,** 269–275.
51. Duich, J. M., B. R. Fleming, and A. E. Dudeck, 1962, "The effect of certain pre-emergence chemicals on grass germination and seedling grasses," *N.E. Weed Control Conf. Proc.* **16,** 479–483.
52. Duich, J. M., B. R. Fleming, A. E. Dudeck, G. J. Schoop, and J. Boyd, 1962, "1961 pre-emergence crabgrass results," *N.E. Weed Control Conf. Proc.* **16,** 495–497.
53. Duich, J. M., G. J. Shoop, and B. R. Fleming, 1965, "1964 preemergence crabgrass control results," *Golf Course Reptr.* **33**(3), 58ff.
54. Engel, R. E., 1965, "Use of pre-emergence herbicides on turf," *Golf Course Reptr.* **33**(4), 16ff.
55. Engel, R. E., 1967, "Is crabgrass here to stay," *Intern. Turfgr. Conf. and Show Proc.* **38,** 60–71.
56. Engel, R. E., 1967, "Temperature requirement for germiation of annual bluegrass and colonial bentgrass," *Golf Supt.* **35**(9), 20ff.
57. Engel, R. E., 1967, "Responses of bentgrass turf to dicamba, mecoprop, and silvex herbicides," *Rutgers Univ. N.J. Agr. Expt. Sta. Bull.* **816,** 85–92.

58. Engel, R. E., and L. M. Callahan, "'Merion' Kentucky bluegrass response to soil residue of pre-emergence herbicides," *Weeds* **15,** 128–130.
59. Engel, R. E., and J. R. Dunn, 1967, "1965 pre-emergence treatments for goosegrass control," *N.J. Agr. Expt. Sta. Bull.* **816,** 92–98.
60. Engel, R. E., R. N. Cook, and R. D. Ilnicki, 1962, "Crabgrass control obtained in established turf with pre-emergence herbicides," *N.E. Weed Control Conf. Proc.* **16,** 543–544.
61. Engel, R. E., R. N. Cook, R. D. Ilnicki, 1962, "The effect of three spring dates of preemergence herbicide application on crabgrass control in established turf," *N.E. Weed Control Conf. Proc.* **16,** 545.
62. Engel, R. E., C. R. Funk, and D. A. Kinney, 1968, "Effect of varied rates of atrazine and simazine on the establishment of several *Zoysia* strains," *Agron. J.* **60,** 261–262.
63. Engel, R. E., R. D. Ilnicki, and R. N. Cook, 1961, "Pre-emergence crabgrass control on turfgrasses," *N.E. Weed Control Conf. Proc.* **15,** 280–283.
64. Engel, R. E., A. Morrison, and R. D. Ilnicki, 1968, "Pre-emergence chemical effects in annual bluegrass," *Golf Supt.* **36**(2), 20ff.
65. Faubion, J. L., and E. C. Holt, 1964, "Purple nutsedge control in bermudagrass with organic arsenicals," *Agron Abstr.*, p. 105.
66. Fortney, W. R., and A. P. Dye, 1962, "Crabgrass control studies," *Ann. Rept. W.•Va. Agr. Expt. Sta.,* 1961/62, Parts 2–3, pp. 5–10.
67. Fryer, J. D., and R. J. Chancellor, 1960, "Effect of dalapon on *Agropyron repens, Agrostis gigantea,* and *A. stolonifera,*" *Br. Weed. Control Conf., 1958 Proc.,* pp. 208–213.
68. Fults, J. L., 1966, "The crabgrass problem—1966," *Intern. Turfgr. Conf. and Show Proc.* **37,** 37–41.
69. Fulwider, J. R., and R. E. Engel, 1960, "Seed characteristics and control of goosegrass, *Elusine indica,*" *U.S.G.A. J. and Turf Management* **12**(7), 24–27.
70. Gallagher, J. E., 1964, "Aquatic weed control," *Golf Course Reptr.* **32**(3), 42ff.
71. Gallagher, J. E., (moderator), 1967, "Weeds are turf problems everywhere," *Turf-grass Times* **2**(6), 3ff.
72. Gallagher, J. E., and R. J. Otten, 1962, "Pre-emergence crabgrass control trials—1961," *N.E. Weed Control Conf. Proc.* **16,** 498–504.
73. Gaskin, T. A., 1964, "Effect of pre-emergence crabgrass herbicides on rhizome development in Kentucky bluegrass," *Agron. J.* **56,** 340–342.
74. Gephart, D. D., 1967, "Dallisgrass control, "Western Lands. News. **7**(3), 16.
75. Gibeault, V. A., 1965, "The selective control of colonial bentgrass (*Agrostis tenuis* L.) with DMPA and trifluralin and the effects of DMPA on turfgrass root growth," M.S. Thesis, Univ. of Rhode Island (abstr. in *J. Sports Turf Res. Inst.* **41,** 1965).
76. Gibeault, V. A., 1966, "Investigation on the control of annual meadowgrass," *J. Sports Turf Res. Inst.* **42,** 17–40 (1967).

77. Giordano, P. M., and C. R. Skogley, 1961, "A study of the effects of various rates and formulations of chlordane on new stands of turfgrass."
78. Goodin, J. R., 1959, "Chemical control of flowering of *Pennisetum clandestinum,* kikuyugrass," *So. Calif. Turfgr. Cult.* **9**(3), 17.
79. Goss, R. L., 1961, "Pre-emergence weed control with soil fumigants," *Wash. State Weed Conf. Proc.,* pp. 10–11.
80. Goss, R. L., "Pre-emergence control of annual bluegrass (*Poa annua* L.)." *Agron. J.* **56,** 479–481; see also *Golf Course Reptr.* **33**(3), 24ff (1965).
81. Hagden, R., and C. Harms, 1966, "Soil fertility levels governing bensulide phytotoxiciity to *Digitaria sanguinalis,*" *Agron. Abstr.,* p. 39.
82. Hamilton, K. C., 1962, "Weed control research in bermudagrass turf,' *Univ. Ari. Agr. Expt. Sta. Rept.* **212,** 23–25.
83. Hamilton, K. C., 1965, "Spurge control in bermudagrass," *Univ. Ariz. Agr. Expt. Sta. Rpt.* **230,** 2.
84. Hamilton, K. C., 1966, "Weed control in dormant bermudagrass," *Univ. Ariz. Agr. Expt. Sta. Rept.* **240,** 7–12.
85. Hansen, C. O., 1964, "Control of winter annual weeds in southern turf with paraquat," *Weed Soc. Am. Abstr.,* p. 93.
86. Hart, G. L., 1966, "Control of poison oak on military reservations with Tordon," *Down to Earth* **22**(3), 6–7.
87. Hart, R. H., and W. S. McGuire, 1963, "Effects of fertilizer on growth of velvetgrass in grass pasture," *Agron. J.* **55,** 414–415.
88. Harrison, R. P., 1966, "Trizone soil fumigant," *Down to Earth* **22**(2), 16–18.
89. Hauser, E. W., 1963, "Response of purple nutsedge to amitrol, 2,4-D, and EPTC," *Weeds* **11,** 251–252.
90. Havis, J. R., 1961, "A test of chemicals for crabgrass control in turf," *N.W. Weed Control Conf. Proc.* **15,** 294–295.
91. Havis, J. R., 1962, "Comparison of chemicals for pre-emergence crabgrass control in turf," *N.E. Weed Control Conf. Proc.* **16,** 493–494.
92. Hemphill, D. D., 1961, "Pre-emergence control of crabgrass," *North Central Weed Control Conf. Res. Rept.* 18:85.
93. Hemphill, D. D., 1965, "Weed control," *Golf Course Reptr.* **33**(3), 36–37.
94. Herron, J. W., 1965, "Pre-emergence crabgrass control," *Golf Course Reptr.* **33**(3), 20–22.
95. Hiltibran, R. C., 1968, "The chemical control of some aquatic plants," *Midwest Reg. Turf Foundn. Turfgr. Conf. Proc.,* pp. 36–41.
96. Holifield, E. L., and R. E. Frans, 1964, "Winter weed removal from dormant turf," *So. Weed Conf. Proc.* **17,** 127–131.
97. Horn, G. C., 1966, "Increasing the effectiveness of turf herbicides by use of oil," *Florida Turfgr. Assoc. Bull.* **13**(4), 1–6; see also *Florida State Hort. Soc. Proc.* **79,** 494–509 (1966).
98. Horn, G. C., 1968, "*Poa annua* in Florida turf," *Univ. Florida Turfgr. Management Conf. Proc.* **16,** 42–45.
99. Hovin, A. W.. 1957, "Variation in annual bluegrass," *Golf Course*

Reptr, **25**(7), 18ff; see also *Am. J. Botany* **45,** 131–138 (1958).

100. Huffaker, C. B., D. W. Ricker, and C. E. Kennett. 1961, "Biological control of puncture vine," *Calif. Agr.* **15**(12), 11.

101. Huffine, W. W., and A. D. West, 1962, "Phytotoxicity studies of herbicides applied to dormant U-3 and Sunturf bermudagrasses," *Agron. Abstr., p. 103.*

102. Jenkins, T. J., 1924, "The artificial hybridization of grasses," *Welch Plant Breeding Sta. Bull. Ser.* **14,** 1–16.

103. Juska, F. V., W. H. Daniel, E. C. Holt, and V. B. Youngner, 1961, "Nomenclature of some plants associated with turfgrass management," *Rept. Turfgr. Nomencl. Comm., Div. XI, Am. Soc. Agron., Mimeo,* 21pp.

104. Juska, F. V., and A. A. Hanson, 1964, "Effect of pre-emergence crabgrass herbicides on seedling emergence of turfgrass species," *Weeds* **12,** 97–100.

105. Juska, F. V., and A. A. Hanson, 1967, "Factors affecting *Poa annua* control," *Weeds* **15,** 98–101.

106. Juhren, M., W. Nobel, and F. W. Went, 1957, "The standardization of *Poa annua* as an indicator of smog concentrations," *Plant Physiol.* **32,** 576.

107. Kemmerer, H. R., and J. D. Butler, 1962, "Establishment of spring seeded lawns," *Illinois Res.* (Summer), p. 5.

108. Kerr, J. A. M., and J. H. Bailie, 1965, "A note on the use of paraquat as a selective herbicide for grassland," *Rept. Agr. Res. N. Ireland* **14** (2), 1–7.

109. Kesler, C. D., R. H. Cole, and C. E. Phillips, 1962, "Pre- and post-emergence crabgrass control in turfgrass," *N.E. Weed Control Conf. Proc.* **16,** 524–527.

110. Klingman, G. C., 1962, "Weed control in *Zoysia,* tall fescue, and bermudagrass turf," *So. Weed Conf. Proc.* **15,** 69–73.

111. Lee, W. O., 1966, "The distribution, growth habit, and control of German velvetgrass (*Holcus mollis* L.) in Western Oregon," Thesis, *Dissertation Abstr.* **26**(9), 4918.

112. Legg, D. C., 1967, "Selective weedkiller for use on young turf," *J. Sports Turf Res. Inst.* **34,** 40–48.

113. Lewis, W. M., and W. B. Gilbert, 1965, "Pre-emergence crabgrass control in golf course turf," *Golf Course Reptr.* **33**(3), 44ff.

114. Lewis, W. M., and G. C. Klingman, "Three evaluation methods for taking weed control data in bermudagrass turf," *So. Weed Conf. Proc.* **16,** 105–109.

115. Limpel, L. E., P. H. Schulat, and F. Batkay, 1961, "The responses of turf and certain turf weeds to Dacthal," *N.E. Weed Control Conf. Proc.* **15,** 296–297.

116. Long, J. A., W. W. Allen, and E. C. Holt, 1962, "Control of nutsedge in bermudagrass turf," *Weeds* **10,** 285–287.

117. Lynd, J. Q., C. E. Rieck, and P. W. Santelmann, 1966, "Soil components determining bensulide phytotoxicity," *Agron. J.* **58,** 508–510.
118. Madden, E. A., 1967, "*Poa annua*, problem weed in sports greens," *Golf Supt.* **35**(1), 13–14.
119. Madison, J. H., 1961, "The effect of pesticides on turfgrass disease incidence," *Plant Disease Reptr.* **45,** 892–893.
120. Madison, J. H., 1962, "The effect of managment practices on invasion of lawn turf by bermudagrass (*Cynodon dactylon* (L.) Pers.)," *Am. Soc. Hort. Sci. Proc.* **80,** 559–564.
121. Mazur, A. R., 1968, "The fate of herbicides," *U.S.G.A. Green Sect. Rec.* **6**(4), 8–9.
122. Miller, C. W., 1964, "Invasion of King ranch bluestem in lawns and turf areas on the southwest," *Agron. Abstr.,* p. 122.
123. Miller, R. W., and R. R. Davis, 1965, "Preemergence herbicides for crabgrass control," *Golf Course Reptr.* **33**(3), 48–49.
124. Mower, R. G., and J. F. Cornman, "Experiments in Pre-emergence crabgrass control," *N.E. Weed Control Conf. Proc.* **15,** 264–267.
125. Mower, R. G., and J. F. Cornman, 1962, "Pre-emergence crabgrass control," *N.E. Weed Control Conf. Proc.* **16,** 489–492.
126. Murphy, W. J., O. H. Fletchall, and E. J. Peters, 1961, "Effect of 2,4-D and related compounds on seedling grasses," *North Central Weed Control Conf. Res. Rept.* **18,** 75–76; see also *Weed Soc. Am. Abstr.,* 1964.
127. Noer, O. J., "As O. J. sees it," *Golf Course Reptr.* **32**(10), 12 (1964); **33**(8), 46ff (1965); **34**(5), 30 (1966).
128. Peabody, D. V., and H. M. Austenson, 1965, "Herbicides and their effect on the yield of grass seed," *Agron. J.* **57,** 633–634.
129. Perkins, A. T., 1968, "Effective turfgrass weed control," *U.S.G.A. Green Sect. Rec.* **6**(1), 11–15.
130. Peters, R. A., H. C. Yocum, and K. C. Stevens, 1962, "Observations on chemical control of crabgrass in turf (1961)," *N.E. Weed Control Conf. Proc.* **16,** 519–523.
131. Pryor, M. R., 1963, "The chemical control of puncture vine," *Calif. Turfgr. Cult.* **13**(4), 29–31.
132. Record, L., 1965, "Long term effects of herbicides," *U.S.G.A. Green Sect. Rec.* **3**(3), 7–9.
133. Rice, E. J., and C. R. Skogley, 1961, "Pre-emergence control of crabgrass in lawn turf," *N.E. Weed Control Conf. Proc.* **15,** 284–288.
134. Rice, E. J., and C. R. Skogley, 1962, "Seed and seedling tolerance of lawngrasses to certain crabgrass herbicides," *N.E. Weed Control Conf. Proc.* **16,** 466–473.
135. Roach, G. W., and W. W. Huffine, 1967, "Herbicide evaluation for the selective control of sandbur in bermudagrass turf," *Agron. Abstr.,* p. 57.
136. Roberts, E. C., and D. R. Brockshus, 1966, "Kind and extent of injury

to greens from pre-emergence herbicides," *Golf Supt.* **34**(5), 13ff.

137. Roberts, E. C., and A. E. Cott, 1963, "Nimblewill threatens Iowa lawns," *Iowa Farm Sci.* **17**(8), 18–19.
138. Roberts, E. C., and J. J. Ptacek, 1962, "Pre-emergence crabgrass control," *Golf Course Reptr.* **30**(3), 18ff.
139. Robinson, B. P., 1956, "A summary of turfgrass weed control tests," *U.S.G.A. Green Sect. J.* **9**(6), 26–28.
140. Robinson, B. P., and J. E. Gallagher, 1958, "Weed control—a problem North and South," *Parks and Rec.* **41**(6), 264ff.
141. Rochecouste, E., 1962, "Studies on the biotypes of *Cynodon dactylon* (L.) Pers. II. Growth response to trichloroacetic acid and 2,2-dichloropropionic acid," *Weed Res.* **2,** 136–145.
142. Rumburg, C. B., R. E. Engel, and W. F. Meggitt, 1960, "Effect of phosphorus concentration on the absorption of arsenate by oats from nutrient solution," *Agron. J.* **52,** 452–453.
143. St. Pierre, L. V., 1968, "An eviction notice for *Poa annua* on fairways," *U.S.G.A. Green Sec. Rec.* **5**(5), 5.
144. Salisbury, E. J., 1963, "Intermittent germination of *Capsella,*" *Nature* **199,** 1303–1304.
145. Santleman, P. W., 1961, "Pre-emergence crabgrass control in Maryland," *N.E. Weed Control Conf. Proc.* **15,** 393–395.
146. Schmidt, R. E., and H. B. Musser, 1958, "Some effects of 2,4-D on turfgrass seedlings, *U.S.G.A. J. and Turf Management* **11**(6), 29–32.
147. Sen, K, M., 1960 "Studies on the influence of some auxin herbicides on grass seed crops," *Versl. Landbouwk Onderz.* **66,** 70pp; see *Herb. Abstr.* **32,** 1386.
148. Shadbolt, C. A., and F.`L. Whiting, 1961, "Urea herbicide breakdown is slow," *Calif. Agr.* **15**(11), 10.
149. Simmons, J. A., and E. O. Burt, 1962, "Tolerance of seedling and established turfgrasses to bandane and chlordane," *North Central Weed Control Conf. Proc.* **19,** 51.
150. Simmons, J. A., and R. Huey, 1964, "The response of Kentucky bluegrass to single and repeat applications of chlordane and polychlorodicyclopentadiene," *Weed Soc. Am. Abstr.,* p. 94.
151. Sinclair, G., 1825, *Hortus Graminicus Woburnensis*, 2nd ed., pp. 400–402.
152. Skirde, W., 1966, "Control of *Polygonum bistorta* on high-altitude pastures," (in German) *Wirtschaftseigene Futter* **12,** 308–315; see *Herb. Abstr.,* **37,** 1300.
153. Skogley, C. R., and J. A. Jagschitz, 1965, "Chemical crabgrass control in turfgrass," *Golf Course Reptr.* **33**(3), 14–16.
154. Smith, W. D., 1960, "Silvex for chickweed control," *North Central Weed Control Conf. Proc.* **17,** 23.
155. Splittstoesser, W. E., and H. J. Hopen, 1967, "Response of bentgrass to Siduron," *Weeds* **15,** 82–83.
156. Sprague, H. B., and G. N. Burton, 1937, "Annual bluegrass (*Poa annua* L.) and its requirements for growth," *N.J. Agr. Expt. Sta. Bull.* **630,** 24pp.

157. Sprague, V. G., 1940, "Germination of freshly harvested seeds of several *Poa* species and of *Dactylis glomerata*," *J. Am. Soc. Agron.* **32,** 715–721.
158. Switzer, C. M., 1961, "Residual effects of some herbicides used for control of crabgrass in turf," *North Central Weed Control Conf. Res. Rept.* **18,** 92–93.
159. Switzer, C. M., 1967, "News report," (original paper not seen), *Weeds, Trees and Turf* **6**(5), 31.
160. Thompson, J. T., and W. S. Hardcastle, 1963, "Control of crab and dallisgrass in narrow leaf turf," *So. Weed Conf. Proc.* **16,** 115.
161. Timm, G., 1965, "Beiträge zur Biologie und Systematica von *Poa annua* L.," *Z. Acker a. Pflbau.* **122,** 3, 267.
162. Troll, J., J. Zak, and D. Waddington, 1962, "Pre-emergence control of crabgrass with chemicals," *N.E. Weed Control Conf. Proc.* **16,** 484–487.
163. Troll, J., J. Zak, and D. Waddington, 1962, "Toxicity of pre-emergence crabgrass killers to some basic grasses," *N.E. Weed Control Conf. Proc.* **16,** 488.
164. Tutin, T. G., 1952, "Origin of *Poa annua* L.," *Nature* **169,** 4291.
165. Tutin, T. G., 1957, "A contribution to the experimental taxonomy of *Poa annua* L.," *Watsonia* **4,** 1.
166. Vandenborn, W. H., 1965, "The effect of dicamba and picloram on quackgrass, bromegrass, and Kentucky bluegrass," *Weeds* **13,** 309–312.
167. Watson, D. P., 1950, "Anatomical modification of velvet bentgrass (*Agrostis canina* L.) caused by soil treatment with 2,4-dichlorophenoxyacetic acid," *Am. J. Botany* **37,** 424–431.
168. White, R. W., Jr., 1964, "Control of broadleaved weeds in Florida turfgrasses," *Univ. Florida Turfgr. Management Conf. Proc.* **12,** 54–58.
169. Youngner, V. B., 1951, "The control of *Poa annua,* annual bluegrass, in putting greens," *So. Calif. Turfgr. Cult.* **9**(4), 27–29.
170. Youngner, V. B., 1959, "Ecological studies of *Poa annua*," *J. Brit. Grasslnds Soc.* **14,** 237.
171. Youngner, V. B., 1961, "Winter survival of *Digitaria sanguinalis* in subtropical climates," *Weeds* **9,** 654–655; see also *Calif. Turfgr. Cult.* **12**(2), 13 (1962).
172. Youngner, V. B., 1965, "Annual bluegrass, *Poa annua*," *Calif. Turfgr. Cult.* **15**(2), 15–16.
173. Youngner, V. B., 1965, "Pre-emergence weed control in turf," *Golf Course Reptr.* **33**(3), 32ff.
174. Youngner, V. B., and F. J. Nudge, 1968, "Chemical control of annual bluegrass as related to vertical mowing," *Calif. Turfgr. Cult.* **18**(3), 17–18.

GLOSSARY

Definitions in the glossary are limited in meaning to the context in which they are used in this book.

Acute (poisoning). Coming to a sharp crisis. An attack of immediate concern.

Aerify. To force circulation of air. Applied to hole punching even if done for other reasons than to affect soil air movement.

Arsenical. Material containing arsenic.

Asexual. Without sex. Propagation by sod, stolons, offshoots, etc.

Back lap. To run a mower reel backwards while dressing with a suspension of a lapping compound, with the object of finely mating the reel to the bed knife.

Biocide. A compound which kills.

Blight. A general term applied to a damaging disease.

Broad leaved. Referring to dicot plants.

Brushing. Running a stiff brush or similar tool over a green to raise stolons so they can be mowed off. Used to reduce grain.

Bulk density. Apparent density of dry soil in the state in which it occurrs in the field. Bulk density is lower on porous soils, higher on compacted ones.

Calibrate. Measure rate of application of a spreader or sprayer under defined conditions.

Carrier. Medium used to spread a pesticide. May be water, oil, vermiculite, diatomaceous earth, etc.

Certified seed (plants). Certification is by a crop improvement society as to variety and purity of the seed, sod, or plant.

Chronic (poisoning). Lingering and often lasting state of poisoning which may have intense symptoms or may be low level or even unrecognized.

Clip (of mower). The forward travel of the mower between cuts.

Clipping height. The height of which the mower bed knife, or impact blade, is set, as measured from a flat surface.

Clone. Collectively, all of the divisions, offshoots, and other vegetatively propagated pieces originating from a single plant.

Colloid. A finely divided material in which surface area is so large in proportion to volume that surface properties predominate.

Compost. A decomposed mixture of plant and animal wastes to which lime, fertilizer, or soil, may have been added.

Control (pests). To limit population and spread of a pest to tolerable levels.

Crown. A region of the plant near the soil surface where tillers, stolons, etc., conjoin.

Cultivar. A line, variety, strain, or distinct subclass of plant.

Damping off. Seedling disease resulting from a variety of organisms.

Dicot. A member of the subclass Dicotyledoneae, characterized by seeds, a pair of seedling leaves, and netted leaf venation.

Emulsion. A dispersion of fine droplets of oil in water, or water in oil. It generally requires an emulsifying agent to stabilize it.

Epidemic. A disease outbreak among a population at one time.

Epiphytotic. A killing disease attack.

Ester. A compound formed by chemical combination between an acid and an alcohol.

Filming agent. A material added to an herbicide to promote its spreading over the leaf surface.

Fumigant. A pesticide that is active in the vapor form and which vaporizes at ordinary growing temperatures.

Fungicide. A material used to kill fungi.

Fungus. A member of a class of plants without chlorophyll that feed on organic matter.

Germinate. To begin to grow.

Grain (of a green). When many leaves and stolons grow in the same horizontal direction they create a grain which favors roll of the ball with the grain, resists the roll of the ball across it.

Granular formulation. Pesticides (or fertilizers) prepared for use as part of a solid granule suitable for spreader application.

Heaving (frost). Displacing a plant out of the ground as a result of frost action accompanying freezing and thawing.

Herbicide. A compound that kills plants (weeds).

Hybrid. A cross between two parents of substantially different genetics.

Hyphae. A thread of fungal growth.

Improved strain. A genetic line of tested superiority in one or more characteristics.

Insecticide. A compound that kills insects.

Interseed. Add seed to existing turf to increase its density or to favor dominance of a particular species.

Mass flow. Hydraulic flow of bulk water solution as opposed to osmotic flow on the molecular level.

Mat. The collection of living stolons covering the soil when stoloniferous grasses are grown.

Mercurial. Containing mercury.

Microorganism. Any of a range of small-sized organisms ranging from protozoa and bacteria to fungi.

Monocot. A plant of the subclass Monocotyledoneae. A seed plant with a single seedling leaf and parallel leaf venation.

Mulch. An inert substance used to protect soil from erosion, and plants and seeds from heat, cold, or drying.

Mycelium. A mass of noninfective fungal hyphae.

Nitrogen. An elemental atmospheric gas unavailable to plants except as it is chemically combined. In talking about fertilizer, nitrogen is used loosely to refer to combined nitrogen as if it were elemental.

Nematocide. A substance that kills nematodes.

Nursery. An area for growing planting stocks (sod, stolons).

Optimum. Most favorable.

Overseed. To seed cold tolerant grasses into a disturbed sod of cold dormant grasses in order to provide winter growth and color.

Parasite. An organism which obtains nourishment from other live organisms.

Pathogen. An organism causing a disease.

Penetrating agent. A substance added to a pesticide formulation to assist the pesticide in penetrating protective layers of cutin, chitin, etc.

Pesticide. A substance that kills pests.

Phloem. Conducting tissue to the outside of a vascular bundle, notably active in moving organic compounds to regions of low concentration.

Plugging. Planting small bits or 'plugs' of sod.

Predator. An organism which preys on other organisms as spiders prey on flies.

Preemergence. Before growth causes emergence from the soil.
Proprietary. The private commercial formulation of a chemical.
Psychrophilic. Cold-loving.
Rejuvenate. Improve a turf by replacing and improving much of the root-zone soil by means of deep hole punching.
Renovate. To rebuild a turf using an existing turf as the seedbed.
Resilience. Ability to recover from impact. A resilient turf is firm rather that soft.
Rhizome. A horizontal underground stem.
Saprophyte. An organism nourished by dead organic matter.
Scalp. To cut the turf from the soil, or to mow overly close, or to cut into the grass crowns.
Seedbed. Soil well prepared for seeding.
Silt. The soil fraction smaller than 0.02 mm and larger than 0.002 mm. Silt particles are too small for good drainage, too large for good aggregation and exchange capacity.
Social parasite. An organism that destroys another by simply occupying its 'home' or its environmental niche.
Sod. Top layer of soil with the plants, roots, and rhizomes binding it together. To plant sod.
Species. An inbreeding group of plants which are morphologically distinct, and genetically isolated.
Sprig. A tuft of plant used as a propagule.
Stolon. A horizontal, above-ground stem. *Stolonize.* To plant pieces of stolon to make a turf.
Strain. A distinct genetic kind of variety.
Susceptible. Lacking inherent ability to resist the stress to which the plant is susceptible.
Sward. An area of land covered with short grass.
Symptom. A change or sign or condition indicating the existance of disease, injury, poisoning, etc.
Syringe. Showering the grass so solar energy will be used in evaporation instead of transpiration.
Systemic. Passing throughout the system; not confined to one part.
Thatch. Layer of dead grass tissues laying above the soil. Thatch is mainly interlaced dead stolons and clippings. In nonstoloniferous grasses, clippings form a thinner felt-like thatch.
Tolerance. Degree to which a plant endures a stress.
Top dressing. A prepared mixture spread over, and worked into, turf. It is apt to be formulated of sand, compost, organic matter, fertilizer, and the like.
Translocate. To move about in the plant in solution.
Turf. A sod of soil with the plants growing in it. A block of peat. A sward of

well-maintained lawn grasses. *Turfgrass.* A grass adapted for and used for growing turf.

Variety. A subclass distinguished by some notable characteristic.

Vascular system. The conducting system of xylem and phloem in which water and dissolved foods move.

Vertical mowing. Cutting perpendicularly into the turf to lift or cut stolons to control grain; or to lift and remove thatch.

Verdure. Living green turf left after mowing. The turf as distinct from the clippings.

Volatile. Changing into or forming vapors.

Weed. A plant you don't want where it is.

Wetting agent. A chemical used to lower the surface tension of water.

Winterkill. Injuries of turf resulting from environmental stresses during the cold part of the year.

Xylem. The inner conducting layer of a bundle, through which bulk water is moved hydraulically under a tension head.

APPENDIX I

Turfgrass Specifications

Specifications are an attempt at communication. Good will and mutual trust of the parties to a contract make specifications work, and specs are most successful when they tell a skilled workman what is to be done. Not all workmen are skilled, and not all men express good will. Ignorance and deceit have lead to bad contracts. As a result, specifications grow and grow, and tell not only what is to be done, but tell how it is to be done, how to judge if it is well done, liabilities and penalties if it is not done well. assignment of responsibilities, and methods of negotiating changes and compromises.

The low-bid system often leads to bad results. Some contractors deliberately underbid jobs with the expectation of using substitute methods and materials to cut costs and return a profit. The poorest contract work is often done by firms that act both as architect and contractor, and who write specs for themselves. Their prices are often irresistably below market. The number of jobs they do is an impressive reference. The work may be second or third class. Repair and reconstruction during the first five years brings the final cost up above the market price for good work. Though I feel strongly about pitfalls in the bid system I shall only note they exist and go on to the goal here of providing checkpoints with respect to turfgrass specifications. The reputation of most contractors is known and will come to light if you really look for it.* The lowest bid of a contractor of impeccable reputation will usually result in good work at a fair price.

Because communication is a difficult art, it is well to discuss all provisions of the specs with the contractor before work begins. This is faster and cheaper than renegotiating when the job is half done.

ELEMENTS OF SPECIFICATIONS

I. General

1. *Definitions*

   Certain words need to be clarified. Who is the owner, the architect, the contractor, or the engineer. Does everyone know what is meant by certified seed, double swing joint, fertilizer, or off-site mixing. If a test is to be made by a "qualified laboratory" you may have to define qualified laboratory by naming the laboratories. Where there is an established authority it may be referred to. For example: "plant names are based on the *Manual of Cultivated Plants* by L. H. Bailey."
2. *Nature of Project*

   The location and purpose of the project should be established. If sod is for erosion control, one would expect lower bids than if it were for a decorative lawn. The contractor needs to know exact locations. Cost will be higher if a rock outcrop is included than if it is excluded, etc.
3. *Responsibilities and Qualifications*
   a. Is the contractor qualified by past experience to do the work? He should supply proof of previous work completed, and his ability to provide suitable equipment and personnel.
   b. Contract bonds. The contractor should provide bond for faithful performance, for payment of claims by labor, and for payment for materials.
   c. Insurance. What insurance is required (liability, workman's compensation), how much, and who bears the cost.
   d. Permits and Standards. Who obtains permits, and who bears the cost? Is work covered by code? Is work to union standards? Sanitary standards, safety precautions, etc., should be noted.

*An example: A plumber got an irrigation contract because he had just done a similar job for a club of good reputation. But no one asked the superintendent, board members, or greens committee members an opinion of his work. A simple phone call would have given the information that the plumber was slow, unreliable, had poor labor relations, required excessive inspection, correction, and supervision, and was not familiar with irrigation work. The reputation of the plumber should have been examined not the reputation of the club that hired him.

e. Who makes utility connections and who bears cost?
f. Utilities. Usually the owner provides an "as is" map of utility locations, after which damage to utilities is the responsibility of the contractor.
g. Errors and conflicts. When prints conflict with specs or various provisions of specs conflict with each other, what is the procedure for determining precedence?
h. Substitution of materials. What is the procedure for substituting materials? Who is the judge of equality when "or equal" is allowed?
i. Change orders. What is the procedure for changing specs by the owner? By the contractor?
j. Supervision. Who is authorized to make decisions for the owner in his absence? The contractor must have a responsible person in charge with authority to make decisions for him.
k. Waste disposal. Are there limitations on burning, burying, etc., and who pays dumping charges?
l. Other. The following may also be considered here: public convenience, public safty, weight limitations of equipment, use of explosives, areas available or off limits to the contractor (e.g., for his use as a corporation yard), control of casual roads and paths arising from contractor use, etc.

   Good relations obtain when responsibilities are defined at every step. Ambiguities lead to negotiation, litigation, and frustration.

4. *Bid and Award of Contract*

   This is largely procedural and provides methods for bidding, selecting, and rejecting any or all bids. It provides for deposit and return of guaranty monies.

5. *Time*

   a. Commencement. Work shall begin within x days of notice to procede.
   b. Number of working days allowed for completion, or target date of completion.
   c. Penalties for late completion; bonuses for early completion.
   d. Delays due to owner and reimbursement to contractor for his loss:

      Contracting parties are ever impatient. Normally the landscape contractor follows after the building contractor. It may help speed his work if some jobs can be done in advance. Often the landscape contractor can be permited to stockpile topsoil, establish certain grades, lay drains and conduits, or do other tasks that normally precede turf construction.

      When planting turf, time takes on a significance beyond that of some other contracts. The best time to sow grass is often limited to a few weeks in the year. When delays by the owner force a contractor to sow at an unfavorable time, I believe he should be allowed to sow under protest, so the expense of any needed reseeding can be assigned to the owner. At present, the contractor is usually held liable irrespective of the time of year he is given his notice to procede.

6. *Prosecution and Progress*
   a. Assignment. The contractor cannot assign his responsibilities to another.
   b. Subcontracting. Subcontractors are regarded as employees of the contractor and he is responsible for their work and their progress.
   c. Progress schedule. The contractor may be asked to provide a progress schedule showing order of jobs and the proposed date of commencement and of completion of each phase of the work.
   d. Temporary suspension. (i) If work is not progressing to standard the owner can stop progress until the work is brought up to standard. This does not extend the deadline for completion of the contract. (ii) If weather or work conditions are unsuitable the owner may suspend work. Such suspension justifies an extension of the time to completion equal to the time of suspension.
   e. Termination. If the contractor fails to provide equipment or a work force adequate for suitable progress for the job he shall be notified. Failure to comply with the notice shall be cause for terminating control by the contractor. The owner may then either: (i) relet the contract; or (ii) provide his own representative to use the contractors equipment and work force, hire additional men, rent additional equipment, purchase materials, and otherwise do what must be done to complete the job. This is done at the contractor's expense.

      The above seems severe, but sometimes an experienced man on small landscape jobs tries for a big job, such as a golf course, and doesn't have the experience or equipment to handle it. Usually, a bookkeeping clause provides for all funds due the contractor to be forfeit into trust. After the job is completed and all bills paid, the contractor has title to any surplus.

7. *Measurement and Payment*

   The contractor is commonly paid for time to time for up to 90% of the value of the work completed to that date. At this point the specs need to define:
   a. Measurement of work accomplished.
   b. Scope of payment. Payment covers work done without release of liability to make good defective work or material.
   c. Acceptance and payment for extra work oredered by the owner beyond the scope of the contract.
   d. Periodic partial payments. When made and for what percent of the value?

e. Acceptance and final payment. When the work is accepted payment is made, except for a percentage which may be retained for thirty to sixty days as a guaranty of work and materials under use.
f. Provision for payment for extra work done within the scope of the contract due to unforeseen circumstances. (For example, a rock ledge may be uncovered and a decision made to blast and remove 50 yd^3 of rock).

II. Doing the Work

On a small job a single set of specs may do. On larger jobs, separate specs are usually written for each unit of work, especially if different subcontractors are involved in the different units. The following outlines several repetitions for different work units.

1. *Staking*

Who does the staking: owner, architect, engineer, or contractor? In some landscape work key features may be placed by eyeball methods. Then the architect does the initial staking, after which the contractor is responsible for conserving the location of the staked spots.

2. *Clearing*
   a. Vegetation. (i) Removal and disposition. What are the restrictions on dumping, burying, and burning) Grass may fail to grow well on fired soil. Who pays dumping fees if a commercial dump is used) (ii) Preservation. Who is responsible for identifying landscape features to be preserved, how are they marked, how are they protected, and how is damage evaluated?
   b. Rock. Is rock (and to what size) removed from the finished grade and what is its disposition? Should it be piled in a certain place for future use? If hidden rock is exposed who decides its disposition.
   c. Rodents. When prairie dog villages, extensive rat nesting sites, or other rodent runs are uncovered, the owner should be notified so control measures can be initiated.
   d. Dust control.
   e. Unique features. Note any special features such as stone walls, springs, Indian mounds, etc., to be preserved or destroyed (wells to be filled and sealed, for example).
3. *Rough grade*
   a. Preservation of topsoil.
   b. Balancing cut and fill.
   c. Source of extra fill or disposition of extra cut.
   d. Replacing topsoil.
   e. Dust control.

f. Grade tolerance.
g. Maintenance of surface drainage. No hollows, basins, or pocks should be left unless specifically designated.
h. Slope. Maximum slope allowed. If execution of the blueprint results in slopes that are too steep, this clause overrides the blueprint. This clause gives operation of mowers, tractors, golf carts, etc., precedence over the sweep of the design as conceived at the drawing table.

4. *Drainage*
   a. Scope. Preservation of grade for surface drainage.
   b. Materials. Kinds of tile, collection lines, drainrock, tile cover, backfill, etc.
   c. Installation. (i) Trenching. Use minimum width trench at full depth. Note minimum radius of turns. (ii) Bedding. Specify bed material. (iii) Laying. Lay tiles with a maximum space between tiles given and with a uniform fall of not less than that given. Are joints to be covered or not? Are ends screened to keep out rodents (see *Principles of Turfgrass Culture,* Chap. 10.)
   d. Backfill. Should be free of stones and fully settled.
   e. Surface drainage. Shall be to plans but with provision for adjustment in the field. Can cart paths be used to hasten surface drainage?
   f. Contractor's obligation. Need for clean up, restoration of grade, preservation and repair of work done previously. When preparing the above section and several other sections, it may be advisable to rewrite the specs separately for greens, tees, and fairways of golf courses and for different use areas in parks, etc.

5. *Reservoirs and Lakes*
   a. Scope of work.
   b. Materials to be used.
   c. Preparation of site. This will vary with the method of sealing. A cultivated soil in fine tilth may be wanted under a plastic lining; a densely compacted soil beneath a bentonite seal; gravel beneath concrete, etc.
   d. Lining and sealing. This is worth a lot of care in writing specs and in supervising the work.
   e. Testing. How is it done and what are the criteria for evaluating)

   Lake and reservoir work should be designed, and specifications written, with the assistance of experts. Limnologists have not been adequately consulted about lake design. Volume-to-surface ratios are very important in determining water temperatures and the kinds of plants, weeds, and fish that will grow. From depth, volume, and surface figures a limnologist can estimate the chances of achieving specific goals. A slight shift in ratios can often shift maintenance costs.

6. *Wells and Pump Stations*

Here again we are out of the realm of turfgrasses, and assistance of an experienced engineer is needed to help write specs and supervise work. An important specification is that providing for testing of the equipment under running conditions. Checks are made for capacity, pressure, vibration, cavitation, cycling, temperature rise, and electrical balance. In a large installation the pump manufacturer should provide the services of an engineer for final adjustments and instruction of operating personnel.

Who makes the electrical connections to the mains? Who makes pump connections to the city mains? (See *Principles of Turfgrass Culture,* Chap. 9.)

7. *Irrigation*

a. Scope of the work.

b. Materials. At this point, the problem of "or eqivalent" equipment becomes most intense. The architect usually designs around a certain line of equipment. The contractor may favor a different brand. If the owner is an impersonal entity, such as a corporation, equipment is selected on a cost basis, and the owner is open to persuasions by salesmen of competing lines. Specifications become unwieldy as they try to define the unique characteristics of each piece of equipment so only the desired brand will fit the specs.

An irrigation system is designed as a whole with the operating characteristics of one part depending on those of other parts. Small differences in performance can result in large differences in efficiency. The decision as to "equivalency" of parts should lie with the engineer or architect, especially as availability of good local service and parts inventories may be important in true equivalency. Even better, the engineer, architect, and owner should sit down together before the specs are written, and reach agreement on the brands of equipment to be used. Equipment can then be specified by catalog number, but often the owner is a public institution, and then every salesman feels that as a taxpayer he is equally entitled to share in the public funds, regardless of limitations of his equipment.

Materials include pressure pipe and fittings; open or nonpressure pipe and fittings; sprinkler heads; valves of all kinds; control wire or tubing; programmers; quick couplings; and miscellany. Valves should be provided with valve boxes having access sleeves. List operating keys and loose parts to be supplied by contractor for operation of the system.

c. General description. (i) Lifting and replacing sod. When an irrigation system is placed in existing turf, provision is made for lifting sod, for maintaining it until replaced, for replacing it, and for giving it special care until it has knit. Contractor replaces dead sod. (ii) Trenching. Trenching should be at the specified depth. Plastic and asbestos cement pipe achieve their strength only when contained in soil of suited depth. Trenching deeper or wider than necessary can increase costs but varying the depth may allow natural flexing of the pipe over a contour and saves costs of fittings.

The contractor shall shore trenches where necessary. The contractor shall light and barricade excavations. Good planning can minimize the time during which hazard from trenches exists. Minimum depths: mains, 20–30 in.; pressure plastic, 18–24 in.; plastic on relief side of valve, 10–18 in. Replace ledge or boulder rock with sand or soil. Replace unstable foundation with firm materials. Keep pipes, valves, wires, etc., out of greens, tees, and bunkers. (iii) Laying pipe. Use the joining method specified by the engineer. Follow manufacurers' directions. (Many makers supply a handbook of instructions for the contractor for efficient and effective construction.) Support asbestos cement and plastic pipe during construction. Recoat metal pipe where assembly has damaged the coating. (iv) Clearance. Horizontal clearance between parallel pipes should be 4–6 in. for secondary pipes and 12 in. for mains over 4 in. Vertical clearance of crossing pipes should be over 2 in. if crossing is 45–90°. With crossings less than 45° allow 4–12 in. clearance depending on size of pipe. (v) Care. Keep pipe clean and plug open ends when work is not in progress. When using plastic avoid scratches, bruises, and direct sunlight. Do not lay plastic when excessively hot. (vi) Anchoring. Provide a concrete anchor for gate valves. Provide specified size thrust blocks for all tees, els, and caps, and for all bends over about 4°. Thrust blocks should be properly placed to receive the thrust of the pipe. (vii) Drains. In cold regions where pipes are drained, provide ball check drains at low points of secondary pipes and hand valves at low points of main lines. In all systems, provide quick-coupler valves at high points for air release when draining or filling the system. (viii) Risers and quick coupler valves (qcv). (1) Description. Detail of double swing joint. Ream galvanized pipe. Coat exposed threads. Set risers more than 4 in. above grade. Set risers vertical or perpendicular to grade. (2) Adjustment. After turf is up and (10) days after notification, heads and qcv shall be lowered flush with the turf. (ix) Automatic valves. Cover a minimum of (6) in. Provide access sleeve and cover unless access is through the head. (x) Control tubing or wire. This should be minimum size or larger. It should be laid with allowance for thermal contraction. Flush tubing before connecting. Provide an 18-in. diameter loop at the valve for ease of maintenance. Lay an extra wire or tube in each group for future repair or modification. Group and tie control lines. Are there any access boxes or other key points where it would be of value to identify individual lines? Lay wire in the same trench as the pipe but (4) in. lower and to the north and/or east side of the pipe. (Then when you dig you strike pipe first and always know where the control lines are. Face north and as the control lines lie to the *right* and *ahead* you can go right ahead with confidence.)

Wire size should never be smaller than specified. All electrical connections must be both soldered (to reduce resistance) and embedded (to make water-tight). To embed, connections may be wrapped with electricians tape and heavily doped, potted in hot asphalt, or, by best current practice, potted in a plastic bag containing a gob of epoxy cement. (xi) Controller. Where is it located? How is it labelled? How is it mounted? Adjust to optimize performance. Fully test and guarantee. (xii) Backfilling. *(1)* Material. Free of rock. In rocky soil the first (4) in. of backfill may need to be of imported materials such as sand. *(2)* Density. Compact to original density. Who repairs settling? When? What is the time limit? When backfill is handled from a tractor seat, i.e., pushed in with a blade and compacted by running the tractor wheel in the trench, the job is apt to be uneven unless very skillfully done. There is likely to be settling, bruising of pipe if the soil is stony, and some pinching of control tubing. *(3)* Stage one. Backfill to hold the pipe firm but leave all joints and fittings exposed. Flush lines, carry out the hydrostatic test, repair leaks, and retest. What is the duration and pressure for the test? *(4)* Stage two. Backfill the rest of the way with suitable compaction or settling. Plastic pipe should be cool and shaded at the time. Compacting pressures should not be excessive. (xiii) Contractor obligation. *(1)* Repair damage caused by his work. Repair settling. *(2)* Clean up. (Disposition of waste.) *(3)* Furnish "as built" drawings (contractor or engineer?) *(4)* Furnish operating instructions. (Contractor or engineer?) *(5)* Failure of equipment and parts. Owner responsible for normal maintenance. Contractor (or engineer?) responsible for malfunction, and for parts or equipment failure.

8. *Construction of Landscape and Site Preparation*
   a. Scope of work.
   b. Materials. Source, kind, and test limits for sand, peat, soil, organic amendments, mineral amendments, soil chemicals (lime, gypsum), and fertilizer.
   c. Description. (i) Order of work. (ii) Limitation on size, weight, and use of equipment to avoid compaction. (Reduced tire pressure helps reduce compaction.) (iii) Staking of features (by owner). (iv) Adding amendments. To what depth? What is the method of incorporation?

d. Special features. (i) Greens (golf, tennis, bowling). Soil construction, ingredients, percentages. Analysis of soils and ingredients. By whom? To what standards? Mixed off site? By what method? Establish subgrade exactly. Place the mix. Consider depth, grade, and degree of compaction (use only light equipment). Collar: directions to extend mix (2?) feet into collar then feather out for (4?) ft. Is feathered area to be mixed with native soil by tillage? (ii) Tees. Note special treatments, special soils or amendments. Is tee to be feathered into landscape so fairway mowers can be pulled over the tee? (iii) Bunkers. Disposition of excavated soil. Spreading soil thinly over the surrounding area usually causes difficulty with the grade and results in impaired drainage. Consider placing excavated soil on top of the bunker or removing it from the site. (iv) Infield areas. Skinned areas are often troublesome and no attempts have been made to standardize mixes (the losing team will find fault with any mix devised). Where blowing dust is a problem, iron sulfate will *help* to stabilize the soil. Lightly rake ca 25 lb/100 ft^2 of industrial grade iron sulfate into the surface, sprinkle lightly, dry, rerake lightly, and sprinkle.

e. Contractors obligation. Clean up, and repair of all damage resulting from execution of the above.

9. *Electrical*

Where lighting of the landscape is used separate specifications need to be written for the electrical contractor. Their scope is extensive and beyond that of this book. Note that with a water system built of nonmetallic materials special attention should be given to grounding the elecrical system.

10. *Tree Planting*

a. Scope.

b. Materials. (i) Trees should be healthy and free from circular, spiral, or kinked roots. (ii) Soil. No "drain rock" or other foreign material should be placed in the bottom of the planting hole. Organic matter used as a mulch is of value as is fertilizer mixed in the backfill.

c. General description. (i) The hole should be 2 times the width and 1 1/4 times the depth of the ball with the bottom cultivated. (ii) Plant the tree so it is (2) in. higher than it was in the field. (iii) Water basin. If used, the water basin should provide a doughnut-shaped pond. The radius of the depression should extend from about one-half the radius to twice the radius of the root system. (iv) Staking. Stakes and ties should be low and permit flexing of the trunk. Stakes should be placed on three or four sides of the tree to prevent mower damage. (v) Water in the same day as planted.

d. Contractors obligation. (i) Replacement of dead trees if survival is related to installation or to an unhealthy condition prior to planting. (ii) Maintenance. What is required and for how long?

11. *Seeding.*
  a. Scope of work.
  b. Materials. This section should contain instructions for receiving and storing materials (see p. 69). Seed, sod, and stolons deteriorate rapidly under poor storage, and sod and stolons have only a short storage life under good conditions. (i) Seed. What kind(s) and percents are used for each area? It is good economy to use certified seed whenever possible. When the seed is received the fully labeled and unopened bags should be inspected by the architect to ascertain that variety and quality meet the specs. Sod, where used, should be of correct species and variety, certified if available, and purchased from a source approved by the architect. Stolons, where used, should be of the correct species and variety and from a source approved by the architect. For turf seed, weed and crop seed should be lumped together and the sum held to less than 0.1% (see p. 63). Specs should be changed year to year to correspond to germination characteristics of the current crop year. For highest quality it is more appropriate to specify pounds per bushel along with germination, since high-weight seed gives both good germination and seedling vigor. Premix seeds to specs unless a large difference is seed weight between species used favors sowing separately. Treat seed for disease control but do not use mercurials much in advance of sowing as they shorten storage life (see pp. 78–81). (ii) Fertilizer. Seedbed fertilizer should contain both nitrogen and phosphorus. This applies to sod and stolons too. Maintenance fertilizer need contain only nitrogen (see p. 71). (iii) Soil amendments. Name kind, amount, depth, and method of mixing. (iv) Soil chemicals. Amounts, purity, and tests for lime and gypsum, are noted (or in alkali areas for soil sulfur or sulfuric acid). Minimum carbonates and particle-size distribution are usually tested, but if dolomitic lime is used for its magnesium content, then percent Mg may be important.
  c. General. (i) Seedbed. Clearing of vegetation, trash, stones over 1 in., wire, stakes, roots, etc., is noted. What is disposition of trash? Grade is to be maintained. Tillage should be to full depth at correct soil moisture (architect determines?). (ii) Fumigation. If used, give materials, rates, conditions of temperature and soil moisture, and whether open or covered. Contractor must protect the public from hazard. (iii) Fertilizer. Name the kind and amount to be tilled down (to 2 lb of N/1000 ft^2). Name the kind and amount for surface applica-

tion in the seedbed (to 1/2 lb N). (iv) Seeding. Give rate, depth, method, and timing (see pp. 75–77.) Seed should not be planted prior to (date) nor later than (date). Reseeding is to be done at a time determined by the owner. If stolons are used give schedule of operation indicating maximum storage time, conditions of storage, rate and method of planting, and maximum time from planting until the first irrigation (see p. 80). Sod to be of uniform quality and thickness with thickness of soil not greater than 3/4 in. Note maximum time to first irrigation. When sod is used, the grade is established lower to allow for sod thickness. As sod is often laid by a separate contractor, specs should indicate that the seedbed is to be established by the contractor before the subcontractor comes in. Clearly state which contractor is responsible for seedbed fertilizer and first irrigation. (v) Germination. Protect from traffic. Protect from drying. (vi) Contractor obligation. Repair and replacement should be done by contractor. If initial seed is sown out of season at insistence of owner he should carry part of the cost of replacement.

12. *Maintenance*
    a. Scope of work. To furnish supplies, materials, labor, equipment, and superintendence of operations to maintain the turf, landscape plantings, and associated features.
    b. General. The contractor is to continuously maintain under any and all circumstances, from the planting of any and every part, during the period of maintenance and until final acceptance, the items in the contract. The owner supplies water and utilities needed for maintenance. (i) Period. Maintain for 45? or 60? 90? days from approval? From sowing? (ii) Equipment and personnel. Maintenance help should be experienced. Tools and mowers should be sharp. Work should conform to best practice. (iii) Weather. Maintenance altered to suit the weather and for the benefit of the landscape, not the convenience of the contractor. (iv) Mowing. When? How High? First mowing at (?) inches when growth has reached (?) inches. Soil must be firm and the mower sharp and the mower should not be tractor pulled. Grass shall be regularly mowed at (?) inches whenever growth reaches (?) inches, or as directed by the architect. When mowing has been delayed, then excess clippings shall be removed immediately following mowing and not allowed to smother the grass. (v) Top dressing. Dress to true greens. Dress sodded areas to level the seams. (vi) Pest and disease control. When growth and establishment are limited by weeds, diseases, insects, etc., appropriate controls should be applied with suitable safeguards. (vii) Fertilization. Amount? Analysis? Frequency? Time (when determined by

the architect?). (viii) Irrigation. Use irrigation to keep plants alive and actively growing. Use the irrigation system; water by hand where needed. Use any means appropriate (e.g., tank truck along highway shoulders).

c. Contractor obligation. To repair or replace any feature damaged or destroyed by work, equipment, goods, or services during execution of the above, or damaged or destroyed by neglect.

13. *Addenda*
   a. Items added in clarification.
   b. Changes and modifications. Be explicit as to the item being changed.
   c. Additions and deletions. Provide for contractor to sign or initial all changes added after the contract is let.

References

1. Musser, H. B., J. M. Duich, and J. C. Harper, 1965, "Guide for preparation of specifications for golf course construction," *Penn. State Univ. Agr. Expt. Sta. Bull.,* 11 pp.

2. Sprinkler Irrigation Association, 1966, "Minimum specifications for turf sprinkler irrigation systems," SIA N- A-66, 8pp.

Acknowledgment:

For assistance with the above thanks is due to: Robert Muir Graves, Golf Course Architect; Mai Arbegast, Landscape Architect; and Ernest Wertheim, Landscape Architect.

APPENDIX II

Equivalents

1 inch	25.4 millimeters (mm)
1 foot	30.5 centimeters (cm)
1 yard	0.91 meters (m)
1 mile	1.6 kilometers (m)
1 decimeter	4 (3.94) inches
1 meter	1.09 yards or 39.4 inches
1 kilometer	0.62 miles
1 ft^2	9.29 dm^2
1 yd^2	0.84 m^2
1000 ft^2	0.93 are
1 acre = 43,560 ft^2	0.40 hectares
1 m^2	1.2 yd^2 or 10.8 ft^2
1 are = 100 m^2	1076 ft^2
1 hectare = 10,000 m^2	2.47 acre
1 oz (fl)	28.3 ml or ca 2 1/2 tbsp
1 cup = 8 oz	226 ml or 1/2 pint
1 quart	0.945 liters
1 U.S. gallon = 0.833 imperial gal	3.78 liters
1 liter	1.06 quarts (U.S.)
1 oz (avoir)	28.3 g
1 lb	454 g
1 kg	2.2 lb

1 lb/acre = 0.37 oz/1000 ft^2 = 10.4 g/1000 ft^2

1 oz/yd^2 = 6.95 lb/1000 ft^2

1 lb/1000 ft^2 = 0.489 kg/are = approx 1/2 kg/are = 48.9 kg/hectare = 1 lb/92.9 m^2 = 1.076 lb/100 m^2

1 kg/are = 2.05 lb/1000 ft^2

A 4-in. cup plug= 1/500,000 acre= 0.804 dm^2

A 1 7/8 circle cut with a *West Point* plugger= 17.77 cm^2

A 7/8-in. core cut with a *Viehmeyer* soil tube (for root analysis) has a surface area of 3.86 $cm.^2$

(°C x 9/5)+ 32= °F (_F— °F x 5/9= °C

Additional equivalents pertinent to irrigation are given in the appendix to Chap. 9 in *Principles of Turfgrass Culture.*

Miscellaneous

100 ft^2 of concrete 4 in. thick requires 8 sacks cement, 18 ft^3 sand, and 24 ft^3 gravel; or 1.3 yd^3 of ready mix.

To estimate the amount of gravel, soil, etc., in a stockpile multiply the area of the base by 1/3 the height.

The following gives the space covered by 100 bedding plants:

Spacing (in.)	*Coverage (ft²)*
4	11
6	25
8	44
10	70
12	100
16	178
20	278
24	400

APPENDIX III

Calibration of Sprayers and Spreaders

1 acre= 43,560 ft^2
1 mph= 88 ft/min

Our problem is to calculate how many gallons or pounds per acre we apply under one set of operating conditions. We begin by finding the conditions. Example: We time our operator and find he walks 220 ft/min. As he is to push a spray boom we multiply 220 by the width of the boom and convert the distance he travels to an area. With a 6-ft boom, 220 ft/min x 6 ft width= 1320 ft^2/min. Then:

$$\frac{43{,}560 \text{ ft}^2 \text{ in 1 acre}}{1320 \text{ ft}^2/\text{min}} = 33 \text{ min/acre}$$

We now know how fast we cover the area. But to get gallons per acre we need to know how long it takes to spray one gallon. Suppose we use a spray pressure of 30 psi for our example. We start the pump and set the pressure at 30 psi. As rate of delivery varies with pressure and nozzle size our results will be good for only this pressure and these nozzles. We place a container under each nozzle and operate the spray for a measured time. (Each nozzle should deliver the same amount of spray. If the amount varies from nozzle to nozzle, replace them all with a new set and begin over.) Suppose we run the spray for 30 sec and collect 1 1/2 pints. This is equivalent to 1 1/2 quarts per minute. In 33 min we will deliver 33 x 1 1/2= 49 1/2 gal, or

$$\frac{33 \text{ min}}{1 \text{ acre}} \times \frac{1\ 1/2 \text{ gal}}{1 \text{ min}} = 49\ 1/2 \text{ gal/acre}$$

If we wish to spray 2,4-D at 2 lb/acre and have a spray formulated to contain 4 lb/gal, we can now put 49 gal of water in the spray tank for each acre, and add 1/2 gal of the herbicide for each acre. Summing, we get:

$$\frac{43{,}560 \text{ ft}^2/\text{acre} \times \text{gal/min}}{220 \text{ ft/min} \times 6 \text{ ft width}} = \text{gal/acre}$$

all provided the pressure remains constant and the man walks with constant speed. We can fully generalize this:

$$\frac{43{,}560 \text{ ft}^2/\text{acre} \times \text{gal delivered in 1 min}}{\text{ft/min of travel} \times \text{ft width of spray boom}} = \text{gal/acre}$$

If we are using a tractor and measuring speed in mph, each mile per hour is 88 ft/min and the general formula is:

$$\frac{43{,}560 \text{ ft}^2/\text{acre} \times \text{gal/min}}{88 \text{ ft/min} \times \text{mph} \times \text{ft width of boom}} = \text{gal/acre}$$

If we want to spray small areas we can convert to units of 1000 ft^2:

$$\frac{1000\ \text{ft}^2 \times \text{gal/min}}{\text{ft/min of travel} \times \text{ft width of boom}} = \text{gal/1000 ft}^2$$

When our calcultaíons show it difficult to apply the amount of biocide we want at the dilution we want, we can change some of the parameters and recalculate the problem.

To apply more material or to apply the same amount of material in more dilute form, you can do any or all of the following: go slower, use a larger nozzle, or use a higher pressure.

To apply less material or to apply the same amount of material in more concentrated solution you may do any or all of the following: go faster, use a smaller nozzle, or reduce the pressure.

Calculations for fertilizer spreaders are essentially the same. With some spreaders rate of delivery varies with speed and is difficult to measure. For large areas, a rough field calibration is usually adequate. The spreader is set approximately right. The time it takes to spread an 80-lb bag of fertilizer is measured. As an example, if we are going 6 mph with an 8-ft spreader and it takes 4 min to spread an 80-lb bag, we can proceed as follows, using the same reasoning: One mph is 88 ft/min so at 6 mph, 88 x 6 = 528 ft/min; 528 ft/min x 8 ft width of spreader = 4224 ft^2/min; 4224 ft^{2}min x 4 min/bag = 16,896 ft^2/80-lb bag.

$$\frac{43{,}560\ \text{ft}^2\text{/acre} \times 80\ \text{lb}}{16{,}896\ \text{ft}^2} = 206\ \text{lb/acre}$$

Putting this all together and generalizing:

$$\frac{43{,}560\ \text{ft}^2\text{/acre} \times \text{lb delivered}}{88\ \text{ft/min} \times \text{mph} \times \text{ft spreader width} \times \text{min to deliver}} = \text{lb/acre}$$

If we have a positive feed spreader where the amount delivered is constant over a unit distance and is unaffected by the speed, we may simplify the calibration. We pull the spreader for a measured distance along a cement floor, and sweep up and weigh the amount delivered. Our general formula then becomes:

$$\frac{43{,}560\ \text{ft}^2\text{/acre} \times \text{lb delivered}}{\text{spreader width} \times \text{ft traveled}} = \text{lb/acre}$$

A Note for Research Workers

A small hopper spreader delivers more when it is full than when it is empty. The error is too large for precise plot work. The following compensation can be made when using uniformly pelleted fertilizer with a pellet size less than the delivery orifice.

By keeping an amount in the hopper an order of magnitude larger than the plot sample, we can provide a constant head while spreading. To illustrate, suppose we are to apply many replications at rates of 400 and 800 g per plot, and have the bags weighed out for each of the plots. Weigh out 8 kg of fertilizer and place it in the hopper. Mark out an area on the floor and bring the spreader into calibration, always keeping 8 kg in it. When it is delivering 400 g per plot area, take it into the field. Add 400 or 800 g to the 8 kg and go over each plot once or twice as appropriate. Continue over the plots. At the end, weight what is left in the hopper and partition the error among the plots.

To an extent the method is self-correcting. If the calibration is low, an amount is left over after each plot. This increases the head and the flow on the next plot, and the spreader comes back into calibration. If the calibration is too high the amount in the hopper decreases, hence the head and rate of delivery decrease and the spreader again comes into calibration.

APPENDIX IV

Measurement of the Area of an Irregular Green

Equipment needed: Measuring tape, 20-d nails, ball of string, and a carpenter's roofing square (optional).

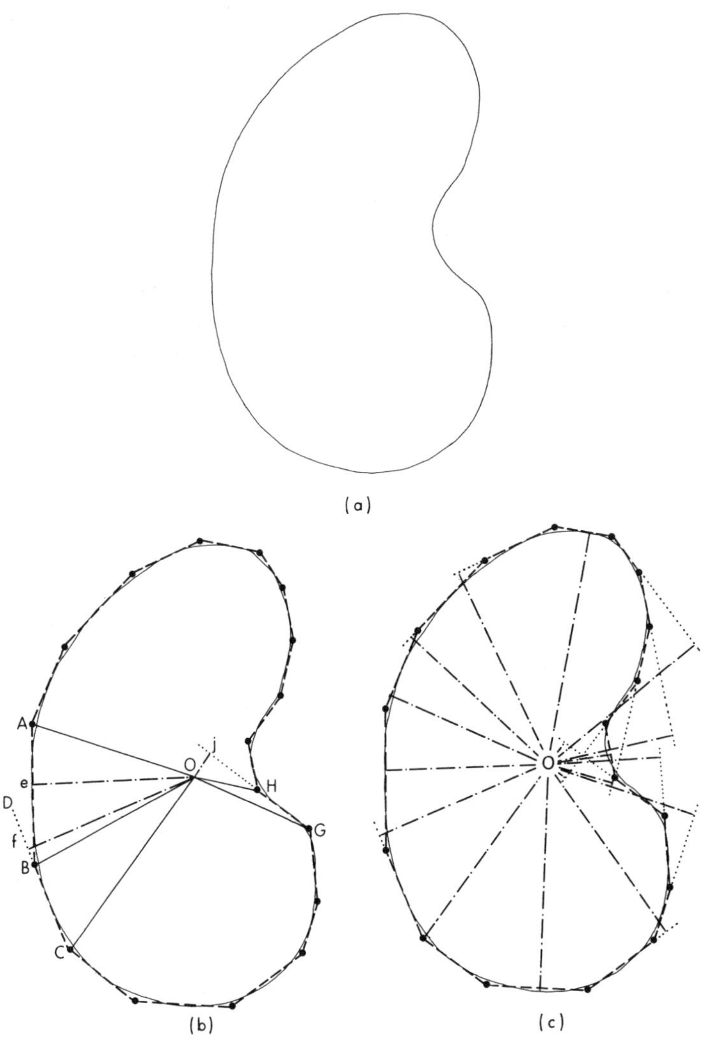

Go around the perimeter of the green and mark it with string stretched between nails pushed into the soil. Match the straight lengths of string to the perimeter of the green as closely as possible (see figure, part *a*). Measure each length of string. Pin one end of the tape somewhere in the center of the green. Go around the green and read the perpendicular distance from the pin to each length of string. The perpendicular distance will be the shortest distance to the string as you swing an arc over the line. The tape will read more a foot on either side of the point you want, but if you wish to check yourself use the square.

You now have the base and altitude of a series of triangles. The area of a triangle is:

$$\text{area} = 1/2\ (\text{base x altitude})$$

Area of the green is the sum of the areas of all the triangles. By using care this method can be made as accurate as you wish.

In the figure (part b), Oe is the perpendicular to line AB and is the altitude of triangle OAB. Line Of is perpendicular to CB extended and is the altitude of triangle OBC. Similarly Oj is the altitude of triangle GOH measured to GH extended. Your helper uses a string on a pin to extend the lines while you measure the altitude. Part c in the figure shows all the altitudes in the example used.

APPENDIX V

Testing Products

Turfgrass managers are continually presented with new products and materials to evaluate. They often fail to get good information from their trials. The usual reason for poor data is that there are too many uncontrolled variables, and no check plot. If we try out a new fungicide on a green, and at the same time re-program our irrigation and then change our fertilizer program, we may get a change in disease incidence. We won't know, however, if the change results from changes in the weather, the fungicide, the irrigation, or the fertilization. All are known to have an effect on disease.

A fundamental principle of scientific induction is this: if every factor in a pair of trials is alike except one, differences between the trials will be due to the difference in that factor. If a single plot is used, there is nothing to compare and no valid information results. When more than one factor varies, complex experimental designs are needed as well as accurate methods of measuring results, and statistical methods of analysis. The professional research man will use these methods along with multiple replications of his test. Without invoking all of the safeguards, checks, and controls of a scientific experiment, the turf manager can still use the above principle of induction to improve his gathering of information.

The first requirement is that he use two plots. One should receive the treatment. The other is treated in a comparable way with a standard known product, or is an untreated check area. The second requirement is that both areas be treated just alike in all respects except for the factor being tested. For example, if we want to test a new fertilizer, we might divide a tee in half the long way; use the new material on one half, and an equivalent amount of the regular fertilizer on the other side. This latter is our check plot. Both plots will get the same mowing the same irrigation, the same traffic, etc. (had we divided the tee across, traffic would be more unevenly divided). If we see a real difference in color or density or growth, we can then say with some assurance that there is a difference in the way the new fertilizer performs.

If instead of using a check plot, we switch from fertilizer A to fertilizer B for two or three months, then switch back again, there is little we can say for sure about their differences unless they are very great—larger than we would usually get from equivalent amounts of a fertilizer element.

The third thing to do in making a test is to make an immediate record. Our mind often plays tricks. If a difference shows up two weeks after we apply the test, and we are relying on memory, we may distinctly remember that the better side is where we applied A, when in fact that is where we used B.

Fourthly, we should mark the exact location of our treatments. Either use markers or measure distances from the plot corners to two permanent features such as trees, sprinkler heads, etc.

Lastly, the size of our plot should be appropriate. In spraying a green with iron, laying down a folded newspaper will keep the spray from about 1 1/2 ft.[2]

This is enough to give a check on whether the spray produced a difference in color or not. With an herbicide spray, a newspaper opened out will protect 5-6 $ft,^2$ a fair test. With all-or-none tests such as these, a fairly small area can serve as a check plot, but for comparisons of equivalent materials, a larger area is usually needed. To compare a finely pelleted fertilizer with the same fertilizer coarsely pelleted could require alternate spreader strips over an acre. The larger test is better in any case, but this must be balanced against appropriateness. In an iron test it would not do to risk having a putting green half dark green and half light green.

Our tests are more accurate when we can repeat them in several different locations. If the fertilizer test above shows a distinct difference we may conclude a difference in product. If we make the same test on three separate tees, and find a difference on only one, we don't have much confidence in that difference. But if we find the same distinct difference in all three tests, then we can have considerable confidence in our results.

Tests may be crude, but if we take care, we can definitely improve the validity of our conclusions. The important points can be summarized as follows: (*1*) Use a treatment and a check on two adjacent areas so you can make a comparison. (*2*) Treat both areas just alike except for the test treatment. (*3*) Make a record of the test. (*4*) Record plot locations. (*5*) Repeat the experiment in several locations if possible.

Author Index

Subject Index*

*Herbicides and weeds are tabulated in the chapter on weed control and are not separately indexed here. For herbicides, see pp. 315-345; for monocot weeds see pp. 347-348; for dicot weeds, pp. 368-370; aquatic weeds, 413. Fertility, irrigation, soils, salinity, drainage, and turfgrass botany including identification and breeding of turfgrasses are treated in *Principles of Turfgrass Culture.*
Page references to figures, charts, and tables are given in italics.

*See Chapter 4, *Principles of Turfgrass Culture*

*For full discussion see *Principles of Turfgrass Culture.*

*Treated fully in *Principles of Turfgrass Culture.*

*See *Principles of Turfgrass Culture.*

*For extensive treatment see chapters 5, 6, and 8 in *Principles of Turfgrass Culture.*